Cognitive

Psychophysiology

principles of covert behavior

F. J. McGUIGAN

Graduate Research Professor
Professor of Psychology
Professor of Psychiatry
Director, Performance Research Laboratory
University of Louisville

PRENTICE-HALL, INC., Englewood Cliffs, New Jersey 07632

Library of Congress Cataloging in Publication Data

McGuigan, Frank J
   Cognitive psychophysiology.

   Bibliography: p.
   Includes index.
   1. Cognition. 2. Psychology, Physiological.
I. Title.
BF311.M15   153   78-18542
ISBN 0-13-139519-X

CENTURY PSYCHOLOGY SERIES

© 1978 by Prentice-Hall, Inc., Englewood Cliffs, N.J. 07632

Printed in the United States of America

10 9 8 7 6 5 4 3 2 1

PRENTICE-HALL INTERNATIONAL, INC., London
PRENTICE-HALL OF AUSTRALIA PTY. LIMITED, Sydney
PRENTICE-HALL OF CANADA, LTD., Toronto
PRENTICE-HALL OF INDIA PRIVATE LIMITED, New Delhi
PRENTICE-HALL OF JAPAN, INC., Tokyo
PRENTICE-HALL OF SOUTHEAST ASIA PTE. LTD., Singapore
WHITEHALL BOOKS LIMITED, Wellington, New Zealand

This book is dedicated to a venerable idea and to some very special teachers.

The idea is that the mind is the activation of neuromuscular circuits:

"The organ of mind is not the brain by itself; it is the brain, nerves, muscles, and organs of sense. . . . We must . . . discard forever the notion of the sensorium commune, the cerebral closed, as a central seat of mind, or receptacle of sensation and imagery . . ." (Alexander Bain, 1855).

"All the endless diversity of the external manifestations of the activity of the brain can be finally regarded as one phenomenon—that of muscular movement . . ." (I. M. Sechenov, 1863).

"It might be naive to say that we think with our muscles, but it would be inaccurate to say that we think without them" (Jacobson, 1967), and as Ralph Lilly stated, Jacobson's studies " . . . proved that the brain had no closed circuits when it came to mental activity" (Edmund Jacobson, 1973).

"The central nervous system no longer appears as a self-contained organ, receiving inputs from the senses and discharging into the muscles. On the contrary, some of its most characteristic activities are explicable only as circular processes, emerging from the system into the muscles, and re-entering the nervous system through the sense organs, whether they be proprioceptors or organs of the special senses" (Norbert Weiner, 1948).

The teachers are:

James Culbertson
W. Horsley Gantt
Howard Gilhousen
William Grings
Edmund Jacobson
Luther Mays
Milton Metfessel

Charles Osgood
Hans Reichenbach
John P. Seward
B. F. Skinner
Kenneth W. Spence
Benton J. Underwood

and for $\mathcal{R}$

Contents

part four
Hypothesized Functions of Covert Processes

part five
Technology of Covert Processes

Preface

The major problem in writing a book on cognitive psychophysiology is how to cover the area adequately. The task is enormous, and obviously impossible for one person to accomplish with thoroughness. A truly complete coverage would include summaries of all psychophysiological measures (GSR, EEG, EMG, etc.) of activated neuromuscular circuits during numerous mental processes, as well as relevant aspects of behavioral cognition (linguistics, information processing systems, etc.). To this is added the technical procedures of measuring covert processes that involve gathering and processing data; this gets us into electronics, computer technology, statistics, neuromuscular anatomy, physiology, psychophysiology, as well as psychology.

One approach to a problem of this magnitude is that of the symposium in which there are cooperative efforts of many. Collaboration perhaps allows more complete coverage with more varied, stimulating ideas but typically lacks uniformity in approach and data bases. The alternative of the individual approach, as in the present instance, leads to restrictions and incompleteness of areas of coverage. (A symposium would not, I think, have come out with Newton's *Principia*, though on the other hand, one person could not have built the atom bomb.) With an apology that I know will be readily accepted by anyone who tries to keep up with the exponentially increasing literature in cognitive psychophysiology, I have restricted the empirical coverage to four data fields: electrooculography (Chapter 5), speech muscle electromyography (Chapter 6), somatic electromyography (Chapter 7), and electroencephalography (Chapter 8). Even so, it was physically (including psychologically) impossible to include the most recent research, and the coverage of these four areas is chronologically uneven since I could not write all four chapters simultaneously, as well as get along with the rest of the book. Without these sacrifices, this book would never have been published; as it is, I feel as though I have just stumbled over the finish line that I set out for in 1960.

Another constraint in covering the topic is book length, and at the sound suggestions of the editor and of Kenneth MacCorquodale (to whom also I owe a special debt for encouragement of this project over many years), I have noticeably shortened the original version sent to the publisher in December 1976—principally, I have removed the technical laboratory chapters on how to measure covert processes, and am publishing them as a separate manual elsewhere. In these days of rapidly rising prices the publisher and author have tried to price the book so that it is especially available to students.

My special hopes for this book are two: For lay thinking, above anything else, that it will help replace the naive Cartesian notion of a cerebral homunculus, of a Donovan's brain model of the mind being solely within the skull. The data to substantiate that we think with our entire body appear to me to be overwhelming, and the numerous extensive measurements of autonomic, cerebral, and muscular events during all cognitive activities fit well with a neuromuscular circuit model of the mind in which there is complex linguistic and nonlinguistic information processing (Chapter 9). What _is_ incredible is that anyone ever did hold the notion that cognition is exclusively a brain function. A close examination of the issue shows that even such staunch "centralists" as Lashley, Hebb, and Osgood did not espouse a strict centralism in which peripheral mechanisms do not serve some function (such as in feedback circuits) during thought. My second hope for the book is a scientific one. We have many varied efforts at studying covert processes (Chapter 2), both theoretically and empirically, but they form such a hodgepodge in our history. I hope that this book will provide some unification and thus a sound foundation for a science of covert behavior which should be at least as scientifically productive as our traditional science of overt behavior. Principally, our effort is to achieve a wedding of behavioral mediation models with empirical psychophysiological efforts to measure directly those hypothetical constructs.

My indebtedness over the many years is to so many that they simply cannot all be named. Collectively, my dedicated and inspiring students, both graduate and undergraduate, deserve the highest ranking, and I think I remember them all starting with the small group of four who met evenings in 1959. My second debt must also be collectively to our colleagues who went before, and I think principally to John Watson (whose great insight on this issue I did not adequately appreciate until many years after graduate school, though I had memorized him thoroughly), and to Edmund Jacobson (who, with a different framework, independently confirmed many of my thoughts about research and about the

mind, as well as having shown me the way in many respects). My colleagues (Black, Chapman, Grings, Hefferline, Jacobson, MacNeilage, Mulholland, Osgood, Paivio, Rechtschaffen, Sperry, and Stoyva) in our Psychophysiology of Thinking Symposium (Academic Press, 1973) were most helpful for our field, and for giving useful direction to my ideas since then.

Of specific individuals, I cannot adequately express the value of my conversations and written interchanges with Charles Osgood, nor to his student, Meredith Richards, for the back-breaking task of improving the verbal presentation of the book. Finally, those who labored so effectively on the typing, clerical, and data-organizing tasks have well earned special thanks. Foremost is Charlotte Collings, whose outstanding help was given for well onto two decades, and to Betty Loving, Bernelle Rich, Fern Greenway, and Elke Thompson for the indices. Others are acknowledged as appropriate within the text.

Finally, I should note that when I first started in this field, having decided that the areas of secondary reinforcement, incidental learning, and knowledge of results in which I was then working showed limited promise, I met with some considerable resistance from some of our colleagues. These notions of directly measuring mediational constructs, of the importance of feedback functions within neuromuscular circuits, of directly explicating mental processes through psychophysiological measures, and in fact of seeking a systematic data base for the entire area of covert behavior evoked little sympathy of understanding some two decades ago. Usually the harshest criticism of a scientific approach to cognitive psychophysiology came from scientific materialists more often than from the mentalists, which has always been surprising to me. Since then, the development of a firm data base and of some primitive guiding theoretical notions have changed all that. I am especially heartened by the enthusiasm about the developing science of covert processes expressed by students and young scientists throughout the world, and I look forward to hearing further from that group over the years. As has been said by a number of individuals, what I refer to as my "science fiction chapter" (Chapter 11) is really not that far away.

F. J. M.

part one

Introduction

The Task of Psychology

The Problem of "Mind," and the Development
of a Natural Science Approach
to "Mental Processes"

If one observes our science in historical and contemporary perspective, one might well wonder how people developed the notion of nonphysical mental processes in the first place. Perhaps early humans invented mentalistic concepts about nonmaterial phenomena and agents in an effort to help them survive in a strange and hostile world. One can, for example, imagine a primitive human being dreaming of the dead and, on awakening, referring to those visited in the dream as "spirits." When faced with threatening events, humans may have postulated mystical gods as causal agents; they could then achieve security by placating the gods with worship and sacrifices. The personal experiences of "self awareness" and of "silently talking to oneself," having no apparent physical origin, might have lead primitive humans to such notions as the homunculus—or a separate entity within oneself capable of monitoring perceptions and thoughts. Eventually, such presumed phenomena became reified when languages incorporated words like "consciousness," "mind," "thoughts," and "ideas" into the vernacular, with no reference to corresponding physicalistic events.

Mentalistic concepts became firmly implanted in Western culture when they were formally developed by the early mental philosophers. The flowering of science in the seventeenth and eighteenth centuries guided some mental philosophers toward the empirical study of mind. Most prominent among these were the British Associationists, from Thomas Hobbes in the early seventeenth century to Alexander Bain into the twentieth. John Locke's reasoning about atoms of the mind, analogous to early models in chemistry, is a good example of the influence of science on the mental philosophy of that period. Scientists, too, started applying observational methods to "mental processes." In particular, physicists began to study the role of sense receptors as necessary instruments of scientific observations in the study of the nonliving world. A classic example is the minute time differences which existed between the astronomical observations reported by Maskelyne and those reported by his assistant Kinnebrook, whom he dismissed; that difference inspired the psychological concept of the "personal equation." At about the same time, physiologists were asking questions about sensation, perception, and the mind itself, particularly when they sought to understand the functioning of the receptor systems. The commonality in the endeavors of such diverse academicians as philosophers, physicists, and physiologists were symptomatic of the *zeitgeist* which, in 1879, led Wundt to found the school of "Structural Psychology"—the first science devoted exclusively to the study of mental phenomena.

Thus, the original task of psychology was that of understanding the mind. However, statements made then about "mind" were untestable (technically meaningless, cf. McGuigan, 1978a). As a requisite for progress psychology had to make a transition from nonmaterial conceptions of mental phenomena to strictly physicalistic ones. The transition was slow and, in many instances, extremely painful. A materialistic conception of mind has historically been unpopular, as it frequently still is. Gall, who held that the brain was the organ of mind, suffered great personal abuse and was even denied a religious burial because of his efforts to advance materialism. Nonmaterialistic conceptions of mind still abound, amazingly, even among scientists. The great Sherrington, in the early part of the century, sought in vain for a special nonmaterial energy of mind. As late as the 1950's, Lashley still found it necessary to vigorously attack nonmaterialistic conceptions held by contemporary neurologists (cf. especially Eccles, 1966).

There were both negative and positive reasons for the eventual transition of scientific psychology to materialism. On the negative side, decades of vigorous introspective investigations followed Wundt's founding of psychology; with these studies the Structuralists and other introspectionists hastened their own demise by accumulating evidence of the sterility of their efforts to introspect on a nonmaterial consciousness. The coupe de grace to Structuralism was delivered none too gently by the classical behaviorists, led by John Watson (1913). The critical argument in their attack was that direct observation of a nonmaterial consciousness through introspection did not satisfy a principle of inter-subjective reliability—one person's observation of his or her own con-sciousness is necessarily private, and only publicly observable events can be scientifically studied. Behavior can be observed by more than one person, and as a phenomenon *does* satisfy a criterion of intersubjective reliability. As a result of the influence of the early behaviorists, psychol-ogy ceased to be the introspective study of "oneself" and became the behavioral study of "the other one."

While it gradually became apparent to psychological scientists that nonmaterialism was a blind alley, on the positive side materialistic ap-proaches became increasingly productive in advancing our understand-ing of the higher mental processes. In proclaiming behavior to be the subject matter of psychology, the early behaviorists still maintained many of the old mentalistic terms. This point requires special attention, for it is often said that theirs was a complete rejection of "mentalistic notions." What the behaviorists actually did was abandon introspec-tionist definitions (in terms of "nonmaterial stuff") and redefined mental terms according to the principles of natural science. Hence, "emotion" ceased to be referred to as "affective quality" and was defined instead as visceral responding. "Consciousness" was redefined as the objectively observable behavior of a person describing the internal and external world (a process denoted by Skinner [1957] as "internal" and "external tacts"). And "thinking" was redefined primarily as implicit language be-havior. Though Lashley eventually diverged theoretically from his teacher, Watson, his brain research on the higher mental processes was instrumental in advancing a staunch psychological materialism.

In short, the combination of (1) the growing awareness of a lack of scientific respectability of nonmaterial conceptions of mind, and (2) the fruitful contributions that followed from materialism, have led to the present renewed interest in the scientific study of cognitive processes.

Even so, an aura of mysticism about the behaviorist's view of higher mental processes persists—but for pragmatic rather than scientific reasons. Essentially, the problem has been one of smallness: the hypothesized implicit reactions equated with thought are minute, and for decades the young behavioral science was not technologically equipped to observe such events directly. The hypothesis was for long untestable. With the development of laboratories for making extremely sensitive psychophysiological measurements, we have acquired the tech-nical capabilities to directly observe small scale responses and thus make suitable tests of early behavioristic theories. By amplifying and display-ing minute muscular and glandular events on cathode-ray oscilloscopes in the psychophysiological laboratory, we succeed in dissolving the mys-ticism about small scale behavior. A response, in short, is activity of muscles and glands; it is irrelevent whether the response is overt (large) or covert (small). It is irrelevant whether a response can be observed with the naked eye (i.e., is overt) or whether specialized laboratory techniques are necessary for its observation (i.e., it is covert). In either case, the behavioral phenomenon can be objectively studied.

Psychology has made considerable progress by means of the classical S-R model. But from the early days behaviorists have been aware of gaps in the statements that can be made with this single stage model. Those gaps have been apparent when dealing with complex behavioral processes, and multiple hypothetical constructs have been proposed to bridge between directly observed external Ss and overt Rs. The variety of proposed rs and ss (inferred covert responses and internal stimuli) in the literature is a reaction to the shortcomings of the classical S-R model and our need to talk about unobserved behavior through traditional methods. One example of a hypothetical construct that intervenes between external stimuli and overt responses is Watson's implicit language habit, i.e., S $\longrightarrow$ (implicit language responses). . $\longrightarrow$ resultant internal stimuli. . $\longrightarrow$ R.

More recent hypothetical constructs are the fractional anticipatory goal response (r_G—s_G) of Hull (1943), the mediational response of Kendler and Kendler (1969), the mediating reaction (r_M) of Osgood (1953), the perceptual response of Schoenfeld and Cumming (1963), and the representational and implicit associative responses of Bousfield, Whitmarsh, and Dannick (1958; also studied by Underwood, 1965). Though such constructs have firm empirical anchorings on the antecedent (stimulus) and consequent (response) sides of the paradigm, their "reality status" is more convincing if they can be directly observed rather than inferred indirectly. By directly (psychophysiologically) measuring the covert bodily events that intervene between external stimuli and overt responses, we should be able to reduce the number and kinds of postulated logical constructs (some will probably turn out to be psychophysiologically impossible) and thus advance more parsimonious theories. One can envision an increasing degree of mutual facilitation between the psychophysiologist and the behavior theorist, in which each guides the other in both empirical research and theory construction.

R. C. Davis and his colleagues have indicated yet another reason for studying covert behavior, namely that overt responses are numerically small in proportion to covert responses: "One has but to observe them on a set of recording instruments to believe that they are by far the most numerous responses of the organism. It is clear that any overt response . . . is surrounded by a wide penumbra of them. . . . In this sea of somatic response an occasional wave breaks into an external response" (Davis, Buchwald, and Frankmann, 1955, p. 1). Related to this fact that covert responses are more numerous than overt responses is the point that covert responses underlie and thus determine overt behavior.

Two points emerge from this brief history: how the notion of "mind" arose in the first place, and how we laboriously arrived at a natural science approach to mental processes. The stage has thus been set for a scientific explication of "mind"—psychologists have provided the principles for explicating "higher mental events" in terms of covert process-es, and psychophysiologists have developed suitable laboratory techniques for measuring these previously unobserved reactions. In short, contemporary study of covert processes can now be related to the original task of psychology, that of understanding the nature of the higher mental processes. Now, however, we are studying publicly ob-servable events and thus proceeding on the natural science basis called for by Watson and his colleagues.

With this general understanding, we shall face some more specific questions about how this study should proceed. These involve the bodily locus of thought and the processes that constitute cognitive activities.

Bodily Locus of Cognitive Activities

Some theorists have considered thought to be strictly a function of brain activity, while others have asserted that thought involves other bodily systems as well. The former position has been referred to as the "centralist" and the latter as the "peripheralist" position. Two represen-tations of the peripheral and central models were presented by Dashiell (1949), based on his 1925 article (Fig. 1.1). The peripheral model most closely corresponds to the principles of classical behaviorism, which stresses primarily response activity.[1] Behaviorists probably overem-phasized the importance of peripheral events (as when they regarded thinking as only responding)—an understandable excess given the con-text of psychology in the early part of this century. At that time, be-haviorists were scrupulously endeavoring to avoid the pitfalls of men-talism by limiting their statements to objectively observable behavior that could provide a sound data base for the development of a truly scientific psychology. Unfortunately, in emphasizing peripheral events, the classi-cal behaviorist frequently paid only lip service to brain phenomena. The brain was little understood, and it was often said that "CNS" stood for the "conceptual nervous system." By concentrating on peripheral sys-tems, behaviorists thus attempted to avoid the pitfalls of merely transfer-ring unseen mental events to unseen brain events. As has often hap-pened in science, positions have been oversimplified and "oversold" in an effort to introduce unpopular ideas. At a time when there was no question about the brain being important for cognition, behaviorists were trying to account for the higher mental processes within the con-straints of their science of observable behavior by calling attention to the role of muscular and glandular events.

---

[1] One common error in understanding the peripheral model results from an over-simplification in Fig. 1.1. As Dashiell pointed out, motor representation A erroneously represents thought as a simple serial order process. Probably, though, no serious theorist ever conceived of thought as a single channel linear process—certainly not Watson who took pains to represent thinking as complex multichannel interaction (see especially our Fig 2.2 taken from page 266 of his 1930 edition of *Behaviorism*).

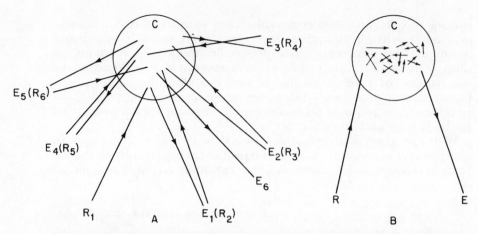

FIG. 1.1 Two extreme views of the role of the brain in thinking. In an extreme motor (peripheral) theory (A) "the original stimulations from a problem situation playing upon receptor R_1 evoke an abbreviated response at effector E_1. This in turn serves to excite receptor R_2 (kinesthetic or other) which evokes a response at effector E_2. And so the nascent abbreviated symbolic responses continue until the thinking eventuates in an overt act, as performed by effector E_6 . . . The neural counterpart of each idea was an excitation in a local spot (cell-cluster) in the brain [B]; and the transitions from idea to idea were referable physiologically to the passage of a neural impulse or train of impulses from cell-cluster to cell-cluster. Now this shooting around of neural currents within the cerebrum is as grossly oversimplified an account as is the story of receptor-effector arcs told above and suggested in part A of the figure" (Dashiell, 1949, pp. 588–89).

If the behaviorists overemphasized responses, the classical centralist neglected them. Extreme centralism has been referred to as "Donovan's Brain Theory," named after the science fiction story in which Donovan arranged to have his brain preserved so that he could continue thinking after his normal life ceased (McGuigan, 1973a). One obvious difficulty with this theory is that, if such an isolated preparation *could* think, without input from the external and internal environment it probably couldn't think very well, and most assuredly it wouldn't have much to think about. On the other hand, the term "peripheralism" is equally unfortunate in that it conjures up an image of thought occurring in a brainless body. One who thinks of thought as only behavior (muscle and gland activity) neglects critical nervous processes. A "peripheral, brainless person," and Donovan's brain model seem equally restrictive in accounting for cognitive processes.

In considering the question of where in the body thoughts occur, an objective scientist would eschew any predisposing biases, considering it possible that any or all bodily systems might serve some function during cognition. Actually, a variety of bodily systems have been empirically implicated in cognitive activities. Excellent accounts of brain functioning during thought may be found in Delafresnaye (1954), Eccles (1966), and more recently Young (1970). The eye has ranked high in importance among bodily organs implicated during cognition. Hebb (1968) held that

8

peripheral activity, especially eye movement, is essential during the formation of images. A general treatment of visual system functioning during cognition may be found in Chase (1973). Visceral activity has been empirically and theoretically implicated in cognitive processes in a variety of ways; we should especially mention work on the esophagus (e.g., Jacobson, 1929), on intestinal activity (e.g., Davis, Garafolow, and Gault, 1957), on electrodermal responding (e.g., Grings, 1973), and on the autonomic system in general (e.g., Lacey and Lacey, 1974). Finally, we note that since the time of the ancient Greeks the skeletal musculature has been held to perform critical functions during thought (cf. Langfeld, 1933, and M. O. Smith, 1969). The importance of cognitive motor responding has been particularly emphasized in Russia and the United States since the latter part of the nineteenth century. As we shall note in Chapter 2, it was Sechenov (1863) who was most responsible for a long line of cognitive psychophysiological theorizing and empirical research in Russia. Sechenov's emphasis was on reflexes and responses, as in his doctrine that "all the endless diversity of the external manifestations of the activity of the brain can be finally regarded as one phenomenon—that of muscular movement . . ." (1965, p. 309). The work of Pavlov (cf. 1941), Bechterev (1923), Leontiev (1959), Galperin (1969), and Vigotsky (1962) carried Sechenov's reasoning into contemporary Soviet psychology.

In the United States, Titchener's (1909) core context theory of meaning placed great emphasis on the skeletal musculature for the development of meaning. But the early behaviorists (Dunlap, 1912, Hunter, 1924a, 1924b, etc.) were probably the primary force advocating theories of thought in which muscle responding was critical.

Our approach, therefore, will be flexible, without predispositions as to whether or not any bodily system should be excluded as at least a partial organ of mind. Later in the book we shall examine data in detail which implicate various bodily systems in cognitive functioning. Our next question now concerns how such bodily systems might interact.

From Localized Center Models
to Circuit Concepts

Early conceptions of brain functioning held to a "center" model. Perhaps the most extreme conception of cerebral localization was advocated by Gall who, in his phrenology, held that there were numerous specific centers in the brain that were identified with particular mental faculties (cf., Gall and Spurzheim, 1809). The most influential attack on Gall's concept of localization was by Flourens. While Flourens also conceived of brain functioning in terms of cerebral localization, his concept was of more widespread and generalized localization than Gall's. Lashley's extensive research, which led him to formulate the principles of equipotentiality and mass action, digressed still further from the rigid concept of brain centers. Major neurophysiological and neuroanatomi-cal advances in tracing pathways throughout the central nervous system facilitated the development of circuit concepts (e.g., Lashley, 1958, Pen-field, 1969). In psychology the circuit concept received notice in early behavioral theories which held thinking to be a function of a total reflex arc (Fig. 1.1). We note too Jacobson's (cf. 1973) pioneering electrical measurement of neuromuscular events which led him to postulate com-plex circuits that function throughout the body. Relevant also is the general use of servo loops and the feedback principle, which received its most vigorous contemporary thrust by Wiener (1948). As he put it, "The central nervous system no longer appears as a self-contained organ, receiving inputs from the senses and discharging into the muscles. On the contrary, some of its most characteristic activities are explicable only as circular processes, emerging from the nervous system into the muscles, and re-entering the nervous system through the sense organs, whether they be proprioceptors or organs of the special senses" (1948, p. 15).

Theorists thus moved from a localized brain center model of the mind to a loop or circuit conception. The issue then became one of specifying the nature of the circuits. Probably the dominant view of mind is that involving strictly intracerebral circuits (as in B of Fig. 1.1) with a major alternative model involving neuromuscular circuits between brain and peripheral systems (as in A of Fig. 1.1 and as in Wiener's description above).

An important issue for our purposes is whether or not there may be strictly intracerebral circuits that do not interact in any way with the musculature. Given the amazing complexity of inner connections among some 10 billion cerebral neurons having an estimated 5×10^{14} (500,000,000,000,000) synapses in the cortex (C. Smith, 1970) it would indeed be surprising if there were not some strictly transcortical circuits as well as some cortical-subcortical ones. Sechenov held that all of the brain's activities are manifested in muscular events. Similarly, Lilly's in-terpretation of Jacobson's early studies was that Jacobson proved "that the brain had no closed circuits when it came to mental activity" (Jacob-son, 1973, p. 8). But they could have been wrong. One could conceive of reasons why critical brain processes that do not result in covert muscle responses might occur. For example, inhibitory stimuli, such as those demonstrated by Hernandez-Peón, Scherrer, and Jouvet (1956), may produce neural activity that prevents efferent discharge, thus inhibiting the occurrence of a particular response. If such closed circuits do exist, the only way they could be studied is directly through brain measures. In this case, science would be an *extremely* long way from understanding the mind, for it would have to await the development of radically new techniques to directly study brain activity. While present electrical techniques for recording brain reactions represent sizeable progress, they still are primitive relative to those which would be needed. If there are some such closed brain circuits there would be some central thought processes that would occur without responses (muscular and glandular components). Psychology, defined strictly as the study of behavior, would then find such events outside its scope (cf. McGuigan, 1966a). To the extent that this is true, Wiener's statement that psychology is like a tape worm that keeps losing segments of its content to physiology would be prophetic.

To determine whether or not there *are* central thoughts in the absence of (peripheral) responses, we need to maintain our flexible strategic position, i.e., we must allow for the possible contribution of any bodily system to the total thought process and attempt to study them all. We thus need to record central nervous system events along with phenomena of noncerebral systems to ascertain their functions in thought. In this way we maximize our chances of arriving at the appropriate model and minimize our chances of missing the truth.

Two complimentary strategies for systematically determining which bodily systems are necessary for cognitive functioning have been suggested (McGuigan, 1966a). Principally, these involve the systematic stimulation of neuromuscular pathways in the manner of Penfield (1958), and the systematic "paralyzing" of various systems (the "curare strategy") as discussed in Chapter 4. However, both the "stimulation" and the "paralysis" strategies are technologically impractical at this time. One alternative which *is* presently realizable, though less than ideal, is to survey data implicating all possible bodily systems and attempt to infer from them the nature of circuits that function during internal information processing. This shall be the strategy of this book, though the task must be circumscribed due to the recent knowledge explosion within the area of cognitive psychophysiology. We shall survey a sizeable sample of the data that implicate various bodily systems in cognitive processing. Priority is given to the eye, the nonoral somatic skeletal musculature, the speech musculature, and the brain, in no particular order. Unfortunately, we shall not cover the autonomic literature. The slow latency of autonomic responses to external and internal stimuli suggests that the autonomic system is not critical for immediate information processing, unlike the rapid actions of the skeletal musculature and the brain. The slow circuits involving autonomic activity *are* probably important for cognitive functioning in providing emotional tone to the information being processed.

Our general assumption is that psychology's task of understanding behavior entails the study of both small and large scale responses—a psychology that confines itself to overt behavior is at best incomplete. As contemporary psychophysiological laboratories continue their success in making covert processes publicly observable, systematization becomes increasingly important. Our progress in theory development should thus be hastened by simultaneously considering overt behavior along with covert reactions. "Covert reactions" (synonymously "covert processes," "covert events") is a generic term referring to all bodily events for which laboratory equipment is required to observe them. There are two major subclasses of covert processes: (1) Covert behavior, which includes strictly peripheral responses of the skeletal musculature, the smooth musculature, and the glands (measured through electromyography, etc.); and (2) Covert neurophysiological processes, which are strictly neural events, principally in the brain (measured through electroencephalogy, etc.). It is important to keep these classifications separate and clear, since we shall study interrelationships among them. More generally, our purpose is to sample available data within the area of overt responses, covert responses, and covert neurophysiological processes. Our objective shall be to develop an integrating structure for these three classes. By focusing on covert events, we should not only find new lawful relations that facilitate the prediction and control of behavior, but should also advance our understanding of many classical and contemporary problems which have thus far been phrased only in terms of overt responses.

This constitutes a statement of our problem and the general plan of attack. In the next chapter we shall further our perspective by summarizing a number of historical and contemporary positions that have implicated response and brain phenomena in the higher mental processes. In Chapter 3, the psychophysiological nature of covert processes is briefly discussed, a preliminary classification system for them is provided, and a view of their formal status in relation to their data bases is offered. In Chapter 4, an effort is made to understand "why covert processes occur" by specifying their antecedents. There we will undertake a number of relevant topics including how covert processes might be acquired through conditioning.

Chapters 5, 6, 7, and 8 reflect our empirical orientation and the general goal of staying close to the data in this preliminary stage of formulating a science of covert processes. With this orientation we summarize a number of studies in which covert processes were measured during various silent cognitive activities. We critically evaluate those studies, and will note the involvement in cognitive activities of eye responses (Chapter 5), of covert oral behavior (Chapter 6), of nonoral (somatic) responses (Chapter 7), and of electrical measures of brain functioning (Chapter 8).

In Chapter 9 the empirical findings are integrated by means of a circuit model, and an hypothesis about the nature of linguistic codes that might be generated within neuromuscular circuits is offered. These verbal codes, one suspects, are not meaningful in themselves, but do make differences in meaning when they function with critical brain events for lexical-semantic processing.

Finally, we consider practical (technological) aspects of covert processes. In particular, in Chapter 10 we attempt to explicate various higher mental processes, such as hallucinations and dreams. Also included are discussions of the psychophysiological nature of a number of related phenomena such as lie detection, biofeedback, tension control, and speed reading. In the last chapter we attempt to view the future and consider the consequences of a fully developed science of covert processes for various institutions of society. As with any scientific development, the social consequences may be beneficial or detrimental, depending on how members of society employ the knowledge. For example, the benefits of a "thought reading machine" would be enormous for certain purposes such as psychotherapy and courtroom proceedings, but used unscrupulously it could be a repressive tool of government.

Let us now attempt to develop a perspective for our problem by turning to a more detailed consideration of its history.

2

Classical Theories of Thinking

In Chapter 1 we attempted to understand how the problem of mind arose, and we examined the question of mental processes within the framework of science. Though it is common in everyday language, and even in the writings of some philosophers, psychologists, physiologists, and physicians, to use terms in a nonmaterialistic sense we here hold strictly to the view that mind is to be understood by specifying physicalistic (bodily) events. Our strategy is that "mental events" are internal information processing phenomena involving the interaction of neural, muscular, and glandular processes—a circuit conception.

An adequate understanding of the history of a problem like ours is necessary for its solution. The efforts of those who have labored before us can provide the perspective necessary for further progress. Often those historically based insights are negative in the sense that they allow us to recognize blind alleys which need not again be explored, but some are positive too in that they direct us toward new knowledge and advanced understanding. Many of the historical statements about our problem sound amazingly contemporary—such historical formulations have guided us in the selection and interpretation of the kinds of data reported later in empirical chapters (5–8). The general conclusion from those chapters is that critical events occur in the eyes, the somatic skeletal musculature, the speech musculature, and in the brain during the internal information processing that we call "verbal thought." The concentration in this chapter, then, will be on theoretical statements that have implicated various peripheral and central covert processes during thinking. After considering some methodological issues (Chapters 3–4) and establishing our empirical bases (Chapters 5–8), in Chapter 9 we shall attempt to interpret the data and classical theories of thought by relating them to critical neuromuscular events through a linguistic processing model.

Thought as a Mediational Process

Scientists and philosophers have dealt with unobserv*ed* (as opposed to unobserv*able*) mental processes in a wide variety of ways, and have formulated an amazing number of terms for them. Goss (1961) ably analyzed formulations of mental phenomena (consciousness, purpose, thought, ideas, and the like) by the classical associationists, the structuralists, and the early functionalists. He then developed a transition to contemporary analyses in terms of complex behavioral phenomena (defined by verbal and nonverbal mediating response paradigms). Goss' generalized mediational paradigm provides a good framework for considering classical and contemporary theories of the higher mental processes.

The psychophysiological data orientation stressed throughout this book makes it clear that the mediating processes in our model are all hypothetical constructs (in the sense of having some kind of "reality status"; cf. MacCorquodale and Meehl, 1948). Alternative formulations, those that regard mediating processes as intervening variables (convenient fictions which have functional relationships with observable events) are certainly defensible approaches. Though we do not emphasize intervening variable approaches, some are mentioned in this chapter.

We shall note two opposing reasons for hypothesizing mediating processes. The more common one (e.g., Hebb, 1949) follows from a principle of parsimony—most psychologists employ a simple behavioral model (such as a single stage S-R model) as far as the simple model can be advanced to explain behavioral phenomena. There is no need, for example, to hypothesize a complex hypothetical construct like a cell assembly to explain reflexive behavior (Hebb, 1949). It is for complex behavior that cannot be explained by a simple S-R model that the parsimonious theorist is forced to hypothesize logical constructs. For example, the mediating process of a holding mechanism within the brain (called "activated cell assemblies") was hypothesized by Hebb (1949) to account for psychological set.

The alternative approach is principally espoused by Osgood (1953): rather than calling on mediating constructs only in the direst of extremities (such as when single stage S-R principles obviously are inadequate) he believed that there are sufficient general phenomena that require a mediational model to make this more elaborate model the appropriate, "natural" one, from which the simpler behavioral phenomena can be derived as special cases. In short, don't send a boy out to do a man's work! Our model in Chapter 9 follows Osgood in that we attempt to develop theoretical mechanisms that realistically account for the data, in preference to more simplistic interpretations.

A mediating process (X) consists of events that intervene between an established stimulus-response connection. When the mediating process is evoked by the external stimulus (S), the probability of the occurrence of the overt response (R) is increased. We have established that many variables (e.g., number of associations) can increase the strength of the S-X-R connection such that there is an increase in the probability that when S occurs, the evocation of X culminates in the overt response. Goss (1961) stated these characteristics of the mediating process essentially as follows: given that the variables S, X, and R occur in the sequences S-X-R, and S-R, two probabilities can be established for R as a function of these two sequences. If the probability of R is different when R is preceded by S-X than when R is preceded by S alone, then X is a mediating process or event. When applied to psychophysiological or physiological mediators, the probability of the overt response (R) varies depending on whether an X, like Hebb's (1949) cell assembly, occurs. For example, in a set experiment, the mediator (the activation of cell assemblies) must occur before a subject can successfully emit the overt response R to a given stimulus S. Similarly, for Watson the implicit language habit (X) that occurs during thinking is a necessary mediator for the solution (R) of a problem (S).

In surveying scientific theories of thought, we shall concentrate on those that hypothesize various kinds of mediating processes as hypothetical constructs. The first class of theory that we shall consider is that in which mediating processes involve events throughout the entire body. Since these theories emphasize muscular and glandular events, in addition to neural ones, we shall now focus on the response aspect of thought. Following that, we shall consider theories in which the brain function of thought has been emphasized.

Before beginning this survey, the more casual reader may wish to merely skim some of the historical sections that follow, then go directly to contemporary statements later in the chapter.

Response Implicated Theories of Thought

Those theories of thought or consciousness in which behavioral events have played a prominent role have often been referred to as "motor" or "peripheral" theories. While there are a number of variations among these theories, they have in common the notion that the higher mental processes are not merely brain phenomena, but are a function of complete sensori-motor arcs involving brain, efferent pathways, muscle and glandular responses, and afferent pathways back to the brain (see Fig. 1.1). Unfortunately, use of terms like "response," "motor," and "peripheral" to identify this class of theory focuses attention on peripheral systems and, as pointed out in Chapter 1, tends to conjure up an image of a skeletal muscle system that is thinking in the absence of a brain. More appropriate descriptive designations would be "wholistic" or "totalistic" theories in that these positions hold that one thinks with systems throughout the body.[1]

EARLY STATEMENTS

Historical antecedents for response-involved interpretations of thinking are rich, dating back to the writings of the ancient Greeks. Perhaps our earliest available description of inner speech related to mental processes was in the fifth century B.C. when Socrates (in Plato's *Theatetus*) described thinking as "discourse when the mind is talking to itself" and judgment as "a statement silently pronounced." Parmenides explicitly identified thought with generalized motor responding when he said "that which thinks is the limbs" and that the highest degree of bodily organization gives the highest degree of thought (from Langfeld, 1933). Because of their observations that pulse and heart activity changed during emotional states, many of the Greeks believed that the heart performed cognitive functions, e.g., "the mind . . . is located in the central region of the breast . . ." (Lucretius, 1965, p. 88). Aristotle held that *pneuma* (ani-

---

[1] I am indebted to William Barry for suggesting this inadequacy of the traditional use of peripheral terms and for the suggestion that "wholistic theory" would be more appropriate. "Neuromuscular circuit model" is the most descriptive term I've been able to come up with (Chapter 9). "Totalistic" was abandoned because it too much resembled a contemporary breakfast food.

mal spirits) transmit impressions of external objects to the mind. The senses, he thought, had a common meeting place in the heart whereby the movements of the *pneuma* were unified. Faint imaginations and memories occur as a result of traces of those sense impressions.

Descartes (1650) emphasized the importance of motor responding for producing the meaning of words: "the habit we have acquired in learning to talk has made us join the action of the mind—which, through the medium of the gland, can move the tongue and lips—with the meaning of the words that follow these motions rather than with the motions themselves" (cited by Herrnstein and Boring, 1965, p. 210).

In 1748, the mechanist La Mettrie (1912) implicated the response in thought when he said that the brain has its muscles for thinking as the legs have muscles for walking—the faculties of the mind are nothing more than the proper organization of the brain and of the whole body. Erasmus Darwin (1794) held that ideas belong to the muscular system. Sir Charles Bell (1842), in his classic experimentation that led to the Bell-Magendie Law, concluded that stimulation of the sensory nerve was not sufficient for a perceptual experience. Rather, Bell found that the total afferent-efferent system is involved in perception so that the response component is necessary for mental activity. This emphasis on the total sensory-central motor systems in perception is a clear forerunner of the central-peripheral circuit model espoused by the early behaviorists (see Fig. 1.1).

BAIN AND THE BASIS OF CONTEMPORARY NEUROMUSCULAR MODELS

We cannot overemphasize the foresight and the far-reaching insights that Alexander Bain had into the nature of mind. With particular reference to thought and language, Bain (see especially 1855) advanced the specific position that thinking is restrained speaking or acting. He explicitly noted that the speech musculature was active during silent reading and, with regard to memory, suggested that suppressed articulation is the material of recollection; he stated that during recall of a word or sentence, if we do not speak (overtly) we feel the twitter of our vocal organs. With regard to volition, Bain (1859) advanced the idea that the striated muscles are instruments of the will and only through them can volition affect other mental and bodily processes. Incipient movements, he held, are necessary to bring an idea into consciousness, for we cannot directly will the appearance of sensations and ideas. Bain's (1855) statement well expresses his wholistic view of mind:

> The organ of mind is not the brain by itself; it is the brain, nerves, muscles, and organs of sense. . . . It is, . . . an entire misconception to talk of a *sensorium* within the brain, a *sanctum sanctorum,* or inner chamber, where impressions are poured in and stored up to be reproduced in a future day. There is no such chamber, no such mode of reception. . . . We must thus discard forever the notion of the *sensorium commune,* the cerebral close, as a central seat of mind, or

receptacle of sensation and imagery. . . . Our present insight enables us to say with great . . . probability, no [nerve-] currents, no mind. The transmission of influence along the nerve fibres from place to place, seems the very essence of cerebral action. This transmission, moreover, must not be confined within the limits of the brain: . . . it is doubtful if even thought, reminiscence, or the emotions of the past and absent, could be sustained without the more distant communications between the brain and the rest of the body—the organs of sense and of movement (cited by Holt, 1937, pp. 38-39).

SECHENOV'S FOUNDATION FOR RUSSIAN REFLEXOLOGY[2]

I. M. Sechenov was influenced by Helmholtz, with whom he worked in Germany, and became the first major Russian scientist to relate muscular and mental activity. (See his widely read "Reflexes of the Brain," 1863.) Sechenov's materialism advocated the objective study of mental activity as reflexes by answering his famous question as to who should develop psychology and how with the answer: "Physiologists, by studying reflexes." Sechenov (1866, 1878) expanded on the reflex character of mental actions by asserting that they involve the highest nervous centers and terminate in one type of event—muscle movement: "All the endless diversity of the external manifestations of the activity of the brain can be finally regarded as one phenomenon—that of muscular movement. . . . Therefore, *all the external manifestations of brain activity can be attributed to muscular movement*" (cited in Herrnstein and Boring, 1965, p. 309). Sechenov presaged contemporary psychophysiology when he said that ". . . the time must come when people will be able to analyze the external manifestations of the activity of the brain just as easily as the physicist now analyzes a musical chord or the phenomena presented by a falling body" (cited by Herrnstein and Boring, 1965, p. 310).

Sechenov developed a circuit model that consisted of a sensory component, a motor component, and a "nervous regulator" in the middle. The nervous regulator was a mechanism which coordinates the activity of the working organs—a conception that anticipated the contemporary concept of feedback. Kinesthesis and sensory feedback arising from covert verbalization was emphasized by Sechenov (1863) as being particularly important for language and thought when he said: "It seems to me even that I never think in words, but always in those muscular sensations which accompany my thought when it is spoken" (Sechenov, 1935, p. 312). He further stated, "At least I know that in my own case while my mouth is closed and motionless my thoughts are often accompanied by internal speech, i.e. by movements of the tongue and oral cavity. In every case when I wish to give priority to one thought over others I invariably express it in a whisper" (cited by Novikova, 1955, p. 210). It was Novikova's assessment that "Sechenov's great achievement consisted in producing the idea of the direct relation between thought and the speech reflexes" (Novikova, 1955, p. 210).

[2] My great appreciation to Boris Segal for providing me with some of the information on Russian scientists discussed in this section.

As we move into the twentieth century we shall briefly mention other theorists who also linked thought to subvocal movement. Ribot (1879) held that each visual perception during silent reading is accompanied by suppressed articulation (cited by Thorson, 1925). On the subject of motor images, Ribot held that all perceptions contain movements of the eyes and limbs, indicating that since movement is an essential factor in seeing an object, it must be an equally essential factor when we see the same object in our imagination. He wrote that "a thought is a word or an act in a nascent state—a commencement of muscular activity" (cited by Dashiell, 1928, p. 538).

It is most impressive that Stricker (1880) conducted a systematic study employing a large number of subjects at a time when such extensive empirical investigation was indeed unusual. As stated by Humphrey (1951), Stricker found that 99 of 100 subjects introspectively reported subvocal speech during thought, and that 58 of 60 other subjects reported speech-like movements during silent reading. His observation that thinking of a tone was accompanied by laryngeal movements indicated to Stricker that pitch perception was produced by laryngeal muscle activity. His general conclusion was that ideas of words are motor ideas in that they consist of conscious awareness of activity in motor nerves and the articulatory muscles.

A variety of other thinkers also implicated kinesthesis in consciousness and similar semantic processes. Egger (1881) reported that he subvocalized during silent reading and during thinking, and Ballet (1886) reported that he inaudibly heard during silent reading (as cited by Pintner, 1913).

Maudsley (1883) held that the contraction of muscles with resultant receptor excitation allows the kinesthetic sense to control central processes. It is interesting that this early speculation received later empirical verification in electroencephalographic research (e.g., Knott, 1939).

Ferrier (1886) developed a theory of attention in which the muscular activity that governs eye movement is essential. (Ferrier's work influenced Wundt, which may in turn have led to Titchener's implication of the muscle system for the development of meaning). Elsewhere Ferrier (1876) held that people call up ideas into their minds by activating motor processes—one's awareness of a sensation or thought is possible only when it succeeds in discharging motor centers.

Külpe (1895) stated that bodily "movements are everywhere important. It is perhaps not too much to say that voluntary recollection never takes place without their assistance" (cited by Jacobson, 1938a, p. 165).

EARLY TWENTIETH-CENTURY THEORIZING

In his famous *Lectures on the Experimental Psychology of the Thought-Processes,* Titchener (1909) suggested that for certain minds all nonverbal conscious meaning is carried by kinesthetic sensations or images. At first, words are motor attitudes, gestures within kinesthetic contexts, so that conscious meaning can be carried by the total kinesthetic attitude. He further suggested that feeling states result from different pressures in the muscle systems throughout the body that could be recorded by instruments and made into objective records (as in our Chapter 11). Titchener suggested that an imagined act is very precisely localized; hence while the original nodding of the head would be rather crude, an imagined nod of the head would be more precise in that excess auxilliary movements during the original overt response would be eliminated.

In developing further his context theory of meaning Titchener (1910) held that when an organism originally faces some situation with a given bodily attitude, the characteristic sensations which that bodily attitude aroused give meaning to the process which is at our conscious focus. Pointing out that we are locomotor organisms and that we are constantly changing our bodily attitudes, T maintained that kinesthetic patterns become engrained in our consciousness. Kinesthetic contexts thus make words contextual so that when we read, the auditory-kinesthetic idea is the meaning of these visual symbols. T held that at least two sensations are necessary to make a meaning. If an animal has only a sensation of light, there is no meaning in its consciousness. But if the sensation of light is accompanied by a strain, the animal perceives light with meaning. The light now becomes "that bright something" due to the strain-context.

As Herrnstein and Boring (1965) point out, T's context theory of meaning anticipated the behavioral theory of meaning, though obviously he would not wish to be classified as a behaviorist (nor would he have been welcomed). In view of their great differences otherwise, it is interesting to note that T shared these notions with Watson (even of a muscle-thought reading machine as in Chapter 11).

The behaviorist Langfeld (1931) espoused a response interpretation of consciousness holding that while a strict S-R behaviorism has no interest in the phenomenon, the phenomenon cannot be neglected. As he cited Smith and Guthrie: "A behavioristic description of man's mind in no way contradicts the common sense assumption that men are conscious. We shall first find out what man *does*, and under what circumstances he does it, because this is open to observation and may be stated exactly. An understanding of behavior is essential to an understanding of consciousness" (in Langfeld, 1931, p. 89.) Langfeld's was an identity theory of the relation of consciousness to physiological processes holding that the two are one and the same. Hence, a change in either afferent or efferent discharges may reproduce a change in conscious content. Furthermore: "Thinking is a great time saver. For the response psychologist, thinking is in all essentials exactly the same as the overt behavior of the individual, condensed into more economical responses" (Langfeld, 1931, p. 106).

In the wake of the behaviorist revolution, Washburn (1916) advanced the doctrine that all mental life is correlated with and dependent upon bodily movement. In elaborating the concept that consciousness is related to movement, she emphasized the role of the covert response:

The kind of consciousness which we call an "image" or "centrally excited sensation," such as a remembered or imagined sensation depends on the simultaneous excitement and inhibition of a motor pathway. The "association of ideas" depends on the fact that when the full motor response to a stimulus is prevented from occurring, a weakened type of response may take place which we call "tentative movement." These movements are actual slight contractions of the muscles which the larger movements would involve (p. 26).

Washburn was explicit: During memorization, articulatory muscles contract; during visual imagery, ocular muscles contract; during kinesthetic imagery, peripherally excited movement sensations result from the slight actual performance of movement. And when mental activity is more complex, numerous different implicit motor responses occur. Finally, the degree to which the motor response is made determines the extent to which mental acts are conscious.

Washburn (perhaps influenced by Dunlap [e.g., 1927]) also considered the possibility of "short circuiting" or "recession" of the response into the central nervous system. She thought that consciousness always initially depends on movement, but after sufficient usage, direct connections might be established in the motor regions of the brain so that the excitation of one could immediately excite the other without the intervention of kinesthestic processes.

Washburn (1916) emphasized the chaining nature of language. During habit formation, movement systems are learned such that one movement provides the stimulus (or part of the stimulus) for another movement. Speech was considered to be a succession of vocal acts in which the kinesthetic impulses from each movement served as unique stimuli for the next in the series. Washburn (1914) also applied chaining to the association of ideas, which occurs when there are associations of movements in which the movements are tentative (incipient) motor processes. Such incipient movements are more economical than full movements because they can be performed far more rapidly and they save energy by producing less fatigue. In short, all associations during consciousness have as their basis association of movements, especially incipient ones. While Washburn (1936) followed rather directly in the behaviorist tradition, she did take issue with the behavioristic principle of strict mechanism. Washburn pointed out that Watson's views followed those of Loeb and Bethe, who held that physical-chemical processes, rather than states of consciousness, are the proper objects of investigation for the psychologist. The mechanist holds that there is no essential difference between living and nonliving things, so that the behavior of living things can be understood in principle as series of chemical reactions. Washburn agreed that so far as animal *behavior* is concerned it is perfectly possible to be a mechanist. However, she thought that the behavior of animals is also accompanied by conscious mental states and psychologists should study animal consciousness too.

Among those who were greatly influenced by Sechenov's ideas (discussed earlier) were especially the eminent Russian psychophysiologists

I. P. Pavlov and V. M. Bechterev. Pavlov held that the "basic component of thought . . . [consists of] . . . kinesthetic impulses [which] pass from the speech apparatus into the cerebral cortex" (in Novikova, 1955, p. 210). Furthermore, "Pavlov . . . pointed out that one had only to think about hand movements for such movements to be initiated and that it was possible to record them by means of appropriate apparatus" (Bassin and Bein, 1961, p. 196).

The contributions of Pavlov are more widely cited in Western countries than are the works of Bechterev, though the latter was also extremely important in developing objective approaches to mental processes. Bechterev (ca. 1903–1905), elaborating on Sechenov's general approach, formulated the notion of the "sochetatelniy" reflex, a concept very similar to Pavlov's "conditional" reflex and based mainly on motorics (motor activity). Bechterev spoke not only about muscle movement, which he regarded as a final product of the highest spheres of human personality, but also about cardiovascular and somatic events in general, about secretoric (that is, hormonal) events, and even about galvanic events on the skin surface, which he thought of as the outer representation of brain reflexes.

Bechterev named his objective approach to mental activity, in turn, "physiological psychology," "objective psychology," "reflexogical psychology," and finally (1923) "reflexology" eliminating the word "psychology." Reflexology was quite similar to Watson's (e.g., 1930) behaviorism although Bechterev's training as a neurologist led him to place greater emphasis on neurophysiological data.

Ideomotor Studies. While William James (1890) was a dualist (as in his ideo-motor theory of consciousness and in the James-Lange Theory of Emotions), his general thesis was that every state of mind is motor in its consequence, i.e., every representation of a movement awakens the actual movement which originally occurred. James recognized the minuteness of the (covert) responses necessarily associated with consciousness when he said that they are perhaps no more than the accomodation of sense organs so that we are typically unconscious of them. He offered an example of his ideo-motor action theory by suggesting that if one thinks of bending fingers, there is automatically a tendency to bend them. If one simultaneously thinks of *not* bending the fingers, then the two opposing thoughts result in a conflict evidenced by the thinker's experience of a tingle in the finger. James held that the feeling of self, when carefully examined, consists mainly of the collection of peculiar motions in the head or between the head and throat. The entire feeling of what people call "spiritual activity" is really a feeling of bodily activities whose exact nature is "by most men overlooked."

In spite of the dualism of James (and others), the motor aspect of the ideo-motor theories perhaps justified their early existence in that they focused attention on incipient, small-scale responses. Münsterberg (1899) in his motor (action) theory of consciousness held that both affer-

ent and efferent innervations were continuous and that the motor discharge is necessary for perception and consciousness to occur. Münsterberg's student, Breese (1899), viewed speech perception as follows:

> The muscles of the vocal cords, throat, and respiratory organs are slightly
> innervated and adjusted, but the process goes no further. Sometimes, however,
> the enunciation is complete so far as the adjustment of the muscles of the vocal
> cords, throat and mouth cavities is concerned. There is a tendency to make these
> adjustments not only when we hear spoken words, but to make them in response
> to other stimuli. We are likely to utter the name of any object upon which the
> attention rests. . . . If, for any reason, the motor apparatus does not respond
> properly, there is an interruption in the conscious stream (p. 49).

Physicalistic Critiques of Idealism and Ideomotor Theories.   While
their implication of incipient responses during higher mental processes
was a positive contribution, ideomotor theories espoused nonmaterial
conceptions of mind. Thorndike (1913) was careful to avoid the accusa-
tion of dualism, in part perhaps because some had criticized his laws of
learning as containing "mentalistic" or "subjective" terms like "satisfying" and "annoying" states of affairs. Though such terms may evoke
subjective connotations, Thorndike defined them objectively, there
being little difference between *his* definitions and contemporary definitions of "reinforcement" and "punishment." In fact, Thorndike attacked
the ideo-motor theories of James, Wundt, McDougall, Washburn, etc.,
and quite colorfully:

> In the present case it teaches us that our belief that an idea tends to produce
> the act which it is like, or represents, or "it is an idea of" or "has as its object," is
> kith and kin with our forebears' belief that dressing to look like a bear will give
> you his strength or that burning an effigy of the foe will make him die, and with
> the modern charlatan's belief that thinking one could walk will mend a broken
> bone. It is kith and kin with them, own grandchild of one and own brother to the
> other—and as false as either. An image, idea or any other mental fact has, apart
> from connections made by heredity, use and satisfying results, no stronger ten-
> dency to produce the movement which it resembles, or represents, or has as its
> object than to produce any other movement whatsoever—no stronger tendency
> to produce it than ideas of dollars and earthquakes have to produce them. Why
> should it? Why should the likeness between John Smith's mental image and an
> event in nature have any greater potency when that event is in the muscles of
> John Smith than when it is in the sky above or the earth beneath him? Why
> should McDougall's "mysterious connection" be allowed to "obtain" just here and
> not elsewhere? It obtains nowhere . . . (1913, p. 105).

Thorndike's attack on the ideo-motor theory is similar to the powerful
criticism by Keller and Schoenfeld (1950) that ideo-motor conceptions
are viciously circular. They point out that a common, fundamental assumption about us and our language is that we have "ideas" which we
then express in language. Why do we express linguistic behavior? Because we have certain antecedent ideas. How do we know that we have

those ideas? Answer: Because of our linguistic behavior. Keller and Schoenfeld assert that such "antecedent ideas" cannot be proved or disproved, and that such a dualism has been a stumbling block for theories of both language and behavior.

Jackson similarly disavowed an ideo-motor theory:

> To say that a man staggers or lies motionless *because* he has lost consciousness . . . is like saying that a man does not speak *because* he has lost the memory of words, which, at the best, is only repeating in technical terms that he does not speak; it is like saying that a man does not move his arm *because* he has lost volition, which is only repeating in technical terms that he does not move it. Nobody is any the wiser for these "explanations"; they explain nothing at all; they are attempts to explain physical states by mental states . . ." (1931-32, p. 159).

In his attack on idealism, Holt stated:

> That all subjective idealists far surpass any materialist in learning, sophistication and general mental acumen, is freely conceded by all subjective idealists. As shown by their printed remarks, they conceive materialists to be a species of filthy Yahoos who eagerly lick up crumbs from the none too festive boards of La Mettrie, Holbach, and Büchner. Since, however, subjectivists, so far as I can discover, limit their own reading to the Sacred Texts (Berkeley, Kant, Hegel, Bradley, etc.), the Proceedings of the Aristotelian Society, and a few stray tracts on deity, prehension among the monads, and holism, they run the risk of not knowing exactly what the materialists have been doing. For materialism since Valhinger, since Freud, since Mauthner, and since the late M. Émile Meyerson is not precisely what it once was . . . Compared with the maledictions of Bishop Berkeley, the following words of the late Fritz Mauthner sound like commendation: ". . . since Kant, materialism can no longer be taken seriously . . . one might call materialism the dunce's philosophy" (Holt, 1937, p. 52).

Certainly a colorful assessment of the idealism-materialism controversy.

EARLY TWENTIETH-CENTURY THEORIZING CONTINUED

McDougall (1902), in his peripheral motor theory, made kinesthesis, among all the sensations, carry the burden of consciousness. Souriau (1907) identified the emotions with responses, asserting for example, that the drop of the mouth is itself sadness. Müller-Freienfels (1912) stated that mental processes are motor processes which are not merely accompanying phenomena, but the essence of all mental activity.

Chronologically, we should now consider Dunlap's motor theory and Watson's theory of thinking, but because of the great importance of these works they will be treated in some detail at the end of this section. Also, Jacobson, who started his lengthy series of studies on mental processes as a student at Harvard about 1908, is especially important for this discussion. His work is extensively discussed in various parts of the book, particularly Chapters 6 and 7.

Thorndike (1898, 1913), in defining the critical terms of his Connectionism, stated that by "impulse" he meant the consciousness that accompanies a muscular innervation. This event is different from the feeling of the act which comes from seeing onself move, or from feeling one's body in a different position. "Impulse" is thus the direct feeling of the doing and is that which becomes associated.

The Hungarian psychologist, Jeno Posch (1915), identified all mental activity with responses, and he vigorously attacked the centralist position by criticizing the notion that mental qualities reside in the brain.[3] Posch held that the higher mental processes were to be explained in terms of verbal and postular responses, muscular tonus and innervation. For him, images are movements, implying especially movements of the eyes. Further emphasis was placed on efferent activity when Posch held that the motor system provides unity for the nervous system since even activity of the sensory nerves results in action. Posch acknowledged his indebtedness to the objective psychology of Spencer and to the motor aspects of the theories of Ribot. Following Spencer, Posch worked out a detailed theory of volition.

Meanwhile, behavioral conceptions of mental processes were gaining ground in American psychology. Kantor (1921) held that concepts originate as perceptual responses, then develop as abstractions from the original contact with the stimulating objects. Weiss (1922) held that the categories of memory, thinking, perception, imagination, etc. are behavioral categories rather than phenomena of the central nervous system. To have the motor pattern is to have the image. According to Weiss the brain is simply a coordinating center for the integration of sensory and motor points so that they act in a harmonious fashion (thus anticipating Sperry, 1952).

Melchior Palágyi (1924) stated that mental content becomes conscious if and only if the physiological process which creates the mental content also activates the speech mechanism—the verbal report that one pronounces prior to a mental state brings about the consciousness.

Carr's (1925) principle of organic behavior states that all sensory stimuli evoke some kind of response. In some cases, such as a change in electrical resistance in the skin or a change of pulse rate, the responses may be so slight that they are detectible only with sensitive recording apparatus.

Dashiell (1925, 1926, 1928), a typical behaviorist, held that the response is critical for thought, that there is a gradual shift from overt speech and gesture to covert abbreviated vocal and manual acts, and that speech, though reduced in intensity to an implicit degree, is still speech. When one thinks, for instance, the operation is a true motor reaction to a situation, not a non-physical and mysterious something. Thinking may be truly objectively observable in some by the tilt of the head, a wrinkle

---

[3] I am indebted to Czabeh Pleh for summarizing and translating this information about Posch.

of nose, a change of breathing, or a twitch of finger. The skillful mind-reader, Dashiell said, is really a muscle-reader.

The staunch behaviorist, Holt (1937), held that when psychologists describe objective action, they are describing consciousness. Experiences of awareness stimulate the speech mechanism, though the action is so slight that one can scarcely know that it has occurred. To study mind and to determine whether an idea has occurred, one should not employ introspection, but should study living tissues with apparatus to ascertain what muscular contractions and what interplay of neuro-motor tensions have taken place. Holt recognized that: "This is a formidable pro-gramme. But it is by no means hopeless. . . . It proceeds, and in my opin-ion successfully, to define mind in terms of matter; or, more specifically, in terms of nerves and muscles" (Holt, 1937, pp. 50-51).

MID-CENTURY STATEMENTS

Briefly, several more recent theorists who implicated responses in thought processes were Humphrey (1951) and Humphrey and Coxon (1963) who contended that muscular tension serves its own special func-tion and is present in much if not all thinking. Bruner, Olver, and Greenfield (e.g., 1966) recognized that motor behavior is essential in the development of perception and thought—in the earliest stage of cogni-tive growth ("the enactive stage") the child knows and reacts to the world with habitual action patterns which are intimately tied to concrete objects and events. Past events are then represented through appropriate motor responding so that bicycle riding or tying knots become represented in our muscles. In later stages of cognitive development, language becomes the principle mode of coping with the world, but enactive modes are still retained. Bruner's theory of cognitive development is similar to Piaget's insofar as motor aspects of children's thoughts are central to early intel-lectual processes (see Piaget and Inhelder, 1971).

Albeit from a completely different point of view, Guilford (1967) put forth some interesting notions concerning motor systems. In his model of the structure of the intellect, Guilford held that information is re-tained in memory in the same form as it was originally committed to storage. Consequently, to the extent that concrete action involved motor components, the memory encoding of them would involve motor com-ponents which would then function in later decoding.

EMERGING MATERIALISM IN RUSSIAN PSYCHOLOGY

Previously we noted that Sechenov had laid the basis for contempo-rary Russian reflexology, in that his line of thought was vigorously de-veloped by both Pavlov and Bechterev in the early part of this century. In Russia following 1917 there was increased vigor of materialistic ap-proaches in psychology as well as in other academic fields—a *zeitgeist* which resulted in widespread acceptance of the principles of Pavlov, Bechterev, and those of behaviorism. For instance, K. N. Kornilov in

1921 made what at the time was a radical declaration that psychology is the science of behavior. Kornilov proposed the concept of "reaction" as an element of behavior, a concept somewhat wider than "reflex" in the usual meaning of the word. The importance of the concept of reaction for psychology in the Soviet Union was that it was the first strictly materialistic concept proposed by a psychologist.

Vigotsky was especially influenced by Bechterev's reflexology, Kornilov's reactology, and Pavlov's concepts of conditioning. Later he elaborated his own doctrine which in turn influenced succeeding Russian psychologists. In accounting for mental functions (memory, attention, perception, thinking, etc.) Vigotsky (1934, 1956) developed a cultural-historical theory of psychological development in which higher psychic functions appear first in society and then develop in the individual through the process of internalization. Language is a social phenomenon which becomes internalized into inner speech. However, thought and speech develop independently up to about three years of age, after which thought begins to occur through verbal speech.

A. N. Leontiev (1959) accounted for mental life by elaborating the ideas of Vigotsky. His most important concept was the motor phenomenon "activity" which occurs when the organism responds to objects in attempts to find those that are appropriate for the satisfaction of needs.

For P. Ya. Galperin (1969), who also followed Vigotsky, the psyche was conceived as a special apparatus in which images play an important part. The function of the psyche is to regulate action (behavior) to the external environment. Psychical activity (dyeatel'nost') results when overt actions are transferred into plans (plans include images, perceptions, etc.). There are several stages of this transfer process, but at each stage there is new reflection and reproduction of an overt action. Firstly, there are overt behavioral actions to objects, then overt speech in the interaction with objects, but there are no overt manipulatory actions. Finally, there is "mental action" with the environment wherein there is no overt behavior (including no overt speech).

The concept of feedback appeared in the mid-thirties in the Soviet Union, particularly through the developments of P. K. Anokhin (one of the last and most prominent of Pavlov's students), and N. A. Bernstein. Both considered their concepts to be natural developments from Pavlov's principles. Bernstein (1966) showed that the regulation of locomotion cannot occur with only two components of a reflex arc. Instead, there has to be a third, final element in which sensory information can be corrected by means of a feedback system. Anokhin's (1969) application of feedback was principally within the neurophysiology of the conditional reflex.

The relationships between motor and verbal development in early stages of life were studied by Koltsova (1958). By psychophysiological research, Koltsova concluded that manipulatory development facilitates verbal development. Luria (1961) and Luria and Polyakova (1959) suggested that the reverse also occurs, viz., that during speech development, verbal responding facilitates motor performance.

More recently, A. N. Sokolov (1967, 1969, 1971, 1972), in his study of the relationship between thought and speech, has followed Russian tradition and emphasized inner soundless speech, which is said to be an internalization of external speech. His principal measure of inner speech has been speech muscle EMG, though he has also taken a variety of other psychophysiological measures. Sokolov's general conclusion is that covert speech muscle activity occurs in all subjects during thought and is ". . . the principal mechanism of thought" (1972, pp. 263-64). To interpret the function of speech muscle activity, Sokolov followed Pavlov in believing that speech proprioception is the basal component of the second signal system. Afferent impulses generated by covert speech reactions relate the first (visual, nonverbal) and the second (verbal) signal systems. Like Pavlov, Sokolov embraced a principle of dynamic functional localization in which there are two-way neural connections among all the speech zones of the brain. The cortical speech areas are excited by afferent impulses, following which speech impulses are transmitted along the efferent speech-motor pathways to the speech musculature which may result in "covert, soundless articulation ('inner speech')" (Sokolov, 1967, p. 6). Covert articulation then generates currents of reverse, proprioceptive afferentation. This proprioceptive (reverse) afferentation from the speech organs is a mechanism of the formation of the verbal code that enters all cerebral speech structures, and regulates cognitive activity. With this emphasis on the importance of the covert oral response, he concluded from electromyographic research that in "the process of mental activity . . . there is a gradual strengthening of muscle tonus—not only in the speech musculature, but elsewhere as well (for example, in the musculature of the forehead, arms, and hand) . . . [with] . . . 'bursts' or 'volleys' of speech motor discharge separated by considerable intervals . . ." (p. 8). Hence the electromyogram reveals a tonic component that

can be looked upon as a relatively generalized "tuning" of the speech mechanisms, while the phasic component is more probably linked with "specific" (local) speech activity (soundless word articulation). . . . In one degree or another all of these forms of electrical activity of the speech musculature are represented in all forms of mental activity . . . [though] . . . in reasoned thought bursts and volleys of electrical activity are more frequently observed . . . (Sokolov, 1967, pp. 8–9).

Such phasic components, also observed in our laboratory, form the basis of our psychophysiologically generated linguistic coding (Chapter 9).

THOUGHTS ABOUT MOTOR ACTIVITY BY "CENTRALISTS"

In concluding this general section of brief summaries about the relevance of muscular responding, it may provide perspective to note that those theorists who concentrate on brain action still implicate muscular phenomena. Even Lashley (1930), who held that peripheral activities are not essential for the maintenance of central events, stated that "... there are continuously maintained central processes which, if they become intense, may irradiate to motor centers and produce expressive movements, implicit speech, and the like" (p. 12). Lashley even attempted to build a thought reading machine which employed the strategy of monitoring tongue movements (see pp. 443–51 in Chapter 11).

Sperry, who concentrated his work on the brain, has held that the primary function of the brain was to regulate behavior. As he put it, "phylogenetic considerations indicate that the vertebrate brain *was designed* primitively for the regulation of overt behavior rather than for mental performance. As one descends the vertebrate scale, purely mental activity becomes increasingly insignificant compared with overt response" (1952, p. 297). In his important book, Malmo (1975) elaborated on Sperry's principles as follows:

> From an objective, analytical standpoint, Sperry (1952) has stated that it is readily apparent that the sole product of brain function is muscular coordination. Of course he includes neurohumoral and glandular components under motor functions, but he assigns them a relatively minor role in his discussion of the mind-brain problem. Putting the matter in another way, Sperry stated that from his studies of the brain, he believes that the entire output of our thinking mechanism goes into the motor system ... (p. 51). It is especially significant that Sperry singled out *thought* in placing stress on the unique importance of the motor system; because in eliminating outmoded concepts of thought based on oversimplified motor theories, psychology has apparently gone too far in the opposite direction, so that now the importance of the motor system is in danger of being understated ... when sensitive electromyography has been used, muscular activity has almost invariably been recorded during thinking.... Electromyography in these instances shows that the motor system is involved in the "silent acts," because the EMGs reflect what is going on upstream in the brain. On the basis of the available evidence it would be premature to say that the feedforward and feedback loops involving, say, the speech muscles, are completely useless (p. 52).

As a final illustration, there is Hebb who equated mind with brain. He established that feedback from muscular responding is necessary for directing the ongoing flow of cell assemblies and stated in 1968 that eye movement is essential in image formation. His theory is discussed extensively in a later section of this chapter.

To conclude this review of the long history of response-involved theories of thought we may observe that the common view that small scale covert responses are involved in some way in mental activity has made strange historical bedfellows indeed—the structuralist Titchener, the functionalists Carr and James, the early behaviorists, and even the centralist Hebb. We shall now consider in greater detail two of the more important theories developed in the early part of this century. That of Knight Dunlap (perhaps the earliest proponent of a behaviorist's type of motor theory of thought) will be considered first, followed by that of Watson. For some general reviews of research relevant to response-involved theories of thought the reader is referred to Clark (1922), Goss (1961), Langfeld (1933), Locke (1970), Max (1934), M. O. Smith (1969).

DUNLAP'S MOTOR THEORY

Dunlap (1912) pointed out that in his time the conventional theory of mental processes held that centrally aroused sensations occurred in the same modality as the original stimulating sensation. In place of the centralist theory, Dunlap put forward "the modern motor theory" in which the motor apparatus is activated during the higher mental processes— when one thinks of a visual object there are movements of accomodation and convergence of the eyes, just as when thinking of sounds there are changes in tension of the tympanum muscles of the ear, or in the neck muscles. When thinking of an object not present there is a faint eye-muscle adjustment as though you were seeing the object. Such conditional reflex muscular responses tense the eyeball, and hence influence the retina, to start faint retinal activity that send optical sensory impulses toward the brain.

For Dunlap, thought and perception involve the total reaction-arc, based on principles of habit formation. No consciousness occurs without the complete reaction. Dunlap (1922) illustrated this concept by means of Fig. 2.1 in terms of learning of a series of nonsense syllables. As he put

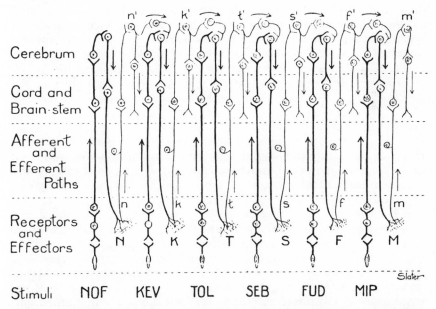

FIG. 2.1 "Scheme of the pathways involved in the learning of a series of nonsense syllables. Assuming the previous development of the reactions perceptual NOF-N, KEV-K, TOL-T, SEB-S, FUD-F, and MIP-M, represented by the heavy lines, the lighter lines indicate the pathways formed from action to action, which eventually enable the successive actions to occur without the primary stimuli" (from Dunlap, 1922, p. 305).

it, "in order that the series of thought reactions may be brought about, after it has been 'learned,' it is necessary to set going the first reaction of the series. This might be done by presenting the first stimulus word again: but ordinarily, after the reactor has 'learned' the series, he demonstrates the fact by reciting it without even this aid" (1922, p. 305).

Dunlap (1922), emphasizing the complexity of muscular activities, pointed out that the vocal muscles are capable of forming hundreds of thousands of definite and distinguishable patterns during the enunciation of words. The multitudes of muscle spindles in which receptors terminate may give rise to numerous internal stimulus patterns so that in the striped muscles are exactly the mechanisms demanded by the known facts of thought processes. Consequently, the conclusion was inescapable that the muscle receptors are receptors for thought reactions.

Dunlap believed that, after a response is well learned and becomes automatized, a short-circuiting mechanism may be interposed. This mechanism then may obviate the necessity for the second reaction in an associated series to await the completion of the first for its initiation. Consequently, while in original learning the complete muscular response is necessary, the overt response is later reduced in size (becomes covert) in the interest of economy. Eventually, the response event may "recede" into the cerebellum, where a physiological mechanism short-circuits the muscular event. Such a short-circuiting mechanism would then have a "point for point" correspondence with the muscular system so that any muscular pattern could then be reproduced within the short-circuiting system. This entire process is an early development of a commonly held "internalization process" (cf. Chapter 4, pp. 111–14).

While Dunlap concentrated upon verbal thought involving the speech musculature, he recognized that there is nonspeech thought too. His notion that "nonverbal" (nonspeech) thought processes involve the nonoral musculature predates Watson (1930) and Max (1937). His notion was that language is not highly developed among children or many primitive peoples, and that even among others such gestures as movements of the hands and shoulders are employed in thinking and communicating thought. Deaf individuals think in words through finger and hand movements and in many cases, he noted, these movements may be observed when the individual is merely "thinking."

It has been said that the early behaviorists "resented the central nervous system." In their efforts not to neglect response activities, some do seem to have been overly zealous, though Dunlap respected the critical functions of the cerebrum. Cerebral cells were important for conscious reactions, he thought, because of their integrative control (or dominance) over the whole organism, believed to be possible because of the multiplicity of the interconnections between them. As he pointed out, afferent impulses that enter the spinal cord or brain stem are reflected back to the effectors without ascending to the hemispheres—such low level reflexes have a limited range of efferent distribution so that the immediate effects upon the organism are necessarily localized. However, afferent currents that ascend to the cerebrum can be reflected to any part of the body. This is because the synaptic connections of the cerebral cells are so complicated that a circuit is possible from any receiving cell in the cerebrum to any of the cells which discharge into the brain stem or spinal cord. Furthermore, Dunlap pointed out that connections may be established in the brain between any afferent/efferent discharges so that any afferent volley that reaches the cerebrum may have a motor effect on (practically) the entire organism. This is an especially important point in principal, for it suggests the need for sampling from many bodily locations in the laboratory study of thought (cf. Chapter 5).

Dunlap emphasized that the superior integrative control exercised through the cerebrum is due to the *arrangement* of neurons, not to their qualitative characteristics. Consciousness, therefore, does not result from the activation of specific nerve cells but is dependent upon the cooperation of large groups of cells, including muscle and gland cells as well as peripheral and central neurons. As to the necessity of the musculature and of glandular activity for consciousness, Dunlap held that the effect of complete elimination of activity of muscle and gland cells on consciousness is "a topic for further investigation" (see "The Curare Strategy" in Chapter 4).

WATSON'S THEORY OF THINKING

John Broadus Watson, destined to become behaviorism's most vigorous spokesman, was nurtured at Chicago with the Functionalists. His doctoral dissertation on maze learning by the white rat was the subject of some frustration due to his efforts to apply the Functionalist's formula for making inferences about consciousness through observation of consequent behavior. He was thus predisposed to take up the behaviorist cause, and all that was needed was for the young psychologist to move to Johns Hopkins University where he came under Knight Dunlap's influence. Dunlap (1932) stated that:

On Stratton's going, the worst I feared did not happen. Instead, Watson was brought from Chicago, and brought into the Department a spirit of energy. As a laboratory director, as well as in our personal relations, Watson was admirable. There was never any hampering of my activities, or any dictation. I only hope that Watson did not find my presence in the laboratory less pleasant than I found his.

Watson, at that time, was primarily an experimentalist. He built apparatus with his own hands; he got the university interested in the laboratory. He stimulated me to put through some of the things I had been maturing.

I had already discarded the old doctrine of "images." Watson, however, still accepted it. He, he said, used visual imagery very effectually in designing his apparatus. Watson had not at that time developed his behaviorism, and his thinking was, to a large extent, along conventional lines. He was violently interested in animal behavior, and was looking for some simplifications of attitude which would align that work with human psychology. Hence, he was interested in the iconoclastic activity I was developing, and was influenced by my views, but carried them out to extremes. I rejected images as psychic objects, and denounced introspection as held by the orthodox psychologists. Watson carried this further, to the excluding from his psychology of everything to which the word "introspection" could be applied, and excluded imagination along with images. I had questioned the possibility of observing "consciousness." Watson carried this to the extreme, also. His first behaviorism, however, was obviously based on the orthodox system by which the mental field was divided into perception, thought, and feeling; and he was merely finding physiological substitutes for these. When I called his attention to this, and urged him to study behavior as behavior, he admitted the apparent Titchenerian basis, but opined that he could get away from that in later writings. He did, eventually but only after the American psychology generally had moved ahead (pp. 44–45).

Watson (1936) acknowledged his indebtedness to Dunlap, especially for his theory of thinking, as follows:

About this time [1909] I began to perfect my point of view about behaviorism. To Dunlap I owe much. In his own biography in this series he has probably stated my indebtedness to him better than I can express it myself. I only want to add that what he says is true (p. 277).

At a time when it was commonly accepted that the proper approach in psychology was to study oneself through introspection, Watson pleaded for the observation of "the other one." To place psychology within the natural sciences, psychologists should observe events external to themselves as the physicist does. The problem of conscious states does not trouble physicists as they make their observations, so why should it hamper psychologists—let them both have the same starting point for building their respective sciences.

Among Watson's many contributions was his position that verbal behavior consists of muscular contractions in the speech (and associated) regions, and hence does not differ in principle from other bodily responses, such as leg or arm movements. This position was remarkable when considered against the views of many of his contemporaries that verbal processes fall outside the scope of science. Goss (1961) suggested that Watson's most important contribution may yet prove to be his theoretical-experimental proposals regarding the role of verbal mediating responses in language and thinking phenomena. Goss formulated Watson's paradigm for the higher mental processes as follows: Initiating stimulus → implicit verbal (primarily vocal) responses and resultant stimuli → overt terminating response.

With specific reference to Watson's theory of thought, Millenson (1967) echoed Bergmann (1956) when he said the theory was an important creative development in the history of behavioral science because it "provides a certain intellectual comfort for the behavioral scientist: thought is given a place in the scheme of things behavioral, and may then be dismissed like other 'mental' ghosts of the past" (p. 284).

Over a period of years Watson elaborated various aspects of his theory of thinking and considered in detail a number of criticisms that were directed against him [see especially the 1920 (volume II) *British Journal of Psychology Symposium* "Is Thinking Merely the Action of Language Mechanisms?"]. While it may seem surprising to some, in a very real sense it is apparent that Watson was humble about his theories, this one in particular. For he was constantly emphasizing that he was laying out a program with many factual gaps to be filled in by research. In this connection, Max (1934) pointed out that Watson's theory of thinking had been "anticipated" by Mueller (1887) and by Dunlap's reaction-arc theory (1912). However, in contrast to others who did not submit their theories to experimental investigation, Watson stressed the importance of empirical tests.

Finally, here, we may point out Watson's contribution as being largely responsible for importing Pavlov's conditioning research into United States' psychology. Watson's emphasis on linguistic processes and thought made it necessary for him to offer an account of language development, which he did largely by employing conditioning principles. At birth, he held, the human is capable of making a large number of unlearned responses, including vocal ones. The unconditional stimuli for vocal responses were not clear, but Watson suggested that they might be of an intraorganic nature (stomach contractions, etc.) or of an external variety (presumably pain or cold stimuli would be examples). Such stimuli evoke muscular contractions in the chest region, thus expelling air from the lungs to produce sounds by vibrating the vocal cords. The continuous action of both extra and intraorganic stimuli produce a flow of changes in the muscles of the throat, tongue, and jaw, which affect the size and shape of the mouth cavities above the larynx as well as the visceral cavities below. In this way the volume, timber, and pitch of emitted sound is continuously modified.

Vocal behavior, of course, commences with birth. As the infant matures, unconditional stimuli evoke unlearned preword sounds ("da," "ma," "a," "u," "wah," etc.), following which unlearned "word" organization commences (e.g., the placing together of two of the above simple responses, such as "dada"). It is important to emphasize that vocal utterances are unlearned—they are produced, according to Watson, as the result of unconditional stimuli in the normal course of maturation. Such unconditional responses, then, can and do serve as the basic raw material of which language is constructed—these unconditional responses are no different in principle from those of the salivary gland and can thus serve as the basis for conditioning. At any stage in the process of speech development, conditioning of the various vocal utterances can occur. In an example furnished by Watson the unconditional response "dada" can become conditioned to the sight of the infant's milk bottle or to the saying of "dada" by a parent. Thus evoked, the conditional response "dada" by the infant may be reinforced by receipt of the bottle. This example, incidentally, is one of a number of instances in which Watson employed trial and error learning ("instrumental" or "operant" conditioning), without distinguishing between classical and instrumental conditioning. It is not surprising that Watson did not make such a distinction, because Pavlov himself did not, and one can find many examples of instrumental conditioning from Pavlov's laboratory. The distinction is perhaps not fruitful for psychology and may be abandoned in favor of a return to Pavlov's mode of thinking about conditioning (McGuigan, 1973b).

Through conditioning, then, all forms of stimuli can become attached to unlearned vocal responses so that numerous stimuli acquire the capacity to evoke any given speech response. Similarly, a verbal (speech) response may be made with a wide variety (dozens or hundreds) of different muscles. The sight of a mother, her clothes, or hearing the word "mother," for example, may lead the infant to say "mama," sometimes screamed, sometimes harshly, sometimes softly, sometimes with a whining tone, or deep down in the throat.

Gradually, the child's verbal responses become shaped into recognizable words. Just how the crude vocal sounds of infancy are shaped into fullblown words is a difficult problem. While in several places Watson paid lip service to imitation (in the popular sense) as facilitating this process, it cannot be said that he really believed in such a phenomenon. Rather, it would seem that he held that a child does not imitate words spoken by adults, for he says that all adult speech is but ". . . unlearned infantile sounds put together by patient conditioning in infancy, childhood and youth" (Watson, 1930, p. 231). A response must already be in an organism's behavioral repertoire before it can be evoked ("imitated") by watching another.

After vocal responses become shaped into recognizable words, the final stage of language development occurs. This is the stage of organization in which a series of oral verbal responses become associated (chained), each providing the stimulus for the next. First two, then three and more words are tied together. The presentation of the father's shoe, for instance, will early lead to the response "shoe-da." Consider Watson's more complicated example of a child learning "Now I lay me down to sleep. . ." Each word stimulus, in the beginning, calls out its associated response:

$$
\begin{array}{cccc}
\text{S}_{(now)} & \text{S}_{(I)} & \text{S}_{(lay)} & \text{S}_{(me)} \\
\downarrow & \downarrow & \downarrow & \downarrow \\
\text{R}_{\text{"now"}} & \text{R}_{\text{"I"}} & \text{R}_{\text{"lay"}} & \text{R}_{\text{"me"}}
\end{array}
$$

But later in the learning process the verbal responses become chained together and the response of saying "now" produces kinesthetic stimuli that lead to the response of "I" then of "lay," and so forth, all having been set off by the initial stimulus word:

$$
\begin{array}{l}
\text{S}_{\text{Now}} \\
\downarrow \\
\text{R}_{\text{"Now"}} \longrightarrow \text{R}_{\text{"I"}} \longrightarrow \text{R}_{\text{"lay"}} \longrightarrow \text{R}_{\text{"me"}}
\end{array}
$$

Once these complex overt language habits develop they can become covert. The pressure of society is responsible for this transition—the child, for instance, is cautioned not to talk aloud. Hence the overt speech is reduced in amplitude to whispered speech with the lips moving. Then another stage typically follows as a result of admonitions of the sort "Can't you read without moving your lips," and the process takes place *behind* the lips. This is implicit, covert or silent speech.

For Watson, the oral response is but one of many which are conditioned to stimuli. He categorized the universe of responses as verbal (speech, or oral-linguistic), manual (nonoral-skeletal muscle) and visceral.[4] Any or all three types of responses can thus be conditioned, resulting in complex chains such that each response can set off additional responses in all three domains (verbal, manual, and visceral, Fig. 2.2).

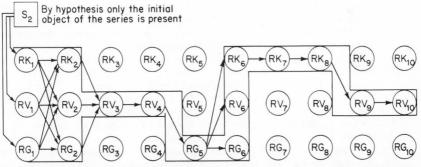

FIG. 2.2 "This diagram shows the behaviorist's theory of thinking. Sometimes we think by using manual, verbal and visceral organizations simultaneously. Sometimes only the verbal, sometimes only the visceral and at other times only the manual. In the diagram the organization taking part in the whole thinking process is enclosed between the two continuous solid lines. The diagram shows clearly that thinking involves all three sets of our organized reaction systems" (Watson, 1930, p. 266).

Watson made an important distinction between *vocal* and *language* habits. The mere saying of a word (the unlearned "dada" by a child or the saying of a word by a parrot[5]) is a vocal habit. A vocal habit is one in which there is no associated bodily response; only the vocal one is made. A language habit, however, is one in which a "verbal" (i.e., speech) response is associated with other responses. When, for instance, a person says "fire," the person is making not only that (oral) response, but also

---

[4] Since I think Watson meant "verbal" to refer to speech or oral-linguistic responses, and since he was clear that there are nonoral language responses too, I suggest that the terms in parentheses be substituted for "verbal." Similarly, I believe "nonoral skeletal muscle responses" is preferable (more precise) to "manual responses."

[5] Or the mynah bird in the Halls of Columbia University who was operantly conditioned to repeatedly tact "I am an organism."

manual responses (one runs) and visceral responses (one contracts the colon), as depicted in Fig. 2.2. These other bodily (manual and visceral) responses are not only associated with the oral language responses but in some instances are substitutable for them (a shrug of the shoulder communicates "I don't know"). In short, a language habit consists of "verbal" responses with associated manual and visceral responses. This discussion makes it clear that Watson has been erroneously accused of espousing a single-channel linear processing model—clearly his was a multi-channel model of parallel processing.

Thinking, to Watson, *is the occurrence of implicit (covert) language habits.* Watson's definition of thinking covers several "varieties" of thought processes, which he classified tentatively into three categories:

1. The lowest level may be thought of as "completely habitized thought" (not Watson's term) in which there is "mere unwinding of vocal habits where the word sequences are invariable" (1920, p. 89). No new learning, no new trial movements are required for the subvocal use of words, as is the case when the organism is placed in a new situation to which adjustment is required— *"you are merely exercising* a verbal function you have already acquired" (Watson 1930, p. 243). This type of thinking corresponds to an extremely simple stimulus-response type of behavior. Examples would include the saying of well-learned rhymes or quotations, or giving the answer to 2 + 2 = ?.

2. At the "semi-habitized" level there is "the solving of problems which are not new, but which are so infrequently met with that trial verbal behavior is demanded" (1920, p. 90). The implicit verbal processes are initiated by a stimulus, but they are not so well exercised that they can function without some learning or relearning. For instance, if one is asked to multiply 333 by 33, one may shortly give the answer, but only after a certain amount of "verbal fumbling."

3. In "non-habitized" thought, one engages in constructive thinking in which the problem is novel and there is the first of a number of learning trials. This is creative thought in which one arrives at new verbal creations such as a poem, painting, or scientific hypothesis. As to how creative responses occur Watson says that *"the answer is that we get them by manipulating words, shifting them about until a new pattern is hit upon"* (1930, p. 247). The *elements* of the new creation (words) are all old (part of the individual's established behavioral repertoire); they just come out in new patterns (combinations), partly as a result of the continuously changing stimulus patterns.

Watson also recognized that the abbreviation of motor acts for increased efficiency during silent talking or thought was problematic for objective recording: "Even if we could roll out the implicit processes and record them on a sensitive plate or phonograph cylinder it is possible that they would be so abbreviated, short-circuited and economized that they would be unrecognizable unless their formation had been watched from the transition" (1919, p. 325). "Such processes are so evanescent and can slip from one motor region into another so rapidly that negative evidence obtained by our present inexact methods is no conclusive argument against our view" (1919 p. 326).

Bound by the technical shortcomings of his era, Watson's hope for the future was that "While our position thus must remain an assumption for the present, we have hopes that refinement of instruments now in use may later prove of service" (1919, p. 327). Finally, with regard to the recording of individual's thoughts, Watson was realistic about the lack of value of typical thought processes when he said that "There is in general no practical need or even scientific need for recording thought, since . . . it finally eventuates in action and . . . most of it in mankind is worthless from the standpoint of society" (1919, p. 327).

In the '30s or '40s it became unpopular to espouse "Watsonian behaviorism." If one takes Watson literally on certain points, the reasons are certainly justifiable. Consider his extreme environmentalism:

Give me a dozen healthy infants, well-formed, and my own specified world to bring them up in and I'll guarantee to take any one at random and train him to become any type of specialist I might select—doctor, lawyer, artist, merchant-chief and, yes, even beggar-man and thief, regardless of his talents, penchants, tendencies, abilities, vocations, and race of his ancestors (1919, p. 248).

Today, we can be more sympathetic toward Watson's views if we consider them against the background of his time, when it was commonly held that child-rearing practices were irrelevant to the later personality and the mind did not emerge until puberty. Watson and Freud (strange bedfellows indeed) were probably the primary forces in replacing that notion with the concept of "as the twig is bent, so grows the tree." Other reasons for Watson's unpopularity among some psychologists might have resulted from an abbreviation of some of his statements. For instance, it was commonly said that Watson defined thinking only as "subvocalization" or "laryngeal responding." An amazingly shortsighted dismissal of his theory of thinking thus resulted by the common sense observation that individuals with excised larynx's could still think (see pages 99–101 for criticism of this reasoning). As much as anyone, Watson emphasized that one thinks with the entire body: "The explicit and implicit language habits are formed along with the explicit bodily habits and are bound up with them and become a part of every total unitary action system that the human organism forms" (Watson, 1919, p. 309). "We would not abstract language, overt or implicit, or other implicit thought processes, from their general setting in bodily integration as a whole" (1919, p. 324). "When we study implicit bodily processes we are studying thought" (1919, p. 326.).

To elaborate his notion that thought is the action of language mechanisms widely distributed throughout the body, he pointed out that during speech and thought there is action of the diaphragm, lungs, and muscles of the thorax, extrinsic and intrinsic muscles of the larynx, muscles of the pharynx, nose and palate, the cheeks, tongue and lips, as well as many manual and visceral responses. Though articulate speech disappears in individuals in whom there is a trachealcannula (so that the air does not flow between the lungs and mouth), the movements necessary for speech remain. Thus, by Watson's view, the individual could still think without a larynx.

NEOBEHAVIORISM

While a distinction between early and later behavioristic theories is arbitrary, it is common to refer to more recent psychological approaches as neobehavioristic. One reason sometimes offered for the distinction is that classical behaviorism employed only single unit S-R laws to explain complex behavior, and that in neobehaviorism multiprocess mediational paradigms, have been developed. That this distinction is too simplistic is a point well made by Goss (1961).

Hull. Clark Hull formulated his long-term research objective to be the understanding of the higher mental processes (see his *Idea Books,* 1962). Hull's strategy was to first establish basic laws of behavior that apply throughout the upper phylogenetic levels—a strategy resembling (and no doubt influenced by) Watson's. After achieving a basic understanding of behavior Hull (1930, 1931) proposed to move on to higher level laws necessary to account for mental processes. In his words:

> Innumerable attempts to derive a satisfactory (i.e., scientific) theory of knowledge and of thought and reason from conscious experience as such have failed. In the place of this I proposed to develop a system which starts from exactly the opposite end. I shall invert the whole historical system. I shall start with action—habit—and proceed to deduce all the rest, including conscious experience, from action, i.e., habit. One thing at least may be said for it: it has never before been given a vigorous trial. Despite some half-hearted suggestions within recent years, no one has dared to challenge the dogma that an organism made up of consciousless particles may not possibly manifest consciousness, or that activity of whatever kind cannot conceivably be conscious. . . . My strategy will be to work on *action*, as such, just as long as possible, leaving the problems of conscious thought and experience . . . to one side. It may well be that, when I have thoroughly worked out the problems of ordinary action, learning of various sorts, symbolism, and so on, I will so far have undermined the matter of conscious experience that it will be relatively easy to attack, there being little left (1962, pp. 837-838).

Unfortunately, Hull was never able to launch a full scale attack on the primary problem of higher processes. He did, though, formulate the basis in the fractional anticipatory goal reaction (r_G), together with its proprioceptive stimulus consequences (s_G). In the complete paradigm, $S\text{-}r_G\text{-}s_G\text{-}R$, the logical constructs r_G and s_G are anchored on the antecedent side by external stimuli and on the consequent side by overt responses. This paradigm allowed Hull (1930, 1931) to reduce the concept of purpose to the pure stimulus act (s_G) and to conceive of ideomotor acts as r_G's. Kendler (1954) illustrated an application of r_G by asking:

How are we to consider language behavior? According to Watson words were merely substitute stimuli for physical objects and situations. Hull later integrated some ideas inherent in Watson's formulation . . . cue-producing behavior, or what Hull labelled the 'pure-stimulus act' . . . would provide a cue for another response. Example of response-produced cues would be the implicit verbalizations of a human counting his change after making a purchase . . . the white rat . . . is capable of making anticipatory-goal responses which produce cues, making possible behavior that otherwise would not occur (p. 348).

Hull's mediating process theory was applied in a number of other ways too, such as response mediated generalization. One of Hull's last statements about r_G-s_G was the prediction of a promising future for this adaptive mechanism: "further study of this major automatic device presumably will lead to the detailed behavioral understanding of thought and reasoning which constitute the highest attainment of organic evolution. Indeed the r_G-s_G mechanism leads in a strictly logical manner into what was formerly regarded as the very heart of the psychic: interest, planning, foresight, foreknowledge, expectancy, purpose, and so on" (1952, p. 350).

Skinner. Skinner's position on thought and the higher mental processes gives a clear cut example of a neobehaviorist who eschews complex mediational paradigms; in fact, in his own work Skinner disregarded *any* mediational processes. To quote Skinner:

The simplest and most satisfactory view is that thought is simply *behavior*— verbal or nonverbal, covert or overt. It is not some mysterious process responsible for behavior but the very behavior itself in all the complexity of its controlling relations, with respect to both man the behaver and the environment in which he lives. The concepts and methods which have emerged from the analysis of behavior, verbal or otherwise, are most appropriate to the study of what has traditionally been called the human mind.
The field of human behavior can be conveniently subdivided with respect to the problems it presents and the corresponding terms and methods to be used. A useful distinction may be made between reflexes, conditioned or otherwise, and the operant behavior generated and maintained by the contingencies of reinforcement in a given environment. Tradition and expedience seem to agree in confining the analysis of human thought to operant behavior. So conceived, thought is not a mystical cause or precursor of action, or an inaccessible ritual, but action itself, subject to analysis with the concepts and techniques of the natural sciences, and ultimately to be accounted for in terms of controlling variables . . . (Skinner, 1957, in McGuigan, 1966a, pp. 17-18).

"When we study human thought, we study behavior. In the broadest possible sense, the thought of Julius Caesar was simply the sum total of his responses to the complex world in which he lived" (Skinner, 1957, in McGuigan, 1966a, p. 20).
Conscious experience is explained by Skinner (1963) as again merely a

certain kind of behavior: "Seeing does not imply something seen. We acquire the behavior of seeing under stimulation from actual objects, but it may occur in the absence of these objects under the control of other variables" (p. 955). The behaviors of seeing, hearing, etc., when the typical evoking stimulus is absent are small scale, not readily observable, covert behaviors.

Osgood.   Osgood (cf. Osgood and McGuigan, 1973) has developed a "three-stage" model that includes both representational mediation processes (S-R principles) and sensory and motor integration processes (S-S and R-R principles). Representational processes are of prime concern here, for they are Osgood's method of handling the traditional higher mental processes (especially perception and meaning.) The representational level was also chronologically the first for Osgood to develop, which he did as a straightforward generalization from Hullian (1943) notions about fractional anticipatory goal responses. Osgood's representational mediation theory, a behavioral associationistic model, is probably the most sophisticated of our theories for handling symbolic processes. Osgood's approach differs from that of the typical linguist because Osgood based his theorizing on objectively observable, systematic behavioral data. Hence Osgood's approach to language is that mediating processes originate in nonlinguistic perceptual motor responses. In particular, as represented at the top of Fig. 2.3, *"a stimulus pattern ($\boxed{S}$) which is not the same physical event as the thing signified ($\dot{S}$) will become a sign of that significate when it becomes conditioned to a mediation process, this process (a) being some distinctive representation of the total behavior (R_T) produced by the significate and (b) serving to mediate overt behaviors (R_X) to the sign which are appropriate to ('take account of') the significate"* (Osgood and McGuigan, 1973, p. 451). For Osgood, r_m's are representations of those aspects of R_T's which have made a difference in appropriateness of behaving with respect to the things signified by signs. As Osgood pointed out, r_m's have been differentially reinforced, e.g., when one moves from place A to place B the locomotor behavior may be *nondistinctive* (one may walk, run, or swim) with respect to avoiding signs of danger at A or of approaching signs of safety at B. There would be, however, common *affective* features of the many ways in which one could avoid A vs. approaching B that could be differentially reinforced, thus becoming components of the signs of A vs. B. For example, assume there is a place A, where there are signs of danger, and a place B, where there are signs of safety. A person at A may move to B through any manner of locomotor behavior (e.g., they may walk, run, swim, etc.). However, these many ways of getting from A to B all share common *affective* features, and these features could be differentially reinforced and thus become components of the mediating response to the perceptual signs of A and B. It is in this way that semantic distinctions originate in the *behaviors* to Things rather than merely in the *perceptions* of Things.

Following an extensive review of the controversy over peripheralist vs. centralist theories of thought Osgood (1953) proposed a compromise position, namely that peripheral mediation is required during the development of symbolic processes but that later peripheral mediation becomes telescoped to a largely central representation.

In 1957, Osgood elaborated on the integration of motor encoding by indicating that at first there is a slow patterning of responses on the basis of exteroceptive controls, such as when one imitates movements of another. Next there occurs a gradual transfer to proprioceptive controls using feedback (and resulting in increased speed of execution of movement) until finally there is a transfer of the overt act to central programming in the integrational motor system. In this respect, Osgood's

COMPONENTIAL r_M = AN "EMIC" PRINCIPLE FOR BEHAVIOR THEORY

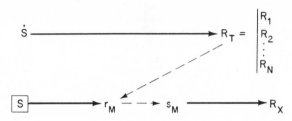

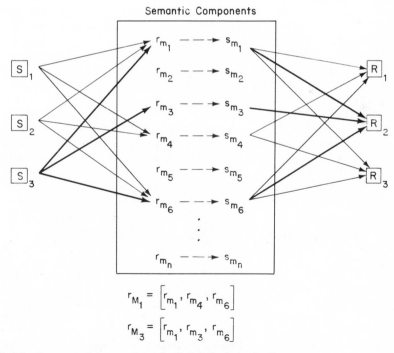

FIG. 2.3 Componential r_M: an "emic" principle for behavior theory.

theory of the development of representational meaning is similar to the response internalization process considered by a number of others (cf. Chapter 4).

As illustrated at the bottom of Fig. 2.3, the total representational mediation process (r_{M1}) elicited by a sign consists of a number of components (r_m's) which are semantic features into which the total meaning can be analyzed. A relatively small number of independent r_m components can combine in a number of patterns to differentiate the meanings of a very large number of distinctive total r_M's. Like the phoneme or the sememe in linguistic theory, the total r_M

(1) *renders functionally equivalent classes of different behavioral events,* either signs having the same significance (like signs 1 and 2) . . . or behaviors expressing the same intention (like behaviors 1 and 3 with respect to intention r_{M1}), (2) *is an abstract entity,* presently unobserved itself but necessary for interpretation of what is observed, and (3) *is resolvable into a "simultaneous bundle" of distinctive features or components* which serve to differentiate among meanings (thus, as shown in Figure [2.3] the meanings of signs 1 and 3 are distinguished by the presence of components 4 vs. 3 respectively) (Osgood and McGuigan, 1973, p. 453).

With regard to the status of r_M as a hypothetical construct, Osgood is clearly a centralist. Referring to the three levels of the nervous system shown in Fig. 2.4, r_M and its component features operate in the highest level and are, by hypothesis, cortical events.

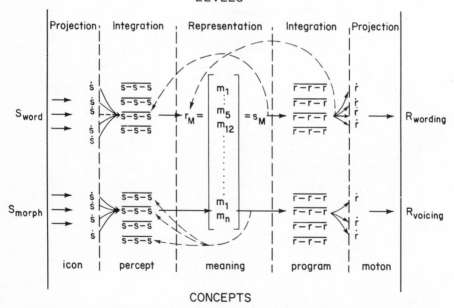

FIG. 2.4   A three-level model of information processing with feedbacks (from Osgood and Hoosain, 1974).

Osgood is aware that anatomical or functional distinctions between sensation (at the projection level of the central nervous system) and more central processes (which he calls perception at the integration level) and meaning (at the representation level) cannot be easily made. Yet on functional grounds (Osgood, 1957a and b, 1963), he held that at least three levels of neural processing must be postulated for both the input (S) and output (R) sides of the behavioral equation (Fig. 2.4). At the most peripheral levels, the projection systems function to transfer input information from receptor surfaces to the sensory cortex, (on the input side) and from the motor cortex to the effector surfaces (on the output side). The projection systems are essentially isomorphic and unmodifiable by experience so that there is a one-to-one relation between sensory stimulations (S) and neural events events ($\hat{s}$), and similarly between motor signals ($\hat{r}$) and responses (R). The signals from the sensory ($\hat{s}$) and motor ($\hat{r}$) projection systems have connections with neurons in the still more central integration systems ($\overline{s\text{-}s\text{-}s}$ and $\overline{r\text{-}r\text{-}r}$). However the relations between projection level signals and integration level events are not isomorphoric and *are* modifiable by experience. In the most central mediating system, the representational level, the total meaning of a sign ($r_M\text{-}s_M$) occurs as a result of the nearly simultaneous activation of a distinctive subset of mediator components ($m_1 \ldots m_n$).

In Chapter 9, intracerebral circuits are important components in our model; they are related to circuit class II, seen in Fig. 9.4. In Fig. 2.4, Osgood represented four types of facilitative effects of intracerebral circuits:

1. $\overline{s\text{-}s\text{-}s} \rightarrow$ M. This "feed-forward" is the encoding of percepts into meanings such that percepts of words are meaningless until they are encoded into semantic feature patterns at the representation level.
2. M $\rightarrow \overline{r\text{-}r\text{-}r}$. This "feed-forward" is the decoding of meanings into programs for overt motor expression.
3. $\overline{r\text{-}r\text{-}r} \rightarrow$ M. Osgood and Hoosain (1974) pointed out that this is a non-obvious potential "feed-backward" from motor programs to the meaning system. Hence, if particular motor programs are set in motion by any means other than the normal "feed-forward" (M $\rightarrow \overline{r\text{-}r\text{-}r}$) route (with or without overt expression) then the individual can also experience meanings appropriate for the program. This type of feedback, incidentally, is quite similar to that hypothesized by Dunlap (1922) and others discussed earlier in this chapter. For example, the phenomenon of "recession into the nervous system" of the original overt response (such as Osgood's r_T), which possibly is accomplished through short-circuiting mechanisms that could eliminate the necessity for kinesthetic feedback from the muscular activity (as proposed by Dunlap), could well be accomodated by Osgood's $\overline{r\text{-}r\text{-}r} \rightarrow$ M relationship. Recall that Dunlap mentioned the cerebellum as the locus of such a short circuiting muscular representation mechanism in the brain. The cerebellum performs primarily motor functions; hence Osgood's placement of these feedback events at the *motor* projection level is consistent with Dunlap's insights.
4. M $\rightarrow \overline{s\text{-}s\text{-}s}$. This "feed-backward" from meanings to percepts can facilitate one of many alternative perceptual integrations so that a particular percept is more likely to be experienced than its many competitors.

The type of feed-forward and feedback circuits discussed here are of great importance for language perception, as well as information processing in general. In Chapter 9 we shall discuss Osgood's model further, with particular reference to muscle circuits which provide what Osgood calls "long-loop" feedback from the speech musculature, thereby facilitating phonemic perception (also see the Gilbert and Sullivan studies pp. 194–202 in Chapter 6).

Schoenfeld and Cumming. Relatively early, these "radical behaviorists" made a frontal attack on the problem of perception. In analyzing the traditional question of perception they concluded that three positions on perception are possible: (1) perception has an independent, noncorporal existence, thus making the affair strictly a metaphysical one; (2) perception is a corporal phenomenon but has no effect on behavior—a position which contradicts the asserted importance of perception and makes it irrelevant to science; (3) perception is a hypothetical construct and behavior is the initial datum of reference.

Adopting position 3, Schoenfeld and Cumming offered the following paradigm for perception as a construct that evidences itself in observable behavior:

$$S \longrightarrow R_1 \cdot R_2$$

Where S is the stimulus event perceived, R_1 is the perceptual response, and R_2 is the reporting response. Hence, when the stimulus event is perceived there are implicit or covert bodily events (their R_1, which in this book we designate by means of r) and the occurrence of these covert bodily events constitute the perception per se. The pattern indicated by R_1 can be described so that the reporting (tacting) response is the overt evidence of the perception.

Representational and Implicit Associative Responses. Underwood and his associates, following Bousfield, Whitmarsh, and Dannick (1958), conducted a series of experiments (e.g., 1965) to test for the presence of verbal mediating responses. The basic paradigm was that verbal stimuli evoke a representational response which is the act of perceiving the verbal unit. The stimulus properties of the representational response (RR) then evoke a chain of implicit associative responses (IAR's) which eventuate in an overt verbal response. For example, if a person is presented with the word "horse," covert responses occur that constitute the representational response of the perception of that particular word. Following the representational response the individual might think of "carriage," the implicit response that is associated with "horse." The particular implicit associative response produced is probably that word which is most frequently associated with the particular representational response, e.g., if the RR to the verbal unit is "long" then the IAR will probably be "short." One particular strategy used by Underwood (1965) was to test for false recognition of overtly presented verbal stimuli. The notion was that the representational response for certain words would evoke specified implicit associative responses, although IAR words were not themselves presented. Then at a later point in the list of words presented to the subjects, the actual implicit associative response words evoked by the earlier representational response words were actually presented to the subject for the first time. The subject would typically (and erroneously) say that the implicit associative response words had been read earlier in the list when it was actually their strong associates. Thus, if the word of the moment was "down," and if it elicits the implicit associative response "up," and if "up" occurred earlier in the list, the subject might falsely believe that "down" had also occurred earlier.

We will note in Chapter 6 that a number of research strategies similar to Underwood's have implicated implicit responses as mediating events for overt responses. These strategies have been very powerful and they serve to supplement the direct psychophysiological measurement of the mediating response.

Now that we have sampled some of the theories which emphasize response events, we shall turn to theories which concentrate on the central nervous system.

Brain Involvement in the Higher Mental Process

BRIEF STATEMENTS

Herrnstein and Boring (1965) pointed out that "the belief that the brain is the chief organ of the mind is quite old" (p. 204) by citing Pythagoras and Plato as having held this view. The word "chief" in their phrase "the brain is the *chief* organ of the mind" is especially interesting for it implies that this ancient conception allowed for there to be other bodily organs of the mind. This flexible conception is probably due in part to the ancients' awareness that other bodily systems were important for psychic activity. In this connection we have noted earlier in this chapter that Parmenides held also that the limbs are important for thinking, and that Lucretius and Aristotle ascribed functions of the soul and emotions to the heart. For Aristotle the brain was but a refrigeration unit for the body. As we now review a sample of prominent historical positions with regard to cerebral localization, in fact, we shall note that there are few who held that the brain is the *sole* organ of the mind—a strict Donovan's brain theory (see p. 8) apparently has little historical precedent.

Galen (A.D. 129-199), the famous Roman physician, was extremely influential in placing the mind within the brain. Albertus Magnus offered an interesting view of the mind within the brain based on an analogy with the judicial system of the Greeks. Just as the Greeks had three law chambers, the first to receive information, the second for adjudication, and the third for carrying out action, Albertus Magnus hypothesized three corresponding ventricles of the brain such that the first received sensations from the receptors, the second interpreted the sensations, the third issued forth motor action.

Perhaps more than anyone else Descartes (1650) implicated the brain in mental processes. Descartes identified the soul with consciousness and believed that the soul interacted with the body through the pineal gland of the brain. Descartes held that thoughts proceed from the soul, and that the body does not think in any way—the heat and movements of the body are merely mechanical. We can thus see the emphasis on the brain for mind, because of the interaction of the soul at the pineal gland.

Despite all his truly great achievements, Descartes' formulation of the mind-body problem probably set the science of psychology back two centuries. A productive science of mind could not seriously commence until a natural science approach to it could be developed, and a prerequisite for this was to discard Cartesian dualism and the notion of a homunculus within the skull. But even Descartes' emphasis on the brain as the organ of mind did not exclude response involvement; as discussed earlier in this chapter, Descartes held that actions of the tongue led to an understanding of the meaning of words.

Cabanis thought that the brain was a special organ whose particular function was to produce thought, just as the stomach and intestines have the special function of carrying on digestion. David Hartley held to an extreme "centralist" position by believing that ideas required only the action of the brain, though sensations of course involve both sensory nerves and the brain.

Phrenology ranks with the work of Descartes in importance for locating the mind in the brain. In his study of the skull, Gall (Gall and Spurzheim, 1809) hypothesized a variety of mental functions at specific regions within the brain. Gall's major tenet was that mental faculties having their seat in highly localized brain regions could be studied by relating skull characteristics with various kinds of aberrant behaviors. He studied hundreds of skulls and obtained numerous anecdotes about individuals with deviant behaviors, measured the cranial deformities, and attempted to correlate those deformities with the extremes of behavior. While he was an excellent anatomist, his psychological data were weak. It eventually became clear that such correlations as Gall sought were not reliable because, among other things, the topographic characteristics of the skull being separated from the brain by the cerebral spinal fluid and the brain meninges, did not accurately reflect underlying brain characteristics. We noted earlier Gall's great contribution in advancing the view of materialism and the social wrath that he experienced, especially that from the church.

Though phrenology was eventually discredited, it did facilitate a long line of empirical research on cerebral localization. Foremost in this trend was the classic work of Flourens who developed an elaborate view of localization, though it was less extreme than Gall's. Flourens' method of ablation—employed by later researchers (e.g., Franz, Lashley)—was based on the logic that any change in behavior which follows excision of a section of the brain indicates that that portion of the brain functions for that particular type of behavior. In Flourens' view, there is not an exact localization of function, but a more general relationship between functions of the brain and behavior, as in the case of the sensory functions of the cortex.

Broca's discovery in 1861 of an important speech center in the left frontal lobe was a classic in the trend toward cerebral localization. At the time, prevailing opinion was that the cortex was inexcitable, but shortly after Broca's discovery, Fritsch and Hitzig in 1870 electrically stimulated the cortex and identified the motor centers. Countering the prevailing view, Fritsch and Hitzig believed that the excitable areas were where the psychic functions entered into the material body.

C. J. Herrick (1924) thought that if the equilibrium of the resting cortex is disturbed, a new pattern of cortical activity develops which modifies all subsequent activity of the system, resulting in the appearance in consciousness of an idea, a judgment, a decision, or a purpose. Herrick believed that consciousness is an important factor in the causative complex that results in behavior. Consciousness thus cannot be ignored in a scientific analysis of the field of behavior.

Reiser (1924) criticized the peripheral approach of the behaviorists as being too simple. It may be true, Reiser granted, that in original learning, the locus of concept and meaning acquisition is peripheral, but in later use that learning is transferred back to central processes. Hence, in the original learning the locus of the concepts of meaning may have to be shifted from the central to the peripheral motor segments of the organism. The response then becomes short-circuited so that overt reaction "drops out." Thinking occurs when stimuli arouse cerebral arcs that include representations of the reaction originally learned through the muscles. That is, neural tissue is capable of being modified by experience and thus the original reactions are preserved through engrams or neurograms. Activation of these central engrams or neurograms produces images, concepts, ideas, etc., which were originally the perceptions; neurologically, having an image is the re-excitation of the neurons originally involved in the perception by only a part of the original stimulating condition.

Head (1926) held that lower functional levels of the nervous system could help us understand the nature of consciousness, though consciousness has a very important relationship to the higher nervous centers. The notion of levels of the nervous system such as espoused by Head has been variously developed by other neurophysiologists too, especially by Hughlings Jackson (1931-32). Jackson was greatly influenced by Cartesian dualism and the evolutionism of Spencer. He accepted a mind-body dualism of such a nature that, in his opinion, no physiologist would ever be able to develop a "physiology of the mind." Jackson thus thought that the mind was, in effect, unknowable. He conceived of the nervous system as consisting of numerous anatomical levels which he categorized into three general groups. These were the highest cerebral centers (which were the physical basis of consciousness) and the lower centers and brain stem (which he tended to ignore as being of subsidiary importance). (We may note in Jackson's grouping of three levels of the nervous system the similarity to Plato's tripartite soul.) As one moves up the hierarchy of levels, one does *not* come upon a level that consists of a different kind of nervous material. Rather, all components of the nervous system have the same constitution, and they all perform the same general sensori-motor function. That is, all cerebral centers serve to coordinate the sensory impressions arising from the receptor organs with movements of all parts of the body. There is thus no single center for mind that is superior to sensori-motor mechanisms since "man himself" is a sensori-motor mechanism. Jackson thus held that the physical basis of mind (consciousness) is a representation of numerous different impressions and movements of all parts of the body. The substrata of consciousness are thus sensori-motor arrangements that rerepresent all lower centers and hence represent the entire organism. Jackson's emphasis on the importance of the brain for coordinating sensori-motor activity, and his stress on the commonality of neural tissue throughout the nervous system, is quite similar to the conception developed by Dunlap discussed earlier in the chapter.

Lashley's work is of sufficient importance to us that we shall devote a separate section to it later, as we do also to the theory of Hebb.

Freeman (1931a) stated that all forms of motor theories agree "that somehow or other afferent stimulation must eventuate in some effector 'response' before consciousness of the afferent stimulation can occur" (p. 430). Freeman (1931b) conducted an empirical investigation using a mechanical device for recording muscular activity during thought and concluded that he had obtained evidence of the general fertility of a motor theory. However, he pressed (1933) for a modification of the motor theory as follows. He contended that motor tonus facilitates higher brain functions because the afferent impulses produced by muscular contraction lower the thresholds of irritability in the higher cortical centers. Consequently, those centers can appropriately process incoming stimuli. Freeman's notion that muscular responding can function to maintain central processes is similar to that of Hebb: "Cortical action is reinforced and sustained by a continuous stream of proprioceptive impulses. Should such stimulation fall below a certain minimum (as during sleep), cortical neurons would be unable to respond adequately to exteroceptive stimulation of moderate intensity" (1931a, p. 447). While he thus recognized that proprioceptive influx from the muscles is of value, Freeman also agreed with Lashley's notion that there were irradiating impulses from central processes that produce motor responses which constitute merely a "leakage" or "motor overflow" phenomenon: "It is indeed highly probable that much overt movement is an incidental consequence rather than a cause of cortical action." (1931b, pp. 430-31).

Brain (1950) linked subcortical structures with consciousness. In particular he suggested that the basal nuclei made their appearance very early in the course of evolution at which time the higher organisms were capable of being conscious. However, it was not until considerably more evolution with the development of the higher brain structures some millions of years later that thought became possible.

Lenneberg (1967) asserted that speech production is under central control by proposing that motor aspects of speech production are governed by a train of elementary neurological events. An enormously complicated firing mechanism which is centrally controlled is superimposed on this train. The central mechanism must plan for smoothly integrated activity of disparate units that require different innervation times. He agreed with Lashley that no simple chain-association theory can account for speech motor activity. In planning the content of utterances the mechanism must have the capacity to rearrange a set of interrelated elements in what is sometimes a very long temporal sequence.

This concludes our brief summary of statements involving the brain with cognitive processes. We shall now consider the works of Lashley and of Hebb in some greater detail.

THEORIES OF LASHLEY

Lashley (1958) continued the materialistic efforts of Gall by attacking dualism and the attendant commensense view of a homunculus: ". . . within the past few years, three leaders in neurology, specialists in different fields, have asserted that mind cannot be explained by the activities of the brain and have sought to reseat the little man on his throne in the pineal gland" (in McGuigan, 1966a, p. 23). Among those leaders was Eccles, who asserted that mind cannot be explained by the activities of the brain, and who "accepts Sherrington's conclusion that the mind is not a form of energy, then evolves an elaborate theory as to how non-energy mind can act on matter, appealing to telepathy as supporting evidence" (Lashley, 1960, p. 530). Lashley also attacked Pavlov on the dualistic grounds that Pavlov regarded mental phenomena as of no concern to the physiologist, a fit subject only for psychologists and philosophers. We thus note the importance of the evolution of materialism within psychology in Russia, as discussed earlier in this chapter.

For Lashley, the problems of thought and conscousness were foremost, and in a number of his writings he put forth the following argument. Watson (1920) maintained that the behaviorist can construct a science disregarding consciousness, just as the physicist does in dealing with other phenomena of the physical world. The role of the observer in the two sciences should be the same, Watson held, so that in studying humans the psychologist should proceed just as the physicist does. Lashley, a former student of Watson's, was not favorably disposed towards this position. He pointed out that, even if one adopts this point of view (or, equally unfortunately, a dualistic position) the question still remains as to how the phenomena described by the subjectivist come into existence in the first place. Whether consciousness is strictly a metaphysical issue or a systematized delusion, it remains a problem for the psychologist and for the neurologist as it does equally for the physicist. Lashley thus attacked the behaviorist school for "not only denying that mental phenomena are relevant in the study of behavior, but asserting that they do not provide a basis for any scientific study whatever. Their position, however, still leaves them with the problem of how man ever developed the delusion that he is conscious" (1960, p. 530).

Lashley thus directly attacked the question of the higher mental processes, holding that the problem requires "a thorough analysis of the phenomena of consciousness, oriented with reference to the phenomena of neural activity. . . . When the questions which are now held to be unanaswerable are properly formulated, they will turn out to be capable of translation into physiological terms and will fall within the competence of present methods of physiological research" (1960, p. 531).

One can infer that Lashley's progressive orientation toward central processes throughout his life was also facilitated by a retreat from Watson, who inspired him: "I once invented a thought-reading machine; a system of levers which magnified and recorded movements of the tongue. I first had my subjects speak a word, then think it silently. Movements of the tongue were minute but otherwise identical with those of speech" (1960, p. 540). His general conclusion was that neural activities and thought are identical with those of action except for lack of facilitation of the final motor path in the former. The function of the pyramidal system is, he believed, to facilitate and thus transform thought into action. Although Lashley's findings in this study are favorable toward a peripheral theory, we must regard them as inconclusive (particularly since they are non-quantitatively reported) due to the limitations of the mechanical methods of measuring tongue activity which were available to him.

Lashley's later conception of mind was as a complex organization held together by the interaction of processes and by the time scales of memory. For him mind has no distinguishing feature other than its organization—there is a complete identity between the organization of the brain and organization of the mind. The billions of neurons in the brain are organized into numerous systems, each of which consists of traces of habits or memories. In his empirical search for the engram Lashley concluded that memory traces do not have a specific localization within the nervous systems. Rather, engrams are laid down (recorded) by means of multiple representations. Trace systems thus consist of numerous neurons that are sensitized to react in certain combinations. An external stimulus may throw a trace system into a state of tonic activity so that, with the synchronized action of the numerous neurons in a given trace system, there may be recall. During the activation of a trace system patterns of neural activity can be observed in which excitation spreads widely throughout the cerebrum.

Some trace systems may be in a tonic state (i.e., they are readily excitable and available for recall), while other trace systems are held in abeyance. For example, when a person is playing chess, memories about chess are readily recalled but if they are interrupted with the question "Who won the pennant last year?" they need to bring the "baseball trace system" into play, and this takes longer than if the person already were thinking about baseball. Thus, a trace system that is in a tonic state dominates the brain field and is relatively impervious to unrelated excitations. That is, when one trace system is activated (is in a state of tonic activity) associations of ideas are limited to the optics included in that group of traces. As to how other stimuli are blocked out so that they do not interfere with the ongoing activity of one trace system, Lashley suggested that there may be an active inhibition for preemption of neurons.

Lashley (1954) discussed the central determinants of perceptual attention, stating that the problem of attention is the problem of the selective dominance of a group of related neural activities with the simultaneous suppression of others. In the total mass of excitation to which a person is subjected, little ever comes to consciousness. Most effects of afferent excitation must be blocked, and Lashley thought that the blocking does not occur at low levels of integration. He concluded that the direction and degree of attention is determined only after considerable organization has been imposed upon the afferent excitations. For example, while listening to a musical composition one can follow the melodic line of one voice while suppressing attention to the sounds of instruments.

Magoun (1954) suggested to Lashley that conscious awareness is simpler than the neuronal processes which subserve it, a view with which Lashley agreed. In Magoun's concept of *summation of input*, when there is consciousness in depth perception, for example, there are numerous inputs, each of which involves hundreds and thousands of nerve impulses, but they are effective only in giving a single unit—visual depth—which we cannot analyze or break down.

Perhaps due to the recent reemergence of interest in linguistic processes, Lashley's (1951) paper on The Problem of Serial Order in Behavior has become a classic. In that paper Lashley's purpose was to account for the logical and orderly arrangement of thought and action, which he regarded as the most complex type of behavior. The integrative functions of the cerebral cortex reach their highest development in human thought processes, and language behavior requires such integration. In this paper Lashley attacked what he referred to as "associative chain theories." At that time (1951) he held that the only "strictly physiological" type of theory to account for temporal integration of language was the type postulated by Washburn (1916) in her motor theory. The notion was that chains of reflexes were activated such that the performance of each element of the series provides excitation of the next element. Speech was thus regarded as a succession of vocal acts wherein kinesthetic impulses from each movement evoke the next in the series.

Lashley argued in several ways against chain theories, holding that the temporal order of letters in words, or words in sentences and of sentences in text or discourse, is not due to direct associations in the sequence of elements. In his famous example of the phonetic sequence pronounced "right," Lashley pointed out that the word is a noun, adjective, adverb, and verb, with four spellings and 10 meanings:

The millwright on my right thinks it right that some conventional rite should symbolize the right of every man to write as he pleases. Meanings, he concluded, are determined by broader relationships than temporal associations. In his example "Rapid righting with his uninjured hand saved from loss the contents of the capsized canoe" Lashley pointed out that the associations which give meaning to "righting" must occur five seconds after the initial stimulus has been received. It is, thus, "certain that any theory of grammatical form which ascribes it to direct associative linkage of the words of the sentence overlooks the essential structure of speech. . . . The order is imposed by some other agent" (1960, p. 540).

What then determines the order? The answer . . . is that the mechanism which determines the serial activation of the motor units is relatively independent, both of the motor units and of the thought structure. . . . Syntax is not inherent in the words employed or in the idea to be expressed. It is a generalized pattern imposed upon the specific acts as they occur (1960, pp. 510-12).

Elsewhere he stated that "grammatical structure and other ordered activities imply some sort of arranging mechanism, active before the words reach overt speech or silent thought. The relations in thought structure are antecedent to consciousness. The tonic background might provide the basis for this preorganization" (1960, p. 535). In the production of speech, at least three, possibly four, major neurological systems are constantly interacting to direct serial order.

Another reason Lashley gave for attacking the "associative chain theory" is that very quick movements are independent of current control. Lashley thought that an entire movement, from initiation to completion, requires less than the reaction time for tactile or kinesthetic stimulation of the arm, which is about one-eighth of a second, even when no discrimination is involved. Such facts "force" the conclusion that an effector mechanism can be present or primed to discharge at a given intensity or for a given duration, independently of sensory control. This independence from sensory control is true not only for contraction of a synergic muscle group, but also for contraction of the different muscles in a complex movement. He gave the example of the finger strokes of a musician, which may be as fast as 16 per second in passages calling for a definite and changing order of successive finger movements. The succession of movements is too quick even for visual reaction time, and sensory control of movements is thus ruled out. Instead, it is necessary to postulate some central nervous mechanism which fires with predetermined intensity and duration, or activates different muscles in predetermined order. The mechanism consists of elaborate systems of interrelated neurons capable of integrating numerous widely spaced effector elements. There are transmitted temporally spaced waves of facilitative excitation, sometimes to all effector elements, sometimes only a directional polarization to receptor and effector elements. These systems contribute to every perception, to every integrated movement.

Furthermore, one neural system may be activated while it is scanned by another, e.g., when one listens to the numbers 3-7-2-9-4, the order can be reassorted to some different sequence. When the memory trace is formed it is integrated with directional characters of a space system. These space characters of the memory trace can be scanned by some other level of the coordinating systems and transformed into succession. The elements of a sentence are readied or partially activated before the order is imposed upon them in expression, suggesting that some scanning mechanism must be at play in regulating their temporal sequence. But Lashley thought that such speculations do little more than illustrate a point of view, and he did not specify the nature of these mechanisms.

Lashley's contributions were great and sizably advanced our understanding of the functioning of the brain. His work (as well as that of many others including the dream researchers) helped to dispell such notions as that "the mind (brain) shuts down at night during sleep." Lashley successfully advanced the thesis that input never enters a quiescent or static system but rather enters one which is already actively excited and organized. Behavior thus is the consequence of the interaction between this background of excitation and the input. Only by specifying the characteristics of the background of excitation can we understand the effects of any given input.

Lashley's attack on the "associative chain theory" does have some limitations. While Washburn's chain theory is too simplistic to account for high speed serial order behavior by itself, Lashley's argument above about the later response to "rapid righting" being incapable of adding meaning to "rapid righting" does not remove this possibility, i.e., one can develop a multiprocess chain model such that the conclusion *could* contribute to the meaning of the verbal response "righting."

With regard to his particular argument that speech cannot function as a succession of vocal acts in which kinesthetic impulses from each movement serve as the stimulus for the next (an argument also invoked by Hebb, 1958) the temporal data they employed must be questioned. Lashley and Hebb argued that since reaction time to tactile or kinesthetic stimulation of the arm is of the order of 125 milliseconds (auditory and visual reaction time being even greater), the feedback from one response is not sufficiently rapid to produce the immediately following response. That is, if as many as 16 responses can occur in one second, "At most there is 60 ms [milliseconds] . . . [for] feedback from the immediately preceding movement . . ." to produce the next (Hebb, 1958, p. 61). In short, the argument is that because the feedback from one response must activate a second response within 60 milliseconds, and since tactile and kinesthetic reaction time is about 125 milliseconds, the "associative chain theory" of temporal integration cannot account for serial order behavior.

There are two major difficulties with Lashley's argument. First, it is not legitimate to use reaction-time data, based on an overt response to an external stimulus, for the purpose of understanding internal feedback phenomena and attendant responses. Second, and of greater importance, is the physiological fact that the feedback from one response *can* produce a second response well within the 60 milliseconds required by Lashley and Hebb. Granit (1955) discussed such rapid loops in detail, and, when presented with Lashley's argument, stated that stretch reflexes do occur in less than 60 milliseconds: "The monosynaptic arc from the muscle spindle and back to its own muscle is fast enough for the purpose that you are considering" (personal communication, August 12, 1962). In a different context, Granit (1955) stated that "Eccles and Sherrington. . . . saw a reflex latency as short as 0.4 msec. (p. 218)." Finally it may be noted that Bickford, Jacobson, and Cody (1964) reported covert (EMG) responses to external stimuli in the neck musculature in about 8 milliseconds, in the arm in about 25 milliseconds, and in the leg in about 50 milliseconds.

These considerations do not, of course, confirm a peripheral feedback hypothesis of serial behavior. But they do limit Lashley's major argument by showing that successive responses may occur within 60 milliseconds of each other so that the variety of theory referred to as the "associative chain theory" remains tenable. Still, there is no particular reason for a contemporary behaviorist to have to hold to a "classical associative chain theory" in attempting to account for high speed serial order behavior. For the preferable model is a parallel channel processing one in which a number of response-central nervous system loops function simultaneously in the temporal integration of behavior (Chapter 9).

Finally, in view of his criticism of a feedback model for high speed serial behavior, it is interesting that Lashley *did* recognize the importance of kinesthetic feedback from the musculature in another context. He explained the moon illusion—that the moon on the horizon appears larger than at its zenith—by saying that this illusion is solely a function of the position of the eyes in their orbits such that the somesthetic impulses from the eyes determine the immediate perception of the size. He further pointed out that one can scan an object with the fingertip and be able to translate the successive tactile and muscular impressions into something very like a visual image of the object. Hence, the visual and kinesthetic systems are very closely interrelated. Perhaps all of the spatial characteristics of vision are dependent upon integration with the postural system. As Fessard (1954) suggested in an interchange with Lashley, there may be a selection of messages from different sources that can meet and interact in an instant in a small space (a few cubic millimeters) where there are electrical forces and chemical and osmotic gradients present that are the determining factors of the resulting excitatory states. On the other hand, in contrast to the visual and kinesthetic systems, the auditory and visual areas are widely separated so that they apparently communicate through long transcortical association pathways. However, Lashley and Sperry showed that destruction of these pathways through the mentioned cortical areas does not change the functional properties of auditory-visual intercortical integration. As a result of such findings, Lashley sketched the transmission of *reduplicated patterns* through a neural network, holding that there is much evidence which implies reduplication of activity throughout extensive cerebral areas. Characteristically, the long intercortical pathways and perhaps loop circuits through subcortical centers have topological arrangements such that the patterns of excitations which are present in any area are transmitted to other areas. There are thus alternative modes of transmission around partial blocks.

Lashley's work constituted a major advance in our understanding of verbal processes, and the thinking of Lashley "the centralist" indeed has a priority position throughout this entire book.

HEBB'S THEORY OF MIND

Hebb took as his explicandum the everyday concept of mental events when he asked, "What does it mean when I say that I have an image of some childhood scene, that I can 'see' the face of an absent friend, or that I can still 'hear' some piece of music after the musician has stopped playing?" (1958, p. 33). It means, Hebb said, that some process occurs in the brain which is in part the same as that which occurred earlier.[6] Hebb thus set himself the task of explicating mind, mental processes, consciousness, etc., in terms of brain activity. The mind, he said, consists of those brain processes that determine complex highly organized behavior.

When the transmission of a neural impulse is relatively direct from the receptor to the effector, the behavior is reflexive or sense dominated. There is no need, in this event, to postulate mediational events of a mental nature. It is when behavior becomes complicated that such a need arises. Here is where Hebb invokes the cell assembly and phase sequence—complicated behavior is under the control of sensory events *and* mediational events (ideas, thinking). It is important to emphasize that complex behavior is controlled by both sensory input and events within the brain that are not at the moment controlled by sensory input—these central events are the cell assemblies, or the ideation that results in higher order behavior. There is, he pointed out, ample evidence that the organism stores information for later use (delayed reaction and set experiments, for example). It is the brain that holds sensory excitation and then delivers it at some later time to the muscles.

To Hebb, reverberating cell assemblies are brain circuits. Two previous researches were especially important in Hebb's development of the primary concept of the cell assembly as a group of neurons arranged as a set of closed pathways. One was the work of Lorente de No concerning closed loops in the brain that become relatively independent of sensory

---

[6] This general notion is of course ancient, and has been employed by numerous thinkers (e.g., Reisser's work discussed on p. 49).

input. Ramon y Cajal had previously described anatomically closed pathways that pervade the central nervous system, but the concept had been largely forgotten. A representation of these closed circuits is presented in Fig. 2.5, which is enormously oversimplified in view of the large number of interconnecting neurons of the cerebral cortex. The principle, however, may be illustrated by noting that when an afferent neural impulse arrives in the cortex along neuron A, neuron B fires, which in turn sets off neuron C. Since C makes junction with B, the firing of C refires B, and so on. B and C make up a cell assembly, which when activated may be thought of as a reverberating circuit. Note that neurons D and E are also activated when B fires, which leads to activity elsewhere in the brain. For example, when E fires, a second cell assembly is activated, i.e., E sets off F, which in turn sets off G, whereupon F refires. The sequential firing of two or more cell assemblies is what Hebb earlier called a *phase sequence,* though he has more recently dropped that term (personal communication, 1974).

The second observation that led Hebb to his concept of cell assemblies was the observation of Von Senden that individuals who have been blind since birth but have their sight restored later in life do not perceive distinct stimulus objects (their world, in James' words, is a "blooming buzzing confusion"). It takes the individuals considerable time to develop distinguishable perceptions of the world. The inference made was that perceptions of the external world have to be built up through laborious experience (though one might consider a "critical period hypothesis equally viable"). Cell assemblies must be slowly formed and Hebb revived the forgotten theory of neurobiotaxis for explaining cell assembly formation, e.g., Kappers (1921). In its general form neurobiotaxis is a description of how repeated simultaneous firings of two adjacent neurons, such as neurons A and B in Fig. 2.5, lead to decreased synaptic resistance. Hence, the greater the frequency with which two

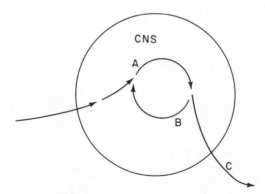

FIG. 2.5 Diagrammatic representation of a re-entrant, closed, or reverberatory pathway. The continuing excitation may then be transmitted to motor organs (from Hebb, 1958, p. 75).

adjacent neurons fire together, the less the synaptic resistance.[7] In developing perceptual acuity as a given stimulus object is repeatedly experienced, a set of cell assemblies is formed in the cortex. When later presentation of the stimulus activates those cell assemblies the resulting reverberating circuit produces perceptual awareness of the external stimulus.

In terms of independent, intervening and dependent variables, Hebb's broad theoretical program can be schematized as follows:

Independent Variables	Intervening Variables	Dependent Variables
Sensory excitations (varying temporal and spatial patterns), direct neural stimulation, content of blood and plasma, nervous system structure and function (varying heredity, surgical injury, disease).	Unobserved function of sense organs, nervous system, effectors, glands, i.e., processes inside the skin. Essentially he relies on cell assemblies.	Observed muscular and glandular activities (to include EMG, GSR, verbal reports, etc.).

In contrast to behaviorists, Hebb employed such anatomical and neurophysiological evidence as he could muster in developing his hypothetical constructs. Perhaps referring to Skinner's refusal to employ physiological data and hypothetical constructs, Hebb held that a refusal to neurologize is discarding a guide to the selection of constructs, and is refusing to look at data that might show that one's theory is wrong. While "psychology cannot be reduced to physiology . . . it seems evident that the psychologist may need every now and then a short bout of physiological psychotherapy, just to permit him to get on with his own business" (1963, p. 26).

To explain mental activity that occurs in the absence of the controlling stimulus that would normally evoke a perception, Hebb developed the concept of images. An image occurs when cell assemblies fire, in the absence of the stimulus, to reinstate the same brain processes that originally occurred during perception of the stimulus. Activation of the cell assemblies can presumably be influenced by internal stimuli which arise from any of thousands of bodily sources. Imagery of everyday life during thought, daydreaming, nocturnal dreams and hallucinations are thus to be understood in terms of central reverberating circuits. The importance of external control of the mental processes is well illustrated by the bizarre nature of dreams and hallucinations since various cell assemblies, not guided by the reality of the external environment, fire in unusual combinations. The hallucination of pain in the phantom limb phenomenon is similarly to be understood—the sensory input might

---

[7] In his more modern version Hebb attributed decreased synaptic resistance to the neuroanatomical observation of the development of boutons at the synapse.

commence at the edge of the amputated limb, the afferent neural volley ascending to the cortex whereupon cell assemblies are activated that give the experience of pain arising in the lower, amputated limb.

With regard to the thought processes, Hebb said that "an 'idea' is the activity of a closed loop, and 'thought' a succession of such activities" (1963, p. 17). Hence, the firing of each cell assembly corresponds to a relatively simple sensory input (or image for that sensory input) such as a particular vowel sound or syllable. The firing of an entire phase sequence then might constitute the thought of an entire word or sentence. Hebb (1954) diagrammed a single phase sequence and contrasting models of thought as shown in Fig. 2.6. Hebb continued by

regarding the train of thought first as a single series of discrete events (top line). We can then represent the classical stimulus-response or motor theory of thought, which Lashley has so effectively criticized, as in the middle line: each "idea" is fully determined by afferent input, and simply amounts to through transmission (as at the right). A significant change is made in the bottom line (if each of the central events in the diagram is a "cell assembly," this embodies the main feature of the theory (Hebb, 1949) published elsewhere). The central event is now determined by *two* influences, one sensory, one central. The central influence is a facilitation from the preceding central activity (Hebb, 1954, p. 408).

The numerous cell assemblies firing in sequence at any given time, directed by antecedent sensory and central events, thus provide composite central activity that is commensurate in complexity with the stream of thought, as represented in Fig. 2.7. There each arrow indicates a single central activity, guided by sensory input (S). Motor consequences of the central activity are not shown. The region denoted by A indicates *concentration* in which all central activities support each other. B and C illustrate *divided attention* with two mental activities occurring concurrently in a parallel fashion.

Hebb defined consciousness per se, as a state of being awake and

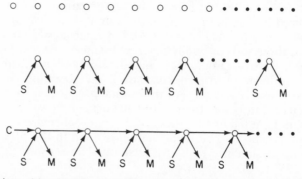

FIG. 2.6   Schematizing thought as a series of discrete events in time, as in the top line: C, central; S, sensory; M, motor. The "motor" theory of thought is in the second line, each central event being determined by sensory input alone. In the bottom line, a central event is determined jointly by sensory and central facilitations (from Hebb, 1954).

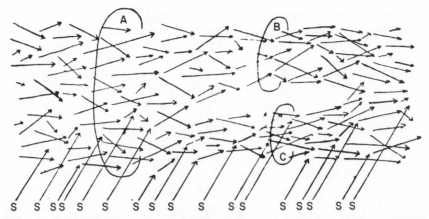

FIG. 2.7. The stream of thought. Each arrow represents a central or sensory activity. A, concentration, with concurrent thoughts supporting each other. B and C, divided attention with two thoughts in parallel (from Hebb, 1954).

responsive. We need the term consciousness, he said, to distinguish between the waking adult animal of a higher species and the same animal under anesthesia, or with a concussion, or in deep sleep. Consciousness is a state of the brain which determines behavior, though the behavioral difference between consciousness and unconsciousness is not clear-cut nor simple. The distinction between unconsciousness and consciousness involves a distinction between sense dominated behavior and behavior in which complex mediating activity occurs, although there is no hard and fast distinction between sense dominated behavior and mediated behavior. An inbetween case is the sleeper who is dreaming but is unresponsive to his external world. At a minimum, mediating processes are present during consciousness, and one normal feature of consciousness is immediate memory, e.g., one remembers what one was thinking about and can produce much of it on request. Unconscious processes exist too in the sense of unreportable and unretained mental events that affect behavior.

Hebb's thoughts on creativity resemble somewhat those of Watson, if one substitutes "cell assemblies" for "responses." Creativity is not the sudden appearance of a whole new process—a new insight consists of a recombination of preexisting mediating reactions. Successful problem solving (a creative endeavor) is a joint product of sensory input and the immediately preceding central processes. If one has not arrived at a correct solution, Hebb's prescription is to first juggle the external stimuli around in order to attempt to change the cell assemblies that are active. If this does not work, drop the problem in order to get away from the immediate environmental situation—this permits changes in the ongoing mediating processes so that the problem can later be approached anew. One can thus prepare for a new idea in advance, but the new idea cannot be commanded at a particular moment.

In considering cognitive learning Hebb explained the association of ideas, perceptual learning, and sensory preconditioning in terms of the build-up and association of cell assemblies. In associating two ideas, two separate stimuli (S_1 and S_2), contiguously presented, build up and evoke with practice their respective cell assemblies that themselves are associated in the cortex. In the future if one cell assembly is evoked it activates the second cell assembly, producing the subjective experience that one idea led to another.

In Pavlov's sensory preconditioning, initially two stimuli (e.g., a light and a sound) are presented contiguously to a subject (Fig. 2.8). Following this, one stimulus (e.g., the light) is conditioned to a given response, whereupon during a test the second stimulus (sound) is found to evoke the conditional response. Hebb's explanation is that the two external stimuli evoke their respective cell assemblies such that there develops cortical chaining leading from the second cell assembly to the first, and the first thereby evokes the conditional response. However, this explanation of Hebb's ignores the assumption that activated cell assemblies result in response events (see Fig. 2.8). An equally plausible explanation is that in the initial stages of conditioning, each stimulus evokes its corresponding evoked response pattern (which may be covert.) Those re-

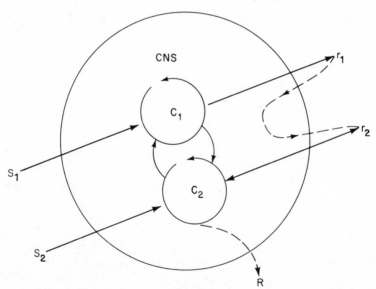

FIG. 2.8   Diagram of a possible mechanism of sensory preconditioning. Stimuli S_1 and S_2 are presented together repeatedly, making the central processes C_1 and C_2 active at the same time so that they establish connections. At this point sensory preconditioning is complete, but demonstrating its existence requires a further step: S_2 is made the conditional stimulus for a response R, and then when S_1 is presented it too can elicit R (from Hebb, 1966, p. 115). This figure has been modified to show the possibility too that sensory preconditioning could equally well be explained through the development of covert responses such that in place of cell assembly 1 r_1 could evoke r_2 which in turn could lead to the evocation of R.

sponses, like the cell assemblies, would become associated too. Hence, in the test situation when sound is presented the resulting covert response produces stimuli that evoke the response for light, which in turn evokes the conditional response.

The nonspecific projection center (the reticular activating system) is quite important in Hebb's (1963) neurologizing. Sensory inputs are transmitted directly to the appropriate sensory nuclei in the thalamus, and thence to their appropriate regions in the cortex. Incoming volleys also enter the reticular activating system which bombards the cortex to keep the cortex aroused. This branching of afferent fibers thus serves a cue function to guide information directly to the cortex, and an arousal function to determine the level of wakefulness. With regard to activation of cell assemblies the arousal function is important because the afferent bombardment supports the firing of cell assemblies. Without sufficient arousal, incoming information would not be processed and mediation would not be possible. Furthermore, the downflow from the cortex to further activate the nonspecific projection center means that thought processes are themselves arousing.

Experimentation in Search of Mediating Processes

The theoretical approaches to mediational processes that we have reviewed are not based on direct psychophysiological measures, nor is it necessary that the mediating processes have empirical reality (they may be intervening variables). Hull held that his constructs were intervening variables, but there is a counter argument that his use of neurophysiological terms ("afferent neural impulses," "reverberation of neural circuits," etc.) implies empirical reality. In locating his mediating processes in different levels of the cerebrum, Osgood is among the more explicit theorists in this respect (cf. especially Osgood and Hoosain, 1974). Schoenfeld and Cumming alluded to the reality status of their perceptual response (R_1) by referring to the electromyographical measures of covert responses by R. C. Davis and his colleagues (Davis, Buchwald, and Frankmann, 1955). The approach in this book is that mediating processes are theoretical attempts to account for cognitive processes (seeing, hearing, thinking) that are directly measurable through psychophysiological means.[8] Hefferline, Keenan, Harford, and

---

[8] In the strict pnysicalism that we are following, we are *not* considering mental processes as a "correlate" of psychophysiological events. That is, it is sometimes argued, as in some of the statements by Titchener, that mental processes are correlated but not equated with the psychophysiological events that we are studying. The position of Müller-Freienfels elaborated by Holt earlier in this chapter is such an interpretation. Our position is that mental processes *are* the activation of selected neuromuscular circuits. To argue that mental processes are correlates of the activation of neuromuscular circuits demands an independent measurement of those mental activities which, in our view, is not possible. In short, mental processes are not correlates of neuromuscular circuit activation. They *are* those events.

Birch (1960) coined the term "electropsychology" which I heartily en-
dorse. Hefferline's proposal was that electropsychology was the application of traditional methods of electrophysiology for the solution of
psychological problems. Through electropsychology we should eventually arrive at a thorough mapping of covert bodily reactions that are
hypothesized to be mediational processes. This wedding of the theoretical strategy of the behaviorists to the empiricism of the
psychophysiologists should be beneficial to both fields. That is, progress
in both psychophysiology and theoretical behaviorism should be enhanced by relating the hypothetical constructs of the theoretician with
the directly measured empirical events of the psychophysiologist's
laboratory. The direct measurement of the hypothetical construct
should guide the further development of our theories that were initially
built on observations of overt behavior alone, just as those theories could
guide the development of a theoretical psychophysiology. We shall illustrate this approach by means of research aimed at measuring
psychophysiological variables within the context of mediational
paradigms.

Volkova (1953) used a differentiation procedure to condition the
word "good" to evoke salivation and the word "bad" for no salivation. He
then found that sentences that had been rated as "good" later evoked
salivation when presented to the subjects while there was no salivation to
sentences that had been rated as "bad." For sentences that had been
rated as intermediate between good and bad, there was an intermediate
amount of salivation. Acker and Edwards (1964) repeated Volkova's
experiment in principle, making certain modifications that improved the
methodology. Their subjects rated words according to whether the
words were "good" or "bad." Some subjects were then conditioned to the
auditory presentation of the word "good," using white noise as the unconditional stimulus and vasoconstriction as the response. Other subjects
were similarly conditioned to the word "bad." For subjects who were
conditioned to "good" both that word and other words that had been
rated as being good evoked vasoconstriction, but words rated by those
subjects as being "bad" did not evoke vasoconstriction. Similarly, for
subjects who had been conditioned to the word "bad" both "bad" and
words rated bad evoked vasoconstriction, but this was not the case for
"good" words. Apparently, words which had a "good meaning" evoked a
generalized mediator for "good" (and similarly for "bad"), and vasoconstriction was in some way related to that mediator. Whether or not
vasoconstriction was an actual component of the mediator, or a response
evoked by a prior mediational process in a complex chain, could be
ascertained through careful psychophysiological research in which temporal relationships among a variety of bodily processes were precisely
ascertained.

Research in which a number of psychophysiological measures were
taken during mediation was reported by McGuigan, Culver, and Kendler (1971). These researchers electromyographically measured re-

sponses from the tongue, right leg, and both arms, together with elec-
trooculographic measures and electroencephalograms from over the
dominant motor area of the brain. Tracy Kendler's (1972) mediational
paradigm was modified to be used for recording covert responses.

These experimenters used three groups of subjects: (1) a verbal mediation group, (2) a non-oral mediation group in which the arms (left vs.
right) were possible loci for mediational behavior, and (3) a nonmedia-
tional control group. It was found that amplitude of tongue EMG significantly increased only for the verbal mediation group, and that the
increase was significantly greater than for the other two control groups
(Fig. 2.9). For the nonoral mediation group, arm EMG and eye activity
was relatively large (and significantly so), these measures being possible
indicators of the right vs. left mediational activity that would be expected
for this condition. There were no other significant differences. The
failure of any psychophysiological measure to increase for the no mediation control group suggests that the oral EMG change for the verbal
mediation group and the arm and eye increases for the nonoral mediation group were possible components of the mediational responses
hypothesized by Tracy Kendler.

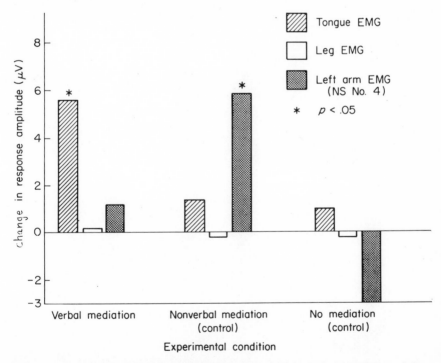

FIG. 2.9 Tongue EMG increased significantly more for an oral-verbal mediation group than
for two control groups. Limb activity was greatest for the directional (right to left) nonverbal
mediation group, as illustrated by reaction to one mediational symbol.

Such positive findings should encourage others to employ the general strategy of psychophysiologically mapping out critical components of neuromuscular circuits that are activated during mediational activities. In this way, we should be able to empirically measure hypothetical constructs that have been developed on the basis of external stimuli and overt responses. In such further direct psychophysiological measures of these patterns, one should employ precise temporal measures in order to specify the patterns not only topographically throughout the body but temporally too. The temporal pattern of approach employed by McGuigan and Pavek (1972) and by McGuigan and Boness (1975), as discussed on pages 363–64, might serve as a useful model in this connection.

part two

Technical and Methodological Considerations of Covert Processes

3

Taxonomy and Theoretical
Status of Covert Processes[1]

The classical distinction between overt and covert behavior is not a sharp one. We recognize events that are clearly overt, such as waving the hand or speaking aloud. Just as clearly, there are events that are hidden from ordinary observation, such as a slight thumb twitch, the brief contraction of a small muscle in the tongue, or an increase in cardiac rate. Between these extremes there is a twilight zone that includes events which are difficult to classify as being either overt or covert—a very slight whisper, a partial blink of the eyes, or an arrested nod of the head, for example.

Whether events are clearly overt, clearly covert, or fall within the "twilight zone," however, is in principle unimportant to us. The fact that

---

[1] This chapter is a selection and abbreviation of a more expanded technical discussion of the laboratory measurement of covert processes published elsewhere (McGuigan, 1978b). It was shortened so that we could concentrate here more on the theoretical aspects of cognitive psychophysiology.

specialized apparatus is required for the observation of small scale behavior does not mean that those behaviors necessarily differ in kind or quality from overt behavior. Nor is it theoretically relevant that events in the "twilight zone" may be studied more effectively by the methods of covert behavior than by the classical methods of observing overt behavior. The important point is that the task of psychology is to understand behavior, *all* behavior. To accomplish this task we must concentrate some of our energies on that sub-realm of behavior that is "covert."

The frequent reference in the psychological literature to "covert behavior" and to similar terms like "implicit response," "subvocalization," and "inner speech" attests to the historical and contemporary importance of concepts of covert events (Chapter 2).

Covert Processes

We use the term "processes" (or equally "reactions," or "events") as in the title of this chapter, instead of "behavior" so that the scope of our inquiry may be increased—we wish to include both behavioral *and* neurological events. Our basic classification, therefore, is a division of covert processes into responses (muscular and glandular events) on the one hand, and central nervous system (CNS) reactions on the other. Muscle responses are best measured through electromyography, while brain events are often electrically studied, as through electroencephalography. This separation of response and CNS reactions is made because the two classes of events operate differently and *are* different components of neuromuscular circuits that function during internal information processing (see Chapter 9). It is also likely that, though we use similar electrical methods for studying the two classes of bodily events, responses simply obey different laws than do neural (nonresponse) events. It is only through their separate study that we can determine whether different laws *do* apply to muscular and neural phenomena. If they do not it will be a simple matter to generalize from one domain to another. It is, then, most efficient to classify systems of responses vs. CNS reactions separately and to study the interactions of these events within neuromuscular circuits. Within the first major classification of covert processes, namely that of muscular and glandular responses, we shall focus on skeletal (as contrasted with smooth) muscle responses, eye responses, and respiration.

MEASUREMENT OF COVERT PROCESSES

There is no problem, of course, in observing overt responses—difficulties arise only insofar as recording and measurement techniques are concerned. Covert events, on the other hand, can only be observed through the use of equipment that, so to speak, extends the scope of our senses. That magnification is required in order to observe is, of course, not unusual, and we have developed numerous kinds of apparatus that allow us to detect phenomena which could not otherwise be studied. The microscope and the telescope are the most obvious examples. It is important to emphasize, that covert processes are in no sense mystical or unusual simply because they must be uniquely sensed, amplified, recorded and quantified.

The various activities of the body involve chemical, mechanical and electrical processes (so far). Measures of chemical reactions are best left to the biochemist and physiologist. In psychological research numerous measures of mechanical reactions have been used. The measurement of mechanical covert behavior started in the early 1900s when experimenters enthusiastically and creatively sought objective evidence of "implicit language habits," a critical concept in behavioristic theories of thinking. Techniques to record covert speech activity during thought involved such devices as inflated balloons and flattened wine glasses placed on or about the tongue; such "sensors" then had mechanical connections to recording systems of tambours and kymographs. The extreme of mechanical measurement was Thorson's (1925) device which magnified tongue movements by a factor of about 4.5 (see McGuigan, 1973a). It is obvious that during the first quarter of this century adequate technology was simply lacking, and it is amazing that early experimenters ever did report successful measurements of small-scale, covert processes. The technological breakthrough came in the twenties with Jacobson's (1927) pioneering electrical measurements of covert behavioral events, and Berger's (1929) electrical measurements of brain events. In developing his methods of progressive relaxation, begun in 1908, Jacobson needed a sensitive measure of muscular tension as a criterion for degree of improvement of his patients. His first valuable index of tension was a kymographic measure of the amplitude of the knee jerk, a reflex which, as with all deep reflexes, does not occur in the well relaxed person. Later Jacobson employed a string galvanometer, the primitive electromyograph believed to have been first used by Forbes and Thatcher in 1921 (cf. Jacobson, 1973). To use the string galvanometer, one inserted electrodes into muscles; the voltage generated by active muscles would produce vibration of a wire whose shadow was recorded on photographic paper.

The string galvanometer lacked sufficient sensitivity for Jacobson, who required a measure of amplitudes less than a microvolt (one-millionth of a volt). His ambitions seemed incredible to physiologists of the 1920s—the accomplished scientist H. S. Gasser, after listening to Jacobson's extremely sensitive equipment requirements, responded by saying, "I take my hat off to a microvolt." In collaboration with Bell Telephone Laboratories, Jacobson eventually developed the integrating neurovoltmeter, which he used successfull in his clinical and scientific work. Contrary to opinion of the time, Jacobson then showed that muscle tonus could be reduced to a level of 0.0 microvolts by the use of progressive relaxation technics (cf. Jacobson, 1973).

In those early days it was important to demonstrate that he was measuring electromyographic activity and not the galvanic skin relfex

(GSR). Among the differences that Jacobson (1932) noted were the greater voltages of GSR readings, the latencies of from 1.0 to 4.0 sec obtained with GSR as contrasted with the fraction of a second which commonly intervened between signal and initiation of the EMG, as well as the differences in frequency, wave form, direction of potential, and tissue of origin of GSR vs. EMG.

Jacobson's pioneering work has led to great advances in electromyography, as has Berger's well known research in electroencephalography. Particularly within the last two decades, extremely versatile electronic systems have been developed to allow sensitive electrical recording of signals generated by bodily processes. As a consequence, the empirical study of covert processes has been progressing exponentially. Let us now turn to a brief consideration of some covert processes, and of a classificatory system for them.

COVERT RESPONSES

Skeletal Muscle Responses. Since electromyography provides the most sensitive measure of muscle activity presently available, covert muscle responses measured through EMG require most of our attention. When we study muscle action potentials (MAP) through electromyography we obtain the electromyogram—a record of the electrical properties of muscles.

The *functional* unit of striate muscle is the motor unit (Fig. 3.1). The motor unit consists of: (1) a nerve cell body which is located in the ventral

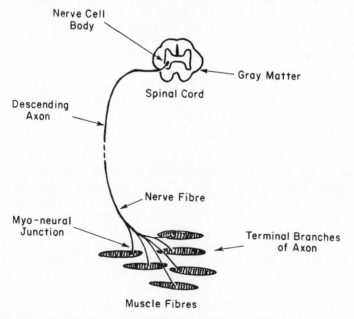

FIG. 3.1   Scheme of a motor unit (modified from Basmajian, 1962).

root of the gray matter of the spinal cord, (2) an axon descending down the motor nerve, (3) the terminal branches of the axon, (4) the myoneural junction, and finally (5) the muscle fibers that are supplied by these branches. The muscle fiber is the *structural* unit of the striate muscle; in appearance it looks like a fine piece of thread. In size, muscle fibers generally vary in length from 1 mm to 10 cm, and in width from 10 to 100 microns. However, muscle fibers may exceed 34 cm in length (Lockhart and Brandt, 1937-38). Muscle fiber components of a muscle are aligned in parallel and probably stretch from the origin as a single entity. The number of fibers per motor unit varies from several (2 or 3) for muscles whose function is fine movement (e.g., muscles in the larynx, those that control movement of the eyeball, the ossicles of ear, etc.) to 2,000 or so for muscles that perform a gross function (e.g., in the leg, the medial head of gastrocnemius).

An efferent neural impulse, which arrives at the central region of a muscle fiber, produces a rapid contraction of the entire fiber (with a latency of perhaps 10 msec), providing that the impulse is above threshold (muscle fibers obey the all-or-none-law).[2] A muscle fiber contraction lasts for approximately 2 msec after which the fiber relaxes. The contraction occurs when the afferent neural impulse produces a localized depolarization which is then transmitted along the membrane that surrounds the fiber. During contraction, the membrane polarity is reversed yielding the major electrical signal that may be recorded. Though the contraction time for each fiber is approximately 2 msec, all fibers of a single motor unit do not contract simultaneously. Hence, the electrical recording of a single motor unit stimulated once is somewhat longer, usually 5 to 10 msec. When observed on a cathode ray oscilloscope, action of a typical motor unit appears as a biphasic spike as in Fig. 3.2.

Visceral Muscle Activity. While not a major focus of this book, visceral activity is of considerable importance in linguistic processing, probably by adding "emotional tone" to semantic interpretation (Chapter 9). Although there has been relatively little psychophysiological research on visceral muscle activity, there have been some interesting findings, and it is likely that much important linguistic processing research will be done on visceral smooth muscle activity. The addition of electrical measures of abdominal activity (electrogastrograms, EGG) during linguistic processing should be strongly encouraged. A wide variety of techniques have been used for the study of visceral events (swallowing a balloon or magnet, fluoroscopy, etc.), but electrical recording techniques are preferable because they reduce the likelihood of artifacts and appear generally more sensitive.

---

[2] For a more thorough discussion of the contraction phenomenon with precise temporal values, see Gatev and Ivanov (1972) whose work is more extensively discussed in Chapter 9.

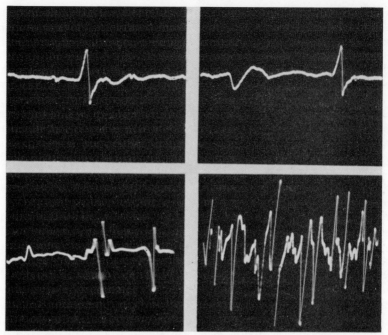

FIG. 3.2 A sample of normal electromyograms showing one, two, and many superimposed motor unit potentials ("interference pattern"). The single potential in the upper left corner had a measured amplitude of 0.8 mv and duration of 7 msec (from Basmajian, 1962, p. 14).

Eye Responses. The wide variety of techniques which have been developed for the study of eye movements may be classified into three fundamental methods for objective recording.[3] The first method, of historical interest only, employs mechanical transducers in which a small rod, for example, is directly attached to the cornea. The second is the optical method in which reflections of a light source onto the cornea are photographically recorded. As Marg (1951) pointed out, the optical method has the disadvantages that the head is immobilized, the subject experiences a strong glare from the light source, the eyes must be kept open (blinking may spoil a part of the record), a complicated optical system is necessary if there is to be registration in two instead of one meridian, and it is time consuming to await photographic development of the film. The third, electrical method of registering eye movements, has none of these disadvantages; consequently it is the most prominently used method in contemporary literature. In discussing electrical measurement of eye activity, we shall exclude consideration of the recording of the illumination potential through electroretinography (cf. Ar-

---

[3] We exclude here discussion of casual observational techniques such as the "peep hole" method in which the eyes are observed through a small hole in the screen that separates the subject from the experimenter.

mington, 1974), and pupillography; the former is relatively unimportant for the study of covert processes during cognition, and while the latter is quite important in this respect, the pupils (with all other autonomic events) are excluded from detailed consideration in this book.

In a valuable history of electrical measurement of eye activity, Marg (1951) pointed out that Jacobson (1930a-d) was the first to use a vacuum tube amplifier for recording the changes of electrical potential during eye movement, thus launching contemporary electrooculography. In 1936 Mowrer, Ruch, and Miller (cited by Marg, 1951) confirmed Jacobson's success in recording eye position with surface electrodes. In addition to the measurement of changes of potential in the eye during mental activity, Jacobson described the functional relationship between eye movements and various kinds of dreams (1938b). After Aserinsky and Kleitman (1953, 1955) elaborated on rapid eye movements during the dream state, electrical measurement of covert processes during dreaming became a major contemporary interest (see Chapter 5).

Respiratory Responses. Sensitive respiration measures can yield valuable covert oral data because of the intimate participation of the breathing mechanism in speech activity. The source of the respiratory signal is the change in the lung capacity that is produced by contraction and relaxation of the intercostal and abdominal muscles.

Common methods of sensing respiration include the rubber bellows and mechanical and temperature systems. The most common measurement is respiration rate, though relative amplitude changes have also been studied and have yielded some valuable findings relating the pneumogram in the study of covert processes and speech (e.g., Ladefoged, 1962).

NEUROPHYSIOLOGICAL PROCESSES

Electrical reactions recorded from the surface of the skull provide the major and most informative direct measure of neurophysiological activity in the normal human (EMG's may be more informative indirect measures of brain activity, as in Sechenov, 1863, and as discussed in Chapter 6). Other approaches (electrical and chemical stimulation techniques, etc.) are not applicable except in specialized instances.

The first tracings of electrical activity from over the human skull were published by Hans Berger in 1929, though his conclusion that they were signals from the brain was not accepted until Lord Adrian independently demonstrated the phenomenon at Cambridge (Adrian and Mathews, 1934). Even then, those who did believe that the signals were generated by the brain still regarded them as rather dull because the alpha frequencies were so constant and thus not indicative of momentary thoughts. Today the controversy as to the source of alpha waves continues. We have, for instance, the startling conclusion by Lippold

(1970a, b, c; Lippold and Novotny, 1970) that alpha waves are generated by the eyes and resonate from the back of the skull. Certainly there is no consensus as to the principles by which some 10 billion cerebral neurons generate the various brain waves, like those in the alpha frequencies. While we appear to be making good progress in electrical measures (see Chapter 8) we must recognize that brain events constitute, in all probability, the most complex phenomena in nature, and probably will be the last to yield to an adequate understanding.

Brain waves have been classified primarily by their frequency range. While the precise values for the defining frequency ranges have varied among authorities, the approximate values in Table 3.1 are common.

TABLE 3.1 Classes of Electroencephalographically Recorded Brain Waves Defined by their Frequency Ranges.

Brain Wave Class	Frequency
Sub-Delta	0-.5 Hz
Delta	.5-4 Hz
Theta	4-8 Hz
Alpha	8-13 Hz
Sigma	13-15 Hz
Beta	15-30 Hz
Gamma	30-50 Hz

Developmental research has indicated that theta rhythms are the earliest to appear in humans, being recordable during the first year of life. Basic alpha rhythms emerge during the second or third year, but the faster components of alpha frequencies usually do not appear until about the 7th or 8th years of life (Kleitman, 1960). The amplitude of EEG signals is usually within 1 to 100 microvolts at the surface of the scalp, though it may reach as high as 500 microvolts.

Efforts to develop lawful relationships involving the ever-changing patterns of electrical gradients generated by the brain have resulted in a wide variety of methods of analysis. Classification of brain waves through complex frequency analyses, the plotting of gradients, and averaging of evoked potentials (see McGuigan, 1978b) are illustrative techniques.

A Summary Classification of Covert Processes

An extended science of covert processes must include numerous measures in addition to those discussed above. In Table 3.2 a systematic taxonomy of the major classes of covert processes is presented, with the primary division separating response events (I) from neurophysiological processes (II) and secondary divisions distinguishing responses in the oral regions of the body (IA), from the nonoral bodily areas (IB). The reference to covert *oral* responses does not commit us to any particular functional interpretation of those response events. An oral response may involve speech in which case it is a *linguistic* oral response or it may serve no internal information processing function, (e.g., a swallow or bite of the lips) in which case it is a nonlinguistic oral response. The discussion in Chapter 9 gives an empirical justification for the conclusion that certain classes of covert oral behavior function linguistically.

TABLE 3.2   A Summary Classification of Psychophysiologically Measured Covert Processes (Estimates of Signal Characteristics Are for Humans)

The two major classes of covert processes are:
I.   covert responses, which consist of, and only of, muscular and glandular events; and
II. neurophysiological processes, principally measured in the normal human through electroencephalography and signal processing techniques.

I.   Covert Responses
   A. Covert oral responses
       1. Skeletal muscle electromyographic measures (2-3000 Hz), principally from the following regions:
           i.   tongue
           ii. lip
           iii. chin
           iv. laryngeal
           v.   jaw
       2. Pneumograms (12-20 respirations/min)
       3. Audio measures of subvocalization ("whispering") (20-20,000 Hz)
       4. Salivation
   B. Covert nonoral responses
       1. Skeletal muscle (2-3000 Hz) electromyographic measures:
           i.   finger
           ii. arm
           iii. leg
           iv. et cetera
       2. Visceral muscle activity (electrogastrogram, DC to .6 Hz; .5-80 mv)
       3. Eye responses
           i.   electrooculogram
           ii. electroretinogram
           iii. pupillogram
       4. Cardiovascular measures
           i.   heart rate (45 to 200 beats/min)
           ii. electrocardiogram (.05 to 8 Hz; 10 μv to 5 mv)
           iii. finger pulse volume (DC to 30 Hz)
           iv. blood pressure (DC to 200 Hz)
       5. Electrodermal measures [galvanic skin response (1 K to 500 K resistance), skin conductance, etc.]
II. Neurophysiological Measures
   In the normal human, electrical activity is studied and recorded with a variety of techniques, e.g., electroencephalograms (DC to 100 Hz; 10 μv to 100 μv), evoked potentials, contingent negative variation (the "expectancy" wave). Other measures should also be considered, such as magnetic sensing systems (e.g., Kolta, 1973).

Most of the available data on covert oral behavior have been gathered through electromyographic recording. During linguistic processing, the tongue yields the most sensitive of these measures, the lips appear to be the next most sensitive region, and the jaw, chin, and laryngeal regions are relatively insensitive (see, for instance, McGuigan, Culver, and Kendler, 1971; and McGuigan and Pinkney, 1973).

As indicated earlier, pneumograms (IA2) are potentially very important measures of covert oral responses but they have not been extensively studied. Breathing rate has generally been found to increase during such linguistic tasks as silent reading, but the interpretation of this finding remains uncertain (e.g., McGuigan, Keller, and Stanton, 1964). Breathing amplitude has been found to increase during auditory hallucinations (cf. McGuigan, 1966b). Audio measures of subvocalization (IA3) have been extremely interesting in the study of covert oral behavior. For example, by monitoring highly amplified sounds issuing from their mouths, it is possible to understand portions of the prose that children silently read (e.g., McGuigan, Keller, and Stanton, 1964), or portions of the verbal content of a paranoid schizophrenic's auditory hallucinations (McGuigan, 1966b). As an indicator of covert oral behavior, the salivation measure (IA4) has not been greatly exploited, but it has led to some interesting findings with regard to verbal processing (e.g., Razran, 1939).

Measures of covert nonoral responses (IB) during linguistic processing are extremely valuable, especially EMGs from such somatic regions as the fingers, the preferred arm, and (for control measures) from the leg. Especially interesting for us is the monitoring of covert finger activity in individuals who are proficient in dactylic language, such as deaf individuals or teachers of the deaf (e.g., Max, 1937; McGuigan, 1971). Similarly, the value of measures of covert eye behavior (especially electrooculography (IB3i), cannot be overemphasized. The last two measures of nonoral behavior, included in Table 3.2 primarily for completeness, (cardiovascular and electrodermal recordings) are quite valuable, but discussion of them is excluded here because of the necessity to limit our coverage.

Various neurophysiological measures (II) should eventually lead to an advanced understanding of the brain during thought, but this exceedingly complex organ will undoubtedly require more advanced techniques of study than we can yet imagine.

We shall now turn to a discussion of the formal or theoretical status of the various covert processes which are classified in Table 3.2.

Formal Status of Covert Processes: Concepts of Covert Reactions

The classical psychophysiological procedures (electroencephalography, electromyography, electrooculography, etc.) specified in Table 3.2 provide us with powerful methods for measuring covert processes

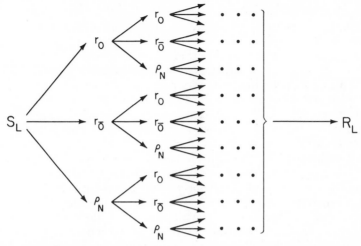

FIG. 3.3 Representation of three classes of linguistic hypothetical constructs: covert oral responses (r_o), covert non-oral responses ($r_{\bar{o}}$), and covert neurophysiological processes (ρ_N). Complex interactions are represented here with arrows, though the representation of them as neuromuscular circuit components in Chapter 9 is more realistic.

and for operationally defining concepts. But empirical psychophysiology lacks a guiding theoretical framework, which is necessary for the development of a mature science of covert processes. In developing a formal theory of covert processes, we must simultaneously consider three hypothetical constructs and their interrelationships. In particular, these are the covert oral language response, the covert nonoral language response, the covert neurophysiological language reaction; they and their interactions are represented in Fig. 3.3. In Fig. 3.3 an external linguistic stimulus (S_L) may evoke a covert oral language response (r_o), a covert nonoral language response (r_o) and a neurophysiological reaction (ρ_N). The enormously complex interactions among these three classes of events are summarized by single arrows indicating that each class of reaction sets off instances of every other class; in Chapter 9 we shall attempt to enlarge upon the nature of these interactions in terms of complex neuromuscular circuits. The ongoing interactions of these three classes of events culminates in an overt response (R_L) that is the termination of this behavioral unit.[4]

At a theoretical level, the covert response has traditionally been considered a hypothetical construct defined according to classical proce-

[4] The question as to how different classes of stimulus events function to produce differences in consequent covert and overt reactions is an important one. In classical cognitive psychology, linguistic stimuli and linguistic responses have been given a priority status, though nonverbal thought has also been considered important too (see especially pp. 382–84 in Chapter 9). Hence, while SL in Fig. 3.3 represents linguistic information input and processing, a similar paradigm could be proposed for nonlinguistic information processing; and there would be additional interactions in a more complex paradigm between verbal and nonverbal thought processes.

dures such as those employed by Hull (1943) or Tolman (1932). Hypothetical constructs are defined by means of functional relationships between external stimuli that anchor them on the antecedent side and overt responses that anchor them on the consequent side. For example, Hull's covert fractional anticipatory goal response (r_G) was defined by readily observable stimuli and responses according to the functional relationships specified by the paradigm: S-r_G-s_G-R. Essentially the same approach to theoretical covert reactions has been used by many others, including Osgood (e.g., Osgood and Hoosain, 1974) and Schoenfeld and Cumming (1963).

While behavioristic paradigms for anchoring constructs of covert processes have been quite successfully employed—the outstanding success of Osgood (e.g., Osgood and Hoosain, 1974) in measuring meaning (r_M) through such techniques as the semantic differential is an excellent example—we seek to compliment this classical approach by means of psychophysiological techniques. In this regard, we note that hypothetical constructs (as distinguished from intervening variables, cf. MacCorquodale and Meehl, 1948) are considered to have "reality status" and thus are (at least) potentially observable. The three major classes of covert linguistic processes (covert oral responses, covert nonoral responses, and covert neurophysiological processes) can thus also be empirically anchored directly through the psychophysiological methods specified in Table 3.2. Fig. 3.4 graphically illustrates the present-day approach in which the hypothetical constructs that intervene between external stimuli and overt responses are operationally defined. We may note in Fig. 3.4 our three hypothetical constructs (ρ_N, r_o, r_o) intervening between the external linguistic stimulus (S_L) and the overt linguistic response (R_L). These intervening hypothetical constructs are directly tied to their psychophysiological data bases, as well as to their indirect data bases (S_L and R_L). Reichenbach (1932) referred to this relationship between the formal constructs and the data level as that of a coordinat-

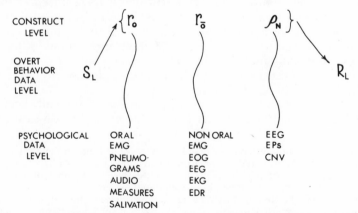

FIG. 3.4 Three hypothetical constructs directly measured through psychophysiological means.

ing definition; Northrop (1948) identified the relation as an epistemic correlation.

More precise speculation at this preliminary stage of the formulation of a science of covert processes is not justified, and we can probably most efficiently proceed by staying extremely close to the data level—though we do need some guiding theoretical notions such as these. While we focus in the coming chapters on linguistic stimuli and consequent linguistic bodily processes, we will consider nonverbal thought in relation to linguistic processes in Chapter 9.

Let us now turn to the general question of "why" covert processes occur and follow that with a survey of data relevant to covert processes that occur as a function of linguistic input. This should provide a data base for the classes of laws hypothesized in Figs. 3.3 and 3.4. After that we shall consider in some detail precisely how linguistic codes function during cognition (information processing).

4

Antecedents of Covert Processes: Learned and Unlearned Responses

In Chapter 3 we discussed a number of covert events, proposed a summary system for classifying them, and considered the formal status of the concepts of the covert oral response, of covert neurophysiological reactions, and of the covert nonoral response. Finally we suggested formal classes of relationships involving these three concepts with the hope that the relationships might guide us in the development of empirical laws. In Chapters 5, 6, 7, and 8 we shall turn our attention to such specific, empirically determined relationships between classes of covert events and their antecedent stimulating conditions. The purpose of the present chapter will be to consider the antecedents of covert processes in a more general way—in a sense, we ask here: "Why do covert responses occur?"[1]

A successful explanation of the occurrence of covert behavior will entail consideration of a difficult methodological question, viz., how we conclude that a *specific* stimulus evokes a *localized* response, as distinguished from more general (nonspecific) relationships between stimuli and widespread bodily reactions to them. For, as we shall see, a number of experimenters have placed importance on the demonstration that a particular, highly localized response was evoked by a stimulus with special characteristics. For example, Jacobson's (1932) subjects made localized covert responses in the speech region (tongue or lip EMG) when asked to think of specific words like "electrical resistance"; heightened activity did not occur to such stimuli in other bodily regions sampled. Jacobson's findings have been used by others to confirm various versions of a motor theory of thinking. These conceptions hold that in imagination (thought, memory, etc.), we covertly use those (localized) muscles that would be employed should we carry out an act overtly, e.g., in imagining the act of walking, the muscles in the legs are covertly used in the same coordinated sequence as if overt walking were taking place. Localized and coordinated responses elsewhere in the body which accompany an overt act (e.g., arm swinging as we walk) also covertly accompany the imagined act.

Jacobson (1967) became convinced of the specificity of neuromuscular patterns as follows: He recalled that, starting in the early 1920s, Hans Berger and he were unknowingly engaged in a race with each other to be the first to measure brain voltages. At that time, both assumed that there was an identifiable specific brain pattern characteristic of each mental act. Jacobson eventually doubted this assumption. As he later said:

Instead, as the result of experiments of others and of myself . . . I am inclined to the opposite belief, surprising as this may at first seem. According to the ultrasensitive measurements during mental activities which have been continued almost daily in my laboratory these past thirty-five years, a specific neuromuscular pattern marks the character of each and every moment of their occurrence. The assumption that there is an equally specific and as readily recordable central pattern has not borne fruit, excepting in a minority of recordings. No one has produced such recordings in convincing measure. . . . In every mental activity what is specific is the neuromuscular pattern (Jacobson, 1967, p. 118).

[1] For elaboration of questions about "why" and the concept of explanation as used here, see McGuigan (1978a, p. 404).

These conclusions have proven especially important in furthering contemporary conceptions of neuro-muscular circuits.

In surveying covert behavior research, we may note that some investigators have studied the effects of one stimulus on a specific response. Others have varied the number of stimuli presented and studied the effects on one or more responses. These two dimensions (number of stimuli and number of responses) may help us to approach this problem of response specificity by using them to classify experiments on covert behavior. In Table 4.1 the number of responses that experimenters simultaneously recorded in their investigations is represented horizontally, while the number of external stimuli they presented is along the vertical dimension. Let us consider types of empirical studies within this framework. The first cell includes those in which the operant level of covert responses is established; in this instance, no stimuli are presented, and only one response is usually recorded (e.g., Hefferline, Keenan, and Harford, 1959). Cell 2 would be for the psychophysiological study of dreams in which external stimuli are not usually presented to the sleeping subject, although typically a number of covert processes are recorded. Cell 3 includes experiments on the conditioning of covert behavior; here the researcher usually attempts to establish a relationship between a single, specific stimulus and a single response class that is localized in one part of the body or within a given bodily system (examples are given later in this chapter).

TABLE 4.1   Studies of Covert Behavior Classified by Typical Experimenter Operations

Number of Responses Simultaneously Recorded

		One	More than One
Number of External Stimuli Presented	Zero	(1) Operant Level	(2) Dreams
	One	(3) Conditioning	(4)
	More than One	(5) Generalization	(6) Orienting Response; Arousal

I cannot readily think of a typical study for cell 4; it is unusual to present a single stimulus and to record several responses, though of course there are some studies in which this has been done (e.g., McGuigan and Bailey, 1969). Cell 5 is represented by conditioning studies in which there is a test for stimulus generalization—several stimuli are presented and the amount of generalization of a single response is measured. Examples for cell 6 are studies of orienting responses and arousal; here the effort has been to specify a variety of responses that occur regardless of the type of stimulus presented to the organism.

One obvious conclusion from the studies classified in Table 4.1 is that a stimulus may serve different functions. To further study stimulus functions, we will need to consider antecedents of covert behavior in greater detail.

Functions of External Stimuli

There are two possible effects of an external stimulus, regardless of the prevailing environmental condition or the operation being performed by the organism. The first type of stimulus effect will be referred to as a *general stimulus function* and the second as a *specific stimulus function*. By "general stimulus function" we mean that a stimulus may produce widespread changes in several regions or systems of the body; two widespread bodily reactions that have been studied are called the *orienting reflex* and the *arousal reaction*. By "specific stimulus function" we mean that a stimulus may evoke only limited bodily changes. For instance, unconditional and conditional stimuli are considered to evoke unconditional and conditional responses that are relatively localized in some bodily region or system. After discussing these two stimulus classes, we can better consider the difficult methodological problem of determining whether a given covert response is a component of a widespread bodily reaction (general stimulus function) or whether it is relatively localized in a given bodily region or system (specific stimulus function).

GENERALIZED FUNCTIONS OF EXTERNAL STIMULI

The Orienting Reflex. The orienting reflex, extensively discussed by Pavlov (1941), is a nonspecific reaction pattern; it is considered to be the first response pattern to any kind of novel external stimulus. E. N. Sokolov (1963) concluded that the orienting reflex facilitates stimulus perception, and that its components include eye movements, dilation of the pupils, suppression of respiration, the galvanic skin response, neck movements, and electroencephalographic changes.

When the orienting reflex commences, there occurs a reduction of the threshold of *all* sense modalities, and hence a generally increasing sensitivity to stimuli. On repetition of the evoking stimulus, the orienting reflex habituates, with the exception of components specifically acted upon by that stimulus, e.g., a local orienting reaction of the organ of vision does not habituate to an adequate light stimulus (Sokolov, 1963). An additional function of the orienting reflex has to do with its role in thought. Maltzman (1971) cited several studies in which it was shown that orienting reflexes can be internally generated as a consequence of thinking. The orienting reflex thus presumably has a perceptual function when evoked by external stimuli, and it functions in thinking when evoked by internal stimuli.

Arousal Reactions.   Neumann and Blanton (1970) suggested that the first statement of an arousal theory was probably that put forth by Fere (ca. 1885) when he proposed that sensations determine the development of psychic energy. Fere thought that all peripheral excitations augment this energy, which in turn activates the effector systems in proportion to its intensity. Consequently, "the intensity of the stimulus, regardless of modality, directly determines muscle output through the effect of the stimulus as a general energizer" (Neumann and Blanton, 1970, p. 460).

There has been considerable research on the generalized stimulus function of increasing the level of activation of an organism. This heightened state of arousal may be reflected by changes in numerous covert measures such as electroencephalograms, electromyograms, galvanic skin responses, or cardiac activity. Extrapolating from (though differing with) Cannon's (1929) energy mobilization system, Duffy (1962) considered activation to refer to the release of energy into various internal physiological systems, in preparation for overt activity rather than to refer to the overt activity itself. Duffy (1962) concluded that although several covert measures generally increase with stimulation, the ". . . organism is not activated as an undifferentiated whole . . . the organism, even when making no overt response, is in a constant state of flux with respect to both its general level of activation and the activation of its several parts" (p. 113).

Duffy's point concerning activational systems is well illustrated by the work of R. C. Davis (1957), whose subjects were told either to press a key at regular intervals or to do nothing and remain as quiet as possible when a given stimulus was presented. He reported four different response patterns as a function of four different types of stimulating conditions (Table 4.2). The E-1 pattern occurred when subjects performed the mild task of paced key pressing. For resting subjects the N pattern was evoked by simple auditory and visual stimuli, the P pattern occurred to complex stimuli (pictures), and the C pattern was the typical reaction to simple cutaneous stimuli. The first two rows of Table 4.2 indicate that palmar sweating and forearm EMG increased under all four stimulus conditions, while the remaining measures in the lower rows may be used to distinguish the four response patterns from each other. This finding is quite important, for it (1) indicates the complexity and widespread nature of covert bodily reactions, (2) shows that there are relatively unique response patterns as a function of the type of stimulus, and (3) indicates that there are response measures that increase regardless of the stimulus class. We shall return to these three points later in this chapter.

In summary, novel external stimuli evoke two related kinds of widespread bodily reaction patterns: (1) the orienting reflex that, among other things, facilitates perceptual sensitivity, and (2) the arousal reaction, an energy mobilizing activity of the organism. Both classes consist of complex, widespread patterns of covert processes, though sometimes covert skeletal responses erupt into overt behavior.

TABLE 4.2 Four Response Patterns Evoked by Four Different Stimulus Conditions (Double Signs Indicate Diphasic Effects)

Response Measure	E-1 (Key Press)	N (Visual and Auditory Stimuli)	P (Complex Stimuli)	C (Cutaneous Stimui)
		Pattern		
Palmar sweating	+	+	+	+
Forearm EMG	+	+	+	+
Pulse rate	+	+ −	−	−
Volume pulse	−	−	−	−
Pressure pulse		− +	−	+
Finger volume	−	−	−	+
Chin volume		+	−	+
Respiration rate	+	−	−	+ −
Amplitude respiration	+	+	−	− +

Adapted from Davis (1957).

SPECIALIZED FUNCTIONS OF EXTERNAL STIMULI: UNCONDITIONAL AND CONDITIONAL REFLEXES

In addition to evoking an orienting reflex and arousing the organism, a stimulus may have a more localized effect. Some relatively specific stimulus-localized response connections are, of course, unconditional reflexes that are effective at birth (e.g., acid in the mouth ⟶ salivation). However, more numerous localized responses seem to be evoked by conditional stimuli (discriminative stimuli are included in the class of conditional stimuli). It is likely that, in the history of any organism, a wide variety of stimuli have acquired the capacity to evoke a multitude of relatively localized covert (as well as overt) responses. Highly localized responses, such as a covert response in the right arm when a person imagines lighting a cigarette or four distinct EMG bursts in the arm when one imagines hitting a nail four times with a hammer (Jacobson, 1932), may be assumed to be the products of learning.

Learning and specific principles of conditioning thus assume considerable importance here. However, when one considers the scope of covert conditioning, including galvanic skin response conditioning, electroencephalographic conditioning, cardiac conditioning, and even phenomena like intestinal conditioning, it becomes immediately apparent that we must establish priorities for our inquiry. Traditionally, psychology has been predominantly concerned with overt skeletal muscle behavior, and I believe rightly so; our priority, therefore, will be to examine issues in the conditioning of skeletal muscle behavior. Since covert muscle behavior can best be studied with the techniques of electromyography, we need to reassess our knowledge about the conditioning of covert responses that are electromyographically recorded. Our hope is that resulting principles will apply to the conditioning of other (also very important) covert systems.

A major value of understanding covert electromyographical conditioning is that the skeletal musculature is the only bodily system that can be voluntarily manipulated. By controlling skeletal muscle activity we can thereby influence other bodily systems such as brain activity, heart reactions, and autonomic responses such as those of the stomach, intestines, and esophagus. With regard to bodily controls, then, skeletal muscle is a critical component in neuromuscular circuits because it may be used to mediate the other systems; a reasonable corollary is that probably only skeletal muscle can be directly conditioned. What appear to be direct autonomic conditioning, brain wave conditioning, and the like may thus be an indirect consequence of skeletal muscle conditioning. We shall shortly follow up this discussion by questioning whether "brain wave conditioning" and "autonomic conditioning" have been found to occur at all. The way in which skeletal muscle influences and interacts with other bodily systems through the generation and transmission of codes will be considered within the context of information transmission in Chapter 9, and technological applications of the principle to tension control will be taken up in Chapters 10 and 11.

While the methodology for establishing the specificity of a stimulus is relatively straightforward, the same question on the response side is much more complex. We have great difficulty in definitively distinguishing between generalized and localized bodily reactions—Duffy, for instance, believed activation to be both general and specific. How nonspecific a bodily event must be before it becomes general, of course, focuses us on the term "relatively" when we speak of "relatively localized events." Miss Duffy and I once discussed this principle. Her contention was that her arousal concept could account for my findings of relatively localized muscle activity during the performance of linguistic tasks (as specified in Chapters 5, 6, and 7). She was extremely agile with her arguments, and the only concession I was able to extract was that highly isolated muscle responses with the great rapidity of a few milliseconds probably were not activational. The problem of distinguishing between localized and widespread bodily reactions is compounded in conditioning experiments because typically only one response class is measured (Table 4.1). This is strange, considering the fantastically large number of responses which occur at the time of presentation of the conditional stimulus. Yet it is common for researchers to conclude that a specific, limited reaction was conditioned to one unique stimulus class, e.g. that a tone as a conditional stimulus evokes a GSR as a conditional response. We have emphasized that at any given instance an organism is making sufficiently numerous responses throughout the various bodily systems that the problem of isolating *the* conditional response (that which the experimenter presumes to condition) is a complex task indeed. We thus need to inquire further into the behavioral (horizontal) dimension of Table 4.2 with special reference to learning studies.

In Classical Conditioning, What Is Conditioned?

This question (sometimes phrased as the problem of "validating" the conditional response) has received considerable attention, indicating its importance to conditioning researchers. We shall consider some instances in which it has been difficult to conclude that "the conditional response" studied was in fact *the* conditional response, the difficulty often arising because of the posssibility of mediational skeletal muscle activity. In these studies we must continually face the possibility that skeletal muscle responses were actually conditioned, and they in turn served as mediating antecedents for the response measured by the conditioning researchers.

EXAMPLES OF THE DIFFICULTY OF ISOLATING A CONDITIONAL RESPONSE

Westcott and Huttenlocher (1961) examined the question of cardiac conditioning, and pointed out that, in previous studies, respiratory activity had not been controlled during the conditioning process. In their first experiment these researchers established ". . . that there are profound and reliable effects on cardiac rate attributable to respiratory patterns" (p. 355). The inference is that, in studies of "cardiac conditioning," a respiratory (skeletal muscle) response was actually conditioned such that respiration mediated heart activity. The work of Skinner and Delabarre (1938) is a case in point. Following the method of Hudgins' (1933) famous experiment on pupillary conditioning, they required the subject to say "contract"

and a gun was fired to produce strong vasoconstriction. Eventually constriction followed the unreinforced saying of "contract" . . . but . . . we found that in the case of an apparently successful result the subject was changing the volume [increasing of the amount of blood flow] of the arm by changing the amount of residual air in the lungs. The depth of breathing was in this case conditioned according to Type R because of the reinforcement of its effect on the volume of the arm. The "successful" result was obtained many times before the intermediate step was discovered by the subject (p. 114).

To establish that changes in cardiac activity are not merely artifacts of respiratory modifications, respiration needs to be controlled; Westcott and Huttenlocher (1961) did this in their second experiment and interpreted their findings as positive evidence for cardiac conditioning.

Respiratory activity, which involves in part the intercostal muscles of the chest, has been similarly implicated as a mediator in other studies. For example, Johnson (1961) found that the nonspecific galvanic skin response is related to changes in respiration. He questioned whether this is a causal relationship or whether both response changes are due to a third factor, such as level of arousal.

The problem of whether or not brain waves can be instrumentally conditioned has long been considered to be an important one. One theoretical reason for its importance concerns the question of whether conditioning is basically a response (muscular or glandular) phenomenon and/or a neural process. Among the positive reports of conditioning brain waves is the work of Kamiya (1968). Through a discrimination procedure in which the subject is furnished feedback, Kamiya reported that subjects can learn to control the presence or absence of alpha waves; this phenomenon is called "alpha wave conditioning." Before concluding that this is, however, actually electroencephalographic conditioning, one should study what else besides brain wave changes might be occurring in the subject during the training trials. Kamiya (1968) reported that ". . . people who were relaxed, comfortable and cooperative tended to produce more alpha waves than those who felt tense, suspicious and fearful . . ." (p. 59). This observation possibly implicates the muscular state and suggests the possibility that Kamiya's subjects learned to control alpha indirectly by learning certain muscular responses—tense people (i.e., those with their skeletal muscle in a chronically contracted state) probably block their alpha rhythms.[2] This interpretation of why alpha waves and alpha blocking occur is an old one. Knott (1939) for example, held that the tensing of muscles with attendant increases in peripheral stimulation produces blocking of the alpha rhythm during "attention." According to this view, then, so called "alpha conditioning" is mediated by antecedent conditional muscular activity. Hence, it is possible that, had Kamiya electromyographically monitored his subjects, he would have found muscular response changes that preceded (and perhaps controlled) the occurrence and nonoccurrence of alpha waves. Dewan (1967, 1968) reported a most interesting finding in this connection. In Dewan's research, the subject voluntarily controlled alpha activity by manipulating eye position and accommodation (cf. Fenwick and Walker, 1969; Mulholland, 1969). The subject was then able to send Morse code signals by means of his electroencephalograms, using short bursts of alpha activity as the dots and longer bursts as the dashes. An example of other work in which eye activity was functionally related to brain events is by Weerts and Lang (1973).

If the eye can effectively control brain waves, feedback from other peripheral systems might also be made to serve the same function; or, in fact, other systems may naturally influence the brain prior to any learning. In a number of studies, it has actually been shown that induced

---

[2] The relationship between antecedent muscle activity and consequent brain wave onset is an extremely complex one. Orne and Paskewitz (1974), for instance, reported that apprehension or heightened arousal does *not* necessarily produce a reduction in alpha activity. They thus challenge a widely accepted rationale for using alpha feedback training to teach one to control anxiety. A technological consequence is their caution against a clinical application of alpha feedback training.

muscular tension enhances evoked potentials from various brain regions, thus empirically implicating the skeletal muscular system as an
antecedent of EEG activity (Andreassi, Mayzner, Beyda, and Davidovics,
1970; Dinges and Klingaman, 1972; Eason, Aiken, White, and Lichtenstein, 1964). The problem of learning to control one's own brain waves is
made even more complex with the report of data by Lynch, Paskewitz,
and Orne (1974) suggesting that alpha increases are not attributable to
brain feedback at all. As they put it:

the data of these experiments do not support the view that the feedback situation
produces levels of alpha activity greater than those seen under natural baseline
conditions or that accurate feedback is necessary to demonstrate gradual trial to
trial increases in this rhythm. The data do suggest that alpha densities observed
in the feedback situation have less to do with feedback per se or a learning
process than with the experimental situation and Ss' own natural alpha densities.
The results support the position that increases in human alpha activity occur in
feedback situations when the individual disinhibits various stimulus, attentional
and arousal factors that normally block this rhythm (p. 399).

The problem of specifying a potential mediator in electroencephalographic or autonomic conditioning is obviously a difficult one. K. Smith
(1954) argued that "galvanic skin response conditioning" is an artifact of
skeletal muscle response conditioning which then produces (mediates)
various types of autonomic activity; among them is the galvanic skin
response. Kimmel and Davidov (1967) sought to test Smith's hypothesis
by monitoring electromyograms from both forearms during galvanic
skin response conditioning. They failed to find a relationship between
electromyograms and galvanic skin responses and thus concluded that
Smith's hypothesis was not confirmed. But in view of the complexity of
the body's musculature, it is premature to dismiss Smith's notion by
merely sampling electromyograms from two localized regions—the critical mediating response may be small and highly localized (conceivably
even a single motor unit) and extremely rapid (several milliseconds).
Finding such a mediating electromyogram in galvanic skin response
conditioning is less likely than finding a needle in the proverbial hay-
stack. It is not that research along the lines of Kimmel and Davidov
(1967) is hopeless, but a more sensitive and extensive search for a
mediating covert response is required before Smith's hypothesis can be
summarily dismissed, particularly in view of the fact that Kimmel and
Davidov used the rather crude electromyographic recording technique
of an ink-writing polygraph (cf. McGuigan, 1978b). The search for
mediating skeletal muscle activity should be encouraged by Maltzman's
(1971) finding of apparent influence from a preparatory motor response on a conditional GSR; this is a positive conclusion for Smith's
hypothesis. Another instance of skeletal muscle affecting the cardiovascular system was reported by Wenger, Baggchi, and Anand (1961), who
found that yogis could control heart rate and pulse to some degree. The
control occurred indirectly and considerable muscular exertion was re-

quired: For the yogis studied there was "retention of breath and considerable muscular tension in the abdomen and thorax. It was concluded that venous return to the heart was retarded but that the heart was not stopped, although heart and radial pulse sounds weakened or disappeared. The fourth subject, with different intervening mechanisms, also presumably under striated muscle control, did markedly slow his heart" (cited by Kimble and Perlmuter, 1970, p. 374).

While much of the focus in "validating" the conditional response has been on galvanic skin response conditioning, "Criticisms of GSR [galvanic skin response] conditioning are not at all unrelated to the validation of conditioned vasomotor change, conditioned cardiac deceleration, the conditioned eyeblink, and conditioned salivation" (Kodman, 1967, p. 813). Kodman continued along the lines that we have developed above: If Smith's hypothesis is true, then the galvanic skin response is "a response from an indivisible sensory-motor system rather than a pure autonomic reaction" (p. 816). I agree completely with Kodman's conclusion. In Chapter 9, conditioning will be shown to involve complex circuits among the skeletal muscle system, the central nervous system, and the autonomic system. These various bodily events are so intimately related that it is difficult to avoid the conclusion that behavior *does* involve the whole person and that conditioning cannot be restricted to one bodily system.

We shall conclude our illustration of the possibility that very rapid skeletal muscle components of neuromuscular circuits mediate autonomic and electroencephalographic events with three final examples. The first example is due to Cohen and Johnson (1971). Using a classical conditioning of heart rate paradigm, they showed that only those groups of subjects who had significant changes in muscular activity exhibited significant heart rate changes. They ruled out respiratory rate and amplitude as relevant variables, but the correlation between heart rate and skeletal muscular activity was high. One implication is that a skeletal muscle response, rather than heart rate, was conditioned.

Simpson and Climan (1971) have indicated that pupil size during the performance of an imagery task is another autonomic variable that apparently is affected by skeletal muscle activity.

The third example is from Belmaker, Proctor, and Feather (1972), who used a different strategy to test the hypothesis that skeletal muscle tension is a mediator for increases in heart rate. They instructed their subjects to generate inconspicuous muscle tension for a 90-second period. Respiratory pattern changes and surface electromyographic changes were not correlated with heart rate increases, nor were any gross muscle movements observed. Nevertheless, during the trials average heart rate increased about 13 beats per minute over baseline. The authors concluded that inconspicuous muscle tension is a possible mediator in human operant heart rate conditioning. Unfortunately, their electromyographic records, made with an ink-writing polyograph, did not indicate the presence of "the inconspicious muscle tension" as a function of the instructions to tense. If, as in all liklihood, tension *was* present, as the experimenters assumed, we have another indication of the limited sensitivity of ink-writing polygraphs for the study of covert behavior. Nevertheless, in absence of confirming evidence of the presence of slight muscular tension, we must be cautious in accepting the conclusion of Belmaker et al.

IS CURARE THE ANSWER?

One approach for ascertaining the role of skeletal muscle contraction (and afferent neural feedback resulting from such contraction) in the conditioning of other systems is to completely paralyze the skeletal musculature, usually attempted pharmacologically by administering neuromuscular junction blocking agents. The process of conditioning can thus be studied when the role of the skeletal musculature has presumably been eliminated. Some examples of reports of successful conditioning with curarized preparations are the works of Solomon and Turner (1962); Black, Carlson, and Solomon (1962); and DiCara and Miller (1968a).[3] Solomon and Turner, for instance, concluded *"that certain types of transfer of training or problem solving can occur without the benefit of mediation by peripheral skeletal responses or their associated feedback mechanisms"* (p. 218, italics in original).

The assumptions upon which this strategy of paralysis is based are that the curare used (1) is actually effective in producing total paralysis of the skeletal musculature, and (2) acts only at the myoneural junction and thus does not affect the central nervous system or peripheral sensory or autonomic mechanisms. The evidence for these assumptions, gained with the use of early impure forms of curare, is ambiguous (Solomon and Turner, 1962). d-tubocurarine, a pure form of curare developed later, was first used in this context by Solomon and Turner (1962), and by Black, Carlson, and Solomon (1962) to conduct improved tests of the central versus peripheral process interpretations of learning and transfer. These experimenters necessarily relied heavily on the pharmacological research available at the time for information about the effects of d-tubocurarine on various bodily systems; we should, therefore, briefly review that pharmacological evidence. The three articles they cited still constitute the bulk of our information on curare derived from the study of humans: Smith, Brown, Toman, and Goodman (1947); Unna and Pelikan (1951); and McIntyre, Bennett, and Hamilton (1951).

The pioneering work of Smith et al. (1947) is of special interest to psychologists because it resulted in a widely accepted (though unjustified) conclusion that individuals remain conscious and can "think" under total muscle paralysis due to curare; therefore, the notion is, muscle activity is not important for thought processes. While one must

---

[3] Richard Solomon informed me that, in his research with Black and with Turner, they did employ EMG controls; I very much appreciate Solomon's and Abe H. Black's helpful thoughts on this curare problem, as expressed to me in personal communications.

greatly admire this pioneering research, the experiment (using but one subject) must be realistically evaluated in light of its methodological inadequacies. Of six shortcomings cited by McGuigan (1966a), the one most immediately relevant to the curare-conditioning studies is that the d-tubocurarine used may not have totally paralyzed the skeletal musculature, a point that could be easily decided through appropriate electromyographic monitoring. Hence, while there may well have been no *overt* responses in the curarized state, important minute (covert) responses still may have occurred (in addition, of course, to autonomic activity).[4,5] Leuba, Birch, and Appleton (1968) conducted a similar experiment but unfortunately it did not include the controls suggested by McGuigan (1966a). Campbell, Sanderson, and Laverty (1964) also performed an experiment similar to that of Smith et al. (1947) in which five human subjects were injected with succinylcholine chloride dihydrate. The authors stated that the drug breaks the connection between the motor neurons and the skeletal musculature to *very nearly* completely paralyze the skeletal musculature, with no anesthetic effect. When subjects were asked after paralysis what they were aware of, they claimed that they were "aware of what was going on around them." The subjects described their attempts to move during paralysis by saying that they were under the impression that their movements were very large, when in actuality they were small and poorly controlled. We should thus be admonished against the uncritical acceptance of subjects' reports. We should also be reluctant to reach broad conclusions about the status of a subject's awareness when there is a lack of *total* muscle paralysis. Our criticism of the Smith et al. (1947) study is also pertinent to the second pharmacological study by Unna and Pelikan (1951). In it, there was no electromyographic monitoring to establish that covert skeletal muscle responses were eliminated. In fact, an amazingly gross measure (viz., grip strength with the hand dynamometer) was used as the index of "muscular paralysis," and even that measure apparently did not decrease to zero under d-tubocurarine. An additional indication of lack of paralysis is that there was never any need for artificial respiration for their subjects. Illustrative of our concern here is Black's (1967) statement that "in experiments on the operant conditioning of heart rate under curare, it may very well be that electromyographic responses were actu-

---

[4] It may also be noted that a subject may not recall events during curare for reasons other than the reduction of muscle activity. Anxiety and trauma, for instance, may have a distracting effect. In this regard, Lewis, Jenkinson, and Wilson (1973) found no evidence of recall of events taking place even during light anesthesia.

[5] We may also note that the work of Zubek and MacNeill (1966) is relevant to this general discussion. These researchers studied the effect of severe restriction of kinesthetic stimulation alone and found that there was a post immobilization effect of slowing occipital EEG activity, an effect that was not present in ambulatory and recumbent control subjects. Furthermore, there were a variety of behavioral deficits including verbal fluency, recall, space relations, cancellation, reversible figures, and color discriminations. Some of these effects were associated with immobilization alone while others appeared to be a function of the combined effects of restricted motor activity and the recumbent position.

ally conditioned and that these led to reflexive changes in heart rate" (p. 202). James Howard (personal communication) suggested a compatible physiological possibility: that the gamma-efferent system may have a significant role in conditioning since it is apparent that the gamma system of fibers has a higher threshold to the blocking effect of curare than the extra-fusal muscle system (Buchwald, Standish, Eldred, and Halas, 1964). If Howard's reasoning is correct, successful conditioning of curarized preparations may have occurred because the covert behavior that remained was due to a still functional gamma-efferent system and its feedback loop. The most sensitive method to determine whether or not the skeletal muscle system *is* actually paralyzed is to extensively monitor it with sufficiently sensitive electromyographic apparatus. When one conducts a sufficiently stringent electromyographical test of the hypothesis that a neuromuscular blocking agent does effectively eliminate the skeletal muscle activity, the subject should attempt to maximally contract the skeletal musculature. For this, the subject could simply be instructed to strongly contract certain muscles, but a more satisfactory procedure would probably be to administer electric shock to the person. Only when the procedures outlined herein are effected, can we reach a firm conclusion as to whether or not curare (or whatever neuromuscular blocking agent is under test) can *totally* eliminate muscle action potentials, i.e., to produce EMG recordings of 0.0 μv throughout the body.

A few autonomic conditioning researchers did monitor EMG when they used curare, but the electromyographic sampling was limited and quite insensitive (the scales used were from 100 to 300 μv/cm).[6] When one considers that important covert responses may be of the amplitude of less than a microvolt, it is apparent that more sensitive measurement techniques than those of ink-writing polygraphs are required. Even so, close inspection of the sample electromyograms offered by the experimenters cited in Table 4.3 often do show variations in the curarized preparation; covert behavior of perhaps as much as 20 μv in amplitude may have been occurring in presumably paralyzed animals. Such covert behavior could have important consequences, such as the possibility considered in this context (though rejected) by Black (1965) that the "full occurrence of a response and its associated feedback is not necessary for the modification of that response by operant reinforcement" (p. 45). In this context, one may recall the discussion above about the possibility that sufficient processing for conditioning may occur strictly through the high threshold gamma-efferent system, even though there is apparent "muscular paralysis." In conclusion, it is hoped that future conditioning research in these areas will include improved methodology, especially by employing sensitive electromyographical monitoring control procedures.

The second assumption stated at the beginning of this section as being

---

[6] I am grateful to Will Millard for helping me in this area of curare and conditioning, and particularly for providing most of the important data in Table 4.3.

TABLE 4.3 Measures Recorded in a Sample of Experiments on Autonomic Conditioning Using d-tubocurarine

Experimenter	Subject Species	Paradigm (response)	Measure		
			EEG	EMG	EKG
Black, Carlson, & Solomon (1962)[a]	Dog	Classical (heart rate)	-	-	+
Black & Lang (1964)	Dog	Classical (heart rate)	-	+	+
Black & Dalton (1965)[a]	Dog	Classical avoidance (heart rate)	-	+	+
Birk, Crider, Shapiro, & Tursky (1966)	Human	Operant (GSR)	-	-	+
Trowill (1967	Rat	Operant (heart Rate)	-	-	+
Miller & DiCara (1967)	Rat	Operant (heart rate)	-	-	+
DiCara & Miller (1968b)	Rat	Operant (vasomotor response)	-	-	+
DiCara & Miller (1968c)	Rat	Operant avoidance (heart rate)	-	-	+
DiCara & Miller (1968c)	Rat	Operant avoidance (blood pressure)	-	-	+
DiCara & Miller (1968d)	Rat	Operant (vasomotor response)	-	-	+
DiCara & Miller (1968a)	Rat	Operant avoidance (heart rate)	-	+	+
Miller & Banuazizi (1968)	Rat	Operant (intestinal contraction)	-	-	+
Miller & DiCara (1968)	Rat	Operant (urine formation and renal blood flow)	-	-	+
DiCara & Miller (1969a)	Rat	Operant (heart rate)	-	-	+
DiCara & Miller (1969b)	Rat	Operant avoidance (heart rate)	-	-	+
DiCara & Weiss (1969)	Rat	Operant avoidance (heart rate)	-	-	+
Hothersall & Brener (1969)	Rat	Operant (heart rate)	-	-	+
DiCara & Stone (1970)	Rat	Operant (heart rate)	-	-	+
Fields (1970)	Rat	Operant (blood pressure)	-	-	+
Pappas, DiCara & Miller (1970)	Rat	Operant (blood pressure)	-	-	+
Slaughter, Hahn, & Rinaldi (1970)	Rat	Operant (blood pressure)	-	-	+
Hahn & Slaughter (1971)	Rat	Operant (blood pressure)	-	-	+

[a] Subjects were "partially" curarized.

necessary for successful application of the curare strategy is that d-tubocurarine affects only the skeletal musculature. Unna and Pelikan (1951) said that following administration of d-tubocurarine in six subjects, "... no evidence was obtained of any action other than on the neuromuscular junction. ... In particular no effects on autonomic organs and also none on cerebral functions could be demonstrated" (p. 480). That appears to be the totality of their offering in this regard— Unna and Pelikan did not present any data (nor were any cited) that substantiate that statement, nor did they further discuss the matter of possible central or autonomic nervous system effects of d-tubocurarine. (They did, though, indicate that Flaxedil affects blood pressure and pulse rate.) The third pharmacological study cited above was that by McIntyre et al. (1951). In their consideration of this matter of possible brain effects, McIntyre et al. first criticized the above cited work of Smith et al. (1947) on the grounds that the Smith et al. results came from subjective observations. A second criticism was that Smith et al. did not make sufficiently sensitive measurements of muscle activity. McIntyre et al. (1951) concluded that "the balance of evidence establishes beyond doubt that d-tubocurarine is capable of modifying central nervous system activity independently of secondary effects due to hypoxia" (p. 301). They did not elaborate however, on the phrase "balance of evidence."

Black, Carlson, and Solomon (1962) summarized evidence indicating that d-tubocurarine affects the brain, as indicated by EEG measures. Other considerable work is consonant with that conclusion. Estable (1959) concluded that curare produces an effect on all cholinergic synapses to varying degrees; Okuma, Fujmori, and Hayashi (1965) reported electrocortical synchronization in animals as a function of the environmental temperature in which the animals received the curare; Amassian and Weiner (1966) and Brinley, Kandel, and Marshall (1958) found an increase in the latency of evoked potentials in curarized animals; and Hodes (1962) reported EEG effects from three different curare compounds (d-tubocurarine, Flaxedil, and succinylcholine). Galindo (1972) implicated both curare and pancuronium. In this same context, I am grateful to James Howard for informing me that curare releases histamine, which causes widespread bodily changes, including increased permeability and dilation of cerebral blood vessels (cf. Douglas, 1970; Koelle, 1960).

Apparently, then, d-tubocurarine does have central nervous system effects. Whether or not these effects are direct, or whether they are produced indirectly by such peripheral mechanisms as inadequate artificial respiration, or reduction of necessary feedback of sensory, especially proprioceptive impulses to the CNS, is unclear. Unfortunately we lack even primitive data here since none of the conditioning researchers cited in Table 4.3 apparently monitored electroencephalograms of their subjects. Consequently we do not know whether or not brain activity of their subjects was, by an EEG index, affected (directly or indirectly) by the d-tubocurarine injected. Finally, with regard to the second assumption for using curare, while curare apparently affects the brain, other data indicate that curare has autonomic effects too (cf. Black, 1971; Grob, 1967; Koelle, 1960).

To summarize our discussion of the two assumptions for the curare strategy:

1. We simply lack sufficient data to decide on the validity of the assumption that the blocking agent produces total muscular paralysis. While under stringent conditions curare might completely eliminate the skeletal muscles as a source of mediation, we do not now possess empirical evidence sufficient to conclude that it does. Researchers who study conditioning of autonomic and central nervous system activity by employing this strategy can add to our knowledge by (a) monitoring electromyograms from *several* bodily sites using sensitive equipment, and (b) monitoring electroencephalograms, preferably from more than one location. In short, skeletal muscle responding has not been excluded by the "curare strategy" as a possible mediator in studies of conditioning of brain and autonomic activity. *Nor has it been shown that thought processes or awareness are or are not affected through injection of curare.*

2. With regard to the requirement that the muscular blocking agent not affect the brain, we should realize that it is methodologically very difficult to establish a *lack of relationship* (like attempting to "prove the null hypothesis"); this is particularly a problem with such complex variables as d-tubocurarine and central nervous system activity. The available evidence indicates that d-tubocurarine does (possibly indirectly) have central nervous system effects. Furthermore, curare apparently has autonomic effects too.

While not the major purpose here, it might be valuable to relate these conclusions to the question of autonomic conditioning. Successful autonomic conditioning of curarized animals has been reported but there have been unsuccessful attempts that apparently defy explanation (e.g., Black, 1971; Ray, 1969). The situation seems to be that, under curare, there is partial functioning and partial nonfunctioning of the autonomic system of the skeletal musculature and of the central nervous system. With this state of affairs, the logical possibilities are sufficiently numerous that one could argue for any of several interpretations. For one, the reported conditioning successes (like the Miller studies in Table 4.3) may have occurred because the autonomic and skeletal muscle systems were still (incompletely) functioning, and the failures may have been due to the autonomic interference caused by the curare (cf. Black, 1971, pp. 36-37). The same interpretation may be applied to the central nervous system. One of the logical possibilities (unlikely as it might be) is that the reverse interpretation holds for the brain—that the successful instances of conditioning occurred *because* of the curare, i.e., curare might directly or indirectly inhibit certain cortical functions such that the inhibition allows lower cerebral mechanisms concerned with autonomic functions to permit conditioning to occur.

In this section we have concentrated on the classical approach, that in which curare has been used. More recently other neuromuscular blocking agents have replaced curare. Nevertheless, the lesson is the same—

these other agents should not be uncritically employed, as has been curare. Whatever the neuromuscular blocking agent used, it should be subjected to the same stringent methodological evaluation discussed above. With regard to several other agents, Wilson and DiCara (1975) studied the effects of a single intraperitoneal injection of three neuro-muscular blockers in rats: succinylcholine, dimethyl d-tubocurarine iodide, and d-tubocurarine chloride. They sampled EMG activity from two bodily regions and measured the EMG recovery time. They con-cluded that they confirmed previous reports of the unpredictable consequences of d-tubocurarine induced paralysis. In particular, their results confirmed the contention by Howard, Galosy, Gaebelein, and Obrist (1974) that d-tubocurarine chloride may be the least desirable choice of the neural blocking agents.

STIMULATION, SURGICAL, AND CLINICAL STRATEGIES

It thus seems that the use of "the curare strategy" has not been adequate to distinguish what the experimenter called "*the* conditional response" from antecedent bodily events that may themselves have mod-ified and consequently controlled that response. Such mediating events might just as well be referred to as the conditional response. Other "strategies" such as electrical stimulation and surgical techniques could conceivably be more successful in isolating relevant bodily systems (cf. McGuigan, 1966a, p. 294). The work of Penfield (1958) illustrates the stimulation approach. Surgical techniques with animal subjects, like those in which Horridge (1965) successfully conditioned an insect with-out a brain, or the peripheral nerve crushing and deafferentation pro-cedures used by Light and Gantt (1936) and by Taub and Berman (1968), might yield valuable, unambiguous information.

In attempting to isolate bodily systems in order to ascertain their func-tions, limited data on pathological cases have sometimes been inappro-priately used to negate broad theories. A criticism of Watson's (1930) theory of thinking is one example. It was argued that individuals with laryngectomies could still think, thus apparently disconfirming Watson's theory. Watson (1930) answered this criticism by saying that concerning "whether the man who cannot talk, cannot think . . . you will find that man both talks and thinks with his whole body—just as he does every-thing else with his whole body" (p. 225). It is important to develop this point in greater detail, particularly because this long-standing methodological error of misusing otherwise valuable clinical data con-tinues despite advances in methodological sophistication and in our knowledge of neuromuscular systems since Watson's time. Shallice (1974), for example, opposed "a modified version of the motor theory of thought" because it holds "that one cannot think well without the in-volvement of the musculature, particularly that concerned with speech." Shallice continued, "It is unfortunate that no clinical neuropsychologist pointed out . . . that peripheral dysarthria, which prevents speech, leaves thought totally unaffected" (p. 1073).

The general conclusion from such reasoning is that the musculature does not have an essential function in cognitive activities. Let us consider six possible errors in this reasoning:

1. *Objective measures of thought under controlled conditions are wanting.* Reliable and valid measures are required to determine whether peripheral dysarthria (or any other pathological condition) in fact affects the thought process. Mere casual observation of a patient is not sufficient. Moreover, one can only make valid inferences regarding *changes* in intellectual proficiency within individuals if both pre- and post-accident measures have been taken. Ideally, too, the effect of the trauma that produced the pathology should be controlled, for any change in thought proficiency may have been produced by emotionality accompanying the trauma and not by the bodily damage *per se* (see also point 5 below).

2. *The extent of the insult to the neural and muscular systems is typically unknown.* Several clinical specialists (neurosurgeons, speech pathologists, etc.) have told me that in pathological cases in which the speech muscles or other linguistic apparatus are malfunctioning, the neuromuscular conditions are seldom (if ever) well defined—there is usually complex damage to muscles and also to associated neural systems. With unknown or poorly determined muscular and neural damage, it is impossible to reach definitive conclusions about the influence of a single aspect of the complex speech system on cognitive functioning.

3. *Internal information processing systems are redundant.* The entire body—not just a single system such as the speech musculature—is used in both verbal and nonverbal thought. Numerous other bodily activities and "parallel" processing systems occur during thought (cf. McGuigan and Schoonover, 1973); the value of such redundant circuits has been pointed out by both Mowrer (1960a and b) and by Adams, McIntyre, and Thorsheim (1969) in other contexts. Hence, even if the *entire* speech musculature were nonfunctional (which seldom occurs), other neuromuscular channels could probably carry on thought. Usually, however, neuromuscular circuits involving portions of the chin, tongue, lips, throat, and jaw muscles remain operative, and these themselves would be sufficient to maintain cognitive proficiency. [See, for instance, Jacobson's (1931b) study in which activity of the phantom limb was apparently imagined through participation of other, intact neuromuscular circuits].

4. *Neuromuscular conditions within a single syndrome are diverse.* Similarly classified individuals seldom exhibit identical symptoms. Shallice for instance stated that dysarthria "prevents speech"; however, this syndrome is more commonly used to include a variety of speech disorders, some involving only lack of coordination of the speech act. Darley, Aronson, and Brown (1969a and b) distinguished five varieties of dysarthria. Such clinically diverse cases hardly form a sound, uniform basis for a generalized conclusion about thought (similar to the misguided efforts to find *the* cause of schizophrenia).

5. *Causal variables are confounded.* Bodily damage, such as that to the speech musculature, is probably accompanied by emotionally traumatic events such as an accident or surgery. The post-shock state of the patient

may thus be a function of the bodily damage, of the trauma that caused the injury, or of a complex interaction between these two variables. One can therefore not reach an unambiguous conclusion about the effects of a somatic damage variable that is so confounded with other variables.

6. *Nonrepresentative sampling.* Finally, one should consider the extent to which generalizations can be made to a normal population from findings on pathological individuals. The lack of random selection of individuals to form a representative data base probably limits the extent to which one can generalize from a sample of unique clinical cases to information processing systems in the normal individual, or even to individuals with different pathologies.

Clinical observations are suggestive sources of hypotheses, but seldom can they furnish a firm foundation for definitive conclusions about the functioning of any single, limited bodily system. Suitable data on these issues might be acquired through rigorous research, but appropriate experiments are methodologically difficult (if not impossible) to conduct given our present level of technical knowledge. The preceding discussion of how to adequately carry out the "curare strategy" in the laboratory illustrates how complex these issues can become. It is hoped that these considerations will help prevent the perpetuation of the methodological error of causal reasoning from clinical cases.

CONDITIONAL COVERT RESPONSE PATTERNS

The preceding discussion leads us to conclude that the problem of isolating "the conditional response" is so complex, particularly in humans, as to be technically unsolvable; the truth may be that a number of bodily processes are indivisible and necessarily participate as a complex conditional event. We may thus be required to talk, not about "the conditional response," but about a number of learned components that form complex conditional response patterns. Hence, when we talk about cardiac conditioning, electroencephalographic conditioning, galvanic skin response conditioning, or even forearm electromyographic conditioning, we should be emphasizing the *patterns* that were conditioned; such patterns may include a number of essentially simultaneous components *and* their mediating antecedent events. To further complicate the problem of separating critical and uncritical components of the conditional response pattern, we can expect that some adventitious covert behavior gains strength during conditioning. Consequently, an experimenter's definition of a conditional covert response pattern probably would necessarily include some adventitious components. An important research problem would be to ascertain the frequency with which such adventitious components "drop out" as conditioning trials continue, and which kinds might remain as stable parts of the conditional pattern.

It thus seems reasonable to stop using the term "the conditional response" because it tends to blind us as to the extent and complexity of covert processes that constitute a conditional pattern.

In contradistinction to the previous discussion, there is one case in which we *might* be able to unambiguously conclude that there was a localized conditional response (though even if true, there must of course be antecedent and consequent neural activity). The exception might be for responses that are topographically limited and well defined. Three brief examples of topographically isolated responses from different fields of research should suffice. The first example is a small "thumb twitch" response which was studied extensively by Hefferline and his associates (e.g., Hefferline, Keenan, and Harford, 1959). This small response is localized in the base of each thumb and is of sufficiently small amplitude that the subject cannot naturally observe or otherwise become aware of its occurrence. The response was studied by placing one electrode at the palmar base of the left thumb and the second at the medial edge of the left hand. An increase of EMG amplitude of from 1 to 3 μv could then be observed approximately every 1 to 2 minutes. Hefferline succeeded in bringing this response under stimulus control through operant conditioning techniques, even though the subjects were unable to verbalize the response contingency relationship. Subjects in this type of conditioning situation, incidentally, develop interesting types of superstitious behaviors, such as one subject in the 1959 Hefferline et al. study who "professed to have discovered an effective response sequence, which consisted of subtle rowing movements with both hands, infinitesimal wriggles of both ankles, a slight displacement of the jaw to the left, breathing out—and then waiting" (p. 1339). This small response isolated in the thumb was successfully conditioned, and since it is such a highly localized event, it may be considered to have been accompanied by a minimum, or perhaps no other, conditional response component.

A second example of a topographically localized response class was laryngeal activity recorded during silent reading in a study by Faaborg-Anderson and Edfeldt (1958). Using needle electrodes in different muscles, it was found that relative to a resting baseline, electrical activity increased in the vocal and mylohyoid muscles but decreased in the posterior cricoarytenoid muscle during reading. Hence, it is possible to specify highly localized response changes by means of needle electrodes. Additionally, it is interesting that laryngeal muscles which are spatially very close nevertheless behave quite differently during reading. Apparently, while some speech muscles are covertly activated during silent linguistic activities, others are simultaneously inhibited in order to achieve high cognitive efficiency. This point has particular value for our information processing discussion in Chapter 9.

Inserted electrodes have been extensively used in EMG work for a variety of purposes. Jacobson (1932) used this technique as more recently has Basmajian (e.g., Basmajian, Baeza, and Fabrigar, 1965). Basmajian et al. demonstrated that a subject can acquire voluntary control over a single motor unit (see Fig. 3.1 on p. 72). By placing inserted electrodes very close together (in the thumb or tongue, for example) EMGs can be visually observed on an oscilloscope and/or heard by means of auditory feedback. By practicing under these feedback conditions, the subject can quite rapidly isolate a single motor unit and "cause it to fire" at will (see pp. 108–10 for further details).

These three examples indicate that some rather localized responses can be specified as a function of experimental conditions, providing that they are topographically limited and recording techniques are sufficiently precise, though they may still be only components of a larger conditional response pattern.

EMPIRICAL SPECIFICATION OF CONDITIONAL RESPONSE PATTERNS

Even though we emphasize *patterns* of conditional responses, such patterns are probably still more localized and limited than widespread arousal reactions. We must thus still consider the second problem stated on p. 85, viz., how to distinguish between conditional response patterns and widespread arousal and orienting reflex reactions. The first step is to ascertain what happens to orienting reflexes and activational patterns during conditioning. Germana's (1968) concept of activational peaking is relevant here. Germana held that the orienting and arousal reactional processes are essentially the same; they differ only because of stimulus requirements. For example, early in conditioning the novel stimulus evokes an activational pattern which is the orienting reflex; this pattern would habituate rapidly if the subject had nothing to do. But when in conditioning the subject *has* to respond, there is a buildup in the generalized activational level over trials—there is an increase in a number of bodily measures like skin conductance, heart rate, breathing rate, and vasoconstriction. Eventually, when the conditional response has been learned, activational peaking occurs; at this point the various psychophysiological measures reach a maximum. As the subject continues to produce the conditional response, the generalized activational level decreases from the peak to baseline level. The behavioral residue constitutes the conditional response pattern. That is, the conditional response pattern includes those responses from localized regions or systems (including the experimenter's target region in the subject) that persist after the leveling out that occurs following diminution from the activational peak.

To empirically define a specific stimulus-response pattern connection that is formed during conditioning, the experimenter obviously needs to sample a variety of stimuli and responses both before and at the conclusion of conditioning. It should first be shown that the response pattern that is to be conditioned does not occur to a sample of disparate test stimuli prior to conditioning. After conditioning, presentation of the test (nonconditional) stimuli again would establish whether or not there was a single conditional stimulus (assuming controls for stimulus generalization and for cross-modal generalization).

Establishing the uniqueness of the conditional stimulus is relatively straightforward. The more complex question is on the response side; that is the problem of unambiguously specifying the conditional response pattern, even after activational peaking. For this, we need to simultaneously monitor a number of covert responses throughout conditioning. After conditioning, those responses that do not systematically change when the conditional stimulus is presented obviously do not belong to the conditional response pattern. Those responses that do systematically change when the conditional stimulus is presented constitute the class of potential conditional responses. From this class we will attempt to define the conditional response pattern. In short, we can solve the problem of distinguishing between conditional response patterns and widespread reactions (problem number 2 above) by an adequate historical account of the conditioning process. Laboratory examples of conditioning can guide us with developmental illustrations of how a specific stimulus can acquire the capacity to evoke a covert response pattern. The classic work of Roessler and Brogden (1943) on vasomotor conditioning is one such valuable guide. Prior to conditioning, the experimenters determined that the unconditional response of vasoconstriction *did* occur to the unconditional stimulus of electric shock, and that vasoconstriction *did not* occur to a buzzer, to the light, or to the overt or subvocal saying of "wek" or "zub." Because the to-be-conditioned response did not occur to a sample of stimuli prior to the experiment it was concluded that there had been no previous conditioning to either the conditional stimulus or to a sample of others, and it also was a pseudoconditioning control procedure. Roessler and Brogden then were successful in the conditioning process so that when a subject said "wek" either overtly or subvocally to a light signal, vasoconstriction occurred. Furthermore, since, after conditioning was completed, the conditional response did not generally occur to the novel stimulus "zub," it may be concluded that a specific stimulus was established as a conditional stimulus. This conclusion is obviously limited since the sampling of novel stimuli could have been more extensive than merely "zub." For example, if the experimenters had tested for the conditional response to novel stimuli that were quite different from the conditional stimulus (more different than merely another nonsense syllable), then stimulus generalization and cross modal generalization could have been ruled out, because there still was some limited responding to "zub." Nevertheless, the Roessler and Brogden study is a good, though rare, demonstration that the effects of a variety of stimuli should be sampled both before and after conditioning, the latter in order to determine whether or not the conditional stimulus has uniquely acquired response-evoking properties.

To summarize this point: in principle, for conditioning studies it is possible to ascertain that a relationship between a specific stimulus and specific response pattern was acquired. This conclusion is possible if one adheres to the following procedures: (1) at the beginning and conclusion of conditioning it is demonstrated that the response is not evoked by irrelevant stimuli (except where we expect the response to be evoked through stimulus generalization); (2) a number of responses are monitored throughout the conditioning process so that a specific conditional

response pattern can be differentiated from other ("irrelevant") responses. When we lack developmental (conditioning) data it is indeed very difficult to distinguish between specific response patterns and more general, widespread reaction patterns.

The general conclusion of the chapter to this point is that covert responses occur because: (1) some stimuli have a generalized evocation function in which widespread bodily reactions occur; and (2) some stimuli have a specialized stimulus evocation function, often due to conditioning, whereby relatively localized response patterns are produced. The next (and most basic) question is whether or not covert skeletal muscle responses *can* actually be learned, as we have been assuming up to this point.

Can Electromyographically Measured Covert Behavior Be Learned?

CLASSES OF ELECTROMYOGRAPHIC LEARNING STUDIES

Table 4.4 represents an attempt to classify the electromyographic conditioning studies (or the electromyographic "conditioning-like" studies). The sample is fairly complete up to this writing date. Those in the first category were presumed to fit the classical conditioning paradigm, those in the second follow Ivanov-Smolensky's (1956) paradigm, those in the third are covert operant conditioning studies, and those in the fourth category include studies of single motor unit training through biofeedback. Category V includes efforts to permanently modify speech muscle activity by providing external auditory feedback. We shall now consider each category in greater detail.

Classical Conditioning. The general purpose of the studies in classical conditioning has been to demonstrate that anticipatory electromyographic responses occur to the conditional stimulus. The typical conclusion is that classical conditioning *has* occurred, but the conditional electromyographic response is usually not well defined, being specified as the probability difference of amplitude during stimulus presentation relative to baseline. Furthermore, these studies suffer from lack of the three appropriate controls. The first is the failure to simultaneously record electromyograms from a number of bodily locations. The purpose of this control, of course, is to distinguish between widespread bodily arousal and a relatively localized conditional response. For example, Fink (1954), in an admirable experiment for its time, paired a sound stimulus (white noise) with an uninstructed arm response and concluded that the sound became a conditional stimulus that elicited localized covert electromyographic activity in the arm. This finding was important, Fink held, because of the relations holding between covert electromyographic activity and overt behavior, viz., that "overt motor response conditioning may be viewed as a consequence of muscle action

TABLE 4.4   Classification of Covert "Conditioning" Studies Using Electromyography

---

I. *Classical conditioning*
    Prosser & Hunter (1936)
    Hunter (1937)
    Hilden (1937)
    Fink & Davis (1951)
    VanLiere (1953)
    Fink (1954)
    Doehring (1957)
II. *Motor method of speech reinforcement*
    Solberg, Tyre, & Stinson (1970)
    McGuigan & Bertera (1973)
III. *Operant conditioning*
    Hefferline, Keenan, & Harford (1959)
    Hefferline & Keenan (1961)
    Hefferline & Keenan (1963)
    Sasmor (1966)
IV. *Biofeedback–motor unit training*
    Harrison & Mortensen (1962)
    Basmajian (1963a)
    Basmajian (1963b)
    Carlsöö & Edfeldt (1963)
    Basmajian, Baeza, & Fabrigar (1965)
    Basmajian (1962)
    Basmajian & Simard (1967)
    Simard & Basmajian (1967)
    Baginsky (1969)
    Fruhling, Basmajian, & Simard (1969)
    Petajan & Philip (1969)
    Scully & Basmajian (1969)
    Simard (1969)
    Simard & Ladd (1969)
    Thysell (1969)
    Sutton & Kimm (1969)
    Lloyd & Leibrecht (1971)
    Basmajian (1972)
    McGuigan, Osgood, & Childress (1973)
V. *Biofeedback–speech muscle learning*
    Hardyck, Petrinovich, & Ellsworth (1966)
    McGuigan (1967)
    Hardyck & Petrinovich (1969)
    McGuigan (1971)

---

potential (EMG) conditioning" (p. 68). To illustrate this control problem, we may note that Fink placed electrodes only on the left arm so that, while he did find that left-arm response electromyograms increased during the conditional stimulus interval, that left-arm response might have been but one component of a generalized reaction. The likelihood of this interpretation is increased when one notes that the unconditional stimulus was a 70-decibel tone which, as Van Liere (1953) showed, produces a widespread startle reaction. While Fink used a control group which received the conditional stimulus and the unconditional stimulus noncontiguously, he measured electromyograms during the conditional stimulus interval only, so that a general startle pattern would go undetected.

The second of the three control problems arises when the experimenter places electrodes only in the locus of the expected conditional response; the obvious suggestion to the subject is that something important is going to happen in the region of the electrodes; e.g., Fink wanted to mask his interest in a noninstructed left-arm response from his subjects, yet he placed electrodes only at that location. By satisfying the first control problem above (using a number of electrode placements), this second control problem is obviously solved. Otherwise, one could simply use dummy electrodes, as Hefferline et al. (1959) did, though that would still leave unsolved the first problem concerning general arousal.

The third control problem with studies in category I of Table 4.4 is that the experimenters typically did not sample the behavioral effects of various nonconditional stimuli before and after conditioning (see p. 104). We have already seen how Roessler and Brogden (1943), in their work on vasomotor conditioning, provided an admirable model of this control principle.

In conclusion, there are a number of studies in which it was reported that classical conditioning of relatively localized electromyographic activity was successful; however, due to failure to include appropriate controls, we can accept this conclusion only tentatively until more comprehensive research is conducted.

Motor Method of Speech Reinforcement. It has been traditionally held that this method of conditioning generally fits the classical conditioning paradigm. For example, Solberg, Tyre, and Stinson (1970) used a 40-watt light as the "conditional stimulus," then projected the word "Press" as the "unconditional stimulus," whereupon the subject pressed a trigger on a pistol grip ("unconditional response"). However, one might better argue that the motor method of speech reinforcement is actually an operant procedure. Hence, the light is a signal that "press" (a discriminative-stimulus) will occur, whereupon the voluntary response of squeezing (an operant) is emitted, followed in some other experiments by an explicit reinforcement. Such classification problems as this raise questions about the generality and universal appropriateness of classical and operant paradigms. There appears to be a growing dissatisfaction among scientists with the distinction between operant and classical conditioning which implies that there are two different kinds of learning. Pavlov extensively studied what we now call operant conditioning, but never interpreted it as a type of learning different from classical conditioning. Regardless of this issue, our immediate interest is a more empirical one—we may note that Solberg et al. report an increasing percentage of electromyographic "conditional responses" as a function of trials. The mean terminal conditional response percentage during acquisition, though, was very low, being about 48% for children and 44% for adults.

There was no evidence of overt response conditioning, leading them to conclude that while their subjects inhibited overt conditional responses, the more sensitive electromyographic response measure *did* indicate conditioning. During extinction, response level for their adult subjects fell to about that of the control groups, but their child subjects showed relatively large resistance to extinction.

There are two major difficulties with their positive conclusion of covert conditioning: (1) they did not report any values of electromyographic increases over baseline during the conditional response interval, nor in any other way did they specify what was counted as a conditional response; (2) electromyograms were measured only from the arm that the subject was instructed to move, so that "the conditional arm response," rather than being a localized conditional response, could have been generalized tension, or even the result of suggestion due to placement of electrodes in a single region.

McGuigan and Bertera (1973) conducted two experiments using the motor method of speech reinforcement. The first, a limited study, was an attempt to confirm the Solberg et al. (1970) experiment, though with multiple bodily measurements. While there was a hint of successful conditioning, the effect was not reliable. In the second study the subjects made a left arm response to one stimulus and a right arm response to another, using the motor method of speech reinforcement paradigm. During the conditioning phase mean maximum amplitude of electromyograms noticeably increased in both arms during the stimulus presentation intervals, the increase over baseline being significant for the left arm. Other group tests for conditioning were negative, though there was especially strong evidence of conditioning in one subject.

There is obviously considerable need for additional research to ascertain whether or not the motor method of speech reinforcement can result in electromyographically measured covert conditional responses.

Operant Conditioning.   The results in Category III with regard to operant conditioning of the thumb twitch response that was discussed on page 102 can be summarized as positive; i.e., Hefferline and his associates (see Table 4.4) have shown that a minute muscle response in the thumb can be brought under control through operant means. Of course, multiple measurements would be desirable in a search for other possible response systems that might mediate the thumb twitch operant. It would also be highly desirable to obtain data relevant to the operant conditioning of other electromyographically defined responses.

Biofeedback: Motor Unit Training.   The typical procedure here is to record (with inserted electrodes) a single motor unit response and transduce the response so that the subject receives external feedback. The feedback is displayed visually and/or auditorally so that, after learning, the single motor unit response appears as a single spike on an oscilloscope and sounds like a "pop" or "click" through a speaker. Within a very few minutes the subject learns to "isolate" the single motor unit (as in response differentiation), produce it "at will," and even emit recognizable patterns for another person, like one of my students who plays "Yankee Doodle Dandy" on his thumb. It is not entirely clear that this learning phenomenon fits any standard conditioning paradigm, though if the feedback functions as what we normally think of as a reinforcement, single motor unit training could conceivably fit the operant paradigm.

The data for bringing single motor units under voluntary control are overwhelmingly positive, though again multiple measurements during the response differentiation procedure are usually absent. Regardless, the response is rapidly acquired and can occur in skeletal muscles throughout the body—in preliminary study we sampled and successfully isolated single motor units from the toe up the body through the tongue.

In contrast to merely bringing the response under internal control, there has apparently been only one effort to bring the single motor unit response under external stimulus control (McGuigan, Osgood, and Childress, 1973). While we were successful in training some pilot subjects to acquire single motor unit control through feedback with the use of surface (as opposed to inserted) electrodes, it is much more laborious than with inserted electrodes. Consequently, we later allowed our subjects to define for themselves a small scale thumb response that often consisted of several motor units, rather than insisting on the isolation of a single motor unit response. Through a discrimination procedure the subjects successfully made the thumb response only to the presentation of a visual stimulus of the word "click," and did not respond to a blank slide. Further analysis indicated that the small scale thumb response, through operant-like conditioning procedures, came under external stimulus controls so that it occurred "automatically" to the projected word "click" during an extinction-like test. Further tests for stimulus generalization indicated that some subjects made "involuntary" thumb response to words similar to "click" ("snap," "smut," "bang," "pop," "glick").

In a second experiment McGuigan, Osgood, and Childress (1973) employed the same general procedure as for the first, except that the subject made the small response in his right thumb to one stimulus (called a "future" slide), the left-thumb response to the second stimulus (a slide coded for "past" meaning), and no response to control (blank) slides. The results indicated that the subjects continued to "automatically" respond to the future and past slides during "extinction" sessions, confirming the results of the previous experiment and indicating that two small scale thumb responses were respectively conditioned to two different stimuli (the future and past slides). There was also some indication that the subjects generalized the thumb responses to time related words (like "tomorrow"). In both experiments, no responses were identified in other regions of the body sampled that were correlated with these thumb responses, somewhat increasing the possibility discussed on page 102 that this type of thumb response is a highly localized event.

The general inference from the studies cited in Table 4.4 is that isolated single and multiple motor unit responses can be brought under both internal and external control through biofeedback learning procedures. Whether or not this type of learning phenomenon can be accounted for by traditional conditioning principles is a matter of future concern.

Biofeedback: Speech Muscle Learning. There have been several studies in which auditory feedback from covert oral behavior was furnished to subjects while they were engaged in silent reading. The strategy in these studies was to attempt to permanently reduce amplitude of covert oral behavior ("subvocalization") during reading to see whether such a reduction would retard or facilitate reading proficiency. The popular view has been, of course, that "subvocalization" retards reading proficiency, while the research literature indicates that the opposite is the case (cf. McGuigan, 1976). Regardless of the implications for the teaching of reading (see Chapter 10) the immediate question is whether or not external feedback from the speech musculature actually can produce learned reduction of response amplitude. The statements offered by Hardyck and his associates (see Category V in Table 4.4) have been that subvocalization can be permanently eliminated within a very short period of time ("about 5 minutes"). It is, of course, technologically and theoretically interesting if speech muscle responses that have been used in silent reading for many years can be so rapidly and permanently "extinguished." McGuigan (1967, 1971) recorded no reduction in amplitude of covert speech electromyograms until subjects were given knowledge of the response-feedback contingency, whereupon the response was shaped downward quite nicely. More important, however, covert oral response amplitude rebounded to about baseline level when subjects later read without feedback. Apparently the subjects did not learn (in any permanent sense) to control covert oral behavior in the absence of feedback. It is interesting to note that when one oral region was controlling the external feedback (e.g., the tongue) other associated oral musculature behaved in a similar, though not so marked a, manner. That is, if the tongue produced the feedback, EMGs from the lips, chin, etc., also were reduced in amplitude, but rebounded once the external feedback was removed. A sample of other covert nonoral response measures did *not* systematically change as a function of the feedback conditions. Consequently, the response changes were apparently localized in the speech region. These results to date thus indicate that feedback techniques applied to the speech muscle region do not result in permanently reduced response amplitude independent of the external feedback, at least under the conditions specified in this section. Until we can permanently modify covert oral behavior during silent reading we will not know the effect of reduced speech muscle activity on reading proficiency. In addition, reduced tension through biofeedback from one muscle does not affect the skeletal muscles throughout the body.

To answer the major question posed in this section, the results of the studies cited in Table 4.4 indicate that we *can* modify covert behavior that is electromyographically defined. A major problem, though, is how to systematically conceptualize these various learning phenomena—it has been difficult to fit all the procedures specified for the five categories of Table 4.4 to standard conditioning paradigms. For example, the motor method of speech reinforcement does not precisely fit either the classical or the operant paradigms. Thus, while the verbal stimulus of "press" has traditionally been referred to as a classical "conditional stimulus," it has more of the properties of the discriminative stimulus in operant conditioning. Yet, because the motor method of speech reinforcement may well not require a contingent event to modify behavior, this method (if further research *does* indicate that it is successful) is not unambigiously an instance of the operant paradigm. Similarly, the procedure for acquiring single motor unit control resembles the operant paradigm, but it has not been independently established that external feedback from the muscles ("biofeedback") has the properties of a reinforcing stimulus. Perhaps the informative function of the feedback is sufficient for learning. This classical problem came to light in the traditional "knowledge of results" studies where the question was to what extent might knowledge of results (as in "biofeedback") function merely to furnish information, to what extent might it function as a secondary reinforcer, or to what extent might it serve both an informative and reinforcing function. Systematic study of the relationship between these two contingency variables is called for. Perhaps with further study of these issues we will be able to apply existing conditioning principles universally to account for the modification of all covert behavior. Otherwise, it may be that some covert responses obey as yet unformulated laws of learning. Regardless of the laws of learning applicable to the acquisition of covert skeletal muscle responses, however, it is clear that new response patterns are acquired. Furthermore, it is reasonable to assume that these specific learned response patterns serve unique functions. The thesis to be developed in Chapter 9 is that these relatively localized muscle response patterns are peripheral components of neuromuscular circuits that function when information is internally processed—in particular, that learned skeletal oral and nonoral muscle response patterns serve unique linguistic thought processing functions. With this emphasis on verbal behavior, particularly that involving the oral musculature, it may be valuable to briefly consider the development of covert speech behavior before concluding this chapter.

Genesis of Covert Oral (and Nonoral) Language Behavior

Verbal (language) behavior may be produced by the oral musculature, resulting in speech, or by the nonoral musculature resulting in communication processes such as gestures (waving the hands, nodding the head), writing, typing with the fingers, Braille, or the dactylic linguistic behavior of the deaf. Such behaviors are all overt, and it is typically assumed that language production is first produced overtly (though this is methodologically difficult to confirm). Once speech develops overtly, it is commonly held that the overt behavior becomes abbreviated and reduced in amplitude, resulting in covert linguistic responses. Much nonspeech behavior can be said to become abbreviated and reduced in amplitude in the same way. For example, on first learning to swim, one makes gross arm and leg movements. Later one can *imagine* that same overt act by making covert arm and leg responses (Jacobson, 1932). Skinner (1957) suggested that such covert verbal behavior is a labor saving practice which is maintained through reinforcement when the speaker is his own listener. We may thus regard the covert response as more efficient and energy-saving than overt behavior, particularly when we symbolically rather than overtly manipulate our world. Millenson (1967) commented on this process as follows, though he makes the common errors of talking about covert behavior as that of "no movement" (it is small yet real movement), and of "behavior" as being only overt (small scale, covert is also behavior):

One of the principal characteristics of language chains is their ability to become covert, so that it is difficult to tell by direct observation what a person is doing, if anything, when he is solving a problem "to himself." . . . By inference, there is every reason to believe that a branching chain . . . is indeed going on, even though close observation . . . reveals no movements of the lips, tongue, eyes or mouth. The value of such an inference . . . lies in its ability to predict and explain other behaviors . . . (p. 282).

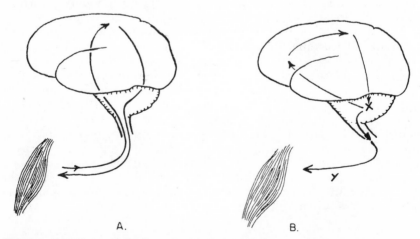

FIG. 4.1 Possible "centralization" of a response. While in the early history of the response, overt and then covert responding were necessary components of the circuit (A), eventually a cerebellar representation (X) of the response would allow more rapid activation of the circuit. There still could also be consequent motor activity (Y).

. . . the notion that chains of behavior can become reduced in magnitude until they are unobservable with the naked eye stands as a scientific proposition capable of generating experiments, whether or not all, some, or no "thought" is to be identified with these chains. It is in this sense that Watson's hypothesis stands as an important creative development in the history of behavioral science (p. 283).

Dunlap (1927) suggested that overt behavior may become short circuited and abbreviated so that the act becomes implicit and might recede into the cerebellum (as we saw in Chapter 2, and as depicted in Fig. 4.1).

Dashiell (1926) noted this aspect of language acquisition by pointing out the slow change from overt speech and gestures to covert behavior: "The movements and gross bodily acts that become conveniently abbreviated and delimited to vocal and manual signs . . . gradually become further condensed and more nascent" (p. 69).

At the heart of Osgood's (e.g., 1957c) semantic theory is the principle that meaning originates in overt responses to stimulus objects, then gradually telescopes to central representation in the mature language user.[7] This motor encoding process begins with an ordering of responses according to exteroceptive controls, as in imitating the observed movements of another person. A transfer to proprioceptive controls—in which the individual employs feedback with a resulting increase in the speed of execution of the response—subsequently occurs.

Eventually, the transfer to central programming in the integrational motor system is accomplished. Bruner, Olver, and Greenfield (1966) refer to the first stage of the enactive stage of cognitive growth, in which a child responds rigidly to concrete objects. There eventually develops a muscular respresentation of the response: "By enactive representation is meant a mode of representing past events through appropriate motor response. . . . Segments of our environment, e.g., bicycle riding, tying knots, etc., get represented in our muscles, so to speak" (1964, p. 2).

The notion of "internalization" in Soviet psychology, as discussed in Chapter 2, (and also employed by Piaget) refers to a process whereby the social use of overt language develops internally in the individual, producing "internal speech." Terms like "inner speech," "silent speech," "subvocalization," "implicit speech," "incipient speech" all refer to this phenomenon of covert oral language behavior.

As to how overt speech becomes covert, Watson suggested that the reduced response amplitude occurs, at least in part, because society punishes the overt response. For instance, the nurse and parents often admonish the child "don't talk aloud" and soon the overt speech dies down to whispered speech such that a good lip reader can still read what

---

[7] An interesting question with regard to the behaviorist's hypothesis that important covert reactions, like Osgood's r_M, originate in overt responses concerns such mental processes as listening and seeing (see especially Skinner, 1957 on this question too). During listening, for instance, there never have been overt responses of the ear. The most one could hypothesize are covert responses produced by contraction of the small muscles within the ears or orienting responses of the entire body.

the child thinks of the world and of himself. (cf. Watson, 1930, pp. 240–41). Skinner (1957) also stated that punishment variables are effective for making overt speech covert, such as when there are aversive consequences for the child's overt speech or when the adult may be overheard and thus may give away his secret.

We have, in this section, briefly considered some thoughts about the process during which overt language behavior becomes covert. Resulting covert linguistic processes are exceptionally complex, involving as they do numerous central and central-peripheral circuits. We shall now turn to a variety of studies of these circuit components in which various covert bodily processes have been measured under a variety of linguistic conditions. In Chapter 5 we shall consider covert eye responses, after which we shall summarize oral skeletal muscle behavior (Chapter 6), covert nonoral behavior (Chapter 7), and electrical measures of brain processes (Chapter 8).

part three

Covert Processes as a Function of Linguistic Conditions: Empirical Studies

5

Nonoral Behavior: Eye Responses[1]

[1] I'm especially indebted to Will Millard for his excellent help with this chapter.

B. Interpretation
    1. Eye Movements During Pre-perception and Perception
    2. Eye Movements During Response Selection and Execution Stages
    3. Visual Neuromuscular Interactions with Bodily Systems
    4. Conclusion
IV. Other Relevant Empirical References on Eye Activity

Eye activity ranks high in importance among covert responses that have been empirically implicated in the performance of cognitive tasks. Eye responses are so important that we have hypothesized them to be critical components of the body's highly complex information processing systems (e.g., McGuigan and Pavek, 1972.) In fact, the data summarized throughout this book indicate that together with the brain and the speech musculature, the eyes are active during essentially every cognitive process. Our assumption is that the eyes function in the formation and transmission of verbal codes within neuromuscular circuits which engage the linguistic regions of the brain. In this chapter we shall critically summarize reports of eye activity during the performance of cognitive processes variously referred to as "imagination," "dreams," "thought," etc.

Methods of studying eye activity date from the time of the Greeks. In early research gross eye movements controlled by the skeletal musculature were principally studied without recording apparatus through direct observation. However, convenient and sensitive electrical response measures like the electrooculogram (EOG) are now in common use (Chapter 3.) Electrical signals result not only from the EOG standing potential between the cornea and the retina, but also from numerous small saccadic movements, (see number 1 below) and grosser movements that can be directly observed. Lindsay and Norman (1972) classified these complex eye movements into four categories: (1) very small and fast responses that occur 30 to 70 each second; (2) large oscillatory movements; (3) slow drifts of a few visual minutes one way or the other; (4) rapid jerks with amplitudes of about five minutes apart, often correcting for the slow drifts. The pupillary response, like all slow autonomic activity, is excluded here. For a review of pupillometry research see Goldwater (1972).

Methodological Criteria

To assess the research on eye responses during the silent performance of various kinds of cognitive tasks, each study will be evaluated by four general criteria. The first two criteria will allow us to determine whether or not the response actually occurred, and if so whether it was a function of the condition of interest (an experimental treatment, for example). The second two criteria are designed to help ascertain the function of the response by providing an index of the degree of general bodily arousal during the condition or experimental treatment. If the response is a localized, relatively unique occurrence it is more likely to serve an information processing function within neuromuscular circuits. However, if it is accompanied by many other responses it probably is but one aspect of a state of generalized bodily arousal, perhaps serving only an energy expenditure function. As noted in Chapter 4, a number of researchers have recognized the importance of this point. Jacobson (1932), for example, found that instructions to imagine certain acts or percepts resulted in localized as contrasted with generalized responses, e.g., when Jacobson asked subjects to imagine the Eiffel Tower, he found increased localized eye activity, leading to the conclusion that image-produced responses are similar to stimulus produced responses. R. C. Davis (1939) was concerned with localized responding during thought when he summarized and interpreted a variety of EMG findings in terms of his principle of focus of muscular responses. This principle, applicable for the inhibition as well as for the excitation of muscular activity, states that, for any psychological process, there is a certain bodily region in which there is a relatively high degree of muscular activity. Furthermore, the amplitude of the response activity decreases as the bodily distance from the focal point increases.

In considering our four criteria, we shall note that they are applicable in the cases of all covert processes and will be employed in Chapters 6, 7, and 8 too.

CRITERION 1

Did the Response Actually Occur? To determine that a response actually occurred, it is necessary to ascertain whether the measure employed by the researcher changed systematically. One method for determining this is for the researcher to first establish a stable, resting baseline level of responding, following which the experimental treatment (or whatever) is administered. The general question is whether some measure of eye behavior changed from the resting baseline condition to the period of administration of the experimental treatment. If the researcher followed this procedure and did determine that the covert response measure systematically changed from baseline, then a "yes" was entered in column 1 of Table 5.1. If the experimenter followed this procedure, but reported that there was no systematic change in the given measure then a "no" was entered in column 1 of Table 5.1. Finally, if the researcher did not compare a covert response measure during the period of the experimental treatment with a previous resting baseline condition, a "?" was entered in column 1, indicating that the experimenter did not successfully employ this criterion as to whether or not the response occurred.

Incidentally, some researchers satisfied Criterion 1 in principle, though they did not employ a resting baseline condition. Such variations in the application of this criterion will be mentioned as appropriate when we discuss the experiments below.

TABLE 5.1 Summary Evaluation of Research on Eye Movements under Cognitive Conditions[a]

Task and Experimenters	(1) change from baseline?	(2) vary as a function of conditions?	Did the Eye Response: (3) occur independently of other covert processes?	(4) specifically relate to a cognitive aspect?
IMAGINATION				
Perky (1910)	Yes	?	?	Yes
Jacobson (1930c, 1932)	Yes	Yes	Yes: arm EMG	Yes
Totten (1935)	?	Yes	?	Yes
Amadeo & Shagass (1963)	Yes	No	?	No
Bergum & Lehr (1966)	?	Yes*	Yes; Pulse rate & pressure; Overt responses No: GSR & pupil size	Yes
Zikmund (1966)	?	Yes	?	Yes
Deckert (1964)	Yes*	No	?	Yes
Brown (1968)	?	No	?	Yes
Reyher & Morishige (1969)	Yes*	Yes	No: EKG, EEG	No
Lenox et al. (1970)	?	Yes	?	Yes
Graham (1970a, b)	?	Yes*	?	Yes
Wietzenhoffer & Brockmeier (1970)	Yes*	?	?	Yes
Antrobus, Antrobus, & Singer (1964)	Yes*	Yes*	No: EEG	Yes
Singer & Antrobus (1965)	?	Yes*	Yes: Heart Rate	Yes
Antrobus (1970)	Yes	?	No: Heart Rate	Yes
Bacon (1970)	?	Yes	?	Yes
Greenberg (1970a)	Yes*	Yes*	?	Yes
Greenberg (1970b)	Yes*	Yes*	?	Yes
Antrobus (1973)	?	Yes*	No: Heart Rate	Yes

[a] In this research survey, we have attempted to specify the results of statistical tests when they were conducted by stating that the effect was "significant" (reliable) or "not significant" (not reliable). Where effects are reported in the absence of these words, together with the absence of asterisks in columns 1, 2, and 3 of the table, the reader may assume that the effects were not subjected to statistical tests. This criterion is not applied to column 4.

Task and Experimenters	(1) change from baseline?	(2) vary as a function of conditions?	Did the Eye Response: (3) occur independently of other covert processes?	(4) specifically relate to a cognitive aspect?
PROBLEM-SOLVING				
Stoy (1930)	?	Yes*	?	Yes
Telford & Thompson (1933)	?	Yes	?	Yes
Clites (1935)	Yes*	Yes*	?	Yes
Collins (1962)	Yes	Yes*	?	Yes
Lorens & Darrow (1962)	Yes*	Yes	No: alpha EEG / Yes: heart rate, CL, GSR	Yes
Amadeo & Gomez (1966)	Yes	?	?	No
Kaplan & Schoenfeld (1966)	Yes	Yes	?	Yes
Rosen & Czech (1966)	Yes*	Yes*	No: GSR	Yes
Sokolov (1966)	Yes	Yes	?	No
Teichner & Price (1966)	?	Yes	?	Yes
Lachman et al. (1968)	Yes	Yes	Yes: GSR	Yes
McGuigan, Culver, & Kendler (1971)	Yes*	Yes*	Yes: Tongue, EEG, Right Leg / No: Arm	Yes
Holland & Tarlow (1972)	?	Yes*	?	Yes
ANSWERING QUESTIONS				
Ellson et al. (1952)	Yes	Yes	?	Yes
Teitelbaum (1954)	Yes	Yes	?	Yes
McGuigan & Pavek (1972)	Yes	Yes*	Yes: EEG, Lips, Neck / No: Arm	Yes
Cutrow et al. (1972)	Yes	Yes*	No: GSR, respiration	Yes
Kinsbourne (1972)	Yes*	Yes*	?	Yes
Day (1964)	Yes			No
Day (1967)	Yes	Yes	No: EEG	Yes
Duke (1968)	Yes	Yes*	?	Yes
Backan (1969)	Yes	Yes*	?	Yes
Backan & Shotland (1969)	Yes	?	?	Yes
Kocel et al. (1972)	Yes	Yes*	?	Yes
Sherrod (1972)	Yes	?	?	Yes

TABLE 5.1 Summary Evaluation of Research on Eye Movements under Cognitive Conditions *(cont.)*

	(1) change from baseline?	(2) vary as a function of conditions?	Did the Eye Response: (3) occur independently of other covert processes?	(4) specifically relate to a cognitive aspect?
Task and Experimenters				
AUTOKINETIC ILLUSION				
Lehman (1965)	Yes*	?	?	Yes
Marshall (1966)	Yes*	?	?	Yes
MEMORY				
Ewert (1933)	Yes	?	?	Yes
Loftus (1972)	?	Yes*	?	Yes
SENSORY DEPRIVATION				
Rossi et al. (1964)	No	Yes	Yes: EEG	No
Rossi et al. (1967)	No	Yes	Yes: EEG	No
HYPNOTIC DREAMS				
Schiff et al. (1961)	Yes	Yes	No: EEG	Yes
Amadeo & Shagass (1963, Exp. 2)	Yes*	Yes*	Yes: EEG	Yes
Brady & Levitt (1964; 1966)	?	Yes	?	Yes
Brady & Rosner (1966)	Yes*	Yes*	Yes*: EEG	Yes
Deckert (1964)	Yes*	No	?	Yes
Graham (1970a)	?	Yes*	?	Yes
Graham (1970b)	?	Yes*	?	Yes
Weitzenhoffer (1971)	Yes	?	?	Yes
Evans et al. (1972)	?	No	?	Yes
NOCTURNAL DREAMS				
Jacobson (1938b)	Yes	Yes	?	Yes
Dement & Kleitman (1957a, b)	Yes	Yes	?	Yes
Dement & Wolpert (1958)	Yes	Yes	?	Yes

| | Did the Eye Response: | | | |
Task and Experimenters	(1) change from baseline?	(2) vary as a function of conditions?	(3) occur independently of other covert processes?	(4) specifically relate to a cognitive aspect?
Berger, Olley, & Oswald (1962)	Yes	Yes	?	Yes
Berger & Oswald (1962)	Yes	Yes	?	Yes
Roffwarg et al. (1962)	Yes	Yes	?	Yes
Gross, Byrne, & Fisher (1965)	Yes	Yes	?	Yes
Amadeo & Gomez (1966)	Yes	Yes	?	No
Arkin, Weitzman, & Hastey (1966)	Yes	Yes	?	Yes
Baldridge, Whitman, Kramer, & Ornstein (1968)	Yes	Yes	?	Yes
Moskowitz & Berger (1969)	Yes	Yes	?	No
Molinari & Foulkes (1969)	Yes	Yes	?	No
Jacobs, Feldman, & Bender (1970a)	Yes	Yes		No
Jacobs, Feldman, & Bender (1970b)	Yes	Yes	?	Yes
Jacobs, Feldman, & Bender (1972)	Yes	Yes	?	Yes
Busciano, Spadetta, Carella, & Caruso (1971)	Yes	Yes	?	Yes
Arkin, Lutzky, & Toth (1972)	Yes	Yes	?	No

Did the Response Occur Because of the Experimental Treatment Per Se?
If it is established by Criterion 1 that the response did occur, a researcher could have ascertained whether or not the response was a direct function of an experimental treatment itself; that is, while one might establish that a response changes from baseline, such a change could have occurred as a function of essentially any stimulation or activity and not because of what was specifically done to or by the subject. Criterion 2 may be satisfied by showing that the covert response systematically changes as a function of two (or more) experimental conditions. For example, one might find that electrical measures from the eyes are greater when the subject imagines looking at the Eiffel Tower versus when one imagines nonvisual activities (Jacobson, 1932). A particularly valuable control in this regard is one in which the response is measured during some nonlinguistic condition and compared with that during a linguistic condition. For example, subjects might have nonlinguistic trials of listening to white noise (McGuigan and Rodier, 1968) or meaningless changing tones (McGuigan and Pavek, 1972) in order to compare response values under those conditions with measures during the condition of special interest.[2] Obviously, if a subject makes a certain response during a linguistic condition which is not made during a nonlinguistic condition, that response is less likely to be a component of a general arousal pattern, and the probability is increased that the response is serving some internal information processing function.

The same notation as for column 1 is used for Criterion 2 in column 2 of Table 5.1, viz., if the experimenter studied the covert response measure as a function of two or more conditions and found that the measure varied systematically, "yes" is written in column 2; if the measure did not systematically vary as a function of conditions, "no" is written in column 2. A question mark indicates that the experimenter did not study the covert response as a function of two or more conditions.

We may note that Criterion 2 is more powerful than Criterion 1 for demonstrating that a response actually occurred. That is, Criterion 2 could substitute for Criterion 1 because a second experimental treatment (or control condition) may serve the same function as that of a baseline measure (and more). To elaborate, a subject told to rest in order to establish a baseline is not "in a vacuum" but is rather in some cognitive state unknown to the experimenter. Hence, rather than allowing subjects to be under their own internal stimulus control ("choosing" their own "cognitive activity") for a baseline condition, the experimenter can bring the subject under external stimulus control by administering a selected experimental treatment. An experimental treatment that is common across subjects should thus produce more uniform behavioral effects than would instructions to rest (wherein "the mind wanders"). Of

---

[2] The problem is difficult, e.g., some subjects still might try to find a systematic pattern to the tones and thus do "mental" work.

course, the more powerful experimental design is one in which it is possible to determine whether or not a response changes: (1) from a baseline condition, and also (2) as a function of two or more experimental treatments.

CRITERION 3

Was the Response a Unique, Localized Event or Was It Only a Component of a Generalized Arousal Pattern? To determine whether a given response is a relatively unique, localized bodily event, it should be shown that the response occurs independently of other covert processes. For this, concomitant measures should be made from a sample of bodily regions or systems. If the researcher successfully employed this criterion and did find that the response was independent of some other bodily reaction(s), a "yes" is entered in column 3 of Table 5.1. If the criterion was employed and it was found that the response was not independent of the other measure(s) taken, "no" is entered in column 3. In either case the concomitant measure taken is specified. If the researcher did not simultaneously record other reactions, a question mark is entered for Criterion 3.

CRITERION 4

Was There a Specific Relationship Between an Independent Variable and a Response Parameter? A final probabilistic indication that a response occurs and serves some information processing function would be the specification of a relationship between a response parameter and a specific aspect of cognition (the latter determined by verbal reports about the subject's "experience," by systematic variation of the subject's conditions or characteristics, etc.). Such specific relationships indicate the intimate involvement of the response with the cognitive activity, e.g., Jacobson (1932) showed specifically that the eyes move *upwards* when one is told to imagine the Eiffel Tower in Paris. We should add, though, that Criterion 4 is rather "loose" and we will take considerable liberty in specifying the kinds of variables involved in specific relationships—the nature of the studies to be considered is so diverse that it is necessary to be flexible in applying this criterion during this exploratory phase of research evaluation. Perhaps after this initial step, we will learn how to improve our application of Criterion 4, the results of which are summarized on pages 152–57.

With these four criteria, we shall now summarize and evaluate relevant empirical research. The studies that we shall consider fall into eight categories as follows: (1) imagination, (2) problem solving, (3) answering questions, (4) autokinetic illusion, (5) memory, (6) sensory deprivation, (7) hypnotic dreams, (8) nocturnal dreams.

Certain other classes of studies will only be sampled (or completely excluded), viz., those in which the eye necessarily functions for visual perception as in reading, e.g., McGuigan and Pinkney (1973), or in paried associate learning, e.g., McCormack and Clemence (1970). Similarly, studies in which there is no direct or objective measure of activity, as in introspective reports, are excluded, e.g., Moore (1896).

Empirical Studies

IMAGINATION TASKS

For one aspect of Perky's (1910) classical study of imagination, subjects first relaxed while they fixated on a central luminous spot within four other spots. Then, when the experimenter spoke a series of words or sentences, the subjects reported eye movements (detected when the peripheral lights flashed into the visual field) and described the images evoked by the words. Perky concluded that "memory images" of sight ("particular and personal ones") typically involve gross movements of eyes, while "imaginations" (images that lack particularity and personal references) generally involve no eye movements. The experiment is evaluated in Table 5.1 where we note that the response *did* occur, as indicated by "yes" under the increase from baseline criterion (though in these early studies we cannot expect confirmation through statistical tests). However, we do not know whether the response occurred because of the imagery task per se since there was no measure of eye movements during another task or control condition; hence a question mark is placed in column 2 (which asks whether the eye response varied as a function of conditions). The question mark in column 3 indicates that we do not know whether or not the eye response was localized, since there were no concomitant measures that would allow an estimate of whether the response occurred "independently of other covert processes." Perky did implicate laryngeal movements during sound images and nostril movements during smell images; however, these measures were not concomitantly taken during any one task. The "yes" in column 4 indicates that Perky reported a specific relationship between an eye movement parameter and specific content of the reported imagery, viz., that the response is a function of "memory" vs. "imagination" (see summary statements on p. 152).

Jacobson's (1930c) subjects first thoroughly relaxed (after receiving prolonged training in progressive relaxation), and subsequently a click-signal instructed them to visually imagine or recollect such visual items as the Eiffel Tower. Several seconds later, another signal instructed them to relax again. Electrically recorded eye movements noticeably increased following the first signal, and then returned to baseline level following the second; hence, a "yes" is entered in column 1 of Table 5.1. Under two control conditions in which the subjects were instructed not to bother to imagine, or to relax the eye muscles, there were neither eye changes nor reports of visual imagery. When asked to visualize the arm there was almost always an absence of EMG in the arms, though if the subject did produce arm EMG, there was no eye response (Jacobson,

1932). Jacobson's interpretation was that when the eye response was absent the subjects imagined bending the arm using muscular sensation. Since the eye response occurred during visual imagination, but typically did not occur during instructions to relax, to the click-signals, or during nonvisual tasks, it appears to be intimately related to visual imagery and the "yes" in column 2 thus indicates that the eye response varied as a function of conditions. Furthermore, the eye response was generally independent of at least one other covert process, as indicated by "yes (arm EMG)" in column 3. Finally, the records during visual imagination showed patterns resembling those that occurred during actual visual perception, e.g., the pattern for imaging the Eiffel Tower was practically identical with the pattern produced when the subject was requested to look upward; the "yes" in column 4 represents this finding.

Totten (1935) confirmed the hypothesis that eye movements required in the perception of an object also occur during imagination of that object. Movements of the right eye during imagination were photographically recorded by the corneal-reflectance method. The question mark in column 1 of Table 5.1 indicates that she did not record a baseline measure. In the majority of the instances (75 vs. 9) the eye movement patterns during imagination corresponded to those that would occur during actual perception; more particularly, the direction of eye movements during imagination involving horizontal or vertical planes generally followed the appropriate plane for each image.

We shall not further elaborate obvious characteristics of Table 5.1, as in the study by Totten that concomitant measures were not taken (indicated by the "?" in column 3) and the directional aspect of the eye movements just reported (indicated by the "yes" in column 4).

In their first experiment, Amadeo and Shagass (1963) sought to determine if eye movements represent scanning of visual images or are merely a nonspecific concomitant of attention. Rapid eye movements (REM) were compared under three waking conditions: rest, directed visual imagery, and during a word-association test which was presumed to produce a state of increased attention. Mean rapid eye movements significantly increased from the resting condition (7.6 per minute) during both experimental conditions. While the frequency was greater during the directed visual imagery task than during the word-association task (20.4 per minute versus 17.7 per minute) the difference was not significant; the "no" in column 2 indicates this lack of significant difference. The authors concluded that rapid eye movement rate increases as a nonspecific concomitant of attention—the inference is that the eye activity they measured is not due to visual imagery content, though the authors recognized that visual content entered into the word-association test; it also seems apparent that heightened attention is also required for the directed visual imagery condition. Consequently, this approach does not appear to be a suitable test for the researcher's question.

Bergum and Lehr (1966) found that frequency of eye movements, recorded by videotape, was significantly lower during the auditory presentation of interesting material than during the auditory presentation both of unpleasant and of dull verbal stimuli. Frequency of eye movement thus discriminated between "levels of affect." The eye movement measure was independent of pulse rate, capillary pulse pressure, and also of latency and duration of the overt key-press evaluative response. However, frequency of eye movements was related to GSR and pupil size.

Zikmund (1966) studied nystagmoid movements while his subjects perceived and then imagined black and white stripes while the stripes were stationary and while they were moving. Nystagmoid eye movements occurred during both visual perception and imagination of the moving stripes, but not during the visual perception or imagination as stationary stimuli. During perception and imagination of movement, though precise frequencies and amplitudes differed, the pattern while imagining the movement to the right resembled the pattern recorded during actual perception to the right. Since the response changed from the condition in which the stripes were imagined as stationary to that in which they were imagined as moving, the "yes" in column 2 of Table 5.1 indicates that the response varied as a function of condition. Finally, since the directions of the perceived and imagined movements were both related to the actual direction of the eye movement, we enter a "yes" in column 4.

In one aspect of his research Deckert (1964) electrically measured eye movements during waking conditions of rest, visual pendulum pursuit, and imagination of pendulum pursuit. Frequency of eye movements did not significantly differ for conditions of actual pursuit and imagined pursuit, whereas pursuit eye movements for these two conditions were significantly above the baseline condition of rest. There were no important differences among conditions as a function of whether the subject's eyes were open or closed. The direction and frequency of eye movements during imagined pursuit corresponded approximately to the actual direction of movement and beat frequency of the pendulum. Similarly, though concomitant EEG and GSR measures were taken, no data on them were reported; hence the question mark in column 3.

Using Deckert's technique, Brown (1968) failed to find a reliable relationship between frequency of eye movements while actually tracking a metronome and frequency of eye movements during visual recall of the tracking. She classified subjects independently as visualizers vs. nonvisualizers and found that eye movements during the recall condition with eyes closed occurred significantly more frequently for the visualizers.

Reyher and Morishige (1969) electrically studied eye movement rate during free visual imagery and while recalling nocturnal dreams. After establishing a resting baseline, the subject signalled the onset and conclusion of free visual imagery and subsequently described the content. The dreams were similarly recalled after a baseline was obtained. Mean rapid eye movement (REM) rates for both conditions were significantly higher than the respective baseline rates, but did not differ from each other. The REM patterns during the experimental conditions were more characteristic (in frequency and amplitude) of a waking state than of nocturnal dreaming. Relative to free visual imagery, dream recall was characterized, by more kinetic imagery and significantly more frequent image episodes of a longer duration. Heart rate significantly increased for the dream recall condition but not for the free imagery condition. Similarly, percent occipital alpha significantly decreased for the dream recall condition but not for the free imagery condition; however this alpha desynchronization was apparently due to a much higher baseline for dream recall relative to the visual imagery condition. REMs increased from baseline during visual imagery, suggesting that REMs are related to the subject's scanning of images. However, the "scanning of image hypothesis" implies that REMs should increase with both the rate and duration of visual episodes, and with the amount of kinetic imagery. Even though the dream recall condition had higher values than the free imagery condition on all three of these characteristics, it did not produce a higher REM rate; hence the authors concluded that REMs represent a nonspecific neural mechanism which is a concomitant of attentive activity, a hypothesis advanced by Amadeo and Shagass (1963).

Lenox, Lange, and Graham (1970) used Deckert's procedure for comparing eye movements during actual pursuit and during imagination of a swinging pendulum. The subjects imagined the pendulum both with eyes open and with eyes closed. There were noticeable regular movements during imagination tasks whose frequencies corresponded in varying degrees to those during perception. During imagination with eyes open, the eye movements were in a square wave form indicating periods of rest interspersed with rapid saccades; with eyes closed, the movements were more sinusoidal and of larger amplitude than during the actual pursuit. The authors concluded that true pursuit movements require the presence of a moving stimulus in the environment and are based on continuous feedback from that external stimulus.

Graham's (1970a) first experiment was an extension of Deckert's work. The subjects observed a horizontal line (designed to elicit saccadic eye movements) and then imagined the line. They also observed a swinging pendulum (used to elicit pursuit eye movements) and then imagined it. The order of the stimulus presentation was counterbalanced. Frequency of pursuit eye movements during imagination of the swinging pendulum approximated that during the actual observation of the pendulum, but as in previous work cited above, electrically recorded eye movement *patterns* during imagination differed from those during perception. In particular the amplitude of the eye movements was significantly smaller during imagery, and there also were more saccades per wave than during the actual observation. These results contrasted with those obtained using the horizontal line, where frequency of saccadic eye movements in the imagination condition was not significantly different from that during actual observation. Graham concluded that eye movements during waking imagery and normal observation may be quite similar for a stimulus that elicits saccadic eye movements but the patterns are different for stimuli that elicit pursuit movements. Since Graham (1970a) did not measure a change from baseline, a question mark is entered in column 1 of Table 5.1.

Graham (1970b) electrically compared eye movements when awake subjects observed the optokinetic stimulus of a slowly moving black stripe with eye movements during a waking imagination condition in which subjects were instructed to "see the stripe on the screen, just as it appeared before." A similar nystagmus-like movement pattern was observed during both the perception and imagination conditions; however, the patterns did differ too in that during waking imagination of the stimulus there were significantly more saccades and fewer oscillations than during actual observation of the stimulus.

Weitzenhoffer and Brockmeier (1970) studied the relationship between listening attention and the rate of rapid eye movements. Baselines were obtained and the subjects were asked to sequentially imagine songs. Baselines and imagination occurred both with eyes open and closed. In another task demanding attention, subjects were asked to listen to one of two voices on a tape recording in which the two voices talked simultaneously but out of phase; this task was also performed with the eyes both open and closed. A significant reduction in rate of rapid eye movement from baseline occurred with eyes open on all attention-producing tasks, but did not occur with eyes closed. The findings indicated a negative relationship between rate of rapid eye movements and attention in a nonvisual modality. Since no comparisons were made for rate of rapid eye movement as a function of the differences in attention-producing tasks, a question mark is entered in Table 5.1 under column 2.

Of direct relevance to this chapter is the series of studies commencing with Antrobus, Antrobus, and Singer (1964) through Greenberg (1971) specified in Table 5.1. Because of the extensive and detailed nature of this work, some of the main findings are merely summarized under Specific Relationships, later in this chapter.

Antrobus (1973), under conditions of lights off and eyes closed, used instructions to "let your mind wander, let your thoughts drift," "make your thoughts shift rapidly from one thing to another. . . ," and "imagine a scene with moving persons and things," all produced larger and more frequent saccads than the three conditions, "concentrate on one specific object," "make your mind blank, don't let any images or thoughts appear," and "picture a stationary object from one vantage point." The results were interpreted as supporting the association of saccadic eye movement suppression with cognitive control. This interpretation was further supported by an auditory signal encoding task with alternating 15-second rest and encoding intervals. Encoding was associated with ocular quiescence and rest with increased saccadic movement. Heart rate variability followed the saccadic activity cycle. In a variation on the auditory encoding task, Antrobus varied the memory

load and complexity of the response while holding stimulus and response rate constant. As predicted, saccadic movements decreased as memory load increased. In conclusion, the decrease in saccads during external information processing is associated with a suppression of interfering thought and imagery. Saccadic movement, then, appears to be associated with switching to alternate information sources, external or internal; saccads are suppressed during the storage and subsequent processing of such information.

PROBLEM SOLVING

Stoy (1930) measured relative size and frequency of horizontal eye movements during problem solving tasks that involved spatial vs. nonspatial relations. Measurements were obtained by viewing the subject's eyes through a Bausch and Lomb Keratometer (a magnification device allowing scaled readings). Although baseline readings were not taken, Stoy found that the frequency and magnitude of eye movements were significantly greater when the subjects imagined and solved spatial problems than when they imagined and solved nonspatial problems.

Telford and Thompson (1933) sought to determine if decreased winking during reading was due to increased mental activity. Subjects were given 5-minute tasks of (1) mentally multiplying two-place numbers that were presented auditorally, (2) reading, and (3) conversing with the experimenter. The eyelid response was recorded mechanically by special "spectacles" supporting a small lever attached to the subjects' eyelid. Closure of the eyelid brought the lever in contact with a switch, actuating a marker on a kymograph. The shortest inter-blink periods occurred during mental arithmetic and the longest occurred for reading. The authors concluded that decreased winking during reading is not due to increased mental activity.

Clites (1935), by direct observation, noted the frequency of eye winks and inter-wink intervals during mental rest (baseline) and during simple and difficult problem solving. He found that subjects successful in solving the problems wink significantly faster during presentation, solving and reporting the solution than during rest. For unsuccessful subjects, the rate of winking decreased in the third quarter of the solving period and then tended to increase just before informing the experimenter that they could not solve the problem. Finally, winking is significantly more rapid during difficult mental work than during simple mental work.

Collins (1962) produced vestibular nystagmus in his subjects by rotating them. During rotation they were instructed to (1) report the subjective experience of a 90° rotation of the body, (2) ignore the effect of rotation and solve silent serial division problems, (3) reproduce the temporal duration of various sound stimuli, and (4) assume a state of reverie by relaxing and daydreaming. Nystagmus duration and degrees of slow-phase eye movements (electrically recorded) were both significantly less during reverie states than during the attention-demanding conditions. Significantly more nystagmus occurred for the mental arithmetic condition than for the other tasks. Collins concluded that the maintenance of vestibular nystagmus is dependent upon continued alertness, vestibular eye movements often being a better indicator of alertness than EEG (see also Collins and Posner, 1963).

Lorens and Darrow (1962) found that electrically recorded eye movement rate significantly increased over baseline during mental multiplication, and was independent of heart rate, skin conductance level, and galvanic skin response. Percent time occipital alpha (EEG) significantly decreased during mental multiplication. Neither random startle stimuli such as horn blasts, shouting, and threats, nor repetitive rhythmic auditory and photic stimulation elicited eye movements of the quantity or duration seen during mental multiplication; furthermore the eye movement rate following these startle stimuli was not observably different from the rate during the baseline periods. In addition, introspective reports suggested that eye movement rate is faster during imagination of vivid as opposed to less clear images.

The conclusion of Amadeo and Shagass (1963) that eye movements in visually normal subjects were indicators of waking attention, rather than of engagement in visual imagery, was followed up in the first experiment of Amadeo and Gomez (1966) using congenitally blind subjects. Rapid eye movements increased from rest more than 200% during a word association task that was designed to induce increased attention. The conclusion was that rapid eye movements are a concomitant of heightened attention since enhanced visual imagery could not be attributed to blind subjects.

Kaplan and Schoenfeld (1966) studied oculomotor behavior during anagram solving. The letters of the anagram to be solved were placed in the same (constant) location throughout each series of trials. The subjects thus necessarily solved the anagrams by rearranging the letters in the same order for each series. There were three series of trials with the locations of letters different in each series. Eye movements were cinematically recorded; in this way the experimenters knew where the eyes were sequentially directed during the solution process. It was reported that similarly formed anagrams tended to condition an oculomotor pattern consistent with the letter ordering. That is, a conditional fixation pattern developed that corresponded to the order of the letters for the anagrams. The order of eye responses was thus consistent within each series but different among series (hence "yes" in column 2). This conditional fixation pattern was considered a behavioral correlate of a "mental set" to perceive the letters in the solution order.

Rosen and Czech (1966) studied sequences of the cognitive process in decision making stiuations. Decisions between two conflicting alternatives had to be made on (1) critical trials, in which the subjects were shocked or not shocked depending on the decision; and (2) non-critical trials, in which the decision did not have a shock-effect. Three phases of each trial were electro-oculographically defined: (1) the predecision phase was measured by ocular latency; (2) the decision phase was measured by ocular avoidance, defined in terms of the largest ocular response to the stimulus and by stimulus viewing time; and (3) the post-decision phase was measured by post-stimulus viewing time. The results, in accord with an earlier, more limited study (Rosen and Czech, 1965), were that pre-decision time (ocular latency) was significantly greater on critical than on non-critical trials. The measures of the decision phase and the post-decision phase were also significantly greater on the critical trials. Finally, skin conductance increased significantly throughout the critical trials but changed negligibly during the non-critical trials. It was concluded that phases of cognitive processes (viz., pre-decision, decision, and post-decision phases) can be identified through electro-oculography.

Sokolov (1966) examined the influence of mental activity and visual fixation as sources of intra-subject variability upon nystagmus that was induced by irrigation of the subject's ear with 44° C water. There were three test conditions: (1) relaxation with eyes lightly closed; (2) fixation on a small distant light while performing a serial subtraction task, and (3) performing a subtraction task with eyes lightly closed. Eight indices of the eye response were recorded, including duration, maximum velocity of slow phase nystagmus movement, amplitude, and total number of nystagmic beats. The greatest nystagmic response, according to all eight indices, occurred during condition 3 in which the subjects performed silent arithmetic with the eyes closed; condition 1, with the eyes closed and relaxing, produced the second largest amount of nystagmic response on all eight indices, while condition 2, mental arithmetic with eyes fixated, produced the smallest response. It appears that the nystagmic response is associated with the performance of mental arithmetic relative to a baseline nystagmic-produced condition, and that visual fixation reduces the size of the nystagmus response during mental arithmetic. Sokolov concluded that experimenters using caloric-induced nystagmus should minimize intra-subject variability by the maintenance of a high level of alertness; mental arithmetic, he held, has been found to be the best method for alerting the subject.

Teichner and Price (1966) obtained eye-movement data while subjects were visually presented a concept formation problem in which the task was to supply the next in a sequence of letters, e.g., ABMCDME-FMGHM__. The sequences were presented under three conditions: (1) unlimited time for inspection of the displayed sequence, (2) mild speed stress—10 seconds for inspection, and (3) blurred image with unlimited time. Eye movements were recorded by camera and measured for position and duration of fixation, and distance between fixations. The measures of duration and distance were largest for (1), the unlimited viewing condition; next largest were for (3), the blurred image-unlimited time condition, and shortest for (2), the speed viewing condition. The conclusion was that under stress, one scans the image less and extracts more information. Or, in other terms, under mild stress one narrows one's attentional field and the mode of processing information becomes more systematic.

Lackman, Aarons, and Erickson (1968) reported a case study suggesting the utility of nystagmus as a parameter of mental function. The patient, diagnosed as a paranoid schizophrenic, exhibited an unusual "spontaneous" nystagmus. Electrical nystagmographic records were collected over a period of 18 months under several conditions including relaxation, graded mental arithmetic, and dermal shock. Sample records showed increased frequency and amplitude of nystagmus over the baseline of relaxation as task difficulty increased. There was little augmentation of the baseline nystagmic response following shock, whereas a simultaneous record of the galvanic skin response indicated a dramatic increase in arousal. Lackman et al. concluded that this measure of eye activity was a sensitive monitor of "mental effort" independent of those processes usually subsumed under alertness or attention. As in many of these studies, one may wonder whether such limited findings of a person's nystagmus is representative of induced nystagmus in the normal population.

McGuigan, Culver, and Kendler (1971) attempted to directly measure covert mediating responses using a variation of Tracy Kendler's (1972) mediation paradigm. There were three independent groups of subjects: a verbal mediation group, a non-oral mediation control, and a no-mediation control group. The non-oral mediation group employed a directional mediating response of pressing a button to the right or to the left. Integrated eye activity significantly increased from the initial to the test phase for this right-left mediation group, but did not significantly change for either of the other two groups. The authors suggested that slight visual glances to the right and to the left were covert response components of right and left mediational activity. Integrated measures of tongue EMG, EEG from over the motor area of the dominant hemisphere, and from the right leg failed to change significantly from the initial to the test phase. There were, however, large arm EMG changes for the right-left non-oral mediation group, being significant for the left arm.

Holland and Tarlow (1972) further examined the previously reported relationship between mental activity and rate of eye blinking (e.g., Clites, 1935; Antrobus, Antrobus, and Singer 1964). Subjects were presented two tasks: (1) repeating sequences of numbers (of four, six, or eight digits) 70 seconds after their initial presentation; and (2) a mental arithmetic task in which the subject heard a two-digit number every 10 seconds and, after 70 seconds, reported the cumulative sum. Eyeblinks were observed directly and recorded on an event marker. For the first task, rate of blinking was inversely (and significantly) related to memory load such that the highest blink rate occurred during the interval of remembering the four-digit stimuli and the lowest blink rate occurred for the eight-digit stimuli (the rate for the six-digit task was intermediate). For the second task, the digits for each trial were classified

according to whether they contained zero or non-zero numbers; blinking rate on the correct trials was significantly greater when the digits contained zeros than when there were no zeros in the numbers. Presumably, the memory load is greater with non-zero numbers. Finally, blinking rate was significantly greater during incorrect trials than during correct trials, regardless of whether the digits to be added contained zeros or non-zeros. In general, then, the greater the memory load, the lower the blinking rate. The conclusion is that increased mental load results in inhibition of blinking, which is an adaptive mechanism for minimizing interference of cognitive processes. This interpretation is similar to that cited by Singer, Greenburg, and Antrobus (1971), in which reduced eye activity is a form of "gating out" other information to "free internal channels for internal information processing."

ANSWERING QUESTIONS

There is an extended sequence of highly interesting research dealing with the cognitive activity that occurs during the processing and answering of question in which unique eye activity has been recorded following the termination of the question. While many of these deal with problem solving, we are placing them within this more specific category of "answering questions."

In one of a series of studies, Ellson, Davis, Saltzman, and Burke (1952) investigated the possibility that eye movements are an indicator of "lying" behavior. They employed a 2 × 2 complete factorial design using the variables of "honesty" and "motivation"—subjects were instructed to be honest or to lie, and motivation was manipulated by monetary reward. The subjects first completed a simple task and were then asked certain critical questions during an interview. Eye movements were recorded cinematically with an American Optical Company opthalmograph. On the critical interview questions, frequency of eye movements for subjects instructed to lie was greater than for "honest" subjects; similarly, subjects motivated by promise of monetary reward exhibited more frequent eye movements than unmotivated subjects.

Teitelbaum (1954) directly observed the occurrence or absence of rhythmic eye movements during silence or during speech activity while fixating on a distant object or gazing into the distance. Eye movements occurred less frequently during speech than during silence. During both speech and silence rhythmic eye movements occurred less frequently when fixating than when gazing into the distance. Teitelbaum considered these results in terms of possible inhibition of eye movements during concentration (e.g., speech) as a means of reducing external interference (an interpretation resembling the gating hypothesis).

McGuigan and Pavek (1972) asked subjects to silently answer questions by thinking either "yes" or "no." In five exploratory experiments, various measures of electrically recorded eye activity seemed to differentiate between silent "yes" and "no" answers. In the final major experiment it was determined that mean duration of the eye response was significantly longer when subjects thought "yes" than when they thought "no." Covert nonoral (EMG) responses were also identified in the two arms; this is an additional index distinguishing silent "yes" from "no" answers. The eye response was independent of EEG reactions from over the left temporal lobe and left motor areas, and also independent of covert (EMG) responses in the lips and neck.

Cutrow, Parks, Lucas, and Thomas (1972) obtained measures of eye-blink latency and rate, breathing amplitude and rate, heart rate, palmar and volar forearm GSR, and voice latency during a deception task. Subjects were instructed to always answer "no" to a number of questions. The results showed that measures of eyeblink rate and latency significantly increased during questions in which the "no" response constituted a lie as contrasted to truthful "no's." Similarly, all other concomitant measures significantly increased during deception. Cutrow et al. concluded that each measure is useful for the detection of deception, but an index combining more than one psychophysiological variable holds advantages over independent measures.

Kinsbourne (1972) used direction of eye and head movements to infer the nature of cerebral lateralization in left- and right-handed subjects. Questions answered were classified as verbal, numerical, or spatial, and initial eye and head movement following the questions was remotely recorded with an audio-visual system. For right-handed subjects, horizontal eye movements were significantly more often to the right for the verbal condition and to the left for the spatial condition (no significant directional effect for the numerical condition). For left-handed subjects directional effects were not prominent. Kinsbourne concluded that, for right-handed subjects, language processes are lateralized in the left hemisphere, while spatial skills are emphasized in the right hemisphere, with numerical thought processes more equally distributed between the hemispheres. For left-handed subjects, the hemispheres are dominant with approximately equal frequency for verbal, numerical, and spatial tasks. These conclusions were confirmed in a second study in which the nature of the task was held constant while the mode of response (verbal or spatial) was varied.

The following studies constitute a subsection within the category "Answering Questions." In these studies subjects have been classified according to whether they consistently move their eyes to the right or to the left following the presentation of a question. The affirmative answers in column 1 for the studies commencing with Day (1964) and running through Kocel, Galin, Ornstein, and Merrin (1972) indicate a directional phenomenon which is measured from a relatively steady ("baseline") eye position.

Day (1964) observed that some subjects, immediately after being asked a question, consistently moved their eyes in only one direction. Day (1967) then measured reaction time to an auditory and visual stimulus as a function of whether the subjects consistently moved their eyes to the left or were consistent "right-movers." Those subjects who moved their eyes to the left showed a reflex eye movement to an auditory stimulus with a latency less than 10 msec and a duration between 50-100 msec to an auditory stimulus, but right-movers did not show this movement. The reflex eye movement to the sound stimulus did not occur under the visual stimulus reaction time condition for the "left-movers." The response for the left-movers thus seems to be related to the auditory modality. "Left-movers" also seemed to show greater amplitude and lower frequency of "general EEG activity" than right-movers. Cerebral and evolutionary speculations were considered.

Following Day (1964), Duke (1968) directly observed lateral eye movements of students while they answered orally administered questions which were either reflective or factual. Lateral eye movements occurred significantly more often to reflective than to factual questions. Furthermore, males moved their eyes significantly more often in a single direction than females, whose direction of eye movement was less consistent; this consistent movement phenomenon was independent of eye dominance. Simple questions seldom elicited eye movement behavior.

Bakan (1969) examined the possible relationships between hypnotizability, laterality of eye movements ("left vs. right movers"), and functional brain asymmetry. "Left-movers" (those who consistently move their eyes to the left following a question) were significantly more hypnotizable than "right-movers"; they were also significantly more likely to be taking a humanistic major in college, they scored significantly higher on the verbal scale of the Scholastic Aptitude Test, and they had a greater tendency to report clear visual imagery. Bakan concluded that the left lateral eye movements were due to a more active right cerebral hemisphere, which implies a syndrome characterized by the greater use of pre-verbal activities for the "left-movers." Hence, these data appear consistent with Day's (1964) characterization of left-movers as imaginative and exhibiting a subjective or internal orientation of attentional processes.

Bakan and Shotland (1969) examined the possible relationship between laterality of eye movement and performance on a task requiring high visual attention. Right- and left-movers were compared for performance on the Stroop color-word test. The subject was visually presented color words printed in conflicting colors. For example, the word "red" was printed in green ink and the correct response was saying the word green. This test provided a measure of visual attentiveness or resistance to distraction. For a second test, black-on-white color names were used to determine reading speed; and a third test presented colored patches to provide a measure of speed of color-naming. All sets contained 80 words or stimuli and the times in seconds to read each set were the dependent measures for each subject. The results indicated that, for the black-on-white condition, right-movers read significantly faster than left-movers. Of particular interest was the result showing that the performance of right-movers was significantly faster than that of left-movers for the condition of color-words printed in conflicting colors. Bakan and Shotland concluded that right-movers exhibit more resistance to distraction than left-movers; and, additionally, that right-movers appear to simply read faster than left-movers, as indicated by their performance on the black-on-white cards.

Kocel et al. (1972) confirmed that the direction of lateral eye movements (observed through a closed circuit television system) prior to overtly answering reflective questions is a reliable individual characteristic. However, as in earlier studies, the phenomenon is not universal, e.g., in this study only nine of 23 subjects made lateral eye movements with "sufficient consistency" in one direction so as to be classified as either "left"- or "right"-movers. These researchers also found that the direction of the eye movement is a function of the cognitive demands of the question. More specifically, the mean percentage of right lateral eye movements to verbal and mathematical questions was significantly greater than the mean for spatial and musical questions (67.5% vs. 45.0%). Thus, these results confirm their hypothesis that questions designed to engage the minor hemisphere (spatial, musical) evoke lateral eye movements to the left, whereas questions engaging the dominant hemisphere (verbal, mathematical) result in lateral eye movements to the right.

Sherrod (1972) tested the hypothesis that individuals who consistently move their eyes to the left following reflective questions—who, according to Day (1964) and Bakan (1969), have an apparent tendency to focus attention internally and are more imaginative—may react more strongly to a persuasive message than individuals who consistently move their eyes to the right. The notion is derived from a study by Festinger and Maccoby(1964) who found that subjects generating more internal arguments exhibit more extreme (positive or negative) attitude-change scores. Sherrod's subjects listened to a persuasive tape recording which argued that only a few hours of sleep are necessary for normal health. They then completed an attitude scale and were asked five reflective questions to classify them as left- or right-movers. Subjects who made five eye movements in the same direction and zero in the other were isolated for separate study. The 100% left-movers were significantly more reactive to the persuasive message than were right-movers as determined by the attitude scale. Sherrod concluded that reactivity to persuasive messages may be yet another correlate of lateral eye movements.

AUTOKINETIC ILLUSION

The relation between eye movements and the autokinetic illusion was studied by Lehman (1965). The subjects fixated the autokinetic point, a red spot of light on the wall of a darkened room, for 90 seconds and verbally reported all starts, stops, and changes in direction of the illusory movement. An American Optical Company opthalmograph, adapted for use with infra-red light, was used to photographically record eye movements. For all subjects the first report of illusory movement was significantly preceded, within ¼ sec, by a large eye movement. Furthermore, maintenance of the movement illusion was significantly often associated with corresponding movements of the eye. Lehman concluded that eye movements are consistently related to starts, stops, and changes in the direction of autokinetic movement.

Marshall (1966) studied the effects of induced eye movements on subjects' reports of the direction of autokinetic movement. A light stimulus viewed by the subjects through a set of Risley rotary prisms was used to effect displacement of the retinal image, causing compensatory eye movements in a given diagonal axis of the visual field. Simultaneously subjects were asked to trace the direction, mark the latency, and measure the magnitude (in seconds) of the autokinetic movement on an electronic tracking device. (While it seems likely that the eye movements actually *were* induced in the direction under experimental control, it would have been advisable to electrically monitor the induced eye movements to confirm that these movements occurred as planned.) Pre-induction control (baseline) data in which there were no induced eye movements indicated no significant differences in the amount of time that the reported autokinetic movement occurred in a particular direction. When eye movements were induced, subjects' reports of the direction of autokinetic movements significantly reflected the direction of the accompanying eye movements. No differences were found in latency or magnitude to different directional eye movements.

MEMORY

Ewert (1933) recorded the frequency of horizontal eye movements through direct observation while his subjects read, learned by dictation, and silently recalled the material read and dictated. He found that frequency of eye movements noticeably increased from baseline while overtly recalling a passage, just as it did while overtly reading that passage. Similarly, frequency of eye movements during silent reading approximated frequency during silent recall of the material read. Finally, frequency while learning by dictation approximated that during both overt and silent recall of the material. He added that data (not presented) indicate that the photographic ocular *pattern*, while reading is reproduced during recall of the same material. Ewert recognized the possibility that the increased frequency during recall is not evoked by the specific recall material, but by a more general factor; however, he argued that, since there are similar frequenices during dictation and recall, the eye movements *are* probably specifically related to the material read. His general conclusion is that eye movements become attached to language symbols (as possibly demonstrated by Kaplan and Schoenfeld, 1966), that they are related to language behavior, and are themselves part of the vocal recall pattern.

Loftus (1972), using a Mackworth stand camera, investigated the extent to which recognition memory proficiency with pictures could be predicted by the number of eye fixations during perception of a picture.

The study consisted of three experiments, each experiment being divided into a study (perception) phase and a test (memory) phase. The subjects were presented 90 pairs of pictures in the study phase and the number of eye fixations on each picture was recorded. In the test phase subjects were to identify from a pool of 180 those 90 picture pairs previously presented. In the first experiment the pictures were assigned different monetary values which were either added to or subtracted from the subject's fee, depending upon whether or not each was correctly identified as having been previously seen. In Experiment II the exposure time to the pictures was controlled by the experimenter rather than by the subject. In the final experiment the subjects viewed pictures either normally or while counting backwards. Eye fixations were recorded during the study phases but not during the test phases.

The results of the first experiment indicated that higher-valued pictures received significantly more eye fixations during the study phase and were remembered better than low-valued pictures.[3] When the exposure time was controlled by the experimenter—the pictures viewed for a fixed amount of time in the study phase—memory performance was a positive function of the number of eye fixations on the picture. (The more the fixations, the better the memory.) This positive function obtained *for each exposure time*—that is, for example, when exposure time was held constant at 3 sec, many short fixations led to better performance than fewer longer fixations. Finally when subjects performed a distracting task while viewing the pictures in the study phase, the eye fixation rate was reduced by about one third; memory performance during the test phase was reliably lower than that of subjects who viewed the pictures under normal conditions.

SENSORY DEPRIVATION

Rossi, Furhman, and Solomon (1964) sought to determine whether rapid eye movements (REMs) during sensory-deprivation are associated with hallucinations as they are with dreams during sleep. Each subject was in sensory-deprivation for three 7-hour sessions; one was a control session and the other two, separated by a week, were experimental sessions. During experimental sessions, when the subjects heard a tone they reported their mental activity; no reports were called for during control sessions. At the conclusion of the study transcriptions of the subjects' narratives were rated by three clinicians on a scale of "type-of-thought-process" (i.e., hallucination, dream, fantasy, day-dream, or reality-oriented). REMs occurred in conjunction with seven of ten rated dreams, but for only one of nine rated hallucinations. A replication of this study (Rossi, Furhman, and Solomon, 1967) yielded similar results, viz., REMs accompanied 70% of the rated dreams and 33% of the rated hallucinations. Additionally, the authors stated in the 1967 study that thought processes rated as fantasies or daydreams during the *sleep state*

---

[3] Note the resemblance to the Rosen and Czech (1966) finding using shock.

were never associated with REMs. Rossi et al. concluded that hallucinations during sensory-deprivation differ from typical dreams of sleep, as indicated by the relative absence of REMs.

Serafetinides, Shurley, Brooks, and Gideon (1971) also electrically measured eye movements during sensory-deprivation, with concomitant measures including EEG, EMG (throat), ECG, and electrodermal activity. There were significant decreases from the first to the second half of the period in EEG voltage and frequency, and ECG rate, and these were accompanied by increases of electrodermal measures (excluding basal and palmar resistance). However, because no information regarding cognitive activity during sensory isolation was reported, we do not enter this study in Table 5.1.

HYPNOTIC DREAMS

Schiff, Bunney, and Freedman (1961) recorded EEG from the parietal and occipital lobes as well as eye movements in one subject during hypnotically induced dreams following normal waking baseline recordings. The instructions controlled the amount of activity within both trance-state dreams and post-hypnotic dreams. In general, the eyes were very active when active dreams were suggested (e.g., dreams about a ping pong match) and inactive when the suggested dreams were inactive in content (e.g., that a mask was put over the eyes). Eye movements were like those occuring in natural dreams, with frequency and amplitude of movement related to the amount of activity in the dreams. EEG recordings during both post-hypnotic and hypnotic dreams were similar to the waking EEG, while the EEG of natural night dreams was similar to the EEG of light sleep. It was concluded that post-hypnotic dreaming, hypnotic dreaming, and natural dreaming share certain characteristics with respect to phenomenal experience and to ocular movements.

Amadeo and Shagass (1963), in their second experiment, electrically studied eye movement frequency in normal and hypnotic states as a function of several conditions: (1) whether the eyes were open or closed; (2) performance of mental arithmetic while hypnotized versus non-hypnotized; and (3) "voluntary control" in which the instructions were to keep the eyes still as opposed to no such instructions. Several aspects of the experiment for which the results are quite complex will not be considered. The main points for us are as follows: in three conditions in which subjects were *not* hypnotized (eyes closed, eyes open, and while performing mental arithmetic), eye movement rate was always significantly greater than during the corresponding three conditions when subjects were hypnotized. Similarly, eye movement rate for subjects not hypnotized was always significantly greater when they exercised voluntary control, regardless of whether the eyes were open, closed, or whether the subjects performed mental arithmetic. Eye movement rate was significantly greater during the arithmetic condition than when the eyes were merely closed, regardless of whether subjects were hypnotized, nonhypnotized, or exercising voluntarily control. Similarly, mean eye movement rate was significantly greater during arithmetic than when the eyes were merely open under both the hypnosis and voluntary control condition. Although not reported in detail, concomitant EEG recordings showed that the reduction in eye movement rate during hypnosis was not associated with sleep wave forms. The finding that increased eye movement rate is associated with mental arithmetic is in accord with the results of Lorens and Darrow; however, the interpretation made by Amadeo and Shagass differs. That is, rate is one indicator of the level of attentive activity and this is apparently reduced following induction of the hypnotic state. Amadeo and Shagass concluded that rapid eye movement changes are a concomitant of increased attention. Lorens and Darrow, however, found that eye movement rate acceleration during mental arithmetic is independent of a variety of other bodily measures, like PGR and heart rate, and that it does not occur merely as a result of stimulation and the like. They therefore concluded that increased eye movement rate is a consistent concomitant of mental arithmetic and is related to the visual images formed during calculation.

Brady and Levitt (1964, 1966) sought to determine whether nystagmic eye movements elicited by an optokinetic stimulus (viz., gazing at a rotating drum having verticle black and white stripes) also occur during hallucination of that stimulus. The combined results of the 1964 and 1966 references are as follows. For the experimental condition, eye movements were (electrically) recorded during (1) waking perception of the optokinetic stimulus, (2) hypnotic perception of the optokinetic stimulus, (3) hypnotic hallucination of the optokinetic stimulus, (4) waking imagination of a situation that oridinarily elicits optokinetic nystagmus, viz., watching telephone poles pass from a moving train, and (5) attempts to feign nystagmic eye movements. Two independent control groups were also used. In the first the subjects (naive as to the nature of the experimental program) perceived the optokinetic stimulus and then attempted to feign nystagmus. Subjects in the second control group also attempted to feign nystagmus, and those susceptible to hypnosis were instructed to hallucinate the optokinetic stimulus while hypnotized. The results showed that four of nine experimental subjects exhibited nystagmus during hypnotic hallucination that was similar to that elicited during waking and hypnotic perception of the optokinetic stimulus. (The amount of nystagmus was positively related to the degree of hallucination clarity.) In general, the nystagmus during hallucination occurred more often than during waking imagination of watching passing telephone poles. In the first control group all subjects showed nystagmus while perceiving the stimulus. In the second control group, subjects susceptible to hypnosis showed nystagmus 30%-80% of the recorded time during the hallucination condition. None of the subjects in any group were able to feign nystagmic eye movements. Brady and Levitt concluded that hypnotically induced visual hallucinations are qualitatively similar to eye movements during perception.

Brady and Rosner (1966) electrically recorded eye movements under baseline conditions during hypnosis, induced dreams, and performance of mental arithmetic. Eye recordings were also taken from control subjects except that they were never hypnotized and were instructed to imagine a dream. Two measures were computed: (1) the range of eye movements, which represented the occurrence of large deflections in the record, was determined by subtracting the largest eye movement from the smallest amplitude of eye movement; (2) amount of activity was computed by determining the average amplitude of eye movement times the rate with which eye movements were made. Mental arithmetic was associated with greater ocular activity relative to resting measures in both the hypnotic and control groups. Additionally, during dreaming, the amount of eye activity for the hypnotized subjects significantly increased above that induced by mental arithmetic in either the waking or hypnotized state. In contrast, the amount of ocular motility was not increased by control subjects who imagined dreaming. Similar results were found for the range of eye movements. Apparently, hypnotic dreaming had more effect on rapid eye movement than imagined dreaming by control subjects. However, the most striking finding relevant to the issue of rapid eye movements in hypnotic dreaming is provided by the correlation of the range of eye movements and the quality of the dreaming reported by the subject. The inference from these data is that the more hypnotized subject's dream experience has the quality of a sleep dream, the greater the ocular activity present.

The following several studies are similar and hence grouped together. While his subjects were hypnotized, Deckert (1964) measured eye movements during conditions of rest, visual pursuit of a moving pendulum, and imagination of pendulum pursuit. The frequency of eye movements for both pursuit conditions significantly increased from the resting baseline, but there was no significant difference between actual and imagined pursuit. A similar analysis of the direction of eye movements showed that during actual and imagined pursuit a 1:1 relationship with the beat frequency of the pendulum was approached. Although concomitant EEG and GSR measures were taken, no data were presented.

In a portion of Graham's 1970a experiment he employed Deckert's 1964 procedures to determine if pursuit eye movements appear during hypnotic imagery of a previously observed stimulus. The subjects first observed the stimulus and were then instructed to imagine the stimulus while in both the waking and the hypnotic state. Two stimuli were used: (1) a horizontal line designed to elicit saccadic eye movements, and (2) a swinging pendulum used to elicit pursuit eye movements. For the horizontal line stimulus, saccadic eye movements were as frequent during actual perception as during imagination in both waking and hypnotic states (as in Deckert's 1964 study). For the swinging pendulum, however, there were certain eye differences between perception and imagination. The electrically recorded eye movements during imagination were more jagged than sine-like, and they exhibited a significantly larger number of saccades. For a stimulus that elicits saccadic eye movements, therefore, eye movements during imagery and actual perception are quite similar. For stimuli that elicit pursuit movements, on the other hand, differences are apparent.

Graham (1970b) recorded eye movements while subjects in the hypnotic state observed an optokinetic stimulus and then imagined it. A nystagmus-like pattern was observed in both conditions, but eye movements during imagery were characterized by a significantly larger number of saccades and a lower frequency of oscillation than eye movements during actual perception. Graham concluded that eye movements during imagination and perception, while similar, differ in some respects.

Weitzenhoffer (1971) hypnotized a subject and instructed him to "sleep and dream" (there were no specific directions regarding content). In a post-session interview, the subject reported "observing" a watch swinging from a chain during the dream. Simultaneous recording of eye movements indicated a period of high amplitude, rectangular-wave activity following the hypnotic instruction, and then a period of relative inactivity. When later instructed to imagine he saw a swinging watch while awake, a record of eye movements similar to those during the hypnotic dream was obtained. Weitzenhoffer concluded that pursuit-*like* eye movements may be obtained in conjunction with imagined or "dreamed" movements of a pendulum; however, the movements during the imagination or "dream" do differ from the perceptual ones that occur when observing a real pendulum in that the movements during the imagined or dreamed experience are not sinusoidal in form. This conclusion is in accord with that of Lenox et al. (1970) on page 129.

Evans, Reich, and Orne (1972) replicated the procedures of Brady and Levitt (1964, 1966) using (1) subjects who were highly susceptible to hypnosis; and (2) subjects insusceptible to hypnosis, but who were instructed to simulate to a "blind" experimenter. If simulating subjects could provide optokinetic nystagmus, its adequacy as a criterion of visual hallucinations would be necessarily questioned. Electrical records analyzed by judges showed that four of 14 hypnotized subjects produced optokinetic nystagmus (during hypnotically induced hallucinations of stimuli normally eliciting optokinetic nystagmus), whereas six of 14 subjects who simulated optokinetic nystagmus were judged to exhibit the nystagmic response. Additionally, hypnotized subjects who experienced subjectively real hallucinations of a revolving drum (a stimulus that usually elicits optokinetic nystagmus) often produced eye movement patterns inconsistent with the content of the hallucination. Evans et al. concluded that eye movement patterns do not provide a reliable method for distinguishing between hallucinatory experiences and actual perception.

NOCTURNAL DREAMS

In this section we will concentrate on those studies in which there were efforts to establish a specific relationship between some eye movement parameter and some cognitive variable such as particular dream content.

An early reference to this phenomenon was made by George Trumbull Ladd, who suggested in 1892 "that the visual elements of dreams were derivations of the 'psychical synthesis' of night-time retinal sense data. This hypothesis led him to speculate that the eyeballs move during dreaming. 'As we look down the street of a strange city, for example, in a dream we probably focus our eyes somewhat as we should do in making the same observation when awake . . .' " (cited by Roffwarg, Dement, Muzio, and Fisher, 1962, pp. 143-44).

Jacobson (1938b) empirically studied eye movements during dreams using his pioneering development of electrooculography (Jacobson, 1930c): "While watching the sleeper, when you note motion in his eyeballs . . . , you may awaken him suddenly and ask whether he was dreaming. If he is a good observer, you may secure an interesting report on what he has been imagining in his dream. Unfortunately, most persons tend to forget their dreams quickly . . ." (1938b, p. 38). He described directional eye movements related to the directional content of the dreams of his subjects as follows:

. . . he winked at a rapid rate, usually without opening his eyes. Under the closed lids, the eyeballs could be seen rolling in one direction or another, sometimes alternately . . . his eyes shifted as if he were seeing things in imagination. At such a moment, if suddenly asked whether they had been thinking about something, some persons replied, "Yes." They added that they had been visualizing. The direction in which the eyeballs had moved seemed to correspond, in sample instances, with the report of the would-be sleeper concerning the direction in which something had appeared to him in imagination. Thus the observer became, in a slight sense, a "mind reader," able to discern when the rester was evidently thinking or reflecting and able to guess a little as to the directions in which the images appeared . . . these crude observations have been carried farther in precise experiments (1938b, pp. 35-36).

Apparently there was no additional psychophysiological study of eye movements and dreams until the early 1950s when Kleitman observed Jacobson's techniques for electrically recording eye activity (personal communication from Jacobson and Kleitman). With a number of colleagues (Azerinski, Dement, Wolpert, etc.) Kleitman reported an extensive series of systematic studies confirming and extending Jacobson's original research. Kleitman and his associates are to be highly commended for initiating, in the 1950s, the major new movement of the objective study of dreams through psychophysiological methods.

Before reviewing the studies in this section, we should note that the question of whether or not the response changed from baseline (Criterion 1 of Table 5.1) is unique here, viz., since the experimenter observes the subject until a change in rate of eye movement response occurs, a change from baseline is always assured. The "Yes" in column 1 of Table 5.1 should be read with this characteristic in mind for all of the dream studies. Similarly, for Criterion 2, the question "did the rapid eye movement response occur because of the dream state?" is trivial because the response is used largely to define the dream state. The affirmative response in column 2 of Table 5.1 should thus be read with this limitation in mind. Our main interests in these studies will then be with the remaining columns of Table 5.1.

Dement and Kleitman (1957a) studied the relation between eye movements and visual imagery during dreams. Of 191 awakenings following rapid eye movements (REMs), 152 instances of dream recall were reported by the subjects. Of awakenings following non-rapid eye movement periods (NREMs), there were only 11 instances of dream recall. The length in seconds of REM periods was significantly correlated with the length in words of dream narratives. To test the hypothesis that specific eye movement patterns are related to visual imagery of dreams, subjects were awakened immediately after the appearance of one of four patterns of eye movements: (1) primarily vertical, (2) primarily horizontal, (3) both vertical and horizontal, and (4) little or no movement. A total of 35 awakenings were accumulated from nine subjects. Comparisons of dream narratives and electroculograms showed that in the four instances of mainly vertical or horizontal movements, the subjects had reported a predominance of activity in the vertical or horizontal plane (e.g., one record of horizontal eye movements was associated with the report of observing two people throwing tomatoes at each other). The 10 instances where subjects were awakened following little or no eye movement were consistently related to reports of the dreamer observing something in the distance. The 21 instances of mixed horizontal and vertical eye movements corresponded to reports of observing proximate objects. To confirm the meaningfulness of these relationships, a number of naive and experimental subjects observed distant and proximate objects or activity while awake. Electrical recordings during these sessions showed similar amplitude and patterns to those obtained during dreaming. There was little movement while subjects observed distant activity and much movement while viewing close-up activity. Dement and Kleitman concluded that these objective data provided confirmation of the hypothesis that REM during sleep closely follow in frequency, duration, amplitude, and pattern the nature of reported visual imagery. This work was generally confirmed by Dement and Kleitman (1957b).

Dement and Wolpert (1958) reported further findings relating eye movements to dream content. A previously accumulated collection of dream narratives and eye movement records were coded and independently classified as "active," "passive," or "unclassifiable due to ambiguity." Large and frequent eye movements were significantly associated with active participation of the dreamer, whereas small and infrequent eye movements were significantly associated with passive participation of the dreamer. Further data from six subjects concerned the relationship of eye movements to the spatial orientation of dream imagery. Of 39 dream narratives recorded after awakenings, 23 were of sufficient clarity to allow specification of the last expected eye movement direction. In 17 of 23 instances the predicted direction of eye movement corresponded to the actual direction as indicated by the recordings. The authors noted that in predicting direction of eye movement one has five choices (up, down, right, left, none), and that the obtained degree of accuracy (74%) was highly improbable by chance.

Berger, Olley, and Oswald (1962) studied the relations among eye movements, frontal EEG, and dream narratives of normal and blind subjects. It was found that a characteristic "saw-toothed" burst (2-3 cycles/sec) of frontal EEG activity reliably preceded (by 5 sec) REMs during dreams of normally sighted subjects. Life-long blind subjects or blind subjects reporting no visual imagery showed no evidence of REMs, whereas blind subjects reporting visual imagery showed REMs associated with reports of visual imagery during dreaming. Berger et al. concluded that the presence of REMs in blind subjects still reporting visual imagery, and their absence in those not reporting visual imagery, appears to confirm the hypothesis that REMs represent scanning of dream visual images.

Berger and Oswald (1962) confirmed Dement and Wolpert's (1958) report of an association between periods of rapid eye movement and active dream content. The narratives were coded and rated as "active" or "passive" according to the events described, while the eye movements were classified as "active" or "passive" on the basis of their frequency and amplitude preceding subject awakenings. Fifty dream narratives were classified as "active," and in 42 instances the matched record of eye movments had been similarly judged. Thirty-nine reports were classified as "passive," and in 23 instances the relevant record of eye movements was also judged to be "passive." Berger and Oswald concluded that there is a significant association between eye movements and the quality (degree of activity) of dream content.

Roffwarg et al. (1962) tested the hypothesis that a 1:1 correlation exists between the direction of eye movements and the gaze of a dreamer during visual imagery. One experimenter continuously observed the EEG and electrical eye movements and awakened the subjects following the appearance of (1) single eye movements, (2) a series of deflections in the same or alternating directions, (3) ocular quiescence, (4) rapid deflections, or (5) other distinctive rapid eye movement sequences. After the awakenings, a second experimenter predicted the pattern of eye movements on the basis of the subjects' reports of their visual dream imagery. Two different experimenters then independently judged the correspondence between predicted and actual eye movement patterns and found that, for dream narratives with the high confidence rating, there was a high (75%-80%) frequency of exact or near exact prediction of eye movement patterns. Dream narratives given intermediate and low confidence ratings yielded successful predictions 66%-75% and 53%-62% of the time, respectively. Roffwarg et al. concluded that accurate descriptions of eye movement patterns may be formulated strictly on the basis of subjective descriptions of recalled visual imagery.

Gross, Byrne, and Fisher (1965) examined the possibility that the reported absence of REMs in eye records of the blind is an artifact of the

"EOG" method. Five blind subjects who reported no visual imagery or recurrent non-visual dreams, were studied for 44 Stage 1 periods (the first of the four cyclical stages of sleep in which dreaming occurs) over 13 night sessions. During these sessions eye movements were electrically recorded, were directly observed, and recorded by use of a sensitive ceramic strain gauge placed on the eyelid over the corneal bulge. No awakenings and dream narrative collections were attempted. The results indicated that the electrical recordings frequently failed to register many smaller horizontal and vertical eye movements detected directly or with the use of the strain gauge. Gross et al. concluded that REMs during sleep are universally present, even in subjects blind for as long as 55 years, and that previously reported negative results were possibly a consequence of the relatively insensitive electrical method of detection.

Amadeo and Gomez (1966, Experiment 2) investigated patterns of eye movements in the sleep of subjects with congenital blindness. All subjects exhibited normal cyclically recurring patterns of EEG and EMG activity during sleep. Rapid eye movement periods in Stage 1 sleep were found for seven of eight blind subjects, though the REM periods were generally fewer in number and of lower amplitude than those found in non-blind subjects. Of the subject awakenings in each stage of sleep, there were seven dream recalls after seven awakenings in Stage 1-REM sleep; 4 dream recalls following five awakenings in Stage 2; and no dream recalls following five awakenings in Stage 3 sleep. A qualitative analysis of the dream narratives showed that no dreams involved the visual modality. Amadeo and Gomez concluded that REMs of blind subjects are not a concomitant of enhanced visual imagery during the dream, but consistent with their first experiment cited earlier, REM rate accelerates during heightened attention.

Previous research had indicated that rapid eye movement periods during dreams of sleep are similar to eye movements during actual perception. Arkin, Weitzman, and Hastey (1966) studied subjects with congenital nystagmus to determine if the characteristic nystagmic movements associated with waking perception were also associated with rapid eye movement patterns during dreams of sleep. Waking (electrical) records were taken during relaxation with eyes open and closed, during tracking of a light, and during "tracking" of an imaginary light with eyes closed. The waking records showed sustained periods of nystagmus while the subjects' eyes were open and closed and during real and imaginary tracking. Records of eye movements during REM and NREM sleep were normal in all respects with the notable *absence* of nystagmus. Arkin et al. concluded that, for subjects with congenital nystagmus, eye movement patterns during REM periods associated with dreams are different from those of normal waking perception and, therefore, the "scanning hypothesis" of eye movements associated with dreams of sleep is questionable.

Baldridge, Whitman, Kramer, and Ornstein (1968) examined during non-REM sleep the effects of eye movement induced by mechanical manipulation, photo stimulation, or caloric stimulation of the semicircular canals. They reported that stimulation resulted in an abrupt change in EEG from prestimulus level to one of light sleep and also produced some clusters of REMs. The induced eye movements influenced the nature of the dream content as reported in subjects' narratives.

Moskowitz and Berger (1969) tested the conclusions of Roffwarg et al. (1962) that there is a correspondence between rapid eye movements and dream content. Their subjects were awakened for dream reports during rapid eye movement periods following one of four distinctive patterns of eye activity: (1) horizontal movements, (2) vertical movements, (3) alternating horizontal and vertical movements, and (4) oblique movements. Fifty-six of 71 reports were selected for analysis on the basis of clarity and descriptiveness of final dream events. Blind matchings of electrical eye records and dream narratives were then completed. Analysis of the decoded matchings indicated 18 of the total 56 were correct. This score was not significantly different than that of 14 expected by chance. A qualitative analysis of nine of the most descriptive narratives showed that only three were correctly paired with eye records. Moskowitz and Berger concluded that these data fail to confirm the previously reported results relating periods of rapid eye movements to dream content, and therefore cast doubt on the validity of the "scanning hypothesis." It is indeed difficult to specify reasons for such different findings as those in this and the Roffwarg et al. study—they could be found in the many differences in techniques and apparatus, or merely due to data sampling fluctuations. We can only rely on future research to lead us to the appropriate conclusion. This state of affairs may be noticed throughout our empirical chapters, as in the work that follows by Jacobs, Feldman, and Bender (1970a, b) vs. the conclusions of Dement and Kleitman (1957a, b).

Molinari and Foulkes (1969) proposed a model of sleep mentation considerably different from that based on the distinction between REM and NREM sleep. They conceived of a tonic-phasic model which contrasts sleep periods of no phasic activation with those of phasic activation, regardless of the status on the REM-NREM dimension. Specifically, it was hypothesized that (1) phasic and nonphasic episodes within stage REM are associated with mental activity qualitatively different and (2) that nonphasic stage REM sleep is associated with mental activity qualitatively similar to that of NREM sleep. For the experiment, dream narratives were collected from 10 subjects for a total of 160 awakenings equally distributed following REM-phasic activity, REM-nonphasic activity, NREM sleep, and sleep onset. The reports were coded and blindly scored for the amount of visual experience and different types of cognitive activity (e.g., interpreting, conceptualization, verbalization, etc). The data indicated that recall of experience immediately prior to awakening was obtained about equally for all awakening categories, with REM-phasic higher but not significantly so. In a further analysis awakenings during REM periods and sleep onset periods yielded a significantly greater recall of earlier dream mentations than NREM awakenings.

Analyses of the qualitative differences in sleep narratives indicated that REM-phasic awakenings were associated with significantly more reports of visual imagery than NREM awakenings; REM-tonic and NREM reports were associated with significantly greater reports of cognitive activity. Molinari and Foulkes concluded that sleep researchers should include additional content analyses of the dream reports to further examine the tonic-phasic conceptualization of sleep mentation.

Jacobs, Feldman, and Bender (1970a) reexamined the hypothesis that eye movements "follow" the action in dreaming during Stage 1—rapid eye movement sleep. Subjects were awakened toward the end of Stage 1 periods, at which time dream narratives were recorded. Electrical recordings and direct visual observation of eye movements failed to correspond to the dream narratives. Although dream action was variable, the pattern of rapid eye movements was found to be similar for all periods observed. The authors noted that eye movements during these periods were different from waking saccades and may indicate an inherent patterned cycle. The authors concluded that rapid eye movements are not responses of subjects "watching" their dreams.

Jacobs, Feldman, and Bender (1970b) awakened subjects from REM periods when any one of the following occurred: (1) a sudden single saccade, (2) a series of saccades, or (3) a period of ocular quiescence. The subject then reported the content of the dream; the subject's confidence level was graded according to the clarity with which the last few events of the dream were reported. For 41 awakenings, eye movements rarely matched the action in the dream report when awakened after a series of saccades or after ocular quiescence. When interruptions followed a single saccade, eye movements matched the dream content 18% of the time; 10% of the time eye movements were exactly opposite to the action in the dream; and 72% of the time there was no relation between dream content and eye movements. The authors concluded that eye movements occasionally match the action in the dream.

Jacobs, Feldman, and Bender (1972) awakened their subjects selected for good dream recall from Stage 1-REM periods following (1) sudden single eye movements, (2) a series of eye movements in the same or alternating directions, or (3) periods of ocular quiescence. The dream narrative was recorded, and the subject rated the clarity of recall. Two independent investigators reviewed the narratives and described the "expected" pattern of eye movements. A third investigator then compared "expected" patterns with actual dc electrooculograms and direct observations by the experimenter. Eighteen percent of the "expected" eye movement descriptions were similar to recorded eye movements. Fifty-two percent were judged to be dissimilar, and the remaining 30% were neither similar nor dissimilar to the actual records. Interpreting the differences between these finding and those of other investigations of eye movement and dream imagery, the authors stated that dc electrooculography measures eye activity more precisely because it records both quick and slow movements, as compared to ac measures which record only relatively slow movement. Differential results might therefore be attributable to differences between ac and dc electrooculography. This point, of course, may be equally applicable to other studies in this chapter.

Busciano, Spadetta, Carella, and Caruso (1971) reported that REMs and reports of visual imagery during dreams were absent in subjects whose ocular motility was temporarily impaired due to various diseases. In two instances the remission of the disease was accompanied by the return of REMs and reports of visual imagery during nocturnal dreams.

Arkin, Lutzky, and Toth (1972) examined the waking and sleeping eye movements of subjects with congenital nystagmus. They held that, according to the "scanning hypothesis," nystagmic eye movements should occur during rapid eye movement periods, as they do in the waking state. Electrical records were made during both actual and imagined fixation and tracking tasks with eyes open and closed. In the sleep sessions the subjects were awakened at 10-, 15-, and 20-minute intervals after the onset of REM periods for the collection of dream narratives. Nystagmus was clearly present during all tasks performed while awake. Although brief nystagmic-like movements were observed in non-REM periods, "no recording of definite sustained nystagmus movements was observed during REMs." In general, the dream narratives and electrooculograms were essentially indistinguishable from those of psychologically and physiologically normal subjects. As Arkin et al. (1966) had concluded earlier, these data fail to conform to the "scanning hypothesis" relating eye movements and dream imagery in subjects with congenital nystagmus.

Summary and Conclusions of Empirical Studies

The conclusions for the four criteria are that the eye response: (1) does reliably occur; and (2) does typically vary as a function of type of cognitive activity. However, for (3) research has been deficient in that it seldom has included concomitant psychophysiological measures; there is some indication that eye responses do occur in isolation from generalized arousal systems and that they thus serve unique functions during information processing. Finally, for (4) an impressive number of specific relationships have been reported between eye movements and specific aspects of "mental contents."

Recall that Criterion 4 (the question of specific relationships involving eye activity) was loosely formulated and developed in a primitive way in the hope that more refined use may be made of it in the future. Our question was whether or not each researcher ascertained a specific relationship between some measure of eye activity and a stimulus or subject variable. In the section on studies of nocturnal dreams in particular, we noted a large number of positive relationships between directional eye movements and the content of visual imagery. However, there have also been some negative findings in this regard (cf. Koulack, 1972). To reach a firm conclusion as to whether or not dream imagery and nature of eye movements are related is indeed difficult, but our general principle in science is to place the greatest emphasis on positive vs. negative results. There are a number of scientific reasons why positive results are more strongly weighted, one being that poor scientific techniques and methods lead to negative results and thus can obscure positive relationships. In an universe with an infinite (or at least indefinitely large) number of variables, it is easy to find zero-order relationships by increasing error variance and it is difificult to find that two variables *are* related. With regard to the specific question of whether or not the nature of eye movements is related to mental content, we are witness to a large number of positive findings. In view of this confirming evidence, it is difficult to conclude that the two variables are not related, at least at this stage of our science of covert processes—attempting to confirm such a negative relationship is like attempting to confirm the null hypothesis. With this emphasis on positive findings of specific relationships gained by researchers in this chapter, we shall summarize those specific relationships below.

SUMMARY OF SPECIFIC RELATIONSHIPS

Imagination Tasks.   Perky (1910): Memory images of sight (defined as particular and personal images) typically involved gross movements of the eyes, whereas imaginations (defined as images that lack particularity in personal references) generally involved no eye movements.

Jacobson (1930c): The direction of the eye response was related to the direction of the content of the visual imagination.

Totten (1935): During imagination, the direction of eye movements involving horizontal or vertical geometrical planes generally followed the appropriate plane for each image, as they would during the actual perceptual task.

Bergum and Lehr (1966): Frequency of eye movements was significantly lower during the auditory presentation of interesting material than during the auditory presentation both of unpleasant and of dull verbal stimuli.

Zikmund (1966): The direction of perceived and imagined movements of moving stripes were both related to the actual direction of the eye movement.

Deckert (1964): The direction and frequency of eye movements during imagination of a moving pendulum corresponded approximately to the actual direction of movement and beat frequency of the pendulum.

Brown (1968): Visual imagination ability (subjects classified as visualizers vs. nonvisualizers) was directly related to frequency of eye movements while recalling a moving metronome.

Lenox et al. (1970): Eye movement frequencies during imagination corresponded to those during perception.

Graham (1970a): Frequency of pursuit eye movements during imagination of a previously observed pendulum were similar to eye movements during perception of that stimulus, although patterns differed during perception and imagination.

Graham (1970b): Eye movements during perception and imagination of an optokinetic stimulus were similar, although there were more saccades and fewer oscillations during imagination.

Weitzenhofer and Brockmeir (1970): Reported a negative relation between rate of rapid eye movement and attention.

Antrobus et al. (1964): During spontaneous day dreaming, internal imagery, and passive thought there was a significant amount of ocular quiescense; ocular motility occurred significantly more often when the subjects' reports concerned their external environment. Instructions to suppress a conscious wish or fantasy were associated with considerable eye movement and blinking. Rapid cognitive change was associated with eye movements and static content was associated with reduced ocular activity. Visualization of motion (like trampoline or tennis scenes) were significantly more frequent when the eyes were open than when closed.

Singer and Antrobus (1965): While pleasant, neutral, or unpleasant imagination of people presumably did not lead to different eye movements, there were significantly more eye movements when the subjects suppressed the image than when they imagined it.

Antrobus (1970): Processing of auditory stimuli was associated with a reduction in ocular motility. Frequency of eye movements increased as a function of increases in information processing (ideational and imagery) demand.

Bacon (1970): Frequency of saccadic (i.e., non-reflexive) eye movements significantly decreased and the duration of ocular quiescense increased as the cognitive operations in a signal detection task increased in difficulty.

Greenberg (1970): Nystagmus (i.e., reflexive eye movements) significantly increased as task complexity increased.

Greenberg (1971): For problem-solving conditions, elicited optokinetic nystagmus significantly increased as a function of task complexity; for nondirected cognitive state conditions nystagmus was greatest for a "Mind Blank" condition, lowest for the "Instructed Daydream" condition, with an intermediate condition called "Cognitive Flexibility."

Antrobus (1973): Saccadic frequency and amplitude vary as a function of cognitive control.

Problem Solving. Stoy (1930): Frequency and magnitude of eye movements were significantly greater when subjects imagined and solved spatial as compared to nonspatial problems.

Telford and Thompson (1933): Blink rate was greatest during mental arithmetic, mixed while conversing with the experimenter, and least during reading.

Clites (1935): Blink rate was significantly faster during difficult mental work than during simple mental work.

Collins (1962): Nystagmus duration and degrees of slow phase eye movements were both significantly less during rotary states than during three attention-demanding conditions. Also, there was significantly more nystagmus during mental arithmetic than for those three conditions.

Lorens and Darrow (1962): Eye movement rate is faster during vivid imagination than during the formation of less clear images.

Kaplan and Schoenfeld (1966): Variations in the location of critical letters in anagram trials produced systematic variations in the order of the eye responses.

Rosen and Czech (1966): Eye activity during three phases (predecision, decision, and post-decision) of cognition during decision making depended on whether the subjects were to be shocked or not shocked.

Sokolov (1966): Apparently, the nystagmus response is associated with proficiency in performing mental arithmetic tasks.

Lackman et al. (1968): "Spontaneous" nystagmus in a schizophrenic increased in frequency and amplitude relative to baseline, as task difficulty increased." Degree of nystagmus is apparently an indication of mental effort or of the content that is being processed.

McGuigan, Culver, and Kendler (1971): Covert eye responses were related to a directional mediation process involving directional concepts of left vs. right.

Holland and Tarlow (1972): The greater the memory load the lower the blinking rate.

Answering Questions.   Ellson et al. (1952): Frequency of eye movements was greater when subjects deliberately lied than when they were being honest. Motivation increased frequency of eye movements.

Teitelbaum (1954): Eye movements occurred less frequently during speech than during silence.

McGuigan and Pavek (1972): Mean duration of the eye response was longer when subjects silently thought "yes" as their answer as opposed to when they thought "no."

Cutrow et al. (1972): Eyeblink rate and latency increased as a function of lying.

Kinsbourne (1972): In right-handed subjects horizontal eye movements are significantly more often to the right for verbal conditions, to the left for spatial tasks with no significant directional effect for numerical thought tasks. For left-handed subjects the directional relationship was not found.

Day (1967): Only left eye movers showed a reflex eye movement to an auditory, but not to a visual, stimulus. The response for left-movers was thus related to the auditory modality.

Duke (1968): Males moved their eyes significantly more often in a single direction then did females. Complex questions elicited eye movements more often than simple questions. Lateral eye movements occurred significantly more often to reflective than to factual questions.

Bakan (1969): Left-movers were significantly more hypnotizable than right-movers; they were also significantly more likely to be humanistic majors in college, score higher on the verbal scale of the SAT, and have a greater tendency to report clear visual imagery.

Bakan and Shotland (1969): Right-movers read significantly faster than left-movers and exhibit more resistance to distraction.

Kocel et al. (1972): Verbal and mathematical questions (which presumably engage the dominant cerebral hemisphere) evoked significantly more right lateral eye movements than did spatial and musical questions (which presumably engage the minor hemisphere).

Sherrod (1972): Left-movers are more reactive to persuasive messages than are right movers.

Autokinetic Illusion. Lehman (1965): The subject's initial report of movement in the autokinetic illusion was significantly often preceded by a large eye movement. Maintenance of the movement illusion was significantly often associated with corresponding movements of the eye. Hence eye movements are consistently related to starts, stops, and changes in the direction of autokinetic movement.

Marshall (1966): autokinetic movement reflected the direction in which the accompanying eye movements were experimentally induced.

Memory. Ewert (1933): Frequency of eye movements during silent reading approximated frequency during silent recall of the material read. Frequency while learning by dictation approximated that during both overt and silent recall of the material.

Loftus (1972): Memory proficiency was positively related to the number of eye fixations.

Hypnotic Dreams. Schiff et al. (1961): The eyes were very active during active hypnotic and post-hypnotic dreams, and inactive when the suggested dreams were inactive in content.

Amadeo and Shagass (1963): Eye movement rate was significantly less when hypnotized than when awake. Eye movement rate while nonhypnotized was always significantly greater than when the subjects exerted voluntary control of the eyes to keep them still, regardless of whether the eyes were open, closed, or while performing mental arithmetic. Eye movement rate was significantly greater during mental arithmetic than when closed.

Brady and Levitt (1964, 1966): Nystagmus during hypnotic hallucination is similar to that during the actual perception of the optokinetic stimulus, regardless of whether the subject is awake or hypnotized. The amount of the nystagmus was positively related to the degree of the clarity of the hallucination. Hypnotically induced visual hallucinations are qualitatively similar to eye movements during perception.

Brady and Rosner (1966): The more a hypnotized subject's dream experience has the quality of a sleep dream, the greater is the ocular activity present.

Deckert (1964): During hypnosis, eye movments while imagining pendulum pursuit corresponded in frequency and direction to those during actual perception of pendulum pursuit.

Graham (1970a): Frequency of saccadic eye movement is approximately the same to the evoking stimulus when perceived during hypnosis and during normal imagination. Frequency of pursuit eye movements to a stimulus designed to elicit them was similar under both hypnotic imagination and perception conditions.

Graham (1970b): During a hypnotic state, nystagmus-like patterns of eye movments to an optokinetic stimulus are similar when actually perceived and imagined.

Weitzenhoffer (1971): The report of observing a watch swinging from a chain during a hypnotic dream was accompanied by corresponding eye pursuit movements.

Evans et al. (1972): Nystagmoid eye movements were made to a rotating drum and also while imagining the rotating drum with black and white stripes, both while awake and while hypnotized (for some subjects).

Nocturnal Dreams.   Jacobson (1938a, b): The direction of eye movements was related to the direction of the movement in the dream images.

Dement and Kleitman (1957a, b): Horizontal movements were related to dream reports with a predominance of activity in the horizontal plane; similarly vertical movements were related to dream content predominantly in the vertical plane. Little or no eye movement during dreams was related to reports of the dreamer observing something in the distance. Mixed horizontal and vertical eye movements corresponded to reports of observing proximate objects. While awake, eye movements during perception showed similar amplitudes and patterns to those obtained during dreaming, i.e., there was little movement when subjects observed distant activity and much movement while viewing close up activity. In general, rapid eye movements during sleep closely followed in frequency, duration, amplitude, and pattern the nature of reported visual imagery.

Dement and Wolpert (1958): Large and frequent eye movements were significantly associated with active dreams whereas small and infrequent eye movements were significantly associated with passive dreams, i.e., amplitude and frequency of eye movements were directly related to the amount of active participation in the dream on the part of the dreamer. Furthermore, the last expected eye movement direction of the dream corresponded in 74% of the cases to the actual direction.

Berger, Olley, and Oswald (1962): Blind subjects reporting no visual imagery showed no REMs during dreams of sleep, whereas blind subjects reporting visual imagery showed REMs during sleep dreams.

Berger and Oswald (1962): Eye movements were directly related to the degree of activity of the dream content.

Roffwarg et al. (1962): Reports of visual dream imagery were used to postdict accurately the corresponding eye movement patterns.

Amadeo and Gomez (1966): REM rate increases during heightened attention.

Baldridge et al. (1968): By experimentally inducing REMs the nature of the dream content was influenced.

Jacobs, Feldman, and Bender (1970b): Eye movements of subjects awakened following a single saccade matched the dream content 18% of the time.

Jacobs, Feldman, and Bender (1972): Using dc electrooculography, 18% of the predicted eye movement descriptions were similar to recorded eye movements.

Busciano et al. (1971): REMs and reports of visual imagery during dreams were absent in subjects whose ocular motility was impaired due to various diseases. In two instances, the remission of the disease was accompanied by the return of REMs and by reports of visual imagery during nocturnal dreams.

INTERPRETATION

The positive conclusion that eye reponses are intimately involved in mental activity leads us to inquire further as to their specific cognitive functions. It is common to consider several stages of information processing, often four stages as represented in Fig. 5.1. First, the impingement of an external stimulus evokes a pre-perceptual (short-term memory) stage, during which all external stimulus input is retained for a brief period. The neuromuscular circuits that function during the pre-perceptual stage include those between the eye and the central nervous

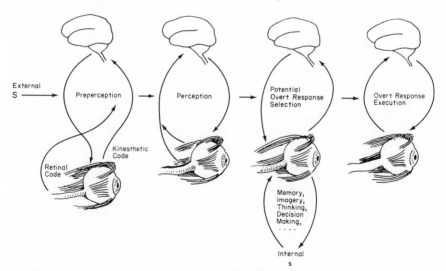

FIG. 5.1 Four commonly represented stages of information processing each represented as eye–brain circuits.

system, wherein coded information from the retina and kinesthetically coded information from the eye musculature are transmitted to the brain. There then follows a perceptual stage during which some of the preceding information from the short-term memory store is attended to by means of further processing within neuromuscular circuits; the selected information that is attended to is then encoded and transmitted for processing at the third, decision-making stage. Decision making is most apparent in an information processing model in which problem solving is the primary concern. A more general cognitive model would represent this third stage as one in which there is not only response selection for potential decisions in problem solving, but also responses relevant to idle thoughts, as in mind-wandering and daydreaming. In addition to the impinging external stimulus, this third stage may be set off by internal stimuli that function within additional neuromuscular circuits (for example, during operations of imagery, thinking, decision making, and memory). Finally, information processing models usually hypothesize a motor stage for execution of the selected response.[4] It is likely that the visual system enters into all four of these phases.

Eye Movements During Pre-Perception and Perception. Certainly during pre-perception and perception (Stages 1 and 2 of Fig. 5.1) the eyes are active to receive external visual information. For valuable findings from studies of eye movements in the initial stages of problem solving in which there is extraction of information, see Pushkin (1969) and Simon and Barenfield (1969).

During the pre-perception and perception stages there are apparently two sources of information transmitted from the eye region: (1) visually sensed information directly from the retina, and (2) kinesthetic information generated by contraction of the sensitive eye muscles. Singer (1974), for instance, indicated that eye movements are important during perception because the eyes are feeding back a complex set of kinesthetic as well as visual information for processing.[5] Components of these two sources of information may be transmitted independently in parallel to the brain while at the same time there is apparently also a complex interaction between the retina and the eye muscles: Eye movements can generate retinal stimulation which may produce both active and suppressive effects on further eye movements, especially of the saccade variety (Martin, 1974). The interaction may be bi-directional: Retinal

---

[4] One may note the similarity of this "modern" model to an early model of brain processes which draws on an analogy with the three courts of the Greek law system. Albertus Magnus (1200-1280) spoke of sensory (information collection), decision (adjudication), and motor (sentencing), functions being sequentially performed in three ventricles of the brain (see pp. 47–48).

[5] As to what kind of information about eye position is used during perception, Festinger and Easton (1974) assumed that information available to the perceptual system about eye position comes only from monitoring efferent commands. They concluded that the efferent command for smooth pursuit eye movements contains good information about the direction of movement but only crude information about speed of movement.

activity may also affect the status of the eye muscles. These resulting complex patterns of afferent neural volleys are then transmitted from the eye for central processing, but always with continuous central-peripheral circuit interactions. The central processing is commonly thought to involve activity of complex feature detectors within neural circuits (cf. Lindsay and Norman, 1972). Feature detectors depend on retinal activity and eye movements which activate certain features so that patterns are "seen" (perceived). With cessation of eye movements, the detector is no longer driven, and perception of the visual pattern ceases (Riggs, Ratliff, Cornsweet, and Cornsweet, 1953). Riggs et al. ingeniously employed an arrangement of sensitive mirrors which held the image on the retina constant in spite of eye movements, whereupon the visual pattern disappeared. From this study, it might appear that the sole function of eye movements in perception is to effect a change of the image on the retina, which then activates the feature detectors.

Hebb, in various of his writings, has concluded that eye movements enter into and make up part of the perception itself. In 1949 he stated that perception is improved by making several glances at a stimulus so that the motor elements (the glances) facilitate the perception. However, the distinctiveness of the perception is not solely or mainly due to distinctive eye movements—while the motor activity is important, it is not all-important. Pointing out that once it was shown that eye movements were not "the whole answer" to account for sensory integration in perception, Hebb stated that it was (unjustly) thereby concluded that the receptor adjustments (head and eye movement) were unimportant for theory. His thesis was that "eye-movements in perception are not adventitious. They contribute, constantly and essentially, to perceptual integration, even though they are not the whole origin of it" (1949, p. 37).

Hebb also emphasized motor activity (including eye responses) during the development of cell assemblies by stating that the arousal of cell assemblies is accompanied by motor activities. The motor activities are then important for sequences of cell assemblies: "Each of these events is associated with two specific motor excitations. One of them at least is subliminal, and one becomes liminal as an event intervening between . . . [cell assemblies]. This 'ideational' series with its motor elements I propose to call a 'phase sequence' " (1949, p. 98).

Eye Movements During Response Selection and Execution Stages. During the post perceptual ("thought") stages of processing externally received visual information, we have seen that further complex eye movements also occur. During the third (decision-making) stage of Fig. 5.1, the eye movements may be used to infer something about the dynamics of problem solving or other cognitive activity. For example, Pushkin (1969) found that the number of eye movements involved in the examination of the problem exceeded those involved in exploring the required solution. Furthermore, he found that success in solving problems was inversely related to number of eye movements. Ruth and Giambra

(1974) concluded that heightened attention during a task increases eye movement rate, regardless of the rate of change of thought content. Furthermore, increased eye movement rate accompanies an increase in the rate of change, but only when the level of attention is high. Their conclusion was that previous researchers who found heightened eye activity did so because attention level was high when rate of change of thought content was increased. We have noted that Koulack (1972), in surveying reported relationships between visual imagery and rapid eye movements, pointed out that in the early studies there was a good correspondence between eye movements and the visual imagery of dreams. These relationships were not confirmed in some later studies, leading him to conclude that eye movements might be related to visual imagery of dreams, but that it is not tenable to conclude that there was a constant isomorphic relationship between the two. Our general conclusion is that there is good reason to believe that the two variables are, in general, related. In this regard, Hall (1974) made the excellent point that while some investigators have concluded there is no relationship between eye movements and imagery (e.g., Paivio, 1973; and Bower, 1972), such a generalization is unsound because it fails to precisely discriminate between different types of imagery. Hall presented positive results confirming previous findings that scanning eye movements are significantly associated with iconic imagery. His discussion of function led him to speculate that eye movements are necessary components of imagery, at least for iconic imagery. Following Mackworth (1963) Hall stated that iconic imagery is imagery that is directly dependent upon a visual stimulus and lasts for approximately a second or two after termination of the stimulus.

The iconic image must be rapidly processed before it fades, and eye movements are a necessary and functionally integral part of the image processing. Hence any attempt to interfere with image processing by manipulating eye movements would probably disrupt that image processing with consequent decrease in accuracy of recall.

We have noted the frequently stated conclusion that during memory, imagery, etc., there is a reinstatement of the processes that occurred during the original perception. In the case of visual imagery these processes of course include eye movements. During the various cognitive activities (memory, imagery, etc.) eye movements function just as they did during perception to generate afferent neural volleys that are transmitted by neuromuscular circuits to and from the brain. Eye movements thus are important as organizing mechanisms for visual imagery—motor activity occurs during imagery just as it did during the original perception—this has also been discussed by Neisser (1970) and Skinner (1953). To Hebb, the visual memory image is a complex of central and motor events. The image is a reinstatement of perception with some loss of detail:

It is not possible to have a clear visual image of a complex object without eye movement, or imagining eye movement (which you may be able to do with some practice; but it is easier just to make the actual movements). In the image, in other words, we have a reinstatement of what happened in perception, *including* the eye movement. It appears that the perception is a complex, with its various parts being linked together by motor processes. We may think of it as a series of cell-assembly activities. One assembly fires, which excites a motor activity, which excites another assembly, and so on. The memory image includes those motor links (1972, p. 243).

Hebb thought that imagery consists of a number of part-images such that one part is excited by the intervening motor link—if one wants to "see" a particular feature of something originally perceived, one makes the eye movement that was originally made during the perception. This helps to reexcite the part-perception that followed the eye movement earlier, when the real stimulus was observed. What Hebb is implying is that *the proprioceptive feedback from the muscular eye response evokes cell assemblies which produce the image of that which was originally perceived.*

Antrobus, Antrobus, and Singer and their colleagues theorized about the nature of the processes that occur during imagery as follows. Singer (1974) suggested that, during perception, kinesthetic and visual information from the eyes may compete with other ongoing fantasy activity. Since the same brain processes deal with external information and long-term memory in a common modality, Singer suggested that we suppress the complex stimulation entering the open eyes when we are lost in reverie. External information is gated out so as to free channel space for internal imagery. Consequently, amount of eye movement is an indication of the presence or absence of ongoing thought or daydreaming. During difficult thought there is amplification of central neural and motor systems to increase the capacity of the perceptual–cognitive operators, as well as reflexive operators. The nystagmus response, which is a reflex, was augmented by increased cognitive demand. When they measured nonreflexive eye movements (saccades) these responses were inhibited as a result of increased cognitive demand. These researchers also considered that imagination is a sequence of discrete images in which a sequence of saccades is generated. During the motionless part of the saccade, the image is processed, and movement occurs as the processing is completed. Thus the control or inhibition of eye movements briefly ceases prior to the development of the next image in the sequence. High cognitive change generates considerable saccadic eye movements.

In short, eye movements are related to a central inhibitory mechanism that can limit the processing of information through the eyes by rendering the eye motionless, thus gating out new information. The processing of short- and long-term memory operations may require different gating rules. During long-term memory operation, as in daydreaming, more gating out of external stimuli may be required than in short-term memory tasks, such as in mental arithmetic.

Some empirical work by others on the nature of eye movements during information processing is particularly relevent to this discussion. For example, Matin (1974) reviewed the literature on saccadic suppression and concluded that eye movement generates retinal stimulation that plays a large role in the suppression effect. The saccadic suppression prevents the perception of stimulation received in the transient period shortly before, during, and after the saccade. Wegmann and Weber (1973) found that blinking was significantly suppressed during imagery. To interpret this finding, they cited a previous finding that reading causes a suppression of visualization and that cognitive activity and human eye blink responses are related. Why, they ask, is blink rate altered during imagery? Perhaps a blink serves an erasure function when one is processing visual information, i.e., after visual information has been taken in and processed, a blink clears the visual registers so that subsequent visual information might be taken in for processing—with higher blink rates, subjects might be clearing out visual information just previously accumulated.

These are some thoughts and findings relevant to the functioning of eye movements during the various stages of information processing. The data and interpretations offered in this chapter make it clear that the eye is of primary importance during cognitive activities. We shall now briefly comment on the interaction of eye–brain circuits with other neuromuscular circuits before moving on to the next response class.

Visual Neuromuscular Circuit Interactions with Bodily Systems.   The visual system interacts closely with other systems for kinesthetic feedback; e.g., J. J. Gibson (1966) argued that vision is a powerful kinesthetic sense, so that it is not purely exteroceptive but is also an autonomous kinesthetic sense. Vision thus affords kinesthetic information independent of mechanical kinesthesis, and furthermore the visual kinesthetic information is rich (cf. Adams, McIntire, and Thorsheim, 1969; Lishman and Lee, 1973). Such kinesthetic circuits no doubt function with others such as those involving the limbs. For instance, Angel, Hollander, and Wesley (1973) concluded that in a visual tracking task, there was an interaction between the hand and the visual system such that manual control affected oculomotor performance. They hypothesized that there is a motor memory in which information concerning hand–eye coordination is stored. The motor memory functions very briefly to ensure the proper coordination—but has little biological utility after the completion of a given motor task. Eye–speech muscle interactions are also of prime importance, as in the complex relationships between visual and verbal thought. A final indication of the complex interaction of eye activity with other bodily processes is in the report of Spreng, Johnson, and Lubin (1968) that there were positive correlations between REM-burst time and respiration rate, and REM-burst time and number of finger impulse responses.

Conclusion.   We have thus seen that the eyes are active during all of the phases of internal information processing, and thus are intimately involved in cognitive functioning. The eyes bring information from the external world directly by means of the retina and through kinesthetic coding from the eye musculature. These coded signals activate central processes as components of neuromuscular circuits to produce perception of those external stimuli. When coded signals from the eyes function in the absence of the controlling external stimuli (having been set off by internal stimuli), they "evoke" (in an unknown way) some kinds of "representations" involving the brain (memories, images and the like). Presumably the coded impulses from the eye primarily "retrieve" ("reinstate," "restructure") visual images, though the different modalities clearly interact during information processing. Some eye movements are no doubt unlearned components of information processing mechanisms, but some are probably modified through experience. Saccadic suppression, inhibition of blinking, etc., may function to some degree in accordance with conditioning principles. In fact, the eye musculature is among the easiest of the body's response systems to condition (cf. Kaplan and Schoenfeld, 1966). Similarly, reading improvement courses indicate that there is modification of eye activity (cf. McGuigan and Pinkney, 1973). The ready conditionability of eye responses may be due in part to the fact that the motor units of the eye muscles consist of only several muscle fibers; consequently, the eye is capable of making numerous, highly differentiated responses.

Schmidt (1966) assumed that efficient eye movements help the complex mental processes of comprehension such that trained and experienced mental processes tend to make eye movement patterns more efficient. Many reading improvement courses are based on this assumption, he pointed out, so that training in eye movement efficiency and in mental aspects of reading are presumed to increase reading proficiency.

Some visual imagery disappears when eye movements cease, and since eye movements are complexly related to the processing of external and internal information, they are most likely involved in cognition through the generation of codes. The coding probably retrieves centrally stored visual images (and may involve both linguistic and nonlinguistic components). We can, however, only speculate as to the precise nature of such codes. In Chapter 9 we shall hypothesize, more specifically, linguistic and nonlinguistic coding systems. Signals from the eyes may be incorporated within those systems and are critical components of neuromuscular circuits, especially during visual thought.

Other Relevant Empirical References
on Eye Activity During Cognition

Breed and Colaiuta (1974)
Gould and Carn (1973)
Griffith and Johnston (1973)
Lehmann, Beeler, and Fender (1967)
Ohtani, Kuchinomachi, and Yagi (1974)

Reder (1973)
A. D. Smith (1973)
Tversky (1974)
Weerts and Lang (1973)
Weiten and Etaugh (1974)

6

Covert Oral Behavior: Studies Under Normal and Interference Conditions

I. Methodological Criteria
 A. Criterion 1: Did the response actually occur?
 B. Criterion 2: Did the response occur because of the experimental treatment per se?
 C. Criterion 3: Was the response a unique, localized event or was it only a component of a generalized arousal pattern?
 D. Criterion 4: Was there a specific relationship between an independent variable and a response parameter?
II. Empirical Measures of Covert Oral Behavior
 A. Mechanical Sensing Studies
 B. Electromyographic Studies
  1. Imagination
  2. Silent Reading
  3. Auditory Hallucinations
  4. Cursive Writing
  5. Learning
  6. Nocturnal Dreams
  7. Miscellaneous
  8. Perceptual Clarification
  9. Additional Citations
 C. Specific Relationships (Criterion 4)
III. Possible Functions of Covert Oral Behavior
IV. Interference with Covert Oral Behavior
 A. The Method of Distraction
  1. Early Studies
  2. Recent Studies
  3. Distraction and Interference—Restraint Methods Compared
  4. Conclusion

As was detailed in Chapter 2, covert oral activity has long been implicated during thinking as the primary response component of implicit language behavior. While previous researchers have employed a number of different terms (inner speech, silent speech, implicit speech, incipient speech, subvocal speech, subvocalization, etc.), the formulations have all implied that the speech system performs critical linguistic functions during the higher mental processes. Covert speech phenomena indeed have a rich historical background, though until this century it has been nonsystematic and almost exclusively nonempirical.

Twentieth century empirical investigations have largely been directed by the theoretical viewpoints of the Russian scientists, e.g., Sechenov (1863) and Pavlov (1941), by the early behaviorists, e.g., Watson (1930), and by the classical research of Jacobson (e.g., 1932). Pavlov held that the basic component of thought is kinesthetic impulses which pass from the speech apparatus into the cerebral cortex (in Novikova, 1961). Watson (1930) held that the term "thinking" should apply to all word behavior, including nonoral behavior, but principally that which goes on "subvocally"; and Jacobson concluded that during imagination, recollection and concrete or abstract thinking involving words or numbers, muscular contractions characteristically appear as specific components of the physiologic process of mental activity. These contractions, he observed, are generally minute but are sometimes grossly visible, and they occur in at least some of the muscles which participate when the same words or numbers are actually whispered or uttered aloud. We shall now review studies relevant to these oral response hypotheses. These researches represent efforts to directly record the activity of the speech mechanism during the silent performance of cognitive language activities.

First, though, a technical problem arises when we seek to ascribe a linguistic function to covert speech muscle behavior, viz., because the speech musculature is also used for non-linguistic functions (swallowing, biting the lips, etc.). As a consequence, we early employed the neutral term "covert oral behavior" to refer to any behavior centered in the speech musculature which occurs during specified experimental treatments—we did not wish to prematurely conclude that the heightened covert speech muscle activity that occurs, say, during silent reading, is serving an information processing function. Suitably well designed experimentation has subsequently led us to conclude that most covert oral behavior measured during the silent performance of language tasks does serve linguistic functions, often justifying the use of the term "covert oral language responses" (cf. McGuigan, 1970a). In such research, of course, covert oral behavior that is clearly nonlinguistic (as in swallowing) is excluded from the experimental records.

Methodological Criteria

To assess research on covert oral responses during the silent performance of various cognitive tasks, we will evaluate each study by the four general criteria presented in detail in Chapter 5 (pp. 118–26).

You will recall that the first two criteria allow us to determine whether or not a response actually occurred, and if so whether it was a function of the condition of interest (an experimental treatment, or whatever), the second two criteria are designed to help ascertain the function of somatic responses by providing an index of the degree of general bodily arousal during the condition of special interest. If the response is a localized, unique occurrence, it is more likely to serve an information processing function within neuromuscular circuits. These four criteria developed in Chapter 5 are as follows.

CRITERION 1

Did the Response Actually Occur? If a measure of the oral musculature changed from the resting baseline condition to the period of administration of the experimental treatment, then a "yes" is entered in column 1 of Table 6.1. If there was no systematic change in the measure, a "no" is entered, and if the researcher did not compare the covert response measure during the period of the experimental treatment with a previous resting baseline condition, a "?" is entered in column 1. An asterisk in Table 6.1 indicates that the researcher employed a statistical test and found a significant effect—in the case of Criterion 1, an asterisk indicates that the covert response reliably changed from the baseline resting condition.

CRITERION 2

Did the Response Occur Because of the Experimental Treatment Per Se? While a response might have changed from baseline, such a change might be due to any stimulation or activity and not because of what was specifically done to or by the subject. Criterion 2 is thus important to show that the covert response changed systematically as a function of two

TABLE 6.1 Summary Evaluation of Covert Oral Behavior Research on the Basis of Four Criteria[a]

| Experimenter | Did the Covert Oral Response: | | | (4) specifically relate to a cognitive aspect? |
	(1) change from baseline?	(2) vary as a function of conditions?	(3) occur independently of other covert processes?	
Mechanical Sensing Studies				
Curtis (1900)	yes	?	?	no
Courten (1902)	yes	?	?	no
Perky (1910)	yes	yes	?	yes
Wyczoikowska (1913)	?	no	?	yes
Reed (1916)	yes	?	yes: pneumogram	no
Golla (1921)	?	yes	?	yes
Clark (1922)	?	?	no: various	no
Scheck (1925)	yes	yes	?	no
Thorson (1925)	yes	yes	yes: pneumogram	yes
Rounds & Poffenberger (1931)	yes	yes	?	no
Electromyographic Studies				
Imagination Tasks				
Jacobson (1932)	yes	yes	yes: various EMG	yes
McGuigan & Straub (see text)	yes	yes	yes	yes
Blumenthal (1959)	yes*	yes*	?	yes
Silent Reading				
Faaborg-Anderson & Edfelt (1958)	yes	yes	?	yes
Edfeldt (1960)	yes*	yes*	?	yes
McGuigan et al. (1964)	yes*	no	no: repiration rate	no
Hardyck et al. (1966)	yes	?	?	no

[a]In this research survey, we have attempted to specify the results of statistical tests when they were conducted by stating that the effect was "significant" (reliable) or "not significant" (not reliable). Where effects are reported in the absence of these words, together with the absence of asterisks in columns 1, 2, and 3 of the table, the reader may assume that the effects were not subjected to statistical tests. This criterion is not applied to column 4.

TABLE 6.1 Summary Evaluation of Covert Oral Behavior Research on the Basis of Four Criteria[a] (cont.)

Experimenter	(1) change from baseline?	(2) vary as a function of conditions?	Did the Covert Oral Response: (3) occur independently of other covert processes?	(4) specifically relate to a cognitive aspect?
Silent Reading (cont.)				
McGuigan & Rodier (1968)	yes*	yes*	yes: arm no: respiration rate	yes
McGuigan & Bailey (1969a)	yes*	no	?	no
McGuigan (In text)	yes*	no	yes: arm, leg	no
McGuigan & Bailey (1969b)	yes*	yes*	no: arm, respiration rate	yes
Auditory Hallucinations				
Gould (1949, 1950)	yes	?	?	no
Roberts et al. (1951)	no	?	?	no
McGuigan (1966b)	yes*	?	yes: arm EMG	yes
Cursive Writing				
McGuigan (1967)	yes*	yes*	yes: arm no: respiration rate	no
McGuigan (1970b)	yes*	yes*	yes: leg, chin, EEG	yes
Learning				
Berry & Davis (1960)	yes*	yes*	yes: arm, GSR no: pulse, EKG	yes
Nocturnal Dreams				
Berger (1961)	yes	yes	no: EEG, eye	no
Larson & Foulkes (1969)		yes	no: EEG	no
Pivik & Dement (1970)	yes	yes	yes: eye no: eye	yes
McGuigan & Tanner (1971)	yes	yes	yes: neck	yes

168

Experimenter	(1) change from baseline?	(2) vary as a function of conditions?	Did the Covert Oral Response: (3) occur independently of other covert processes?	(4) specifically relate to a cognitive aspect?
Miscellaneous				
Bassin & Bein (1961)	yes	yes	yes: arm	yes
Novikova (1961)	yes	yes	no: EEG	yes
Sokolov (1967)	yes	?	yes: GSR and EEG	yes
Sokolov (1969)	yes	yes	yes: right finger, etc.	yes
Perceptual Clarification				
McGuigan, Osgood, & Hadley (1973)	yes	yes*	yes: lip, arm, leg	yes
McGuigan, Osgood, & Schoonover (in text)	yes	yes*	yes: lip, arm, leg	yes

169

(or more) experimental conditions, e.g., electromyograms from the speech musculature are greater when one imagines Ohm's Law than when imagining lighting a cigarette (Jacobson, 1932). A particularly valuable control in this regard is one in which the response is measured during some nonlinguistic condition (white noise, or meaningless changing tones, etc.) and compared with that during a linguistic condition.

The same notation ("yes," "no," "?") as for column 1 is used for the other criteria of Table 6.1.

CRITERION 3

Was the Response a Unique, Localized Event or Was It Only a Component of a Generalized Arousal Pattern?   This criterion requires that the response occur independently of most other covert processes. For this, concomitant measures should be made from a sample of bodily regions or systems. As described in Chapter 2, various psychophysiological theories of thought have hypothesized that localized changes occur in the speech musculature during the silent performance of language tasks so that Criterion 3 will be especially important for this chapter.

CRITERION 4

Was There a Specific Relationship Between an Independent Variable and a Response Parameter?   A final probabilistic indication that a response is a localized event is the specification of a relationship between a response parameter and a specific aspect of cognition (the latter determined by verbal reports about the subject's "experience," by systematic variation of the subject's conditions or characteristics, etc.). Such specific relationships indicate the intimate involvement of the response with the cognitive activity. We emphasize that this is a rather "loose" criterion and considerable liberty will be taken in specifying the kinds of variables involved in specific relationships. We will note in this chapter that Criterion 4 has not been extensively employed in this area.

Empirical Measures of Covert Oral Behavior

The enthusiasm generated in the early part of this century for the empirical study of psychophysiological phenomena and the direct recording of thoughts by measuring speech muscle responses led to a number of ingenious mechanical measuring systems (e.g., Lashley, as discussed in Chapter 2). However, these studies were premature in that experimenters attempted to substitute their enthusiasm for apparatus sensitivity (Chapter 3). Sufficiently sensitive measurement techniques did not arrive until the technological development of electronics and Jacobson's (1927) application of the vacuum tube for the precise measurement of higher mental processes. Consequently, empirical conclusions from the early studies employing mechanical sensing devices have little value, but the efforts are historically interesting and important because they led to contemporary psychophysiological study of the higher mental processes. We shall review these early studies first, after which electromyographic research will be considered.

MECHANICAL SENSING STUDIES

In 1895, Hansen and Lehmann (in Dashiell, 1928, and in Edfeldt, 1960) sought to understand the nature of "mind reading" ("thought transference") by placing subjects in a room with especially good acoustics, and asking them to think intently of a number or word. They arranged for two subjects to be seated with their heads at the foci of concave mirrors placed with the principle axes falling in a straight line and the foci 2 meters apart. One subject selected a number from a bag and concentrated on it with closed lips. The other subject waited until he found himself ready to write down a selected number. The recipient's guesses as to which number was transmitted were better than chance and many of the errors were confusions of similar sounds (e.g., 14 was confused with 40). The mirrors allowed the sounds to be transmitted from focus to focus about 14 times more intensely than without the mirrors. The conclusion was that minimal sound productions on the part of the implicit speaker were fairly adequately received by the perceiver, although neither the recipient nor the sender reported lip movement. Apparently there was unconscious whispering which could be heard by the observer. Covert oral behavior was thus thought to occur during thinking, and these findings helped to stimulate later, more objective experimentation.

Curtis (1900) placed a tambour on the larynx and asked his subjects to (1) rest, (2) silently read, (3) silently recite, and (4) whisper one of the same passages. Kymograph records indicated that laryngeal activity increased over baseline level during the 20 silent language conditions for 15 out of 20 subjects. Curtis discounted the five "failures" since four of these subjects did not show laryngeal activity during whispering, and the fifth said that he intentionally suppressed his speech movements. Courten (1902) used a rubber bulb placed on the tongue to monitor tongue movements and generally confirmed Curtis' findings.

Perkey (1910, Experiment VIII) recorded laryngeal movements (by means of a Verdin Laryngograph) from three subjects who were selected for their ability "to obtain auditory imagery." After relaxation the subjects were given a signal indicating that a word was to be spoken. If the subjects had an auditory image to a word, they were to signal with a minimal hand movement. Perky classified the subjects' introspective reports according to whether they were "images of memory" or "images of imagination." The former were "distinguished by particularity and personal reference," and the latter by "lack of particularity . . . in the sense of a particular sample, placed and dated . . . and absence of personal reference" (p. 436). The analysis indicated that laryngeal movements occured in 84% of the 155 memory images, whereas 91% of the 214 imagination images were not accompanied by laryngeal activity. Perky stated that the experiment was repeated "with like result." Apparently, Perky measured an increase in laryngeal activity over baseline when words were presented. Because amplitude of covert oral behavior varied directly with the degree of concreteness of the word, a "yes" appears in Column 2. Though Perky did not record concurrently from other bodily regions she did ascertain that the laryngeal response did not occur to the signal alone. This, incidentally, is a valuable control which is quite important for this field; it was also employed in later work by Jacobson (1932).

Wyczoikowska's (1913) subjects thought about words, remembered melodies that had words or no words, listened to words and melodies, and so forth, while a flattened wine glass was placed about the end of the tongue. Tongue reponses were then recorded on a kymograph. She concluded that every activity produced some movement of the tongue and that thinking words (in contrast to hearing them) produced responses of comparable shape but reduced in amplitude. Unfortunately Wyczoikowska reported her data only in the form of sample tracings. Since she did not report any baseline data, it cannot be assumed that the tongue responses were specifically related to the experimental conditions; consequently we enter a question mark in Column 1 of Table 6.1. Furthermore, since she obtained reponses to melodies for which there were no associated words, it cannot be concluded that the tongue activity was specifically related to the language conditions. Hence, we enter a "no" under Column 2 of Table 6.1.

Reed (1916) had subjects hold a block in the mouth cavity within closed lips and teeth. A thin rubber condom was within the block, and a rubber tube emerged forming an air passage between the speech receptor and a tambour. Air pressure variations within the mouth due to tongue movements and to breathing were thus recorded on a kymograph. Independent breathing curves were also recorded from the nose, chest, and abdomen. The subjects were instructed to (1) not think of anything, (2) silently read, (3) silently write, (4) whisper, (5) read aloud, (6) silently count, and (7) solve arithmetic problems. Reed attempted to separate inner speech from breathing by comparing the independent breathing curves with his covert speech measures. Results were positive for from one-fourth to three-fourths of his 13 subjects in that he found evidence of inner speech during thought: "The first conclusion that appears from this is that inner speech is not a universal but an individual trait" (p. 380). In some instances Reed found that the curves from the mouth during silent reading corresponded in form to the curves obtained during whispering and overt reading, and that they were independent of the breathing curves. Results on one subject were sufficiently striking to conclude that "the objective certainty of inner speech in silent reading and writing . . . is established" (p. 370). Because Reed obtained positive evidence of increased covert oral behavior over baseline, a "yes" appears in Column 1 of Table 6.1. Because the oral behavior was independent of the form of the breathing records we enter "yes pneumogram" in Column 3.

Golla (1921) attached one end of a small spring to the thyroid cartilage and the other end to a leather collar about the neck. A small button, attached at a right angle to the spring impinged on the membrane of a tambour. The vibrations of the tambour were pneumatically conveyed by a rubber tube to another tambour which actuated an optical lever. A beam of light was projected on the optical lever, so that magnified excursions were photographically recorded. The subject was asked to sing up and down an octave, and then to think the notes of the octave. Similar ascending and descending curves were obtained under both conditions, as indicated by a sample record, though the amplitude of the curve for the thinking condition was about one-third of that for overt singing. The finding that similar curves, differing in amplitude, occurred for the overt as compared to covert conditions leads us to enter a "yes" in Column 2. No baseline data were reported; no other bodily measures were taken; it is not clear just what the subject did for the thinking condition, and records were not obtained for other tasks. Nevertheless, the remarkable similarity of the curves (from a single subject) for the overt and covert conditions is striking.

In the fifth of a series of studies, Clark (1922) recorded respiration, arm volume, and laryngeal and tongue movements while four subjects solved a series of novel problems. A small cup-shaped object with a rubber membrane was attached to the throat, and a mechanical system of levers registered horizontal and vertical laryngeal movements. Tongue movements were recorded by means of a small flat frame inserted into the mouth in such a way that a rubber membrane fit on top of the tongue. Though the subjects first relaxed, the results of the kymograph tracings are reported only during problem solving, and only as follows: the total time spent in thinking was 513.3 seconds. Tongue movements were present 34.7% of this time; vertical laryngeal movements were present 22.4%. A complex of changes in the other measures occurred during the experimental session, indicating rather widespread bodily activity during thinking. Thus, because of the manner in which these results were reported, it is difficult to reach any firm conclusions about oral behavior.

Scheck (1925) inserted a small inflated rubber balloon into the subject's mouth so that it rested lightly on the top of the tongue. Tongue movements and thoracic pneumograms were recorded by a system of tambours and a kymograph. Records during rest were made, following which subjects wrote scientific prose which was dictated to them, read silently, and listened to a march, a ballad, and a jig. Scheck reported results only on himself, regarding them as "typical" of those obtained from a small group of senior and graduate students. Visual observation of the sample records suggested that some noticeable tongue activity appeared during rest, that there were several periods of heightened tongue movement during writing and reading, and that relatively little tongue activity occurred while listening to the ballad and to the march. Tongue movements were clearly greater while listening to the jig than during rest. Because the tongue response was larger during writing and reading than while listening to the ballad and to the march, we write "yes" in Column 2 of Table 6.1.

Thorson (1925) recorded thoracic respiration, and vertical and horizontal tongue movements on a kymograph. The tongue measurements were made by attaching a small suction cup to the tongue, and, with a system of levers, she achieved amplification of 3.5 or 4.5 times. One purpose of the study was to determine whether "internal speech" during the performance of various language tasks produced curves similar in form to those that occurred during the whispered performance of the same task. Using 18 subjects, she compared the tongue records under these two conditions. The conclusion was negative: only "4.4% of the total cases show some similarities . . . between pattern of movement in thinking as compared with whispering" (p. 13). Because this conclusion is so frequently cited, it is valuable to note that the mean is based on 10 subjects, 7 of whom showed 0% similarity, and 3 who showed 29%, 15%, and 17% similarity. While one might accept Thorson's conclusion that tongue movements during thinking do not resemble those during whispering (but note the conclusions of Wyczoikowska, 1913, and Reed, 1916), the generalized rejection of a motor theory of thinking should be reexamined. She concluded, for instance: "Movements of the tongue are not universal in internal speech or verbal thought . . . [and] . . . are not so much dependent upon the content of internal speech as they are upon conditions of nervous irradiation and muscular tonus" (p. 27). This conclusion disturbed Watson (1930, p. 240) who criticized her experiment because of the lack of sensitivity of her apparatus (×3.5 or ×4.5 amplification). Her work, however, actually provided positive support for Watson's theory since she *did* obtain heightened tongue activity during the performance of language tasks, relative to tongue amplitude during control periods when subjects were told to keep their thoughts "blank." To understand this, note that Thorson (1925) rank ordered the various tasks according to relative amount of tongue movement during each as follows:

1.   Reciting silently the alphabet as rapidly as possible. . . .
2.   Thinking "experimental psychology" while singing "ah" and tapping the table. . . .
3.   Reciting silently the multiplication tables of 7's and 9's while singing "ah" and tapping with the fingers. . . .
4.   Thinking following whispering. . . .
5.   Mental multiplication during filing distraction. . . .
6.   Reciting silently the mulitplication tables of 7's and 9's after doing so under distraction. . . .
7.   Thinking "experimental psychology" after doing so under distraction. . . .
8.5   Writing a passage from dictation. . . .
8.5   Thinking without any distraction and following no distraction. . . .
10.   Reading silently a Polish passage alternating with whispering of it. . . .
11.   Blank . . . (p. 25).

It appears that little or no effort was made to achieve minimal resting levels between conditions, for subjects evidently changed conditions rather rapidly, and there were only three base-line periods in which instructions were to "keep their thoughts blank." It is thus remarkable that all tasks, on the average, resulted in more tongue movements than did the blank periods. Furthermore, Thorson demonstrated that distraction increased the amount of tongue activity (the first five tasks in rank order). Hence, rather than the typically cited negative conclusion, her following statement seems more appropriate: "the records show continuous irregular movements of the tongue, varying in amount in different situations" (Thorson, 1925, p. 18). Because amplitude of covert oral behavior did vary as a function of conditions, we enter "yes" in Column 2.

Rounds and Poffenberger (1931) placed a face mask on their subjects, and recorded variations in oral air pressure by leading a small tube to a tambour, and then to a kymograph. In this way, movements within the chest, larynx, tongue, etc., were recorded. Sample records were reported for an unspecified number of subjects during a resting period. The baseline records indicate uniform activity, but during mental work periods the curves are quite erratic and irregular, perhaps indicating the occurrence of covert speech reactions. As a comparison, records obtained on an individual who had been incapable of speaking since birth showed no noticeable change in covert oral activity during the silent addition period. It is in this sense that the Rounds and Poffenberger (1931) study is affirmatively classified according to the second criterion of Table 6.1.

As a general comment on these early studies, it is quite apparent that controls, by today's standards, were inadequate, that the apparatus was quite crude, that findings were not evaluated statistically, that conclusions were often justified merely on the basis of selected sample traces, that a small number of subjects was often used, and so forth. In view of the lack of experimental sensitivity, it is therefore surprising that positive evidence of increased oral activity ever was obtained. But they were grand!

ELECTROMYOGRAPHIC STUDIES

Imagination. In 1932 Jacobson summarized extensive work to that time in which he collected electromyographic data during a variety of mental acts Jacobson (1925; 1927; 1930a, b, c, d; 1931a, b). His general procedure was to extensively train his subjects in progressive relaxation after which they could achieve a remarkably low baseline level (sometimes even down to zero microvolts). During experimental sessions two signals (clicks of a telegraph key) were presented: the first to instruct the subject to engage in a particular "mental activity," and the second (occurring several seconds later) to relax any muscular tensions present. Needle electrodes were inserted into the tip of the tongue or into the upper lip. Electrodes were also placed elsewhere (see subsequent discussion), apparently during successive sessions. Signals from the electrodes produced vibrations of a string galvanometer. These deflections were photographically recorded, allowing the measurement of response amplitudes less than 1 microvolt. Tasks included "imagine counting," "imagine telling your friend the date," "recall a poem," "multiply [certain numbers]," "think of [abstract matters such as 'eternity,' 'electrical resistance,' 'Ohm's Law']." For five subjects, the overwhelming number of tests were positive in the sense that oral behavior noticeably increased following the first signal, and then returned to base-line level following the second. Data on the sixth (see next paragraph) and seventh subject (who was unable to relax) were not reported. Jacobson employed the control procedure of instructing subjects: "Upon hearing the first signal do not bother to think." Since the first signal produced no EMG changes under this condition, it was concluded that the oral response did not occur merely because the click-signal was presented. In addition, Jacobson showed that no response changes occurred in remote ("irrelevant") bodily locations sampled when the above tasks were presented. For example, when the subject imagined lighting a cigarette, no change in tongue EMG occurred; instead, heightened EMG was recorded in the arm. Other control tests were similarly negative with regard to the tongue, (e.g., "Imagine the Eiffel Tower in Paris") although this instruction evoked eye potentials. These findings indicate that covert responses are highly localized, are evoked as a function of the particular kind of stimulus, and occur in the part of the body that one would use should the response have been overtly made.

The above results were also obtained in subjects who were not trained to relax (as in his sixth subject), indicating that the responses to the stimuli were "not artifacts resulting from training." When subjects were extremely relaxed (as indicated by minimal EMG levels), they reported an absence of "mental activities involving words and numbers. . . ." On the other hand, introspective reports, while performing activities involving words or numbers, indicated tenseness in the oral region (as also reported by Perky, 1910).

Jacobson's work has occasionally been criticized. For instance, with regard to the condition in which the subject is told not to bother to think, Humphrey (1951) has stated: "But the understanding of the instructions is just as much a mental process as the understanding of the former instructions . . . there should have been some peripheral action corresponding to the content of the instructions . . ." (p. 216). Max (1937) criticized the procedure of announcing the subject's problem in advance: "Such a method entails the subject's awareness of the problem throughout the foreperiod, which therefore is not truly a 'control' for the subsequent thinking response" (pp. 303–4). In evaluating such criticisms of Jacobson's work, one should not lose sight of how thoroughly relaxed his subjects were. Jacobson's extensive relaxation program probably produced the most relaxed subjects in the history of this kind of psychological research. One would expect, with Humphrey, peripheral activity sometime during the "Do not bother to think" test. But, recognizing the possibly fleeting nature of the covert response, particularly in such well-relaxed subjects, such a minute event could easily be missed. The fact is that Jacobson's research, conducted with such apparent carefulness, yielded remarkable results, and the appropriate criticism of it should only be found in countering data.

We repeated one aspect of Jacobson's work in our laboratory, with some differences in methodology. I very much appreciate the help of Steven Straub in conducting this work (McGuigan and Straub in Table 6.1). Ten normal-awake and four hypnotized female undergraduate college students were given three imagination instructions for each of the following bodily areas: speech, both arms, eyes, legs, nonpreferred arm, preferred arm, and none (control). Group means for the 10 awake subjects are plotted in Fig. 6.1 such that the higher the value, the greater the increase in response amplitude during the imagination period over baseline. The mean amplitude values for the EMGs measured during each target task are compared with means for all other (non-target) tasks. For example, the lips and the tongue should be intimately involved for the Speech Category of imagination tasks. We can see that the lip and tongue EMG values were in fact somewhat higher for the critical target tasks (in this case speech) than for the other tasks. Similarly, the arms, eyes, leg, and preferred arm were always more active during the target tasks. But the effect in general is quite small. Only 11 out of the 126 statistical tests were significant at the .05 level, which is about chance. Viewed as a whole, these results indicate only minor success, at best, in

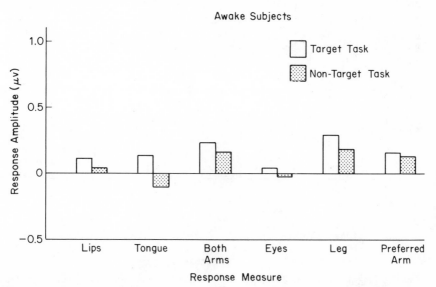

FIG. 6.1 Group mean EMG changes from baseline during imagination periods for ten awake subjects.

confirming the findings of Jacobson. One obviously crucial reason was that Jacobson used subjects trained over a long period to relax, whereas our untrained subjects perhaps had elevated baselines. One possible solution was to attempt to rapidly relax our subjects by means of hypnotism, which also might enhance the localized bodily response to the selective imagination instructions. Consequently, the experiment was repeated using four college students who-imagined the tasks under hypnosis. The results, following the methods used for Fig. 6.1 are presented in Fig. 6.2. While there were too few subjects to justify statistical tests, the mean results are more consonant with Jacobson's, that is, the relevant bodily areas for the target tasks reacted much more in conformity with expectations when subjects were hypnotized. Hence, for speech tasks, the lips and tongue are dramatically more active than for the nonspeech tasks. When both arms were supposed to be used in imagination, the mean activity for both arms also was relatively high. The leg and arm regions also covertly responded according to Jacobson's hypothesis. Only for vision was the effect not so pronounced. It seems

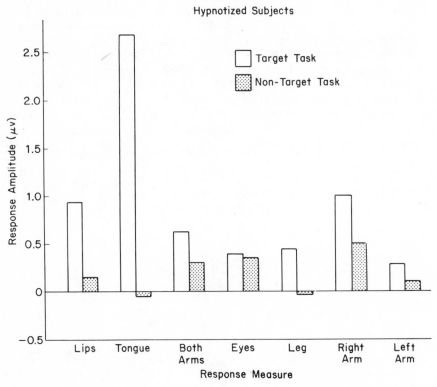

FIG. 6.2 Group mean EMG changes from baseline during imagination periods for four hypnotized subjects.

that the effect reported by Jacobson appears more prominently in our hypnotized than our awake subjects, perhaps because they were better relaxed, which lowered baseline levels, and/or because of a general imagination-facilitating hypnotic effect. To separate the reasons, the experiment should be repeated with subjects trained in progressive relaxation.

Blumenthal (1959) pretested 81 subjects, and selected 11 who evidenced noticeable tongue EMG during thinking. The subjects were given the following requirements: to rest; to listen to each of a series of words, and upon hearing each word to think of saying the word back to the experimenter; to imagine licking a postage stamp and to suck a lemon; to listen to words, but to try to keep the tongue relaxed and still; to listen to a bell, but to do nothing. Among the results, Blumenthal reported that maximum magnitude of tongue EMG when thinking of words was significantly higher than during the two control conditions of resting and listening to a bell; furthermore, mean tongue movement was significantly greater for lingual than for labial words. Tongue movements during the two control conditions did not differ significantly. The motor imagination tasks of licking a postage stamp and sucking a lemon resulted in significantly greater tongue activity than during the control conditions, and also than when hearing and thinking of saying words. The response inhibition condition of keeping the tongue relaxed while merely listening to words did not result in significantly different amounts of tongue activity. Blumenthal's purpose in selecting his subjects was to enhance the possibility of discovering specific relationships between class of vocal movements and word class (as in the lingual versus labial difference). Nevertheless, this selection obviously limits the extent to which the findings can be generalized.

Silent Reading. Faaborg-Andersen and Edfeldt (1958) inserted needle electrodes in three locations in the laryngeal musculature, namely, the vocal, the posterior crico-arytenoid, and the mylohyoid muscles. They recorded EMGs and sound records when the subjects rested, read silently, and read aloud. The subjects read their native prose (Danish) and foreign prose (Swedish). Though they studied 10 subjects, only sample records of two are presented. Their conclusions were: (1) vocal and mylohyoid EMG increased during silent and overt reading of both Danish and Swedish prose, but posterior crico-arytenoid EMG was inhibited, (2) the EMG was substantially greater for subjects unaccustomed to reading foreign prose during the reading of that foreign prose than when reading their native language, but this effect was not present for subjects accustomed to reading the foreign text; and (3) the EMG activity started .3 to .5 seconds before onset of an audible signal during overt reading.

Edfeldt (1960) used 84 Swedish college subjects who had indicated an interest in possible improvement of their reading ability. He first administered a battery of objective tests. During the experiment, 30-second relaxation periods were alternated with five 30-second reading periods. Edfeldt varied the difficulty of the text ("easy" versus "difficult"), the clarity of the text ("clear" versus "blurred"), and classified his subjects according to whether they were "good," "medium," or "poor" readers. Laryngeal EMG (recorded from needle electrodes in the mylohyoid muscle) was continuously integrated, and amplitude was sampled during relaxation and during silent reading; amount of silent speech was measured by comparing EMG amplitude during reading with base-line levels. Edfeldt reported that "good" readers engage in significantly less silent speech during silent reading than do "poor" readers; that the reading of an easy text results in significantly less silent speech than does the reading of a difficult text; and that the reading of a clear text produces significantly less silent speech than does the reading of a blurred one. Edfeldt (1960) concluded "that silent speech cannot be a habit which is, in itself, detrimental to the reading performance . . . it appears likely that . . . silent speech actually constitutes an aid toward better reading comprehension . . ." (p. 154). Furthermore, he claimed that silent speech occurs in the reading of all persons.

McGuigan, Keller, and Stanton (1964) reported two investigations using children (N=36 and N=60) and one using college subjects (N=24). They found that mean maximum amplitude of lip and chin EMG was significantly greater during silent reading than during rest periods for both kinds of subjects. Increased EMG occurred in the college subjects regardless of whether they read English or a foreign language (French). Pneumograms were also recorded, and it was found that respiration rate significantly increased from a resting level during silent reading for children, and for college subjects when reading both native and foreign prose. A sensitive sound and magnetic tape system allowed the experimenters to record subvocalization during silent reading, and they reported means of 1.53 and .43 subvocalizations per minute for the two samples of children, but none for the adult subjects. The authors also attempted to record arm EMG, but apparatus failure prevented the attainment of useful data on this measure.

Hardyck, Petrinovich, and Ellsworth (1966) selected 17 subjects from a college reading-improvement class on the basis that they subvocalized during silent reading. They placed electrodes on the throat, and transduced the electrical signals to provide the subjects with auditory feedback that varied with EMG amplitude. The subject was asked to relax, and then to read while attempting to keep the EMG feedback to a minimum. Only sample records of one subject are reported, but Hardyck et al. indicated that EMG increased during reading, relative to the relaxation period, and they reported: "In all cases one session of the feedback was sufficient to produce complete cessation of subvocalization. Most of the subjects showed a reduction of speech muscle activity to resting levels within a 5-minute period . . . after 3 months . . . none of the subjects gave any evidence of subvocalization . . ." (p. 1468). Contrary to the conclusions of Edfeldt, these authors regarded subvocal speech as detrimental to reading proficiency, and thus regarded the feedback condition as therapeutic: "This *treatment* resulted in immediate and long lasting cessation of the subvocalization . . . [and] . . . should prove valuable in *treating* some reading problems" (p. 1467, italics added). Unlike Edfeldt, no quantitative data are reported on EMG activity, nor for the reading proficiency of their subjects before or after "treatment." McGuigan (1967) used a feedback paradigm based on operant principles in which a relatively large amplitude of covert oral behavior during silent reading was punished by a slightly noxious auditory stimulus, and a reduction in response amplitude was negatively reinforced by cessation of the auditory feedback. McGuigan's results demonstrated that the problem was not methodologically as simple as Hardyck et al. (1966) had implied, for covert oral response changes during reading occurred as a result of both feedback *and* nonfeedback (control) conditions; these response changes occurred even with sensors placed in a variety of locations and with the subjects unable to verbalize the response-feedback contingency. Hardyck (1969) reported further work on this problem, but failure to present systematic data on response changes, modifications in reading proficiency, and unclear control procedures precludes any clearcut conclusions.

Luria (1966a, b) placed great emphasis on the role of verbal kinesthesia in intellectual functions, but because his data are either clinical in nature or were collected under conditions of speech interference, the present review does not dwell on them. Yet, Luria's work is sufficiently relevant to observe that he offered such interesting hypotheses as that aphasia may be due to impaired kinesthesis of the speech musculature.

McGuigan and Rodier (1968) conducted two experiments in which college subjects (N=45 and N=36) first rested, then engaged in a listening condition, and finally read silently while the listening condition continued. The listening conditions were silence, prose, prose played backwards, and white noise, presented in counterbalanced order for each subject. The EMGs were recorded from the chin, tongue, and forearm, and breathing rate was quantified. Of 14 comparisons of the listening-only conditions with baseline level, only two significant differences occurred: chin EMG and breathing rate significantly increased while listening to prose. Hence, there is some indication that covert oral behavior and breathing rate increase during the auditory presentation of language stimuli ("speech perception"). With regard to oral EMG during reading, the findings "confirm those previously reported (McGuigan et al., 1964) and we can confidently conclude that covert oral behavior and breathing rate significantly increase during silent reading, relative to rest" (McGuigan and Rodier, 1968, p. 651). As to the effects of auditory stimulation, it was found that

. . . auditory presentation of prose and of backward prose during reading leads to a significantly greater amplitude of covert oral behavior than occurs during silence, but noise does not have this effect. It is concluded that the increased covert oral behavior is beneficial to S, perhaps by facilitating the reception and/or processing of language stimuli in the presence of auditory interference; or alternately, that Ss simultaneously respond to visual and auditory (language) stimuli (p. 649).

McGuigan and Bailey (1969a) selected 16 children who showed pronounced covert oral behavior during silent reading from the subjects used by McGuigan et al. (1964), and retested 13 of them after two and after three years; three subjects were retested only after three years. During the original test, the 16 subjects exhibited a significant amount of covert oral behavior (lip or chin EMG) during silent reading, relative to a baseline period. The mean amplitude of the covert oral response noticeably decreased from the original to the second and third tests; amplitude after three years was significantly lower than during the original test, and at that time was approximately of the same value as for college subjects who had been tested but once. Furthermore no subvocalizations during silent reading were detected during the second test, in contrast to the means of 1.53 and .43 subvocalizations per minute reported in the original study. It was concluded that covert oral behavior during the performance of a language task "naturally" decreases in amplitude with age, but that it still persists at a significantly high level in the adult.

One possible problem with the McGuigan and Bailey (1969b) longitudinal study concerns the effects of repeated testing on covert behavior. If repeated testing reduced the amplitude of the covert response, heightened covert oral behavior during silent reading could be an artifact of a novel laboratory environment that habituates with time. To study this issue we plotted variations of EMG amplitude during silent reading over a nine month period, and also studied the relationship between reading proficiency and silent speech as a function of testing frequency.

Thirteen male and female children from grades 2, 3, and 4 were classified as "subvocalizers" by their teachers and by chin and lip EMG data, following the general procedures of McGuigan, Keller, and Stanton (1964). The three other children were similarly classified as low subvocalizers. The 13 subvocalizers were randomly assigned to one of three groups: Group 18 (n=5) was assessed for amplitude of covert oral behavior during silent reading bi-monthly in laboratory situations for a total of 18 times; Group 9 (n = 4) was assessed monthly for a total of nine times; and subjects in Group 2 (n = 4) were assessed twice, at the beginning and at the conclusion of the experiment. The low subvocalizers were treated as were those in Group 9.

Group mean differences of integrated EMGs are shown in Table 6.2, as are overall means obtained by computing the mean of group averages for each EMG locus. The mean increases from baseline during silent reading in lip EMGs were significant ($p < .05$) for groups 18 and 9 only. When the lip EMG values were averaged over all groups, they were found to have significantly increased during silent reading, with a mean of 1.4 μv. The chin EMG mean differences did not significantly increase for any of the individual groups ($p > .05$), but when these means were pooled across all 16 subjects, the mean difference of 2.8 μv was found to be significant. Left and right arm EMG and leg EMG significantly increased over baseline during silent reading only for Group 18. The overall average of the leg and arm mean differences was significant only for the right arm EMG measure, which was expected since this measure typically increases in the preferred arm placement (Chapter 7).

TABLE 6.2   Mean Response Changes (μv) over Baseline During Silent Reading as a Function of the Number of Test Sessions During a Nine-Month Test Interval

EMG Response	"Subvocalizers"			Low-"Subvocalizers"	
	Group 18 (18 sessions)	Group 9 (9 sessions)	Group 2 (2 sessions)	Group 9 (9 sessions)	Overall
Lips	1.1*	.9*	2.1	1.9	1.4*
Chin	1.1	1.8	4.8	4.0	2.8*
Right arm	.8*	.4	2.0	0.0	.7*
Left arm	.2*	−.5	1.1	.1	.3
Right leg	.2*	−.5	.2	0.0	0.0

*$p < .05$

The possible operation of an habituation effect caused by repeated testing was examined by plotting the difference between reading and rest as a function of the number of testing sessions. In Figs. 6.3 through 6.6, the EMG means from each of the four conditions are presented. Figure 6.3 shows the EMG differences across sessions obtained for group 18. With the exception of session 2, lip EMGs remained above zero and were relatively stable. The same held for the right arm, left arm, and right leg. The chin EMG values fluctuated more dramatically above and below zero. In Fig. 6.4 it can be seen that the chin and lip EMGs for group 9 remained above zero and were more or less stable across sessions. As presented in Fig. 6.5, for subjects who were tested twice, there was a slight decrease in EMG differences across all EMG loci, though the differences are not significant. In Fig. 6.6 it is evident that chin and lip EMG values remained above zero throughout; EMG values for the right arm, left arm, and right leg hovered (nonsignificantly) around zero. It is especially interesting to note the high chin and lip EMG values for this group, selected for absence of noticeable "subvocalization" by the teachers with the naked eye.

The group mean differences of Table 6.2 were compared separately for each EMG locus; the only significant differences between groups were the larger right leg and arm EMGs for group 2, relative to the low subvocalizers.

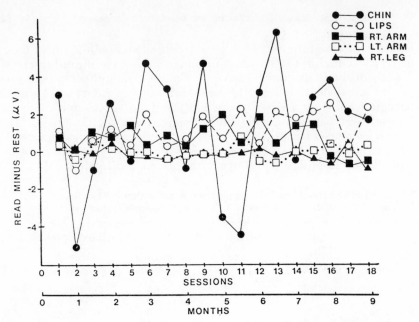

FIG. 6.3   Mean covert response changes over baseline as a function of testing sessions for Group 18.

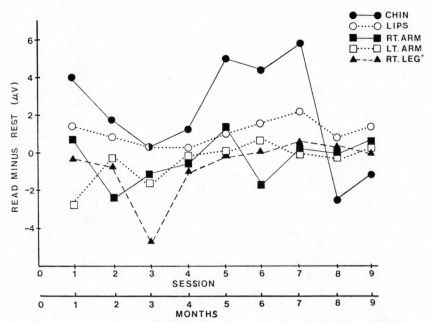

FIG. 6.4   Mean covert response changes over baseline as a function of testing sessions for Group 9.

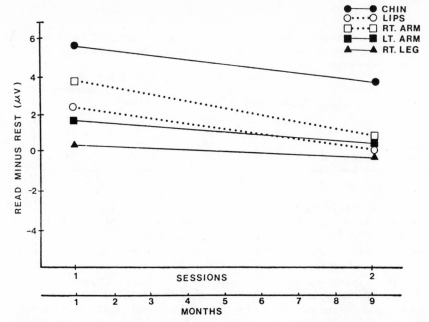

FIG. 6.5   Mean covert response changes over baseline as a function of testing sessions for Group 2.

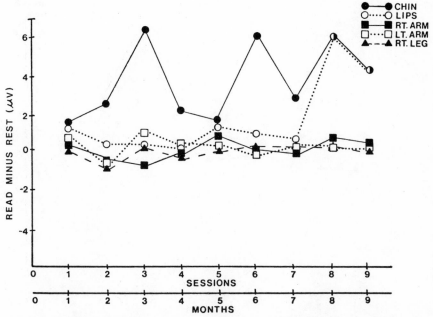

FIG. 6.6   Mean covert response changes over baseline as a function of testing sessions for low subvocalizers.

185

TABLE 6.3 Mean Reading Rate (words per min) and the Number of Subvocalizations During Pre-Experimental Sessions and at the Conclusion of the Experiment

| | Reading Rate | | Number of Subvocalizations | |
| | Before | 9 Months | Before | 9 Months |
Condition	Experiment	Later	Experiment	Later
Group 18	63	124	52	3
Group 9	73	128	7	20
Group 2	69	106	74	47
Low Subvocalizers	85	106	0	7

The mean reading rate (words per minute) and the mean number of subvocalizations are presented in Table 6.3. For example, the group that was tested 18 times read at a rate of 63 WPM prior to the experiment and 124 WPM at the end of the nine-month period. This increase of 61 WPM in reading rate for group 18 was significant as was the 37 WPM increase in reading speed for group 2. The average increments in reading rate for the other groups were not significant. When the scores were pooled and the subjects in the four conditions were evaluated as a single group, the increase in reading rate of 46 WPM was significant. As can be seen in Fig. 6.7 the number of times tested did not have an apparent effect on reading rate.

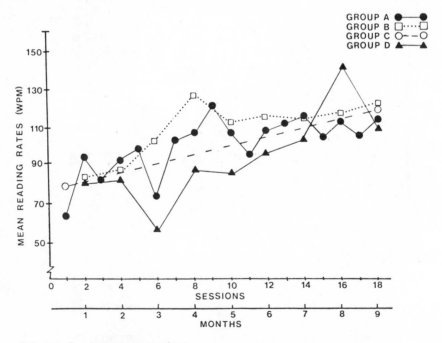

FIG. 6.7 Reading rate vs. sessions.

In summary, significant increases in integrated lip EMGs from baseline levels were found for groups 18 and 9, the subvocalizers, but not for the low subvocalizers. The number of subvocalizations emitted did not appear to change consistently across groups. Chin EMGs did not significantly increase for any of the four conditions separately, probably because the chin musculature is less sensitive as a locus of information processing. However, the chin muscle *is* part of the general speech musculature and does participate in internal information processing (as indicated by other studies in this chapter) and by the fact that when the data from the present study were pooled for all four groups, the mean increase in chin EMG throughout the experiment was significant.

In conclusion, it does not appear that repeated testing resulted in a sizable reduction of covert behavior. Lip EMGs, in fact, increased over rest levels during the performance of a language task whether subjects were tested on a monthly or bi-monthly basis. This situation was not as clear cut for chin EMG measures. In contrast, the nonpreferred arm and leg EMGs did not consistently increase above baseline as a function of the number of testing sessions. The frequency of audible subvocalizations did not change consistently as a function of exposure time to training material. A significant habituation effect due to repeated testing thus does not appear. Consequently, the fact that some electromyographic measures of covert oral behavior remain above baseline regardless of repeated testing suggests that even if there is a habituation effect, which did not clearly manifest itself through these data, covert oral behavior still occurs in the silent reader. These data are thus consistent with the more general interpretation that covert oral behavior serves a linguistic function during internal information processing.

McGuigan and Bailey (1969b) had their subjects silently read, memorize prose, listen to the auditory presentation of prose, listen to music, and attentively listen to "nothing" (a blank tape on a tape recorder), with instructions to relax before each task. The experiment was repeated three times (N=36, N=40, and N=25). Measures taken were EMG from the chin, preferred forearm, tongue, breathing rate, and EEG from the right motor area. It was found that chin and tongue EMGs during silent reading and memorization significantly increased from base-line level, and that the amounts of these increases were significantly greater than for the two non-language conditions (listening to music and to nothing). Respiration rate and preferred forearm EMG significantly increased from base-line level during silent reading, memorization, and listening to prose, and the increases for these three language conditions were significantly greater than for the two non-language conditions. The EEG amplitude significantly decreased during attentive listening to "nothing." Covert oral behavior increased in all three experiments while listening to prose, but in no case was this measure significantly higher than base line. It was concluded that increased covert oral behavior, preferred forearm responses, and breathing rate are associated with the processing of language stimuli.

Auditory Hallucinations.   The successful recording of subvocal speech during auditory hallucinations is of striking importance to the general topic of this paper. The first work was by Gould (1949, 1950). He studied psychotics who emitted subvocal speech, selecting them by means of a stethoscope over the larynx and studying them by means of a sensitive microphone close to the mouth and by chin EMG. Gould (1949) reported that "there was marked correspondence between the subvocal speech as heard by the investigator and the voices as heard by the subject" (p. 425), and numerous examples of this correspondence are given. One patient was asked to think a story and to imagine lecturing; Gould reported that the amplitude of EMG from the vocal organs increased from a sustained resting level of 27.5 microvolts to 66.0 microvolts and 50.5 microvolts, respectively. A second patient showed an increase to 66.0 microvolts and 55.0 microvolts from a resting level of 27.5 microvolts, when asked to imagine that she heard her husband calling her, and hearing someone recite a poem, respectively.

Roberts, Greenblatt, and Solomon (1951) studied six psychotics who experienced auditory hallucinations during the test, four who did not hallucinate during the test, and three nonpsychotic comparison subjects. The EMGs were recorded on an inkwriting polygraph from the anterior neck, chin, and temporomandibular joints on both sides. The subjects relaxed, and then signaled the beginning and ending of an hallucination by raising and lowering the little finger. Records were taken for 10 minutes. No relevant gross EMG changes were noted for the seven nonhallucinating subjects. The six remaining subjects reported a total of 43 hallucinations. The amplitudes of EMG records were quantified by millimeters of pen deflection into three classes ("slight," "moderate," or "marked"). Nineteen instances of moderate to marked EMG occurred, but only four of these instances coincided with the raising of the finger, leading to the conclusion that auditory hallucinations are "not consistently accompanied by vocal myographic discharges . . ." (p. 914). These relatively negative findings might be tempered by the fact that EMGs were recorded by means of relatively insensitive equipment (viz., an inkwriting polygraph that apparently registered only 19 responses from four body locations of six subjects during 10 minutes, which is amazingly low even for a normal subject during a total of 240 minutes of records), and that the criterion of the occurrence of a hallucination was unobjective. That is, one cannot be sure that the subjects in fact hallucinated when (and only when) they raised their fingers.

McGuigan (1966b) had a schizophrenic subject relax, and depress a button each time that voices were heard. Pneumograms, sound production (from a sensitive microphone placed before the lips), and EMG from the chin, tongue, and (nonpressing) arm were continuously recorded. For 15 of the reported hallucinations, the subject was asked to remain silent after their occurrence; for the remaining 10, the subject was asked to report the content of the hallucinations. It was found that chin EMG and breathing amplitude significantly increased during a

2-second interval just prior to the report of hallucinations, relative to a comparable time interval 6 seconds prior to the button press, while there was no noticeable change in arm EMG. A significant number of slight whisperings were detected immediately before the hallucinations were reported: in two instances, the whisperings were sufficiently clear that they could be identified as part of the content of the overtly reported hallucinations. Control measures were taken prior to overt speech and pressing the button; these curves showed no resemblance to those obtained for actual hallucinations. Similar results have also been reported by Malmo (personal communication, December 19, 1967, and 1975) and others, e.g., Inouye and Shimizu (1970).

Cursive Writing. McGuigan (1967) selected a group of college subjects who had excellent handwriting (n = 7), and a group who had poor handwriting (n = 4), from a larger group of 117. The subjects wrote a list of words, and drew ovals with a rest period preceding each task. Tongue, chin, and non-writing arm EMGs were recorded, as was respiration rate. The group mean of tongue and chin EMG for all 11 subjects significantly increased from rest while writing words, but not when drawing ovals. The amount of increase while writing words was significantly greater than when drawing ovals. Arm EMG did not significantly increase during either experimental condition, nor was there a significant difference between the amount of increase in arm EMG while writing or while drawing ovals. Respiration rate significantly increased under both conditions, but the amount of increase between conditions was not significant. The increase in amplitude of covert oral behavior during writing, relative to that while drawing ovals, was greater for the poor writers than for the excellent writers, but the difference was not significant; only minor differences between groups occurred for the arm and respiration measures. The experiment was repeated (McGuigan, 1970b), using eight excellent writers and eight poor writers, and also groups of eight subjects who said that they did or did not subvocalize during writing. The same measures as those employed in the 1967 study were taken, except that lower leg EMG was substituted for arm EMG, and the electroencephalogram (EEG) was recorded from the right motor area. The subjects wrote words, and drew ovals in counterbalanced order with relaxation periods preceding each task. The results generally confirmed those of the previous study. In this study, though tongue EMG was *significantly* higher in amplitude for the poor writers than for the excellent writers, no differences between the groups who said that they did or did not subvocalize were significant. A third control study was conducted using six subjects who wrote words, drew ovals, or drew clefs in counterbalanced order. The number of subjects was too small to allow statistical tests of significance to be meaningfully conducted, but the amplitude of tongue EMG was noticeably greater while writing words than while drawing clefs or ovals. Among the conclusions were the following: (1) amplitude of covert oral behavior increased significantly more during cursive writing than during a nonlanguage task (but this was not the case for the nonoral processes sampled); (2) amplitude of covert oral behavior during writing varies inversely with the quality of one's writing; (3) respiration rate increased significantly during the performance of the language and the nonlanguage task, but it increased above base line significantly more during the former.

Learning. In a sequel to a previous study (Berry and Davis, 1958), Berry and Davis (1960) recorded jaw and right arm EMGs during a serial learning task consisting of nine two-place numbers. The memory drum was programmed to allow anticipation, delay, and information intervals, all of two seconds duration. Concomitant measures of heart rate, EKG, volume pulse, and palmar GSR were also recorded. The results indicated that speed of learning was significantly correlated with the magnitude of jaw EMG and of the volume pulse. Generally, the rapid learners exhibited high skeletal muscle activity in the head region. Although not significant, a tendency was noted for jaw EMG and EKG patterns for correct and incorrect responses to vary systematically with individual differences in learning speed. Additionally, EKG magnitudes during the information interval following incorrect responses showed a significant positive correlation with speed of learning. The measures of arm EMG, palmar GSR, and heart rate were not found to be systematically related to speed of learning. As a general conclusion, Berry and Davis suggested that the rate of verbal learning is associated with increased physiological activity in the head region, and further, that this activity is most important in the interval when a correcting response is made following an incorrect anticipatory response.

Nocturnal Dreams. Berger (1961) studied the tonus of extrinsic laryngeal muscles, EEGs, and eye responses from nine subjects for a total of 17 night sleep sessions. Laryngeal EMG muscle tonus decreased with the onset of sleep and remained constant, except for rapid further decreases preceding the onset of EEG stage 1-REM periods. Berger concluded that this EMG suppression preceding REMs is characteristic of a generalized inhibition of somatic musculature, or is a peculiarity of the laryngeal muscles. In evaluating this study and the conclusions, it should be recognized that the sampling of the skeletal musculature was extremely limited, was studied with surface electrodes over the complex laryngeal musculature, and only recorded on an ink-writing polygraph.

Larson and Foulkes (1969) studied the relation between pre-REM EMG suppression, previously reported by Berger (1961) and Jacobson, Kales, Lehmann, and Hoedemaker (1964), to dream recall. Eye, EEGs and submental EMGs were obtained from five subjects for a total of 42 nights. Awakenings and collections of dream reports were scheduled during (1) high-EMG, nonrapid eye movements (NREM) sleep, (2) low-EMG, NREM sleep, and (3) low-EMG, REM sleep (i.e., Stage 1 EEG). The dream reports were blindly scored for dreamlike fantasy and latency measure from time of awakening to time of coherent report (orientation time) was noted. For the two NREM awakening categories it was found that recall and fantasy scores were significantly higher during high-EMG NREM sleep than during low-EMG NREM sleep. Comparisons between REM awakenings and NREM awakenings indicated that mean fantasy and mean recall scores were significantly higher during REM awakenings than during low-ENG NREM awakenings, but not significantly different for comparisons between REM awakenings and high-EMG NREM awakenings. Mean time to orientation was significantly higher for low-EMG NREM awakenings as compared to high-EMG NREM awakenings, whereas the latter two did not significantly differ, suggesting that decreased cognitive functioning is associated with pre-REM EMG suppression. Larson and Foulkes concluded that these data indicate a reduction in reportable mentation and cognitive efficiency at the point of NREM EMG suppression preceding the onset of REM sleep; and that this characteristic NREM event should not be considered a part of the presumed monotonic increase in activation from NREM to REM sleep.

Pivik and Dement (1970) recorded EEGs, eye responses, and mylohyoid EMGs for a total of 107 sleep sessions in order to examine phasic motor inhibition during NREM sleep. Additional procedures of electrical stimulation of the calf muscle afferents (H reflex), which synapse directly on spinal motoneurons, were completed to assess the possible inhibition of this reflex during NREM sleep. Analyses of the EMG data indicated that phasic EMG suppressions occurred without exception in all subjects during all stages of NREM sleep in every sleep session. Suppression appeared with the greatest frequency in stages 2 and 4, averaged 250 msec in duration, and exhibited a higher frequency in the 10 minutes preceding REM periods than in the same interval of time following REM periods. Study of the H reflex data indicated a tonic reduction during NREM sleep, relative to wakefulness, and a tonic and phasic inhibition of the H reflex during REM sleep. Additionally, a complete phasic inhibition of the reflex was noted simultaneously with the NREM phasic EMG suppression. Insofar as a positive correlation has been established between qualities of sleep mentation and phasic events during REM sleep, Pivik and Dement concluded that the NREM phasic EMG suppressions noted in this experiment might provide a suitable electrophysiological event for the study of NREM mentation.

McGuigan and Tanner (1971) found that covert oral behavior (lip and chin electromyograms) was significantly higher during rapid eye movement (REM) periods in which there were conversational dreams than during nonrapid eye movement (NREM) periods. On the other hand, REM periods for the visual dreams showed only minor and nonsignificant changes in overt oral behavior, relative to the NREM periods. Little change occurred for neck responses, suggesting that behavioral changes were localized in the speech region. It is especially important to note that very rapid phasic activity was recorded. The general conclusion often offered by dream researchers that "EMG decreases during REM periods" thus should be tempered with the suggestion that while EMG tonus does decrease, phasic activity increases in dreams involving speech processes. The locus from which the sleep researcher is recording is also important, though often unspecified or thought irrelevant.

Miscellaneous. Smith, Malmo, and Shagass (1954) had 22 subjects with pathological behavior and 11 college subjects listen to prose as the volume was decreased at intervals, so that the sound was periodically almost inaudible. The EMGs were continuously recorded from the forehead, neck, chin, and both forearms. Smith et al. reported that chin EMG and EMG from both forearms significantly increased from a baseline level during listening, but that forehead and neck EMG were unaffected. The patients had a significantly higher level of chin EMG during listening than did the normal subjects, with no other response measures differing between groups. It is possible that the increase in chin EMG was produced by listening to the prose, but it may also have been caused by the subjects "straining" when the volume was reduced. Two similar studies were also conducted in the same laboratory, these without a reduction in volume (Bartoshuk, 1956; Wallerstein, 1954); however, no data are reported for comparing covert oral behavior during listening with a baseline level. The main purpose in all three of these investigations was to study gradients from the first through the tenth minute of listening (cf. Malmo, 1965). Consequently, the results are not directly relevant to the present problem.

Bassin and Bein (1961) recorded EMG from the lower lip and distal part of one arm using "more than" 50 subjects. They recorded a baseline level, following which subjects engaged in a "simple verbal task" (e.g., silent arithmetic). Only sample tracings are reported, but they indicate that during the performance of the verbal task there are slight increases in lip EMG with no readily apparent changes in (an unspecified) arm EMG. Increasing the difficulty of the task (reading a list of jumbled words and letters) greatly increased the amplitude of lip EMG. Bassin and Bein also studied a number of pathological speech subjects, and concluded that a considerable increase in lip EMG occurred if the subject was asked to perform a verbal task that involved the critical defect. If the task is beyond the subject's powers, there may be a reduction in lip EMG with a marked increase in right-hand EMG: for example, subjects with hysterical mutism produce normal baselines for the lip and right hand, but, when asked to mentally pronounce a word that they are unable to overtly say, there is a dramatic increase in right arm EMG, thus indicating that subjects were "using writing as a method of compensation for a speech defect" (p. 200).

Novikova (1961) placed electrodes on the tongue and on the dorsal surface of the right forearm of 11 normal subjects. Sample records indicated that tasks such as silently reciting the months, days of the week, and a poem, or memorizing figures and words, all led to increases in tongue EMG, relative to a baseline level. As the difficulty of the verbal task was increased, amplitude of tongue EMG proportionately increased. Increase in tongue EMG while listening to instructions is also reported. During the solution of a difficult arithmetical problem, depression in "electrical activity of the cerebral cortex . . . could be seen to coincide with the period of activity in the tongue" (p. 215). Three illiterate subjects showed especially high tongue EMG relative to literate subjects. No results on arm EMG are reported for normal subjects. Novikova also presented sample records on deaf mutes, and concluded that subjects who knew both oral and manual speech showed EMG increases in both regions while performing arithmetical tasks. The same phenomenon was demonstrated in normal subjects who were proficient in manual speech, and it was noted that tongue EMG increased prior to the onset of an increase in arm EMG. Novikova concluded that a single functional system develops which includes control of both fingers and tongue.

In a general theoretical article, Sokolov (1967) presented sample tracings, and briefly summarized some of his empirical findings. During the solution of an arithmetical problem, there was a tonic increase in lip EMG from baseline level, with bursts of phasic activity: "Tongue electromyograms always show increase in integrated electrical activity of 150-180% in comparison with 'background level (rest state)' " (p. 12). During the writing of familiar material (the subject's name) Sokolov demonstrated that there was no increase in lip EMG from baseline level, but that there was a dramatic increase in tonic and phasic activity when the subject listened to a story for 260 seconds; there was a gradual increase in tonic lip EMG (similar to findings summarized by Malmo, 1965), again with individual (phasic) bursts of electrical activity. Citing previous findings that the galvanic skin response (GSR) and alpha-rhythm depression are indicators of general activation of the cortex by the brainstem reticular formation, Sokolov stated that comparisons of speech electromyograms with GSR and alpha depression "allows for a fairly precise differentiation in the electromyograms between the general tonic and the special speech components" (p. 11). This independence of covert speech activity during the performance of language tasks led Sokolov to attribute a unique function to the covert oral response, as is seen later in this review.

In a later translation, Sokolov (1969) summarized a series of studies in which subjects were given both verbal and nonverbal (visual) tasks, under the following conditions. The subjects (school children, students, and laboratory assistants) underwent preliminary extinction of orienting responses to the electrical apparatus, were relaxed to obtain baseline levels, and simultaneous recordings were taken from various areas of the speech and nonspeech musculature. Sokolov presented a variety of individual records, one to illustrate each of his general conclusions. The various tasks included counting to oneself, thinking about previous events, solving arithmetic problems, silent reading of native and foreign prose, listening to phrases and then recalling these phrases, solving Raven Matrices, and so forth. The general finding is that speech motor activity increases from baseline level during the performance of these tasks, regardless of whether they are language or non-language. Furthermore, response amplitude increases as the difficulty of the task increases, and decreases as the task becomes more automatic and its solution becomes sterotyped.

Perceptual Clarification.   Osgood and McGuigan (1973) posed two theoretical issues concerning the possible function of covert oral behavior:

1. Is such demonstrable covert oral activity *necessary* for linguistic processing? It is conceivable that sub-vocal activity is nothing more than excitatory overflow along those pathways ordinarily involved in overt execution—and like the noise of an engine, not essential to its functioning. A compromise view would be that while peripheral involvement is necessary for the *development* of language, including both phonological and semantic codes, it is no longer necessary for adult linguistic performance (cf. Osgood, 1953, pp. 653-55).

2. Is such demonstrable covert oral activity *sufficient* for linguistic processing? If proprioceptive feedback from the vocal musculature were to provide anything more than a generalized tonic effect upon language perception or meaning, it would have to display precisely particularized relationships to the auditory linguistic stimuli. This is certainly true for *overt* speech, but it must be shown to hold as well for *covert* speech.

Although it is not required that covert speech be a miniature of overt speech—resemble it in every way except amplitude—there is some evidence for a reasonably close resemblance. For example, heightened covert oral EMG during silent reading and during auditory hallucinations were often accompanied by slight "whispering" that would be understood as English words by the experimenter (Gould, 1949; McGuigan et al., 1964; McGuigan, 1966b). McGuigan and Winstead (1974) concluded that individuals silently (covertly) processing words characterized by the presence of letters representing labial phonemes exhibited heightened lip EMG; furthermore lingual alveolar words (which, when overtly spoken, require considerable tongue action) were accompanied with heightened tongue EMG. Their conclusion was that there is a discriminative relation between covert oral behavior and the phonemic system during internal information processing. To the extent that these issues can be resolved affirmatively, then, an affirmative answer to issue (1) becomes more likely.

Osgood and McGuigan (1973) planned a series of four experiments to get at the "truth" of the matter. The idea behind the first of their joint studies came from a phenomenon Osgood once observed while listening to a recording of a Gilbert and Sullivan operetta with his wife. As Osgood reported it, his wife ". . . was following the printed libretto. In the midst of a many-voiced male chorus—which I found completely

unintelligible—I happened to glance down to where her finger was tracing the music. I also started following the test, and suddenly the words
became perfectly intelligible. It wasn't simply that I now "understood"
what was auditorily fuzzy; the words being sung *sounded* clear. Repeated
tests gave the same subjective effect. I have since checked with other
people, and many report the same observation" (p. 470). The first question thus was whether this Gilbert-and-Sullivan Effect (as we have come
to call it) can be demonstrated under controlled laboratory conditions. If
so, then we face the question of the basis of the phenomenon.

There are three possible types of feedback which are relevant here
(refer to Fig. 9.13 on p. 385). The first is long-loop proprioceptive feedback from the peripheral speech musculature to the other sensory integration systems (particularly hearing and vision); this is McGuigan's
prime candidate for explaining this type of perceptual phenomenon.
The second is short-loop, purely central feedback from the representational (meaning) level into the integration (perceptual) level; this, of
course, is Osgood's prime candidate for explanation of the same
phenomena. The third is perhaps better described as "short circuiting"
than as "feedback"; it is a possible centralizing process itself, the pulling
back up into the representational level of processes that begin as overt
reactions in muscles and glands, lose their overtness as they gain programming in the motor integration system, and finally become directly
elicitable as meaningful r_M's by signs as stimuli. As discussed in Chapter
4, Dunlap (1927) and Watson (1919) referred to this possibility as a
"recession" into the nervous system, especially into the motor regions
such as the cerebellum. Some such centralizing process is implicitly assumed in Osgood's interpretation of other (semantic) phenomena we are
studying. A similar type of short-circuiting was proposed by Greenwald
(1970) in his rejuvenation of William James' notion of ideomotor
action—the principle that the perceptual image or idea of an action
initiates execution of that action. In Greenwald's behavioristic transcription of this notion, it is proposed that the peripheral feedbacks (visual,
etc., as well as proprioceptive) of actions, thus *images of actions,* become
conditioned to sign-produced input stimuli and thereby can become
anticipatory to and serve to initiate the very actions from which they
were derived. It should be noted that this proposal explicitly involves the
formation of Osgood's *s-s* associations.

The four experiments planned by Osgood and McGuigan may be
summarized as follows. Experiment I used Gilbert and Sullivan choral
materials and was designed to merely demonstrate the empirical validity
of the phenomenon, but it does not allow choice among the alternative
interpretations. Experiment II used Finnish linguistic materials—a language which, though easily and fluently pronounceable after surface
training, is still meaningless to the subjects; persistence of the G-S Effect
with r_M (meaning) removed favors McGuigan's oral muscle interpretation, and a central feedback interpretation is disfavored. Experiment III
would use the operetta materials again, but with oral proprioceptive

feedback prevented; if the G-S Effect still appears, the central feedback interpretation is favored as against the speech muscle one. And Experiment IV would again use the Finnish materials but also with prevention of proprioceptive feedback; if the G-S Effect still appears, then we must obviously look elsewhere for an explanation. The first two of these planned experiments have been completed, and we are gaining some information on techniques for the third and fourth experiments (see the next section on Interference with Covert Oral Behavior). Unfortunately, at this stage of our technological development, it may be impossible to remove proprioceptive feedback (cf. p. 220).

The first experiment, that on the Gilbert and Sullivan effect, was conducted by McGuigan, Osgood, and Hadley (1973). Prior to that study, it had been amply demonstrated that perception in one modality may be facilitated by increasing stimulation in another (see, for example: Hartman, 1933; Kekcheev, Kravkov, and Shvarts, 1947; Zwosta and Zenhausern, 1969). However, these are all cases of generalized, noninformational facilitation. The only studies we have been able to locate in which specific facilitation across auditory and visual modalities is investigated are reported by W. M. Smith (1965a, b). Smith found that near-synchronous presentation of auditory verbal stimuli facilitates tachistoscopic recognition of the "same" verbal stimuli in the visual mode. According to Smith (1965b), the fact that the effect occurs when another's voice (the experimenter's) is heard synchronously with the visual display, as well as when the subject himself speaks the words (repeating the experimenter), eliminates feedback from the speech musculature as an explanation. However, the possibility that the subjects were *sub-vocalizing* while listening to the experimenter is not eliminated. Therefore, Smith's results offer another instance of the G-S Effect (albeit in reverse, hearing upon reading), but they do not help to differentiate between covert oral and cerebral sources of facilitation.

The subjects in our G-S experiment listened to several pieces of choral music while simultaneously viewing slides containing printed passages. The slides sometimes helped them understand the words being sung (when they matched) and sometimes not (unmatched). The subjects *did* reliably report the subjective G-S Effect: they signalled understanding of the choral material significantly more often when the accompanying slides matched the sung words than when nonmatching slides accompanied the music, and also significantly more often than a control (auditory presentation only) condition. Overall veracity of the *subjective* reports of understanding was indicated by the fact that *objective* recognition scores were significantly higher for choral passages signalled "understood" than for those signalled "not understood." Furthermore, amplitude of tongue EMG (typically the most sensitive measure of covert oral behavior) was significantly higher under the condition in which the perceptual integration effect occurred. Further, control data indicated that the behavioral change was localized in the speech region. We, therefore, have some reason to believe that covert oral activity (in the tongue, where one would most expect it) does occur with higher amplitudes when the G-S Effect is present than when it is absent.

The result of this first experiment in the planned series of four thus gives us reasonable confidence that the Gilbert-and-Sullivan Effect is a valid phenomenon—that presentation of synonymous material in one communication modality can clarify perception in another modality. But at this point both covert oral response and central feedback mechanisms remain as possible explanations.

The second experiment in the series is fundamentally a replication of the first, with Finnish materials substituted for the Gilbert and Sullivan operetta selections. This experiment will be referred to as having been conducted by McGuigan, Osgood, and Schoonover. The only other important design difference was that this study had no music-only condition, as explained by Osgood and McGuigan (1973). The reason for using Finnish materials, it will be recalled, is that Finnish is easily pronounceable with little training, thus providing *meaningless,* yet phonetically specific, verbal stimuli. If the G-S Effect is obtained with Finnish materials, then the central representational-level feedback explanation of the perceptual facilitation phenomenon is disfavored, and the peripheral feedback mechanism is favored. If the effect obtains *and* concomitant covert oral behavior increases as compared to nonoral measures, then there is further, but still not conclusive, evidence for the peripheral interpretation.[1] Because of its importance and because it has not been previously reported, the Finnish study will be reported in more than usual detail in this chapter. Eventually, all four studies will be available (we hope) as a cohesive monograph.

We will consider the effects of presenting unintelligible (LoI) and intelligibile (HiI) spoken Finnish passages to subjects, while simultaneously presenting specific matching (synonymous) visual Finnish material, specific nonmatching visual Finnish material, or non-specific (blank slide) noninformational material. The results are compared to the findings of the G-S study in an attempt to clarify the feedback mechanisms involved in the G-S Effect, as well as to confirm the reliability of this perceptual-integration phenomenon.

Seven female college students were trained in two one-hour sessions to satisfactorily pronounce Finnish. No translation into English of either the training or experimental materials was provided, thereby preventing the learning of semantic content of the Finnish prose.

---

[1] Furthermore, if the G-S Effect occurs with the meaningless materials concomitant with heightened covert oral behavior, we might suppose that while covert oral responses are important for linguistic processing their function is not directly with semantic processing per se. Consequently, as we shall note especially in Chapter 9, we hypothesize that covert oral responses function in the generation of phonetic coding which, while in itself is not meaningful, plays a major role in determining the precise nature of the consequent semantic processes.

Audio-visual materials used were:

1. Five different 40-sec passages of spoken Finnish material tape recorded for auditory presentation. In order to prevent any "inherent" meaning, no syntactic structure existed in the passages. Two passages were LoI material, over-dubbed with white noise so as to be auditorily unintelligible. Two passages were HiI selections, and one passage was used in a practice session preceding each complete experimental presentation.
2. Slides of Finnish prose accompanied the spoken passages, such that there were two slides that matched the auditory prose, and one nonmatching slide for each passage.
3. Recognition tests for each experimental condition included eight "phrases" from the spoken passages, four from the nonmatching slide, and eight extraneous Finnish "phrases."

   After a practice session, four spoken (40-sec) passages (two HiI and two LoI were presented to each subject in incompletely counterbalanced order (Underwood, 1966, p. 464). The order of slide presentations accompanying the auditory material was: blank slide (10-sec), matching *or* nonmatching slide (10-sec), blank slide (10-sec), and matching *or* nonmatching slide (10-sec). After each 40-sec presentation, the subject was given a recognition test for that passage. An interval of about one minute occurred between each experimental condition to allow the subject to relax.

To anticipate briefly, the overall results of this experiment were consistent with the findings of the original G-S study. First, the subjective G-S Effect was reliably established: For LoI material, when the accompanying slides matched the spoken words, the subjects signaled auditory clarity during 53% of its presentation time, as against 15% of the time when the nonmatching slides accompanied the passages ($t = 5.04$, $p <$ .05; $\alpha = .05$ throughout), as against 25% of the time for the LoI/Blank-slide condition ($t = 6.97$, $p < .05$). The subjects signaled auditory clarity for HiI material 100% of the time when the slides matched, and 80% of the time when the slides did not match, while corresponding LoI reports were much lower (viz., 53% vs. 15%), thus indicating that they followed the instructions to signal when the words actually being spoken were clear to them. It does not appear that the G-S Effect could have been due to the presentation of visual materials, per se, since the subjects signaled auditory clarity more often in the LoI/Blank-slide condition (25%) than in the LoI/Nonmatching-slide condition (15%); and, in any event, this difference was not significant.

In order to assess the accuracy of the subjective reports of clarity, recognition scores were computed as the percentage of items from the actual spoken passages that were correctly identified. These recognition scores served as an objective measure of auditory clarity, and were grouped according to visual condition and subjective report. Objective recognition scores were significantly higher ($t = 8.42$, $p < .05$) for spoken passages signaled subjectively clear (39% correct) than for those not so-signaled (12% correct), thus verifying the overall subjective reports of clarity.

The data shown in Table 6.4 provide a more sensitive test of the G-S Effect. Recognition scores for the LoI/Matching-slide/Subjectively-clear condition (27%) are more than twice as high as for the LoI/Blank-slide/ Not-clear condition (11%); these results are thus clearly in the direction established by the G-S study. However, these means do not differ significantly ($t = 1.28$, $df = 5$). For all visual conditions, the HiI selections have higher recognition scores than LoI selections, thereby supporting the classification of selections as to their intelligibility.

TABLE 6.4   Recognition Scores for Spoken Finnish Passages (Percentage of Items That Are Correct) as Functions of Visual Conditions and Subjective Reports

Report of Subject	Matching Slide (%)	Nonmatching Slide (%)	Blank Slide (%)
Subjectively clear			
HiI selections	50 (n=7)	40 (n=7)	33 (n=7)
	(69 [n=8])	(46 [n=8])	(26 [n=8])
LoI selections	27 (n=7)	00 (n=2)	00 (n=4)
	(54 [n=8])	(50 [n=2])[a]	(20 [n=6])
Not subjectively clear			
HiI selections	—[b]	33 (n=3)[c]	33 (n=3)
	(67 [n=3])	(00 [n=2])	(47 [n=8])
LoI selections	28 (n=6)	4 (n=7)	11 (n=6)
	(44 [n=6])	(10 [n=8])	(10 [n=8])

Note: For comparison, corresponding values obtained in the G-S study are given enclosed in parentheses.
[a] Based on two subjects, one of whom scored 100% and the other 00%. Hence, the average is meaningless.
[b] No subjects were in this category.
[c] Based on three subjects, one of whom scored 100%, and two of whom scored 0%.

It was suggested in the G-S study that a perseveration effect occurred in the Blank-slide condition that directly followed a Matching-slide presentation; i.e., when subjects were actually hearing clearly (during the Matching-slide condition), they continued in an illusion of clarity when the blank slide was presented. The data for the present study were examined to determine if a perseveration effect occurred. As shown in Table 6.5, signaled clarity for the second LoI/Blank-slide condition was somewhat higher (30% and 27%) than for the first LoI/Blank-slide condition (21%), the latter having had no warm-up period. Also, signaled clarity of the LoI passages for the second Blank-slide condition, when immediately following a matching slide, was much higher (30%) than the recognition scores (0%); and, when the Blank-slide condition followed a nonmatching slide, the signaled clarity (27%) was higher than the recognition scores (14%). Thus there is some evidence to indicate a perseveration effect in the Blank-slide condition, but it apparently was more a function of the warm-up period in general than of whether the preceding slide matched or not.

TABLE 6.5 Signaled Subjective Clarity (% Time Signaled) and Recognition Scores (% Correct) for Blank-Slide Periods, the Second Following Either Matching or Nonmatching Visual Materials

| | First Blank-Slide Period | Second Blank-Slide Period Following | |
| | | Matched Visual Material | Nonmatched Visual Material |
Report of Subject	(%)	(%)	(%)
Subjective Clarity			
Hil selections	89 (55)	81 (64)	97 (54)
Lol selections	21 (2)	30 (64)	27 (2)
Recognition scores			
Hil selections	25 (28)	43 (44)	43 (50)
Lol selections	11 (12)	00 (12)	14 (00)

Note: For comparison, corresponding values obtained in the G-S study are given enclosed in paretheses.

As noted in the G-S study, and as suggested above, there is a possible alternative explanation for the G-S Effect: namely, that the subjects may have been attending to the visual material rather than to the auditory material. According to this argument, the subjects might have deluded themselves into reporting subjective clarity in the Matching-slide condition. This possibility was disconfirmed in the G-S study and there is some evidence here too that discounts this explanation (see Appendix to this chapter for details).

In the G-S study, increased covert oral behavior occurred during perceptual clarification, and no real differences in nonoral covert activity were found between the LoI/Matching-slide/Clear condition and the control presentation. Hence, the remaining hypothesis for the present study is that the G-S Effect should be accompanied by increased covert oral behavior, while simultaneous measures of nonoral activity should show no significant increases during perceptual clarification. The integrated EMG measurements (obtained from tongue, lip, arm, and leg placements) were reduced to means for each subject, and these mean values were transformed into ratios (as described by Lykken, Rose, Luther, and Maley, 1966) that correct for individual differences. The ratios were then used to compare covert activity during the G-S Effect (LoI/Matching-slide/Clear condition) with the presentation that controlled for general activation (LoI/Blank-slide/Not Clear condition). As can be clearly seen in Table 6.6, the amplitude of tongue EMG was significantly higher ($t = 2.60$, $p < .05$) when LoI material was accompanied by a matching slide and subjective clarity was signaled (.25) than when LoI passages were accompanied by a blank slide and no clear hearing was reported (.21). Note also that both arm and leg EMG amplitude remained low in both conditions, and did not significantly differ as a function of the two conditions; had the covert activity been

200

due to a general arousal effect, these nonoral measures should have increased with the tongue amplitude. The results presented in Table 6.6 thus indicate that increased covert activity during the G-S effect was localized in the speech region and they confirm that the tongue EMG is generally the most sensitive measure of covert oral behavior.

TABLE 6.6   Mean Ratios of Covert Response Amplitudes for LoI Selections as Functions of Slide Conditions and Signaled Clarity of Spoken Finnish Passages

Measures	Matching Slide Clear	Blank Slide Not clear	t
Tongue EMG	.25	.21	2.60*
Lip EMG	.08	.09	0.56
Arm EMG	.05	.04	0.94
Leg EMG	.01	.01	0.00

*$p < .05$

Since the results of this experiment are essentially consistent with those of the original G-S study, there is good reason to believe that the G-S Effect occurs *even in the absence of semantic information*. Specific auxiliary stimulation (matching slides) facilitated more perceptual clarification than non-specific stimulation (blank slides), thereby discounting the generalized cortical excitation theory (Zwosta and Zenhausern, 1969) *as an explanation of the G-S phenomenon*. Moreover, the absence of meaning content in the visual and auditory materials seems to preclude cerebral representational-level feedback (Osgood's r_M) as mediating the perceptual integration demonstrated *in this study* (if in fact r_M is totally a central process—it *could* be a brain-muscle loop process). The heightened covert oral behavior that accompanied the G-S Effect strongly implicates peripheral feedback mechanisms in the processing of even meaningless linguistic materials. Although the results do suggest *sufficiency* of oral feedback (and hence a peripheral-central loop interpretation of the G-S phenomenon), the design of the present experiment does not permit any conclusion as to the *necessity* of such peripheral feedback in linguistic processing. Feedback from a central representational system may also be shown to be sufficient in planned Experiment III of this series. As discussed in footnote 1 and in Chapter 9, the fact that covert oral behavior accompanies perceptual clarification of both meaningful *and* meaningless material suggests that, while it may have a verbal function, the covert oral response may not itself have a semantic function.

Additional Citations.   Among the other relevant articles that it was not possible to include here, one should especially note the work by Locke and his associates. His research has contributed especially to the development of the hypothesis that the speech musculature participates in internal linguistic processing (see Chapter 9): Locke (1969); Locke (1970a, b); Locke (1971a, b, c); Locke and Fehr (1970a, b); Locke and Fehr (1971); Locke & Fehr (1976); Locke and Ginsburg (1975); Locke and Kutz (1975); and Locke and Locke (1971a, b).

Also of particular interest to us are the following works: Aarons (1971); Adatia and Gehring (1971); Boros (1972) Fair, Schwartz, Friedman, Greenberg, Klerman, and Gardner (1974); Garrity (1975a, b); Inouye and Shimizu (1970); Inouye and Shimizu (1972); Putnoky (1975, 1976); Schwartz (1975); Schwartz, Fair, Greenberg, Friedman, and Klerman (1973); Schwartz, Fair, Greenberg, Mandel, and Klerman (1974); and Szegal (1973).

SUMMARY AND CONCLUSION

The results summarized under column 1 of Table 6.1 lead to the conclusion that covert oral behavior increases over baseline during the covert performance of a wide variety of language tasks. It would appear, from column 3, that increased respiration rate and preferred (writing) arm EMG also increase from baseline during the covert performance of language tasks; however, it has not been established that systematic changes occur in various other measures, and, in fact, the indication is that such behavior as nonpreferred arm EMG and leg EMG do not significantly increase over baseline levels.

Column 2 summarizes rather inconclusive evidence that covert oral behavior may not significantly increase under nonlanguage conditions. In column 4 we note that a number of specific relationships between various subject and experimental variables were established as a function of covert oral behavior. Those relationships are summarized below.

SPECIFIC RELATIONSHIPS (CRITERION 4)

Mechanical Sensing Studies.   Perky (1910): Laryngeal movements occured in 84% of 155 memory images whereas 91% of 214 imagination images were not accompanied by laryngeal activity.

Wyczoikowska (1913): Thinking of words produced tongue responses comparable in shape to hearing the words, but of reduced amplitude.

Golla (1921): Subjects gave similar ascending and descending curves for a measure from the thyroid cartilage for thinking and for overt singing.

Thorson (1925): Tongue movements were greater during a variety of tasks than they were during non-task conditions. Furthermore, distraction systematically increased the amount of tongue activity.

Imagination.   Jacobson (1932): Covert responses were highly localized when evoked as a function of a particular class of stimulus and they occurred in the part of the body that would be used should the response be made overtly instead of "in imagination" (confirmed in part by McGuigan and Straub).

Blumenthal (1959): Maximum magnitude of tongue EMG was significantly greater when thinking of lingual as compared to labial words. Also, motor imagination tasks of licking a postage stamp and sucking a lemon resulted in significantly greater tongue activity than during control conditions (e.g., listening to a bell, hearing and thinking the same words).

Silent Reading. Faaborg-Andersen and Edfeldt (1958): Laryngeal EMG was substantially greater for subjects reading unfamiliar foreign prose (Swedish) than when reading their native language (Danish), but this effect was not present for subjects accustomed to reading the foreign text.

Edfeldt (1960): Laryngeal EMG during silent reading was significantly larger for poor readers than for good readers, for difficult text than for easy text, and for blurred text than for clear text.

McGuigan and Rodier (1968): Silent reading during the auditory presentation of prose and backward prose resulted in a significantly greater amplitude of covert oral behavior than during silence, but reading during white noise does not have that effect.

McGuigan and Bailey (1969b): Tongue and chin EMGs were significantly higher during silent reading and memorization than during two nonlanguage conditions (listening to music and to nothing).

Auditory Hallucinations. McGuigan (1966b): In a schizophrenic, chin EMG and subvocal whisperings significantly increased when hallucinations were reported; more particularly, some of the subvocalizations were auditorally identifiable as part of the content of the overtly reported hallucinations.

Cursive Writing. McGuigan (1970b): Tongue EMG was significantly higher while writing words than while drawing ovals, and it was significantly higher in amplitude for poor writers than for excellent writers.

Learning. Berry and Davis (1960): Rate of verbal learning is associated with increased EMG activity in the head region.

Nocturnal Dreams. Pivik and Dement (1970): Qualities of sleep mentation and phasic events during REM sleep are positively related.

McGuigan and Tanner (1971): Phasic covert oral behavior occurs during linguistic dreams.

Miscellaneous. Bassin and Bein (1961): As the difficulty of a verbal task increased, amplitude of lip EMG increased.

Novikova (1961): As the difficulty of problems increased, tongue EMG proportionately increased.

Sokolov (1967, 1969): Speech muscle EMG increases as the difficulty of a task increases, and decreases as the task becomes more automatic and its solution becomes stereotyped.

Perceptual Clarification. McGuigan, Osgood, and Hadley (1973): Perceptual clarification of meaningful material in the auditory modality occurred as a function of simultaneous matching visual input. The perceptual clarification was accompanied by significant increase in tongue EMG.

McGuigan, Osgood, and Schoonover (in text): Confirmed the above study of perceptual clarification with meaningless auditory and visual input. The perceptual clarification also was accompanied by significant increases in tongue EMG.

Possible Functions of Covert Oral Behavior

In considering the broad range of possible interpretations of the phenomenon of increased covert oral behavior during the silent performance of language tasks, the following five points span the spectrum of interpretations:

1. Such covert behavior has no special significance or consequence in itself—it may be: (a) simply one aspect of a widespread state of heightened bodily arousal, evoked by essentially any form of stimulation; (b) merely "motor leakage" from critical brain processes; and so forth. This interpretation follows from extreme centralist theory which holds that information processing, thinking, and other cognitive processes occur exclusively in the brain (the "Donovan's Brain Theory," McGuigan, 1973a).

2. While the covert response may have no language function, its occurrence may produce neural feedback to the central nervous system which, in turn, evokes some critical brain events, and helps to guide the flow of ongoing central activity. This centralist intepretation thus grants some limited value to peripheral events, but holds that central events are far more significant.

3. A less extreme centralist position holds that each critical central event results in efferent discharge which produces a (peripheral) response. Hebb (1949), for example, hypothesized that the firing of cell assemblies results in (covert or overt) responses. The response, as in Interpretation 2 above, then may set off additional cell assemblies. But, in contrast to Interpretation 2, this theory states that there is a one-to-one correspondence between central and peripheral events; hence, the measurement of a response may be used as an indirect index of the important central ("thought") event (cf. McGuigan, 1966a, p. 295).

4. The covert response is part of an arc in which efferent neural impulses produce a response, which in time sets off afferent impulses back to the brain. Each of the three aspects of this sequence is necessary (though not sufficient) for the performance of language tasks. This is the standard motor theory of thinking (or consciousness), and holds that covert responses serve some critical language function.

5. "Man Thinking Is Simply Man Behaving" (Skinner, 1957, p. 452). This is an extreme peripheralist position in which neurological events (central, afferent, and efferent impulses) are considered psychologically irrelevant or unimportant, and are thus largely ignored. Hence, response events (primarily oral behavior) are both necessary and sufficient for the performance of language tasks; they, in fact, define the "cognitive" process.

To decide among these possible interpretations is, of course, a difficult task. We shall hypothesize that the covert oral response functions in the generation of a phonetic code which is itself not meaningful but which may be responsible for differences in meaning, a model developed in Chapter 9. In the meantime, we shall consider one additional strategy for ascertaining the function of covert oral behavior—attempting to "damp" covert oral behavior to determine the possible effects on information processing.

Interference with Covert Oral Behavior

In the previous section results of the research strategy of studying covert oral behavior as a function of various experimental (and other) conditions were reviewed. In this section we shall summarize and evaluate the results of empirical investigations in which the reverse strategy has been employed, viz., to attempt to eliminate, or otherwise interfere with, covert oral behavior and note any effects on cognitive functioning. Five techniques have been employed to reduce or interfere with normal covert articulation, commonly for the purpose of studying effects on silently performed linguistic activities: (1) distraction, (2) mechanical interference or restraint, (3) anesthetization, (4) voluntary ("conscious") control, and (5) biofeedback from the speech musculature. In considering the following research in which these techniques have been employed, it will be clear that many studies lack methodological sophistication and therefore are mentioned primarily for historical purposes.

THE METHOD OF DISTRACTION

In this method the subject engages in some irrelevant and presumably interfering behavior, such as counting aloud, while silently performing a given cognitive task.

Early Studies. Murray (1967) summarized several early studies, such as Münsterberg's (1890) attempt to observe lists of letters while simultaneously counting aloud. He reported that, as compared to when he overtly spoke the letters, his recall of the letters was reduced by half. This finding was confirmed by T. L. Smith in 1896. W. G. Smith (1895) reported a severe decrement in recall if subjects said "la . . . la . . ." in time to a metronome as matrices of letters were viewed. In 1915 Arnold reported that inhibition of breathing resulted in reduced recall. He inhibited breathing by inserting plugs into the nostrils; hollow plugs permitted breathing under other conditions as a control for the distraction effects due to blocking the nostrils.

Münsterberg's student Breese (1899) had his subjects count while learning nonsense syllables, reporting that learning was thereby detrimentally affected. Secor (1900) attempted to produce articulatory interference by having his subjects recite the alphabet aloud, whistle, sing, or listen to a xylophone while they were silently reading. Based on introspective reports, he concluded that articulatory interference eliminated inner speech. Binet (1903) reported that the recitation of verses did not interfere with thinking in that his subjects were able to understand and answer questions posed during the recitation. Pintner (1913) studied reading speed and comprehension while the subjects repeated numbers aloud and concluded that, with training under such distracting conditions, one may eventually read as effectively with as without interference. Reed (1916) asked whether inner speech facilitates understanding or is merely incidental during thought. His subjects read, wrote, and added while simultaneously repeating "Jack and Jill ran down the hill." For comparison the subjects performed the same tasks without distraction. He reported that the distraction had a debilitating effect for some subjects but not for others. Reed's general conclusion was that inner speech has no important function for reading, writing, or for the additional process.

Meumann (1917) reported that stimultaneous counting while silently reading made reading difficult but not impossible.

Thorson (1925) had her subjects engage in a variety of thought tasks such as silently reciting the alphabet, thinking "experimental psychology," and performing mental multiplication during distracting conditions (singing "ah" while tapping the table with a finger). She found that distraction increased the amount of tongue activity during the performance of the thought tasks, relative to amount of tongue activity when the tasks were performed under normal (non-distracting) conditions.

Recent Studies.   Zhinkin's (1960, 1964) subjects tapped their fingers with a constant rhythm while solving problems, the notion being that there would be interference with the variable rhythm of speech movements of inner speech. For certain problems and certain subjects there was strong interference, with less for others. The effect of interference gradually lessened for all with practice.

Robinson (1964) had children read silently without distraction, overtly, and overtly while masking the sound of their voices. Practice while overtly reading led to significantly faster increase in speed of reading than practice with overt reading during masking of the voice. These results would suggest that reduction of the feedback from the voice reduces reading speed. Alternatively, there may be merely a distracting effect of the masking.

McGuigan and Rodier (1968) had subjects rest, then engage in a listening condition, and finally read silently while the listening condition continued. There were four listening conditions: (1) silence, (2) non-matching auditory prose, (3) prose played backwards, and (4) white noise. Chin EMG and breathing rate significantly increased while listening to prose (forward or backward), but not under the other listening conditions, indicating that these response patterns may have a function during speech perception. As to the effects of auditory stimulation, it was concluded that the auditory presentation of prose and of prose played backwards significantly increased amplitude of covert oral behavior, relative to reading in the absence of external stimulation; white noise does not have this effect. It was concluded that the increased covert oral behavior perhaps facilitates the linguistic processing in the presence of (specifically linguistic) auditory interference; or alternatively that the subjects may simultaneously respond to the nonmatching visual and auditory language stimuli, resulting in an overall summative response rate that is higher than for either type of stimulation alone.

Distraction and Interference-Restraint Methods Compared. Adams, McIntyre, and Thorsheim (1969) studied impaired auditory feedback and impaired proprioceptive feedback as methods for interfering with short-term memory. To impair auditory feedback, white noise was delivered through earphones to prevent the subject from hearing the sound of his own voice when pronouncing a tetragram aloud. To impair proprioceptive feedback, each subject was required to clamp the tongue between the teeth and hold a deep breath. There was also a combined condition of impaired auditory and proprioceptive feedback in which the subject experienced the white noise and the tongue-breath methods together. These distraction-interference methods were used during acquisition, while recall was normal under test conditions. Poorer recall was found for all feedback-impaired conditions than for a control condition. Subjects who had auditory or proprioceptive impairment had equivalent recall, while subjects with combined impairment had the lowest recall. Hence, interference with feedback, regardless of the type studied here, reduced retention. The authors cite three other studies in which noise did (or tended to) interfere with recall using a short term memory paradigm (Dallett, 1964; Murdock, 1967; Murray, 1965).

In the discussion of the following work reported by Sokolov, both the method of distraction and the method of mechanical restraint are considered. For continuity we shall include both methods here but the results for the method of restraint will again be mentioned in the next section. Sokolov (1956) compared four interference techniques during thinking: (1) pressing the lips together and holding the tongue between the teeth, (2) simultaneously reciting a verse, (3) simultaneously repeating "lia" and (4) listening to sentences uttered by the experimenter. He concluded that none of the methods were effective in interfering with cognitive functioning.

Sokolov (1972) cited the conclusions of Blonskii that listening to speech was difficult during the enunciation of verses. Sokolov employed four test series as subjects listened to texts while they simultaneously (1) recited verses, (2) counted, (3) recited verses learned at different stages of the study, and (4) freely listened. The instructions were to reproduce the contents of each text later. Simultaneous recitation of verses interfered with the understanding and memorization of the texts read, though as the recitation of the verses became more automatic, comprehension of the speech increased. For the counting test series, the subjects were able to understand and memorize what they heard; Sokolov's interpretation was that counting was more automatic than recitation of verses; hence the subjects could still process the materials heard. Other results are not of immediate relevance.

Sokolov (1972) also reported some experiments carried out by M.B. Makhalevskaya in which subjects performed arithmetical calculations under the following conditions: (1) with free articulation, performing the calculations silently; (2) with lips and tongue clamped between the teeth; (3) while simultaneously reciting a poem; (4) while pressing the hand on a rubber balloon. Clamping the tongue and lips had a small short-term negative effect on arithmetical problem solving, with a larger amount of interference produced by the recitation of the poem.

With regard to the method of distraction, Sokolov concluded in general that extraneous motor speech and verbal-auditory stimuli have a strong adverse effect on the performance of mental tasks; however, with repetition, the interference effect of the external verbal stimuli decreases so that mental tasks can be performed as competently as under control conditions in which articulation is free. He further concluded that sometimes extraneous verbal materal does not have a negative effect on mental operations, and occasionally it accelerates them.

Conclusion.   Many of the studies reported in this section are methodologically unsound in that objective data are often lacking. Further, the assumption that external distracting stimuli interfere with or eliminate the covert oral behavior required for the performance of the primary cognitive task is probably false. Rather than blocking out covert oral behavior, the subjects probably respond to both the primary and the distracting tasks by increasing the amount of their speech muscle activity. That is, it is quite probable that subjects continue to process the primary cognitive tasks covertly, while adding additional covert responses to process the presumably distracting tasks. This seems reasonable when one recognizes that covert oral responses are extremely short in duration, often as short as several milliseconds, so that covert responding in any given muscle locus can occur to the "distracting task" in the intervals between the critical processing responses to the primary tasks. If the subjects in fact do learn to do this, they therefore improve performance on the task, as noted directly above in Sokolov's conclusion.

Another possibility is that some muscle fibers can respond to the primary task while another set responds simultaneously to the distracting task, so that cognitive processing of two activities can proceeed "in parallel," as is assumed in Chapter 9. The findings of McGuigan and Rodier (1968) are relevant here, viz., that the auditory presentation of prose and of the same prose played backward during silent reading led to significantly greater amplitude of covert oral behavior than merely reading in silence. The greater amount of muscle activity during the "distracting condition" may reflect an increased rate and number of muscle fibers responding, some to one task, others to the second task. Their further finding that the external presentation of white noise during silent reading does not lead to a significantly greater increase of covert oral behavior than does reading in silence suggests that the covert oral responding was actually linguistic in nature. Sokolov (1972) suggested a similar possibility—namely, that when there is presumed interference of one muscle group, other muscle groups not participating at a given instant may, in effect, take on the processing load. Only in the McGuigan and Rodier research, however, was direct EMG recording of the musculature made to ascertain the effects of the experimental conditions on covert oral behavior. We are left with the possibility that speech muscle fibers can participate in the processing of different kinds of externally presented information, perhaps by an increase in the rate of firing some fibers and/or an increase in the number of fibers participating in the processing activity.

Finally, the lack of consistent conclusions among the experimenters leads to the general inference that the method of distraction has not been shown to detrimentally affect cognitive processing of the primary task, or, at the most, that detriments which occur are temporary.

MECHANICAL RESTRAINT

In this method, the experimenter attempts to interfere with or minimize covert oral behavior by restricting action of the speech musculature, principally of the tongue and/or lips.

Early Studies. Barlow (1928), for instance, used the method of mechanical restraint by having the subjects hold a pencil crosswise between their teeth, thus restraining or interfering with normal movements of the tongue. He found that verbal learning was less efficient with mechanical restraint than when full articulation was possible. A variation of the mechanical restraint method is the "force" method, which had been recommended for "eliminating silent speech" to supposedly improve silent reading. Cole (1938), for example, suggested that one keep the lips and jaws apart and hold the tongue against the bottom of the mouth by means of two fingers, a ruler or large eraser. (Presumably a large pickle would do as well, if the subject did not eat it.) Durrell (1940) advocated use of the force method by having subjects bite on a pencil or paper clip while reading. Gates (1947) suggested that the subject attempt to keep the tongue still by pushing it hard against the roof of the mouth, by compressing the lips, by holding the tongue between the teeth, or by putting a clean spoon or lollipop in the mouth. For other advocates of the "force" method see Bond and Tinker (1957).

Underwood (1964) reported a general conclusion from several studies (Breese, 1899; Colvin and Meyer, 1909; Mould, Treadwell, and Washburn, 1915; and Smith, 1896) that inhibition of articulation causes learning to be less efficient. However, in another study he reported by Henmon (1912) there was no effect on learning.

Underwood (1964) inserted a wooden tongue blade crosswise in the mouth of the subject with lips closed over the blade. He found no evidence that this technique affects rate of learning. Cole and Maltzman (1969) reported studies by the Soviets Nazarova (1952), Kadochkin (1955), and Luria (1962) in which the tongue and lips held between the teeth interfered with verbal cognitive operations. In Nazarova's research, the spelling proficiency of young children was reduced when holding their tongues between their teeth. Luria's aphasic patient, who had damage to the left fronto-temporoparietal region, could spell words correctly when his tongue was free but had difficulty when he held his tongue in his teeth.

More Recent Studies.   As reported in the previous section, Sokolov (1956, 1972) discussed results when subjects placed the tongue and lips between the teeth. His general conclusion was that restraining speech movements of the lips and tongue had an insignificant effect (often none at all) on the performance of mental tasks for adults; however, restraint did have a noticable negative effect for children. Further, as cognitive actions became automatic the interference ceased to have a negative influence and may even have become a positive factor that accelerated thought. Apparently adults can better learn to adjust to a negative influence than can children. Sokolov pointed out that while articulation may be restrained, it is still concealed and implemented through imperceptible movements of the speech apparatus which no mechanical interference technique is capable of inhibiting.

McGuigan and Keller (1962) disrupted normal muscular activity by mechanically vibrating the speech, arm, and hand musculature continuously while children solved problems from the Binet Intelligence Tests. Relative to control groups they found a significantly: (1) greater latency of responses for subjects who received arm-hand vibration than for those who did not; (2) greater response latency for subjects who received laryngeal vibration than for those who did not; and (3) longer latency of response for subjects who had received both laryngeal and arm vibration than for those who received only laryngeal or arm vibration.

Colle (1972) inserted a tongue depressor crosswise between the teeth of children during a short-term memory task, with no sizeable impairment of performance.

In our laboratory, we recently completed a study on the mechanical interference of covert oral behavior during silent reading.[2] In this study nine female college students silently read under three counterbalanced conditions: (1) normally, with no interference; (2) when the tongue was held between the teeth; and (3) with the tongue wrapped around a tongue depressor that was inserted across the mouth between the teeth. Prior to each reading session the subjects relaxed for baseline recording. The condition for the baseline recording depended upon the reading condition to follow so that if the subject was going to read with the tongue between the teeth, she attempted to relax during baseline with the tongue between the teeth; similarly if she was going to read with a tongue depressor inserted, baseline recording was taken under that condition and, finally, if the subject was going to read naturally (with no interference) she relaxed for baseline under that condition. For each of the three sessions each subject read, in counterbalanced order, equated passages of prose, and her reading rate was determined. On completion of reading, a 10-item multiple choice test for comprehension was administered for each passage.

Mean integrated amplitude values for EMG, quantified as in McGuigan (1967), are presented in Table 6.7 as a function of the various reading conditions. Note that the amplitude of the tongue during baseline rest without interference was 3.7 μV and that it increased to 6.8 μV during silent reading; the difference of 3.1 μV with an asterisk indi-

TABLE 6.7   Mean EMG Amplitude (μV) for Each Response Measure as a Function of three Silent Reading Conditions.

	Condition								
	Without Interference			Tongue-Between-the-Teeth			Tongue-Depressor		
Covert Response	Baseline	Read-ing	Dif-ference	Baseline	Read-ing	Dif-ference	Baseline	Read-ing	Dif-ference
Tongue	3.7	6.8	3.1*	12.1*	13.3	1.2	9.7*	13.0	3.3*
Lips	10.8	15.1	4.3*	6.1	10.6	4.5*	8.8	10.1	1.4*
Chin	8.5	11.4	2.9*	7.7	9.2	1.4*	8.6	10.0	1.4*
Right arm	5.3	5.6	0.3*	5.3	5.6	0.3*	5.4	5.9	0.4
Left arm	1.8	1.9	0.1	2.3	2.2	−0.1	2.2	2.1	−0.1

* $p < .05$

[2] My research assistants, Billy Jefferson and Regis Magyar, assisted with this study and with the anesthetization study reported on page 215. The data were reanalyzed for confirmation by Marilyn Kaplinski.

cates that the increase during silent reading over baseline was statistically significant.

Tongue amplitude was noticeably higher during baseline recording for the two interference conditions than while reading normally; in particular, the values of 12.1 μV and 9.7 μV were significantly larger than the normal resting value of 3.7 μV (t = 2.49 and 2.34, p < .05, respectively). It is especially interesting that the amplitude of tongue EMG increased even from the high baseline values to silent reading during the conditions of interference, the increase of 3.3 μV with the tongue depressor being significant (t = 2.60). Lip and chin EMG were not noticeably affected by two interference conditions. Baseline resting values were similar (and not significantly different) for both lips and chin under all three conditions and both significantly increased under all three reading conditions. As is commonly found (see Chapter 7), right arm EMG significantly increased under two reading conditions, in contrast to left arm EMG, which did not.

To determine whether interference with covert oral behavior during silent reading affected reading proficiency, consider the two measures of reading rate (The Pearson Product Moment Correlation between the two measures of reading rate was .74) and one measure of reading comprehension in Table 6.8. There were no significant differences in reading rate, measured by words per minute, or in comprehension among the three conditions. Reading rate measured by number of end-of-line eye movements per minute (cf. McGuigan and Pinkney, 1973) when reading with tongue between the teeth was significantly faster than when reading with the tongue depressor; no other differences were significant.

TABLE 6.8   Reading Proficiency as a Function of Silent Reading Condition

Reading Condition	Mean Number of End-of-Line Eye-Movements per Minute	Mean Number of Words per Minute	Mean Number of Errors per Ten Questions
Without interference	20.4	198.1	3.0
Tongue between the teeth	22.1	226.2	3.3
Tongue depressor	19.1	214.3	3.2

It thus appears that the two methods of interference studied raised the baseline level of tongue EMG, relative to normal, nonrestrained baseline level. Neither condition of reading with tongue restrained resulted in a significant decrease in any of the three measures of covert oral behavior, relative to reading without tongue restraint; we cannot, therefore, conclude that the restraining techniques depressed activity of the oral musculature. Nor can we conclude that the interference techniques affected reading proficiency, since the restraining techniques were not accompanied by reading rate or comprehension values significantly different from those without restraint. The suggestion, in fact, is that tongue restraint was effective in raising general baseline (tonic) resting level, quite as one would expect, but it did not decrease covert oral behavior during silent reading, so that the speech musculature still functioned for cognitive processing "on top" of the high tonic baseline level. Finally, as would also be expected, the continued presence of covert oral behavior during silent reading even with tongue restraint allowed for normal cognitive functioning (as indicated by the lack of a significant difference in reading rate and comprehension during restraint relative to reading during non-restraint).

There is however one somewhat tenuous relationship that might be pointed out for further study: (1) baseline tongue EMG for reading with the tongue between the teeth was larger than for reading with the tongue depressor, but not significantly so; (2) reading with the tongue depressor showed a significantly greater increase over baseline for tongue EMG than for reading with the tongue between the teeth; (3) reading with the tongue between the teeth led to a significantly faster reading rate by the eye measure than reading with the tongue depressor; (4) reading with the tongue between the teeth had a slightly (not significantly) lower comprehension measure. There thus seem to be hints of differences in behavior due to the two interference conditions, but it is difficult to interpret what these differences might mean. The possibility exists that the tongue between the teeth led to more rapid reading with less covert oral behavior and less comprehension than did the tongue depressor condition.

Conclusion. Methodological difficulties with the restraint paradigm prevent any firm conclusions. For example, if it should be shown that cognitive proficiency is reduced when there is mechanical interference of the oral musculature, one still does not know whether this is due to distraction per se or to its actual interference with covert oral behavior—vibrating the knees or restraining the toes may have a similar depressing effect. In any event, the literature summarized above makes it clear that the results are not uniform as far as cognitive interference is concerned.

Another difficulty is that if you restrain one speech group muscle, other groups can still function,[3] as shown in our laboratory work discussed above. Only in that study was there an attempt to independently verify through electromyography that covert oral behavior was interfered with. Our general conclusion was that, instead of reducing covert oral behavior, the methods of restraint actually increased baseline tongue EMG amplitude; further increases during silent reading still oc-

[3] For example, even if the tongue were "completely restrained," processing could still continue in redundant channels involving the lips, the jaw, the larynx, etc. Furthermore, the techniques we studied in the research reported above in our laboratory indicate that "restraining" actually increases amount of muscle activity.

curred, thus allowing cognitive processing to continue despite the application of an interference method.

In summary, it cannot be said that the method of mechanical restraint is effective in disturbing normal processing in the speech musculature, or in reducing cognitive proficiency.

ANESTHETIZATION

In this method the attempt is to reduce or eliminate functioning of some part or parts of the peripheral speech apparatus through topical application or injection of an anesthetic to produce nerve blocking. Although most research of this type is of more recent origin, Dodge (1896) anesthetized his tongue and lips, using a 20% cocaine solution, and reported that his inner speech was not disturbed. Consequently, he reasoned that inner speech is independent of peripheral elements.

Effects on Language Production. McCroskey (1958) reported that anesthetization of the oral region with Xylocaine resulted in decreased levels of overt articulatory accuracy. Ringel and Steer (1963) administered Xylocaine to the oral region by the topical and by the nerve blocking technique and reported that the resulting deprivation in the tactal sense produced auditory alterations of the speech output. Schliesser and Coleman (1968) anesthetized the oral region of their subjects by performing a bilateral mandibular nerve block and a nerve block in the area of the incisive foramen of the anterior hard palate, employing Xylocaine HOL 2%. They also applied a topical anesthetic to the entire surface of the hard palate. Their report was that, although articulation was somewhat less adequate in the absence of auditory or oral tactical sensation, a degree of accuracy in articulation was maintained. Abbs (1973) selectively anesthetized the gamma efferent nerve fibers that innervated the muscle spindles of the jaw. He found that with this type of sensory feedback blockage there was a gross loss of fine positional control with a reduction in jaw velocity and in jaw acceleration, and the entire temporal pattern of jaw movements was significantly altered. The muscle spindle receptors, he believed, are important for bringing about precise finely coordinated neuromotor control of the speech musculature. Sussman (1970) topically applied 10% Xylocaine on the anterior half of the tongue including the sides and the undersurface. He found that the anesthetic alone did not produce interference with overt speech, but that the anesthetic in conjunction with delayed auditory feedback did produce a disruptive effect.

Scott applied a local anesthetic to block sensation from surface receptors in the tongue, palate, lips, teeth, and oral mucosa and reported minimal effects on speech intelligibility; however, the anesthetic impaired the "naturalness" of the speech produced (in MacNeilage and MacNeilage, 1973).

Scott and Ringel (1971) reported that bilateral mandibular, infraorbital, posterior palatine, and nasal nasopalatine nerve block injections of

2% Xylocaine eliminated sensation from the surface receptors in all supraglottal structures except for the pharynx and the posterior third of the tongue. Gammon, Smith, Daniloff, and Kim (1971) produced bilateral infra-orbital blocks that affected the anterior and middle superior alveolar nerves, thus apparently anesthetizing the upper lip, alveolar ridge, and anterior maxillary teeth by means of a 2% Xylocaine solution. This procedure did not produce a great amount of articulatory interference; the most disruption occurred as a function of anesthesia and a masking condition.

Borden, Harris, and Catena (1972) attempted to produce a nerve block on the lingual nerve without affecting the motor fibers of the mylohoid nerve. Electromyographic monitoring indicated that muscles which were innervated by motor fibers from the blocked nerve were consistently inactive. On the other hand those muscles which are innervated by the sensory fibers from the blocked nerve, and those muscles which should be independent of the blocked nerve, were active to an inconsistent extent depending upon where the EMG electrodes were placed and upon individual differences between subjects.

Galzigna, Manani, Mammano, Gasparetto, and Deana (1972) recorded changes in EMG activity from a dog's flexor radialis muscle induced by nerve stimulation under the condition of procaine administration. EMG levels were recorded during the "fast evolutionary phase" and the recovery phase. Anesthetization with procaine amide resulted in an EMG block about 2 min after its administration. In the "fast evolutionary phase" the twitch showed little decrease in frequency and the tetanic response progressively faded. No tetanic facilitation occurred, and during recovery the twitch became normal.

Effects on Language Comprehension. Apparently the only attempt to date to interfere with speech perception or comprehension was in our laboratory, where the effects of topical application of lidocaine to the tongue and lips on silent reading proficiency and EMG levels were studied. For this study we were fortunate to have the cooperation of 12 right-handed male and female college students. The general procedures and the specific materials reported by McGuigan and Winstead (1974) were followed here, except that certain modifications were necessary to study the effects of the drug, as discussed below. Briefly, there was first a nondrug baseline recording period, after which electrodes were removed from the tongue and lips. Then, for half of the subjects a 5% lidocaine solution was topically applied only to the surface of the tongue, and a placebo consisting of the lidocaine solvent was applied only to the lips. For the remaining (counterbalanced) subjects lidocaine was topically placed only on the lips and the placebo was applied only to the tongue.

Following administration of the drug, electrodes were replaced and three sets of slides were shown to the subjects in counterbalanced order, a resting baseline condition preceding each set. The slides contained: (1) bilabial words which, if overtly spoken, would maximally engage the lips; (2) lingual alveolar words which, if overtly spoken, would maximally engage the tongue, and (3) meaningless items equated for light reflection and size. During stimulus presentation the subjects silently memorized the items, then silently rehearsed them for a 20-sec period, and finally wrote the words on paper. The maximum amplitude of each EMG tracing was measured during 700 msec periods which were selected at random from each baseline, slide presentation, and rehearsal period. The mean EMG values for each condition were computed for each subject, and group means are entered in Table 6.9.

TABLE 6.9   Mean Maximum Amplitude of Tongue and Lip EMG (μV) During Rest with and without Lidocaine

Lidocaine on Tongue	Resting Baseline Condition	
	Predrug	Postdrug
Tongue EMG	44	41
Lip EMG	43	44
Lidocaine on Lips		
Tongue EMG	72	75
Lip EMG	51	56

The first question we shall consider is whether or not the application of lidocaine affected oral EMG. In the first data column of Table 6.9 we can study the mean maximum amplitude values during rest before the drug was applied, and compare those values with the mean of the three baseline conditions that were prior to each experimental treatment after the drug was applied. For instance, mean (pre-drug) tongue EMG was 44 μV during rest, and 41 μV during rest when lidocaine was applied to the tongue. None of the 4 differences between pre-drug and post-drug conditions in Table 6.9 approached significance. Though we must recognize that there is the necessary confound in this comparison due to pre- and post-drug order effects, it seems likely that application of the 5% lidocaine solution to these two oral regions did not affect EMG amplitude during rest.

Before application of the electrodes, subjects had been asked to read aloud a single passage; they then read an equated passage at the end of the experiment. Three raters judged the number of disfluencies (errors of mispronounciation, slurring of words, deletions, and the like) for each (tape recorded) reading. The mean number of speech errors detected by the three raters did not significantly change from before to after the administration of the drug. In particular, when lidocaine was applied to the tongue, the mean number of errors detected was a 3.0 before vs. 2.7 after the drug had been applied; with lidocaine on the lips, the relative number of errors was 3.4 vs. 2.2. Again, although there is a necessary order effect that must temper the conclusion, it seems that the drug did not adversely affect the overt speech processes.

Mean post-drug EMG resting values were subtracted from mean values during stimulus presentation and during rehearsal, allowing us to study increases in covert behavior from baseline as a function of presentation and rehearsal of the bilabial and lingual-alveolar items. The resulting group means are presented in Table 6.10. With lidocaine on the tongue, presentation of the lingual-alveolar materials produced a significant (p < .05) increase in tongue EMG, while presentation of the bilabial items produced an increase which was nonsignificant. Tongue EMG also increased significantly under the two rehearsal conditions.

With lidocaine on the tongue, lip EMG increased significantly only for the bilabial conditions during stimulus presentation and during rehearsal. Other response changes when lidocaine was on the tongue were generally small and nonsignificant. When lidocaine was applied to the lips, tongue EMG increased significantly during all four conditions. Lip EMG also increased during all four conditions, but never significantly.

TABLE 6.10   Mean EMG Response Increases (μV) from Post-drug Resting for Bilabial and Lingual Alveolar Words

	Stimulus Presentation		Rehearsal	
	Bilabial	Lingual	Bilabial	Lingual
Lidocaine on Tongue				
Tongue EMG	6.6	6.0*	20.2*	15.5*
Lip EMG	12.7*	6.5	14.2*	4.0
Right Arm EMG	7.7	−1.0	9.2	2.0
Left Arm EMG	2.5	3.5	4.7*	−2.7
Right Leg EMG	0.0	−1.0	.7	−.2
Lidocaine on Lips				
Tongue EMG	31.2*	23.8*	38.7*	47.0*
Lip EMG	3.2	.2	10.5	5.3
Right Arm EMG	1.3	−1.6	9.2	6.8
Left Arm EMG	3.3	2.8*	−2.1	4.2
Right Leg EMG	−2.0	−.7	2.2*	−.5

* $p < .05$

It is interesting to note that when lidocaine was placed on the tongue, amplitude of tongue EMG was lower than when lidocaine was placed on the lips for all four entries in Table 6.10. However, none of these differences was significant under any experimental condition. Lip EMG was lower when lidocaine was on the lips than when it was on the tongue for three of the four comparisons, the largest difference being for the bilabial presentation where the relative amplitudes were 3.2 versus 12.7 μV. However, as with the comparison of tongue EMG with and without lidocaine on the tongue, none of these lip EMG differences were significant. Nevertheless, the direction of the means in seven of the eight comparisons does suggest a possible depressing effect of lidocaine on EMG values at the location where it is applied.

We shall now consider possible effects of lidocaine within the paradigm reported by McGuigan and Winstead (1974). The results of their study indicated that when subjects processed bilabial material, covert oral behavior in the lip region was relatively heightened; similarly, when subjects processed lingual-alveolar material, covert oral behavior in the tongue region was relatively heightened. This led to the conclusion that there is a discriminative relationship between the phonemic system and class of covert oral behavior. Note from Table 6.10 that when lidocaine was on the tongue, tongue EMG significantly increased during presentation of the lingual-alveolar material, but not during the presentation of the bilabial material. Lip EMG increased significantly only for the bilabial presentation, and not during the presentation of the lingual material. During rehearsal, tongue EMG increased significantly while silently processing both kinds of materials, whereas lip EMG increased significantly only for the bilabial rehearsal condition. These results are in general agreement with the discriminative relationships reported by McGuigan and Winstead; however, by themselves they do not indicate any particular effect of the lidocaine.

The results are somewhat more complicated when lidocaine was placed on the lips. Then, tongue EMG significantly increased for all four conditions; the increase was larger for the two bilabial conditions than for the lingual conditions. One possible interpretation is that lidocaine placed on the tongue *might* have had some debilitating effect; being a very strong muscle, however, the tongue still could function relatively normally. With lidocaine on the lips, a depressing effect on the weaker lip muscle forced the tongue to take on a greater share of the information-processing load.

These results indicate that the topical application of 5% lidocaine still allows the speech muscle to function adequately during internal information processing. However, this preliminary experiment using EMG as the dependent variable should be followed up with more extensive investigation.

Conclusion. A major difficulty with studies summarized in this section is that relatively few have featured extensive electromyographical monitoring of the various oral regions; thorough objective testing of cognitive proficiency during the silent performance of a linguistic task has also been lacking. Furthermore, because of the great complexity of the speech musculature and of the afferent and efferent neural systems, it would be technically difficult (if not impossible) to paralyze all of the speech musculature while maintaining an otherwise normally functioning human being. Partial paralysis would still allow the remaining musculature to function covertly, allowing the remaining functioning muscle to maintain cognitive processing at a normal level. Thus, we do not have sufficient data to conclude that anesthetization of selected parts of the oral musculature reduces cognitive functioning.

VOLUNTARY ("CONSCIOUS") SUPPRESSION OF SPEECH MUSCULATURE

Studies. In this technique subjects are merely instructed to perform or restrain a given speech muscle act. Bird and Beers (1933) instructed subjects to read silently with "maximum inner speech" (articulating every word with lip and tongue movements) and "minimum inner speech" (suppressing articulation). The maximum inner speech condition was said to produce poor reading, leading to the conclusion that an increase in inner speech decreased reading rate. Actually, this result was predictable, since in normal reading, the tongue and lip movements which occur are highly efficient, and these would certainly be slowed by intentionally accentuating the lip and tongue movements. In the minimum inner speech condition, the subjects were free to achieve their normal level of efficiency, yielding normal reading performance.[4]

Gates (1947) suggested that silent speech could be reduced by keeping the tongue still—pushing it hard against the roof of the mouth while compressing the lips. Fryer (1941) reported that the conscious suppression of articulation was detrimental to performance in adding. Bond and Tinker (1957) suggested informing subjects of the supposed negative effects of silent speech on reading proficiency and encouraging them to avoid silent speech as much as possible. A variation of this "information method" is when special training is given to reduce or eliminate covert oral behavior during silent reading. For example, O'Brien (1921) had one group of subjects perform exercises to eliminate silent speech during silent reading, although he found that this group did not differ in reading proficiency from a normally treated group. McDade (1937) had his pupils follow the method of "nonoral reading" in which the pupils read silently (instead of overtly) from their first day of school. McDade concluded that the nonoral method led to superior reading ability, compared to that of pupils taught "normally." A very obvious problem is the "Hawthorne effect" which probably occurred due to the special stimulation provided by the teachers and to the use of special teaching materials produced by McDade for the nonoral group, thus calling any positive conclusion into serious question.

Conclusion. The general methodological unsoundness of the studies cited, including obvious confounds, lack of objective measures of cogni-

---

[4] Though not directly concerned with speech muscle, R. C. Davis (1939) reported that instructions to keep the right arm relaxed during mental work reduced EMG activity in the three bodily areas being monitored (both arms and the leg) and also reduced the amount of work output.

tive proficiency, and lack of EMG monitoring to assess the effects of instruction on the oral musculature, renders the value of this technique highly questionable.

SPEECH MUSCLE BIOFEEDBACK

Studies. The strategy here is to transduce electromyographic signals from the speech musculature so that they can be heard by the subject, who is engaged in silent reading. One can thus employ the external representation of one's own speech muscle activity to monitor the amplitude of covert oral behavior. The task is to use the biofeedback signal to reduce the amplitude of covert oral behavior so that any effects on reading proficiency could be studied by the experimenter (McGuigan, 1967, 1971). Our data indicate that, while subjects were able to employ the auditory feedback signal to reduce the amplitude of covert oral behavior during silent reading, the effect is not permanent, i.e., when the feedback signal is removed, the amplitude of covert oral behavior returns to baseline level. Although Hardyck, Petrinovich, and Ellsworth (1966) concluded that the heightened speech muscle activity during silent reading could be permanently eliminated within 5 minutes of "treatment" (sic), no systematic data were reported to substantiate their conclusion. In a somewhat sounder study,[5] Hardyck and Petrinovich (1970) did conclude that reduced amplitude of laryngeal EMG affected reading performance. Relative to two groups who did not receive laryngeal feedback, feedback subjects did less well on comprehension of the difficult material, leading Hardyck and Petrinovich to conclude that ". . . subvocal speech . . . is a useful stimulus input capable of mediating a cognitive response" (p. 651).

These and other speech muscle biofeedback studies are also discussed in Chapter 4 and earlier in Chapter 6.

Conclusion. Since available results to date indicate that speech muscle activity has not been more than temporarily reduced with the biofeedback technique, it is not possible to ascertain the long-term effects on cognitive processing of such reduction. However, the method itself is obtrusive. When the biofeedback signal is present and covert oral behavior is thereby reduced, the signal itself is a distracting influence. Consequently, even if experimentation had been reported as reducing cognitive efficiency, we would not know whether it was due to the reduced amplitude of covert oral behavior or to the distracting (interfering) effect of the external feedback signal.

GENERAL CONCLUSION

None of the methods for reducing or interfering with covert oral behavior during the silent performance of cognitive tasks have been shown to be effective in actually reducing or interfering with covert oral

---

[5] For an incisive methodological critique of the Hardyck and Petrinovich work, see Wells (1976).

behavior, or in affecting cognitive efficiency in performing the primary task. In the typical non-medical psychology laboratory, the most promising possibility for damping covert oral behavior (without the severe and extensive disruption of normal functioning that extensive nerve blocking would entail) would be to topically apply Lidocaine throughout the oral cavity. This would include especially the entire accessible surface of the tongue and the lips; for this, concentration of Lidocaine at least as high as the 10% concentration used by Sussman (1970) should be employed. Nevertheless, at the present primitive level of technological development, the general strategy of hampering covert oral behavior is not promising. It seems unlikely that efforts to understand the function of covert oral behavior during information processing will be sizeably advanced in the immediate future through this strategy. Other approaches should thus be given a higher priority. On the basis of available data, we will consider the function of covert oral language behavior in detail in Chapter 9. For now we should turn to an assessment of covert nonoral language responses.

Appendix[6]

With regard to the question of interpretation raised on page 200 of this chapter, to the effect that the subjects in the Finnish experiment might have been reading, rather than listening, the following points indicate that they were in fact following instructions to listen.

(1) It was previously shown that signal clarity was reported in the HiI/Nonmatching-slide passages very often (80%), just as for the HiI/Matching-slide passages (100%); much less clarity was signaled for the LoI conditions (viz., 53% and 15%). Had the subjects been reading, and not listening, the signaled clarity should have been nearly the same for both HiI and LoI material. (2) It will be recalled that subjects signaled clarity in the LoI/Matching-slide condition significantly more often than in the LoI/Nonmatching-slide passages. If they had been deluding themselves into clear hearing by reading the slides, they should have continued the delusion in the Nonmatching-slide condition and reported clarity there. In fact, only two subjects reported any clarity at all when the slides did not match the auditory material, and that was only 15% of the time. Most often, the subjects signaled no clarity at all during the LoI/Nonmatching slide presentations, and their very low recognition scores (4% correct) support that they did in fact not hear clearly (Table 6.2). (3) If the subjects had not been attending to the spoken passages, then their recognition of that material should not have been as high as it was (40% correct) for the HiI/Nonmatching-slide condition; note that this is nearly the same as the recognition of HiI/Matching-slide material, again indicating that subjects were listening and not reading. (4) As can be seen in Table 6.11 the overall recognition scores for the HiI/Nonmatching-slide condition were about the same for visual material

[6] Addition to the Gilbert and Sullivan Experiment discussed on page 200.

(34% correct) as for auditory material (36% correct). During the LoI/ Nonmatching-slide presentations, however, the recognition of visual materials (23% correct) was significantly higher than for auditory materials (4% correct) presented in the same condition ($t = 3.61, p < .05$). These differences indicate that, during Nonmatching-slide presentations, an interaction occurred between intelligibility of spoken passages and the type of materials presented (i.e., visual or auditory). Apparently, during the difficult LoI/Nonmatching-slide condition (when subjects signaled clarity only 15% of the time), subjects paid more attention to the slide than to the auditory material in an attempt to facilitate clear hearing. This seems plausible since the visual materials in the Matching-slide presentations *do* facilitate subjective clarity of the auditory material.

TABLE 6.11   Recognition Scores for Visual and Auditory Materials (Percentage of Items Correct) Presented During Nonmatching-Slide Condition

Subject No.	Items from Visual Presentations		Items from Auditory Presentations	
	Hil (N=8)[a] (%)	Lol (N=8) (%)	Hil (N=4) (%)	Lol (N=4) (%)
1	38	25	50	00
2	25	00	25	00
3	00	38	75	00
4	25	12	00	00
5	50	12	50	00
6	75	38	25	25
7	25	38	25	00
Means	34	23	36	4

[a] Indicates number of possible correct items.

A comparison of covert activity during the LoI/Nonmatching-slide/ Not-clear presentations with the covert activity during the control (LoI/ Blank-slide/Not-clear presentations) is a further test of the localization of covert activity in the speech region during the G-S Effect. Increased covert oral activity *without* concomitant increases in nonoral measures *during the LoI/Nonmatching-slide/Not-clear condition* would place the validity of the G-S Effect in serious doubt; such a finding would mean that increased covert activity was localized in the speech region regardless of whether matching or nonmatching slides were presented. If, however, increases in oral *and* nonoral measures were found, the heightened covert activity would be indicative of a general arousal effect, and the results suggest that this effect does, indeed, occur: When LoI material was accompanied by nonmatching slides and no subjective clarity was reported, mean ratios of covert response amplitudes of tongue (.24), arm (.06) and leg (.02) EMGs were higher than when LoI material was accompanied by a blank slide and no clear hearing was reported; the amplitude of lip EMG was the same (.09) in both conditions. Although these differences were not significant, covert oral *and* nonoral response amplitudes increased *concomitantly* during a condition (LoI/Non-matching-slide/Not-clear) which, as previously discussed, was difficult for the subjects. Thus it seems reasonable to suppose that, during this demanding condition, a general arousal effect occurred as subjects shifted their attention to the visual materials in an attempt to facilitate clear hearing of the auditory passages.

7

Covert Nonoral Behavior: Somatic Responses

I. Methodological Criteria
    A. Criterion 1: Did the response actually occur?
    B. Criterion 2: Did the response occur because of the experimental treatment per se?
    C. Criterion 3: Was the response a unique, localized event or was it only a component of a generalized arousal pattern?
    D. Criterion 4: Was there a specific relationship between an independent variable and a response parameter?
II. Empirical Studies
    A. Problem Solving
    B. Imagination
    C. Silent Reading
    D. Speech Perception
    E. Learning
    F. Nocturnal Dreams
III. Summary and Conclusions
IV. Interpretation

Throughout the first eight chapters of this book we attempt to stay close to the empirical level, reviewing the numerous studies and historical observations which indicate that a variety of bodily systems are covertly activated during cognition. Among the more important bodily systems that have been empirically implicated in the silent performance of cognitive tasks are the eyes, covert speech behavior—already consid-

amplitude of lip EMG was the same (.09) in both conditions. Although these differences were not significant, covert oral *and* nonoral response amplitudes increased *concomitantly* during a condition (LoI/Non-matching-slide/Not-clear) which, as previously discussed, was difficult for the subjects. Thus it seems reasonable to suppose that, during this demanding condition, a general arousal effect occurred as subjects shifted their attention to the visual materials in an attempt to facilitate clear hearing of the auditory passages.

7

Covert Nonoral Behavior: Somatic Responses

Throughout the first eight chapters of this book we attempt to stay close to the empirical level, reviewing the numerous studies and historical observations which indicate that a variety of bodily systems are covertly activated during cognition. Among the more important bodily systems that have been empirically implicated in the silent performance of cognitive tasks are the eyes, covert speech behavior—already considered in Chapters 5 and 6—electroencephalographic measures of brain functioning (Chapter 8), and visceral activity.[1]

While the function of these several bodily systems during thought has been appreciated (to varying degrees) for some time, relatively little attention has been paid to the nonoral skeletal musculature, despite the attention which some prominent individuals have devoted to it since the time of the ancient Greeks (see Chapter 2). Over a hundred years ago Sechenov (1863) held that muscular movement was the external manifestation of all the activity of the brain. In 1909, Titchener emphasized the role of the skeletal musculature in the development of meaning, and later Jacobson (1932) empirically confirmed a circuit model of neuromuscular functioning. Also in Chapter 2 we discussed extensively how muscle responding was critical in the theoretical formulations of the early behaviorists, for example Watson's (1930) claim that manual (nonoral) responses were necessary components of implicit language habits (which he defined as "thought"). Indeed, there is ample, if little noticed, precedent for the position that a person thinks with the entire body, *including* the nonoral skeletal muscle system. Covert nonoral responses generated by the somatic skeletal muscle systems are thus instrumental components of cognitive neuro-muscular circuits; we shall now assess the data on which this conclusion is based. To do this, we shall critically summarize findings (principally electromyographic) involving skeletal muscle activity during the silent performance of language tasks (often referred to by the investigators as such cognitive activities as "imagination" or "thinking"). Laborious as it may be, this step is necessary to assure that there *is* sufficient empirical justification for the position that the motor system serves important cognitive functions. Readers will vary as to how they will process these empirical studies. For some, a thorough reading will be important, while others may prefer to use the empirical chapters selectively for reference materials.

Methodological Criteria

To assess the cognitive research on nonoral, somatic responses, we will evaluate each study by the four general criteria presented in detail in Chapter 5 on pages 118–26. Recall that the first two criteria allow us to determine whether or not a response actually occurred, and if so whether it was a function of the condition of interest (an experimental treatment, or whatever). The second two criteria are designed to help ascertain the function of somatic responses by providing an index of the degree of general bodily arousal during the condition or experimental

[1] We should mention especially work on the esophagus (e.g., Jacobson, 1929), on intestinal activity (e.g., Davis, Garafolo, and Gault, 1957), on electrodermal responding (e.g., Grings, 1973a, b), and on the autonomic system in general (e.g., Lacey and Lacey, 1974).

treatment. If the response is a localized, relatively unique occurrence it is more likely to serve an information processing function within neuromuscular circuits.

CRITERION 1

Did the Response Actually Occur? If the researcher did determine that the covert response measure systematically changed from baseline, then a "yes" is entered in column 1 of Table 7.1. If the experimenter reported that there was no systematic change in the measure, then a "no" is entered in column 1 of Table 7.1. Finally, if the researcher did not compare the covert response measure during the period of the experimental treatment with a previous resting baseline, a "?" is entered in column 1 of Table 7.1, indicating that the experimenter did not successfully employ this criterion.

CRITERION 2

Did the Response Occur Because of the Experimental Treatment Per Se? Criterion 2 may be satisfied by showing that the covert response changes systematically as a function of two (or more) experimental conditions, e.g., one might show that electromyograms from the preferred arm are greater when the subject imagines lighting a cigarette than when imagining the Eiffel Tower (Jacobson, 1932).

CRITERION 3

Was the Response a Unique, Localized Event or Was It Only a Component of a Generalized Arousal Pattern? A relatively unique, localized response occurs independently of other covert processes, as shown by concomitant measures from a sample of bodily regions or systems. We thus: (1) distinguish the response of interest from a state of general bodily arousal, and (2) control for demand characteristics resulting from a single measurement device attached at a single bodily location. In column 3 of Table 7.1, a "yes" or "no" entry is accompanied by a list of the other bodily regions or systems for which concomitant measures were reported.

CRITERION 4

Was There a Specific Relationship Between an Independent Variable and a Response Parameter? A relationship between a response parameter and verbal reports, systematic variation of the subject's conditions or characteristics, indicates the intimate involvement of the response with cognitive activity.

The studies to be considered fall into six task-specification categories, as follows: (1) problem solving, (2) imagination, (3) silent reading, (4) speech perception, (5) learning, (6) nocturnal dreams.

TABLE 7.1 Summary of Nonoral Skeletal Muscle Activity During Cognitive Tasks[a]

Task and Experimenter	Did the Specified Muscle Response:			
	(1) change from baseline?	(2) vary as a function of conditions?	(3) occur independently of other covert processes?	(4) specifically relate to a cognitive aspect?
Problem Solving				
Golla (1921)	Yes (arm)	Yes	?	Yes
Tuttle (1924)	Yes (patellar reflex)	Yes	?	Yes
Bills (1927)	Yes (general)	Yes*	?	No
Golla & Antonovitch (1929)	Yes (arm, leg, patellar reflex)	No	Yes: respiration	No
Freeman (1930)	Yes (leg)	Yes	?	Yes
Freeman (1931b)	Yes (arms & legs)	?	?	No
Max (1933)	Yes (arm & hand)	Yes	?	No
Clites (1936)	Yes (rt. arm)	?	?	Yes
Davis (1937)	Yes* (rt. arm)	?	?	Yes
Max (1937)	Yes (arms)	Yes	Yes: leg	Yes
Davis (1938)	Yes* (rt. arm)	Yes*	No: neck	Yes
Davis (1939)	Yes (leg, arms)	Yes	Yes: arms, leg	Yes
Ellson et al. (1952)	Yes (rt. arm)	Yes*	?	Yes
Reuder (1956)	Yes* (rt. arm)	Yes*	?	Yes
Stennett (1957)	Yes* (arms)	Yes*	No: palmar conductance	Yes
Leshner (1961)	Yes* (arms)	Yes*	?	Yes
Novikova (1961)	Yes (hand, tongue)	?	?	No
Pishkin (1964)	? (preferred arm)	?	?	Yes
MacNeilage (1966a)	Yes* (forehead, rt. arm)	Yes*	Yes and No: see text	Yes
Pishkin & Shurley (1968)	Yes* (forehead)	Yes*	No: GSR	Yes
Vaughn & McDaniel (1969)	Yes* (frontalis)	Yes*	?	Yes
McGuigan (1971)	Yes* (left arm)	Yes*	No*: lip, EEG; Yes: leg, respiration rate	Yes

[a]In this research survey, we have attempted to specify the results of statistical tests when they were conducted by stating that the effect was "significant" (reliable) or "not significant" (not reliable). Where effects are reported in the absence of these words, together with the absence of asterisks in columns 1, 2, and 3 of the table, the reader may assume that the effects were'nt subjected to statistical tests. This criterion is not applied to column 4.

227

TABLE 7.1 Summary of Nonoral Skeletal Muscle Activity During Cognitive Tasks (cont.)

Task and Experimenter	(1) change from baseline?	(2) vary as a function of conditions?	Did the Specified Muscle Response: (3) occur independently of other covert processes?	(4) specifically relate to a cognitive aspect?
Imagination				
Jacobson (1927)	Yes (biceps)	?	?	Yes
Jacobson (1930a)	Yes (rt. biceps)	Yes	?	Yes
Jacobson (1930b)	Yes (rt. arm)	Yes	?	Yes
Jacobson (1930c)	Yes (rt. arm)	Yes	?	Yes
Jacobson (1931a)	Yes (rt. biceps)	Yes	Yes: eye	Yes
Jacobson (1931b)	Yes (lft. arm)	Yes	No: right arm	Yes
Shaw (1938)	Yes* (various)	No	?	No
Shaw (1940)	Yes (rt. arm)	Yes	?	Yes
Wolpert (1960)	No (various)	?	?	No
Silent Reading				
Jacobson & Kraft (1942)	Yes (leg)	?	?	Yes
Strother (1949)	Yes* (arms, legs)	Yes*	Yes: right arm	Yes
McGuigan & Rodier (1968)	No (left arm)	No	Yes: left arm	No
Hardyck & Petrinovich (1970)	Yes (right arm)	Yes*	No: chin-lip, laryngeal	Yes
Speech Perception				
Smith et al. (1954)	Yes (arms, neck, and forehead)	Yes*	No: arms, chin	Yes
Wallerstein (1954)	Yes* (forehead, arms)	Yes*	Yes: neck, forehead Yes: chin, forehead, arms,	Yes
Bartoshuk (1956)	Yes* (forehead arms)	Yes*	Yes: chin, arms, forehead No: frontalis, EEG	Yes

Task and Experimenter	(1) change from baseline?	(2) vary as a function of conditions?	(3) occur independently of other covert processes?	(4) specifically relate to a cognitive aspect?
Learning				
Travis & Kennedy (1947)	Yes (brow)	Yes	?	Yes
Berry & Davis (1958)	Yes* (forehead & left arm)	Yes*	No: masseter	No
Berger, Irwin, & Frommer (1970)	Yes (rt. wrist, arm)	Yes*	Yes: forehead masseter	Yes
Petrinovich & Hardyck (1970)	Yes (Laryngeal, chin-lip, rt. arm)	Yes*	?	Yes
Beh & Hawkins (1973)	Yes (arm)	?	?	Yes
Nocturnal Dreams				
Max (1935)	Yes (arms)	Yes	Yes: leg	Yes
Stoyva (1965)	Yes (fingers)	Yes	No: eye	Yes
Wolpert & Trosman (1958)	Yes (general)	?	?	Yes
Wolpert (1960)	Yes (wrist)	Yes (?)	No: EEG, eye (various)	Yes
Jacobson et al. (1964)	Yes (29 muscle groups)	?		Yes
Baldridge et al. (1965)	Yes (hand, foot)	?	No: eye	Yes
Sassin & Johnson (1968)	Yes (arm, leg)	?	No: EEG	Yes
Larson & Foulkes (1969)	Yes (forehead)	?	No: eye EEG	Yes
Pessah & Roffwarg (1972)	Yes (middle ear muscle)	Yes*	No: eye	Yes
Gardner et al. (1973)	Yes (various)	—	No: eye	Yes

PROBLEM SOLVING

Golla (1921) measured tonic muscle activity of an unspecified forearm with a mechanical apparatus during a mental arithmetic task. Records obtained from one "unsophisticated" subject indicated that muscle tonicity increased during the task and was positively related to the difficulty of the problem. Golla concluded that such muscle activity may not only be a manifestation of cerebral activity but a necessary concomitant of it. In Table 7.1, because the arm measure changed from baseline we enter "yes" in column 1 (the lack of an asterisk indicating that no statistical test was applied.) The "yes" in column 2 is indicative of his finding that muscle tonicity increased as a function of difficulty of the problem, this specific relationship also accounting for the "yes" in column 4. The question mark in column 3 indicates that no other bodily measures were concomitantly made with arm activity.

Tuttle (1924) tapped subject's patellar tendons with a constant force at constant intervals and obtained measures of muscle tonus during conditions of rest, problem solving, and conversation. Muscle tonus was measured as the distance of leg deflection during the knee jerk. The records from all subjects showed that mental activity increased muscle tonus, with reflex activity being highest during problem solving, next highest for conversation, and lowest for the relaxation condition. Agreeing with A. P. Weiss, Tuttle concluded that "attention" is increased tonicity of the muscles which adjusts the body for the favorable reception of stimuli. Furthermore, amount of muscle tonus seemed to be positively associated with the degree of attention. Because the assessments in Table 7.1 for each article should be fairly apparent from this point on, the reader should be able to relate each study to the four criteria without further comment here, except as necessary.

Bills' (1927) approach was unique. He asked, "Will an increase in the total amount of muscular tension in the body increase mental efficiency and thus reverse the usual order of dependent and independent variables in the experiment?" Muscle tension was increased by having the subjects squeeze a spring dynamometer, and the increased tension was confirmed by kymographic records. Mental work included the learning of nonsense syllables, the learning of meaningful paired associates, adding columns of numbers, and a rapid perception task. Learning efficiency (average learning time) was measured under normal and increased muscular tension. During all types of mental work, learning efficiency was significantly greater under increased muscular tension, with no sizable differences among the various mental tasks.

The effect of fatigue upon adding numbers and upon the perception task indicated that learning speed was less susceptible to decrement under increased muscular tension than under normal tension; however, during fatigue the decrement in accuracy of performance did not differ between the two muscle conditions. After a thoughtful analysis of various ways in which heightened muscular tension might facilitate mental

work, Bills implied a confirmation of Washburn's (1916) hypothesis that motor innervations are not mere accompaniments of directed thought, but are essential parts of the cause of directed thought. Bills also presented a most interesting historical summary of previous research on the influence of muscular tension on the efficiency of mental work, citing the positive findings of Lombard in 1887, Dresslar in 1891, and so forth. The "yes" in column 1 for this study may be somewhat misleading because Bills employed degree of muscle tension as the independent variable, thus intentionally increasing tension from a resting condition. In column 2, the "yes" indicates the successful use of a control (normal muscle tension) condition, and the "no" in column 4 reflects the finding that there were no sizable differences in learning efficiency as a function of the various mental tasks. (This same comment applies to several other studies too, particularly to S. M. Smith et al., 1947 and to Beh and Hawkins, 1973.)

Golla and Antonovitch (1929) measured tonus of arm and leg extensor muscles and the patellar reflex by means of an optical myograph while subjects performed various cognitive tasks (mental arithmetic, pursuit tasks, etc.). In general, there was an immediate rise of tonus or reactivity at the inception of mental work, an increase that remained for a brief period before returning to the original level. No relation between efficiency or task difficulty and amount of muscle activity was found. Golla and Antonovitch concluded that these *involuntary* responses serve a preparatory function in the performance of cognitive tasks. The inconsistency between these results and those summarized by Bills (1927) which show that increased muscular tension improves mental efficiency may be due to the fact that the previous work dealt with voluntary innervation and thus may have no direct bearing on the involuntary responses studied by Golla and Antonovitch. Two experiments in which muscle tension changed with the performance of "mental work" were reported by Freeman (1930). In the first experiment, tension of the quadriceps muscle group of the right leg was measured during conditions of rest and during various counting operations that varied in difficulty. Tension was measured with an optical lever attached to the patellar tendon; a beam of light was reflected from the lever upon a millimeter scale so that the higher the reading, the greater the quadriceps tension. The result was that tension increased upon presentation of the problem and decreased as the task was completed. Tension during the first part of the problem varied directly as a function of task difficulty. Diminution of the tension in this muscle group appeared to be a positive function of the correctness of the response.

In a second and similar experiment, subjects were interrupted during the performance of their tasks. The findings were in accord with those of the first experiment, though there were additional tension increments following task interruption. Freeman concluded that increased muscle tonus occurs during mental work because it has been previously reinforced by the successful completion of the task.

In further work, Freeman (1931b) obtained records of muscle thickening of the arms and legs while his subjects engaged in a mental arithmetic task. The subjects sat in a device resembling a pillory or "stock," and displacements of levers resting on the arm and leg muscles were photographically recorded. The data indicate that muscle thickening increased from baseline during performance of the task, although the loci of these movements varied from subject to subject. Freeman concluded that the peripheral neuromuscular "flux" during this cognitive activity provides evidence of the general fertility of a motor theory of consciousness.

Using deaf-mute subjects, Max (1933)[2] recorded covert (EMG) contractions of the arm and hand muscles during "simpler types of consciousness" (sleep, dreams, and sensation) and during thought problems (verbal, visual, kinesthetic, and arithmetic). The results indicated (1) that arm and hand action-currents increase during dreams, (2) that sensory stimulation is associated with action-current responses of the peripheral musculature, (3) that the subjective experience of a kinesthetic image is a correlate of actual muscular contraction, and (4) that in deaf subjects, responses in the hand muscles are associated with thinking, and appear to be present during vocalization by deaf subjects able to speak. Max stated that hand EMG varies with the type of problem; hence the "yes" in column 2.

Clites (1936) examined the relation between involuntary muscle contractions, grip tension, and action potentials during successful and unsuccessful problem solving. Grip tension, as measured by an arrangement of tambours and a kymograph, and right forearm muscle action potentials (EMG) were recorded during periods of relaxation and during attempts to solve the second water dipping problem of the Binet Test. Comparisons of performance between successful and unsuccessful subjects indicated that successful subjects show significantly greater right forearm-EMG, and significantly less overt movement of the arm; they also manifested greater relaxation of the grip, but this change was not significant. Unsuccessful subjects exhibited relatively consistent forearm-EMG, grip pressure, and overt movement from rest periods to solution periods. Disregarding task performance, no significant correlations were found between EMG, grip tension, and overt involuntary movement of the arm. Clites concluded that the superior performance of the successful subjects may be attributed to increased muscle activity. The general conclusion from his entire series of studies was that muscle activity is either increased during problem solving or problem solving is identical with increased muscle activity. Either explanation is offered as a substitute for the hypothesis that there is a mere "overflow" of efferent impulses from the brain.

R. C. Davis (1937) investigated the relationship between "mental work" and muscular phenomena (EMG recorded from the right forearm with an electron oscillograph). Three types of "mental work" were

---

[2] These data are further described in Max (1935).

studied: memorization of poetry, rotational addition, and multiplication. Baseline action potentials were obtained during relaxed rest preceding each task. Significant EMG increases from baseline were found during poetry reading, and multiplication. During addition there was also an EMG increase, but the effect was not statistically significant. No EMG comparisons were made as a function of type of mental work. For all three types of "mental work" there tended to be a negative correlation between the amount of right arm action potentials and the amount of work accomplished.

Investigating the motor theory of consciousness (in which cognitive activity is related to motor activity of the linguistic apparatus), Max (1937) hypothesized that the activity of the linguistic mechanisms of deaf subjects should increase relative to hearing subjects during the solution of "thought problems." His measure was electromyographic activity of the musculature of both forearms that controlled finger movements (the locus of the subject's "speech"). A response was implicitly defined as any measureable voltage during problem solving; response amplitude ranged between .1 and $9\mu v$ (microvolts). He found that abstract thought problems elicited action-current responses more frequently and to a greater extent in the arms of the deaf individuals than in the legs. Some particular findings were as follows: (1) the subjective experience of a kinesthetic image was accompanied by peripheral EMGs in 73% of the instances for hearing subjects and in 84% for deaf subjects; (2) for deaf subjects, abstract thought problems produced heightened EMGs in 84% of the cases as compared with 31% for hearing subjects; (3) simultaneous recording of EMGs from the arms and legs of the deaf produced 73% positive responses in the arms and 19% in the legs; (4) for deaf subjects, simple silent reading and repetition of verbal material produced smaller and less frequent EMGs than reading with the intent to remember or engaging in relatively complex thought problems; (5) in general, the more intelligent and better educated the deaf subjects, the less the EMG response to problem situations; (6) vocalized speech was accompanied by manual currents more frequently in deaf than in hearing subjects. His conclusion was that these manual responses in the deaf are more than adventitious effects of irradiated tensions, and that they have some specific connection with the thinking process. His results thus supported the behavioristic form of a motor theory of consciousness.

Davis (1938) recorded muscle action potentials from the right forearm and side of the neck near the thyroid gland while his subjects mentally solved five series of graded number problems. Baseline recordings were obtained preceding and following each series. Forearm EMG was significantly lower than neck EMG during the baseline period. Both significantly increased during problem-solving from the baseline levels. Forearm EMG exhibited a significantly greater percentage increase than neck EMG, although Davis suggested that this difference may be attributed to a greater sensitivity of the arm apparatus. Although no differential EMG responses were associated with success or failure, there was a corresponding increase in action potentials of the arm and neck as task difficulty increased. Davis concluded that these results confirm the hypothesis that muscular tensions form a part of the ordinary psychological processes and that further attempts should be made to relate such processes and muscle action.

In further work, Davis (1939) had two independent groups of subjects engage in mental arithmetic and in memorizing nonsense syllables, respectively. EMGs were recorded from the left and right forearms and from the calf of the left leg. The subjects worked under normal conditions and also with instructions to relax the right arm. There were increases (as measured by percent increase during work relative to resting) that were not statistically evaluated in all three bodily locations during normal work conditions. During multiplication, the focus of activity was in the right arm (with the least activity in the leg), while in learning nonsense syllables neither arm dominated the other. The subjects spontaneously reported that there was a strong tendency to write during multiplication but not while memorizing nonsense syllables. There was little difference while learning nonsense syllables among these three locations, leading Davis to speculate that activity during the nonsense syllable condition was concentrated in some other part of the body, such as in the speech musculature. Instructions to relax the right arm during work reduced EMG activity in all three bodily regions for both conditions. Furthermore, there was "definite evidence" that work output decreased when the subjects tried to keep their arm relaxed.

Interpreting his own current and previous findings, and also the work of Shaw (1938) and others, Davis put forth a "principle of focus of muscular responses," applicable to both the inhibition and excitation of muscular activity. The principle is that, for any psychological process, there is some region in which there is a relatively high degree of muscular activity. A corollary of this principle is that the amplitude of activity decreases as the bodily distance from the focal point increases.

In their eighth experiment, Ellson et al. (1952) recorded EMG from opposed muscle groups in the arm during "lying" and "non-lying." The subjects were provided the opportunity to take fifty cents in various coin denominations. During a subsequent interrogation period, crucial questions were presented visually concerning the denominations of the particular coins taken. Subjects then responded to these questions by making "yes" or "no" movements of a key. They were instructed that they could keep the money if they successfully escaped detection. The results indicated that EMG response *amplitude* did not significantly discriminate lies from truths. However, EMG response *latencies* were significantly shorter for critical lying responses than for critical non-lying responses.

In the following three studies, the investigators attempted to manipulate the subject's subjective approach to the problem-solving task in order to assess the relationship of this variable to the degree of covert muscle activity occurring during the task. The focus of these studies is upon general bodily arousal, rather than on localizing specific bodily areas of responding.

Reuder (1956) studied the differential effects of ego- and task-orienting instructions on muscle tension during problem solving. She factorially combined two types of instruction (ego-orienting vs. task-orienting) with two levels of difficulty of mathematical progressions. Right forearm EMGs were obtained during rest, presentation of instructions, and problem solving. The results indicated that no significant increases in EMG from initial rest occurred during instruction or inter-problem rest periods; but that right forearm EMG did significantly increase during the problem solving. The effect of increased problem difficulty significantly increased EMG activity. A significant instruction-by-difficulty interaction indicated that task-oriented subjects exhibited higher EMG levels on the more difficult problems than they did on the easy problems, whereas the ego-oriented subjects showed higher EMG levels for the easy problems than for the difficult ones. Reuder concluded that ego- and task-orienting instructions interact with task difficulty and therefore this experimental variable must be considered in the design of experiments relating muscle tension and performance.

The hypothesis that an inverted-U relationship exists between level of arousal and performance on an auditory tracking task was tested by Stennett (1957). As a measure of arousal, right and left arm EMGs and palmar conductance were recorded during a baseline condition of rest and while performing the tracking task under various incentive conditions. Incentive was varied widely from one condition where the subject thought performance was not recorded to another where performance determined the avoidance of 100-150 v shock. The results indicated that the hypothesized relation between performance and arousal was generally appropriate, regardless of the measure considered. Stennett concluded that incentive is the most important experimental variable determining the steepness of the EMG gradient during task performance. The "yes" in column 4 refers to the relationship between levels of incentive and arousal. It could be argued that this is not a specific cognitive relationship and should therefore read a "no" for this study.

Leshner (1961) studied the effects of levels of aspiration on muscle action potentials during a problem solving task. Subjects were assigned to four groups designated as Expect-Success, Hope-Success, Expect-Failure, and Hope-Failure. All groups were given figure-pattern problems during two task sessions which were preceded and separated by rest periods. "Expect" groups stated aspirations in terms of scores they expected to obtain; "Hope" groups stated the scores they wanted to achieve. Following the task, half of each group were given fictitious scores and norms indicating they had failed while the other half received fictitious information indicating success. EMG from both forearms were recorded throughout the entire experimental session. The results indicated a general (though non-significant) trend for all groups of an increase in EMG above resting levels during aspiration periods, followed by a further increase during the task. Muscle activity decreased from the task level when subjects were informed of their success or failure. A significant aspiration by achievement interaction indicated that for subjects who failed, the rate of tension increase was greater for subjects who stated expectations than for those with unrealistic aspiratione; but for subjects who succeeded, EMGs of the unrealistic were significantly higher than those of the realistic. Regardless of aspiration, EMGs during work significantly decreased among successful subjects and significantly increased among those who failed.

Seeking to localize covert responding in deaf mutes during problem-solving, Novikova (1961) recorded (unspecified) arm and tongue EMGs as the subjects solved mental arithmetic problems. Sample records showed increased EMG from both regions above rest while the subjects were engaged in the tasks. The same phenomenon was reported for normal subjects who were proficient in manual speech. Novikova concluded that a single functional system develops which apparently includes control of both fingers and the tongue.

Using chronic schizophrenics, Pishkin (1964) investigated the intercorrelations between concept identification performance, number of trials to criterion, time per response, learning rate, and EMG, with the focus on the relationship between EMG and concept identification performance. Subjects categorized geometric patterns as "A" or "B," following which a light came on above either A or B to indicate correct response. There was a significant positive correlation between preferred arm EMG amplitude and learning rate, and a negative correlation between preferred arm EMG amplitude and time per trial. These relationships suggested that some motivational influence was involved and that the general tension level was lower in those subjects who produced more errors.

Although specifically interested in studying changes in EEG amplitude, MacNeilage (1966a) also obtained records of various other indices of activation including right arm- and forehead-EMG, EKG, and palmar conductance during a spaced auditory serial addition task. Baseline recordings were taken during rest; following that there were two experimental conditions in which the subjects simply wrote numbers or silently performed serial addition of numbers that were auditorally presented. These two conditions were then repeated and followed by a final rest period. The results showed that all indices of activation significantly increased from rest during both of the experimental conditions, but no reliable differences were found between the two experimental conditions. Difficulty of the serial addition task (varied by speed of presentation) significantly increased only forehead and right arm EMG in the first part of the experiment; however, in the second part of the experiment, difficulty of the task significantly increased heart rate, respiration, and right arm-EMG, while significantly reducing EEG alpha. Forehead EMG was not significantly affected by task difficulty in the second part. A description of the within-trials effects for the addition task indicated that, as percentage correct responses, EKG, and palmar conductance decreased, the EEG alpha amplitude increased. However, arm-and forehead-EMG showed no similar gradients. MacNeilage concluded that all measures excepting EMG show a high concordance and that this exception presents difficulty for an activation theory of mental performance. (cf. p. 86 for a discussion of activation theory.)

Pishkin and Shurley (1968) studied the effects of cognitive stress upon subsequent performance of a concept identification task and on level of arousal. Three levels of task complexity were factorially combined with two sets given to the subjects (solvable and unsolvable). The concept identification tasks required classification of geometric patterns in accordance with the relevant dimension (size, color, or shape) by pressing one of two response keys. In the first stage of the procedure the subjects were given a set-task that established either a solvable or unsolvable set. For the solvable set, subjects received accurate feedback; in the unsolvable set, subjects were given incorrect feedback on 50% on the trials. In the second stage of the experiment the subjects were presented a similar series of concept identification problems while spontaneous galvanic skin response (GSR) and forehead EMG were recorded. The results were that task complexity and the effects of cognitive stress induced by the unsolvable set significantly increased the number of errors on the concept identification task and forehead EMG, while spontaneous GSR significantly decreased. Significant Task-Set interactions indicated that increases of muscle tension and number of errors and decreases in spontaneous GSR are of lesser degree for the unsolvable than for solvable conditions. Correlational analyses showed a significant positive relationship between EMG and number of errors, and significant negative relationships between these measures and the GSR. Pishkin and Shurley interpreted these data as indicating that increased muscle activity is associated with the inability to process information, while spontaneous GSRs indicate successful information intake.

Vaughn and McDaniel (1969) recorded frontalis muscle activity ("forehead" EMG) during a match-to-sample visual discrimination task. Control recordings during relaxation, viewing a sample stimulus, and performance of the manual response were followed by six experimental trials. The results showed a significantly higher EMG amplitude associated with correct to incorrect responses, with attenuation of muscle tension following errors for all but the first and last trial. Phasic EMG responses were typically superimposed on a progressively rising and then falling gradient of frontalis muscle activity. Vaughn and McDaniel concluded that these data support E. N. Sokolov's (1963) conception of the orienting relfex, in that phasic increments and decrements are dependent upon tonic adjustments (see our discussion of Sokolov's work in Chapter 2). Thus habituation of the phasic orienting reactions explains the downward trend of this response during the final trials.

Max's classical conclusion that covert finger movements occur in deaf subjects during thinking was tested by McGuigan (1971) using six subjects proficient in manual speech and who were learning oral speech. It was found that amplitude of left-arm and lip electromyograms significantly increased during problem solving. Left-arm EMG increased significantly more during problem solving than during a nonverbal control task; integrated electroencephalograms from the left motor area decreased significantly more during the problem solving. No significant differences occurred for leg EMG, but respiration rate increased significantly during all tasks. In conformity with the findings of Max (1937) and Novikova (1961), McGuigan concluded that the manual and oral regions were covertly functioning as a single linguistic system during thinking.

The two studies which follow are typical examples of a research paradigm which is important for studying the function of the skeletal muscle system during thought and has a long history (e.g., Jacobson, 1911). Rather than measuring muscle activity, the effort is to eliminate muscular responding. While these studies are thus atypical of those in this chapter, they are important for us from the perspective of a different research paradigm. Smith, Brown, Toman, and Goodman (1947) administered *d*-tubocurarine, a neuromuscular blocking agent, to a healthy trained adult observer not undergoing an operation. The dosage was two and one-half times that necessary for respiratory paralysis and was therefore considered adequate (though not verified) for complete paralysis of the skeletal musculature. During the 54-min period of paralysis it was reported that no changes occurred in the EEG, consciousness, sensory functions, or in any aspect of the higher central nervous system, although objective tests of CNS functioning were not conducted. Smith et al. concluded that paralysis of the skeletal musculature did not affect central processes; this evidence has been used by others to disconfirm a motor theory of consciousness. For six methodological shortcomings of this study, see McGuigan (1966a, p. 219) and page 93 of this book.

As a study of the motor theory of consciousness, Leuba, Birch, and Appleton (1968) tested the problem solving ability of a subject during paralysis of the voluntary musculature by *d*-tubocurarine. The subject was paralyzed during two experimental sessions and presented with arithmetical, verbal, and mechanical problems after the injections of the paralytic agent. Upon reversal of the paralysis this subject orally answered the problems presented during the experimental sessions. The results indicated that the subject solved the problems during paralysis as he would in the normal state. Additional subjective reports indicated he was as alert and mentally effective during paralysis as he was in the normal state. Leuba et al. concluded that muscles and their afferent impulses were not required during paralysis for the successful solution of these problems. While some methodological improvements were made in this repetition of the Smith et al. (1947) experiment, the critical improvements—such as the lack of EMG monitoring to assure complete paralysis—were unfortunately missing. Lack of EMG monitoring is not a minor criticism (a point that becomes apparent under thorough examination of the data). It has not been demonstrated that curare produces *complete* paralysis without leaving critical aspects of the skeletal musculature intact (c.f. McGuigan, 1973b). The important point is that we do not know what effect *total* paralysis of the skeletal musculature would have on cognition, as the proper study has not yet been conducted. The results of Jacobson (1929), in which totally relaxed subjects report lack of consciousness, suggest that complete muscular paralysis with a neuromuscular blocking agent would eliminate cognitive processes.

IMAGINATION

The classical work in this section has been conducted primarily by Jacobson. On pages 175–79 we have discussed Jacobson's development of this research area—perhaps a review of that section would facilitate perspective of the following articles. Principally, Jacobson was interested in the psychophysiological measurement of mental activities as a basic science endeavor and for clinical application (to measure progress with progressive relaxation as in the elimination of phobias).

Jacobson (1927) reported the effects of progressive relaxation training on various conscious processes including imagery, attention, reflection, and emotion. His observations indicated that extreme relaxation was incompatible with the simultaneous presence of these activities. To test this conclusion using another approach, Jacobson employed a string galvonometer to measure electrical activity of brachial-biceps muscle of the arm while the subject engaged in imagined activities using the same arm. Nonamplified readings from this instrument indicate that muscle action potentials increased from rest during the period of imagination. Jacobson suggested that a clear-cut interpretation of these preliminary data would require recordings from several muscle groups during a variety of tasks. Jacobson (1930a) conducted an experiment to determine if imagination of a specific motor act is associated with an increase of muscle action potentials of the muscles that would be involved in the overt performance of that act. EMGs were recorded from the right biceps-brachial muscles of the arm by use of a string galvonometer and vacuum tube amplifiers. The subjects first relaxed and then, at a tone signal, imagined that they voluntarily flexed their right arm. For control conditions subjects were either presented the tone signal and instructed not to imagine, or asked to imagine movements of the body other than the right arm. The results indicated that during imagination of right arm flexion 96% of the (141) tests were associated with EMG increments from the right arm; whereas 93% of the (149) control tests of imagination of other than right arm movement showed no increase of right arm EMG. Additionally, EMG levels during imagination of right arm flexion were consistently above relaxation levels and of the same form and duration, but lower in amplitude, than during actual overt right arm flexion. Jacobson concluded that imagination of voluntary movement is associated with neuromuscular activity in the locale of the imagined act.

The next report in this series by Jacobson (1930b) replicated and extended his previous finding that localized EMG increments characterize imagination of voluntary motor acts. The subjects were instructed to imagine various acts commonly performed with the right arm: "imagine lifting a cigarette to your mouth"; "imagine throwing a ball"; "imagine pulling on your socks." EMGs were recorded from the right arm during the experimental conditions as well as during control periods of relaxation, when subjects were under instructions either not to imagine at all or to imagine performing motor acts with the *left* arm following the auditory signal. The results indicated that EMG increments of 186 to 550 percent above resting baseline occurred in 159 of 163 tests. All control tests were negative. In a second part of the experiment, subjects were asked to recollect any previous muscular acts commonly performed with the right arm. Recording and control procedures were similar to those of the first experiment. EMG increments were found in 60 of 90 experimental tests. Post-session interviews indicated that some subjects recalled these past experiences *visually*. Hence, Jacobson reasoned that the negative instances in the right arm may have been accompanied by increases in other body locations (e.g., the eyes), thus accounting for this relatively low percentage of positive findings. In any event, Jacobson did extend the base for his general conclusion that imagination and recollection of voluntary acts is accompanied by localized electrical changes in appropriate neuromuscular regions.

In a replication of previous procedures (1930a, b), Jacobson (1930c) used platinum iridium wire electrodes for more precise measurement of muscle action potentials. Electrode insertion was in the biceps muscle of the right arm. EMG records were made during baseline relaxation, while imagining lifting a ten pound weight in the right hand, and while imagining lifting the weight in the left hand (control tests). To corroborate the EMG data a mechanical device composed of a system of levers was attached to the supported right forearm, allowing the measurement of microscopic flexions. All records obtained during experimental conditions of imagined movement of the right arm did show a correspondence between microscopic flexion and increased muscle action potentials. The 19 control tests (imagining lifting the weight with the left hand) were all negative for both measures of muscle activity. To further specify the relation between muscular activity and imagination, subjects were instructed to cease imagining or to relax upon hearing an auditory signal. Comparisons of records for each condition showed that both instructions returned muscle activity to resting levels, suggesting to Jacobson that muscle activity is required for imagination. In another procedure, subjects were instructed to relax the right arm and simultaneously to imagine lifting a weight with the same arm. In one condition the instruction was added that if this was impossible then the subject should engage in imagination; in the other condition the subject was instructed to relax if he could not perform the simultaneous tasks. EMG records showed that all subjects in the first condition had increased muscle activity, while subjects in the second condition showed resting levels of right arm activity. Jacobson concluded that imagination of movement of a part of the body cannot occur if the muscles of that area are relaxed. Generally, these data confirm previous findings of Jacobson (1930a, b) that contraction of specific muscles occurs following instructions to imagine an act that involves those muscles during overt performance.

Jacobson (1931a) further examined the differential activity of arm and ocular muscles during imagination by instructing relaxation-trained subjects to either "imagine" or "visually imagine" lifting a weight with the right arm. EMGs were recorded by use of inserted electrodes during the experimental conditions and also during a control condition in which subjects were instructed not to imagine following the signal. After the instructions to simply imagine the action, all subjects showed EMG increases from rest of the right biceps muscle, whereas instructions to *visually* imagine the action produced increased biceps activity in only one of 17 tests. When EMG was simultaneously recorded from the ocular region following instructions to visually imagine, voltage changes from rest were observed in 29 of 31 tests. No changes from rest of arm or ocular muscle activity were recorded during the control condition. Further tests indicated that subjects instructed to "imagine" the arm action consistently showed increased biceps activity and occasionally showed ocular muscle activity. Jacobson concluded that imagination involves specific neuromuscular activities and that the locus of this activity is dependent upon the type of imagery (i.e., visual vs. non-visual).

Jacobson (1931b) conducted a series of tests to determine if a subject could imagine flexion of a left arm amputated 32 years previous to the experiment. EMG during instructed imagination of left-hand flexion was recorded from the partly amputated biceps muscle and from the muscles that flex the right hand. When instructed to imagine left-hand flexion the biceps stump EMG showed increased activity in 13 of 14 trials for the subject while recordings of right arm EMG showed increases in 6 of 6 cases. Control tests to imagine nothing showed no increased activity from either electrode placement. In other control tests the subject was instructed to overtly bend the left and right foot or the right arm. Unlike normal subjects, left-arm EMG was usually found to increase during imagination of these activities. These latter data suggested to Jacobson that activities of the arms are not clearly dissociated in this subject. However, of particular interest was the voluntary report of the subject at the conclusion of the experiment that he could not imagine left-hand activity independent of the right hand. That is, no independent imagination apparently existed for this subject's left hand. Jacobson concluded that imagination or recalled use of the lost muscles that flex the left hand are associated with a "substitute-reaction" of the corresponding muscles of the right arm or in the remnant muscles of the upper left arm. It would be of interest to conduct further work with more recent (or double) amputees, since building up substitute circuits presumably takes time.

In work which is related closely to Jacobson's, Shaw (1938) investigated the distribution of muscle activity during various tasks of imagination to determine if there is a localization in the muscle groups involved in the actual performance of the imagined activity. EMG was recorded from those muscle groups expected to increase in activity during imagination of various tasks including typing, singing, playing a wind instrument, and squeezing a hand dynamometer. The results indicated that there were significant increments in EMG for all subjects, although localization was not always consistent. Furthermore, there was an absence of increased EMG in subjects unable to imagine the instructed actions. Shaw concluded that muscle activity is a necessary concomitant for the imagination of various activities.

In subsequent work, Shaw (1940) studied the relation between muscle action potentials and imagination by instructing subjects to first lift a series of weights with the right arm and then imagine lifting the same weights with the same arm. At no time was the subject allowed to see the weights. Action potentials were recorded from the right forearm during actual and imagined lifting. The results indicated that increments in right arm-EMG occurred during actual and imagined lifting of the weights and that the magnitude of the muscle response in *both* conditions increased linearly with the magnitude of the weight. Of particular importance is that these muscle responses did not decrease with repeated imaginations—since the responses did not habituate, they are more likely to be critical for the imagination process. Shaw concluded that muscular activity during imagination appears to increase with the amount of difficulty associated with the imagined task.

Wolpert (1960) recorded EMG from a variety of electrode placements while subjects imagined actions that had, upon previous overt performance, yielded measurable potentials. No increased EMG responses were noted during imagination. Wolpert attributed this failure to confirm Jacobson's (1930) findings to his use of surface electrodes (rather than needle-electrodes) and to the use of subjects untrained in progressive relaxation. These non-trained subjects were probably tenser than trained, relaxed subjects, so that the small potentials that accompanied thought may have been swamped by generalized tension potentials generated by nervous subjects anticipating instructions.

SILENT READING

Jacobson and Kraft (1942) electromyographically measured muscle activity of the leg (right quadriceps femoris) with wire electrodes while (100) subjects engaged in a task of silent reading. The results indicated that the mean leg EMG curve ran between the values of 1.5 to 2.0 μv for the duration of the 30 min reading period. The highest levels occurred during the first two minutes of reading and during the last four minutes of reading; the lowest EMG level occurred during the interval of 16 to 18 minutes of reading. Post-experimental session recordings indicate that the average EMG level of the quadriceps muscle dropped to less than .5 μv during relaxation. Jacobson and Kraft concluded that the level of quadriceps-EMG during reading is consistently above the level of rest.

Strother (1949) monitored arm- and leg-EMGs while subjects read interpretive material expressive of happiness, hate-anger, tranquility-reverence, and fear. Readings were taken on arm and leg muscles on either the left or right side at any one time and counterbalanced with readings on the contralateral side in subsequent trials. The results showed that, regardless of location, muscle activity differed significantly as a function of the four different kinds of emotional material read. The order of EMG magnitude of the different emotions in descending order were: fear, hate-anger, happiness, and tranquility-reverence.

By comparing naive subjects with subjects trained in dramatic reading the expectation was that the mere effects of reading could be further distinguished from the effects of simulated emotion. Analysis of variance supported two related hypotheses: (1) that differential tension patterns, as well as magnitude of response, distinguished between the emotions simulated; and (2) that experienced readers showed more generalized tension patterns whereas naive subjects showed concentration of activity more in the right arm only. However, the number of subjects was too small to lend itself to statistical treatment.

In two experiments McGuigan and Rodier (1968) systematically manipulated the amplitude of covert oral behavior during silent reading. There were four reading conditions: (1) silence, (2) auditory presentation of prose, (3) backward prose, and (4) white noise. Oral activity (chin and tongue EMG) generally increased under the reading conditions, as did breathing rate. However, non-oral responding was inconsistent: Left arm EMG increased slightly in 13 statistical tests (only one of which was significant), decreased in four tests (none of which were significant), and did not change in one.

Hardyck and Petrinovich (1970) studied the relationship of subvocal speech to difficulty of reading material and to comprehension. Three groups of subjects read two passages, varied as to level of difficulty, while laryngeal, chin-lip, and right forearm flexor EMGs were recorded. Subjects in the *Normal* group simply read the passages, whereas in a laryngeal *Feedback* group, subjects heard a tone following any increase in the amplitude of the integrated laryngeal-EMG. To control for the added complexity of this task, a *Control* group received the same tone if the right forearm flexor-EMG exceeded a predetermined relaxation level. All measures of EMG activity were found to increase from baseline during the reading tasks, although no statistical analyses were conducted. All three EMG measures did significantly increase as the difficulty of the prose read increased. There were also two significant interactions: Experimental condition interacted with muscle group, and difficulty level interacted with muscle group. Specifically, laryngeal-EMG increased for "easy" vs. "hard" reading material for the Normal and Control groups but remained near zero for the Feedback group, whereas chin-lip and forearm flexor activity showed no systematic change in relation to the experimental condition. The interaction between difficulty level and muscle group indicated that laryngeal and chin-lip activity were correlated with difficulty, while the forearm flexor group showed little change. Comprehension was significantly and inversely related to difficulty, with the Feedback condition exhibiting a significantly greater decrement in comprehension relative to the experimental and control conditions. Hardyck and Petrinovich concluded that subvocal speech serves as a vital stimulus input capable of mediating a cognitive response—an extension of a proposal by Osgood (1957b).

The internal processing that occurs during listening is no doubt unique in some important respects. By systematically recording various covert processes, we should be able to specify the critical neuromuscular circuits that function during speech perception. Unfortunately, as we shall see, much additional research is necessary on this important problem. Smith, Malmo, and Shagass (1954) studied listening and talking. Two groups of subjects—psychiatric patients and college students—heard a tape-recorded article on sleep. Subsequently, they were asked to verbally recall what the article was about. EMG activity was recorded during a period of quiescence both preceding and following the tape-recording. No sizable differences in amount of muscle tension were measured between the periods before and after listening. However, significant increases in muscle activity were found in both forearms and the chin during listening. During talking significant increases in EMG activity occurred in all sites monitored. When amount of muscle tension between the patients and the students was compared the patients showed a significantly higher amount of tension in the chin only during both reading and talking. These muscle tension changes were thought to be related to attention. However, the tape recording the subjects listened to sounded in places "like a bad radio" so that the subjects evidently had to generally strain to be able to comprehend the words; consequently, the EMG changes in this study are not unequivocally related to the process of speech perception, and should be evaluated with that caution in mind.

Wallerstein (1954) recorded EMG from the chin, forehead, and both forearm extensors during tasks of attentive listening that were varied in ease of comprehension. His subjects listened to a detective story ("easy") and then to a philosophical essay ("difficult") of about 10 minutes length. Each was preceded and followed by rest (baseline) intervals, and each was repeated three times. The results indicated that frontalis-EMG significantly increased from the baseline during all listening periods, whereas a significant increase in chin-EMG was found for only the second and third hearings of the story, but not similarly for the essay. During the listening period, frontalis-EMG exhibited a nonsignificant rising gradient of tension while chin-EMG showed no clear pattern. Wallerstein concluded that rising gradients of muscle tension reflect the amount of information processed, rather than task difficulty or level of arousal. Theoretically, (after Hebb, 1949) these gradients may be viewed as the interaction of central and motor events constituting the thought process.

Wallerstein also found that pre-rest tension of the frontalis significantly decreased from the first to third hearings of the story and the essay, while a similar pattern for chin-EMG was not significant. Right and left arm-EMGs were not observed to systematically vary during the rest and listening periods. Examining the relationship between motivation (as indicated by the slope of EMG gradients) and arousal (measured by EEG amplitude), Bartoshuk (1956) obtained frontalis, chin, and both

244

forearm extensor EMG as well as EEG recordings preceding, during, and following three successive auditory presentations of a story. Significant frontalis EMG gradients above baseline occurred during all three presentations; the EMG slope and EEG amplitude were inversely related for the first presentation only. Recordings from the chin revealed positive EMG gradients above baseline in approximately half the subjects whereas the forearm extensors showed a significant decrease from baseline during the initial hearing. Both chin and forearm EMGs were independent of EEG voltage. Considering the data of his experiment together with the similar one by Wallerstein (1954), Bartoshuk provided three empirical conclusions: (1) positive frontalis EMG gradients are significantly associated with listening to either a story or an essay; (2) the slope of the frontalis EMG gradient is positively associated with interest in the material listened to, suggesting that this gradient is indicative of motivation to listen; (3) frontalis EMGs are more closely associated with listening than are either forearm or chin EMG. In both studies forearm extensor EMG failed to show positive gradients during listening; although positive chin EMG gradients did appear during the three listening sessions, they were found to be unrelated to interest, frontalis EMG, and EEG amplitude.

LEARNING

Travis and Kennedy (1947) studied the effect of external feedback from supraorbital ("brow") muscle tension during a simulated "lookout" task in which the subjects signalled the perception of visual or auditory stimuli. Visual or auditory stimuli were presented contingent upon the reduction of the supraorbital muscle tension (EMG) with the criterion being successively reduced as a function of trials. The results showed that rate and amplitude of supraorbital-EMG and reaction time are inversely related. The authors noted that alertness often decreased to the point of somnolence. Travis and Kennedy concluded that this technique may be practically applied to maintain alertness. We indicate in column 2 of Table 7.1 that there was a change of brow EMG from baseline during the task; this conclusion seems reasonable because the procedure used produced EMG decrease, though this is not a typical baseline procedure.

Berry and Davis (1958) recorded EMGs from the right forearm extensor, masseter (jaw), and the frontalis muscles of subjects engaged in a serial learning task. Nonsense syllables were presented so that there was a 3-second information interval and a 3-second intersyllable or the response interval. A learning score was computed as the total number of correct responses for 20 trials. The results indicated that the sum of jaw and forehead EMGs for response and information intervals was significantly and nonlinearly related to learning scores. The best and poorest learners had higher potentials than mediocre. In order to assess the differential behavior after right and wrong responses, a measure representing the difference between the drop in EMG following a right response and the drop following a wrong response was computed for each subject. It was found that these changes were also non-linearly related to learning scores, the differences being larger for the best and poorest subjects. For all analyses, arm EMG and learning scores were not significantly related. Berry and Davis noted that the non-monotonic relations between muscle tension and learning are more complex than usually thought and therefore require further study before firm conclusions may be arrived at. Their preference, however, was for the following interpretation. The muscle activity recorded during superior learning represents responses such as pronunciation of the syllable vocally and subvocally. This type of action would favor learning especially as there was more of it following an incorrect response that needed to be replaced than following a correct response which did not need to be replaced. For poor learners, the heightened EMG represented tendencies to escape, to make subvocal ejaculations of surprise or dismay, or other indiscernable activity; thus when the subject is shown to be wrong, such responses probably interfere with learning.

Berger, Irwin, and Frommer (1970) measured EMGs during two different observational learning tasks: (1) to learn eight hand signals from the manual alphabet for the deaf by observing pictorial models; and (2) to memorize eight word-number pairs presented on a card. EMGs were recorded from the right wrist and right forearm flexor positions during the two learning periods. Baseline recordings were taken during rest periods preceding each observational learning task. The results indicated that muscle activity at both electrode placements was significantly greater during the hand-signal task than during the word-number task. No tests of differences between baselines and experimental periods were reported. Berger et al. concluded that their data support previous results relating localized muscular activity and cognitive activity. For confirmation and extension of these findings see Berger and Hadley (1975) and Bernal and Berger (1976).

Petrinovich and Hardyck (1970) studied the relative amount of generalization of an instrumental response from words to pictures and from pictures to words. The picture and word training stimuli were presented to subjects who were instructed to press a key when each stimulus appeared. During the test series, each subject pressed the key only when a slide that had been included in the training series was detected. During testing, EMGs were recorded from the muscle group active in the performance of the overt response (viz., forearm flexor). Consequently overt and covert EMG response records were obtained. Considering only overt responses, the results indicate that retention for the picture stimuli was significantly higher than that for the words, that the retention for both pictures and words was significantly higher than for the generalization from either words to pictures or from pictures to words, and that there was no significant difference between the number of generalized responses from either words to pictures or from pictures to words. A similar analysis of overt *and* covert responses yielded the same results except that the mean number of generalized responses from pictures to words was significantly higher than from words to pictures. Petrinovich and Hardyck suggested that the relatively higher generalization from pictures to words is possible because subjects verbally coded the name of the object shown in the picture when the training slide was presented. Thus, the greater generalization during testing may be understandable because the relevant covert response was made earlier during training.

In a procedure reminiscent of Bills' (1927), Beh and Hawkins (1973) examined the effect of induced muscle tension on the acquisition and retention of a serial list of 12 words. They used four groups of subjects in a 2 × 2 factorial design of tension-relaxation during acquisition, with tension-relaxation during recall. Tension was induced by the use of a hand dynamometer with an EMG feedback system that signalled the subject when the prescribed level of tension had not been achieved. The results indicated that the subjects who learned under tension required significantly fewer trials to learn the list; furthermore, groups who learned under tension demonstrated significantly better recall one week after training. Beh and Hawkins concluded that their data are in essential agreement with those reported by Bills (1927). An increase in arm EMG is indicated in column 2 of Table 7.1 although, because it was induced by the dynamometer, this is not a typical response increase over baseline.

NOCTURNAL DREAMS

Mental activity occurs throughout sleep, being most vivid during dreams. While the eyes have been the major focus of study during dreaming (as discussed in Chapter 5), nonoral muscle responding has received attention too. Max (1935) conducted an experimental study of the motor theory of consciousness by recording EMG from the arms and legs of "deaf-mute" subjects during sleep, dreaming, and external stimulation during sleep. Since "speech" was produced by activity of the hands and arms of his deaf subjects, Max hypothesized that increased EMGs in these regions would be associated with dreaming, and with consciousness in general. The records showed that the transition from the waking to the sleeping state was associated with a progressive diminution of arm EMG for both deaf-mute and normal subjects. When awakened from periods of increased arm EMG activity it was found for 30 of 33 instances that the subjects reported dream activity. There was no leg EMG response during dreaming. As a control, deaf subjects were also wakened during periods of electrical "silence," and for only 10 of 62 such awakenings were dreams reported. Similar procedures for hearing subjects indicated that, although dreams were reported, arm EMG activity remained constant throughout sleep. When other stimuli were presented during sleep it was found that they elicited increased arm EMG activity more frequently for deaf subjects than for normal subjects. Max concluded that the dreams of deaf-mute subjects appear to be associated with increased EMG activity of the arm, and are therefore consistent with the motor theory of consciousness. The increase from baseline in Table 7.1 is interpreted here as an observation that was monitored by Max and related to dream reports; it is thus atypical in that it was not produced by an experimental treatment. The same reasoning applies to most of the other articles in this section on sleep research.

Stoyva (1965) repeated Max's (1935) study on the association between finger activity and mental activity during the sleep of deaf subjects. EEG, eye movements, and finger-EMG were recorded from deaf and normal hearing subjects during sleep. The subjects were awakened for dream narrative collections following bursts of finger activity or prolonged quiescence in the EMG record. The results showed that the mean rate of finger EMG bursts for deaf and hearing subjects during REM and non-REM sleep was essentially the same. A replication of these procedures employing more sensitive apparatus and scoring techniques yielded similar results. Stoyva concluded that these data fail to confirm Max's (1935) earlier findings and therefore refute the motor theory of thinking in which cognitive activity is related to motor activity of the linguistic apparatus.

In evaluating Stoyva's (1965) study, it should be pointed out that he employed an ink-writing polygraph for recording EMG, a technique that is probaby not as sensitive as that used by Max. Furthermore, Stoyva's conclusion that there was "no difference between deaf and normal subjects with respect to amount of finger EMG activity in any stage of sleep. Accordingly, finger movements during sleep on the part of deaf persons cannot be taken to substantiate the motor theory of thinking" (1965, p. 348) is based on the assumption that the fingers of normal hearing dreamers are inactive during the mental activity of dreaming. We have noted in this chapter considerable evidence that the arms (including finger activity) are quite active during thought. Hence, Stoyva's findings may actually be quite positive ones that indicate peripheral finger activity in deafs and normals during dreaming. Finally, it should be noted that Stoyva measured "mean rate of finger EMG bursts," based on whether an amplitude of 20 μv was exceeded. Many of the covert responses with amplitudes of less than 20 μv might also have yielded interesting findings.

Wolpert and Trosman (1958) recorded eye movements, frontal and parietal EEG, and gross body movements (as EEG artifacts) of 10 subjects over 51 nights of experimental sleep. The results indicated that detailed dream recall occurred significantly beyond chance when the subjects were awakened during gross body movements of Stage 1 sleep. Wolpert and Trosman concluded that sleep researchers should awaken subjects for narrative collection during periods of gross body movement rather than rapid eye movement in order to obtain maximum recall of completed dream episodes. The significant point thus is that "gross body movement" signalled the end of a dream episode. Consequently, awakening during a REM period without bodily movement would interrupt the dream episode. These researchers did not, however, present a comparison of the effectiveness of the two techniques for "diagnosing" dream periods.

Wolpert (1960) recorded EEG, eye movements, and (preferred) arm and wrist EMG of subjects over a series of 20 experimental sleep sessions. His subjects were awakened for dream narrative collections from Stage 1-rapid eye movement periods following distinctive EMG patterns; he also awakened them during sleep Stages 2-4. Independent judges rated the dream narratives and EMG records, and subsequently compared ratings of the decoded pairs. The results of this procedure indicated that wrist EMG was significantly greater during Stage 1-REM periods than during Stages 2, 3, and 4 ("nondreaming") periods of sleep. Additionally, significant associations between EMG activity and dream narrative content were found for some subjects.

As one example, a subject was awakened when there was an isolated muscle action potential in his right arm, at which time he reported that as the dream was interrupted he was reaching for a jacket. In another instance there was a combined bodily movement, following which the subject reported that, at the end of the dream he jumped over a line of fish with sharp dorsal fins by extending his arms, legs and trunk. Wolpert concluded that motor expression of dream content is greatly inhibited but not absent.

The tonic activity of the body musculature of six humans during natural sleep was studied systematically by Jacobson, Kales, Lehmann, and Hoedemaker (1964). EMG activity was measured in 29 muscle groups of the six subjects for a total of 24 subject-sleep sessions. There was also simultaneous recording of EEG and eye movement. To emphasize the difference between tonic and phasic activity of skeletal muscle, tonic responding is sustained and continuous. Phasic muscle activity is rapidly changing, occurring in bursts. Hence, while it is common to find that tonus decreases during dreaming, there still is much rapid phasic activity. The distinction is especially important for us because we hypothesize in Chapter 9 that linguistic coding is carried in large part by phasic bursts of the skeletal musculature (rather than by tonic activity). During sleep, tonus of most head and neck muscles typically decreased at the onset of Stage 1-REM periods. As an example, hyoid-EMG was found to decrease in 47 of 61 REM periods observed. Muscle tonus of the trunk and limbs was found to remain unchanged in all of 487 REM periods observed, although frequent bursts of activity were noted. Jacobson et al. concluded that muscle tonus of the neck and head is related to EEG Stage 1-REM periods while tonus of the trunk and limbs exhibits a relatively constant level. It should be noted that there was little concentration on phasic activity in this study, yet phasic activity is the more important for studying mental content, whether awake or during dreaming (e.g., McGuigan and Tanner, 1971; Sokolov, 1972). This point is also well made below by Baldridge et al. (1965). In fact, Dement and Kleitman (1957b) reported an increase in fine muscle movements during the dream phase which was essentially absent in non-dream phases. They reported that these fine movements were observable directly but were not recorded with their electromyographic techniques, which were apparently not sufficiently sensitive for covert response research. The importance of the value of studying phasic muscle activity during dreaming should thus be underscored and kept independent from the often made statement that EMG *decreases* during dreaming—while apparently tonic EMG *does* decrease, phasic activity does *not*.

Baldridge, Whitman, and Kramer (1965) further examined Aserinsky and Kleitman's (1953) original report of an association between rapid eye movements and body movements during dreams of sleep. By the use of highly sensitive strain gauges, continuous measurements of eye, throat, hand, and foot movements were recorded during undisturbed sleep. The results indicated that movements appeared simultaneously from all locations and that this activity was significantly correlated with REMs. Body movement patterns correctly identified 32 of 41 peaks of eye movement activity, the typical criterion of when the subject was dreaming. Based on this and previous work, Baldridge et al. point out that the strain gauge method for detecting eye movement is "many times more sensitive than that recorded by means of the corneoretinal potential" (1965, p. 25). They emphasized that previous negative findings with regard to increased muscle activity during dreams have been based on very crude measurement techniques. Based on the previously reported association of REMs and dreams Baldridge et al. concluded that fine muscle activity is associated with nocturnal dreams. They suggested three possible interpretations of the concurrence of fine body movments with dreaming: (1) that the dreamer is attemping to carry out the action of the dream as the dream unfolds; (2) that the covert responses provide increased proprioceptive input into the brain which is then interpreted as a dream; or (3) that the dream and muscle activity occur simultaneously as a result of some independent mechanism such as heightened activity in the reticular formation.

Sassin and Johnson (1968) measured EEG, eye responses, and arm, leg, and submental EMG while their five subjects slept in the laboratory for two consecutive nights. The object of the study was to specify the relationship between body motility (any "detectable" movement) and K-complexes (i.e., sharp reversed wave forms interspersed with slow components) of Stage 2 sleep, the latter often considered an indicator of arousal. The results showed that K-complexes preceded body movements (significantly) during Stage 2 sleep; the mean latency for 396 movements was 2.52 sec. The rate of body movements per minute was significantly lower in slow wave (Stages 3 and 4) sleep than in Stages 1 and 2; rate of body movements was not significantly different in Stage 2 vs. Stage 1-REM periods. Analysis of the type and duration of muscle movements indicated that 80% of Stage 3 and Stage 4 movements were global, involving the head, extremities, and trunk. Movements during Stages 1 and 2 were evenly divided between movements of the head, face, or mouth and global movements; a significant number of phasic limb movements occurred during Stage 1-REM periods. Sassin and Johnson concluded that body motility during sleep is not a random phenomenon and appears to be systematically related to characteristic K-complexes of Stage 2 sleep. Their finding of a significant number of *phasic* limb movements during dreaming is to be emphasized and related to our previous discussion of this point.

Larson and Foulkes (1969) examined the reported association between EMG suppression and passage from NREM sleep to REM sleep (cf. Berger, 1961; Jacobson et al., 1964). They recorded nocturnal EEG, eye responses and submental EMG from 5 subjects for a total of 42 nights. A total of 196 awakenings for the collection of dream narratives was classified among three awakening categories: NREM sleep preceding EMG suppression and REM onset; NREM sleep immediately following the EMG suppression; and early moments of REM sleep accompanied by EMG suppression. The researchers also recorded the time from calling the subject's name to the time at which he gave a coherent reply to the first questions following the awakening ("orientation time"). The results indicated that suppressed-EMG-NREM awakenings tended (not significantly) to be associated with lower dream recall frequency and lower Dreamlike Fantasy Scale ratings than did high EMG-NREM awakenings. Two of five subjects showed significantly longer orientation times on suppressed EMG pre-REM awakenings than on high EMG-pre-REM awakenings. Contrary to the traditional view of a monotonic transition from NREM sleep to REM sleep, Larson and Foulkes concluded that a momentary "deepening" of sleep (in terms of vivid mental content and decreased reactivity to the awakening stimulus) appears to accompany the pre-REM suppression of submental EMG potentials.

Experiments demonstrating an association between rapid eye movements (REMs) and middle ear muscle activity during sleep were described by Pessah and Roffwarg (1972). By use of acoustic impedance techniques the authors continuously monitored the stapedius and tensor tympani muscles. The experimenters then observed whether or not REM periods followed middle ear muscle activity (dream narratives were not called for). The results showed that middle ear activity typically precedes, and continues throughout, REM periods. Eighty percent of all middle ear muscle activity occurred within REM periods and half of the remaining 20% occurred in 10-min intervals prior to REM sleep onset. Pessah and Roffwarg concluded that this phenomenon requires further examination, with particular focus on the possible association of middle ear muscle activity and auditory imagery.

Gardner, Grossman, Roffwarg, and Weiner (1973) studied the relation between fine limb movements and dream actions of REM sleep. The subjects, selected for good dream recall, were awakened for dream reports following EMG activity of the four extremities. They were awakened at four different times: (1) when there was no movement; (2) when there was upper limb activity with an absence of lower limb activation; (3) when there was lower limb activity with an absence of upper limb activation; and (4) when there was mixed upper and lower limb activation. The total of 209 dream reports and EMG records were coded, scored blindly, and then decoded for statistical analysis. The results indicated that a significant correlation existed in good dream recallers between the location of actual bodily movement and location and amount of dreamed action.

Summary and Conclusions

On the basis of the data and analyses in the preceding section, we may conclude:

1. that a variety of covert nonoral skeletal muscle responses *did* occur under a number of cognitive conditions in that the response measure changed from baseline (Criterion 1);
2. to a large extent those responses appear to have occurred because of the cognitive conditions studied by the researchers, since those responses often varied systematically as a function of the cognitive conditions (Criterion 2);
3. the most apparent conclusion with regard to Criterion 3 is that researchers generally did not make concurrent measures of other covert processes. The implication is obvious that researchers should more extensively apply this criterion. When this criterion *was* successfully applied, the nonoral response classes of interest (those specified in column 1 of Table 7.1) co-varied about as frequently with other response measures as they were independent of other covert reactions;
4. to a very large extent, the responses specified in column 1 in some way specifically related to a cognitive condition. The various specific relationships are abstracted below.

SUMMARY OF SPECIFIC RELATIONSHIPS
IDENTIFIED IN COLUMN 4 OF TABLE 7.1

Problem Solving. Golla (1921): increases in forearm tonicity were positively related to the difficulty of the problem to be solved.

Tuttle (1924): muscle tonus (patellar reflex) increased from relaxation to conversation to problem solving.

Freeman (1930): leg tension increased during the first part of mental tasks directly as a function of task difficulty.

Clites (1936): successful problem solvers showed greater right forearm EMG and significantly less overt movement of that arm than did unsuccessful problem solvers.

Davis (1937): amount of right arm EMG was negatively related to amount of mental work accomplished.

Max (1937): the more intelligent and better educated subjects gave smaller amplitude of manual arm responses to problem solving situations.

Davis (1938): right arm and neck EMG increased as the difficulty of the problem solving task increased.

Davis (1939): there is a bodily focus of muscular activity for various psychological processes, e.g., during multiplication the focus is in the right arm (relatively greater activity there than in the left arm which, in turn, is greater than in the left leg). During learning of nonsense syllables the focus was thought to be in the speech musculature. Response amplitude decreases as distance from the point of focus increases.

Ellson et al. (1952): arm EMG response latencies were significantly shorter for critical lying responses than for critical non-lying responses.

Reuder (1956): subjects under a task-oriented instruction exhibited higher EMG levels on the relatively difficult problems than they did on easy problems, whereas subjects who received ego-oriented instructions showed higher EMG levels for easy problems than they did for difficult problems.

Stennett (1957): as the subject's incentive is increased, there is an inverted U relationship with integrated amplitude of EMGs from the left and right arms, and also with Palmar conductance.

Leshner (1961): during problem solving, EMGs decreased significantly for successful subjects and significantly increased for subjects who failed.

Pishkin (1964): amplitude of EMG in the preferred arm significantly and positively increased with learning rate, and there was a negative correlation between preferred arm EMG amplitude and time required per trial.

MacNeilage (1966a): as difficulty of serial addition tasks increased, forehead and arm EMG significantly increased.

Pishkin and Shurley (1968): there was a positive correlation between number of errors made on a concept identification task and forehead EMG; furthermore that EMG activity increased significantly as a function of task complexity when the subjects were given both solvable and unsolvable sets.

Vaughn and McDaniel (1969): amplitude of frontalis EMG during a match to sample visual discrimination task significantly increased when the subjects made correct responses, and decreased following errors. Phasic responses were typically superimposed on a rising and falling EMG gradient.

McGuigan (1971): amplitude of left arm and lip EMG significantly increased over baseline during problem solving, with the arm EMG being significantly greater than during a nonverbal control task. Integrated EEG from the left motor area decreased significantly more during problem solving than during the control task.

Imagination. Jacobson (1927): reduction in EMG tension prevented the subject from engaging in conscious processes like imagery, attention, reflection, and emotion.

Jacobson (1927, 1930a): imagination of a right arm flexion produced heightened EMG in the right arm, whereas imagination of activity of other parts of the body did not produce right arm EMG increase. His general conclusion was that imagination of voluntary movement is associated with neuromuscular activity in the locale of the imagined act. For his succeeding studies we will maintain this general conclusion and cite only the specific findings.

Jacobson (1930b): confirmed his (1930a) findings except that he used a variety of specific imagination instructions such as "imagine lifting a cigarette to your mouth," "imagine throwing a ball," etc. The same relationship was found when the subjects were asked to recollect other muscular acts commonly performed with the right arm.

Jacobson (1930c): imagining lifting a 10-pound weight produced EMG increases in the right biceps, but imagining lifting with the left did not. Furthermore, subjects could not simultaneously imagine lifting a weight and keep their arms relaxed, i.e., they either had to disregard the relaxation instructions and imagine, or disregard the imagination instructions in order to keep their arm relaxed.

Jacobson (1931a): imagining lifting a weight with the right arm produced EMG increases in the right arm. On the other hand, to *visually* imagine lifting the weight with the right arm typically increased EMG from the *ocular* region, but did not typically increase biceps activity in the right arm.

Jacobson (1931b): imagination of left hand flexion in an amputated arm is associated with a substitute reaction in the corresponding muscles of the right arm, and in the remanent muscles of the upper left arm.

Shaw (1940): the magnitude of right arm EMG linearly increased as the magnitude of weights increased; this was during actual lifting of the weights and while imagining lifting those weights.

Silent Reading. Jacobson and Kraft (1942): right leg muscle EMG increased during a 30-minute silent reading period, the highest EMG level occurring during the first and last several minutes of reading.

Strother (1949): EMG level in the forelimbs while reading various kinds of emotional material was in order of descending magnitude when reading the following kinds of prose: fear, hate-anger, happiness, tranquility-reverence.

Hardyck and Petrinovich (1970): laryngeal, chin-lip, and right arm EMG measures increased as a function of difficulty level of material read.

Speech Perception. Smith et al. (1954): EMG increased in the forearms and chin while listening to a recording. When overtly recalling there were significant increases from the forehead, neck, both arms and chin.

Wallerstein (1954): frontalis EMG significantly increased from baseline while listening to a detective story and to a philosophical essay. Chin EMG increased significantly for the second and third hearings of the story but not for the essay.

Bartoshuk (1956): frontalis EMG is associated with interest in the material listened to and is more closely associated with listening than are forearm or chin EMGs.

Learning. Travis and Kennedy (1947): rate and amplitude of super orbital EMGs are inversely related to reaction time during an external feedback lookout task.

Berger et al. (1970): right wrist EMG was higher while learning the manual alphabet for the deaf through observation than when memorizing work-number pairs visually presented. They concluded that there was a relationship between cognitive activity and localized muscle activity.

Petrinovich and Hardyck (1970): the mean number of generalized EMG responses from pictures to words was significantly higher than from words to pictures, suggesting that covert responses made during learning to pictures involved verbally coding the names of the objects shown in the pictures.

Beh and Hawkins (1973): subjects with induced muscle tensions in the arm learned significantly faster than subjects who did not have such induced tensions. Furthermore, delayed recall was significantly greater for those who learned under tension.

Nocturnal Dreams. Max (1935): arm EMG increased during the dreams of deaf mute subjects.

Stoyva (1965): in both deaf and hearing subjects, REM periods showed a consistently accelerated rate of finger EMG activity in comparison with other stages of sleep.

Wolpert and Trosman (1958): there was a strong relationship between frequency of recall of a dream if the dreamer awakened during gross bodily movement.

Wolpert (1960): EMG was significantly greater during REM sleep than during Stages 2, 3, and 4. Additionally, there were significant associations between EMG activity and dream narrative content for some subjects, but not for others.

Jacobson et al. (1964): muscle tonus of the neck and head is related to EEG Stage 1-REM periods.

Baldridge et al. (1965): fine muscle activity in various parts of the body is associated with REM periods.

Sassin and Johnson (1968): phasic limb movements occur during Stage 1-REM.

Larson and Foulkes (1969): momentary deepening of sleep is accompanied by pre-REM suppression of submental EMG.

Pessah and Roffwarg (1972): middle ear muscle responses typically precedes and continues throughout REM periods.

Gardner et al. (1973): there is a significant correlation between location of actual bodily movement and location and amount of dreamed action.

In general, it seems clear that numerous covert nonoral skeletal muscle responses occur when individuals silently engage in a wide variety of cognitive activities. The problem now is to speculate about how these covert responses function during cognition.

Relative to our understanding of covert nonoral behavior, we can entertain a more refined model of the function of covert oral (speech) behavior (McGuigan, 1976). That model has been based to a large extent on the conclusions that (1) there is a discriminative relationship between class of covert oral behavior and the phonemic system, and (2) that the speech musculature is physiologically capable of generating and transmitting such distinctive phonetic information to the linguistic regions of the brain.

The great versatility of verbal symbolism has led us to recognize a priority for linguistic thought involving principally the speech musculature and the linguistic regions of the brain (McGuigan, 1966a). Just as clearly, however, nonoral behavior can also serve linguistic functions. How often do we substitute gestures for spoken words, as in waving goodbye to a friend, or shrugging the shoulders? More refined nonoral language functioning occurs when deaf individuals communicate with dactylic language, when the blind read by Braille, when people engage in cursive handwriting; and we may note in this context the ability of the cutaneous senses to receive and process linguistic input (cf. Geldard, 1966). [With speech we presume that there is commonality in production and perception processes (Chapter 9). We make the same assumption here too.] No doubt the responding of the nonoral musculature is involved in some way in processing information necessary for understanding the meaning of the stimulus input. There is considerable precedent for this statement, as in Titchener's context theory of meaning (1909) in which he held that the meaning of words in part originates in bodily attitudes of the muscle systems. Jacobson (1929) held that localized bodily tensions literally *mean* the imagined act. When contractions in a given bodily region are recognized by a person who has been trained in Progressive Relaxation, they are then qualitatively interpreted, e.g., tension signals in the right arm might mean to one individual that they are covertly behaving (imagining) "as if" to overtly light a cigarette, or tensions in the shoulders and back may be interpreted by a busy executive "as if" hurrying to get the day's work done. Jacobson (1929) maintained the "... *working hypothesis that any report of the experience of muscular tenseness is incomplete until a function is stated.* The subject is simply asked, if necessary, 'A tension to do what?'. . . Sherrington (1915) goes so far as to believe that tonus is always to be understood in the light of its aim or function. He states, 'Every reflex can, therefore, be regarded from the point of view of what may be called its 'aim.' To glimpse at the aim of a reflex is to gain hints for future experimentation on it. Such a clue to purpose is often difficult to get . . .' " (pp. 78-79).

It has been previously argued that, during linguistic processing (when "thoughts" occur), both oral and nonoral responses interact in some complex but supportive fashion (McGuigan, 1976). When one imagines lighting a cigarette with the right hand, for example, one covertly responds symbolically in the oral region (perhaps subvocally by saying "cigarette" or "fire,") and almost simultaneously responds with the nonoral skeletal musculature with contractions of muscles in the right arm and hand (Jacobson, 1932). These oral and nonoral responses are hypothesized to interact in carrying information to the linguistic regions of the brain. (And we must not forget that there also follows an emotional component to thoughts through circuits that engage the autonomic system.)

Granting that the nonoral skeletal musculature has a linguistic capacity, whether or not it functions discriminatively in the generation and transmission of verbal coding, as the speech musculature apparently does, is still open to question. At first glance one is inclined to answer this question in the negative. It is clear that the speech musculature—being an extremely complex and flexible system in which motor units of only several muscle fibers can be differentially activated—is physiologically capable of very precise discriminative reactions (Chapter 3). In contrast, the nonoral skeletal musculature (with the exception of that in the eyes and the middle ears) is not as physiologically capable of precise differential responding (e.g., in gastrocnemius there are typically some 2,000 muscle fibers that must react in concert when each motor neuron is activated). Nevertheless, language *is* processed to at least some extent nonorally, often quite efficiently and in great detail. It may be that there exist discriminative relationships between linguistic categories and classes of nonoral responding. A specialized example of this is the deaf individual proficient in dactylic language who, when silently processing a linguistic unit, exhibits heightened activity in exactly those fingers which would be engaged during overt communication of that particular linguistic unit.

If the nonoral musculature does not function in the generation and transmission of a verbal code of the degree of complexity and precision as the code carried by the oral musculature, what kind of code might reasonably be involved? We shall hypothesize two kinds of codes: first, a nonoral linguistic code, the nature of which is dependent upon the individual's verbal learning experiences, and second, a nonlinguistic code which has developed as a result of conditioning to various stimulus objects and events. The distinction is thus based on the difference between the learning of linguistic symbols vs. non-linguistic referents.

We shall designate the hypothesized linguistic code generated and transmitted by the nonoral skeletal musculature as an *allographic code*. The term "allogram" is analogous to "allophone" in that an allogram is a written linguistic unit, just as an allophone is a spoken linguistic unit. Similarly, an allogram is an instance of a grapheme class, as an allophone is an instance of a phoneme class. In the Latin alphabet a grapheme would consist of many letters and letter combinations, each of which is an allogram (e.g., the "p" in "pin," the "pp" in "hopping," and the "gh" in "hiccough" are all allograms of the same grapheme).

What is the relationship between graphemes and phonemes? Certainly there is not a one-to-one relationship between spoken language and written language, but just as assuredly there is a considerable overlap. Osgood (personal communication), in effect, has suggested that graphemes are more ambiguous than phonemes.[3] Such a difference might be related to the previous argument that the speech musculature is capable of more highly refined differential responding than most of the other muscles of the body, especially the writing arm and hand.

The notion put forward here is that activation of a pattern of nonoral skeletal muscle responses generates afferent neural impulses that carry an allographic code, as we hypothesize that the speech musculature generates and transmits a phonetic code. The allographic codes are transmitted through neuromuscular circuits to the linguistic regions of the brain. The particular linguistic units of the allographic code, as we said, would depend on the learning history of the individual. We would suppose that one who has learned cursive writing with the Latin alphabet might generate linguistic units consisting of letters or combinations of letters (syllables, etc.) from that alphabet. Those who have learned other languages (Braille, Arabic, Chinese, symbolic logic, or dactylic language of the blind) might generate afferent neural volleys coded appropriately for that language by means of particular nonoral muscle patterns. In this way, then, we could have parallel linguistic information processing involving the speech muscle and the non-speech muscle. When one thinks "bicycle riding," for example, a person: (1) covertly says the words, or some minute fractional component of the words, (as suggested by heightened EMG speech muscle records); (2) covertly writes the words (as suggested by increased EMG in the preferred arm); (3) and also responds elsewhere in the body (particularly, in this instance, the legs). This last point brings us to the second kind of code which might be generated by the nonoral skeletal musculature.

The hypothesized nonlinguistic coding generated by the nonoral skeletal muscles involves a more primitive kind of symbolism than that needed for language—what may be called "referent coding." It is feasible that referent coding also functions at the subhuman level. An animal who has had sufficient experience in responding to a given stimulus object may generate an afferent neural volley in the absence of that stimulus object by reinstating the conditional response pattern, as in dreaming. The precise status of the skeletal muscle fibers during the evocation of the conditional response would then be representative of the conditional stimulus such that the resulting afferent neural volley

---

[3] I am certainly grateful to Charles E. Osgood for his many contributions to my work that have grown out of our ongoing friendly debate (cf. Osgood and McGuigan, 1973), but here especially for guiding me in the direction of the "grapheme concept."

would be coded for that stimulus. Referent coding would thus consist of neuro-muscular states that represent corresponding external conditional stimuli. The view of a ball, for instance, would evoke complex muscle reactions throughout the body, but principally in the throwing arm. When those covert reactions generate neural impulses, coding for the object *ball* would be transmitted to the brain. Conceivably, this non-linguistic coding may be directed through neural circuits to the minor ("nonverbal") hemisphere. Such circuits for referent coding could help us to understand "nonverbal thought," a concept that Sperry (1973) found quite important in his split brain experimentation.[4] Referent coding is relevant also to other considerations of "verbal vs. nonverbal thought" e.g., Pavlov's second and first signal systems; the first signal system may function through referent coding with the minor hemisphere, while linguistic coding involving phonetic and allographic neuromuscular events may underlie the second signal system. Accordingly, while the nonoral skeletal musculature generates a verbal (allographic) code which functions with linguistic regions of the brain, additional circuits might function directly between the nonoral skeletal musculature and, principally, the minor hemisphere.

In summary, during such cognitive acts as perception, imagery, thought, and dreams, we hypothesize for further consideration that the complex muscle response patterns include (1) those speech muscle components that function in the generation of a phonetic code; (2) those nonoral skeletal muscle components that function in the generation of an allographic code; (3) those nonoral skeletal muscle components that function in a nonlinguistic referent code; and (4) circuits involving the autonomic system for adding emotional tone. In conjunction, these various volleys are transmitted to their appropriate regions of the brain (the verbal coding to the linguistic regions for lexical-semantic processing, the nonverbal coding regions of the brain for nonlinguistic processing).

With Watson (1930) and many others, it is here proposed that there are critical nonoral muscular components of cognitive activity. A high priority next step is to seek additional data relevant to nonoral coding systems. Our expectation is that further experimentation would specify highly differentiated covert responding in the nonoral musculature as a function of class of linguistic input. While it is unreasonable to expect covert nonoral responding to be as differentiated as that of the oral musculature (with the exception of eye activity, which we treat separately) we should expect to find some relationship between classes of bodily locations and linguistic input. Specification of those relationships should greatly contribute to our understanding of information processing in the nonoral musculature, and hence of the functioning of the motor system during cognitive activities. In Chapter 9 we shall develop our notions about coding in greater detail.

---

[4] See also the important work of Malmo (e.g., 1965, 1975) for related phenomena and interpretations.

8

Electrical Measures of Brain Processes

Historical Development

We have previously discussed some of the important historical developments and contemporary theories about brain functioning (Chapter 2) and have noted that the most effective and most widely used measures of central neurophysiological processes are electrical ones. It was Caton in 1875 who first recorded spontaneous electrical activity in the absence of stimulation, and he also recorded evoked potentials from the exposed cortex of an animal while stimulating the eyes with a lamp. Lindsley (1969) suggested that Caton might even have observed the contingent negative variation (CNV) first systematically described by Walter in 1964 (a, b, c). Following Caton's work, there was a certain amount of relevant research in Europe, but nothing of any great significance until Berger's (1929) landmark recording of spontaneous brain activity (the electroencephalogram) from the skull of the normal human. Berger's difficulties in finding acceptance for his findings among the scientific community are well known: As Lindsley (1969) pointed out neurophysiologists of the day were reluctant to think that any events other than the well-known spike potentials occurred in the nervous systems. Acceptance of the slow alpha potentials occurred only through the prestige of Lord Adrian and the confirmation of alpha waves by Adrian and Matthews (1934). [Cf. Lindsley (1969, pp. 2-15) for some of these important historical developments in electroencephalography.]

A method for readily observing average evoked potentials from the human scalp, a much more difficult event to record than the spontaneous EEG, was developed by Dawson in 1947. Briefly, Dawson's method was to superimpose a number of synchronized EEG traces on a cathode ray oscilloscope and record them on a single photographic record. In this way a consistent time-locked relationship appears as a consequence of the commonality of the individual traces in the group traces, revealing the average evoked potential. The importance of Dawson's work was that it led to improved methods for recording evoked potentials, viz., signal averaging with the use of small commercial computers which calculated average transients. A veritable flood of research on the average evoked potential has followed, as will be reported in this chapter.

Another major advance in electrical measurement of brain activity was the recording of the contingent negative variation, which is not readily observable in the raw trace. Typically, the signal-to-noise ratio must be increased, which is possible through the computer averaging technique. The CNV is a slow negative shift in the EEG baseline that occurs when there is a contingency between two successive stimuli. The first stimulus is followed after a constant time interval by the second stimulus to which one must make a response. An example of the CNV can be seen in the EEG trace shown in Fig. 8.1 where we may note that a light flash (S_1) was followed in 1.5 seconds by a continuous tone (S_2). The slow negative potential (CNV) can be observed within the S_1-S_2 interval. The subject's key press terminated the tone and also the negativity of the CNV. For further information about average evoked potentials see especially Donchin (1969); Goff, Matsumiya, Allison, and Goff (1969); Lindsey (1971); Lindsley (1969); Regan (1972); Shagass (1972); Sutton (1969); Vaughn (1969); and for further consideration of the CNV see Cohen (1969) and Tecce (1971, 1972).

The widespread interest in electrical potentials may be witnessed in such disparate fields as psychiatry, neurology, electroencephalography, psychology, ophthalmology, audiology, computer science, and engineering. The early promise of advancing our understanding of brain functioning through these electrical techniques has been realized to some extent, as we shall note in this chapter. While these findings will be of interest to us for the central linguistic aspects of the model developed in Chapter 9, we should recognize that the field is still in its infancy, as can be noted from general reviews of the literature (Lindsley, 1944; Ellingson, 1956; Karlin, 1970; Schmitt, 1970; and the Society Proceedings of the American Electroencephalographic Society, 1972). Ellingson (1956), for instance, concluded that too many functions have been attributed to the alpha rhythm, as in understanding the higher mental processes. Similarly, Lindsley (1969) said "I am afraid, unfortunately, that we don't know so very much more about the nature of the alpha rhythm or the other rhythms than Berger so ably described . . ." (p. 3). Our lack of advanced understanding of electrical cerebral rhythms is

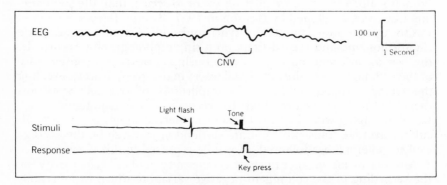

FIG. 8.1   Example of contingent negative variation (CNV) in the raw EEG trace. CNV is the upward shift in EEG baseline occurring between light and tone. Scalp placements are vertex (Cz) and the right mastoid; relative negativity at Cz is upward (from Tecce, 1971).

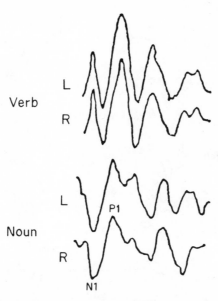

FIG. 8.2 Mean scalp-recorded click-evoked activity from a subject. Each response is an average of 10 trials. Right (R) and left-hemisphere (L) responses using the noun and verb meanings of the single stimulus word "rock" are shown. Calibration: 200 msec, 5 μV. Note lack of baseline (from Teyler, Roemer, Harrison, and Thompson, 1973).

also revealed through the critical review of the literature by Brumlik, Richeson, and Arbit (1966/1967) in which they categorize existing theories as being of the neuronal, mechanical, or combined variety.

A Methodological Note

One particular methodological problem with electrical studies (particularly average evoked potentials) concerns the definition of the reaction by the change from baseline criterion. Researchers in this area typically do not present an extended baseline from which average evoked potentials can be noted. The position taken here is that this criterion is as important for brain studies as it is for the study of other bodily processes. In Fig. 8.2 a set of wave forms that lack baselines may be contrasted with the curves in Fig. 8.3 where the long baseline prior to the open arrow (stimulus onset) may be observed. We are more confident with the data of Fig. 8.3 that the cortical average evoked potentials did occur, as indicated by a change in baseline.

Authors often conclude that their experimental treatments produced distinctive wave forms, as in Fig. 8.4. Such findings warrant a "yes" in column 2 of Table 8.1, but as we have noted especially in Chapter 5, the stronger reasoning results when we evaluate experimental effects as the function of both criteria number 1 (a change from baseline) and 2 (varia-

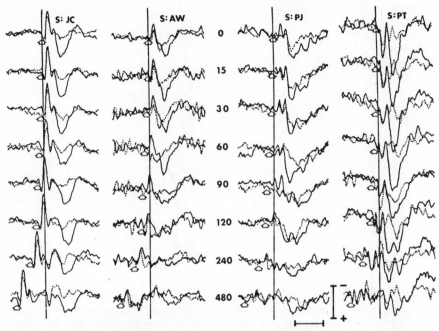

FIG. 8.3 Average evoked potentials for two different experimental conditions. The onset of S1 is indicated by the outline arrow and S2 by the vertical line. Each column is from a different subject. The two left columns were recorded from the occiput and those on the right from the vertex. Vertical calibration: 10 μv. Horizontal calibration: 500 msec. Positivity is indicated by a downward deflection. Note stable baselines prior to first stimulus (S1) (from Rohrbaugh, Donchin, and Eriksen, 1974).

tion as a function of condition). Perhaps experimenters assume that the pre-stimulus baseline would average to essentially a straight line, but it is preferable to actually demonstrate a stable baseline for many reasons (e.g., to assure that the equipment was operating properly, or that the subject was in fact relaxed). Examples of short pre-stimulus intervals where the assumption of stable baselines that is questionable may be found in Rosenfeld, Rudell, and Fox (1969, Fig. 2 on their p. 822) and in Cohn (1971, Fig. 1d on his p. 600).

With these considerations, we shall now turn to a summary of data on brain processes during various cognitive activities. Each study will be evaluated by the four general criteria presented in detail on pages 118–26 of Chapter 5.

Methodological Criteria

Recall from page 118 that the first two criteria allow us to determine whether or not a reaction actually occurred, and if so whether it was a function of the condition of interest (an experimental treatment, etc.).

The second two criteria help us ascertain the function of brain reactions by providing an index of the degree of general bodily arousal during the experimental condition. If the reaction is a localized, relatively unique occurrence it is more likely to serve an information processing function within neuromuscular circuits.

CRITERION 1

Did the Response Actually Occur? If the researcher determined that the electrical brain measure systematically changed from baseline, then "yes" is entered in column 1 of Table 8.1; if there was no systematic change from baseline, then "no" is marked; and if there was no attempt to establish a baseline prior to the experimental treatment, a "?" is entered in column 1 of Table 8.1. An asterisk indicates a statistically significant effect—in the case of Criterion 1, an asterisk indicates that the brain activity reliably changed from the baseline resting condition.

CRITERION 2

Did the Response Occur Because of the Experimental Treatment Per Se? Criterion 2 may be satisfied by showing that the covert reaction systematically changes as a function of two (or more) experimental conditions, e.g., one might show that the evoked potentials differ from when the subject processes taboo words than when processing neutral words (as in Fig. 8.4 on p. 000). A particularly valuable control in this regard is one in which the reaction is measured during some nonlinguistic condition (as

CORTICAL EVOKED POTENTIALS TO SEMANTIC STIMULI

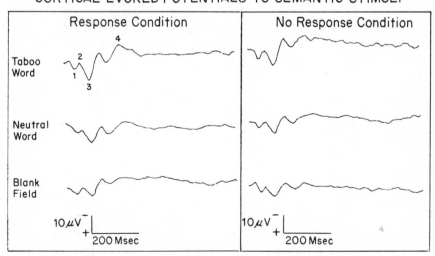

FIG. 8.4 Individual recording illustrating the cortical evoked response under the different stimulus and response conditions. Amplitudes were significantly greater to the taboo words, and greater under the response conditions than under the no response condition (upward deflections are negative) (from Begleiter and Platz, 1969).

TABLE 8.1 Summary of Electrical Neurophysiological Activity During Cognitive Tasks[a]

Task and Experimenter	Electrode Placement	Did the EEG Reaction:			
		(1) Change from Baseline?	(2) Vary as a Function of Conditions?	(3) Occur Independently of Other Covert Processes?	(4) Specifically Relate to a Cognitive Aspect?
Mental Arithmetic					
Kennedy et al. (1948)	External Ianthi	Yes	?	Yes: alpha, eye	Yes
Ford (1954)	Frontal lobe	Yes	?	Yes: EKG	Yes
Johnson et al. (1960)	Occipital, parietal and frontal areas	Yes	No	?	No
Lorens & Darrow (1962)	Frontal, parietal, occipital and temporal	Yes*: % alpha decrease	?	Yes: heart rate, eye, GSR	No
Chapman & Bragdon (1964)	At midline 2.5 cm below vertex and 2.5 cm above inion	Yes	Yes	Yes: eye, ERG, alpha, pupil dilation, accommodation	Yes
Glanzer et al. (1964)	Parietal, temporal, and occipital	?	Yes*	?	Yes
Chapman (1965)	Parietal	?	Yes	?	Yes
Chapman (1971a)	Parietal	?	Yes	?	Yes
Giannitrapani (1966)	Left & right frontal, temporal, parietal & occipital areas	Yes*	Yes*	?	Yes
MacNeilage (1966b)	Parietal lobe	Yes*	No	Yes: heart rate, GSR	No
Shevrin & Rennick (1967)	Bilateral, parietal	Yes	Yes*	?	Yes
Volavka et al. (1967)	Parieto-temporal	Yes	Yes	No: GSR	Yes
Glass & Kwiatkowski (1968)	Occipital	Yes	Yes	?	Yes

[a]In this research survey, we have attempted to specify the results of statistical tests when they were conducted by stating that the effect was "significant" (reliable) or "not significant" (not reliable). Where effects are reported in the absence of these words, together with the absence of asterisks in columns 1, 2, and 3 of the table, the reader may assume that the effects were not subjected to statistical tests. This criterion is not applied to Column 4.

Did the EEG Reaction:

Task and Experimenter	Electrode Placement	(1) Change from Baseline?	(2) Vary as a Function of Conditions?	(3) Occur Independently of Other Covert Processes?	(4) Specifically Relate to a Cognitive Aspect?
Mental Arithmetic (cont.)					
Sokolov (1968)	Frontal, parietal, and occipital	?	No	Yes: EMG (speech)	No
Vogel et al. (1968)	Parietal and occipital	Yes	Yes*	?	Yes
Vogel et al. (1969)	Occipital	?	Yes*	?	Yes
Elul (1969)	Midline, fronto-occipital	?	Yes*	?	Yes
Chapman (1971b), Exp. I	Frontal, occipital	?	Yes*	?	Yes
Chapman (1971b), Exp. II	Frontal, occipital	?	Yes	?	Yes
Chapman et al. (1971)	Frontal, occipital	Yes	Yes	Yes: eye	Yes
Ishihara & Yoshii (1972)	Fz-Cz	?	Yes*	?	Yes
Learning					
Hillyard & Galambos (1967)	?	Yes	Yes	?	Yes
Rosenfeld et al. (1969)	Vertex	Yes*	Yes*	?	Yes
Begleiter et al. (1967, 1969)	O₂	Yes	Yes*	?	Yes
Brown (1970)	Parieto-occipital	Yes*	Yes*	Yes: eye	Yes
Rosenfeld & Hetzler (1973)	Visual cortex (rats)	Yes*	Yes*	?	Yes
Imagination					
Golla et al. (1943)	Parietal-occipital	?	Yes	No: respiration	Yes
Slatter (1960)	Parietal, occipital	Yes*	Yes*	?	Yes
Antrobus et al. (1964)	Occipital	?	Yes*	No: eye	Yes

TABLE 8.1 Summary of Electrical Neurophysiological Activity During Cognitive Tasks (cont.)

Task and Experimenter	Electrode Placement	Did the EEG Reaction:			
		(1) Change from Baseline?	(2) Vary as a Function of Conditions?	(3) Occur Independently of Other Covert Processes?	(4) Specifically Relate to a Cognitive Aspect?
Reading (Visual Linguistic Input)					
Travis & Knott (1937)	Occipital	Yes	Yes	?	Yes
Knott (1938)	Frontal, parietal, occipital(?)	Yes*	Yes*	?	Yes
Pepin et al. (1952)	Frontal, parietal, occipital	Yes	?	?	Yes
Lifshitz (1966)	Parietal, occipital, frontal	?	Yes	Yes: eye	Yes
John et al. (1967)	Occipital, frontal, frontal	?	Yes	Yes: eye	Yes
Lille et al. (1968)	?	Yes	Yes	?	Yes
Shevrin & Fritzler (1968)	Frontal, vertex, occipital	Yes	Yes*	?	Yes
Weinberg & Cole (1968)	Occipital	?	Yes*	?	Yes
Begleiter & Platz (1969)	Inion	Yes*	Yes*	?	Yes
Buchsbaum & Fedio (1969)	Occipital	?	Yes*	?	Yes
Sharrard (1969)	?	?	Yes*	?	Yes
Buchsbaum & Fedio (1970)	Occipital	Yes*	Yes*	?	Yes
Heinemann & Emrich (1971)	Fronto-occipital	?	Yes*	No: EKG	Yes
Fedio & Buchsbaum (1971)	Occipital	?	Yes*	?	Yes
Shelburne (1972)	Parietal	?	Yes	Yes*: eye	Yes
Shelburne (1973)	Vertex, parietal	Yes	?	?	Yes

Did the EEG Reaction:

Task and Experimenter	Electrode Placement	(1) Change from Baseline?	(2) Vary as a Function of Conditions?	(3) Occur Independently of Other Covert Processes?	(4) Specifically Relate to a Cognitive Aspect?
Speech Perception (Auditory Linguistic Input)					
Darrow & Hicks (1965)	Parietal, motor, occipital	Yes*	Yes*	?	Yes
Feldman & Goldstein (1967)	Vertex	?	Yes	?	Yes
Koukkou & Lehman (1968)	Frontal, central, parieto-occipital	Yes*	Yes*	?	Yes
Evans et al. (1970)	Frontal, parietal, occipital	Yes*	Yes*	?	Yes
Roth et al. (1970)	Vertex	?	No	?	No
Smith et al. (1970)	Vertex	?	Yes*	Yes*: eye	Yes
Hirsh (1971)	Vertex	Yes	Yes	Yes: EEG	Yes
Morrell & Salamy (1971)	Frontal, central, tempero-parietal	?	Yes*	?	Yes
Picton & Low (1971)	Vertex	Yes	Yes*	Yes: eye, GSR	Yes
Wood, Goff, & Day (1971)	Temporal central	?	Yes*	?	Yes
Cohn (1971)	Anterior to ear	Yes	Yes	?	Yes
Matsumiya et al. (1972)	Parietal	?	Yes*	?	Yes
Teyler et al. (1973)	Fronto-parietal	?	Yes*	?	Yes
Neville (1974)	Temporal	Yes	Yes*	Yes: eye	Yes
Attention					
Haider (1967)	Occipital temporal, vertex	?	Yes	?	Yes
Ritter & Vaughan (1969)	Supraorbital vertex, right occipital, vertex	No / Yes / Yes / No	No / Yes / Yes / No	?	Yes

TABLE 8.1 Summary of Electrical Neurophysiological Activity During Cognitive Tasks *(cont.)*

		Did the EEG Reaction:			
Task and Experimenter	Electrode Placement	(1) Change from Baseline?	(2) Vary as a Function of Conditions?	(3) Occur Independently of Other Covert Processes?	(4) Specifically Relate to a Cognitive Aspect?
Brenner, Moritz & Benignus (1972)	?	Yes	Yes	?	No
Ohman & Lader (1972)	Vertex	Yes	Yes	Yes: GSR	Yes
Hillyard et al. (1973)	Vertex	?	Yes*	?	Yes
Visual, Nonverbal Thought Tasks					
Cohen & Walter (1966)	Association cortex	?	Yes	?	Yes
Shevrin et al. (1971)	Frontal, vertex, occipital	Yes*	Yes*	Yes: eye and alpha bursts.	Yes
Symmes & Eisengart (1971)	Vertex	?	Yes	?	Yes
Ruchkin & Sutton (1973)	Vertex, occipital	?	Yes*	?	Yes
Rohrbaugh et al. (1974)	Vertex, temple	Yes	Yes*	?	Yes
Auditory Nonverbal Thought Tasks					
Sheatz & Chapman (1969)	Vertex	Yes*	Yes*	?	Yes
Waszak & Obrist (1969)	Right	Yes	Yes*	No: eye	Yes
Jenness (1972)	Vertex	Yes	Yes	Yes: eye	Yes
Speech Production					
Ertl & Schafer (1967a)	Motor area	Yes	No	?	Yes
Ertl & Schafer (1967b)	Frontal, temporal	Yes	?	No: EMG (lip)	Yes
McAdam & Whitaker (1971a)	Precentral gyri and inferior frontal areas	?	?	?	Yes

Did the EEG Reaction:

Task and Experimenter	Electrode Placement	(1) Change from Baseline?	(2) Vary as a Function of Conditions?	(3) Occur Independently of Other Covert Processes?	(4) Specifically Relate to a Cognitive Aspect?
Miscellaneous Thought Tasks					
Smith et al. (1947)	Fronto-occipital	No	No	No: EKG	No
Morgan et al. (1971)	Vertex	?	Yes*	?	Yes
Galin & Ornstein (1972)	Temporal, parietal	?	Yes*	?	Yes
McGuigan & Pavek (1972)	Temporal, motor area	Yes*	No	No: both arms, lips, neck, eyes	Yes
McKee et al. (1973)	Temporal-parietal	?	Yes*	?	Yes
Miscellaneous					
Knott (1939)	Occipital	Yes	Yes	?	Yes
Sutton et al. (1965)	Vertex	?	Yes	?	Yes
Gullickson & Darrow (1968)	?	Yes*	Yes	?	Yes
Ulett et al. (1972)	Occipital	Yes*	Yes*	?	Yes
Lewis et al. (1973)	Lateral ring montage	?	No	?	No

the blank field condition of Fig. 8.4) and compared with that during a linguistic condition.

The notation ("yes," "no," "?") as for column 1 is used for the other criteria of Table 8.1

CRITERION 3

Was the Response a Unique, Localized Event or Was It Only a Component of a Generalized Arousal Pattern? To determine whether a given reaction is a relatively unique, localized bodily event, it should be shown that the reaction occurs independently of other covert processes. For this, concomitant measures should be made from a sample of bodily nonbrain regions or systems.

CRITERION 4

Was There a Specific Relationship Between an Independent Variable and a Response Parameter? This criterion indicates that a reaction is a localized event and that the event is intimately involved in the cognitive activity.

Using these four criteria, we shall now summarize and evaluate eleven categories of empirical research: (1) Mental Arithmetic, (2) Learning, (3) Imagination, (4) Reading (Visual Linguistic Input), (5) Speech Perception (Auditory Linguistic Input), (6) Attention, (7) Visual, Non-verbal Thought Tasks, (8) Auditory, Nonverbal Thought Tasks, (9) Speech Production, (10) Miscellaneous Thought Tasks, and (11) Miscellaneous.

Empirical Studies

Before starting this section, kindly note that we are summarizing a sample of the literature relevant to various kinds of cognitive activity. For most readers' purposes it may be sufficient to merely skim the research to gain a general appreciation of the empirical (often conflicting) conclusions. Others may wish to study the research in some detail, while yet others may prefer to use the section merely for selected references.

MENTAL ARITHMETIC

Kennedy, Gottsdanker, Armington, and Gray (1948) reported previously unobserved spindles in respect to locus and facilitating conditions, yielded by subjects engaged in thinking tasks. The intermittent spindle-shaped EEG with a frequency of 8-12 Hz and a maximum amplitude of 20-30 μv was recorded from bipolar electrodes placed just in back of the external canthi of the eyes. This "kappa" wave appeared in about half of the subjects tested during "thinking" tasks (e.g., discrimination, choice reaction, mental arithmetic, etc.) and was thought to be independent of occipital alpha activity. The authors held that kappa waves are not an artifact of eye movements, although the latter point has been the subject of controversy (cf. Lorens and Darrow, 1962; Ford, 1954; see also, McGuigan, 1966a, p. 237). Kennedy et al. suggested that the source of the new EEG may be the temporal lobes of the brain. In 1953, Ford showed that mental effort was accompanied by increased cardiac strain. Later (1954) he examined the effects of mental arithmetic on bioelectric potentials of the frontal lobes. EKG and monopolar EEG were recorded from the left frontal lobe of right-handed subjects and right frontal lobe of left-handed subjects as they were engaged in alternating periods of rest and mental arithmetic performance. Results indicated that the mean amplitude of integrated bioelectric potentials was greater during mental effort than during rest for 18 of the 19 subjects. A slightly higher (not significant) mean amplitude of potentials during the second experimental period as compared to the first suggests the absence of an "adaptation" effect. No significant association was found for the EEG means and degree of success on the mental arithmetic problems. Although EKG also increased during problem solving, it was not significantly correlated with EEG amplitude. Some EEG records were contaminated by the tonus of the facialis muscle; however Ford indicated that EEG frequency increases were independent of such muscle activity. He therefore concluded that mental effort is usually accompanied by low frequency, high-amplitude EEG increases in the frontal lobes.

Johnson, Ulett, Sines, and Stern (1960) investigated the effects of photically induced EEG disruption on cognitive functioning by evaluating subject performance on a variety of cognitive tasks. The degree of occipital, parietal, and frontal EEG activiation present during the performance of each cognitive task was classified using a scale previously developed by Ulett and Johnson (1958). It was found that the degree of EEG disruption in response to photic stimulation was not related to quality of performance on any of the tasks used. Marked to extreme disruption of EEG activity during the actual learning of each task did not impair recall or memory of that material nor did it interfere with the cognitive processes involved in solving arithmetic problems. Johnson et al. suggested that cognitive functions involved in learning, retention, and recall, as shown by these tests, are not necessarily impaired by disruption of the usual patterns of neural activity, by an EEG criterion.

Lorens and Darrow (1962) examined the relation between eye movement rate, heart rate (EKG), conductance level (GSR), and EEG (frontal, parietal, temporal, and occipital) during a baseline period and during a task of mental multiplication of two digit numbers. All subjects showed a significant increase in eye movement rate, and a significant decrease in the percent time alpha during mental multiplication, although these two measures were not significantly related. Heart rate and conductance level were not significantly associated with problem solving or with eye movement rate. Further analysis indicated that kappa waves, previously associated with mental activity (Kennedy et al., 1948), were present in records obtained from temporal and external canthi electrode placements; however these waves were not observed in the absence of alpha waves and were not limited to the problem-solving period. Other wave forms reportedly associated with mental activity, such as "augmented theta" (Mundy-Castle, 1957) and the "slow frontal wave" (Ford, 1954), could not be differentiated due to EEG alterations associated with the corneo-retinal potential. Lorens and Darrow concluded that eye movements are a consistent concomitant of mental multiplication but that a characteristic EEG wave form is not.

Chapman and Bragdon (1964) examined the effect on visual average evoked potentials of (relevant) numerical and (irrelevant) nonnumerical visual stimuli. On the left of two adjacent screens were projected sequentially two one digit numbers, each for .75 sec and each followed by a bright blank field for .75 sec. The luminance of the blank was four times that of the numbers. After each sequence the subject was to say which of the two numbers was numerically smaller, or were they "even." The correct answer then appeared in the right screen as a green luminous figure; otherwise, the right screen was a green blank. Average evoked potentials were via electrodes and averaged. These reactions revealed consistently larger average evoked potentials to the numbers than to the blanks. Substituting for the blank a plus sign of approximately the same intensity as the numbers, Chapman and Bragdon found average evoked responses to both, but consistently larger average evoked potentials to the numbers, except in instances where the plus sign initiated a stimulus sequence. (No mention was made of whether sequences initiated with a blank would show the same result.) This was interpreted as resulting from increased task relevance, since the plus sign signalled an upcoming number sequence.

Glanzer, Chapman, Clark, and Bragdon (1964) studied two sets of tasks—mental addition and concept tasks. Electrode placements were over the parietal (P_z) and occipital regions (O_z) to record alpha; and over the right and left temporal fossae (F_7 and F_8) to record kappa rhythms. On the mental addition tasks the difficulty of the task significantly increased the output of kappa but not alpha. On the concept task, however, the difficulty of the task depressed the output of alpha significantly. Kappa rhythms during the concept task varied considerably among subjects but remained consistent within subjects. Glanzer et al. concluded that kappa rhythms are not simply related to task difficulty but appear to be a function of a number of complex variables. The authors suggested that since in the concept task, input was primarily visual and in the addition task, input was primarily auditory, the EEG effects may be related to a modality-by-difficulty interaction. They added that this seems to be a reasonable hypothesis because alpha is recorded near visual centers and kappa is recorded near auditory centers.

Chapman (1965) examined the effects of task relevancy on average evoked potentials recorded from the Cz location (10-20 system). He presented letters and numbers in an alternating temporal sequence (i.e., #, L, #, L). and told the subject which would be the relevant stimuli. The task was either to report which number was smaller or which letter came first in the alphabet, depending upon which were the relevant stimuli. The results were that when the stimuli are task relevant the amplitudes of the average evoked potentials which they elicit are greater than those elicited by the same stimuli when they are not task relevant. Average evoked potentials apparently reflect cognitive aspects of stimuli when the task concerns the relevance of the stimuli to a subsequent task.

A further study by Chapman (1969) also addressed itself to the relevance question. A sequence of number and letter stimuli were presented with numbers relevant on some runs and letters relevant on the others. Monopolar and bipolar recordings of average evoked potentials were made simultaneously on the midline 2.5 cm below the vertex and 2.5 cm above the inion C_z^P and O_z. The study consists of two experiments. In the first, resembling Chapman's 1965 study, two numbers (#) and two letters (L) were presented on each run, with some runs in the order #, L, #, L and the other runs, L, #, L, #. The numbers were relevant on half the runs and the letters relevant on half. The task was such that the subject had to perceive both relevant stimuli on any given trial. The results showed that the average evoked potentials tended to be larger to the same stimulus when it was relevant than when it was irrelevant, and that the first response in a sequence was larger than the later ones. In addition, the number responses were larger than the letter responses. The second experiment concerned the effect of stimulus shape on size of average evoked potentials. The relevant stimuli were 1 and 2; the irrelevant stimuli were −, +, and a large blank area (B). The order of presentation of the stimuli was B, #, +, −, #, B. The results were that both relevant stimuli evoked larger average evoked potentials than the irrelevant stimuli; and the response to 2 was larger than the response to 1 in both presentation orders.

Giannitrapani (1966) studied EEG differences between resting and thinking (mental multiplication). Recordings were made from the left and right frontal, left and right temporal, left and right parietal, and left and right occipital areas. A significant increase of average frequency in all areas during mental arithmetic over baseline was found; furthermore the increase was the greatest in the two frontal and in the left temporal areas. Giannitrapani, concluded that these differential findings are a result of the differential involvement of the areas studied and are an indication of their functional role for the conditions studied. However, since the left-right difference was also present during resting, Giannitrapani also allowed for the possibility that the left-right difference is an intrinsic characteristic of brain activity which may be correlated with the fact that most of his subjects were right handed. Mean frequencies also differed significantly as a function of the time periods—the first period being the greatest with a general decrease through the last. This difference occurred in both "resting" and "thinking" periods.

In an earlier study, MacNeilage (1966a) had failed to find cognitive effects on EEG. He speculated that motor effects were so great that any cognitive effects would not have been found if they did exist. MacNeil-age (1966b) then used tasks involving varied activities but similar stimuli and motor responses in a renewed attempt to successfully demonstrate cognitive effects on EEG. EEG was recorded from the parietal lobe and quantified into alpha and beta frequencies. Heart rate and GSR were also recorded. The three tasks included (1) continuous adding of num-bers in groups of four and writing the answers after each group (add-ing), (2) writing down every fourth number (writing), and (3) writing down every "7" and "9" (7s and 9s). Adding requires continuous mental work, writing requires little more than counting the stimuli, and count-ing 7s and 9s demands continuous visual monitoring of the stimuli. Analysis indicated that there were no reliable amplitude differences in EEG among the three cognitive tasks. However, significant differences were obtained in heart rate and GSR, both physiological measures being reliably higher during adding than during the other two tasks. The author suggested that the lack of differences in overall EEG amplitude indicated that the effect of difficulty was too slight to show in this exper-iment. Reliable short term changes in EEG were found in both alpha and beta measures, but these appeared to be related to motor activity. These results suggest that we should measure motor effects in EEG studies to a greater extent than we have in the past.

Shevrin and Rennick (1967) studied the changes in amplitude and latency of the cortical average evoked potentials (CEP) from symmetrical parietal electrode placements in response to the same tactile stimulus (finger tap) during three conditions: attention, free association, and mental arithmetic. In the attention condition the subjects were in-structed to estimate varying time intervals between tactile stimuli. The results indicated that the amplitudes of two negative electrocortical po-tentials were significantly greater when the subjects were estimating time intervals than during free association or mental arithmetic. Peak latency of the second negative potential was also significantly greater in the attention condition than in the other two conditions. Free association conditions were distinguished by the occurrence of alpha bursts. Shevrin and Rennick concluded that attention is associated with the increased amplitude of negative components of the CEP and greater peak latency of the second negative component of the CEP.

Volavka, Matousek, and Roubicek (1967) investigated the differences between the simple opening of the eye and two problem-solving situa-tions at different levels of general activation. Pairs of GSR electrodes were used on the second and fourth finger of the left hand, and EEG recordings were taken from the right parieto-temporal region. The con-ditions of the experiment were as follows: C: eyes closed; O: eyes opened; A: eyes closed, mental arithmetic; and M: eyes closed, mental arithmetic with financial reward. Two sequences of these conditions were used: C-O-A-M and C-O-M-A. There was a significantly greater number of GSRs in Condition M in which eyes were closed while the subjects performed mental arithmetic with financial reward than there were in any other condition. The EEG frequency analysis showed that (1) in condition O relative quantities of all frequency bands were lower than in conditions A and M; (2) in conditions O, A, and M there was less theta and alpha activity than in condition C; (3) while suppressed in condition O, beta activity increased in conditions A and M; (4) differences between conditions A and M were not significant. It was also found that mental activity is accompanied by decreased variability of beta activity. Volavka et al. suggested that beta activity (both its amount and variability) is more closely related to the general level of activation than are the brain waves in any other frequency band under study.

Glass and Kwiatkowski (1968) studied occipital EEG during a condition of mental arithmetic (with eyes closed) and periods in which the subjects sat with eyes opened. Power spectral analyses (changes in energy present at different frequencies) were performed on the obtained EEG record. Maximum amplitude in the power spectrum with eyes closed occurred in the region of 10 Hz. However, the power at 10 Hz during mental arithmetic was usually up to 50% less than that during the condition of eyes open. In contrast to the mental arithmetic condition, eye opening enhanced the power at low frequencies. The authors concluded that these results support the impression that there are differences in the effect on EEG of eye opening and mental arithmetic other than those associated strictly with ocular factors.

Sokolov (1968) obtained measurements of speech muscle activity (EMG), EEG (frontal, temporal, and occipital), and GSR while subjects were engaged in a task of mental arithmetic that varied in difficulty. Speech EMG was found to increase from rest during solution of the problems and was related to problem difficulty. Records of the GSR and occipital and temporal EEG were not significantly related to EMG activity and thus were not specific to thinking activity. Sokolov observed irregular discharges resembling "kappa waves" at the moment of problem solution but suggested that these were a result of corneoretinal potentials rather than electrical activity of the cortex. Sokolov concluded that such EEG reactions do not yet suffice as indices of verbal thought.

In an attempt to relate individual differences in ability and performance to EEG activity, Vogel, Broverman, and Klaiber (1968) studied parietal and occipital EEG during conditions of rest and mental arithmetic of varying difficulty. Specific relationships were investigated between EEG slow waves (7 Hz or less), the amount of time (sec) alpha and beta rhythms were present, the frequency (Hz) of alpha and beta rhythms, and three separate indices of mental ability: (1) general level of mental ability as defined by mean performance on a battery of 17 cognitive tests; (2) Automatization Cognitive Style, defined as ability to perform simple or repetitive tasks better (Strong Automatization) or worse (Weak Automatization) than expected from the subject's mean level of performance on the battery of tests; and (3) performance on the mental arithmetic tasks.

No significant correlations were found for general level of cognitive ability and any index of the EEG. However, slow waves and slow alpha frequencies were significantly and positively correlated with both automatization ability and with efficient performance under conditions of mental effort; and automatization was inversely and significantly related to time in beta rhythms during periods of mental effort. These data corroborate the findings of Mundy-Castle (1957) where slow waves were found during periods of mental effort. Vogel et al. concluded that these slow rhythms may indicate a type of selective inhibition that facilitiates performance during mental effort.

In a follow-up study Vogel, Broverman, Klaiber, and Kun (1969) classified college students as strong or weak automatizers. Occipital EEG recordings were obtained at rest and during photic stimulation. EEG "driving" responses to photic stimulation were defined as two consecutive seconds of EEG waves at the fundamental frequency of the photic stimulation, or at one of its harmonics or subharmonics. The mean number of driving responses of the weak automatizers was significantly greater than for the strong automatizers. Weak automatizers also tended to yield two different types of alpha "driving" responses to photic stimulation: alpha provocation (the tendency of alpha to be elicited regardless of the frequency of the flickering light), and alpha "following" (a tendency of alpha to be evoked at the frequency of the flickering light). These findings were interpreted to mean that strong automatizers possess a relatively greater degree of central adrenergic dominance than do weak automatizers.

Elul (1969) investigated the differences between Gaussian behavior of the EEG in the idle state and during performance of a mental arithmetic task. Recording was bipolar, with a midline, fronto-occipital electrode configuration. Extensive samplings of EEG from one subject followed a Gaussian (normal) probability function in the idle state 66% of the time; during performance of arithmetic, the portion of Gaussian EEG decreased to 32%. The interpretation was that the cooperative activity of cortical neuronal elements increased during performance of a mental task.

Chapman (1972) reported two studies relating EEG kappa rhythms (7-13 c/sec) to periods of problem solving. In the first experiment, EEGs were recorded during tasks in a $2 \times 2 \times 2$ factorial design: the two levels of task difficulty were arithmetic vs. counting, with eyes either open or closed, and speech either aloud or silent. The results of the analysis of EEG (frontal occipital) records obtained from 150 subjects indicated that significantly more kappa activity occurred during difficult tasks and with eyes closed, whereas the speech variable did not have a reliable systematic effect. The amount of kappa was correlated with several subject variables, e.g., anxiety, height, weight, and education.

In the second experiment, kappa activity was studied during the learning and overlearning of lists of nonsense syllables by the method of serial anticipation. During learning trials, the amount of kappa activity increased compared to a control task. With a large number of overlearning trials over a number of sessions, kappa activity gradually decreased to the control level. In a second part of this experiment, subjects were engaged in the solution of concept problems while (frontal and occipital) EEG records were obtained. All 12 subjects showed a similar pattern of alpha wave decrease during the stages of memory storage and selection of relevant information. However, there was considerable variation from subject to subject in the kappa activity data—some subjects consistently showed increased kappa activity during problem solving, whereas there was less frequently observed kappa activity in others.

Chapman, Cavonious, and Ernest (1971) examined EEG records obtained from eyeless subjects engaged in mental arithmetic to determine if alpha and kappa waves forms were artifacts of ocular activity or were of cerebral origin. For one experiment, a subject who had both ocular globes removed was alternately instructed to do mental arithmetic problems of varying difficulty and then to rest with his "mind blank" while EEG activity was recorded. The results showed that time in alpha decreased from rest to the periods of mental computation and appeared to be related inversely to the difficulty of the problem; kappa waves (thought to be related to mental effort) increased from rest to periods of mental computation and appeared to be positively related to task difficulty. These data indicate that alpha and kappa wave activity are independent of the corneoretinal potential.

In a second experiment the possible relation between alpha activity and activity of extraocular muscles was studied. Bilateral EEGs were recorded from subjects who had had one orbit and the corresponding extraocular muscles removed. It was hypothesized that if EEG alpha was dependent upon the activity of these muscles then the records should markedly differ from that of normal subjects. The results indicated that both alpha and kappa wave forms were normally present during tasks of mental arithmetic and periods of rest. Subjects showed more alpha activity on hard tasks than on easy tasks, more with eyes closed than open, and similar patterns of alpha activity on both sides. Chapman et al. concluded that the presence of normal alpha and kappa EEG activity in these eyeless subjects refutes the explanations of alpha and kappa EEG activity in terms of ocular artifacts.

Ishihara and Yoshii (1972) attempted to study the relationships between EEG and factors of mental activity by use of multivariate statistical analysis. A frequency analysis was carried out on EEGs from a Fz-Cz lead (10/20 system). Fifteen kinds of mental task subtests, designed to interfere minimally with the EEG recording, were used. The findings of Ishihara and Yoshii included: (1) the Θ activity during mental performance seemed to originate in the frontal midline area (Fm Θ) and tended to appear in the subtests that required continuous concentration of attention; (2) four significant factors were extracted as the result of factor analysis of the subtest scores: simple arithmetic and mechanical memory, complex arithmetic and rule identification, discrimination and indication, and perception of simple visual patterns; (3) factor analysis of the EEG band scores indicates that each δ, $\alpha-$, $\beta-$ and β_2- band components was of one-factor structure; (4) factor analysis of the Θ-band scores of EEG yielded two significant factors pertaining to thinking and work speed.

The authors questioned why 30% of the subjects did not induce Fm Θ activity during mental work. It should be noted, however, that in a previous study (Tani, Atsushi, and Nakai, 1968), only 50% of the subjects showed Fm Θ activity during mental work. Ishihara (personal communication September 14, 1977) informs me that there has been much research recently on Fm Θ in Japan (e.g., Yamaguchi and Niwa 1974), but most of them have been written only in Japanese.

LEARNING

Hillyard and Galambos (1967), using the basic paradigm to produce CNV (Fig. 8.1), investigated how prior exposure to two stimuli, which are paired without a required motor response, would affect subsequent acquisition of CNV. They compared two groups: one experienced S_1 and S_2 paired and the other experienced both stimuli, but unpaired. The subjects also experienced a "probability dilution" condition, in which S_1 was not followed by S_2 for 50% of the trials. Finally, there was an extinction condition. In the analysis of their data, they used a baseline which consisted of the 0.2 sec interval before the presentation of S_1. Their results show that while a CNV appeared for subjects in the paired-no response group, when the reaction was required the CNV was acquired more rapidly. The group whose previous training was with nonpaired stimulus presentations took longer to reach their maximum value of CNV, indicating that the previous paired training without the motor response did enhance acquisition of CNV. The probability dilution condition was not accompanied by a decrease in CNV for either group, a finding not in agreement with the results of other investigators; e.g., Tecce (1972) indicated that there is usually a reduction in amplitude under these conditions (which has been called an "equivocation effect") and pointed out that Hillyard and Galambos' study is the only one not to find this reduction. Hillyard and Galambos also found that there is a negative correlation between reaction time and CNV.

Rosenfeld, Rudell, and Fox (1969) repeatedly presented a tone to subjects and computed the average evoked potential. A baseline was determined by computing the difference between the average voltages preceding the tone and the average voltages following the tone by 200 msec. One group of subjects observed their own EEGs on an ocilloscope while a second group merely sat in a dim light. Each time subjects' average evoked potential to the tone exceeded their computed baselines by 1 standard deviation, they received a light flash indicating that they had acquired 10¢. In the next phase of the experiment however, the subjects in both groups lost 10¢ each time their average evoked potential exceeded the criterion. Then, the earlier reward condition was reinstated. Finally, to control for possible artifacts the tone was removed for the first group but a corresponding signal was presented on the ocilloscope; for the second group, the tone was attenuated so that the evoked potential was essentially minimized or absent. For both groups there was a significant difference between the sum of the scores of the rewarded phases and the sum of the scores of the baseline and the punished phases, suggesting that the subjects had achieved control over the amplitude of their own brain waves.

Differences in mean amplitude of baseline and punishment vs. the two rewarded phases "approached" significance. The operant effect was not large, however, averaging only about 30% success as opposed to 16% during baseline. There was no uniform brain pattern among subjects— some seemingly generated a new component in the critical segment, others increased the amplitude of all components, and so forth. Likewise, there was no uniformity of verbal report when subjects were asked how they had altered their brain waves. The authors maintained that their data argue against both selective attention and the notion of learning a simple motor response whose somaesthetic feedback or efferent impulse generates the desired amplitude change, as explanations of the operant effect upon EEG. They held that perhaps subjects are learning to generate some internal state which may mediate an altered evoked potential by either increasing the overall excitability of many (or perhaps particular) neuron populations, and when the population is activated, its greater effective size yields an enhanced voltage. Subjects' verbal reports suggest that behavior they call "imagining" can bring the relevant state about.

Begleiter, Gross, and Kissin (1967) had earlier demonstrated that it was possible to condition affective meanings to meaningless stimuli, thereby altering amplitudes and latencies of the visual evoked potentials to those previously meaningless stimuli. The CS was a transparent outline of a pentagon, which was rotated into "three distinguishably different positions." Each position of this figure was conditioned to one of three affectively homogeneous sets of twenty words, which were of either positive, negative, or neutral meaning value. In this experment (Experiment I) the conditioning occurred without the subjects' knowledge of the conditioning procedure. Begleiter, Gross, Porjesz, and Kissin (1969) conducted a further study to determine if the subject's awareness of the conditioning process would reliably alter the results obtained in the previous study. The subjects were told prior to conditioning that there was a relationship between the CS and the UCS, but were not informed as to what this relationship was or the exact purpose of the experiment (this is "Experiment II"). The subjects for Experiment III were "totally" aware of the conditioning procedure, i.e., they were informed prior to conditioning of the explicit relationship between the CS and the UCS, and they were also informed of the explicit purpose of the experiment. Both amplitudes and latencies of the visual average evoked potentials were analyzed. Considering the amplitudes, when the subjects were conditioned without awareness (Experiment I), there seemed to be a suppression of average evoked potentials to the positive and negative

CSs, so that amplitude levels were lower than for the neutral condition, and this decrease in amplitudes was more marked to the negative figures. In Experiment II, there was an overall enhancement of the amplitudes of the average evoked potentials to the affective stimuli, again more marked in the case of the negative stimuli. In Experiment III, the amplitudes of both the positive and negative stimuli approximated those for the neutral figures in all three experiments, with no reliable differences occurring among the three affective conditions.

In Experiment I, all five latencies for the negative stimuli were significantly shorter than for the positive and neutral stimuli (which did not significantly differ), implying a possible vigilance effect. In Experiments II and III, however, corresponding latencies did not differ significantly among any of the stimuli. The experimenters concluded that levels of awareness of the CS-UCS contingency might be reflected in a physiological index (amplitude) of conditioning. (See also Begleiter and Platz, 1969; Begleiter, Porjesz, Yerre, and Kissin, 1973; Porjesz and Begleiter, 1975; and Begleiter and Porjesz, 1975).

Brown (1970) attempted to enhance alpha activity through the use of a closed feedback loop incorporating a lamp, the intensity of which was directly proportional to the alpha abundance over the right parieto-occipital region. Sessions consisted of alternating rest and experimental periods. The greatest degree of alpha enhancement occurred during the first experimental session, an effect which was interpreted as being a function of insight rather than conditioning. Sixty percent of the subjects showed specificity of alpha response to the experimental sessions as compared to the rest periods. Significant increases in alpha activity occurred within as well as across sessions, although after a certain point further training did not produce increases across sessions. Voluntary control of alpha occurred in the absence of eye movements. The subjects uniformly reported that enhanced alpha appeared to be related to "narrowing of perceptual awareness and pleasant feeling states."

Rosenfeld and Hetzler (1973) determined a median amplitude at a 30-msec criterion segment of the wave form of each visual average evoked potential of 9 rats. They then made available to the rat's medial forebrain bundle stimulation on one bar if the rat's average evoked potential was larger than the median, or, alternatively stimulation on the other bar if the average evoked potential was smaller than the median. The percentage of correct responses for all rats was significantly greater than chance. Analysis of individual data indicated that only one rat learned the discrimination without attempting to selectively generate either large or small average evoked potentials; one rat learned to generate small average evoked potentials; two rats did not show increases in correct responses appreciably greater than chance; and five animals learned to generate large average evoked potentials. Extreme values of both conditional-large average evoked potentials and conditional-small average evoked potentials were significantly more extreme in their values on the best day for each subject than the most extreme large and small average evoked potentials obtained during baseline, indicating to the authors that conditional neural events are not the same events as those regularly occurring, say, in the baseline period. Additional evidence of operant conditional potentials was offered by Rosenfeld, Hetzler, Birkel, Kowatch, and Antoinetti (1976), and by Rosenfeld (1977).

IMAGINATION

Golla, Hutton, and Walter (1943) studied the relationship between mode of habitual imagery and the extent to which alpha rhythms were present in parieto-occipital EEGs. The subjects were initially instructed to engage in a variety of cognitive tasks (mental arithmetic, recollection of a past event, "thinking over" past or future activities, etc.) On the basis of the subject's reported activity during such tasks, each was classified as engaging in primarily verbal imagery, visual imagery, or a mixture of the two types. EEGs were then collected with eyes closed during mental arithmetic. The records were then classified according to the extent of alpha waves present: (1) "M," when the alpha rhythm was extremely small in amplitude; (2) "R," for responsive when the rhythm was attenuated during later eye opening or mental exertion; and (3) "P," for persistent alpha rhythm, regardless of whether the eyes were open, closed, or regardless of nature of mental activity. A correlational analysis indicated that all 22 subjects classified as "M" EEG-type exhibited primarily visual imagery, while 8 of 11 "P"-types exhibited primarily verbal imagery. Twenty-seven "R" subjects were evenly distributed between visual and verbal imagination categories. EEG rhythms were also correlated with records of respiratory rhythm. Members of the "P" group showed predominantly irregular respiration patterns while members of the "M" group showed predominantly regular respiration patterns. Golla et al. concluded that these data support the hypothesis that people who make greater use of visual imagery also have greater activity in the visual association areas and thus less alpha rhythms.

Slatter (1960) examined the relation between alpha rhythms and mental imagery by recording parieto-occipital EEGs from 60 subjects during various mental tasks (mental mulitiplication, recollection of past activities, imagination of manual activities, imagination of "thinking over" written texts, and active vision and visual recall). Following the series of tasks subjects were interviewed to ascertain the nature and mode of habitual imagery (visual vs. verbal). Unlike the report of Golla, Hutton, and Walter (1943) that subjects' modes of habitual imagery were amenable to unequivocal classification, Slatter found that no one subject could be unequivocally classified as to their habitual mode of imagery. Analyses of the EEG data indicated that subjects classified as predominantly visual imaginers exhibited alpha blocking during imagination in 249 of 264 tests; whereas subjects classified as predominantly verbal imaginers exhibited alpha blocking in 24 of 148 tests. When subjects were instructed to actively inspect a picture (active vision) alpha was blocked in all instances. When instructed to visually recall the picture, alpha was usually blocked but less than during active vision. Further analyses of the EEG data indicated that the degree of alpha suppression during active vision and visual recall was significantly and positively related to the amplitude of the alpha waves during rest. The extent to which a subject reported habitually engaging in visual imagination was inversely related to the amplitude of alpha during rest and positively related to the degree of alpha blockage during imagination, both relationships being significant. Slatter concluded that researchers attempting to correlate EEG and mental activity must attend to individual differences in the predominant mode of imagery.

Antrobus, Antrobus, and Singer (1964) asked relaxed subjects to report "what was just going through their minds" immediately following each 4-second period of either ocular motility or ocular quiescence. The results indicated that while subjects reported imagery involving their external environment there was a supression of time in alpha activity and a significant increase in ocular motility. Whereas while subjects were engaged in daydreaming, internal imagery, or passive thought there was a significant amount of ocular quiescence and a significant increase in time in alpha activity. These data were accepted as consistent with previous reports of the relation between eye movements and alpha suppression.

READING (VISUAL LINGUISTIC INPUT)

In a search for objective manifestations of cognitive processes, Travis and Knott (1937) recorded brain potentials from above the left occipital area. By means of a translucent screen, subjects were presented with words, nonsense words, and blank cards for .25 seconds duration. The perseveration time of the subjects, defined as the length of time between the removal of the stimulus and the return of the brain potentials to their pre-stimulus values, was recorded. The results indicated that both words and nonsense words gave greater perseveration times than blank cards. Two possible explanations are: (1) the difference is a function of a structured versus a non-structured stimulus; and (2) the words and nonsense words evoked some meaning, and processing meaningful stimuli required more time. The authors preferred the latter interpretation because subject reports indicated that they had "types of imagery, trains of thought, and in some instances affective states associated with the words . . ." (Travis and Knott, 1937, p. 356). The authors also noted that, with repeated presentations, a word lost its perseverative value, indicating that adaptation seems related to repetition. Finally, perseveration time for standard words having a known meaning was 4.6 sec, nonsense words was 4.8 sec, blank cards was 3.1 sec.

Knott (1938) recorded brain potentials while subjects read overtly and silently. Preceding each experimental session, baseline recordings were obtained while the subject rested with eyes closed. EEGs were recorded from unspecified electrode placements but, as indicated in Pepin, Kibbee, and Wells (1952), they were probably from frontal, parietal, and occipital placements. For the results, there was a significant increase in mean EEG frequency from each baseline period, to the following reading period; mean EEG frequency also increased significantly from the silent reading period to the oral reading period. No frequency difference was found between the two baseline periods. Although quantitative measures of EEG amplitude were not conducted, the author indicated that alpha waves were reduced relative to baseline values by 10 to 90 percent during the reading sessions. Knott concluded that the higher EEG frequency during oral reading as compared to silent reading is attributable to the increased complexity necessary to initiate motor sequences of speech.

Pepin, Kibbee, and Wells (1952) repeated Knott's (1938) experiment, recording frontal, parietal, and occipital EEG during conditions of rest, and overt and silent reading. The obtained records showed the decreased amplitude and increased frequency during reading reported by Knott. However, the increased frequency during oral reading as compared to silent reading was difficult to observe due to the general pattern of cortical activity. Pepin et al. suggested that the difference between EEGs of overt and silent reading may be attributable to muscular artifact rather than to a characteristic pattern of cortical functioning, because overt reading involves more complex sensory-motor events.

Lifshitz (1966) examined the effects of two classes of visual stimuli on the average evoked cortical response potentials of ten 18- to 33-year-old males. The first stimulus class consisted of photographs which were either positive (female nudes), negative (repulsive medical), or neutral (scenic) in affective content. The second stimulus class consisted of (1) four or five lettered words, (2) these same words with their letters scrambled, (3) the same stimuli with recall reward, or (4) a series of "dirty words." The stimuli were presented either focused or unfocused. No consistent eye movements were found as a function of the type of stimulus. The wave form of the averaged evoked potentials (recorded from frontal, occipital, and occipito-parietal leads) from the neutral, the positive, and the negative affective photographs were different, most markedly for the nudes. The average evoked potentials to projected words and letters showed lesser differences. The average evoked potentials of the focused photographs were different in components after 75 ms, most notably in a larger peak at 250 to 400 ms. The average evoked potentials to focused four-or five-lettered "dirty" and "scrambled" words differed in wave form in some individuals. It was further concluded that the average evoked potential patterns of the focused photographic stimuli and the word stimuli were quite dissimilar, while the pattern of responses to the unfocused stimuli and the words were similar.

In an attempt to show that the average evoked potential is affected by the perceived content as well as by the physical parameters of a stimulus, John, Herrington, and Sutton (1967) presented subjects with stimuli of different geometric shape and size, and also with different words. The geometric shapes were a circle, a square, and the square rotated to appear as a diamond. The words used were "square" and "circle." No baseline data were reported. Visual inspection of the data led to the following conclusions: (1) the response to just a flash of light was different than that which occurred to the presentation of a geometric form, (2) different shapes of equal area elicited different responses, (3) similar shapes of different sizes elicited similar responses, (4) different words equated for area elicited different responses. This last result may not be so clear, though, as different responses to different words were obtained from one subject but not from another. The differences between average evoked potentials elicited by stimuli of different shapes, and the similarity of average evoked potentials to stimuli of the same shape but different sizes. indicates that average evoked potentials are related more to the shape of the stimulus than to its size. John et al. suggested that average evoked potentials constitute a physiological correlate of perceptual rather than sensory processes.

Lille, Pottier, and Scherrer (1968) studied the effects of distracting mental activity on the average evoked potential employing three different conditions: (1) discrimination of two different low intensity signals, visual when the average evoked potentials were produced by auditory stimuli and acoustic when they were produced by visual stimuli; (2) a test of the same type at a higher frequency of stimulus presentation; and (3) a discrimination task as in 1 and 2 while reading a difficult text. The average evoked potentials of 40 tests with 27 subjects were compared to those obtained during periods of rest preceding and following the experimental tasks. The results showed that the average evoked potential, either visual or auditory, decreased during mental activity (the discrimination task); the decrease was greater when the frequency of the discrimination task was raised, and was maximal during discrimination while reading the text. During the rest period following the mental task the amplitude of the average evoked potential progressively increased to its initial level. Lille et al. concluded that the amplitude of the average evoked potential is inversely related to level of mental activity.

Shevrin and Fritzler (1968) exposed subjects to two visual subliminal stimuli which differed in content and contour-complexity, while recording average evoked responses and accompanying verbal free-associations. Both the content of verbal associations and the latency of average evoked responses were found to vary with the two stimulus conditions. The average evoked response apparently reflected stimulus differences at subliminal speeds of exposure in the absence of conscious discrimination. The authors believed that the average evoked responses may contain a complex coding for conscious and unconscious psychological processes of a symbolic nature.

Weinberg and Cole (1968) studied differences in average evoked potentials as a function of neutral vs. emotional stimuli. The neutral stimuli were neutral words, letters, and blank flashes, while the emotional stimuli were taboo words. All subjects were presented both types of stimuli an equal number of times (the order of stimulus presentation was the same for all subjects). The mean density of estimated frequency was determined for frequencies between 2 and 16 Hz; the only reliable differences were between the average evoked potentials of the neutral words and those of the taboo words, blank stimuli, and letter stimuli. It was suggested by the authors that the results reflect differences in classes of stimuli. Their explanation was that some form of active inhibition was occurring so that the taboo words tended to register as relatively meaningless stimuli, like blank and letter stimuli. Considering that parameters such as stimulus structure, area, contrast, and brightness were not controlled, it is difficult to know exactly what effects were being measured in this study. Additional data in which differences in evoked potentials were demonstrated when subjects respond to identical stimuli for different reasons were reported by Weinberg, Walter, Cooper, and Aldridge (1974). For example, when the response to a triangle occurs because the stimulus is a triangle, the evoked potential is different than when the subject makes a response to the same stimulus because it is an unfilled figure.

Begleiter and Platz (1969) recorded average evoked potentials from the occipital lobe while the subjects viewed the stimuli of taboo words, neutral words, and a flash of light. There were two response conditions: (1) the subject did not have to respond, and (2) the subject was required to say the word which was presented. Both latencies and amplitudes of the average evoked potentials were recorded.

With regard to amplitudes, reliable differences for the later components of the average evoked potentials existed as a function of both the type of stimulus and the response condition. Specifically, the affective words produced a significantly greater amplitude than either the neutral words or the light flash, with no reliable difference between the latter two conditions. The amplitude of the average evoked potentials was also reliably greater when the subject was required to make the oral response, and the amplitudes for negative words was less than those for either positive or neutral words. These results (as well as those of Begleiter et al., 1969, Experiment II) do not agree with those of earlier work by the same investigators (Begleiter et al., 1967) where the amplitudes for affective stimuli were found to be *less* than those for neutral stimuli for all components.

With regard to latencies, both the taboo and neutral words produced reliably shorter latencies for the fourth component of the average evoked potentials than did the light flash. Shorter latencies for the second component occurred when the subject was required to make the oral response. The authors concluded that there were no "consistent differences in the latencies of the major amplitudes," and none were reported in Experiments II and III of Begleiter et al. (1969).

Buchsbaum and Fedio (1969) examined whether or not linguistic and non-linguistic stimuli produce different average evoked potentials. The average evoked potentials were recorded from over the right and left occipital lobes. The stimuli were words, random dot patterns, and designs generated by a Linc computer so as to keep the physical parameters of the stimuli constant. There were two experimental conditions: (1) a word-random dot comparison condition in which a series of 32 words and 32 random dot patterns (each stimulus presented eight times in a random order) were presented at a rate of one stimulus per second, and (2) a word-design condition, which consisted of the same procedure as the word-random dot condition except that the design stimuli were used in place of random dot stimuli. During each of the stimulus conditions a pair of average evoked potentials, one for each recording point (left or right occipital cortex), was obtained. Standardized correlation coefficients were then calculated within and between pairs for statistical comparison.

The results indicated that reliable differences in the average evoked potentials elicited by linguistic and nonlinguistic stimuli were obtained in both hemispheres. Furthermore the wave forms for the two types of stimuli showed a significantly greater difference in the left hemisphere than in the right. Also the latency of a major positive component of the average evoked potentials was shorter for words than for either the random dot or design stimuli; this was true for both hemispheres, but the latency differences between linguistic and nonlinguistic stimuli were greater in the left hemisphere. These findings are consistent with the general hypothesis that verbal information is processed primarily in the left hemisphere. The fact that the wave form of the average evoked potentials was different for the two types of stimuli when their physical characteristics were kept constant lends support to the concept that the average evoked potentials do reflect, in some way, cognitive dimensions of stimuli.

Sharrard (1969) conducted three experiments which were directed towards the investigation of the possibility of using EEG recordings to diagnose language and hearing disorders. In these three experiments EEG amplitudes and latencies were measured to pure tones (Experiment I), to words read in normal order (Experiment II), and to the same words read in reverse order or backwards (Experiment III). The experimenter concluded that: (1) inter-subject differences in magnitude were statistically significant, (2) the magnitude of EEG reactions to words read forward was significantly greater than to words read in reverse order. Sharrard further concluded that the analysis of EEG reactions to pure tones could be used to distinguish normal adults and children from children with hearing disorders, but that language disorders could not be positively identified. No electrode placements were given by the experimenter, and no changes from any baseline condition were included in the report of this study.

Buchsbaum and Fedio (1970) examined hemispheric differences in the waveform of average evoked potentials to verbal and nonverbal stimuli presented to the left and right visual fields. Thirty-two three-letter words and their nonsense correlates (obtained by randomly shifting the letter forms, thus controlling for stimulus brightness) were pre-

sented every 900 msec in random succession for 50 msec each. Position to the left or right of a fixation point was randomly determined. Each subject had 384 stimulus presentations. Average potentials were recorded simultaneously over the left and right occipital cortex (monopolar placements). For each of the four stimulus conditions (verbal or nonverbal × left or right visual field) and for each recording point (left or right occipital cortex) a pair of average evoked potentials was obtained based on replicate stimulus presentations. Standardized correlation coefficients were then calculated within and between replicate evoked reaction pairs for statistical comparison.

The authors concluded that verbal material and nonsense patterns produce significantly different evoked waveforms from left and right occipital cortex. Also, average evoked potentials recorded from events involving primary pathways (e.g., left hemiretina, i.e., right visual field, to left occipital cortex) differed significantly from those involving secondary pathways (e.g., left hemiretina to right occipital cortex). Evoked responses with primary pathway involvement were also more stable (or had higher signal-to-noise ratios). Average evoked potential waveforms from the right hemisphere appeared to be more stable than those from the left. Also, nonsense stimuli apparently elicited greater average evoked potential stability than the words, regardless of visual field of projection or hemisphere recording. Both retinal presentation and hemisphere of recording significantly altered average evoked potential waveforms.

Heinemann and Emrich (1971) presented neutral and emotional words at slowly increasing light intensities while fronto-parietal EEGs were recorded in conjunction with EKG recordings. The subjects were instructed to press a button to signal when they first perceived any light; when the shapes of the letters were just distinguishable; when they thought they could guess the word stimulus; and when they were able to correctly read the word. The EEG records were scored to determine the percent time in alpha as a function of word class (neutral vs. emotional) and as a function of recognition time interval. The results indicated that all subjects exhibited significantly more alpha waves during the perception of emotionally significant words than during the perception of neutral words. The EKG also showed a significantly lower cardiac frequency for emotional words than for neutral words. Heinemann and Emrich concluded that: ". . . the presence of a differential reaction provides that the meaning of the word must have been recognized before the subjects became aware of the presence of the stimulus. The alpha activity was highest between the time when the information became available but was not reaching conscious awareness and the time when the inhibition was overcome by the increase in stimulus intensity and stepwise recognition of the word began" (1971, p. 449).

Fedio and Buchsbaum (1971) studied the average evoked potentials of left and right unilateral temporal lobectomized subjects, and of normal subjects. The stimuli were three-letter words and nonverbal material (random dot patterns) presented tachistoscopically in either the left or the right visual field. The average evoked potential for each subject was computed separately for the left and right occipital lead during randomly intermixed presentation of the four stimulus conditions. The results of the statistical analysis indicated that in both hemispheres, both the words and the dot patterns produced significantly more dissimilar average evoked activity when the visual material was projected along the primary rather than the secondary or indirect visual pathway to each hemisphere. The greatest difference in average evoked potentials as a function of stimulus class was found when stimuli were flashed in the right visual field (left hemiretina) and EEG was recorded from the left occipital cortex (of the presumed dominant speech hemisphere). Transmission via the direct or primary route (i.e., left hemiretina-left hemisphere; right hemiretina-right hemisphere) to each occipital lobe elicited significantly more stable average evoked potential waveforms than activation by means of the indirect or secondary pathways. For the left-temporal lobectomy group the verbal-nonverbal discrimination index was higher for the primary visual pathways but lower for the secondary pathway, for both hemispheres. For the right-temporal lobectomy group, this index was severely reduced compared to normals for both the primary and secondary visual pathways, and for both hemispheres.

While among normals, the left-right hemiretina discrimination index was significantly greater than zero for both words and dots for both hemispheres, it was only significant for dots for the left-temporal lobectomized subjects and only for words in the right-temporal lobectomized subjects (again for both hemispheres).

Waveform stability was about the same in all groups for words, but while it was also about the same in normal and left-temporal lobectomized patients for dots, it was markedly reduced in the right-temporal lobectomized patients, especially for the left hemisphere. ". . . for each patient group, more stable average evoked response activity was recorded from the operative rather than the intact hemisphere . . . (1971, p. 267). Furthermore, the [verbal-nonverbal discrimination] score for the left temporal patients was greatest for average evoked responses calculated from left hemisphere leads, the measure being larger than that obtained for the normal group. These findings may be interpreted to mean that temporal lobe lesions modify inhibitory or attentional factors in perceptual behavior, resulting in larger amplitude in cortical activity, less 'noise' and more stable average evoked responses . . . the data also extend earlier findings that the temporal lobes facilitate visual perception and deal with stimulus adequacy or the elaboration of information in guiding visual behavior" (1971, 269). The authors believed it particularly significant that the average evoked potentials derived from left cerebral activity were different regardless of routing stimuli via the primary or secondary visual pathways; this did not occur with right hemisphere recordings. It appears then that interhemispheric exchange via cerebral commissures and/or subcortical structures favors left hemisphere reception and transference. This view is consistent with a dominant role for the left hemisphere as a comparator mechanism. But one might ask how their data could determine whether this difference has to do with transcommissural "reception and transference" or with differences in hemispheric processing (see also Buchsbaum and Drago, 1977).

Shelburne (1972) compared the visual evoked reactions (VERs) elicited by words and nonsense syllables from both the left and right hemispheres. Shelburne also included a condition in which the stimulus was relevant in the making of a decision. The stimuli used were words and nonsense syllables consisting of three-letter consonant-vowel-consonant trigrams. Each letter was presented separately in sequence, and the first two letters of each word and its matched nonsense syllable were the same, with only the third letter being different. The subject's task was to determine whether or not the stimulus formed a word, and to make a motor response. In a second experiment, the stimuli were changed so that the first letter of the trigram was the only letter that was different between the nonsense syllables and the words. The evoked potential for each letter was analyzed separately.

Shelburne reported no consistently reliable differences between the VERs to word stimuli and to nonsense stimuli. He did analyze evoked potentials to individual letters separately, and differences were found between some letters, so that his conclusion is somewhat unclear. The amplitude of responses to third position stimuli was significantly greater than of those to first position stimuli in all subjects. These differences were maximal at 450-550 msec following stimulus presentation, and were characterized by a larger amplitude for the third letter when it was the only different letter between the word and the nonsense syllable. In the second experiment, in which the first letter was the only different letter, the amplitude of the average evoked potential for the first letter was reliably larger than that for the second or third letters. No differences were indicated between average evoked potentials from the right and left hemispheres.

The increased positive amplitudes of the late components of the VER were related to the subject's decision-making process. For example, when the last letter determined whether the stimulus was a word or a nonsense syllable, and a subsequent answering response was required, that letter became functional in the making of a choice. The use of these techniques holds promise for making objective neurophysiological evaluations of patients with reading disabilities.

Shelburne (1973) investigated visual average evoked responses to language stimuli in normal children. The stimuli were letters of the alphabet presented in sequences as consonant-vowel-consonant (CVC) trigrams. The subject was instructed to decide whether or not the CVC formed a word or a nonsense syllable. As in Shelburne (1972), the third letter was critical for making this decision. EEG recordings were taken from electrodes placed on the vertex, and from the right and left parietal areas. Shelburne found that if the children performed well on the discrimination task, then reactions from third position stimuli (the last consonants) had a significantly greater positive amplitude than reactions from first position (the initial consonants) and second position stimuli (the vowels). These statistically significant differences were most prominent at the vertex electrode, and maximal differences were noted at latencies of 450-600 msec after stimulus presentation. If the subject performed poorly on the task or was unable to make a correct decision, then no such differences were observed. The average evoked potential differences that were obtained appeared to be related to the subject's decision making after visualization of the third stimulus, the last consonant.

SPEECH PERCEPTION (AUDITORY LINGUISTIC INPUT)

Darrow and Hicks (1965) examined the phase relationships (relative timing) of EEG records from the left motor, parietal, and occipital areas of the brain while subjects were presented either non-linguistic simuli or linguistic stimuli of variable emotional content. The three classes of stimuli used were: (1) "sensory," e.g., unexpected non-linguistic noises; (2) "indifferent ideational," having little emotional import; and (3) "disturbing ideational," having high emotional impact on the subjects. These stimuli were presented in irregular order, and with varying intervals between presentation, to reduce anticipatory and adaptive effects. The experimenters concluded that diphasic phase reversals occurred significantly more often after the disturbing-ideational stimuli than before their presenations, and that for the presentation of indifferent-ideational stimuli the reverse is true. Darrow and Hicks further concluded that the higher frequency of phase reversals following the disturbing-ideational stimuli suggests the interaction of different areas of the brain due to the additional requirement of "perceptual and ideational evaluation."

Feldman and Goldstein (1967) studied average evoked reactions to synthetic syntax sentences presented into one ear, and related these patterns to behavioral performances. Synthetic syntax sentences are constructed such that each succeeding word in a three-word phrase is selected on the basis of its conditional probability of occurrence with respect to the syntactic structure of the English language. In order to complicate the task, a secondary message (from the life of Davy Crockett) was also presented in the non-test ear. When presented with a synthetic syntax sentence, the subject was to press a button on a response board placed in front of him in order to match the sentence which the subject had heard. All of the subjects received the three-word sentences at 30, 50, 60, and 70 dB sound pressure level. The experimenters stated that as the intensity in dBs of the presented words decreased, there was a progressive increase in the latency of all of the components of the evoked response, and that this degree of latency change was greater in the later components of the response. That is, the lower the intensity of the signal, the greater the latency of all components of the reaction. It was also noted that all subjects scored 100% correct answers when the intensity level was at either 70, 60, or 50 dB. The experimenters concluded from this analysis that what they considered a lack of a reliable difference in performance, even when there was a noted latency change, indicates that intensity and not intelligibility is the crucial factor governing the latency. The authors concluded that the average evoked responses to these synthetic syntax sentences are closely related to non-semantic stimuli both with respect to the absolute latency of the response components as well as the relative change in the latency of the components with intensity.

Koukkou and Lehmann (1968) sought to describe the duration and wave frequency of EEG patterns induced during sleep by meaningful test sentences, to correlate the EEG activity with the quality of the retrievable memory storage of the stimulus, and to investigate (in a second series of experiments) the effects of training on the characteristics of the EEG activation associated with learning.

In the first series of experiments, subjects were presented with short test sentences during sleep. For 110 of the 156 presentations of test sentences, the subjects were provided with a small hand key which put a mark on the EEG recording when pressed. All subjects were instructed to remember the test sentences, and that after being awakened they were to spontaneously report the sentences which they could recall. The sentences were presented during Stage 2 sleep, and an EEG analysis was made from a parieto-occipital recording. The durations of the EEG activation periods which followed the presentation of the test sentences were correlated with the quality of the recall of sentences after the subject had been awakened. The degrees of quality of recall of sentences were divided into classifications of four different scores. It was found that the durations associated with the four recall scores were significantly different except for the two better scores; decrease of quality of recall was associated with shortening of the EEG activations. The longest durations of EEG activation were associated with a correct spontaneous recall, the intermediate durations with possibility to recognize, and the shortest durations with lack of recall. Higher frequencies of the alpha waves during the first 2 sec of the activation were associated with better recall. The subject averages of duration of activation for a given recall score obtained when key responses were required and the same averages when key responses were not required were not significiantly different.

In the second series of 18 experiments (performed on one subject over a period of eight months) there was again a systematic trend to higher frequencies associated with better recall scores, but the systematic increase in frequency from the first nine to the second nine experiments was not statistically significant. Koukkou and Lehmann suggested that the duration of the EEG wakefulness pattern after presentation of test sentences reflects the time available for long-term storage of the memory material in retrievable form.

Evans, Gustafson, O'Connell, Orne, and Shor (1970) studied the possibility of eliciting overt movement responses from sleeping subjects. The criterion for sleep was absence of alpha, as determined by monitoring frontal, parietal, and occipital EEGs. Suggestions, such as "whenever I say the word 'itch,' your nose will feel itchy until you scratch it," were administered during alpha-free emergent Stage I sleep periods. The cue word (e.g., "itch") was presented during subsequent alpha-free emergent Stage I REM periods on the same night or the following night. Subjects made "correct" overt responses to 89 of 416 answers. In most cases EEG-defined arousal was not present before or after the suggestion, the cue word that followed and the appropriate response. For those cues that elicited a correct response when alpha did occur, the alpha frequency was significantly slower than waking alpha (as found in a two-minute control period prior to sleep) and significantly faster than transient Stage I alpha occurring spontaneously (as counted in three segments of one second duration). When divided into more responsive and less responsive subjects, evoked alpha appeared similar to waking alpha for nonresponders and similar to spontaneous sleep-elicited alpha for responders. The average latency of the overt response following presentation of the cue word was 32 seconds; this latency increased as the temporal dissociation between the administration of the suggestion and the cue word increased. During post-sleep testing, there was only fragmentary recall of suggestions and cue words, with no recall of responses. However, correct responses were elicited by the presentation of the cue word (e.g., "itch") the following night during REM sleep, even up to six months later. Evans et al. concluded that subjects are capable of some interaction with their environment while asleep.

Roth, Kopell and Bertozzi (1970) compared amplitude of cortical (vertex) average evoked potentials to aural presentations of meaningful and meaningless material under either memory (attention) or non-memory (non-attention) conditions. The average evoked potential to the first syllable of each sentence was significantly greater than to subsequent syllables. The authors considered that this may be due to the duration of the silent interval between the last word of a preceding sentence and the first word or syllable of the following sentence. Attention and non-attention conditions were not significantly different for either sentences or words when a simple peak-to-peak measure was used. However, for sentences, the shapes of attention curves were alike, and the shapes of non-attention curves were alike when comparisons were made within individual subjects. The experimenters concluded that sense and non-sense words were not distinguished in EEG wave form.

Smith, Donchin, Cohen, and Starr (1970) compared the effects of listening to verbal versus nonverbal stimuli presented to each ear as follows: (1) numbers at the rate of one per second, (2) letters substituting for one of the numbers at the average rate of one every 15 seconds, and (3) clicks at the average rate of one every 5 seconds. The intensity of the numbers and letters was approximately 55 dB sound pressure level. At no time did the same letter or number appear in both earphones nor did stimuli arrive stimultaneously to the two ears. The experimental session was divided into four conditions which differed from one another only in the instructions given to the subject. The four conditions and their order of presentation were to:

1. report letters in the right (left) earphone.
2. report letters in the left (right) earphone.
3. report clicks in the right (left) earphone.
4. report clicks in the left (right) earphone.

Task relevance of the clicks affected the amplitude of the auditory average evoked potentials (as measured from the vertex). In six of the eight subjects, there was a significant enhancement of the auditory average evoked potential P300 component when the subjects were told to report clicks as compared to letters. Analysis of concomittant eye movement recordings revealed that averaging the potentials derived from the eye movement electrodes showed no time-locked activity in relation to the click onset. Thus, it was found that when the subject was instructed to respond to clicks delivered to one ear, all clicks, regardless of the ear in which they are presented, elicited a P300 component in the auditory average evoked potential which was larger than the P300 elicited by clicks when attending to a verbal message. When the subject was asked to report the letters presented to one ear, the P300 component was significantly enhanced only for the attended ear. Comparison baseline data are absent in this experiment.

Hirsh (1971) recorded auditory average evoked potentials from the vertex, 50 msec of baseline preceding stimulus onset, and 550 msec following the stimulus. The stimuli consisted of a 600 Hz tone pip followed by three 1200 Hz tone bursts (20 msec, with 1.5 msec rise and fall times), all presented at approximately 60 dB. The stimuli were presented in cycles of four tones such that a cycle was made up of: A, a warning (600 Hz) that a cycle was beginning; B, the standard 1200 Hz tone; C, the test tone (also 1200 Hz), which was either the same intensity as B or plus/minus 3dB; and D, a control (1200 Hz), always the same intensity as B. The tones were presented at equal intervals 2.5 seconds apart. Reactions to the four tones were averaged separately.

The first two series of cycle presentations were identical to those used by Davis (1964), namely, a control with the subjects reading, and a button press-response series. A third series of cycle presentations constituted a "counting trial" in which the subject was asked to count the number of times a tone was presented. The fourth series of cycles comprised the decision trials in which the subject signaled with the button press after the presentation of the "C" third tone. Three different types of decision trials were used: (1) the subject responded if C was different from B, (2) the subject responded if C was stronger than B, (3) the subject responded if C was weaker than B. Subject concensus was that detection of a decrement in C was more difficult than either of the other two tasks.

In general, the overall response to the test tone, C, in the decision trials was enhanced, supporting findings by Davis (1964). Only a slight relation was found between the level of performance and enhancement of response to the test tone, C, in the decision trials. The overall responses in the three control conditions were quite similar. The mean amplitude of all responses in the decision trials was 5.5% above the overall mean, whereas all other conditions had means below the overall average. The appearance of a late positive component, P300, was evident in 11 of the 15 subjects.

Morrell and Salamy (1971) conducted an experiment in which right-handed subjects monitored an audio tape and reported each stimulus heard. Five different verbal stimuli were repeated 50 times in a quasi-randomized order. The most consistently observed feature of the electrocortical average evoked potential to the speech stimuli was a prominent negative wave (N_1) occurring at 40 to 50 msec, reaching a maximum around 90 msec after the signal onset, and a subsequent positive going event peaking at a mean latency around 160 msec (P_2). Systematic differences between the various speech stimuli were not detected. The amplitude of the N_1 component was reliably larger in the left than in the right hemisphere. In the left hemisphere, the largests N_1 response occurred in the temporal-parietal region, and these average evoked were significantly larger than those of the frontal region. In the right hemisphere, the largest response occurred in the Rolandicsite, and this amplitude was significantly larger than those in the frontal or posterior regions. The information which distinguished between the two hemispheres in electrical responses to speech stimuli was basically carried by the amplitude of the N_1 rather than the P_2 component. The authors concluded that specialized neural pathways are activated in the left temporo-parietal cortex when speech sounds are perceived.

Picton and Low (1971) used a contingent negative variation paradigm, requiring subjects to make an auditory discrimination, and to respond to the second stimulus, but with the modification that a feedback stimulus was added after the response. Recording at the vertex revealed that, as the discrimination became more difficult, (1) the contingent negative variation apparently was prolonged until the feedback stimulus occurred, (2) this negative signal that occurred between the second stimulus and the feedback stimulus significantly increased in area, and (3) the amplitude of the evoked response to the feedback signal significantly increased. The authors suggested that the discharge of contingent negative variation occurs at the time of significant informational feedback, usually at the second stimulus in the traditional paradigm; however it occurred to the feedback stimulus in this modified design. The increasing average evoked potentials to the feedback stimulus lend support to the notion that components of an average evoked potential reflect the psychological significance of the stimulus. The eye showed no systematic variation, and palmar galvanic skin response occurred 2 sec after the first stimulus. Respiration, heart rate, facial GSR, and trans-cephalic potentials were recorded in some subjects but were not reported.

Wood, Goff, and Day (1971) recorded auditory average evoked potentials as a function of linguistic versus nonlinguistic processing conditions. In a linguistic task, right-handed subjects discriminated between two possible stimuli (/ba/ or /da/) which differed only in those acoustic cues important for distinguishing between voiced stop consonants. In a nonlinguistic information task, right-handed subjects discriminated between two identical linguistic stimuli (/ba/) that differed only in fundamental frequency. The binaural stimulus presentations (descriptions of which are abbreviated here) were counterbalanced. Signals were recorded over temporal and central locations of both hemispheres. Average evoked potentials for the two tasks significantly differed only over the left hemisphere indicating specific involvement of the left hemisphere during auditory linguistic processing. These results have been extended by showing (1) that similar average evoked potential differences do not occur when subjects are required to process auditory dimensions which convey no linguistic information; and (2) that such differences are not accompanied by differences in background EEG, pre-stimulus baseline shifts, or movement-synchronized activity.

Cohn (1971) simultaneously presented either verbal (one-syllable words) or nonverbal (click) stimuli to both ears, and recorded summated average evoked potentials at homologous locations over each hemisphere. Bipolar electrodes were anterior to the external acoustic meatus. All subjects showed greater amplitude of initial output of summated average evoked potentials to non-verbal stimuli over the right hemisphere. Half showed greater amplitude of initial output of summated average evoked potentials to verbal stimuli over the left cerebral hemisphere; for remaining subjects reactions were similar for left and right recordings. All subjects for all conditions of stimulus presentation showed average evoked potentials compared to a resting baseline. Preferred-handedness had no noticeable effect.

Matsumiya, Tagliasco, Lombroso, and Goodglass (1972) examined interhemispheric asymmetries in transcranial auditory evoked reaction in human subjects who processed various verbal and nonverbal stimuli of high and low meaningfulness (defined as relevance to the subject's task). Measurements of asymmetry were obtained by comparison of two bipolar recordings from the left and right parietal locations, including a location above Wernicke's area. Average evoked reactions were obtained under four conditions that were designed to contrast low and high significance levels of noise and low and high significance levels of words: (1) undiscriminated words; (2) undiscriminated, nonlinguistic sounds; (3) discrimination of the sounds in condition 2; and (4) meaningful speech. The magnitude of asymmetry was expressed by a ratio involving peak-to-peak amplitude of a wave recorded from the left hemisphere with the corresponding amplitude of a wave recorded from the right hemisphere. The ratio values under condition 4 (meaningful speech) was significantly larger than for the three other conditions. Furthermore, under condition 3 (discrimination of sounds) ratio values were significantly larger than those obtained under condition 2 (non-discrimination between the sounds). When the subjects had to use the meaning or significance of each stimulus maximally, the asymmetry of average evoked potentials was large, but when the subject did not have to rely on meaning or significance to process the stimuli, the stimuli did not produce such large asymmetry. The same sound effects produced different magnitudes of asymmetry when different tasks were imposed on the subjects (condition 2 versus condition 3). The authors suggested that this indicates that the relationship between the significance of the auditory input to the subject's task and the difference in magnitude of the average evoked potential may be more relevant to the occurrence of interhemispheric asymmetry in average evoked potentials than is the difference between verbal and nonverbal materials without regard to task relevance.

Teyler, Roemer, Harrison, and Thompson (1973) recorded click-average evoked potentials (fronto-parietal EEG) during the presentation of ambiguous linguistic stimuli. In each of three phases homonyms were aurally presented preceding the click stimulus. In Phase 1 (disambiguated stimulus, verbal response) right-handed subjects repeated the noun or verb form of the word (e.g., "to rock" vs. "a rock") after the click was presented. In Phase 2 (ambiguous stimulus, verbal response) the word was presented without a modifier and the subjects repeated the same word after the sound of the click. They then reported whether they had thought of the word as a noun or as a verb. Phase 3 (ambiguous stimulus, nonverbal response) was the same as Phase 2 except that the subjects were instructed to silently "think" of the word stimulus after the sound of the click. For nouns and verbs the dominant (left) hemisphere average evoked potential was significantly larger in amplitude than was the right hemisphere reaction. The mean right-left difference was twice as large, and significantly so, in the noun as opposed to the verb category. Each of the three phases of the experiment was separately analyzed for overall (pooling reactions to nouns and verbs) right-left hemisphere differences, and it was found that the left hemisphere response was of reliably greater amplitude for all three phases. Additionally, the latency of the click-evoked wave form did not vary significantly as a function of hemisphere. However, latency of Phase 1 was significantly shorter for verbs compared to nouns. Teyler et al. concluded that these data demonstrate a significant influence of linguistic meaning on human scalp-recorded average evoked potentials.

Neville (1974) aurally presented subjects with verbal (digits) and nonverbal (clicks) both dichotically and monaurally through earphones. More dichotically presented verbal stimuli were identified correctly from the right ear than from the left, while there was no significant difference for the perception of nonverbal clicks. Averaged evoked potentials for dichotic verbal stimuli showed early components of greater amplitude, and later components of shorter latency, from the left hemisphere compared to the right. No such difference was apparent for nonverbal stimuli. The results are interpreted to indicate assymmetry of hemispheric functioning with respect to verbal processing.

ATTENTION

Haider (1967) described a series of studies of variation in average evoked cortical potentials corresponding to signal detection in vigilance tasks, selective attention to visual or auditory stimuli, and of expectation of stimulus occurrence. In the first, Haider, Spong, and Lindsley (1964) reported that the magnitude and latency of visual average evoked potentials from the right occipital cortex and vertex correlated .75 with fluctuations in attentiveness during a prolonged visual vigilance task. In a second study, Spong, Haider, and Lindsley (1965) recorded average evoked potentials from temporal occipital areas of the cortex and found that when subjects are required to perform an active discrimination between visual and auditory stimuli, amplitude varies according to whether the subject is attending specifically to one, and not the other, of the two stimulis. The amplitude to visual or auditory stimuli was greater when the subjects were attending to the corresponding stimulus modalities than when they were attending to the opposite stimulus modality. In a third experiment the effects of correct and incorrect expectancies on average evoked potential amplitude were measured, and it was found that the incorrect pre-occurence stimulus expectation diminished the magnitude of the average evoked potentials by 35%. The results of these studies indicated that central effects of attention and expectation produce characteristic changes in average evoked potentials.

Ritter and Vaughan (1969) examined the generality of the late positive component (LPC) of average evoked potentials during both auditory and visual discrimination tasks. In the visual task, the subject pressed a switch whenever a standard periodic flash was replaced by a dimmer one at irregular intervals. In the auditory task, the subject pressed a switch whenever a standard periodic tone was replaced by a different one at irregular intervals. Recordings were made from a supra orbital position to the chin, vertex to the chin, right occipital to the chin, and, in the manner of Haider et al. (1964), vertex to right occipital.

The results for all subjects for both tasks were similar in that vertex and occipital recordings showed a prominent LPC. Since the LPC was common to the two leads, the bipolar linkage of the two failed to show the LPC, possibly explaining the negative results of Haider et al. (1964). Further, in the auditory task the LPC came later than the range measured by Davis (1964), who had also reported negative results. The authors concluded that their data obviated the possibility that the LPC was a motor potential and that it represents cerebral processes associated with evaluation of unpredictable changes in stimulation.

Brenner, Moritz, and Benignus (1972) attempted to determine

whether EEG measures of alpha would be sensitive to various types of "attention" in humans. Baseline alpha readings were taken on two randomized groups of subjects. One group then underwent "Silva Mind Control" training (suggested to be a combination of "relaxation" and meditation) while the other group was conditioned to produce increased alpha through classical conditioning (CC) techniques. An auditory click was presented to the CC group, followed after 10 seconds by a flashing strobe light set at the subject's eyes-closed alpha frequency. Results showed that the CC group did produce increased alpha when later presented with the click stimulus, and the authors concluded that an "expectancy" attentional set was thereby demonstrated. The Silva group also showed increased alpha after their training, which the authors described as evidence of "internal focus" of attention. A peak shift in alpha was noted for both groups following CC and Silva training.

Ohman and Lader (1972) studied direction of attention and interstimulus interval as possible factors governing attenuation of the average evoked response. The basic design was a 2×2 factorial, with attending versus nonattending to auditory stimuli as one factor, and two different interstimulus intervals as the other. In the attending conditions, the subject was instructed to respond to each click by closing a microswitch as quickly as possible. In the nonattending conditions, clicks were presented but were irrelevant to the subject's task. In all conditions, auditory average evoked potentials from the vertex were measured to clicks of about 70 dB intensity and 1 msec in duration. The auditory average evoked potentials were sampled every 2 msec starting 20 msec before each click stimulus (baseline) and continuing for 500 msec after the stimulus onset. The effect of attention directed towards the stimuli was very clear, producing larger reactions than the nonattention condition for both P1-N1 and N1-P2 components. Higher response amplitudes were found for the long interstimulus intervals. Furthermore, a strong decremental effect over time was found: The auditory evoked potential decreased with stimulus repetition even when the subject paid attention. The effect of attention on the auditory evoked potential was not attributed to a more rapid amplitude decrement in the non-attending conditions. Skin conductance level was monitored throughout the study and was found not to exhibit a general decrement, as did the auditory evoked potential.

Hillyard, Hink, Schwent, and Picton (1973) investigated selective attention by having subjects listen to tone pips in one ear and ignore concurrent tone pips in the other ear. Auditory average evoked potentials, recorded from the vertex, had a negative component (peaking at 80 to 110 milliseconds) when evoked by tones in the attended ear that were substantially larger than those evoked by tones in the opposite ear. According to Hillyard et al., this was the first definite evidence that changes in an average evoked potential component can specifically reflect selective attention as opposed to a preparatory or reactive change of nonselective state. A late positive component peaking at 250 to 400 milliseconds reflected the response set established to recognize infrequent, higher pitched tone pips in the attended series.

VISUAL, NON-VERBAL THOUGHT TASKS

Cohen and Walter (1966) studied differences in the CNV as a function of class of tachistoscopically presented stimuli. Average evoked responses to geometric or pictorial stimuli were more elaborate than to clicks and flashes—the usual stimuli in CNV procedures. When the imperative stimulus was a different symbol or picture requiring interpretation, the first and second negative components of the average visual evoked potential were of higher amplitude compared to those for repeated exposures to the same stimulus. Cohen and Walter suggested that this reaction is a function of the diversity of the stimuli and the corresponding increment in information.

Shevrin, Smith, and Fritzler (1971) sought to determine if discrimination between two subliminal stimuli could be detected by examining average evoked potentials. Two methods of analysis were: (1) a sequence method, in which the component was identified as the first positive-going component 90 msec post-stimulus; and (2) an amplitude method, in which the component of interest was the largest positive-going wave (measured from the previous negative-going component) within a broad range (40-260 msec in this case). Stimuli were matched in size, color, general configuration, and brightness, but differed in internal contours so that one stimulus (R) was easily distinguishable as a pen or a knee, while the other (matched) stimulus (D) consisted of geometric shapes similar to the meaningful stimulus in form. Bipolar recordings were between frontal, vertex, and left occipital placements, with frontal-occipital leads providing the main findings. Stimuli were randomly presented for series of 1 msec, 30 msec, and again 1 msec. EEG reactions were eliminated by the experimenters if eye movements, blinks, or alpha bursts occurred during stimulus presentation. The authors found that for both the sequence and the amplitude methods, evoked responses to stimulus R were significantly greater than to stimulus D for the *first* 1-msec presentation. Average evoked potential to stimulus R were significantly greater than to D for the 30-msec presentation, but not for the second 1-msec presentations (due possibly, the authors believed, to habituation and/or fatigue). When the data from a similar study (Shevrin and Fritzler, 1968) were included, it was found that the responses to R were significantly greater than to D across all conditions, using both the sequence and amplitude methods. By the sequence method the positive-going component was significantly later for the 30-msec condition than for either 1-msec condition, while the reverse was found (also significant) by the amplitude method.

No subjects described seeing any stimuli following the 1-msec exposures, while all subjects reported two stimuli during the 30-msec exposure although they could not be verbally identified. Following stimulus exposures subjects were told to free-associate, and those associations were scored for occurences of the following three categories: (1) words conceptually related to "pen" and/or "knee," such as ink, leg, etc., (2) words homophonically related to pen and/or knee, such as *pen*nant, a*ny*, etc., and (3) words associated to the homophonic combination of pen and knee (penny), such as coin, round, etc. It was found that for both the sequence and the amplitude methods average evoked potentials to stimulus R were significantly greater than to stimulus D for the *first* 1-msec presentation. Free association revealed that verbal effects of the type described by category 1, above, were significantly associated with an average evoked potential amplitude component, while effects of the types 2 and 3 above were significantly associated with alpha bursts approximately 1½-sec poststimulus.

For older subjects (17-20) the sequence and peak methods' components coincided: for younger subjects (12-16) they differed. Younger subjects had significantly larger amplitudes than older subjects for all conditions using the amplitude method and for the 30 msec condition using the sequence method. The authors offered the notion that "unconscious attention" parallels "conscious attention" electrophysiologically except that stimulus perception is subliminal. In column 3 of Table 8.1 it is indicated that the reaction was independent of eye blinks and alpha bursts because EEG responses were eliminated from the data if delivered during eye movement blink or alpha burst.

Symmes and Eisengart (1971) studied average evoked potential correlates of meaningful visual stimuli in children by tachistoscopically presenting photographic slides of familiar objects or cartoons to a group of normal children. Control stimuli consisted of blank slides or unfocused cartoons matched for brightness, and a warning flash preceded the slides by 1 sec. Electrodes placed at E_Z, C_Z, and O_Z (international 10-20 system) yielded a vertex negative slow potential peaking about 500 msec after slide presentation, which correlated with reports of interest in and recall of both objects and cartoons. Reactions in the occipital region changed less consistently with pictorial material, and were the same to the warning flash whether it preceded control or test stimuli.

Ruchkin and Sutton (1973) investigated the relationship between visual average evoked and emitted potentials and stimulus significance. It had been previously found by Sutton, Tueting, Zubin, and John (1967) that an emitted potential would occur in the absence of an auditory stimulus when the absence provided significant information. In the Ruchkin and Sutton (1973) investigation, the stimuli were 10-msec light flashes. In the control condition, the subject was informed prior to each trial whether there would be one or two flashes ("certain condition"). In the experimental condition, the subject guessed prior to each trial whether there would be one or two flashes ("uncertain condition"). Correct guesses were rewarded financially and incorrect guesses were penalized. EEGs were from vertex (C_Z) and occipital (O_Z) regions, both referred to the left earlobe (A_1). There was a significant difference in P3 between the uncertain and the certain condition, leading Ruchkin and Sutton (1973) to generalize the finding of Sutton et al. (1967) to visual stimuli.

Rohrbaugh, Donchin, and Eriksen (1974) had subjects manually respond to two rapidly successive visual patterns. In one set of conditions, both stimuli were needed for the formation of a correct choice, while for the other set of conditions the patterns were presented in such a predictable order that only simple reaction time was actually measured. Electrodes were placed at the vertex and right occiput referred to linked earlobes, and on the left temple and inferior orbit. Signal averaging indicated that P300 was enhanced significantly above other components during the "choice" conditions only, implicating P300 in poststimulus processing, such as in decision making, and not in terms of preparatory adjustments or anticipation.

AUDITORY, NON-VERBAL THOUGHT TASKS

Sheatz and Chapman (1969) investigated the effects of task relevance on average evoked potentials to auditory stimuli during problem solving. Recording was from the vertex referred to the right mastoid. Stimuli were three noises and three pure tones maintained at approximately 75 dB sound pressure level. On each trial, two noises and two tones were presented with an inter-stimulus interval of 0.8 seconds. The pitch of each tone and noise stimulus was randomly selected from one of three possible values. The subject's task on each trial was to compare the two relevant stimuli and determine which was lower in frequency. On some trials, the subject was told that the tones were the relevant stimuli while on other trials, the noises were relevant. The auditory average evoked potentials contained positive peaks at approximately 150 and 300 msec. These peaks, especially the P2 component, tended to be larger when the stimuli were relevant than when the stimuli were irrelevant. Statistical analysis showed significant differences to exist from baseline recordings and between averaged evoked potentials to relevant versus irrelevant stimuli. Therefore, when stimuli are relevant to the subject's task, they evoke larger positive peaks than when the identical stimuli are irrelevant. Whether or not the enhanced potentials occurred independently of other electrophysiological measures was not determined.

Waszak and Obrist (1969) investigated the CNV during the performance of a disjunctive reaction task with two motivational states. The subjects were either to make or withhold a motor response depending on a tone presented as S_2. Half of the trials were performed under a speed condition and the other half were under a relaxed condition. The CNV was determined by comparison with a prestimulus baseline. In the beginning of the experiment, subjects performed the task with their eyes closed, but measurements of eye movement taken by EEG electrodes indicated that eye movement potential was exerting a major influence on the CNV. Because of this finding, seven subjects were excluded and the remaining subjects performed the task while fixating on a spot 2 m away. The authors also suggested that eye potentials be summated by computer, as they (like the CNV) may not be of large enough amplitude to be detected trial by trial. The results of this study indicate that all subjects developed CNV irrespective of motivational state, and there was no difference in CNV amplitude that was dependent upon motivational state. As in Hillyard and Galambos (1967), faster reaction times (within subject only) were preceded by CNVs with significantly larger amplitudes than slower reaction times.

Jenness (1972) studied the effects on the auditory average evoked potential of stimuli that were equally informational but of different value. The task was of the discrimination learning type where one of two clicks followed a ready signal (a flash). Another flash informed the subject to push a button to indicate whether the click was high or low in tone. Two seconds later, the same click occurred if the response was correct, or no stimulus occurred if it was incorrect. EEG (vertex) waveforms were recorded throughout all trials. In addition to hourly pay, subjects received a five cent reward for each correct identification of the high click; no reward was given for correct identification of the low click. Based upon sample waveforms evoked during the presentation of the two "task" clicks, the author states that slight amplitude differences occurred in early training, while later, at higher levels of accuracy, the wave-form differences were larger, typically associated with components later than P_2. Potentials evoked by the feedback click—physically identical to the task click—were 30% to 100% larger in amplitude in the first negative-positive component than those evoked by the task click. Jenness concluded that the waveform of average evoked potentials may depend upon the functional role of the stimulus and the experimental operations employed.

SPEECH PRODUCTION

The occurrence of cortical activity preceding voluntary speech was reported by Ertl and Schafer (1967a). Ertl referred to this activity as the "cortical command potential" which "commanded" speech muscle responding. In a conversation with him I asked what "commanded" the cortical command potential, suggesting in the same sense that it could be a "speech muscle command potential." Ertl and Schafer (1967b) then recorded EEG from the F_7-T_5 location (10-20 system) and EMG activity was monitored from the upper lip while subjects voluntarily spoke the letter "T." From a figure in their report, it appears that an increase in EMG begins about 200 msec preceding the onset of voice activity and 30-50 msec before the increased cortical activity. This increased EMG in the lips is probably the very beginning of the speech activity. The authors reported that lip EMG "contaminated" the cortical activity preceding speech, though the lip response may be the measurement of a muscle component of a neuromuscular processing circuit.

McAdam and Whitaker (1971a; see also 1971b) studied localization of language production in the normal human brain, taking recordings from over the left and right precentral gyri and over inferior frontal areas. Each subject was told to produce four sets of responses in the following order: a spitting gesture, a set of words beginning with the phoneme [k] and having at least three syllables, a coughing gesture, and a set of words beginning with the phoneme [p] and having at least three syllables. Salient features of the electrical activity preceding language production may be summarized as follows: (1) larger negative potentials are recorded from the left hemisphere (Broca's area) than from the right hemisphere; and (2) inferior frontal and precentral potentials show significant differences between hemispheres, which is suggestive evidence for within-hemispheric localization. McAdam and Whitaker advanced these data as the first direct physiological evidence for localization of language production functions in the intact, normal human brain.

MISCELLANEOUS THOUGHT TASKS

Smith, Brown, Toman, and Goodman (1947) sought to obtain a subjective report of the physiological and psychological effects of d-Tubocurarine on bodily processes (as verified by EEG, EKG, and pulmonary ventilation). Curare was administered intravenously in small dosages until a final dose totalling two and one-half times the normal dosage sufficient to induce respiratory paralysis was reached. EEG was recorded from the fronto-occipital area of the brain pre-, during, and post-administration of d-Tubocurarine. The EEG recordings (alpha) remained within normal limits in all respects in all conditions. No significant changes in amplitude, frequency, or percentage time of alpha activity occurred even at the maximum dosage of curare. The authors concluded that curare does not possess central stimulant, depressant, or analgesic properties. The large dosage failed to significantly affect EEG or to impair consciousness, memory, or sensorium (but see p. 93).

Morgan, McDonald, and MacDonald (1971) investigated differences in bilateral alpha activity while subjects engaged in two sets of tasks: left hemisphere tasks involving verbalization and arithmetic calculation, and right hemisphere tasks involving visual imagination. One electrode was placed on the vertex of the head, and one on either side above the center of the occipital ridge. Reflective eye movements were observed by the experimenter and sensed by horizontal eye electrodes. Subjects were selected on the basis of hypnotic susceptibility in order to compare reactions between high and low hypnotizables. In addition, subjects were classified as left-movers or right-movers according to the direction of their reflective lateral eye movements. It was found that: (1) there was more alpha activity in the right hemisphere than in the left for both groups; (2) there was a significant difference in the proportion of right hemisphere alpha, depending on the task in which the subject was engaged; (3) the left-movers had a higher mean hypnotic susceptibility score than the right-movers, though it reached statistical significance only when seven pilot subjects were added; and (4) there were no sizable differences for the alpha laterality measure (i.e., left-right asymmetry of alpha) between either the high and low hypnotizable groups, or between the left- and right-movers. Morgan et al. (1971) suggested that the results were encouraging for bilateral alpha recording as a technique for studying hemispheric localization of function in the human brain. In a later study (Morgan, MacDonald, and Hilgard, 1974) high and low hypnotizable subjects differed significantly in absolute amplitude, but no difference in laterality was found.

Galin and Ornstein (1972) tested the hypothesis that the ratio of right to left hemisphere power would be greater during performance of verbal tasks than spatial tasks. Recordings were made from the left and right temporal and parietal areas. Each subject performed a series of four cognitive tasks—two verbal tasks and two spatial tasks. The verbal tasks included writing a letter and mentally composing a letter with eyes open and fixated at the central spot on the table. The spatial tasks included one in which the subject is given a two/dimensional geometrical pattern to memorize, and then must construct the pattern with multicolored blocks (modified Kohs block design), and one in which the subject is presented with a sectioned figure and is instructed to choose which of five assembled figures could be constructed from the sections (Modified Minnesota Paper Form Board Test). Galin and Ornstein found that the ratio (right over left) was significantly greater in the verbal tasks than in the spatial tasks, and that it is possible to distinguish between these two cognitive modes as they occur in normal subjects, using simple scalp recording.

McGuigan and Pavek (1972) sought "to psychophysiologically differentiate covert linguistic behavioral patterns when one silently answers 'yes' versus 'no' to questions" (p. 237). Electrodes were placed over the left temporal lobe and the left motor area, as well as on both forearms, the lips, the neck, and at the external canthi of the eyes. It was found that in general no meaningful trends as a function of condition were determined for EEG, neck, or lips. However, responding to questions by either (1) thinking "yes," then signalling "yes," or (2) thinking "no," then signalling "no" was accompanied by significantly earlier events over the left temporal region than over the left motor region. Overtly responding "yes" to a tone did not produce differential latencies between EEG sites. Also, latencies of the left temporal EEG reaction to the tone did not differ from latencies of reaction to the linguistic tasks just mentioned. However, the linguistic tasks produced longer left motor EEG latencies than did signalling at the tone.

Duration of horizontal eye movement was significantly greater when subjects thought "yes" than when they thought "no." On the average EMG activity was greater in the active arm when subjects thought "yes" and signalled "yes" than when they thought and signalled "no." Also, covert responses more frequently occurred earlier in the passive arm than in the active arm.

The authors speculated that complex feedback loops involving the left temporal region, the passive arm, the neck, the eyes, (all of which gave similar latencies of covert events), and other areas are concomitants of information processing, followed after a decision is made, by activation of the left motor cortex, which then "commands" the active arm to respond (see Fig. 9.6).

Morgan et al. (1971) and Galin and Ornstein (1972) had shown that there was relatively less alpha in a hemisphere when it was primarily responsible for information processing during the performance of linguistic or spatial tasks. McKee, Humphrey, and McAdam (1973) attempted to confirm and extend these findings for musical or linguistic tasks; they also scaled their linguistic tasks in difficulty, anticipating that the more difficult the task, the more alpha suppression would be seen over the left hemisphere. The subjects were given four parallel tasks; three of these were linguistic in nature and constructed to vary in difficulty, and the fourth task was a musical one. The linguistic tasks involved: (1) reporting each instance of a specific item, "NAACP"; (2) reporting all instances of the words "liberal" and "conservative," whatever their form; and (3) reporting all instances of the usage of the verb "to be" in any of its forms. The musical task was to note the occurrence of a particular irregularly repeated two measure theme in an unfamiliar Bach concerto. Left-right ratios of alpha activity were recorded from left and right temporal-parietal sites and were computed for each task. A significantly greater amount of alpha activity was seen over the right than over the left hemisphere, regardless of the task. Left-right alpha ratios were significantly highest for the musical task, and tended to significantly decrease progressively with increasingly difficult linguistic tasks.

MISCELLANEOUS

Knott (1939) required subjects in a variety of conditions to respond to either or both of two flashing lights placed in front of them, during which EEG measures of the latent time of blockage of alpha rhythm were taken. The various experimental conditions introduced motor tasks (such as lifting weights) in an effort to determine whether "peripheral" kinesthetic stimuli would affect the "central" phenomenon of latency of alpha blockage being measured. Results led to the conclusion that "the reduction in mean latent time of blocking is peripherally determined" rather than being owed to such central factors as mental set.

Sutton, Braren, Zubin, and John (1965) investigated evoked potential correlates of stimulus uncertainty. Average evoked potential waveforms to sound and light stimuli were recorded with the active electrode one-third of the distance along the line from the vertex to the external auditory meatus. The stimuli, clicks or brief light flashes, were presented in pairs; the first member of the pair served as a cueing stimulus and the second stimulus, which followed after a random interval of 3-5 seconds, was the test stimulus. There were two types of stimulus pairs presented: in one type of pair, a cueing stimulus was followed by a test stimulus which was always a sound or always a light flash—the subject was certain of the sensory quality of the test stimulus before it occurred. In the second type of pair, a different cueing stimulus was followed by a test stimulus which was either a sound or a light—the subject was uncertain as to the sensory quality of the test stimulus. These pairs of stimuli were presented in a random order. During the interval between the cueing and test stimuli, the subject stated a guess as to the sensory modality of the next stimulus. The most dramatic effect was the difference between certain and uncertain waveforms. The amplitude of the P300 component was significantly larger for the uncertain stimulus than for the certain stimulus in all cases.

In an additional experiment, the degree of uncertainty was manipulated by presenting two types of uncertain pairs: in one type of pair, a cueing stimulus was followed one-third of the time by a sound stimulus and two-thirds of the time by a light stimulus. In the other type of pair, a different cueing stimulus was followed by the inverse ratio. In all instances, the late positive component deflection occurred, but was greater in amplitude for the lower probability stimulus. This late positive component was of significantly higher amplitude for the wrong guesses than for the correct guesses.

Gullickson and Darrow (1968) examined the rapidity of EEG time changes during a variety of mental functions. A wave-by-wave analysis procedure yielded registration of the time and phase relationships. This analytic procedure indicated an increase in rapid reversals of time relationships during orienting and semantic processes, suggesting reverberation between various brain areas. The effect was greater during the presentation of unfamiliar versus familiar stimuli, taboo verbal stimuli versus indifferent verbal stimuli, and during the period of "expectancy" associated with the contingent negative variation. Gullickson and Darrow suggested that such activities attending higher mental functioning are of a different nature than the anterior leading effects that accompany conditions of simple organic mobilization or arousal.

Ulett, Akpinar, and Itil (1972), using digital computer period analysis and analog frequency analyzer techniques, found significant occipital EEG changes from resting during both hypnotic induction and hypnotic trance. These changes differed from drowsiness or sleep EEG patterns. During hypnotic induction there was a "significant decrease of slow and an increase of alpha and beta waves accompanied by an increase in amplitude and decrease in amplitude variability, in the best hypnotic subjects. Both the best and the poorest hypnotic subjects exhibited similar changes during the hypnotic trance period, although the best hypnotic subjects showed greater EEG changes, in particular, significantly more alpha activity, than the poorest ones" (p. 366). Due to this increased alpha, the authors likened hypnosis to meditative states and alpha training.

Lewis, Jenkinson, and Wilson (1973) investigated awareness during anesthesia. Previous studies of awareness during anesthesia used patients undergoing surgery, thus involving complications of premedications and anxiety due to, and stimuli from, surgery. Anesthesia was induced with thiophentone and maintained with N_2O and O_2. EEG electrodes were attached with collodion in a lateral ring montage using the International "10/20" system, omitting electrodes O_1 and O_2 because of the face-mask harness. Electrodes were also attached about 1 cm lateral to the outer canthi to monitor eye movements. Stimuli presented during anesthesia included a pre-recorded tape containing the reading of a poem, the ringing of a fire-bell, and a list of 15 low-frequency words. No alteration was found in the ongoing EEG pattern on visual inspection when the tape was switched on and off. No apparent reception of sensory input, and no recall or recognition, could be demonstrated in this study.

Conclusions and Summary

On the basis of the data considered in this chapter, as summarized in Table 8.1, we can conclude that:

1. Electrical measures of neurophysiological activity quite often have changed from a baseline condition. However, as indicated by the rather large number of question marks in column 1, frequently this criterion was not employed.
2. Quite often the experimenters established that their measure of brain activity did vary as a function of conditions, as indicated by the relatively large number of "yesses" in column 2.
3. With regard to the question as to whether or not the brain reactions systematically occurred independently of other covert processes, the main conclusion is that researchers in this area typically do not record simultaneous measures of other bodily activity. To some small extent we do note that other covert processes have been identified as occurring independently of brain activity, while some other measures have co-varied with the dependent variable employed by the researcher.
4. A rather large number of specific relationships have been established, and these are summarized below.

Mental Arithmetic. Kennedy et al. (1948): Kappa waves occurred in about half of the subjects during various thinking tasks.

Ford (1954): Mental effort is accompanied by low frequency high amplitude EEG increases in the frontal lobes, independent of facialis muscle tonus and EKG measures.

Chapman and Bragdon (1964): The evoked reaction to visual material appears positively correlated with meaningfulness of the stimuli for the problem.

Glanzer et al. (1964): As the difficulty of mental multiplication tasks increased, output of kappa waves significantly increased but not the output of alpha. As difficulty of concept tasks increased, alpha output significantly decreased.

Chapman (1965): When stimuli are relevant to a task, they evoke larger amplitudes of evoked potentials than the amplitudes evoked by the same stimuli when those stimuli are not relevant to the task.

Chapman (1969): Evoked responses tended to be larger to a stimulus when it was relevant than when it was irrelevant.

Giannitrapani (1966). A significant increase of average frequency in eight EEG locations from rest to the performance of mental arithmetic; the increase was significantly greater in the frontal and in the temporal areas than in the other areas.

Shevrin and Rennick (1967): Amplitudes of two negative electrocortical potentials of the cortical evoked potential were significantly smaller during free association and mental arithmetic than during attention in estimating time intervals.

Volavka et al. (1967): Eye opening and mental arithmetic suppressed theta and alpha waves. Beta activity decreased with eyes open and increased with mental arithmetic. Increase in beta activity in connection with mental arithmetic is in agreement with the observation of Mundy-Castle (1957).

Glass and Kwiatkowski (1968): Performance of mental arithmetic suppressed alpha rhythms up to 50% more than when the subjects merely sat with their eyes open doing "nothing." The conclusion was that mental arithmetic affects EEG in a way that cannot be accounted for by strictly ocular factors.

Vogel et al. (1968): Slow waves were significantly and positively correlated with efficient performance under conditions of mental effort (mental arithmetic). These slow rhythms may indicate a type of selective inhibition that facilitates performance during mental effort.

Vogel et al. (1969): Individuals who were weak automatizers (those who have poor ability to perform simple or repetitive tasks) emit significantly more driving EEG responses to photic stimulation than do strong automatizers.

Elul (1969): The EEG followed a Gaussian probability function while the subject was idle more often than while engaged in a mental task.

Chapman (1972): Kappa waves significantly increase during difficult tasks with the eyes closed, but not on other tasks. The amount of kappa was correlated with a number of subject variables such as anxiety, height, weight, and education. Amount of kappa activity increased during learning nonsense syllables relative to a control task.

Chapman et al. (1972): Alpha and kappa waves are normally present during mental arithmetic and rest. There is more alpha on hard vs. easy tasks, and more with eyes closed than opened.

Ishihara and Yoshii (1972): Two significant EEG factors during mental tasks concern thinking and work speed.

Learning.   Hillyard and Galambos (1967): Pairing of stimuli affects CNV. There is a negative correlation between reaction time and CNV.

Rosenfeld et al. (1969): Operant reinforcement significantly increased auditory evoked potentials over those for both baseline and punishment (loss of reward) conditions.

Begleiter et al. (1969): Absolute and relative differences in amplitudes and latencies for conditioned-positive, conditioned-negative, and neutral stimuli were found, depending upon the degree of awareness of the true nature of the experiment. Level of awareness of the CS-UCS contingency thus seems to be reflected by the amplitude of the evoked potential.

Brown (1970): Enhanced alpha appeared related to narrowing of perceptual awareness and pleasant feeling states."

Rosenfeld and Hetzler (1973): Successfully conditioned in rats extremely large and extremely small evoked potentials significantly greater and lesser, respectively, than corresponding extremes of baseline periods.

Imagination. Golla et al. (1943): Subjects who had small alpha waves engaged primarily in visual imagery during a variety of cognitive tasks; subjects generally classified as having persistent alpha rhythms exhibited primarily verbal imagery.

Slatter (1960): The degree of alpha blocking during imagination was significantly and positively related to the extent to which a subject engages in visual imagination. During rest the amplitude of alpha is significantly and inversely related to the extent to which a subject habitually engages in visual imagination.

Antrobus et al. (1964): Imagery involving external environment is accompanied by a suppression of alpha activity (and a significant increase in ocular motility). During day-dreaming, internal imagery, or passive thought there was a significant increase in alpha activity (and a significant amount of ocular quiescence).

Reading (Visual Linguistic Input). Travis and Knott (1937): Perseveration time (the length of time between the removal of a stimulus and the return of brain potentials to their prestimulus values) was greater when subjects were visually presented words and nonsense words than when presented with blank cards.

Knott (1938): EEG frequencies increased during both silent and overt reading relative to rest; and also were higher during overt versus silent reading.

Pepin et al. (1952): Frequency of EEG waves increased from rest to reading, both silent and oral; however, it was not clear that there was a difference between oral and silent reading.

Lifshitz (1966): "Dirty words" evoked a larger cortical response and different wave form than scrambled words.

John et al. (1967): Evoked potentials are related more to the shape of the visual stimulus than to its size.

Lille et al. (1968): Amplitude of evoked potentials produced by simple auditory or visual stimuli is inversely related to the level of mental activity being performed while the potentials are being evoked.

Shevrin and Fritzler (1968): Latency of average evoked potentials discriminates between two types of subliminal stimuli.

Weinberg and Cole (1968): Evoked potentials reliably differ as a result of viewing neutral words compared to taboo words, single letters, or blank flashes.

Begleiter and Platz (1969): Affective (taboo) words produced a significantly greater amplitude than either neutral words or a light flash in the evoked potential. The amplitude was significantly greater when the subject had to repeat the word than when remaining silent. The fourth component of the evoked potential was at a reliable shorter latency for taboo and neutral words than for the light flash. Shorter latencies of the second component occurred when the subject was required to make a response.

Buchsbaum and Fedio (1969): There are significant differences in wave form from both hemispheres between words and random dot patterns and between words and designs, with the differences being greater in the left hemisphere.

Sharrard (1969): Magnitude of EEG amplitude in a listener is significantly greater to words read forward than to words read in reverse.

Buchsbaum and Fedio (1970): There are differing waveforms for words and nonsense figures.

Heinemann and Emrich (1971): There are significantly more alpha waves during the perception of emotionally significant words than during the perception of neutral words.

Fedio and Buchsbaum (1971): Averaged evoked responses in lobectomized subjects had a general wave form during tachistoscopic recognition that was in part dependent upon whether the stimulus was verbal or nonverbal, and also on which hemisphere the stimulus was directed to through the eyes.

Shelburne (1972): The amplitude of VERs is reliably larger to the first letter of a word than for the second or third letters.

Shelburne (1973): Poor vs. good decision-making performance is related to VER differences as a function of letter position.

Speech Perception (Auditory Linguistic Input). Darrow and Hicks (1965): Emotional stimulus words that required perceptual and ideational evaluation are characterized by rapid diphasic reversals of inter-area EEG phase relations, suggestive of interaction between brain areas.

Feldman and Goldstein (1967): There was a progressive increase in the latency of all components of an average evoked reaction to meaningful sentences as the intensity of the presented stimuli decreased, and this degree of latency change was greater in the later components of the reaction.

Koukkou and Lehmann (1968): Duration of alpha and higher frequency of alpha was directly associated with better recall.

Evans et al. (1970): Subjects overtly responded to suggestions during Stage 1 sleep when alpha waves were not being elicited, indicating that the subject interacts with the environment during sleep.

Smith et al. (1970): There was a significant enhancement of the P300 component of the auditory evoked potential when subjects were told to report heard clicks as compared to heard letters.

Hirsh (1971): The auditory evoked potential was enhanced when subjects had to make a decision.

Morrell and Salamy (1971): A negative wave was recorded at about 40 to 50 msecs of the auditory evoked potential to speech stimuli; this component was reliably larger in the left hemisphere than in the right. Furthermore, this wave was significantly larger over the temporo-parietal region than over the frontal region for the left hemisphere.

Picton and Low (1971): The contingent negative variation was prolonged as the difficulty of the discrimination increased. Furthermore the contingent negative variation between the second stimulus and a later feedback stimulus significantly increased in area, and the amplitude of the evoked response to the feedback signal following the response significantly increased.

Wood, Goff, and Day (1971): Average evoked potentials significantly differed for auditory linguistic tasks over the left hemisphere, but not over the right hemisphere.

Cohn (1971): Nonverbal auditory stimuli showed a greater amplitude of initial output over right brain while verbal auditory stimuli produced similar or higher amplitude over the left.

Matsumiya et al. (1972): Interhemispheric asymmetry of auditory evoked potentials reliably differed during presentation of meaningful task relevant vs. meaningless undiscriminated sounds and words.

Teyler et al. (1973): Linguistic stimuli elicited larger evoked potential reactions in the dominant hemisphere. These hemispheric differences in amplitude were significantly greater for nouns than for verbs. Over both hemispheres, latency for verbs in the evoked wave form was reliably shorter than for nouns, and the latency to verb forms was significantly shorter than to noun forms in the left hemisphere.

Neville (1974): Average evoked potentials for verbal stimuli showed earlier components of greater amplitude and later components of shorter latency from the left than from the right hemisphere.

Attention. Haider (1967): Characteristic changes in cortical evoked responses correspond to varying conditions of attention and expectation.

Ritter and Vaughan (1969): The late positive component of the auditory evoked reaction appears to be a correlate of central processes for evaluation of unpredictable changes in stimulation.

Ohman and Lader (1972): The P1-N1 amplitudes of the average evoked potentials were larger when directing attention toward as opposed to away from stimuli.

Hillyard et al. (1973): The negative component of auditory evoked potentials was significantly larger when evoked by tones in one ear which were attended to than when evoked by tones in the other ear which were not attended to.

Visual, Nonverbal Thought Tasks.   Cohen and Walter (1966): Geometric and pictorial visual stimuli produced more elaborate evoked responses than clicks and flashes. Interpolation of a different stimulus resulted in higher amplitude of first and second negative components than did repetition of the same stimulus.

Shevrin et al. (1971): Verbal associations conceptually and veridically related to a subliminal meaningful stimulus related to a specific average evoked response component, while homophonic, unveridical associations were related to later alpha bursts.

Symmes and Eisengart (1971): Vertex negative slow potentials correlated with reports of interest in and recall of pictorial stimuli in children.

Ruchkin and Sutton (1973): When subjects were required to accurately guess about the oncoming visual stimulus, evoked potentials were significantly different than when the subject knew the nature of the stimulus in advance.

Rohrbaugh et al. (1974): When a motor response required integration of the properties of two successive stimuli, P300 was significantly increased.

Auditory Nonverbal Thought.   Sheatz and Chapman (1969): Relevant stimuli evoke larger evoked potential peaks than when the identical stimuli are irrelevant.

Waszak and Obrist (1969): Significantly larger CNVs preceded fast vs. slow reaction times.

Jenness (1972): Feedback stimuli evoked different wave forms than "task" clicks that were physically identical.

Speech Production.   Ertl and Schafer (1967a): A "cortical command potential" occurs prior to voluntary speech and left fist contractions.

Ertl and Schafer (1967b): Lip EMG preceded the cortical command potential which was followed by voice activity.

McAdam and Whitaker (1971a): Larger negative potentials while the subject is overtly speaking were recorded from over Broca's area in the left hemisphere than over the homologous area in the right hemisphere.

Miscellaneous Thought Tasks.   Morgan et al. (1971): Amount of alpha in the two hemispheres differs significantly as a function of type of task.

Galin and Ornstein (1972): The ratio of right to left hemisphere power is significantly greater during performance of verbal tasks than during performance of spatial tasks.

McGuigan and Pavek (1972): Thinking "yes" and signalling "yes," or thinking "no" and signalling "no" were accompanied by significantly earlier EEG reactions over the left temporal area than in the left motor area.

McKee et al. (1973): Left-to-right alpha ratio decreases as linguistic task increases in difficulty.

Miscellaneous. Knott (1939): There is a specific relationship between peripheral kinesthetic stimuli and latency of alpha blockage during attention to flashing lights.

Sutton et al. (1965): Amplitude of the P300 component was significantly larger for uncertain than for certain stimuli.

Gullickson and Darrow (1968): There were rapid reversals of time relationships during orienting and semantic processes that suggested reverberation between various brain areas. The effect was greater during the presentation of unfamiliar vs. familiar stimuli, greater for taboo verbal stimuli vs. indifferent verbal stimuli, and during expectancy (CNV).

Ulett et al. (1972): Hypnosis, both induction and trance, differs from rest, though greater change is evident in trance than in induction, and for good than for poor hypnotic subjects.

Concerning Interpretations
of Electrical Measures of Brain Activity

In the introduction to this chapter we have considered a number of thoughts about brain activity, and have made reference here and in Chapter 2 to various theories of central nervous system functioning. Now we shall more explicitly consider neural processes, particularly in linguistic regions of the brain, as they function in neuromuscular circuits with other parts of the body. In Chapters 5, 6, and 7 we considered how linguistic coding might be generated by the skeletal musculature as it functions within neuromuscular circuits. We presume that coded afferent neural volleys ascend to the linguistic brain regions whereupon phonemic processing occurs, following which there is lexical-semantic processing. These latter processes involve the integration of phonemes into words. Just how these phonemic engrams are stored and combined into words constitutes a major issue in memorial and neurophysiological research. An additional complex matter is how semantic processing occurs whereby the meaning of the words is perceived. Let us now consider some of the stages of linguistic processing involving the nervous systems in greater detail.

AFFERENT NEURAL VOLLEYS

When specific patterns of phasic muscle activity, on the background of tonic muscle activity, generate afferent neural volleys, linguistic information is transmitted to critical regions of the brain (Chapters 5, 6, and 7).

It is widely held that such information is carried in trains of afferent neural spikes (Perkel, 1970; Stein, 1970; and Terzuolo, 1970).[1] When the discrete spike trains arrive at a synapse, the binary signal is transformed to analog by the release of synaptic transmitters which transmit the information to the next neuron in the circuit. Bullock (1967) considered the relationship between neural spikes and various stimulus parameters in some detail. One interesting coding possibility he suggested is that the intervals between spikes are continuously variable so that those intervals may function as an analog system. Concerning other possible coding systems, Bullock said:

"The finding of broad general interest is that there is not one code but several. The average frequency is doubtless the code in some fibers. In others a number code is employed—the number of spikes following each stimulus measures its intensity; the individual intervals do not systematically vary, and the average frequency is contaminated by the variable rate of recurrence of stimuli. A latency or phase code (these two can be distinguished in some cases) is found in several preparations in which regular events are measured in intensity by the time between some invariant signal of their happening and a delayed second signal (whose frequency is therefore constant). Some fibers appear to be like doorbells and simply carry presence or absence signal (1967, p. 351).

Bullock thus considered a common notion among neurophysiologists that there is a functional yes-no system that depends on *which* neural fibers are activated. Such a binary system could form the neural basis of a binary processing model involving neuromuscular circuits. In the preceding chapters we considered an "on-off" (binary) model for muscle fibers, and the same reasoning could apply to the resultant afferent neural impulses. This issue is relevant to Müller's law of specific energies of nerves in that coding and processing throughout the nervous systems may depend upon which neurons are activated. Similarly, within any given neuron we have the all or none law which may also be described in binary arithmetic. In short, internal information processing could involve both coded spiked trains within any given neuron and a system of which neurons are activated, both of which may be represented in binary form.

SEMANTIC PROCESSING
IN CIRCUITS INVOLVING THE CENTRAL NERVOUS SYTEM

On arriving at the brain, the coded information carried by the afferent neural spike trains generated by the skeletal musculature is processed in some complex manner. It is reasonable to suppose that semantic proces-

---

[1] Schmidt (1972, 1973) reported considerable evidence supporting the view that a subject uses the inflow of proprioceptive feedback from an earlier portion of a movement sequence to cue the timing of a later portion. Furthermore, characteristics of the proprioceptive feedback in short term memory may cue the timing of a later movement, a view for which there has been clear support. In an exchange with Jones (1973) Schmidt concluded that the proprioceptive feedback explanation is favored over a motor outflow hypothesis.

sing involves the activation of cerebral circuits that include both trans-cortical and cortical-subcortical loops. Quite possibly, specific parameters of afferent neural volleys determine the precise nature of patterns of evoked potentials, of contingent negative variations, and of various other electrical measures of activity of the brain, as detailed in the empirical findings of this chapter. Variations in these patterns could conceivably be the neurophysiological basis of phonemic differences which produce semantic differences. For instance, should the speech musculature generate volleys phonetically for /p/, followed by /i/ /t/, there might be an evoked potential or CNV with one set of parameters; however, should the speech musculature set off a volley coded for /b/ followed by /i/ /t/, somewhat different neural parameters would be measured. In the first case, "pit" would be lexically and semantically processed, while in the latter it would be "bit." The findings of Ertl and Schaffer (1967b) are an illustration of the possible transmission of a verbal code from the speech musculature to activate central events such as transcortical circuits. As noted earlier in this chapter these researchers electromyographically recorded a lip response prior to the recording of a central phenomenon which they referred to as a cortical command potential. This brain event thus might constitute the cortical component of a neuromuscular loop that is critical for semantic processing.

Some specific studies that suggest the existence of transcortical loops are as follows. Darrow and Hicks (1965) recorded from the left parietal, motor, and occipital regions. They found that emotional stimulus words that required perceptual and ideational evaluation are characterized by rapid diphasic reversals of inter-area EEG phase relations, suggestive of interaction between brain areas. Gulickson and Darrow (1968) reported similar rapid reversals of time relationships during orienting and semantic processing, suggesting reverberation between various brain areas. Giannitrapani (1966) found that during mental arithmetic, average EEG frequencies in the frontal lobes and in the left temporal lobes were greater than in the right temporal, left and right parietal, and left and right occipital areas. This corresponds to Hicks and Darrow's findings and is further suggestive of transcortical loops. McGuigan and Pavek (1972) measured a cortical event over the left temporal lobe that occurred significantly earlier than a similar event over the left motor area. A highly speculative interpretation is that there was cerebral transmission from the language regions of the temporal lobe to the motor area for response execution.

These neuro-physiological recordings suggest that transcortical circuits might be actual hypothetical contructs, such as Hebb's (1949) cell assembly or Osgood's (cf. Osgood and Hoosain, 1974) posit of the storage of linguistic units, in particular of phonemes at the motor projection level. Feedback from the skeletal musculature may thus activate (reverberate) these circuits so that phonemes are retrieved (reconstructed, etc).

An important question is whether or not there are strictly cerebral circuits that do not involve peripheral mechanisms. The principal hypothesis about such circuits would be that there are central representations of response events which resulted from the original overt responding. The overt response eventually became covert and ultimately might even have been short circuited and thus eliminated. The early behaviorists referred to this process as the response receding into the nervous system, and Dunlap (1927) suggested the cerebellum as the central site of such possible peripheral representations. In this event, there could be critical cerebral circuits involving representations of the original muscular response which can be run off more rapidly than those involving longer circuits with the musculature (Fig. 4.1). If there are some exclusively central processes in which there is representation of responding there would be "thoughts" that could not be studied behaviorally. Such an occurrence would place a severe limitation on psychology, defined as it is as the study of behavior (i.e., of muscular and glandular events). Our science would thus be confronted with an agonizing dilemma. "Thinking" is, of course, part of our traditional content, but if there are some crucial brain events that do not entail consequent (or have antecedent), associated responses, the central processes could not be universally studied by means of stimulus-response laws. Hence, the dilemma: psychology would either have to exclude, at least partially, thinking phenomena from its subject matter, or it would have to redefine its domain to include not only behavioral (muscular and glandular events) but also neurophysiological phenomena. One consequence of this latter possibility is that psychologists would have to seek laws that bear little or no resemblance to those currently occurring in psychological (behavioral) theories.

To empirically test for the existence of such an exclusively central processing system, one might longitudinally trace the history of an overt response as it recedes, using some suitable means for both peripheral and central recording. In the meantime, we do know that covert responses abound in all linguistic activities, and possibly there are cognitive activities with covert responses only as consequences of cerebral circuits, (see Fig. 4.1). In this case there would always be a muscular component along with the central component, so that the higher mental processes *could* always be behaviorally studied. We shall maintain our working assumption that during language perception and other cognitive acts, covert responses generate afferent neural impulses coded for the externally impinging linguistic units; when they enter the brain they in some sense "match" the appropriate lexical and semantic representations. Certain findings and theories about those representations, selected for their relevance to the theoretical perspective we have developed, should now be reviewed.

NATURE OF MEMORY TRACES

When the phonetic coding carried by afferent neural volleys from the skeletal musculature ascend to the linguistic regions of the brain, we have supposed that centrally stored memories are thereby "tapped." Contemporary scientific literature is inundated about memorial phenomena, including considerable controversy about processes by

which verbal and nonverbal information is processed, stored, and retrieved. To guide us in how afferent coding accesses well-organized,
stored information, let us sample some relevant findings and notions,
such as those concerned with processes of matching sensory input
against stored representations, or more constructive processes.[2] We do
not here have to take a position on these issues, but we should consider
how our model of muscle-generated coding might function in conjunction with various memorial models.

Storage Representations.   In an early study of short-term visual memory, Averback and Coriell (1961) concluded that a buffer storage
mechanism which is local in character tends to erase stored information
when new information enters. The storage time of short-term memory
in vision was estimated to be of the order of 250 msec (see also
Mackworth, 1962; Sperling, 1960).[3]

Rubenstein et al. (1971), in considering lexical retrieval, concluded
that recognition of a visually presented word entails phonemic recoding.
The phonemic form of the stimulus is compared against the representations of the entries in the internal lexicon to achieve the recognition of a
word.

Smith and Jones (1974) concluded that verbal memory is like a real
dictionary, one that is organized on the basis of initial phonemes.

In proposing an active model of speech perception, Stevens and
House (1972) suggested that children at an early age build up a catalog
of relations between auditory patterns and articulatory gestures; the
gestures may include such components as tactual and kinesthetic sensations, and motor commands. The items in the catalog represent gestures
of approximately syllabic length; the length of the segment that they
consider forms a unit for peripheral analysis. Some attributes of an
incoming auditory pattern are then "looked up" in the dictionary of
auditory-articulatory correspondences. If a correspondence is found between the stimulus and a dictionary item that could have been produced
by the human articulatory mechanism, then speech perception occurs.
They cite a number of proponents of the concept that reference to
articulation plays a role in speech perception (Cooper, Harris, MacNeilage, and Studdert-Kennedy, 1967; Halle and Stevens, 1962; Liberman,
1967; Liberman, Cooper, Shankweiler, and Studdert-Kennedy, 1967;
Stevens and Halle, 1967). It may be noted that this theorizing is quite
compatable with our model of muscle-generated coding, especially from
the speech musculature, as developed in Chapters 6 and 9.

Pylyshyn (1973) argued against a memory representation system

---

[2] The classic reference for consolidation theory is McGaugh (1966). This interpretation
has been updated by Mah and Albert (1973). The best statement of the possibility that
amnesia is a retrieval rather than a storage problem is in Lewis (in press). Also refer to
Lewis (1969) (personal communication from Donald J. Lewis, March 30, 1976).

[3] Wickelgren and Berian (1971) concluded that long-term memory did not begin until
about 10 sec after the study period in which their subjects engaged, and that it is
substantially complete at about 30 sec after the study period.

which is sensory and pictorial, saying that the picture metaphor (which suggests that images are entities to be perceived) is misleading. Rather, he suggested that "what we know" (memory) is essentially conceptual and propositional, so that, for instance, a memory representation is a proposition.

Following Conrad (1964), Cohen (1973) suggested that registration of verbal material is typically accomplished by acoustic recoding and rehearsal, while pictorial recognition is dependent upon the re-presented item being exactly identical with the first presentation. The implication is that what is stored visually is a replica (not a transform) that the subject does not recode. Hence, the differences between memory for verbal and visual material. Cohen's research suggested to him that while rehearsal may be important for verbal memory, it is inappropriate for pictorial memory: "To state the case metaphorically, while verbal memory may resemble a tape-recording with a re-circulation loop, pictorial memory is more like a one-shot photocopy" (1973, p. 564). He believed that pictorial memory might be a function of one's referent coding system, while verbal memory might be evoked by one's phonetic coding system.

Rollins and Thibadeau (1973) found that a shadowing task interfered more with information received auditorily than with information received visually, suggesting to them that information received visually is stored independently of the auditory modality.

Strømmes (1974) developed a schematic model for the storage of meaningful verbal material; in it, the storage of words and of meaningful symbols is assumed to be separate, implying that lexical processing is separate from semantic processing. Strømmes also indicated that transformational grammar may be in error since symbols which carry meaning must be isomorphs of the real states—this is in accord with our Chapter 6 notion of "referent level coding" generated by the nonoral skeletal musculature.

Memory as a Process.   Wechsler's (1963) view of memory is in contrast to a "dictionary" model. The brain, he suggested, does not store or permanently record anything. Its essential function is to code and transmit information as needed. Hence, memory is like the melody realized by striking the keys on a piano, rather than like a filing cabinet. Not being like a computer that stores, the brain is more like a matching machine.

Runquist and Blackmore (1973) found that subjects use phonemic attributes for auditory recognition; semantic and lexical processing, they concluded, might more realistically be a complex, constructive process rather than the relatively simple mechanical retrieval from a permanent "store."

Osgood, in his work on semantic processing, has postulated a series of processing levels, the highest being the Representation Level (see our Fig. 9.13, p. 385). The first component of the Representation Level is a Lexicon, which is a "process" (not a storage) type of memory. The Lexicon is analogous to the long dial bank of an old-fashioned desk calculator which spins to a particular set of readings dependent upon the momentary key-punched input. These readings are the multicomponential codings that are literally the meaning of the word. This system can be re-used very rapidly as new perceptually integrated forms are received from the Integration Level. Once formed, the word exits from the Lexicon into an Operator (the second type of memory) where cognitive interactions occur. The Operator is a type of short term memory which is wiped clean, making it ready for further operations by outputting into memory or into behavior or sentence production. In a sense, the Lexicon is a short-term and immediately reusable *word* meaning mechanism, whereas the Operator is a short-term and reusable *sentence* meaning mechanism. Finally, Osgood postulates a Memory in the lay sense of storage. The memory contains representations of code strips for previously cognized output from the Lexicon. This is a long-term memory such that when code strips are drawn from the memory this information is *re*-cognized (rather than freshly cognized) (cf. Osgood, 1957a, b, 1971, and personal communication).

Conclusion. This sampling of views and data makes it clear that memory concepts are sufficiently complex that any psychophysiological model must be consonant with models of a number of memorial functions. Osgood (personal communication) has suggested at least five kinds (components) of memories: (1) a very short term memory which reverberates in area 17, referred to as iconic; (2) a short term memory which involves reverberation in Osgood's sensory integration level ($\overline{s}$-$\overline{s}$), like Hebbs' cell assemblies; (3) a process memory which takes the form of a semantic code (Osgood's Lexicon); (4) a long term memory in which there is storage of cognized sets, including semantic feature codes; this memory functions after interactions between simple cognitions have occurred; (Osgood's concept of $[m_1 \longrightarrow M_2]$); and (5) an as yet little understood nonlinguistic, long-term memory for location and for times of events.

NEUROPHYSIOLOGY OF MEMORY

As to the neurophysiological locus of memory representations, Lashley's trace system that grew out of his long search for the engram suggests to us that lexical and semantic systems extend throughout the entire cerebrum. However, it is possible that a lexical store may have primary representation in the dominant cerebral hemisphere while a referent level store may have primary representation in the minor hemisphere, an inference following from split brain research (Sperry, 1973; Nebes, 1974). In support of this possibility we may note that Seamon and Gazzaniga (1973) in studying cerebral laterality effects found that subjects who employed a verbal rehearsal strategy yielded significantly faster response latencies for probes to the left than to the right hemisphere. On the other hand, there were significantly faster latencies for probes to the right than to the left hemisphere when using an imagery code. Their conclusion was that there are separate processing systems for verbally and visually coded information. Of particular relevance for us is that their characterization of visually coded information is quite similar to our referent level coding in the case of the eyes (see Chapter 5).

Pribram (1971) suggested that, in effect, Lashley's trace system operates through a holographic-like process. If so, when the afferent impulses for a linguistic unit make a holographic match there would be retrieval of the impinging linguistic unit. Other possible retrieval processes could involve electro-chemical matching of a central representation, resonance matching, or some system that is as yet almost completely unexplored, such as matching magnetic signals within the brain. Recent research in which magnetic field variations from the human brain have been recorded are of especial interest in this connection (cf. Kolta, 1973; and Brenner, Williamson, and Kaufman, 1975).

Kesner (1973) presented a neurological analysis of memory from an information processing viewpoint. He suggested that the cue-access to memory involves a matching between sensory system and the cerebral cortex, that the midbrain reticular formation and association cortex function in the short term memory system, and that the hippocampus is critically involved in consolidation and readout of information in the long-term memory system.

In various places throughout the book, but especially in Chapter 9, we note the potential value of representing various neuromuscular and cognitive processes in binary arithmetic—the all or none character of muscle fiber contraction, of neural impulse firing, of binary representation of aspects of semantic processing as in Osgood's semantic feature matrix (see especially Osgood and Hoosain, 1974), as examples. The binary representation of an afferent neural linguistic code could well relate to a binary representation of central neural structures and processes. This conception conforms well with the "module-concept" of cortical architecture developed by Szentagothai (1975). Szentagothai pointed out that the relative simplicity and regularity of the cortical architecture allows it to be reduced to a three dimensional lattice. The network of cortical neurons can thus be interpreted in terms of excitatory and inhibitory neuronal actions, an interpretation that is confirmed by data that he summarized. Szentagothai also summarized recent advances which have been made in describing cerebral cortical networks statistically and geometrically. Using a sample of the entire neocortex, he developed a straightforward arcform connection between specific cortical input and output for the major sensory areas, holding that the concept applies to the remainder of the neocortex.

Szentagothai elucidated the possible mode of connection between the primary and secondary sensory areas. The integrative unit of primary sensory cortices would consist of a finite block of lamina IV (see Fig. 8.5)

where a group of afferents belonging to the same receptive field terminate. The visual cortex, as an instance, is subdivided into alternating
ocular dominance columns of about 350 μm wide—well in correspondence to the observed span of the terminal arborizations of specific
afferents. Afferent impulses are delivered to spiny stellates with axons
that deliver volleys to vertical columnar spaces ascending to layers III
and II, and descending through layers V and VI. The spiny stellates in

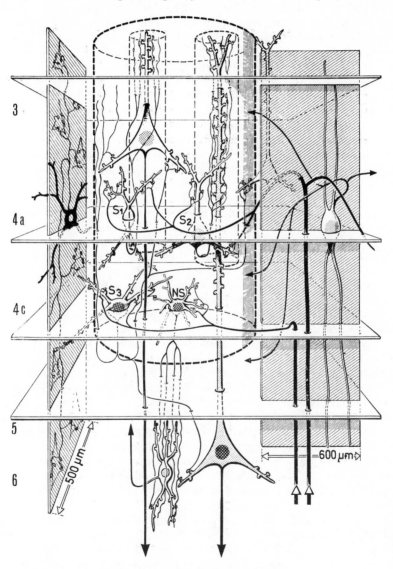

FIG. 8.5 A network of cortical neurons (from Szentagothai, 1975).

the lower strata of lamina IV may act on a wide column (perhaps 500 μm wide) by their scattered ascending branches, possibly acting on somewhat distant pyramidal cells, conceivably providing the basis of binocular interaction (this would be sensory integration which we hypothesize in chapter 9 to be accomplished by our circuit class II.)

The axonal arborizations of pyramidal cells are distributed in thin, extended vertical discs. The considerable frequency of these cells led Szentagothai to the notion that the cortex may be built up of parallel vertical slices, each under the control of a basket cell (or set of basket cells). The basket cells (activated by afferents) might superimpose an inhibitory bias upon the array of pyramidal cells. The combination of active afferents might then lead some basket cells to remain silent so that the pyramidal cells of the respective slices might become activated; conversely, other basket cells might be activated inhibiting the pyramidal cells in these slices. In this way we have the skeleton of a functional chain through which any specific afferent pattern is processed in the primary sensory regions. It is thus possible to represent the sensory areas in terms of a complex lattice whose function may be represented in binary form (excitatory-inhibitory units) which is in some way activated by the afferent volleys ascending to the sensory and linguistic cortex. Szentagothai hypothesized that the remainder of the neocortex is structured in the same way, so it may also be that the afferent volleys arising from the skeletal musculature to the language cortex function in a similar manner. In short, muscle status that generates afferent neural impulses may be represented by a binary code which enters the brain, wherein Szentagothai's lattice may neurally represent semantic processing. We hope to eventually make progress in more precisely specifying possible neural and lexical-semantic processes, such as relating Osgood's semantic feature matrix (Osgood and Hoosain, 1974) to Szentagothai's module-concept of cortical architecture.

In considering neuromuscular models of internal information processing, the relationship of channel capacities from one system to another is of primary importance. The parameters of rate and amount of information transmission must be specified between various receptor, neural, and muscular systems. There may be, for instance, a "shrinkage" or loss of information when signals are transduced at junctions between these various systems. For example, a larger number of muscle fibers contract than there are muscle spindle receptors, so that there could be a reduction of information when muscular contraction generates afferent neural impulses. The kinds of computations made between input-throughput and output units that McCulloch (1951) made in his excellent article entitled, "Why the Mind Is in the Head" may help guide us toward an understanding of receptor neuromuscular information, tranduction, and transmission, particularly by establishing constraints. While I disagree with McCulloch's conclusion, his reasoning processes provide us with an excellent model. For example, one of the reasons that McCulloch put the mind in the head is that, in effect, information delivered through the nervous systems cannot be adequately transferred to the muscles, due to limitations of the muscles: Part of the corruption ("loss of information") is "referable to the coupling of our nervous system to our muscles . . . so that the rate at which impulses can come over the nerves is wasted by the inability of muscle to follow. In us a nerve of a thousand axons can be in 2^{1000} possible states, whereas the muscle, because it can only add tensions, has only a thousand possible states. 1000 is about 2^{10}; so the corruption in passing from nerve to brain is 100 to 1" (1951, p. 45).

There are several problems with McCulloch's argument. For one there are between about 2 to 2000 muscle fibers in each human motor unit (Basmajian, 1962). Hence, each efferent neural impulse may activate many muscle fibers. Furthermore, a muscle fiber takes about 1 or 2 msec to contract: in strong contractions, it may contract as rapidly as about 50/sec, which "seems to be the upper physiological limit for the frequency of propagation of axonal impulses" (Basmajian, 1962, p. 8).[4] Granit (1970, p. 252) made a similar point when he stated that the extrinsic eye muscles can respond with discrete contractions at a rate of 300 to 400 per second, and that motorneurons are unlikely to be able to discharge at such rates. In other words, the facts may actually support McCulloch's argument in the reverse—activity of muscle fibers may be limited by the ability of the nervous system to transmit information.

Furthermore, what may appear to be constraints on information transmission processes throughout the body in the form of information loss (corruption) in various transducing events may actually not be a loss—there may be compensating factors in the transduction processes, like increased number, rate, or probability of neural or muscular contraction.

This matter of transferring information from one bodily system to another is obviously extremely complicated, but with regard to the possibility of the skeletal musculature generating linguistic codes, there is no apriori reason to suppose that it is limited in such a way that it cannot perform that function. Cherry (1957, pp. 288-89) presented some additional relevant information on this topic.

In this chapter we have reviewed a number of studies in which brain activity was implicated in various thought processes. The technological advances in studying brain action have been great indeed in recent years, and we can expect further advance in the immediate future. Among the more important recent technological advances have been the study of the contingent negative variation which has been shown to systematically vary with a number of stimulus parameters that are important for mental events. For example, the study by Costell, Lunde, Kopell, and Wittner (1972) showed that CNV amplitude was proportional to sexual interest

---

[4] However, according to Kiang (1966) spontaneous neural impulses have been measured at the rate of 100 spikes per second, and they have been driven by external stimuli to a rate of 150 spikes per second.

in visual exposures of male nudes, female nudes, and sexually neutral silhouettes.

It is entirely possible that cognitive linguistic processing may be represented in binary arithmetic to include the following: (1) generation of a verbal code according to the state of contraction of the skeletal musculature; (2) resulting volleys of afferently coded linguistic neural impulses; (3) evoking semantic-lexical processes in the brain wherein semantic features (Osgood and Hoosain, 1974) are produced through complex patterns of excitatory-inhibitory neural processes transmitted along latices, as Szentagothai's module concept. These resultant cognitive processes may then be neurophysiologically measured through electrical techniques, as in our recording of differential patterns of evoked potentials and contingent negative variations as a function of cognitive content.

Appendix

Other relevant works that it was not possible to include in this chapter are as follows: Cutting (1974); Dorman (1974); Glass and Kwiatkowski (1970); Grabow and Elliott (1974); Mundy-Castle (1957); Poon, Thompson, Williams, and Marsh (1974); Sandler and Schwartz (1971); Sussman (1971); and Tepas (1974).

9

Linguistic Coding
and
Internal Information Processing

In this chapter we shall explore the possible routes and mechanisms by which impinging linguistic stimuli are transduced and transmitted through the various bodily systems during what has traditionally been called the process of language perception. Language perception most frequently (but not exclusively) occurs in the auditory modality (for speech perception) and in the visual modality (for reading). We shall also consider the roles of the somatic skeletal musculature in linguistic processing.

The earliest and most prominent form of external transmission of information was by (oral) speech; later the members of some cultures were sufficiently ingenious to invent written language. By formulating systems of symbols for writing the spoken sounds of speech, such cultures sizeably increased their rate of knowledge acquisition—the development of a link between writing and speech was of such importance that it probably ranks above the invention of the wheel. The value of being able to write spoken language can be underscored by noting that those cultures which have not yet made the transition from spoken to written language remain today in relatively primitive states. Also, rate of illiteracy is an accepted sociological index of the degree of technological advancement of nations/cultures. The advantages of written language are many; but two obvious ones are that writing gives us the ability to increase our symbolic manipulation of our world, and that the accumulation of knowledge over the years is more efficient and reliable by written than by auditory means. The following discussion primarily concerns speech, although the principles which evolve should be generally applicable to our later discussion of reading.

External and Internal Linguistic Coding

The stream of speech emitted by a speaker is an acoustic analog signal. The problem of reliably analyzing acoustic speech sounds in terms of linguistic units is far from being adequately solved; we will not consider this problem in any detail, but merely note that the topic has received considerable attention (e.g., Foss and Swinney, 1973; Fujimura, 1972; and also later in this chapter). Analog analysis of speech has been pro-

part four

Hypothesized Functions
of
Covert Processes

ductive for some purposes, whereas the quanitification of the analog speech signal by means of binary arithmetic has been fruitful for others. It is especially interesting in this context to note that some *bodily processes,* including those intimately involved in speech, are more effectively represented in binary than in analog form for some purposes. Contraction of a muscle fiber and firing of nerve impulses are relatively discrete (on-off) events that obey the all-or-none law. Thus they are not well suited to an analog model in which electrical signals convey information primarily by amplitude or rate of change. Hence we shall attempt to represent selected neuromuscular speech events in binary form and to relate these to binary representations of analog speech and other language signals.

SPEECH SIGNALS PHONEMICALLY REPRESENTED BY DISTINCTIVE FEATURES

One prominent characteristic of natural languages is that many bipolar word pairs can be represented by "yes-no" binary symbols. Obvious examples are antonymic terms which are relativistic (relative to some standard, e.g., high-low), and those which are absolute and hence mutually exclusive (inside-outside). Phonemes also have bipolar characteristics, and it is not surprising that the early descriptions of phonemes (dating from the Hindus about 300 B.C.) carried a notion of binary opposition (Cherry, 1957). Roman Jakobson and his colleagues have successfully used these binary characteristics of language and offered a complete binary description of phonemes (e.g., Jakobson, Fant, and Halle, 1952). Jakobson et al. (1952) regarded phonemes as bundles of *attributes,* a notion similar to that of Twadell's (1935) "micro-phonemes." These attributes are "detected" as the listener monitors the stream of speech. For example, one detects such attributes as "the buzzing vibrations of the chords of the larynx, (called *voicing*) heard during all English vowels (hard, moon, see, etc.) and certain consonants (z, v, etc); the hissing breath sounds (as in hard) ... the explosive sounds (like) boy ... the nasal quality ... (new) ..." (Cherry, 1957, p. 92).

In 1952, Jakobson et al. proposed 12 possible attributes (distinctive features) of phonemes that may be represented as 12 binary oppositions; for example, a phoneme may have the distinctive feature of being either nasal or oral (it cannot be both)—the binary opposition "nasal/oral" may thus be used to specify one distinctive feature of a phoneme. In any language, every distinct phoneme may be uniquely described with reference to the complete set of 12 distinctive features. Since distinctive features have been empirically determined, they are subject to modification; consequently the number has varied, depending on the stage of the research, and on the authority (for example, see Chomsky and Halle, 1968; Ladefoged, 1967; Small, 1973).

Distinctive features may be represented in an acoustical speech stimulus model as a set of twelve orthogonal axes that form a phonemic feature space. A simplified phonemic feature representation is presented in Table 9.1 where two distinctive features are represented as a two-way matrix: the "nasal/oral" feature is represented by rows, while the "vocalic/non-vocalic" feature is represented by columns. The cells of this two-dimensional space thus specify four possible phonemes although only incompletely since other features are needed to exhaustively specify a phoneme. For example, the shaded cell in Table 9.1 specifies a phoneme that has the distinctive feature of being nasal (vs. oral) and vocalic (vs. nonvocalic). A more complete breakdown is presented in Table 9.2 in which nine distinctive features make up the rows and 28 English phonemes make up the columns. In any cell in the table a + entry signifies that the distinctive feature represented by that row *is* an attribute of the phoneme represented by that column, while a − entry indicates the feature that *is not* an attribute of that phoneme. Each phoneme of spoken speech is thus uniquely described in Table 9.2 by a binary chain of plus and minus feature oppositions. (The blanks in Table 9.2 indicate that a plus or minus is not necessary for that cell since that information would be nondistinctive; Table 9.2 is thus a specification of the *minimal* distinctive features necessary to distinguish each phoneme.)

Acoustic evidence of phonemes may be collected in the form of physical measurements. By sampling a number of speakers, a distribution of emitted sounds for each phoneme could be accumulated, one data point for each speaker. The resulting cluster of points may be plotted, as Cherry (1957) has indicated, so that the central tendency of the distribution specifies acoustically the phoneme cell (Fig. 9.1). The speech of a speaker can then be plotted as a continuous phonemic trajectory from cell to cell (from phoneme to phoneme). However, it should be emphasized that this is a binary phonemic representation of what is in fact an analog signal (a speaker's voice obviously does not operate in a binary fashion). As Cherry suggested, however, even though the acoustic signal is analog, the listener probably interprets each feature in a binary manner, simply identifying whether particular phonemes were "intended" or

TABLE 9.1   A Two-Dimensional Phonemic Feature Space

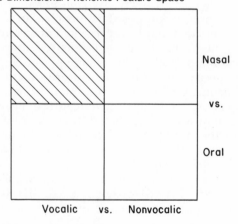

Vocalic   vs.   Nonvocalic

TABLE 9.2 The Phoneme Pattern of English (Received Pronunciation) after Jakobson, Fant, and Halle (from Cherry, 1957)

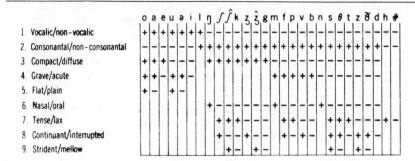

	o	a	e	u	ə	i	l	ŋ	ʃ	ʃ̂	k	ʒ	ʒ̂	g	m	f	p	v	b	n	s	θ	t	z	ð	d	h	#
1. Vocalic/non-vocalic	+	+	+	+	+	+	+	−	−	−	−	−	−	−	−	−	−	−	−	−	−	−	−	−	−	−	−	−
2. Consonantal/non-consonantal	−	−	−	−	−	−	+	+	+	+	+	+	+	+	+	+	+	+	+	+	+	+	+	+	+	+	−	−
3. Compact/diffuse	+	+	+	−	−	−		+	+	+	+	+	+	−	−	−	−	−	−	−	−	−	−	−	−	−	−	−
4. Grave/acute	+	+	−	+	+	−						+	+	+	+	+	−	−	−	−	−	−	−					
5. Flat/plain	+	−		+	−																							
6. Nasal/oral								+	−	−	−	−	−	−	+	−	−	−	+	−	−	−	−	−	−	−		
7. Tense/lax									+	+	+	−	−	−		+	+	−	−		+	+	+	−	−	−	+	−
8. Continuant/interrupted									+	−	−	+	−	−		+	−	+	−		+	+	−	+	+	−		
9. Strident/mellow									+	−		+	−			+	−				+	−		+	−			

Key to phonemic transcription: /o/–p*o*t, /a/–p*a*t, /e/–p*e*t, /u/–p*u*t, /ə/–p*u*tt, /i/–p*i*t, /l/–*l*ull, /ŋ/–lu*ng*, /ʃ/–*sh*ip, /ʃ̂/–*ch*ip, /k/–*k*ip, /ʒ/–a*z*ure, /ʒ̂/–*j*uice, /g/–*g*oose, /m/–*m*ill, /f/–*f*ill, /p/–*p*ill, /v/–*v*im, /b/–*b*ill, /n/–*n*il, /s/–*s*ill, /θ/–*th*ill, /t/, –*t*ill, /z/–*z*ip, ð/–*th*is, /d/–*d*ill, /h/–*h*ill. The prosodic opposition, stressed vs. unstressed, splits each of the vowel phonemes into two.

were "not intended" by the speaker. A good example of this, offered informally by Charles Osgood, is "He is a trader/traitor." When spoken in the dialects of many people, the two sentences sound acoustically identical, yet the listener interprets one or the other as having occurred in a binary manner. Referring to Table 9.2 we can note that the phonemes /t/ vs. /d/ differ on the tense/lax feature, so that the listener who interprets the phoneme as being /+/ (tense) on feature 7 perceives

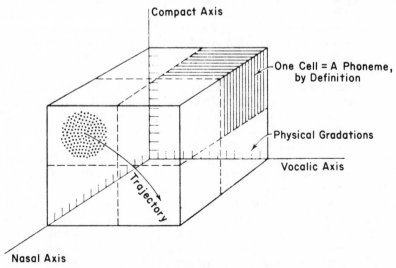

FIG. 9.1 Three features as general coordinates. Phonemes are quantal cells, and speech is a trajectory of system points (from Cherry, 1957).

"He is a traitor," but the listener who interprets it as /−/ (lax) on feature 7 perceives "He is a trader." The interpretation, of course, can be *independent* of the speaker's actual intent. Experiments in auditory psychophysics support this notion that speech perception occurs in binary form. For example, Pollack and Ficks (1954) showed that correct identification of multidimensional auditory signals occurs when each of a number of dimensions can assume only two values. We shall have more to say about speakers' semantic intentions and listeners' interpretations later.

Specifying the units of speech perception is a priority research problem. The major difficulty is that acoustic signals have not yet been adequately analyzed into functional linguistic units. Some have suggested that the unit is the word (cf., Osgood and Hoosain, 1974, for a discussion of this topic, especially regarding visual perception); and others that they are the smaller units of syllables or phonemes (cf., Cole, 1973; Harris, 1971; Massaro, 1974). Massaro (1972) concluded that the syllable and not the phoneme is implicated as the perceptual unit for speech perception. Savin and Bever (1970) concluded that phonemes are perceived only by an analysis of already perceived syllables—once the syllable is recognized, then the information about its components can be "recovered." But Foss and Swinney (1973) disagreed and argued that it is uneconomical to represent input in terms of phonetic syllables. On the side of phonemic analysis, Cole and Scott (1972) showed empirically that phonemes are identified in terms of their distinctive features, and they concluded that phonemes were distinguished on the basis of a serialized, self-terminating scan of distinctive feature differences. And Mattingly and Kavanagh (1972) held that, even though speech cues are not discrete events, a listener perceives segmental sounds; they held that speech perception is not a purely acoustic event, but that the listener hears speech phonetically. Also, perceptual units may be different from production units, e.g., Osgood and Hoosain (1974) held that while the word is the unit of speech perception, the syllable is the unit of speech production.

Fortunately, this particular controversy about the minimal size of linguistic units does not materially affect the principles of internal information processing that follow here. This is because minimal distinctions between syllables or words, as well as between phonemes, may also be achieved by using the oppositions of Table 9.1, e.g., the word "pit" is distinguished from "bit" by the initial phoneme /p/ vs. /b/, and these two phonemes are distinguishable by opposition 7, "tense/lax" of Table 9.1. As long as the larger units of words and syllables may thus be distinguished by phonemic units, the following principles do not depend on the size of the perceptual units. It may well be, too, that units of speech perception differ among people, depending on their conditioning history. Persons who learned to read by the "word method," for example, may perceive by word units when reading, while those who learned by "sounding out" may perceive phonetically.

To clarify some linguistic terms and principles, we note that linguistic theory includes rules for specifying a language and for accounting for linguistic structure of speech sounds. There are three levels of analysis of acoustic stimuli:

The Physical Phonetic Level. At this most concrete level the phonologist describes and measures acoustic stimuli through the use of wave form analysis on oscilloscopes, sound spectograms, etc. Phonological *theory* specifies relationships between physical analyses at this level and the next highest level of abstraction, the systematic phonetic level—the phonological representation of an acoustic stimulus is transformed through those relationships into its *phonetic* representation.

The Systematic Phonetic Level. Here, the phonetician represents speech utterances by means of phonetic transcriptions, as in the international phonetic alphabet (e.g., [P], [B]). Speech sounds like the [P] in "pill" are described by the distinctive *and* non-distinctive features which fill all of the cells in Table 9.2. Phonetic features describe speech sounds and are also responsible for making differences in meaning at the next higher linguistic level (the phonemic level). That is, while phonetic features are not in themselves meaningful they do make for different meanings at the phonemic level because they play a role in distinguishing between words, e.g., [P] vs. [B] distinguish the "minimal word pairs" "pill" vs. "Bill" (Twaddell, 1935). In "pill" vs. "Bill" the initial sounds are both bilabial stops, the only difference being that when articulating [B] the vocal folds are in vibration whereas in articulating [P] they are not. Hence, a feature called "voicing" distinguishes [P] vs. [B], and thus "pill" vs. "Bill." As we shall hypothesize later, the difference between perceiving the two acoustic stimuli "pill" vs. "Bill," is embodied physiologically in a *phonetic* stimulus code which is carried by afferent neural impulses from the laryngeal region to the linguistic regions of the brain. This code would be generated when perceiving "Bill," but a neural volley from the laryngeal region would be absent or reduced for "pill." In short, speech sounds are described in terms of phonetic features which consist of distinctive and non-distinctive features. And these features, while not themselves meaningful, make for a difference in meaning at the phonemic level.

The Phonemic Level. Here speech sounds are represented only by means of distinctive features (thus excluding the non-distinctive features). A segment of a speech sound may thus define a phoneme as a bundle of distinctive features. The phoneme, as we shall see, is intimately involved in lexical and semantic processing.

With these understandings, let us now consider broader aspects of speech than merely the level of the acoustic stimulus.

The system of distinctive features may be applied, in principle, to several "levels" of speech analysis. Cherry (1957) and Jakobson and Halle (1956), for instance, described five levels of speech (Fig. 9.2): (1) the physiological level of speech production where nerve impulses are sent from (it should be "to and from") the sender's brain to the speech organs; (2) the articulatory level at which the positions, shapings, dimensions of the organs, vocal cavities are observable by means of EMG, X-rays, etc.; (3) the acoustic level, at which physical sounds are analyzed; (4) in reception, involving the physiology of the ear and subsequent neural activity; and (5) in reception, the "psychological level" at which there is word recogntion. Each level may be further analyzed into numerous sublevels, e.g., Studdert-Kennedy (1974) specified a model of speech perception (involving Cherry's levels four and five above) as having auditory, phonetic, phonological, lexical, syntactic, and semantic components.

In principle, distinctive features may be specified for all five levels or phases of Fig. 9.2, facilitating our development of relationships among those levels (Cherry, 1957; Twaddell, 1935). However, a relatively refined matrix of distinctive features has only been worked out for level 3, the acoustic level, at which auditory stimuli are transmitted as air vibrations. There has been considerable description of distinctive features at the articulatory level (level 2), but only in prose form. Certainly a priority research effort is to specify phonemes by defining distinctive feature matrices for the other levels.

We shall now consider two response classes underlying aspects of speech: first that class produced by the speaker (levels 1 and 2) and later the second response class, viz., linguistic reactions within the listener (levels 4 and 5).

RESPONSE ASPECTS OF SPEECH PRODUCTION AS DISTINCTIVE FEATURES

Activities within the speaker are specified in terms of neural and response parameters for spoken phonemes, words, and the like. Phonemic response states are thus classified into characteristic forms of articulation

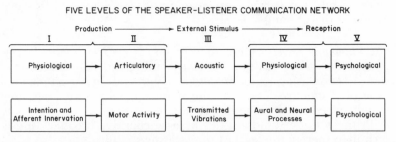

FIVE LEVELS OF THE SPEAKER-LISTENER COMMUNICATION NETWORK

FIG. 9.2 Two similar representations of the speaker-listener communication network—Cherry, 1957 (above), and Jacobson and Halle, 1956 (below).

(closure, opening, voicing, etc.), though only rather crudely, e.g., the vocalic (+) feature is ". . . primary or only excitation at the glottis together with a free passage through the buccal tract" (Jakobson and Halle, 1971, p. 40). However, we should eventually be able to *very* precisely specify unique muscular states electromyographically for each phoneme, as we shall consider later in this chapter. Table 9.2 may thus constitute the principle not only to define the external stimulus characteristics of speech, but also to electromyographically define response aspects of phonemes during speech production. The nine feature oppositions of Table 9.2 should thus correspond to nine unique electromyographically definable states, e.g., nasality (#6) would in part be defined as large EMG tongue amplitude, which occurs when the tongue is placed against the soft palate (velum) as in /n/. It should be added, however, that the acoustic speech stimulus model of Table 9.2 would be related to a (muscular) response state matrix (level 2) only through a complex transformation.

RELATIONSHIPS BETWEEN SPEECH PRODUCTION RESPONDING AND EMITTED PHONETIC STIMULI

The principles of Table 9.2 which enable us to uniquely define elements of (acoustic) speech in a stimulus matrix and (eventually) of speech production in a corresponding response matrix can now be used to consider relationships between speech production responses and the resulting external stimuli (level 2 to level 3 of Fig. 9.2). In the production of speech (levels 1 and 2) there probably is a rather stable and unique relationship between each response state in the speaker and the speaker's emitted phonetic stimulus (level 3). As the response state for speech production changes, the resulting stimulus also systematically changes, such that both the response and the emitted stimuli can be (independently) characterized as a speech stream trajectory from cell to cell, as pictured in Fig. 9.1. Harris (1974) made reference several times to the response-stimulus relationship, as when she considered a prediction from Lindblom's undershoot model that electromyographic signals associated with phonemes should remain constant, though the spacing between them should be altered; or that articulators tend to adopt a fixed position for a given phoneme. However, Harris made it clear that empirical studies have not yet firmly established general relationships between response states (be they defined as articulatory, electromyographic or whatever) and unique utterances that are characterized phonemically.

SPEECH PERCEPTION RESPONSES AND DISTINCTIVE FEATURES

When speech stimuli impinge on the listener, they produce internal events wherein there is perception of that linguistic input (levels 4 and 5). Speech perception occurs when stimulus elements, represented by a matrix like that in Table 9.2, evoke events within the listener for which we may develop some kind of corresponding representation as a reaction matrix. The continuous speech perception within the listener, like the acoustic stream, can also be represented as a trajectory from cell to cell in a space like that pictured in Fig. 9.1. However, as with the relation between levels 2 and 3, the perceptual reaction matrix cannot be literally the same as the stimulus matrix but must be a complex transformation of it.

The problem of how a linguistic stimulus comes to evoke a given linguistic reaction pattern has, of course, received considerable attention. The position among some linguists (cf. Chomsky and Halle, 1968) is that there may well be innate characteristics in the development of speech production and comprehension (given what we know about human speech neuromuscular physiology, it would be surprising if there were not). Nevertheless, the connections between *specific* speech stimuli and internal reactions *must* be learned. The laws governing language learning are obviously highly complex but it would be a stroke of good fortune if in view of the relatively advanced state of our knowledge about conditioning, speech phenomena were to obey (at least in part) conditioning laws. Considering only the processing of small linguistic units (phonemes, words), each acoustically represented phoneme (level 3) might function as a conditional (discriminative) stimulus that evokes the corresponding phoneme in a reactional matrix system within the listener. Such a stimulus-response relationship is characterized in Fig. 9.3, using but three dimensions. To the left of Fig. 9.3 we represent the external language stimulus (S_L) that is emitted by the speaker; when the stimulus impinges on the listener it evokes the language response pattern, a portion of which (r_L) is represented to the right.

There is, incidentally, good evidence that discrete binary contrasts in language (as in Table 9.2) *can* be differentially conditioned, e.g., words that have been naturally or experimentally conditioned as "good" vs. "bad" differentially evoke psychophysiologically measured covert conditional responses (Volkova, 1953; Acker and Edwards, 1964). Perhaps of even greater importance are the findings that conditional language re-

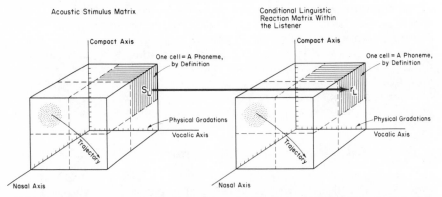

FIG. 9.3 Representation of a phoneme as a conditional acoustic linguistic stimulus (S_L). The external stimulus evokes a corresponding perceived phoneme within the listener, represented as a conditional linguistic response (r_L) (adapted from Cherry, 1957).

sponses generalize to other words along complex stimulus dimensions (cf. Razran, 1939a, b), and generalize between stimulus objects and corresponding words (Cofer and Foley, 1942), etc.

Neuromuscular Events in Internal Information Processing

We have developed the general notions that continuous linguistic signals can be represented in binary code; and that these stimuli evoke perceptual covert response processes within the listener that may also be represented by a systematically related system. We shall now sketch out some neuromuscular processes by which linguistic codes might be generated and transmitted within the language recipient.

We have accumulated abundant anatomical and physiological evidence about specific circuits (loops) between the brain and a wide variety of peripheral mechanisms (Chapters 5, 6, 7, and 8). Some of these circuits may function as servo loops, providing some kind of feedback as they facilitate internal information processing. But, because we lack sufficient knowledge about what mechanisms within the circuits control what, we shall use the noncommital term "circuit" without qualifying them as servo or feedback circuits. Furthermore, it may be wise to avoid the analogy in psychology with the engineer's "feedback"—in contrast to the instantaneous feedback in electronic circuits, consequences in the organism take relatively more time to "feedback."

There is abundant anatomical and physiological evidence about specific circuits (loops) between the brain and a wide variety of peripheral mechanisms (e.g., McGuigan and Schoonover, 1973). A paradigm for specifying classes of circuits which might serve linguistic functions during information processing is presented in Fig. 9.4.

The first kind of circuit (designated Ia) occurs when stimuli excite receptors, wherepon afferent neural impulses evoke brain events that result in efferent impulses back to the receptor. Such loops must reverberate for some time following stimulus reception. There is also the probability of extra-CNS loops between receptors and other peripheral mechanisms, like receptor-speech muscle-brain circuits (circuit class Ib and Ib') (cf. Tomatis, 1970).

The second general class of circuit (which would function for sensory integration) would consist of strictly intercerebral loops (II). These may include circuits between the cortex and subcortical regions (cf. Penfield, 1969) as well as complex transcortical loops, such as Hebb's (1949) cell assemblies.

Finally, there are three possible loops between the brain and effectors: circuit class IIIa in which one covert response class ($r_{1, 2} \ldots n$) leads to a series of additional covert responses; IIIb, in which one covert response (r_2) is an antecedent ("determiner") of an overt response (R); and IIIc, where the consequences of an overt response (R) include both internal signals (to the central nervous system) and external signals that interact

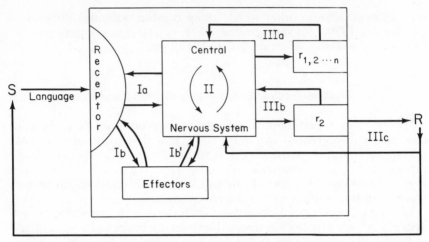

FIG. 9.4 Schematic representation of potential circuits during internal information processing. Covert processes in the receptors, brain, muscles, and glands (measured by EEG, EMG, GSR, etc.) serve as the basis for inferences about these hypothesized loops within a person.

with stimulus input (S_L); as in overt speech. Circuits IIIa and IIIb involve only internal signals from the response, while in circuit IIIc the response produces both internal *and* external signals.

We shall now consider circuits of the classes I, II, and III in greater detail. It is important in the following discussion to emphasize that when we refer to circuits and loops, we mean *classes* of these circuits. That is, we do not imply that there is a single neuron conducting a single impulse along a single channel circuit. Rather, circuits must carry complex volleys of numerous neural impulses simultaneously along parallel channels all throughout the body. Hassler (1966) has detailed some neural circuits that function in parallel. Tomatis (1970) pointed out that auditory stimuli influence the vagus nerve which widely distributes signals, including those that are transmitted to the viscera. For other research in which it has been concluded that there is parallel processing of information see Wood (1974), Saraga and Shallice (1973), Burrows and Okada (1973), and P.J. Smith (1973).

Fig. 9.5 is a somewhat expanded representation of the internal information processing circuits that are hypothesized in Fig. 9.4. To begin to appreciate the complexity of the neuromuscular systems with which we shall deal, and to gain an indication of their ability to meet the processing requirements of our model, we may note, as an example, that there are 130 million rods and cones in the eye. These cells make junction with one million nerve fibers; this ratio of 130 to 1 indicates that exceedingly complex events must occur in the transfer of information from the receptor to the optic nerve. On the motor side, the oculomotor nerve contains 25 thousand fibers, and the muscles that produce eye movements have approximately 3 muscle fibers for each nerve fiber. This ratio of 1 neural fiber to 3 muscle fibers invites thought about the transfer of information back from the brain to the eye musculature. For comparison with the optic and oculomotor nerves, other cranial nerves contain about 70,000 fibers, and motor roots of spinal nerves contain about 100,000 fibers. Estimates are of some 10 billion cerebral neurons. These neurons make perhaps 5×10^{14} (i.e., 500,000,000,000,000) synapses in the cortex (Smith, 1970). Although unestimated, numerous muscle fibers constitute about half of the weight of human bodies.

But to proceed, we may note that all internal linguistic events following stimulus input necessarily are "abstract," since phonemic and semantic entities are obviously not present in the acoustic signal. Consequently, the assertion of such linguistic entities as phonemes and meaning reactions requires processing of the stimulus input. After considering the initial processing of the signal in the periphery, we shall turn to systems involving central events.

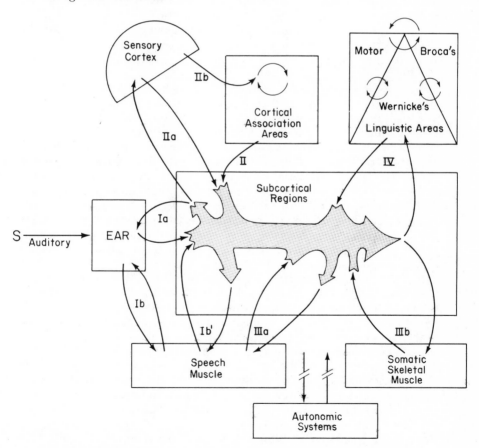

FIG. 9.5 Possible neuromuscular circuit classes in internal information processing.

Peripheral Processing. How might the peripheral events represented in Figs. 9.4 and 9.5 function linguistically? First, there are receptor mechanisms per se which transduce input signals during initial stimulus processing. Stevens and House (1972) considered the role of this peripheral receptor analysis in speech perception by citing a number of neurophysiological studies which indicate that "fairly complex processing takes place peripherally. Therefore, the peripheral auditory mechanism must impose on the input signal a much more radical transformation than a simple frequency analysis. The processing probably provides considerable information concerning attributes of the signal that are relevant to the discrimination of various linguistic categories or features" (p. 48). Another indication that there is peripheral processing of the external stimulus in the ear is that the electrical response from the hair cells follows the acoustic wave, while that from the first nerve cell does not (cf. Alpern, Lawrence, and Wolsk, 1967).

More important than the linguistic processing in which auditory stimuli are transduced to neural impulses, however, are those receptor processes that might function as components of circuits of the classes Ia and Ib.

Receptor-Subcortical Circuits (Class Ia). Once the auditory signal enters the ear, nerve cells in the cochlea of the inner ear are activated as a function of the vibration frequencies that have impinged on the external auditory meatus and on the eardrum. The resulting afferent neural impulses are conducted along the auditory nerve (that consists of some 30,000 afferent neurons) to subcortical levels of the cerebrum, following which efferent impulses return to the receptor; the continuous operation of this loop forms the class of circuit designated Ia. Lawrence (1957) cited findings that indicate that there is efferent feedback from the brain to the ears. This well-described type of receptor-brain-receptor circuit could function during short term memory by temporarily holding linguistic units so that the perceiver can form the units into a grammatical string (as discussed later in this paper).

Receptor-Speech Muscle-Brain Circuits (Class Ib). The second possible loop might serve a peripheral speech function by involving the ear directly with the speech musculature. Wyczoikowska (1913) implicitly hypothesized such a loop in explaining why her subjects reported that they felt strong impulses in the tongue when listening to auditory stimuli. Her subjects reported, for instance, that they heard words with "vibrating motions" in the tongue during thought. She specified the physiological basis of this phenomenon to be the lingual and the glossopharyngeal nerves between the ear and the tongue, so that stimulation of the ear might directly innervate the tongue facilitating the perception of external speech: "The chorda tympani . . . modified by the stimuli of the ear, can promote simultaneously an innervation of the tongue for the purpose of the speech heard" (p. 44 in McGuigan, 1966a). Stevens and House (1972) cited an even earlier reference to a speech perception

342

model that is based on the active internal replication of the external stimulus, viz., von Humboldt in 1836 held that the human being immediately repeats that which has just been heard. They then proposed an elaborate, active model of speech perception in which the listener participates equally with the talker—the listener internally generates the speaker's message as if to operate as the speaker (rather than as the listener). As Stevens and House pointed out, this is the concept of "analysis by synthesis" put forward by Halle and Stevens (1959). A similar view, put forth by Cherry (1957), is discussed later in this chapter.

Tomatis, in Sidlauskas (1970), suggested a circuit somewhat like the class Ib, though with the difference that the auditory stimulus is transduced *prior* to the tympanic membrane:

The auditory nerve is protected by a bony pyramid structure. Before the sound reaches it, the sound has to pass through a long and eventful journey. First, as soon as it enters the external ear, before it reaches the tympanic membrane, it touches upon the cartilaginous and skin lined passages of the meatus. This is not a dead surface. It is innervated by different nerves, i.e., the facial, which is at the back of the pavilion and comes from the auricular branch; then the trigeminal, which descends through the temple auricular and enters in front; and the pneumogastric, which is at the back of the meatus and reaches the tympanic membrane. This region of auditory canal disposes the ear to listen. The tympanic membrane, which is the barrier to the entering sound wave, gathers the sound. This sound, already marked by all these imprints, is transmitted to the cochlea. It is, therefore, of importance to see what has happened to the sound wave before it has reached the ear itself. *It is certain that many parts of the organism have been alerted to the sound in the meantime* (in Sidlauskas, 1970, p. 3, italics mine).

Tomatis' point emphasizes the extremely complex interaction of the numerous receptor-neural-muscular circuits of the body. Long past are the days in which a simple unidirectional linear telephone system model of neurophysiological functioning can serve any positive purpose. Tomatis has emphasized the complex interaction of numerous bodily mechanisms by tracing their embryological development. Though the various bodily organs are very different from each other, he held that they functionally form one unit, so that the functional oneness is to be understood by retracing the phylogenetic and ontogenetic origin of each organ, a concept that Tomatis also attributes to Arey (1965): "Groups of organs associate as *organ systems* within the *organism*, or embryo as a whole. The development of an organ is brought about by the cooperative activities of morphogenesis of histogenesis" (pp. 24–27). Particularly relevant for us is Tomatis' reference to the common origin of the body's bony parts and of the respective bodily muscles which enable the inferior mandibule and the hammer/anvil to function together. That is, the musculature controlling the activity of the mandibule (the jaw) and the hammer and anvil of the middle ear derive from the same first arch of the mesodermal embryonic structure. Furthermore, the masseter (jaw) and temporal muscles are both innervated by the trigeminal nerve (interestingly, within the context of tension control, discussed in Chapter 10 we can understand why tension in the jaws—such as in clinching or grinding the teeth—allows for the detection of muscular tension in the temple). Tomatis continued by pointing out that the facial nerve (VIIth) innervates all of the musculature of the face except that of the eyelid; and that the second arch of the first embryonic layer leads to the development of the upper part of the larynx, from which comes the hyoid bone to which the muscles controlling the tongue are attached, and from which develops the third ossicle of the middle ear (the stirrup), which is equipped with its own musculature (cf. Arey, 1965). In short, Tomatis pointed out that the same embryology establishes the close connection between the audio-vocal complex and helps us to understand the interactions between the constituents of the middle ear and the speech musculature. Tomatis implied that it is important to understand these interrelated neuromuscular mechanics in order to adequately understand language functioning. The vagus nerve is also of extreme importance because it proceeds from the cephalo-thoracic area and extends far into the abdomen. Tomatis suggested that the vagus is thus the visceral nerve par excellence because it functions to, in effect, conduct incoming auditory linguistic stimuli widely throughout the body including especially the viscera. It is in this way that, as linguistic functions develop, visceral components of language also develop. This autonomic circuit for adding emotional tone to linguistic stimuli is depicted in Fig. 9.5.

Other relevant neurophysiological findings include those by McCall and Rabuzzi (1973) who stimulated the laryngeal nerve and demonstrated a reflex connection between the middle ear muscles and the sensory nervous supply to the larynx. One interpretation, they suggested, is that this tympanic muscle reflex may have a function in vocalization—there may be middle ear muscle contraction in association with speaking. Their findings accord with the results of a number of previous researchers who have shown that contraction of the middle ear muscles precedes the production of sound (cf. McCall and Rabuzzi, 1973, p. 56). Other evidence for afferent pathways from the speech muscle has been presented by Bowman and Combs (1968) and Sussman (1972); since these studies are especially relevant for the entire set of circuits Ib'-IIa, they will be discussed in the next section.

With regard to circuit class Ib, we should also note that there is direct functioning between the retina and the skeletal musculature of the eye. In Chapter 5, for instance, we saw how eye movements produce retinal activity that generates volleys of afferent neural impulses to the brain. Sherrington (1947) pointed out that there is activity in the reverse direction too, suggesting a loop between the retina and the eye musculature. Hence, when the eye is stimulated, in addition to the nervous electrical propagation directly to the brain, "some of this electrical reaction generated in the eye does not reach the brain-cortex but diverges by a side-path into nerve-threads which relay it to a small muscle, which . . . activates . . . the pupillary muscle . . ." (1947, p. xvi). Sherrington continued that the "psychical" can influence the body's acts due to the retina's extreme sensitivity; by reacting, as few "as six photons can be perceived; and a visual reaction can release motor behavior of the whole body" (p. xviii).

A sample of nonphysiological, principally psychological-information processing, research that indicates that the speech muscle is intimately involved in the processing of linguistic stimuli within the listener during perception provides data that also are consistent with the interpretation of a class of circuits like Ib. For instance, Boros (1972) recorded significant increases in tongue EMG while his subjects listened to tape recordings of various types of auditory prose. Goto (1968a, b), in his studies of inner speech, implicated speech movements during silent reading and hearing. Zhinkin (1968) used cineradiography to record movements of the speech musculature (tonic vibration of the pharynx in the area of the superior constrictor) during language perception.

Brown and Bellugi (1964) indicated that linguistic stimuli spoken in a child's environment are, in a sense, automatically (involuntarily) reproduced by the child—it is as if the spoken stimulus "mechanically" evokes the same response, with a minimum (if any) of central "holding" or mediational activity.

Kimble and Perlmuter (1970) discussed the "tip of the tongue" phenomenon reported by Brown and McNeill (1966) in which it was found that subjects with an item on the tip of the tongue produced responses that sounded like the sought-for term much more frequently than the subjects produced words of similar meaning. Kimble and Perlmuter thought that "It seems very likely that an image of the sound of a word is what mediates its recall and production" (p. 373). This interpretation is consistent with our hypothesis of a phonetic (nonmeaningful) code ascending from the tongue to the brain where *semantic* processing occurs.

Eriksen, Pollack, and Montague (1970) summarized several lines of evidence that suggest that encoding in visual perception may consist of implicit speech or naming. The suggestion is that information is stored in a temporary sensory store and transformed into another representation during the read-out—the read-out is possibly implicit verbalization. A compatible suggestion by Hintzman (1965, 1967) is that the re-coding in short term memory is subvocal rehearsal, though Cole and Young (1975) concluded that encoding of speech sounds and short term memory occur independently of any subvocalization during the memory task. In any event, Eriksen et al. (1970) concluded from a series of studies that in order to perceive a word one must implicitly speak the word to oneself before it can be overtly vocalized. This conclusion was based on the major finding that the more syllables a word contains, the longer it takes a subject to implicitly speak the word. (Incidentally, this type of experiment is typical of a number in which reaction time is measured with apparatus like a voice key. Since reaction time values are important for making such inferences, the more precise measurement of the overt response by electromyographical means might facilitate such theorizing [cf., McGuigan and Boness, 1975].)

DiVesta and Rickards (1971), using a concept formation task, concluded that the process of labeling is an encoding mechanism, and that articulation increases the saliency of the appropriate code for the task.

These are some of the positive assertions alluding to circuits like the class Ib, and some of the data consonant with this class of circuit.[1] More generally in this section we have noted that during peripheral linguistic processing, signals are continuously transmitted from the ears to subcortical levels and return back again by way of the circuit class Ia of Fig. 9.5. Signals also possibly arrive at subcortical levels from an ear to speech muscle circuit (pathways Ib and Ib' that are in parallel with loop Ia). We shall now consider the next "step" in internal linguistic processing, viz., how signals from external stimuli that enter two ears become integrated into one perceptual phenomenon—a problem that has concerned us for many millennia. Decartes' solution was, for instance, to ascribe the integrational function to the pineal gland.

Sensory Integration Circuits (Class II).   The acoustic signals that arrive at the thalamic-brainstem-midbrain regions by the class of circuit designated Ia may interact with impulses that ascend from the speech muscle by path Ib'. Hence, once the speech muscle is activated by Loop Ib', afferent impulses are also generated which direct information to the subcortical regions by circuit Ib'. This afferent flow then interacts with the incoming information Ia directing neural volleys to the sensory cortex by circuit IIa. Regardless of whether one or both of these classes of loops function linguistically, afferent flow into the subcortical region simultaneously sets off additional ascending and descending loops. The ascending circuit is to the sensory (in this case auditory) cortex by way of loop class IIa of Fig. 9.5. (A number of specifications of auditory pathways through the brain stem and midbrain are available, e.g., Goldstein, 1968.) The descending loops from subcortical levels to the skeletal musculature (loop classes IIIa and IIIb) will be considered in the next section.

Some evidence for the existence of a pathway Ib' from the speech muscle to the cortex (II) is the work of Bowman and Combs (1969), who stimulated the distal portion of the hypoglossal nerve, which arises in the tongue, and recorded evoked potentials in the contralateral sensory motor cortex with a latency of only 4 to 5 msec. These hypoglossal fibers are thus rapidly conducting and may well carry signals that function in circuit II for sensory integration. In fact, Sussman (1972) concluded that there may be a one-to-one mapping of the oral area on the corresponding cortical areas. Sussman's conclusion was based on the findings of

---

[1] There are, of course, data which are not consonant with this circuit class Ib. For example, Henderson (1972) presented some behavioral evidence suggesting that an auditory-verbal loop cannot play a mandatory role in the coding and storage of visual information for a short-term memory store.

Bowman and Combs (1968) that each nerve unit of the lingual nerve is associated with a discrete receptive field on the dorsal surface of the tongue, and that the sensory and motor areas of the cortex contain relatively large regions devoted to the lip and tongue.

Penfield (1969) presented evidence for thalamic-cortical circuits (like II) on the basis of his findings with electrical stimulation procedures. For example, he showed that stimulation of the sensory area of the cortex activates specific ganglion cells in the thalamodiencephalic target. The entire circuit consists of nerve fibers running from the lower brain stem through the thalamus to the sensory cortex and back down to the thalamus (Penfield and Jasper, 1954, p. 474). Each afferent auditory train from the two ears (as we have seen, these are afferent signals which are already linguistically processed to some degree) arrives at the thalamic nuclei and ascends by neural pathway II to the audio-sensory cortex in both hemispheres.

Hassler's (1966) work is especially relevant here. He stated that the anterior basal part of the ventrolateral nucleus (V.o.a.) is a neuronal station of the afferent pathway to the motor cortex. V.o.p. is the terminal nucleus of the dentatothalamic fibers. V.o.a. and V.o.p. together form the basal part of the ventrolateral nucleus. If single electrical stimuli are applied in V.o.a. or V.o.p. single twitches of the face and tongue occur. Since these are afferent neuronal stations to the motor cortex, the impulses must ascend to the cortex and then descend to the speech muscle. The internal pallidum also belongs to the afferent neuronal circuit to the motor cortex, but it is only one of the afferent systems to the motor cortex. This may be taken as further anatomical and functional neurophysiological evidence for the existence of multiple channels for internal processing.

Hassler found that if patients were asked to move during stimulation, they reported a variety of interesting experiences, depending upon the precise nature of the stimulation. For example, zhen hetents are asked to count backwards, stimulation of V.o.p. produces an acceleration of speaking or counting. The patients usually seem to be in a hurry or under an impelling force, so that they omit some numbers or miss the correct sequence. Sometimes they rush to count in such a manner that they repeat the same word until it can no longer be understood. Sometimes stimulation in the pallidum slows down the counting to the point of complete blockage. The patients report inhibition, e.g., "I could not think so well," "My voice did not go as I wanted." Stimulation in V.o.a. typically slackens the backward counting or speaking, while stimulation in V.o.p. produces an acceleration before there is blocking. Subjects report "There was such a pressure on me that I had to speak faster and faster." "My thoughts were driven even until thinking was interrupted." "I know I counted faster; my thoughts were going faster even to the vanishing point."

Hassler specified two afferent neuronal systems to the motor cortex: (1) from the dentate nucleus through V.o.p. to area 4 ; (2) one that originates from pallidum internum, passes through the H_2 and H_1 bundles of Forel through V.o.a. of the thalamus, and to the primary motor cortex (Brodmann's area 6aα). The stimulation of this second system usually elicits retardation of speaking and of purposive movements.

Each sense system and each modality of each sense system has its own specific relay nucleus, as well as two layers of its own specific integrative nuclei in the thalamus. These are specified in detail by Hassler. Sensory motor activities are not integrated in the thalamus, but some of the thalamic nuclei participate in that integration. There are projections from the thalamus to the different primary sensory or motor fields, and from the latter to the association fields. The secondary or tertiary sensory areas of the cortex are called "areas of integration." Let us now consider a possible function for such integration areas, namely that integration of different modalities contributes to the meaning process.

Goldstein (1968) indicated that a precise representation of the peripheral sensory stimulus is preserved through at least some early stage of cortical processing and that the region where the representation arrives is the first auditory area of the cerebral cortex. In human beings the auditory cortex occupies the anterior transverse temporal gyrus of Heschl (Brodmann's areas 41 and 42) which is located on the superior bank of the first temporal convolution.

Goldstein suggested that a peripheral stimulus delivered to any portion of the auditory, visual, or somesthetic receptive fields activates one and the same central "association" system (specified in Goldstein, 1968, p. 1517) in an undifferentiated way; this he holds constitutes part of a generalized thalamocortical system, but its function is unclear: "Little is known about what sort of associations between diverse sensory inputs might be accomplished by a system conveying no information other than that *some* stimulus has been presented *somewhere* . . ." (Goldstein, 1968, p. 1519).

Such an undifferentiated central association system could prove extremely important to the present discussion. One reason is that a system like this might function to transfer signals from one modality to another. If the cortical association system is activated by a visual stimulus, for example, it could direct impulses into somasthetic channels to activate the body musculature. Hence, when one silently reads prose, this central neurophysiological system might direct the internal visual stimuli into muscle channels to covertly activate the oral skeletal muscle, a possibility which is further detailed in McGuigan (1970a). Edmund Jacobson (personal communication) has held that an external stimulus becomes meaningful when it is transferred into another modality; perhaps the central association system performs such an intermodal transfer function. It is thus indicated in Fig. 9.5 that impulses from the sensory (auditory) cortex descend in parallel back to the subcortical regions, first directly (IIa) and secondly through the cortical association areas (IIb). As these subcortical-sensory cortex-association cortex loops continue to reverberate in *both* hemispheres, the incoming auditory signals from the two ears may be integrated into one perceptual phenomenon; additional integration of the auditory signals with internal signals arriving from various other bodily sources (speech muscle, viscera, etc.) may occur in the central association areas.

Linguistic Processing Circuits: Cortical-Covert Behavior Interactions (Classes IIIa, IIIb, IV).　In Fig. 9.5, circuits of the classes IIIa and IIIb reverberate simultaneously with circuits of class II. That is, while sensory integration is occurring (II) subcortical-skeletal muscle circuits run simultaneously (and in parallel) between (1) the subcortex and the speech musculature (IIIa), and (2) from the subcortex to and from the other skeletal muscles of the body (IIIb). By hypothesis (McGuigan, 1970a), a function of loops IIIa and IIIb in Fig. 9.5 is to produce conditional (muscle) response patterns that participate in the formation of verbal codes that are afferently carried back to the brain by loop class IV. When circuit IV is activated, there is lexical-semantic processing wherein the listener understands (perceives) the incoming linguistic stimuli.

Several kinds of evidence for circuits from the speech muscle to the brain are as follows: Sauerland and Mizuno (1968) found evidence for a specific reflex between the tongue and laryngeal musculature such that afferent impulses are carried by hypoglossal fibers from extrinsic and intrinsic portions of the tongue to the brain stem, following which the intrinsic laryngeal musculature is activated. Presumably, impulses from the brain stem then ascend to the cortex. We have already noted Bowman and Combs (1969) specified an afferent pathway from the tongue to the sensory-motor cortex by way of the hypoglossal nerve. Sussman (1972) offered the general conclusion that there is a centripetal pathway that conveys sensory information from the muscle-spindle end organs in the tongue to the brainstem by a hypoglossal-to-cervical nerve route and hypoglossal-to-lingual. Ojemann (1975) recently showed that the lateral thalamus is an integrating center for various activites concerned with speech. Relevant here also are the works of Van Riper and Irwin (1962) and of Mysak (1966) in which an oral tactile sensory system was established as an important component of the speech monitoring mechanism; this system presumably employs sensory receptors that function in a closed-loop feedback system during overt speech. Speakers evidently track their speech by the emitted sound patterns and also by somesthetic processes resulting from articulation (Smith and Henry, 1967). Fucci (1972) implied that individuals with low vibrotactile thresholds in the lips and tongue are speech-defective because there is an interruption in the sensory feedback mechanism used to control the articulators.

Further indication that closed loops involving muscle response feedback are important comes from Mowrer (1960a, b) and from the work of Adams and his associates (Adams, McIntyre, and Thorsheim, 1969; Adams, 1971; Adams, Goetz, and Marshall, 1972). The work of Adams et al. indicates that, in verbal and motor learning, sensory feedback from the response lays down the reference against which the correctness of future occurrences of the response is tested. These data that support Adams' closed loop theory of learning were interpreted as being negative for Lashley's hypothesis of motor programming (cf. our discussion of this topic in Chapter 2, p. 55).

Quite relevant here is the research of Siengenthaler and Hochberg (1965) on the measurement of reaction time of the tongue to auditory and tactile stimulation. They found that tactile stimulation produced the shortest reaction time (viz., 123 msec). Auditory reaction time varied as a function of sound intensity from 129 msec to 209 msec. They concluded that tactile feedback from the oral region is important for monitoring speech, and hypothesized that a speech mechanism which operates on a servo system probably uses the most efficient sensory channels available in monitoring speech output.

Kleitman (1951) also emphasized the importance of neuromuscular circuits and of proprioceptive impulses in his discussion of the sleep-wakefulness cycle. His reasoning is thus consonant with our general circuit model. In particular, Kleitman held that afferent impulses generated by the muscles are thought to be the primary neural factors that maintain wakefulness, while absence of the afferent impulses leads to sleep. In this way, the amount of afferent neuromuscular activity determines one's level of consciousness (where Kleitman considers consciousness in terms of sleep-wakefulness phenomena.) The occurrence of muscle tension, he says, "seems to stimulate cortical activity and cortical activity, in turn, raises the tension of the muscles" (1951, p. 18). During muscular relaxation, with a diminution in the stream of proprioceptive impulses to the brain, this feedback circuit results in the fall of bodily temperature. Hence, the causal sequence can be summarized as follows: the temperature of the blood is determined mainly by muscular tension; as the change of temperature of the blood reaches the brain it results in consequent brain activity having to do with regulation of the body's temperature. Consequently, Kleitman has used bodily temperature as an index of muscular relaxation.

Fremont-Smith (1951) also emphasized the importance of afferent neural impulses for determining the degree of consciousness, e.g., in order to be conscious of what a speaker is saying, you must exclude impulses that arise from mechanisms in your body that are irrelevant for the listening activity.

Goto (1971) conducted an interesting study in which he found that Japanese subjects were far less accurate than Americans in their auditory discrimination of words containing the sounds of "L" vs. "R," even when the words were spoken by American voices. Even those Japanese subjects who were most proficient in English and had relatively good pronunciation of "L" and "R" had poor auditory discrimination of these sounds. The auditory discrimination of syllables, Goto concluded, is made possible through practice in speech and hearing from early childhood; without such early practice, there is considerable difficulty in perceptually discriminating between them, even when they come under productive control in later life. Goto emphasized the importance of kinesthetic sensation arising from a person's own speech when one is in the process of learning to articulate.

Regarding the peripheral components of circuits IIIa and IIIb, we have already reviewed the abundant evidence that numerous covert skeletal muscle responses occur throughout the body during the silent performance of linguistic tasks (McGuigan, Chs. 5, 6, and 7, 1973a). We may expect the speech musculature to be the most prominent in linguistic coding processes—the generalization is that covert oral language responses occur in *all* linguistically competent individuals, even though the amplitude may be extremely low in highly proficient readers (e.g., Edfeldt, 1960; McGuigan, 1973c). Nonoral skeletal muscle responses during linguistic processing are also critical; prominent examples are heightened covert behavior in the preferred arm during reading, memorizing, and listening (McGuigan and Bailey, 1969a; McGuigan and Winstead, 1974), and covert dactylic responses in the deaf while thinking (Max, 1937; McGuigan, 1971).

Fjeld (1965) measured arm EMG, as a measure of covert responding, during a visual signal detection experiment in order to determine the relation between covert responding and threshold values. Visual stimuli following a ready signal were presented to the subjects at or below their threshold and detection was simultaneously measured by overt arm movements and covert arm EMG activity. The results indicated a significant improvement in detection when measured by the gross response *and* the covert EMG response, as opposed to gross responses alone. It was additionally noted that the EMG response measure became relatively more useful as an indicator of accuracy at the weaker than the brighter light values, whereas the overt response measure became relatively less useful. Fjeld concluded that covert responses reliably convey information about performance of which the subject is "unaware."

The work of Goodwin, McCloskey, and Matthews (1972) has specific relevance to circuit types III and IV. These researchers studied the possibility that muscle spindle afferent discharges contribute to the perception of limb position. An alternative view attributes the position sense solely to extramuscular mechanoreceptors, e.g., Pacinian corpuscles and Golgi tendon organs. The triceps or biceps muscle of the "experimental" arm was stimulated with a constant frequency vibrator while the experimenter simultaneously repositioned this arm. The blindfolded subjects were instructed to keep the contralateral or "tracking" arm constantly aligned with the stimulated arm. Thus the relative difference in position of the arms provided an objective measure of the proprioceptive illusion. The results showed that all subjects consistently misjudged the position of the experimental arm during vibratory stimulation. Goodwin et al. concluded that these data are compatible with the interpretation that intramuscular afferent discharges of the spindles are perceived by higher neural centers and thus contribute to limb position sensibility. Finally, the authors concluded that there was equally strong support for a role for muscle receptors provided by the finding that position and movement sense at a joint could be preserved following anesthesia of the skin and tissues of the joint itself.

Capability of Speech Muscles for Refined Differential Activity. We must now consider the critical question of whether or not the speech musculature can actually function in the generation and transmission of a verbal code, as we have hypothesized in the interaction of circuits IIIa and IV. The following evidence, added to that previously cited, suggests an affirmative answer.

Sussman (1972) considered the nature of the information carried by the afferent pathways from the tongue and, relying on the work of Bowman and Combs (1968), concluded that "Not only can the higher brain centers be kept informed as to the *initiation* of a high-speed consonantal gesture of the tongue but also as to the *attainment* and subsequent *release* of that gesture. . . . The neuromuscular system of the tongue has been shown to be a built-in feedback system that can signal the length and rate of movement of a muscle" (p. 266). Consequently ". . . it is logical to assume that the *afferent discharge pattern emanating from the tongue should contain high-level distinctive information.* Such discriminative information can be provided by the differential frequency discharge patterning of the muscle spindles due to the orientation of the extrafusal fibers relative to the direction of movement" (p. 267, italics mine).

Another line of research that supports the hypothesis that speech muscles function in the generation of a verbal code has resulted in evidence of a discriminative relationship between speech muscle behavior and the phonemic system during various cognitive processes. For example, Blumenthal (1959) showed that tongue electromyograms were of significantly greater magnitude when subjects thought of saying lingual-alveolar verbal materials (that would require major tongue movements during *overt* speech), as compared to when they thought of saying bi-labials. In a series of experiments, Locke and Fehr (e.g., 1970b, see also Chapter 6) reported more covert lip activity during the subvocal rehearsal of labial words, relative to nonlabials. More recently, McGuigan and Winstead (1974) reported that covert responses in the tongue are relatively pronounced when the subject is reading, memorizing, and rehearsing prose that is heavily loaded with lingual-alveolar material, while covert lip behavior is especially pronounced while reading, memorizing, and rehearsing prose that is dominated by bi-labial material. Of more direct significance to speech perception, one extremely well relaxed subject listened to sentences and words loaded with either labial or nonlabial verbal material. This subject significantly increased lip electromyograms while listening to labial material but not while listening to comparable nonlabial material (McGuigan, 1973a). In short, it seems that the particular class of verbal material (bilabial, lingual-alveolar, etc.) silently processed evokes relatively heightened covert activity in the speech musculature that would be used for the overt production of that class of verbal material. One possible interpretation is that the speech muscle covertly generates a verbal code that is related to the phonemic system.

Other relevant data are that there is heightened tongue EMG during perceptual clarification ("The Gilbert and Sullivan effect" as reported by Osgood and McGuigan, 1973, and in Chapter 6). In the second in a series of four studies planned by Osgood and McGuigan, meaningless auditory prose (spoken to the subjects in the Finnish language) was used. Even with the meaning reactions removed, there was still auditory perceptual clarification accompanied by heightened tongue EMG. These data are consonant with the conclusion that the speech musculature does carry distinctive information to the brain, but that the information is not itself meaningful. Our interpretation is that speech muscle-generated coding is phonetic (see p. 375).

Penfield's (1969) work also substantiates the kind of loop diagrammed as IV in Fig. 9.5. There are, Penfield said, three major speech areas: Wernicke's area, Broca's area, and that in the supplementary motor-area. (Wernicke's area is the major and indispensable one, Penfield concluded, because it is the only one that leads to permanent aphasia when removed.) These three areas, we hypothesize, form the cortical components of loop IV. Interactions among these language regions and other cortical areas may constitute the transcortical loops (II) of Fig. 9.4, analogous to Hebb's (1949) cell assemblies.

Penfield electrically stimulated these three speech areas and concluded that all three have effective axonal connections into the thalamic nuclei. Furthermore, he concluded that conduction is not a generalized spread of current (such as a "field force") but is highly localized axonal conduction from the cortex to the thalamus. The afferent (and efferent) components of this loop are specified in Penfield and Jasper (1954, p. 474). Penfield believed that the circuit between the pulvinar and Wernicke's area is of special importance. He suggested that when afferent impulses reach Wernicke's area, "translation" occurs—that is, words become connected to the corresponding concepts. Impulses descending from Wernicke's area were thought to activate the central integration circuits, whereupon the "idea" of the linguistic input is experienced. For example, if the acoustic language stimulus is "apple" the activation of the subcortical components (of what we are labeling loop class IV) produce in the listener the "idea" of the "familiar rounded colored edible fruit." Penfield's "translation" and "idea" concepts will be related to our later discussion of lexical-semantic processing, and are relevant to our earlier discussion of meaning and central integration.

In a series of studies Ojemann and his associates electrically stimulated various locations of the human thalamus during and after stereotaxic thalamotomy, and found that left thalamic stimulation evokes a specific alerting response that affects both short- and long-term memory (Ojemann, 1975). Ojemann et al. concluded that within the left lateral thalamus there is an anatomical substrate for speech which ". . . includes pulvinar and *en passage* fibres related to the central medianum and dorsal medial thalamic nuclei. This finding supports the proposal of Penfield and Roberts (1959) concerning intrathalamic localization of speech function. The overlap of sites within the lateral thalamus from which anomia and perseveration, respiratory inhibitions, and alterations in short-term verbal memory can be evoked supports the concept of the lateral thalamus as an integrating centre for various activities concerned with speech" (Ojemann and Ward, 1971, p. 679).

Ojemann's work on the thalamus, together with that of Penfield and his associates, places special emphasis on this region for language transmission comprehension, and subcortical integration (as in Fig. 9.5). Nevertheless, it would be premature to unequivocally subscribe to Penfield's interpretations. Osgood (1957b), for instance, placed and representational (meaning) reactions (his r_M's), as well as his $\overline{s\text{-}s}$ and $\overline{r\text{-}r}$ (basically integrational) events at the cortical level; certainly this contrasts with Penfields' thoughts. I think we simply do not yet know which components of circuit IV are the most critical (if there are, in fact, isolated critical components) for "semantic interpretation," "ideas," "translation" or the like, and that we must await extremely deft research for these most important answers.

The next question to be asked is whether a system of distinctive feature oppositions can be fruitfully employed to describe the information generated during the complex interaction of muscle fiber contraction, muscle receptor stimulation, and consequent discharge of afferent neural impulses. An empirical specification of precise patterns of muscle fibers responding as a function of patterns of distinctive feature oppositions (like those to be presented later on p. 000 in Fig. 9.11) would be fantastically complex. No electromyographic work to date has even approached the refined laboratory analysis that would be required for measuring speech muscle activity for coding distinctive features during language reception. Even the much simpler problem of specifying relationships between muscle activity and distinctive features during speech *production* (vs. perception) has not led to extremely impressive results. Harris (1974) reported one line of research, for example, that followed from the proposal of Jakobson, Fant, and Halle (1963) that the "tense" member of the opposition pair (tense/lax, #7 in Fig. 9.11 on p.377) leads to more forceful articulation than does the "lax" member. As Harris pointed out, the "tense-lax" distinction is meant to be the primary one between "voiced" and "voiceless" consonants so that instances of the phoneme class /p/ should demand greater muscular tension when produced than for /b/. Harris cited four studies in which this expectation was examined by measuring force of orbicularis oris contraction in the lips. In three studies, she stated that the differences between /p/ and /b/ were not significant, while a small difference was found in the fourth. However, there is later, more encouraging evidence. For example, Hirose and Gay (1971) found that the posterior cricoarytenoid muscle participates in laryngeal articulatory adjustments, particularly for the voiced/voiceless distinction. They stated that "there is a consistent increase in PCA (posterior cricoarytenoid) activity for voiceless consonant production regardless of phoneme environment" (pp. 135–138). They also reported that vocalis and the lateral cricoarytenoid muscles both appear to be activated in the production of vowel segments, but rather suppressed for consonantal segments.

Raphael (1971) also tested the view that tongue muscles are physiologically more tense for tense symbols of the tense-lax opposition in production, than for the lax instances of this opposition. Raphael found that there is consistently greater activity, as hypothesized, on the part of the genioglossus muscle (a flat triangular muscle, the strongest of the extrinsic tongue muscles that forms most of the substance of the tongue) for the items linguistically classified as tense, than for their counterparts that were hypothesized to correspond to the "lax" members of the oppositions.

Researchers have apparently concentrated more on electromyographic recording of speech muscle patterns during speech production because of the relatively greater difficulty of studying such patterns during speech perception. It is likely that the muscle pattern-distinctive feature relationships are the same or very similar during both processes, so that inferences can be made from data during speech production to speech perception. We would only expect greatly reduced amplitude during perception. As Dashiell (1928, p. 483) has said, "when speech is reduced in intensity to an implicit degree, it is still speech—much mystery has been needlessly attached to speaking that goes on within one silently." Just because speech is inaudible, he said, we should not jump to the conclusion that there is a new non-physical process of some new-non-material entity at work. To call it a "psychic" process only adds to our problems, explaining nothing.

Because they are learned together, Cherry (1957) even suggested that speech perception and speech production are one and the same phenomenon: ". . . that when we listen to someone speaking, we are also preparing to move our own vocal organs in sympathy—not necessarily motor responses, but subthreshold—and that our imitative instincts of childhood never leave us. Piaget, for instance, comments upon our instinctive recognition of mouth position when hearing speech" (p. 293). On this point Cherry also said that "the representations we carry in our heads, of speech sounds, are likely to be formed of data concerning vocal organ configurations, the cavity resonances (formants), the larnyx frequencies, et cetera" (p. 294). In this context, Lashley (1960) said that ". . . the understanding of speech involves essentially the same problems as the production of speech . . . comprehension and production of speech have too much in common to depend on wholly different mechanisms" (p. 513). MacNeilage (1970) and MacNeilage and MacNeilage (1973) offered the related suggestion that the phoneme may be a basic unit stored in the nervous system as a fixed articulatory position, a positional target, uniquely related to fixed positions of the articulators for a given phoneme. These statements closely resemble those of Wyczoikowska (1913) and others presented earlier in this chapter.

Electromyographical research of speech muscles is in its infancy, and there has been but limited success. Yet we should eventually be able to specify unique speech muscle response patterns as a function of distinctive features, not only during production but also during perception. To achieve this highly refined level of analysis, we will require much more sensitive and precise techniques than those previously or currently used. One promising approach is that of Isley and Basmajian (1973); by implanting fine wire electrodes these researchers were able to quite precisely specify various speech muscle patterns during the performance of a variety of oral tasks (but unfortunately for us they did not include speech activities).

It *would* be fortunate if the relationships between muscle states and distinctive features were the same for all the five speech levels previously mentioned including those for speech production and speech perception. In developing our model for perception, we shall make this assumption and consider that speech muscle response patterns produce distinctive feature codes.

The implication of the following section is that such codes are carried by circuit classes III, interact with circuit class IV, and could thereby produce "semantic interpretation," "ideas," and the like.

Muscle Patterning and Generation of Neural Codes. Anatomists, neurophysiologists, and similar scientists have contributed notably to our relatively advanced state of understanding of the functioning of the skeletal musculature and consequent neural coding of volleys of afferent neural impulses that carry information to the brain. In fact, the area of neural coding is one of the more active and productive areas of recent scientific activity (cf. especially Fitts and Posner, 1967; Granit, 1955, 1972; Melton and Martin, 1972; Quarton, Melnechuk, and Schmitt, 1967; Tobias, 1972; Uttal, 1965, 1972).

Phasic Muscle Patterns. The patterns of afferent neural impulses generated by muscle activity depend on the precise combination of muscle fibers that contract.[2] The skeletal muscles of vertebrates (including humans) contain fibers designated as tonic and as phasic. (Keul, Doll, and Keppler, 1972.) Each muscle in the body consists of different numbers of each type—some muscles are composed primarily of tonic fibers while others are composed primarily of phasic fibers. The relative number of each type of fiber presumably depends on the function of the muscle. However, while muscles are mixtures of the two types, all muscle fibers of any given motor unit are of the same type.

---

[2] We emphasize the muscular aspects of this peripheral complex because through electromyography muscle activity has been relatively more susceptible to study in the normal human and has probably yielded more valuable empirical findings during cognitive processing.

Structurally, tonic fibers are thinner and dark-colored (sometimes referred to as "red fibers" or Type I). Phasic fibers are thicker and pale ("white fibers" or Type II). The coloring of the fibers depends upon the amount of myoglobin content, which indicates differences in the oxidating metabolic processes. For us, the important differences between phasic and tonic fibers depends on their twitch time; tonic fibers have the slower twitch time, and they fatigue more slowly than do phasic fibers. Consequently, continuous tonic actions (such as when a stork stands on one leg for hours at a time) are controlled primarily by tonic fibers. The phasic fibers have low latencies and contract rapidly (using, incidentally, larger amounts of creatine phosphate). The tonic fibers are less excitable and use lower amounts of creatine phosphate. Hence, while tonic fibers function primarily for endurance work, phasic fibers function more efficiently in rapid, short lasting, high intensive work. The predominantly phasic muscle (those composed primarily of white fibers) also have a higher resting membrane potential, higher irritability, and a higher conduction velocity of excitation. A variety of other differences (especially biochemical) between the two types of fibers are discussed by Keul et al. (1972).

In 1968, A. N. Sokolov suggested that it is primarily the phasic muscle fibers which are involved in internal linguistic coding, which observations in our laboratory confirm. Rapid changes in the patterns of contraction of phasic muscle fibers may thus rapidly generate different parameters for stimulating muscle spindles (and other receptors). Consequently, coded afferent neural impulses are continuously generated as a function of the changing states of the musculature.

To speculate about the possible involvement of the tonic muscles, perhaps sustained tonic muscle activity functions to maintain general bodily arousal. It is possible that tonic activity influences the reticular activating system which functions in circuits with the cortex for purposes of cerebral arousal. The present notion that the skeletal musculature functions in the generation of verbal codes that are afferently carried to the brain reminds us especially of references in Chapter 2, such as that by Pavlov that the "basic component of thought . . . [consists of] . . . kinesthetic impulses [which] pass from the speech apparatus into the cerebral cortex" (in Novikova, 1961, p. 210).

Other researchers who have considered the importance of coded neural impulses and the activity of muscle systems for the retrieval of thoughts or memories include Penfield whose electrical stimulation of the brain led to reports of memories of past events. Penfield first stimulated on the surface of the temporal cortex and obtained reports of "double awareness" in which the subject (patient) remembered past events while at the same time reporting awareness of the present circumstances. In later work, Penfield obtained verbal reports while stimulating the patient subcortically, leading him to theorize about subcortical memory processes (Berger and Thompson, 1977, for evidence of subcortical memory processes). Many years ago I asked Penfield about the possibility of stimulating even further peripherally, perhaps even at the neuromuscular junction while obtaining the patient's verbal report. His answer was enthusiastically negative. More recently, however, the verbal reports of subjects engaged in Rolfing (a technique in which the "patient" experiences intense manual stimulation of the muscles for prolonged periods of time) appear to be similar to those of Penfield's patients. A sample of the "recalled memory" thus produced is given by Keen (1970): "In the seventh hour of processing, pressure on a muscle in my shoulder released the memory of childhood conflict with a person I loved deeply—a memory that had become encysted in my chest" (p. 60). It is entirely possible, though far from being satisfactorily confirmed, that we could systematically stimulate the muscles to generate afferent verbal neural codes that could retrieve distant memories. If we knew the proper stimulus patterning to apply at the brain, at the muscles, or anywhere within the neuromuscular circuits diagramed in Fig. 9.5, we could, by this line of reasoning, retrieve whatever memories we designated.

Of interest in the context of the muscular generation of coded neural volleys is the work of Marteniuk, Shields, and Campbell (1972) and Marteniuk and Ryan (1972) on the psychophysics of kinesthesis, in which positional cues and starting and terminal positions of a movement provide important kinesthetic cues. Finally, Pishkin (1973) also noted that nonoral muscular activity may be important for linguistic functioning. Pishkin reported a linear relationship between muscle action potentials and amount of information input, defined as problem difficulty, in concept identification by psychiatric patients.

Afferent Neural Volleys.   When specific patterns of phasic muscle activity, on the background of tonic muscle activity, generate afferent neural volleys, the linguistic information is transmitted to critical regions of the brain. It is widely held that trains of afferent neural spikes carry the generated information (Chapter 8). When the discrete spike trains arrive at a synapse, the binary signal is transformed to analog by the release of synaptic transmitters which carry the information to the next neuron in the circuit (oversimplified). On arriving at the brain, the coded information carried by spike trains is complexly processed. We have noted in Chapter 8 a number of measures of brain processes as a function of linguistic input, and it is reasonable to conclude that the information carried by the afferent neural volleys determines the patterns of evoked potentials, of the contingent negative variation, and of other electrical measures of brain activity that constitute linguistic processing events.

Semantic Processing in Circuits Involving the Central Nervous System.   As far as the central nervous system aspects of the model are concerned, we do not have sufficient knowledge to say much about neurophysiological functioning of lexical-semantic storage systems—in fact, as noted in Chapter 8 it is difficult today to go much farther than Lashley's (1960) trace system. It is reasonable to suppose, however, that semantic processing involves the activation of cerebral circuits, particu-

larly that transcortical loops are set off through circuit class IV of Fig. 9.5, as discussed in Chapter 8. The suggestion here is that a speech code is transmitted from the speech musculature by way of circuit class IIIa to activate circuit class IV, within which cortical components of semantic processing circuits are activated in the cerebrum. It is thus our working assumption that during language perception, covert responses generate afferent neural impulses coded for the externally impinging linguistic units; when they enter the brain they in some sense "match" the appropriate lexical and semantic representations. This is the process represented by loop IV of Fig. 9.5. We have hypothesized that perception occurs when the afferent neural volleys represented by a binary chain, such as the −, +, −, +, −, −, + for /p/ in Table 9.1 and in Fig. 9.11, complexly interact with critical linguistic regions of the brain. In Chapter 8 we suggested that the afferent volleys from circuit class III which activate circuit class IV function cortically in a similar manner. In short, *the muscle status that generates afferent neural impulses may be represented by a binary code which enters the brain, wherein Szentagothai's (1975) lattice may neurally allow semantic processing that is represented by Osgood and Hoosain's (1974) semantic feature matrix. Further, all of these events may be represented in binary arithmetic, forming a single compatible binary system.*

PROCESSING VISUAL LINGUISTIC STIMULI

The preceding discussion has centered on auditory processing, with the understanding that the principles were generally applicable to other modalities too. We shall briefly consider visual processing here, and merely note that other modalities are also important (and interesting), as in cutaneous coding (Geldard, 1960). Kirman (1973), incidentally, reviewed efforts to present acoustic speech to the skin, and concluded that it is possible to structure speech stimuli for effective tactile perception so that tactile displays of speech can be comprehended at rapid rates. One effective method is the vibration method in which the subject places the hands on the speaker's face (as Helen Keller did); Kirman suggested that this method's success is partly due to the perceiver's ability to relate the vibration cues to the articulatory movements of the speaker (as a result of the perceiver's own experience as a speaker?).

There is evidence, too, that the visual modality is an aid to auditory speech perception. For example, in their discussion of speech communication, Morgan, Cook, Chapanis, and Lund (1963), pointed out that listeners can obtain information by watching the lips and face of a speaker. They cited the finding that "listeners obtain higher scores on speech intelligibility tests when they can see the lips and face of the talker than when they cannot, even though all other factors such as the intensity of the received speech and the noise are the same under both conditions of listening. The reason for this is that the average person is able to obtain some information by so-called "lip reading." "The increment in intelligibility contributed by visual cues is a function of the prevailing speech-to-noise ratio; if the speech-to-noise ratio is high, the listeners hear the words clearly and therefore cannot take advantage of the cues provided by lip reading; if the speech-to-noise ratio is low, they need, and they in fact use, the visual cues" (Morgan et al., 1963, p. 180). We have informally observed a number of "unconscious shadowers" (individuals who move their lips almost in unison with the speaker they are observing) visibly shadowing the verbal content from the speaker.

Lyakh (1968) studied 34 babies of 2 to 8 months of age and electrically recorded a winking response as a conditional reflex during the perception of speech sounds. He found that the infants made the conditional responses to visually perceived auditory speech stimuli, as they did to the isolated sounds of speech. However, the infants did not adequately respond to the sounds of the vowels when their view of the speaking individual was obstructed. Lyakh concluded that the visual perception process is dominant over the acoustic components in the perception of speech sounds by the very young. These considerations suggest that the speaker's speech muscle activity helps the perceiver to understand the language being spoken. Perhaps the perceiver refers the visual input to his or her own articulation and thence reproduces the acoustic stimuli through his or her own covert oral behavior.

Let us now consider visual processing within the context of Fig. 9.5. With regard to written language, when light waves reflected by text enter the eyes, the visual pattern falling on the retina excites the rods and cones to produce afferent neural impulses that carry the input information as transduced signals. We have also noted that kinesthetic information is generated by eye movements (Chapter 5). These afferent patterns then ascend, presenting the signals for half of each image to each hemisphere—referring to Fig. 9.5, Loop class Ia produces reverberation in Loop class II. Simultaneous with the activation of Loop class II, neural impulses descend from the thalamus to the speech muscle, actuating Loop class IIIa, and to the other skeletal muscles in the body, activating Loop class IIIb. As the impulses reverberate from the two hemispheres with the thalamus, by loop class II, integration of the two patterned halves of the visual image occurs, just as for auditory processing. There is also integration of Loop II impulses with the returning impulses from the skeletal muscle throughout the body (Loops IIIa and IIIb). As in the case of auditory linguistic perception, the product of this complex thalamic-cortical integration is the neural linguistic coding that activates Loop IV; and Loop IV is intimately involved in processing representations of the linguistic input stimuli in central memory storage.

In brief, then, visual linguistic stimuli are processed in the same general way as are auditory linguistic stimuli, with some obvious differences. One major difference may be the lack of a circuit that functions directly between the eye and the speech musculature (loop Ib), without going through the more complex regions of the brain. Still, the neuroanatomy and neurophysiology need to be carefully studied for this circuit *is* possible. Speech, vision, and hearing are intimately related. As a case in point, persons well trained in intrapersonal observation and progressive relaxation invariably report simultaneous muscular tensions in the eyes and in the speech region during imagery (Jacobson, 1929); and we have abundant evidence of covert eye and speech reponse components of behavioral patterns during thought (Chapters 5 and 6). Neural pathways connect these three regions by way of the facial nerve and geniculate ganglion, the greater superficial petrisaln for the eye, the stapedius branch for the stapes and stapedius muscle, and the chorda tympani for the tongue. The intimate interconnections among the various response systems, how activity in one influences the response of others, and further evidence of parallel processing are illustrated also by the work of Roland (1972) who showed that during silent, oral, and choral reading conditions, stutterers made significantly more eye movement retraces than did non-stutterers. Furthermore, the stutterers made significantly more retraces during choral than either silent or oral reading. In this regard note also that the oculomotor system has access to the efference (outflow) from the hand that produces target movements during visual tracking, i.e., there is proprioceptive input from the arm of use of the pursuit eye movement system (Angel, Hollander, and Wesley, 1973; Steinbach, 1969).

A second difference between processing visual and auditory stimuli is that, while there is substantial evidence of heightened covert oral behavior during reading, there are limited data of covert oral responding while listening to auditory linguistic stimuli. The lack of impressive data during listening may be simply because there have been relatively few studies directed at the problem (McGuigan, 1970a, 1973a). Mankin suggested another reason: "Concerning the function of subvocal speech, assume . . . that the medium for short-term memory is acoustic or auditory; might one of the functions of subvocal speech be to perform this transformation of visual stimuli into this acoustic, or auditory medium? If so, then it will answer the question . . . as to why reading results in more covert activity than listening" (in McGuigan and Schoonover, 1973, pp. 379–80). While the point is controversial, there is evidence that short-term memory does function in an acoustic medium (e.g., Hintzman, 1965, 1967); and since peripheral processing has been implicated in short term memory (Averback and Coriell, 1961) a (possible) lack of loop class Ib in visual processing, in contrast to auditory processing, may account for the larger amount of covert oral behavior during reading relative to listening—it may be that lack of loop Ib prevents involvement of the speech muscle during the early stages of visual linguistic processing, and thus a heavier demand is placed on the speech muscle for transformation of the visual code to an auditory one later in the processing. If this is so, after short-term memory is terminated, covert oral behavior is accentuated, making it easier to measure. In short, during speech perception slight covert oral behavior may occur early through loop Ib and also later through circuit IIIa; but in silent reading covert oral behavior mainly occurs later than loop Ib, and with greater reliance on loop III.

From a more commonsense point of view, we note that reading is more difficult for a child than listening—children apparently expend little effort in learning to speak, engaging primarily only the auditory-speech systems. However, in reading, the child must learn to change from a visual modality into the more basic original auditory modality. Perhaps the cortical association areas discussed on page 348 function in the exchange of modalities engaging the skeletal musculature thus producing the covert speech acts necessary for the comprehension of written prose.

Another reason that the speech musculature responds covertly to a greater degree to visual stimuli in reading than to auditory stimuli in listening may be that it is more difficult for auditory stimuli to become conditional stimuli for speech responses; that is, during self-generated speech the child manipulates the speech musculature (the response) *following* which the child perceives the auditory speech stimuli that were emitted. Hence, the response occurs prior to the stimulus so that it would be difficult for the child's spoken auditory stimulus to acquire response evoking properties for the speech musculature (if there were conditioning under this arrangement, it would be backward and the data indicate that backward conditioning is difficult to achieve; even when and if it occurs conditioning it seems unstable.)

On the other hand, speech stimuli emitted by other speakers can occur prior to the child's speech responding; but, for successful conditioning, the temporal relationship between the impinging stimulus and the child's speech response would have to be rather precise, and the child would have to repeat units of the received speech stream. This type of learning is possible—Brown and Bellugi (1964) indicate that young children do, more or less automatically, repeat what is spoken to them.

INTERNAL INFORMATION PROCESSING
IN THE ABSENCE OF DIRECT CONTROLLING STIMULATION

The emphasis to this point has been on processes immediately following external stimulation, processes that are traditionally referred to as "perceptive." We shall now briefly consider information processing when there apparently is no immediate external stimulus in control, as when one is "lost in thought" or "dreaming." Such internal events are not directly anchored on the stimulus side, but they may eventuate in overt behavior. We thus commence this discussion "in the middle" of the behavioral unit of Fig. 3.3 on page 79, well after the impingement of the external stimulus and prior to the overt response. Within the context of Fig. 9.5, the events that we now consider are schematized as loops IIIa and IIIb, the type of circuit in which covert responses eventuate in overt behavior.

Penfield (1969) described a loop in which afferent neural impulses arise within the higher brain stem, ascend to the motor cortex and descend through the medulla to the musculature. He suggested that activation of this circuit links the diencephalon to the cerebral cortex and constitutes an action that precedes the sending out of impulses to produce an overt response. Penfield suggested that this neuronal action selects data from sensory input and formulates the pattern, an action that is an accompaniment of consciousness and thought. According to Penfield, a person makes a decision when loops reverberate between the diencephalon and the motor cortex. The activity during the decision then produces efferent neural impulses that evoke an overt response (R_L of Fig. 3.3).

In support, Penfield cited the following experiment: A patient with exposed cortex was asked to squeeze his own hand while neuronal activity was recorded along the precentral gyrus of the motor cortex; activity was disturbed only in the hand region of the precentral gyrus. The subject was then told to get ready to clinch his hand at the word "now" but to not actually clinch. When the surgeon said "now" the same disturbance of rhythm occurred at the electrode placement on the hand region of the motor cortex, just as when the hand was actually squeezed. The disturbance was only at that locus, and there was no overt hand movement. Penfield's interpretation was that the word "now" produced a conscious thought for controlling the hand in the way the patient had in mind; hence, nerve impulses were dispatched along a selected path in the brain to that part of the motor gyrus which controlled the hand—this was a controlling message that ascended from the diencephalon. Because the patient did not overtly squeeze his hand, there must have been a countermanding inhibitory message. Otherwise, a command message would have followed the disturbance in the precentral gyrus that would have resulted in the overt hand response. This is an instance of the more general phenomenon of why intentions don't always overflow into actions—also relevant is Osgood's interesting discussion of this matter in terms of convergent hierarchies (Osgood, personal communication).

Incidentally, Penfield offered as another example of neural events prior to an overt response, an individual overtly repeating *a word stimulus*. In this case, patterned nerve impulses ascend from the central integrating complex to the voice control portion of the motor cortex in both hemispheres. From the cortex, impulses descend, down to the appropriate motor nuclei in the pons and medulla oblongata, and then presumably to the speech musculature where the overt response of speaking the word is made. Penfield's two examples thus offer us some interesting cues about neural activity while "planning," prior to overt responding. These neural events would no doubt have covert responses as antecedents (see Erickson et al., 1970) and consequences and thus be neural components between the (muscular) responses of the behavioral unit of Fig. 3.3.

McGuigan and Pavek (1972) psychophysiologically measured covert behavior prior to overt responding while a subject was making a decision (answering a question silently by thinking yes or no); following the thought, subjects indicated their yes or no response overtly by pressing one of two buttons (left or right). The psychophysiologically recorded events during the decision period are presented in Fig. 9.6. McGuigan and Pavek offered the interpretation that during the thought period, loops that involved the left temporal lobe, the passive arm, the lips, the neck and the eye were simultaneously run off. They interpreted the finding of a covert response in the passive arm prior to that in the active arm as being inhibitor in nature—in effect, the subject had to "tell" themselves *not* to respond overtly in the passive arm, before they could overtly respond in the active arm. Following that processing a motor "command" through the cortical motor area may have activated the responding arm for the overt response. Using a set of very simple tasks (reaction time tasks) McGuigan and Boness (1975) confirmed McGuigan and Pavek's finding of a covert response in the passive arm, a finding that is consonant with the interpretation that the response serves an inhibitory function. McGuigan and Boness also measured covert events intervening between the external stimulus and the overt response and plotted temporal patterns that resembled those of Fig. 9.6.

The events discussed in this section that are anticipatory to overt behavior, are probable determiners of overt responses that no doubt serve important information processing functions. These events intervening between the external stimuli and the overt response are likely components of the loops of Fig. 9.5. During perception, loops I through IV occur, but after external stimulus are perceived there can be considerable additional internal processing. For example, the external stimulus

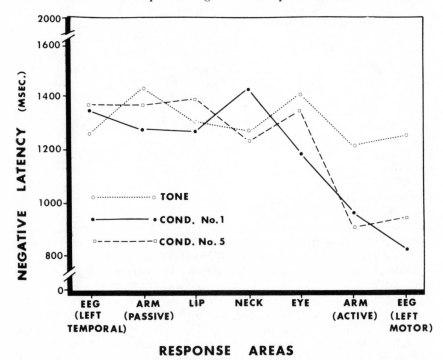

FIG. 9.6   Relative mean latencies of responses identified in various bodily regions. (The higher the data point on the vertical scale, the earlier the response followed stimulus termination.)

may pose an arithmetic problem which, once perceived, entails the continuous running off of the circuits of Fig. 9.5 until a solution is rendered in the form of an overt response (R_L of Fig. 3.3).

However, the circuits II, III, and IV of Fig. 9.5 may be continuously activated even when not set off by an immediate controlling external stimulus (as when "lost in thought")—while external stimuli may influence the circuits, the human organism no doubt has the ability to relatively isolate itself symbolically from the external world for considerable periods of time. It is during such self-imposed periods of sensory isolation that we engage in thought processes, much of which was described by Watson as worthless and not worth the trouble of publicably recording through psychophysiological instrumentation; on the other hand much self-generated internal semantic activity has no doubt been valuable, resulting in great creativity and problem solving (like Archimedes' "eureka" episode).

Environmental stimulation no doubt exerts influence on thought processes, even though the stimuli often are not apparent. Skinner (1957) took up the interesting problem of why a person will emit a verbal response in the absence of the controlling stimulus, e.g., the child who comes to the breakfast table and emits the word "orange" even though no orange is present. One answer is that other stimuli (tablecloths, etc.) have been associated previously with oranges and thus themselves have acquired response evoking properties (a tablecloth may become a discriminative stimulus for the response "orange"). A much more elaborate example of verbal behavior emitted in the apparent absence of a controlling stimulus was Professor Whitehead's challenge to the young behaviorist in 1934 to account for the fact that he (Whitehead) said "No black scorpion is falling upon this table." Skinner's (1957) answer, somewhat delayed, appears in *A Personal Epilog* (1957).

NEUROMUSCULAR EVENTS AND LOOP TIMES

We have identified a number of reactions that occur at various locations throughout the body and have hypothesized that they are components of circuits like those of Fig. 9.5. We have, furthermore, suggested a temporal order for these various neuromuscular events, sequentially labeled by the symbols I, II, III, and IV. The circuits I, II, III, and IV, however, have been merely hypothesized to serve the linguistic functions we have specified. Furthermore, the empirical findings employed to sketch out such circuits were almost exclusively lacking in temporal information—while the previously cited data indicated that such circuits quite possibly do exist, they do not show that they actually perform such linguistic processing functions in the hypothesized temporal sequence. We are, in fact, far from the highly inventive physiological experimentation that would allow precise specification of such internal information processing circuits with confidence. One step toward that goal is to bring to bear relevant temporal data that already do exist—while such a step still will not answer the question as to whether or not those circuits function linguistically, such temporal data could at least indicate which circuits are and are not possible.

The approach that we propose will be based on a rather limited sample of data relevant to the duration of and temporal relationships among the events specified in Fig. 9.5. If this limited effort helps to establish some empirical guidelines and constraints for our information processing model, a more extensive effort could be considered. Hopefully, this approach will eventually increase the probability of making successful indirect inferences (but nothing more than that) about actual linguistic neuromuscular circuits. However, even the relatively small sample of data that we consider are complex and difficult to relate precisely to the model of Fig. 9.5. The results of our efforts on this topic might therefore be diligently studied in the appendix to this chapter by the especially interested reader. The reader less interested in such psychophysiological detail might review Fig. 9.7 more generally, considering primarily the principle of relating such temporal information to the circuits of Fig. 9.5, and remembering that such extremely rapidly firing circuits as we have hypothesized apparently *are* physical possibilities.

The estimates, based on simple reaction times discussed in the appendix to this chapter, suggest an approximate temporal interval of some 100 msec between an external stimulus and an overt response for the simplest input-output situations. It is within some such interval that at least some of the internal information processing circuits of Fig. 9.5 might function and result in one of the three classes of response circuits specified in Fig. 9.4.

The attempt made in Fig. 9.7 and in the appendix to this chapter to specify some of the temporal values for components of our hypothetical neuromuscular circuits led us to first calculate that minimal value of approximately 100 msec for processing of an external stimulus to an overt response unit. Apparently circuits of the nature discussed on page 390 under references 8, 9, and 10 of Table 9.3 (in which some 80 msec are consumed between the arm to sensory-motor cortex to ventral root to arm) could function within this time period, perhaps for sensory integration as in our circuits Ib'-II. Presumably circuits like our II-IV that serve lexical-semantic functions would reverberate for some additional time; perhaps such ongoing circuit processes are represented in the "Projection, Secondary Association Language Cortex" region of Fig. 9.7 with values for events following stimulus impingement of several hundred milliseconds. However, as we have well recognized it is difficult to do more than establish approximate contraints for a linguistic processing model with this approach. Nevertheless, even these very approximate estimates suggest that the extremely rapid brain-muscle-brain-muscle circuits that we have hypothesized *are* physical possibilities—one must be impressed with the finding, for instance, that stimulation at the tongue produces a contralateral cortical event with only a 4 or 5 msec latency. In short, while we have only been able to illustrate this approach

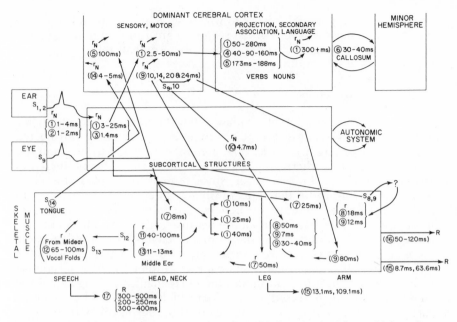

FIG. 9.7 A sample of temporal values of events within hypothesized internal information processing circuits (discussed in the appendix to this chapter).

here, it does appear promising; with considerably more information which is suitably organized, it might be possible to more precisely specify these neuromuscular circuits and their temporal order of activation in internal information processing.

Conditional Linguistic Response Patterns and Coding

We have assumed that in learning a language, some auditory linguistic unit (perhaps an allophone) acquires the stimulus function of evoking a complex bodily reaction. Assuming optimistically that the acquisition of this stimulus-response relationship obeys the laws of conditioning, we shall refer to the stimulus pattern as a conditional (discriminiative) stimulus and to the response pattern as a conditional linguistic response pattern. In this section we consider the question of what it means to ascribe a linguistic function to the conditional covert behavior that occurs during the performance of cognitive tasks.

Earlier, the potential importance of being able to represent the analog speech stream in binary phonemic coding was emphasized and it was noted that many neuromuscular processes are discrete, on-off events, so that, at a molecular level, they too can be represented in binary form. The principal neuromuscular events that are on-off are single nerve impulses and single muscle fiber contractions, both of which obey the

367

all-or-none law. The major issue to which we shall now turn is how the skeletal musculature in the speech region might function in the generation of internal linguistic codes. After that we shall take up nonoral skeletal muscle responding.

COVERT SPEECH RESPONSES

We have cited considerable evidence that the peripheral components of loops IIIa and IIIb in Fig. 9.5 become especially active during the performance of linguistic tasks. The general conclusion throughout the literature has been that "amplitude of covert oral behavior increases during 'thought' tasks." However, since muscle fibers obey the all or none law, it cannot be that muscle fiber responses per se increase in amplitude. Rather, it must be that electromyographical measures of muscle activity increase in amplitude because the muscle fibers are contracting more rapidly and/or the number activated per unit time has increased. Therefore, a more precise statement is that an increase in the *rate* with which oral muscle fibers contract and/or in the total *number* contracting per unit time facilitates the performance of language tasks. In either case, the increased muscle fiber activity increases the excitation rate of the receptors embedded in the muscles, causing an increase in the afferent neural activity fed back from the musculature. This increased neuromuscular activity, we assume, is evoked by external conditional language stimuli, and constitutes a conditional response pattern, as represented by the matrices of Fig. 9.3. It is this conditional muscle responding which in theory facilitates internal information processing by generating a linguistic code that is carried to the brain (by circuit IIIa of Fig. 9.5). Furthermore, the amount of muscle fiber-afferent neural impulse activity should be indicative of the amount of information generated and transmitted. Consider, for example, a person who experiences difficulty in performing some linguistic task, e.g., one who does not adequately comprehend the prose being read. Under such circumstances there is an ("automatic") increase in the amount of speech muscle activity (commonly called "subvocalization") with consequent increases of afferent neural impulses. Hence the individual experiencing a need for a larger amount of internal information generates that increase primarily in the speech muscle and transmits it to the brain, especially to the cortical linguistic regions. The amount of covert speech muscle activity generated should therefore be related to linguistic proficiency, the difficulty of the task, and so on. An accomplished reader or writer would need to generate a minimum amount of verbal information in the oral region (this being sufficient to allow adequate task performance). But a poor reader, or a good reader under distracting conditions, needs to send a greater amount of verbal information, presumably with some redundancy, to the brain (redundancy is often necessary in various avenues of life to achieve understanding, e.g., the effective teacher makes the same point in different ways, and more than once).

The relevant data support the above reasoning (McGuigan, 1973c).

More particularly, previous research has indicated that amplitude of covert oral behavior is inversely related to reading proficiency when proficient vs. unproficient subjects are *selected* for comparison; but amplitude increases when proficiency is *experimentally* increased. Experimentally produced decreases of covert oral behavior possibly reduce reading proficiency. Amplitude of covert oral behavior also increases as textual and environmental demands increase. The general empirical conclusion, then, is that increased covert speech muscle activity is beneficial in the performance of language tasks, and our interpretation has been that such responses are beneficial because they perform a linguistic function, thus justifying the term "covert oral *linguistic* behavior" (McGuigan, 1970a). We now need to consider the kind of linguistic code that might be generated by the skeletal musculature during linguistic behavior. We also need to consider how such an afferently carried code might interact with the brain; that is, how circuit class IIIa functions with circuit IV.

We have seen that linguistic stimuli evoke, by hypothesis, complex patterns of conditional covert oral and non-oral responses, and we have placed emphasis on the oral responses produced by the speech musculature. These conditional response patterns must consist of an enormous number of spatially distributed muscle fibers which at any given instant may be categorized as those in a state of contraction and those that are relaxed (lengthened). To represent the state of the skeletal muscle fiber system, we can employ a response matrix like that to the right of Fig. 9.8. In such a complex three-dimensional matrix, each cubic cell in the matrix could represent one speech muscle fiber. A conditional response pattern can then be represented in a large matrix whose cells, at any instant, are in the state of on or off. Following the principle of Fig. 9.3 a discrete conditional stimulus input would evoke a complex discrete pattern of covert oral and covert non-oral conditional linguistic responses. This binary pattern would be the muscular events at the periphery of loops IIIa and IIIb of Fig. 9.5.

Each speech muscle is represented in the three-dimensional space of Fig. 9.8 such that the a dimension is height, b is depth (into the body), and c is breadth or width (across the body). For instance, the muscles of the lips are systematically represented in terms of motor units, and each motor unit is subdivided into the appropriate number of muscle fibers. For example, the first cube, (a_1, b_1, c_1) is the cell in a three-dimensional space for one particular muscle fiber; the cube a_1, b_1, c_2 represents a spatially adjacent muscle fiber. The state of each muscle fiber at any given time t_1 is represented by /+/if the fiber is in contraction, or by /−/ if it is relaxed; 0 indicates the absence of a muscle fiber at that particular spatial location. Coded afferent volleys are set off from each set of speech muscles (the lips, the tongue, the chin, etc.). The precise nature of these afferent neural impulses is determined by the complex state of the muscle fibers in the set of three dimensional matrices, e.g., by the entire set of the three values /+/, 0, and /−/.

Let me offer a brief summary and preview of the notions being de-

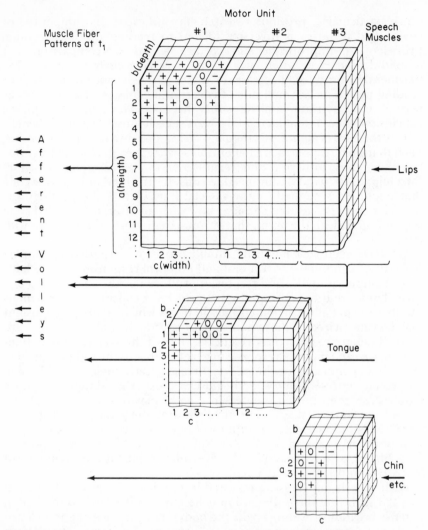

FIG. 9.8 Muscle fiber patterns and resultant afferent neural volleys at time t_1.

veloped. External linguistic stimuli become discriminative stimuli that evoke spatially distributed responses in the oral musculature. These responses may be described in binary form as consisting of muscle fibers throughout the entire speech musculature; each fiber may be in an on or off state. Once evoked, a given muscle fiber pattern activates the system of receptors embedded in the muscles and tendons to generate a unique afferent neural impulse volley that is coded for a given allophone, such as $[p_1]$ (recall that an allophone is a concrete instance of an abstract phoneme class). Another similar, afferent neural volley would be coded for another allophone of the same phoneme class that differed in some

370

specifics (e.g., [p₂]). While the two volleys would be produced by two different patterns of muscle fiber contraction, there would be a considerable number of muscle fibers in common on-off states. That is, two such neural volleys would be coded for the same phoneme class because of the commonality of antecedent muscle fiber contractions. But there would be slight differences in their coding because the muscle fiber patterns for the slightly different allophones of the same phoneme class would also slightly differ. In short, differences between neural codings for different allophones are due to slight instantaneous differences in muscle fiber states.

The neural volleys that result from muscular contraction transmit a phonetic code that contains distinctive features and nondistinctive features; the nondistinctive features, in effect, constitute "noise," being events unique for each allophone. The common characteristics of the muscle fiber patterns and the resulting neural impulses produce the coding for distinctive features. That is, the muscle fibers which can only have an on-off function still can generate an unique event (a distinctive feature) within a phonetic code. The unique event (coding) depends on the precise fiber combination that contracts at any instant, and similarly for the resulting on-off neural events of the afferent neural volley.

Once the ascending phonetic code interacts with the linguistic regions of the brain, in some (unknown) sense the appropriate phoneme is perceived ("produced," "restructured," "retrieved"). For instance, if the afferent neural volley is coded for the allophone [p], the distinctive features carried in a neural code may match those distinctive features for the phoneme /p/, producing ("retrieving," or whatever) that phoneme; the nondistinctive features of the afferent volley might in some sense be ignored by such a central processor (though they might not be ignored in another volley since what may be nondistinctive for one phoneme pair may be distinctive for another—the central processor would have to have a property that allows it to identify distinctive vs. nondistinctive features as a function of class of phonetic input, probably making such decisions within a grammatical context).

We have previously concluded that covert oral behavior ("silent speech") occurs in everyone, but is more pronounced in some people, and under certain environmental conditions. When covert oral behavior becomes especially pronounced, there is an "eruption" into "subvocalization"; consequently, external speech stimuli are emitted in the form of slight "whispering" which can be amplified and to some extent understood by a listening experimenter (Gould, 1950; McGuigan, Keller, and Stanton, 1964; McGuigan, 1966b). Such exaggerated covert oral behavior produces additional coding beyond what is normally required, so that semantic processing is facilitated. The additional coding is probably redundant to that which is normally generated. A precise analysis of increased neuromuscular activity might yield a large number of parameters that could function in the generation and transmission of this additional, redundant coding. One could be a spatial system so that different combinations of cells of Fig. 9.8, with considerable overlap, could generate simultaneously two allophones of the same phoneme class, like [p_1], and [p_2]. These two generated afferent volleys could then be transmitted simultaneously, in parallel, to the brain. Or, the heightened covert oral muscle responding when reading prose could be temporally, instead of spatially, redundant. In temporal redundancy, the same muscle fiber patterns for a given allophone contract more than once, in succession, transmitting identical, but successive, volleys to the brain.

If the amount of redundancy produced by subvocalization is *still* insufficient to produce comprehension, the information processor may "break into" overt speech, pronouncing aloud the word or words that are difficult to comprehend; hence, as often happens in everyday life, an individual will overtly repeat what is said or read, adding a further redundant, externally generated auditory signal which impinges on the eardrum (this would be loop IIIc of Fig. 9.4).

We should also not forget that any given oral pattern is also associated with a complex covert nonoral response pattern. Hence, a conditional linguistic stimulus evokes *both* oral and nonoral components. Especially prominent components of nonoral patterns occur in the preferred arm and hand, possibly due to conditioning while learning cursive writing of prose. Other localized conditional muscle patterns may also be evoked, such as heightened behavior in the left wrist during processing of a word like "wristwatch."

The body thus also has information processing redundancy in the sense that an external linguistic stimulus may have several symbolic representations in different parts of the body, so that several oral and nonoral regions may generate coded afferent neural patterns. When the neural volleys reach the language regions of the brain they may activate some kind of representation of the external stimulus (by way of loops IIIa and IIIb to loop IV of Fig. 9.5). In exploring the coding principle further we shall for simplicity continue to consider only the speech musculature.

Complex conditional patterns in the autonomic system must also occur; though we are not considering such responses here, they *have* received considerable attention (e.g., Grings, 1973a, b). Circuits involving the autonomic no doubt add much richness to internal behavior, adding "emotional tone" to linguistic units (certain words evoke "feelings in the pit of the stomach").

To continue with Fig. 9.8, the on-off status of speech muscle fibers constitutes a pattern during speech perception at a given instant, time t_1. By adding a temporal dimension to the matrix, we can represent continuously changing covert response patterns as a function of the changing linguistic input. Such a matrix appears in Fig. 9.9; in the column to the right the various speech muscles are specified, along with fibers of each motor unit. Hence, the first cell in Fig. 9.8, which we labeled as a_1, b_1, c_1 at time t_1 was in an "on" state, as indicated by the /+/ in the first cell of the top row of Fig. 9.9. In the first time column (under t_1) the status of the other muscle fibers of Fig. 9.8 are represented for all of the speech musculature. Columns t_2, t_3, ... t_n indicate the status of the speech musculature at times following t_1. For instance, the first fiber a_1, b_1, c_1 is contracted at time t_1; it is also contracted at time t_2; but is relaxed at time t_3.

To the left of these spatial-temporal matrices, we summarize (under "Coded Muscle Pattern at Times:") the coded status for each muscle fiber in binary arithmetic. Hence, for fiber a_1, b_1, c_1, the spatial-temporal status is specified by "110," and so on. In short, we now have a spatial-temporal matrix which determines the coded afferent impulses, the latter being represented to the far left of Fig. 9.9. Once in this binary form, we are now in a position to treat a code in a powerful fashion, using formal models that have far reaching consequences, such as those employed by Rouvray (1973) and Fienberg (1974).

In short, as the covert linguistic response pattern changes in the ongo-

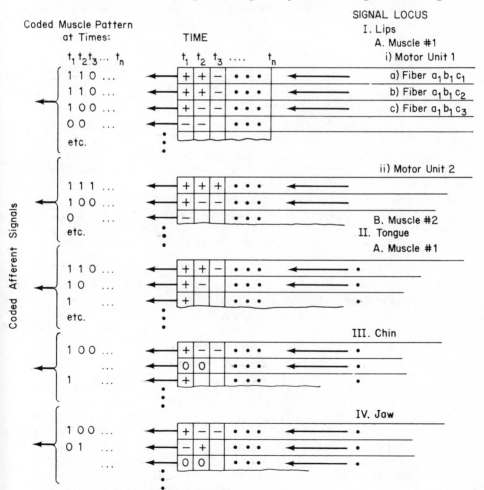

FIG. 9.9 Myoneural patterns as a function of time.

ing generation of a verbal code, Loops IIIa and IIIb of Fig. 9.5 reverberate—the muscle pattern activity is transduced from a spatially represented binary code (that changes as a function of time) into an afferent neural code that ascends to the language regions of the brain.

To briefly emphasize some points: The patterns of neural impulses generated by the continuous firing of muscle fibers ascend from the speech muscle (circuit IIIa) and from the non-speech muscle (circuit IIIb); these volleys are integrated at the thalamic level above the thalamic relay stations (Hassler, 1966), and are also integrated at the thalamic level with impulses descending from the sensory cortex (II). The consequence of this processing and integration is the activation of loop class IV of Fig. 9.5 that ascends to the language regions of the brain.

This general hypothesis, incidentally, would appear to accord with the work of others who have taken totally different points of view from ours. For one, Studdert-Kennedy (1974) proposed processes that convert the neuroacoustic input into neurophonetic representations, and that additional processes transform entities at the neurophonetic level into neurophonemic representations. When there is transfer from the neurophonetic level to the neurophonemic level, external speech is perceived. By our model, the neuroacoustic input (in Studdert-Kennedy's terms) is converted, at least in part, by covert activation of the speech musculature; when the resulting afferent neural volleys, phonetically coded, reach the linguistic and motor regions of the brain, the phonetic code is processed to reproduce the appropriate phonemes "stored" there. Our coding function of oral behavior is also consistent with the finding by Estes (1973) that phonemic encoding of visually presented letters was obtained when vocalization was permitted at input, but phonemic encoding was not present when vocalization was supressed. Similarly, Rubenstein, Lewis, and Rubenstein (1971) concluded that visual word recognition entails phonemic recording through auditory/articulatory processes. Hintzman (1967) held the relevant view that subvocal rehearsal has a recoding function in short-term memory.

Liberman, Cooper, Harris, MacNeilage, and Studdert-Kennedy (1967) suggested that during perception, the listener generates speech to transform auditory stimuli into instructions to the vocal mechanism that give rise to those patterns. The production of sounds is made with different articulatory maneuvers so that the listener makes a natural division of acoustic stimuli into articulatory categories. In perceiving sounds the listener transforms the auditory stimuli to articulatory patterns so that the listener makes sharp discriminations phonemically. For example, if an allophone of the phoneme class /p/ enters the ear, the listener transforms the auditory stimulus to an articulatory category for that phoneme. Such reasoning could well involve covert oral behavior along the general lines of our model, though the authors do not suppose that. They suppose only that there is some link by an unknown abstract mechanism between the perception and the production of speech in regard to those aspects of speech articulation that are phonetically significant (Liberman, personal communication, September 14, 1977). For the most recent comprehensive presentation of this position see Liberman and Studdert-Kennedy (1977).

Jakobson and Halle (1971) speculated about relationships between linguistic and physiological functioning, particularly motor events during speech perception. In particular, they suggested that sonority features might be related to the amount, density, and spread of nervous excitation, while tonality features relate to the location of this excitation; they expected that neural reactions to sound stimuli will eventually supply a differential picture of distinctive features at this level, which would certainly be an impressive accomplishment. At the "psychological" level, which they considered to be the study of speech sounds that illuminate the "perceptual correlates of the diverse distinctive features," the perception of each feature is independent of the other as if separate channels were involved. This conclusion, based on the work of Miller and Nicely (1955), is consistent with our assumption that internal linguistic processing proceeds in "parallel" channels. During perception, listeners correlate the incoming message with a code that is common to themselves and to the speaker, leading Jakobson and Halle to study relationships between motor acoustic and perceptual coding rules. In decoding a message, the listener thus extracts distinctive features from the perceptual data. Jakobson and Halle held that during perception kinesthetic feedback (our circuit IIIa) of the listener plays a role in this decoding process.

A summary and expansion of the events in Fig. 9.9 is presented in Fig. 9.10, with illustrative phonetic coding for the afferent volley of neural impulses. The changing status of the speech muscle is represented in binary form to the right of Fig. 9.10, as a function of time. For instance, the first set of coded muscle fiber patterns, represented at the top of Fig. 9.10 as occurring at times t_1 through t_n (designated Series 1), are from the first column of Fig. 9.9 labeled "Coded Muscle Pattern at Times: t_1." Hence, pattern t_1 is represented in Fig. 9.9 as a column of 1 1 1 0, etc., and that pattern is also depicted behind the t_1 of Fig. 9.10. Similarly, the pattern under the second column of Fig. 9.9, labeled t_2, is 1 1 0 0, etc.; this pattern is represented behind t_2 of Fig. 9.10; and likewise for t_3. This first series of muscle fiber patterns occurring at times t_1 through t_n includes the *entire* speech musculature. That muscle pattern then generates the afferent neural volley that is represented in Fig. 9.10 as being coded (through a transformation represented by the broken line) for the distinctive features 1 through 9 that describe a particular phoneme, as listed in Fig. 9.11. This transformed code (the result of an *exceedingly* complex transformation) carried by the neural volley is coded /−/ for feature 1 (the nonvocalic feature), /+/ for feature 2 (the consonantal feature); /−/ for feature 3 (the diffuse feature), etc. This particular neural coding for features 1 through 9 is for the allophone [p] which matches the coding for the phoneme /p/ (Jakobson and Halle, 1971). In short, in series 1 of Fig. 9.10 the afferent neural impulses transmit the distinctive and nondistinctive features for the allophone [p], and this allophone instance of the phoneme class /p/ is indicated by the nine /−/,

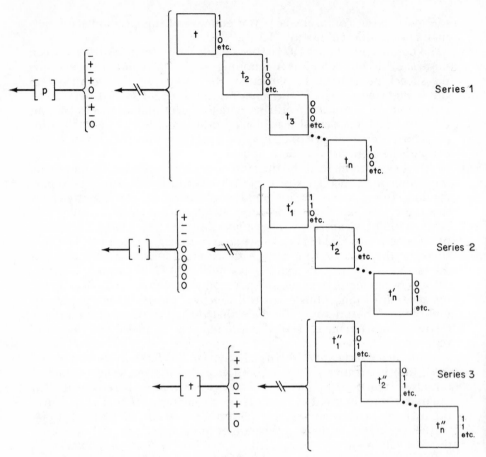

FIG. 9.10 Phonemic coding as a function of temporal-spatial afferent neural patterns.

/+/, and 0 (for nondistinctive features) symbols. This phonetic coding for the allophone [p] is then transmitted to the brain for central processing, whereupon the phoneme /p/ is produced (retrieved, perceived).

The second in the series (Series 2) of muscular states (labeled t_1' through t_n' in Fig. 9.10) generates the afferent neural patterns representing the features /+/, /−/, /−/, /−/, 0, 0, 0, 0, etc.—the neural coding for the allophone [i]. The still later neural volley (series 3) represented by T_1'' through t_n'' represents the neural coding for the allophone [t]. In short, the status of Jakobson and Halle's nine feature oppositions listed in Fig. 9.11 are for the allophones [p], [i], and [t] as specified in the three series of Fig. 9.10. When this coded phonetic volley reaches the language regions of the brain, the phonemes /p/, /i/ and /t/ are successively (?) processed. With the perception and integration of these three phonemes, the word "pit" is "perceived." Let us see how this entire process might work according to this hypothesis.

Nine distinctive features are listed in the left column of Fig. 9.11. As

376

we have noted, at any given instant an acoustic language stimulus may be characterized, as in column I, by the members of the oppositions specified by the binary chain of pluses and minuses (as well as by the blanks). To distinguish /p/ from, say, /b/, number 7 is the critical feature. We emphasize this distinction by placing feature 7 toward the bottom of Fig. 9.11. That is, by including the "tense" feature (/+/), the stimulus is coded as a member of the class /p/; however, should opposition 7 be the "lax" feature (/−/), the stimulus would be coded as an instance of the phoneme /b/.

The acoustic stimulus that impinges on a person then evokes a speech muscle pattern (through circuits Ib and/or IIIa of Fig. 9.5) as indicated in column II of Fig. 9.11. In the example of perceiving the phoneme /p/, the acoustic stimulus evokes the topmost pattern of muscle fiber contraction indicated as series 1 in Fig. 9.10 at the times "$t_1, t_2 \ldots t_n$" for the allophone [p]. While there is a complex transformation between the binary chain for the acoustic stimulus (column I) and the binary chain that represents the speech muscle response pattern (column II), for simplicity shall we assume constant, nontransformed feature relationships between these and the remaining columns of Fig. 9.11.

Once the acoustic stimuli (column I) evoke a pattern of speech muscle fiber contraction (column II), there results a unique afferent neural volley characterized in column III of Fig. 9.11. This volley represents the coding in Fig. 9.8 carried by the loop class IIIa that activates loop class IV. The coded afferent volley in this example then produces perception of ("retrieves") a phoneme (like /p/) in the central processing represented by column IV; perhaps the phoneme is a central motor program, as suggested by Osgood (personal communication).

The issue of the unit of linguistic perception is a complex one, but as

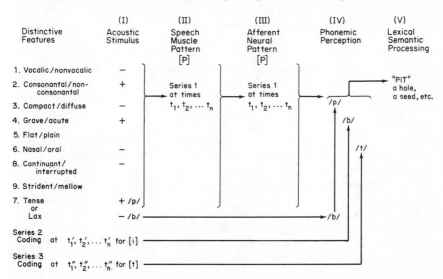

FIG. 9.11 Coding processes within the listener that lead to word perception.

we noted earlier the principles developed here probably do not depend on the outcome of the issue. It is possible that the perceptual unit is the phoneme, following which words are perceived. This possibility is represented in column IV as the process by which the internal phonetic stimuli from the speech musculature evoke the phoneme /p/. The remainder of some specifiable acoustic language unit, like a word, may then be similarly processed with additional afferent volleys arriving in the brain almost simultaneously with that for [p]—in this example, the phonetic neural stimuli that evoke the phoneme /p/ are followed by the neural volleys that evoke the phonemes /i/ and /t/. As represented at the bottom of Fig. 9.11, when the Series 2 and Series 3 neural volleys coded for [i] and [t] follow [p], the word "pit" is evoked, perhaps from a lexical store; lexical and semantic processing is represented in column V of Fig. 9.11. Had, however, the "lax" member of opposition 7 been a component of the external language stimulus (in place of the "tense" member) the phoneme /b/ instead of /p/ would have been perceived. "Perception" of /b/ when followed by /i/ and /t/ would produce the word "bit" instead of "pit" from a lexical store.

How a word (like "pit") is processed is, of course, an enormously complex matter (and a subject of lively controversy). In some way during processing, the units of a word must be integrated, following which a representation of the word is evoked so that the word is recognized and meanings are associated with it (e.g., for "pit," the listener thinks of a depression in the ground, or whatever). This is the process that Penfield (1969) called "translation" in which "ideas" occur. In column 5 of Fig. 9.11 we merely note this semantic and lexical processing. It is certain, however, that the meaning of a perceived word within a sentence is not specified unambiguously when in isolation—the meaning of a word also depends upon context. In this instance "pit" could refer to a depression in the ground; or if the sentence concerns fruit, the listener would interpret a meaning related to seed; a member of a commodity exchange may interpret it as a locus for selling wheat, or a bettor as an opportunity to "pit" one horse against another, etc. Perhaps words and their units are partially processed, and then held in some kind of short-term memory until a grammatical and semantic context is formed, thus allowing a final decision as to which of several meanings each word in a sentence will take. By thus involving words and their meanings with short-term memory, we can consider possible interactions between central storage system and receptor processes. In this context Averback and Coriell (1961) related receptor processes to short term memory; perhaps such a central-receptor memory relationship is a result of activation of a circuit like loop Ia in Fig. 9.5.

We shall conclude with a summary of our development of the phonemic processing that leads to the perception of a word as we have developed it in this chapter. When a stimulus impinges, it is transduced and transmitted so that eventually a verbal code is generated with the intimate involvement of the skeletal musculature. This neuromuscular processing results in phonetic coding that is neurally transmitted from the speech muscles to the central nervous system; arrival of the afferent neural volleys leads to the central evocation of phonemes, and to lexical and semantic processing. This is circuit class IIIa interacting with circuit class IV of Fig. 9.5.

We thus make progress toward the solution of the difficult problem of how centrally stored phonemes are evoked with the hypothesis that the covert muscle activity generated during silent linguistic processing produces a phonetic neuromuscular code that is centrally processed to evoke phonemes from central storage—a word (in this example, "pit") is thus perceived and interpreted.[3] There is then efferent flow back to the musculature that involves a meaning reaction (r_M). According to Osgood (cf. Osgood and McGuigan, 1973; Osgood and Hoosain, 1974) r_M is represented as a complex code of *semantic features* (componential mediator components, $\pm r_{m_1} M \pm r_{mn}$) which initiates complex, continuing muscle-brain-muscle-brain circuit reverberation. However, in Osgood's view, although mediator components (r_m) and complexes (r_M) have their origins in overt behavior in the history of the organism, in contemporary mature language performers they are purely central mediation processes, not requiring motor activation and feedback.

I should mention here that part of the collaborative argument between Osgood and McGuigan (e.g., 1973) stems from Osgood's model as presented in Osgood and Hoosain (1974, our Fig. 2.4). That figure is modified in Fig. 9.12 to include peripheral levels. This modification seems reasonable to Osgood (personal communication), but, of course, it does not commit him to any modified aspects of his theory. First, in the case of linguistic processing of words, circuit 1 is represented from the muscle back to the sensory projection level (Osgood calls this "long-loop feedback") through the sensory integration level directly to the motor integration level, where phonemic perception (retrieval, or whatever) occurs. Finally circuit 1 continues into the representational level for semantic processing by means of the feedback circuit in the original Osgood and Hoosain diagram. The other possible circuits are sufficiently numerous that it would not be possible to detail them here. Merely for illustration we represent one alternative in which there might be no muscle involvement and in which there would be a direct circuit between the sensory integration level to the motor integration level for phonemic perception prior to activation of the representation level; this is represented by the added circuit II in Fig. 9.12. In any event, once phonemes are restructured there is activation of the appropriate representational processes, as indicated by Osgood's feedback circuits. The foregoing theoretical integration of skeletal muscle coding processes

---

[3] Hebb's (1949) cell assemblies would thus be evoked by the phonetic code ascending by circuit IIIa (together with other central and peripheral antecedents), leading to word perception. The phonetic coding from IIIa would, in Osgood's (1957b) system, evoke phonemes represented within the motor and nervous system that function at Osgood's program ($\overline{r}\text{-}\overline{r}$) level.

LEVEL

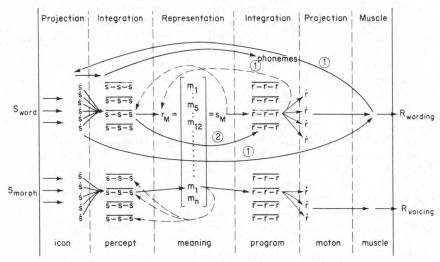

FIG. 9.12 A modification of Osgood's semantic processing model to include linguistic functioning of the skeletal musculature.

with what is probably the most sophisticated model of semantic processing available today is about as far as we can progress at this time in explaining language processes at a psychophysiological level. Consequences of this integrated model should be explored and related to various neurophysiological models. In particular several classes of neuromuscular loops involved in semantic information processing include: loops between brain and receptors, between brain and effectors, and intracerebral circuits. The latter include circuits between cortex and subcortical regions as well as complex transcortical loops. The classical extreme centralist position considers intercerebral loops as the only significant type. Thus the extreme centralist (Donovan's Brain) model fits as one part of a more comprehensive overall theoretical framework, but by itself is probably inadequate to account for cognitive phenomena. The proposed modification of Osgood's models might provide the requisite increase in generality.

It is important to emphasize that the phonetic code generated by the speech muscles, while not itself meaningful, is responsible for making differences in meaning. For instance, if one perceives the letter D, followed by the letters AD, the tongue is primarily responsible for generating an afferent neural volley phonetically coded for [D], and "DAD" is perceived. Had "M" been sensed, however, the lips would be the primary agent for generating a phonetic coding for [M] which, when followed by AD, leads to the perception of "MAD." In this way the speech muscle can be responsible for semantic differences.

We have considered events during linguistic perception in which the impinging linguistic stimulus unit is recognized (by evocation from a lexical store) and interpreted (through semantic processes). Once a meaning reaction is evoked it may then produce mediating stimulation that leads to additional verbal units in complexly concatenated linguistic chains. These concatenated response sequences include associations, perhaps like the implicit associative responses discussed by Bousfield, Whitmarsh, and Danick (1958) and Underwood (1965). The interactions among such implicit associative reactions must be *exceedingly* complex,[4] and we again emphasize that internal information processing must proceeed simultaneously in a number of "channels," and not according to a straw man single channel chaining model.

We must conclude by emphasizing that our attempts to represent these extremely complex, reverberating neuromuscular events in discrete form and in diagrams is highly artificial and a great oversimplification. The most complex neuromuscular diagrams of the human mind that we could offer would still fall far short of an adequate account of internal language processing, probably the most complex phenomenon in nature.

COVERT NONORAL LINGUISTIC PROCESSING

The great versatility of verbal symbolism has led us to recognize a priority for linguistic thought involving, principally, the speech musculature and the linguistic regions of the brain (Chapter 6). But we have also hypothesized that nonoral behavior can serve linguistic functions (Chapter 7).

Linguistic (Verbal) Processing. We noted previously that during linguistic processing in which there is cognitive activity (McGuigan, 1970a) both oral and nonoral responses interact in some complex but supportive fashion (see Fig. 3.3). When one imagines an act involving the legs, for example, one covertly responds symbolically in the oral region and almost simtulaneously responds with the nonoral skeletal musculature involving contractions of muscles in the legs. The oral and nonoral responses then interact in directing information to the linguistic regions of the brain. And there also follows an emotional component to thoughts through circuits that engage the autonomic system.

Granting that the nonoral skeletal musculature has a linguistic capacity, we also tentatively assumed that, like the speech musculature, it functions discriminatively in the generation and transmission of verbal coding. However, since the speech musculature is physiologically more capable of precise discriminative reactions than is the nonoral skeletal musculature (with the exception of that in the eyes and the middle ears) the latter cannot function *as* discriminatively. Nevertheless, language *is* processed, at least to some extent, nonorally, often quite efficiently and in great detail, and there probably is some kind of discriminative relationship between linguistic category and class of nonoral responding. In Chapter 7 we hypothesized two kinds of such codes: first, a nonoral

---

[4] Though nothing approaching the complexities of understanding and creating *novel* sentences, which we do most of the time.

linguistic code, the nature of which is dependent upon the individual's verbal learning experiences; and second, a nonlinguistic code which has developed as a result of conditioning to various stimulus objects and events. This distinction was based on the difference between learning *symbols* vs. learning *referents*. The linguistic code generated and transmitted by the nonoral skeletal musculature was hypothesized to be an allographic code in which allograms (instances of a grapheme class) are generated by the activation of patterns of nonoral skeletal musculature. The resulting afferent neural impulses then carry the allographic code, as the speech musculature generates and transmits a phonetic code. The allographic codes are transmitted from circuit class IIIb of Fig. 9.5 to the linguistic regions of the brain by circuit class IV. In this way, then, we can have parallel linguistic information processing involving the speech muscle and the nonspeech muscle. According to this view, then, when one thinks "bicycle riding," for example, one covertly says the words (as suggested by EMG speech muscle records), covertly writes the words (as suggested by increased EMG in the preferred arm), and also responds elsewhere in the body (particularly the legs in this instance). We shall now mention the second kind of code generated by the nonoral skeletal muscle.

Nonlinguistic (Nonverbal) Processing. The hypothesized nonlinguistic coding generated by the nonoral skeletal muscles involves a more primitive kind of symbolism than that for language, which also functions at the subhuman level. With "referent coding," in responding to a given stimulus object, we generate a coded afferent neural volley by reinstating the conditional response pattern. In short, the nonoral skeletal musculature generates verbal (allographic) codes that function through circuits IIIb of Fig. 9.5. Perhaps additional circuits (IIIc) would also function directly between the nonoral skeletal musculature and the minor hemisphere for the nonverbal referent level code.

VERBAL AND NONVERBAL THOUGHT

Since the circuit from the midbrain to the cortical speech areas, which we designated as loop IV in Fig. 9.5, functions to transmit verbal codes for linguistic processing, this circuit must be intimately involved in "verbal thought." Our priority for verbal thought processes does not deny the existence of so called nonverbal mental processes. Some circuits in Fig. 9.5 would also function for nonverbal processes, as in the case of the ear which receives both linguistic and non-linguistic stimuli; but there are probably other circuits that function uniquely for non-linguistic processing (as for music). Perhaps some of the non-oral musculature would serve a major function in non-verbal thought; and we know that the minor cerebral hemisphere is implicated in non-verbal thought (cf. Davis and Schmit, 1973; Nebes, 1974; and Sperry, 1973).

Verbal and nonverbal mental processes cannot conceivably function independently, and the interelationships must be exceedingly complex. To the extent to which verbal and nonverbal processing occur respectively in the two hemispheres, the corpus callosum would be a primary neurophysiological mechanism for relating the two kinds of thought. Such an intercerebral circuit would be sufficiently complex to relate verbal and non-verbal processes, and could function sufficiently rapidly—Filbey and Gazzaniga (1969) estimated transmission time across the corpus callosum to be in the neighborhood of 30-40 ms. On the basis of reaction times for making "same vs. different" decisions on visual stimuli presented to one or both of the cerebral hemispheres, Davis and Schmit (1973) discussed some fascinating possibilities for interaction of visual and verbal processing systems. For one, they inferred that the right hemisphere can compare and analyze signals only on the basis of visual information, but the left can function both visually and verbally.

Soviet psychologists have considered the relationship between verbal and nonverbal thought in terms of the first (visual, nonverbal) signal system and the second (verbal) signal system. Sokolov (1972), for instance, following Pavlov, held that proprioceptive speech impulses form the basal component of the second signal system. Sokolov (1972) pointed out that the articulation of words is at the same time a motor speech process and auditory process.

> . . . The presence of a constant coupling and interaction on the part of the motor speech and speech-auditory analyzers permits us to assert that every kind of speech kinesthesis is "wired for sound," i.e., linked with auditory speech stimuli, whereas auditory (and, in reading, visual as well) perception of words is linked with speech kinesthesis. When speech movements are inhibited, residual kinesthetic impulses are capable, therefore, of activating verbal connections in the auditory analyzer despite their weak intensity, compensating thereby for inhibited speech movements (p. 153).

Furthermore, these neural impulses that arise from the speech musculature function to relate the two signal systems. Following our discussion above, it may be that the second signal system has primary location in the dominant hemisphere, that the first signal system has primary locus in the minor hemisphere, and that afferent neural impulses from the speech musculature relate the two signal systems by initiating impulses that cross the callosum.

Penfield's (1969) work is also relevant to these considerations. For instance, Penfield reported a connection between the pulvinar thalamus and Wernicke's area. A lesion in Wernicke's area produces aphasia, but if the lesion is in the upper brain stem, the effect is more pronounced in that it produces unconsciousness (thanks to William Feindel for pointing that out to me). There is a similar connection between the thalamus and the cortex in the minor hemisphere; a lesion in this circuit produces loss of perception of space relationships; Penfield concluded that there are two cortical-thalamic mechanisms, one in each hemisphere: the circuit in the dominant hemisphere serves a speech function while that in the minor hemisphere has a (nonverbal) spatial orientation function. When activated (from the diencephalon) these two circuits consitute "the neurophysiological mechanisms that form the *physical basis of thought*" (Penfield, 1969, p. 147).

Paivio's (1971) postulation of two independent coding systems involves a distinction similar to that between verbal and non-verbal thought: his nonverbal system is based on imagery, and his verbal system is based on acoustic storage. There are, though, some data not consonant with Paivio's distinction, e.g., Runquist and Blackmore (1973) found no evidence to clearly support the notion of two coding systems in which the memory codes do not interact between the systems. And, Nelson and Brooks (1973) failed to find differential effects of phonemic similarity on image-coded and non-image-coded words. While there may be different coding systems, they may not be independent but rather, complexly interacting as we suggested above.

Steven and House (1972) have summarized results of dichotic experiments that have relevance for verbal as opposed to nonverbal thought. The data indicate that the left temporal lobe plays a greater part in speech perception than does the right temporal lobe, whereas the opposite is true for nonspeech stimuli. Furthermore, isolated steady state vowels apparently function between these two extremes. Osgood (in press) concluded that there is a cognitive system that is shared by cognitions set up via both "perceptual" (i.e., non-linguistic) and linguistic channels and in which the two types of cognitions interact. This cognitive system is a deeper mental grammar than that characterized by the linguistic grammar. He then concluded that the purely linguistic construct, and rules of the competence grammar inferred from the intuitions of linguists about sentences, could not possibly be an adequate (sufficient) representation of the deeper mental grammar.

In conclusion, there seems to be sufficient reason to postulate separate concepts for what we loosely call verbal and nonverbal thought and to study their interelationships. Two such concepts would be based on the two signal systems (Pavlov, Sokolov, etc.), on results from split brain preparations (e.g., Sperry, 1973), on the electrical stimulation and clinical work of Penfield, on Paivio's (1971) research, on dichotic experiments (Stevens and House, 1972), and on Osgood's (1957b) theoretical position.

Summary and Conclusion

During cognitive acts the complex muscle response patterns include (1) those speech muscle components that function in the generation of a phonetic code; (2) those nonoral skeletal muscle components that function in the generation of an allographic code; (3) those nonoral skeletal muscle components that function in a nonlinguistic referent code; and (4) circuits involving the autonomic system for adding emotional tone

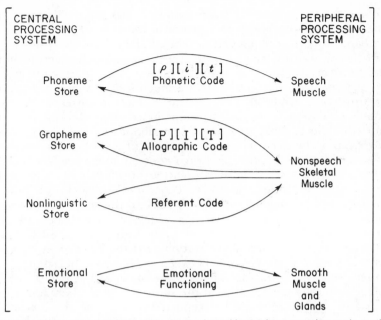

FIG. 9.13 Peripheral-central linguistic processing with resultant meaning and emotional reactions.

(Fig. 9.13). In conjunction these various volleys are transmitted to their appropriate regions of the brain (the verbal coding to the linguistic regions for lexical-semantic processing, the nonverbal coding to other regions of the brain for nonlinguistic processing).

Appendix

To establish perspective for the temporal problem on page 366, consider the time required for running off a total S-R unit, using as a simplification values for simple (as opposed to choice) reaction time. Reaction time estimates (when the stimulus is a light and the overt response is such as a key press) vary between 170 msec and 260 msec (Bartlett, 1963; McGuigan and Boness, 1975; Teichner and Krebs, 1974a; and Woodworth and Schlosberg, 1954). Numerous variables affect reaction time and thus help to account for these differences (Woodworth and Schlosberg, 1954), though one classically neglected variable that is immediately relevant here concerns variations in operational definitions of "the overt response." With different criteria of the overt response, we are forced to question the concept of a standard temporal value of *the* reaction time to light, as classically reported in our textbooks. For instance, when McGuigan and Boness (1975) electromyographically measured an overt response, they ascertained that the overt response actually started at about 185 msec following stimulus onset, while the value for the actual closing of the microswitch was about 225 msec. That is, the more sensitive electromyographical measure of the *onset* of the overt behavior provides a reaction time of about 40 msec, prior to the switch closing measure. Hence if the mechanism for the overt response could be a very sensitive microswitch or a slow reacting, cumbersome piece of apparatus that would yield a much longer value, a degree of arbitrariness is introduced into the time values measured in this way. Bartlett's (1963) work makes this point more incisively—the overt response that he studied commenced at about 101 msec when electromyographically measured; but by means of a sensitive strain gauge Bartlett ascertained that the key switch *started* to move at approximately 125 msec and that the key itself reacted at about 175 msec; hence perhaps 50 msec of the subject's "reaction time" was artifactual, due to the mechanical lag of the key, and 75 msec of the classically measured reaction time is apparently artifactually due to failure to measure reaction time from the onset of the (EMG) muscle response itself.

"Reaction time" is even more complicated than indicated here, for there is a sizeable period of time between the onset of the action potential that occurs with muscle membrane depolarization (which is electromyographically measured) and the start of muscle fiber contraction, e.g., Gatev and Ivanov (1972) reported values for this excitation-contraction latency of around 8 to 13 ms. Furthermore, in the case of light, while the stimulus impinges on the receptor essentially instantaneously, a measure of auditory reaction time is artifactually delayed—with sound traveling approximately 1100 feet per second, a stimulus several feet away from the subject would take perhaps 3 msec from stimulus onset to impinge on the eardrum.

Another important consideration is that the motor period (the time from the onset of the covert response to the onset of the overt response) depends on the muscle group employed for making the overt response (cf. Weiss, 1965). Variations in motor periods can be illustrated by noting that the durations reported by McGuigan and Boness (1975) using a sidewise finger movement were approximately 80 msec and 100 msec for simple and choice reaction time respectively. In contrast, Botwinick and Thompson (1966) and Hilden (1937) reported motor periods of approximately 50 to 60 msec using a fingerlift response in a simple reaction time situation; Hathaway (1935) reported values ranging between 60 to 120 msec for a forearm response; Barlett (1963) measured a motor period of about 50 to 60 msec for the hand. With respect to a voice response three estimates of the time by which covert (EMG) onset in speech muscles occurred prior to the audible speech sound were (1) 300 to 500 msec by Faaborg-Anderson and Edfeldt (1958), (2) approximately 200 to 250 msec by Ertl and Schafer (1967a), and (3) from 300 to 400 msec by Hirano and Ohala (1969).

One valuable conclusion for information processing research, then, is that we should specify events within the interval from stimulus onset to *start* of the electromyographically measured overt response. And it *is* important that we accurately measure reaction time since these data form the bases of inferences about events intervening between external stimuli and overt responses (e.g., Erickson, Pollack, and Montague, 1970; E. Smith, 1968; Teichner and Krebs, 1974a, b). More generally, classical reaction time measures which included the apparatus processing time of voice keys, switches, and the like should be discarded and replaced by the more accurate values that can be obtained through electromyography. The implication of this conclusion is that the commonly held textbook concept of a standard reaction time as general over many experimental conditions and essentially constant for any given modality is a myth.

Our initial guidelines thus suggest an approximate temporal interval of some 100 msec between the external stimulus and the overt response for the simplest input-output situations; it is during some such interval that at least some of the internal information processing circuits of Fig. 9.5 might function, eventuating in one or more of the three classes of response circuits specified in Fig. 9.4. Of course, many circuits are still "looping" *after* this simple response is made.

In attempting to temporally specify events between the external stimulus and the overt response, we can rely on several kinds of studies. For one, there are studies of internal events immediately following onset of the external stimulus (prior to the overt response), such as evoked brain potentials. We can also use various "internal reaction time measures" in which a stimulus was applied at a point within some internal system and consequent reactions in other regions within the body were measured prior to an overt response. Similarly, there are studies in which covert events immediately prior to the overt response have been studied. By integrating the results of such classes of studies we may be able to, in a sense, put together some of the pieces of the "internal information processing jig saw puzzle" so that we can make sensible inferences about these very rapid, complex, interacting, events that occur between external stimuli and overt responses. Continued accumulation and integration of such temporal information might eventually allow us to specify with some precision complex classes of circuits like those of Fig. 9.5.

Figure 9.7 includes a sample of temporal values for potential circuit components. We note that input from both the ear and the eye enter subcortical regions that include the thalamus, brainstem, midbrain, etc. These afferent neural impulses are then transmitted downward to the oral and nonoral skeletal musculature (represented at the bottom of Fig. 9.7) and simultaneously "upward" to the sensory and motor cortex of the dominant cerebral hemisphere (represented at the top of Fig. 9.7. Later, various other cortical regions (the projection areas, secondary cortex, association areas, and especially the language regions) become involved in the processing. At the upper right of Fig. 9.7 intercerebral transmission is indicated through the corpus callosum; ascending neural impulses from the thalamic level are also transmitted directly to the minor

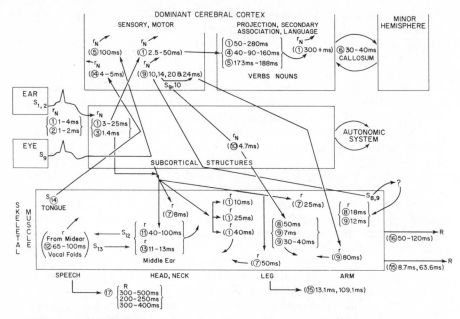

FIG. 9.7 A sample of temporal values of events within hypothesized internal information processing circuits (discussed in the appendix to this chapter).

hemisphere. Additionally, complex, but slow, circuits between the central nervous system and the autonomic nervous systems are represented to the right of Fig. 9.7; these circuits are of great behavioral importance, but are excluded from detailed consideration here. Finally, when the skeletal musculature is sufficiently contracted, overt responses result, as indicated by the Rs to the right of the skeletal muscle representation at the bottom of Fig. 9.7. We now turn to a sample of time values for the various events hypothesized as circuit components.

The initial event in Fig. 9.7 is receptor processing. However, we cannot offer a unitary, constant estimate of receptor processing time since this event is a complex of a number of subprocesses and also a function of a number of variables. [One subprocess in the ear for example is the cochlear microphonic wave which takes about 3 msec to traverse the length of the human cochlea (Goldstein, 1968).]

Total receptor processing time for the ear is shorter than for the eye. Chapman (1961, 1962) held light flashes constant at 500 mμ and a duration of 100 msec, while recording with microelectrodes inserted into the retina of the intact bullfrog. He reported latencies of the first spike varying in the neighborhood of 60 to over 800 msec. He concluded that measures of frequency and number of spikes recorded at the eye may be good indices of the neural messages which reach higher centers (Chapman, 1961). Because of the difficulty (or impossibility) of specifying a

388

standard value for receptor processing time, this first processing event is not quantitatively represented in Fig. 9.7.

H. Davis' (1973) summary of latencies for various auditory evoked potentials has some overall organizational value for us. Evidently realizing the above stated difficulty about specifying receptor processing time, Davis reported events measured temporally following the cochlear microphonic. He reported that the first neural reaction after the external stimulus is processed in the ear has a latency of 1 to 4 msec. This initial neural event is depicted in Fig. 9.7 beneath the term "nerve impulse" and is identified as being from our first reference (Davis) by means of the reference symbol ① ; the event that initiates this neural reaction in the ear is identified by S_1 (S is for stimulus and the subscript "1" relates the stimulus to the neural reaction time ① by means of reference ① , viz., Davis). The recorded event is specified as a *neural* reaction in the auditory nerve by the symbol r_N. A listing of all of the references to be considered here is offered in Table 9.3, with the references completely given in the Reference section.

The second time given below "nerve impulse" is identified by the symbol ② referring to the work of Amadeo and Shagass (1973) who measured an evoked potential over the sensory cortex at approximately 1 to 2 msec following stimulus impingement. They reasoned that this was too fast to actually be a cortical event and that it was possibly from the auditory nerve. Hence, this event appears in Fig. 9.7 as an extremely rapid potential following stimulus impingement (the stimulus is specified as the subscript 2 in $S_{1,2}$ within the ear). A similar phenomenon was recorded by Hasselt (1972) as a short latency visual evoked potential from the auricle and mastoid process with a latency of 10 msec (3 msec longer than that of the ERG wave), which he thought originated from the optic nerve. Next in time following the auditory nerve event are evoked potentials from the brainstem and midbrain—H. Davis (1973) stated that reactions from the cochlear nucleus to the medial geniculate body can be grouped together, and occupy a time zone of about 3 to 25 msec (after the cochlear microphonic). Since the Davis reference for this event is the same as before, we also refer to this subcortical event by ① . Below that for Davis is reference ③ in which Jewett, Romano, and Williston (1970) reported widely distributed potentials from the scalp with an initial peak latency as short as 1.4 msec. They interpreted these potentials as being generated in brainstem auditory structures. Perhaps these occur because external auditory stimuli may be transduced and transmitted through the body prior to the tympanic membrane (cf. Tomatis, 1970). We shall also note later that Bickford, Jacobson, and Cody (1964) reported a muscle response to an auditory stimulus with a latency as short as 8 ms. Such data make it clear that these neuromuscular circuits function with great rapidity, far more rapidly than the relatively slow time values of about 60 ms on which Lashley (1951) based some of his reasoning about high speed serial order behavior. They also indicate some apparent contradictions.

TABLE 9.3   Citations for Time Values in Fig. 9.7. r$_N$ in Fig. 9.7 Refers to a Neural Reaction, While r Is a Skeletal Muscle Response.

① Davis (1973
② Amadeo and Shagass (1973)
③ Jewett, Romano, and Williston (1970)
④ Morell and Salamy (1971)
⑤ Teyler, Roemer, Harrison, and Thompson (1973)
⑥ Filbey and Gazzaniga (1969)
⑦ Bickford, Jacobson, and Cody (1964)
⑧ Hammond (1955)
⑨ Evarts (1966, 1973)
⑩ Bernhard, Bohm, and Petersen (1953)
⑪ Goldstein (1968)
⑫ Shearer and Simmons (1965)
⑬ McCall and Rabuzzi (1973)
⑭ Bowman and Combs (1969)
⑮ Gatev and Ivanov (1972)
⑯ Bartlett (1963)
   Botwinick and Thompson (1966)
   Hathaway (1935)
   Hilden (1937)
⑰ Ertl and Schafer (1967a)
   Faaborg-Anderson and Edfelt (1958)
   Hirano and Ohala (1968)

Each neural and muscular event in Fig. 9.7 obviously does not cease at that point; rather, each is but one component of a complex neuromuscular circuit with additional consequences. This continuous nature of each event is, in each case, represented by an ongoing arrow.

Most interestingly for us, Davis discussed "sonomotor" muscle responses that occur with a latency between 10 and 50 msec. Sonomotor muscle responses are reactions to acoustic stimuli that are especially prominent when recorded at the inion, over the temporalis, or the post-auricular muscle. Davis added that "the response may be a reproducible sequence of waves with peaks separated by about 15 msec" (1973, pp. 466–67). These findings suggest central-peripheral loops such as we have indicated in the head-neck muscle region of Fig. 9.7 by the reference symbol ① , for Davis (1973), at 15 msec intervals, viz., at 10 msec, 25 msec, and 40 msec. Davis added: "The presence of myogenic responses, if consistent, is the valid sign of activity in the acoustic centers and reflex pathways of the brainstem . . ." (p. 467).

Following the brainstem and midbrain potentials of 3-25 msec, we represent in the sensory motor cortex (by the Davis symbol ①), fast vertex potentials with latencies of 25 to 50 msec; for simplicity, this event class is indicated only in the dominant hemisphere of Fig. 9.7.

The next temporal event reported by Davis is the class of slow vertex potentials (N_{100}-P_{200}-N_{280}) that constitute a complex generated by the primary project areas and in the surrounding secondary association areas. This complex is indicated as issuing from the 25 to 50 msec class of events in the sensory and motor cortex running to the projection, etc. areas; it is specified by the time region 50-280 msec in the upper middle representation of the cortex. Still later than the 50-280 msec events are reactions (P_{300}) diffuse in origin that occur at 300 msec or greater latency.

Morrell and Salamy (1971) reported events with latencies similar to those of Davis' 50-280 msec cortical events, and these are represented below ① in the projection (etc.) areas by ④ ; in particular, they measured the onset of a negative wave that was especially prominent in the left temporoparietal region with a latency of about 40 to 50 msec. This wave reached a maximum at about 90 msec after signal onset, following which there was a positive going event that peaked at about 160 msec.

Also within the general time interval of Davis' 50-280 msec were some interesting values reported by Teyler, Roemer, Harrison, and Thompson (1973), as indicated by their reference symbol ⑤ . They found that auditory linguistic stimuli elicited larger evoked potential reactions in the dominant (as opposed to the minor) hemisphere. The latency to verb forms was significantly shorter than to noun forms in the left hemisphere, verb latency = 173 msec, noun latency = 188 msec. That is, evoked response latencies showed not only hemispheric asymmetries but also significant linguistic form-class differences, with verbs having a shorter latency than nouns. The latency of an evoked wave form to clicks did not vary significantly as a function of hemisphere.

Finally, to the upper far right of Fig. 9.7, interhemispheric transmission time was estimated as 30 to 40 msec by Filbey and Gazzaniga (1969).

Let us now concentrate more extensively on circuits involving the skeletal musculature represented at the bottom of Fig. 9.7. We have already noted the rapid responses at 10, 25, and 40 msec in the head and neck that issue from the subcortical region, 3-25 msec temporal interval (Davis, 1973). Perhaps related to that 10 msec response is the 8 msec neck response to auditory stimulation reported by Bickford et al. (1964), as represented by ⑦ . Bickford also reported latencies from auditory stimulus impingement to responses to be 25 msec in the arm, and 40 msec in the leg, as indicated in those muscle regions by ⑦ .[5] These responses emanate from the neural pathways at the thalamic region from the ear (the events indicated at the 3-25 msec portion of the subcortex).

Hammond (1955) applied the stimulus of a sudden pull that stretched the biceps, and recorded human biceps EMG responses with a latency of 18 msec, represented as ⑧ in the arm muscle region. There was a second biceps response to the same stimulus with a latency of about 50 msec. The stimulus S_8 in the upper right arm region is represented as setting off a circuit of unknown nature (indicated by the "?") returning to the arm to produce the 18 msec response. We also represent a stimulus, S_8, below the Hammond reference for the work of Evarts

---

[5] Donald B. Lindsley (1951) cited research by R. C. Davis in which the very rapid muscle tension response to a sudden unexpected stimulus was recorded with a latency of 40 msec or less, values which are consonant with these.

(1966, 1973) on the monkey. Evarts stimulated the hand and recorded arm EMG responses with latencies of 12 msec, of 30-40 msec, and a third phase at about 80 msec. We represent by ⑨ the fastest (12 msec) response as being similar to that recorded by Hammond at 18 msec, with unspecified mediators because Evarts suggests that these reactions were too rapid to involve the sensory-motor cortex. We also represent the afferent neural impulse from the stimulus in the hand ($S_{8,9}$) as continuing to the sensory cortex (⑨) where Evarts measured neural reactions (r_N) with latencies of 10, 14, 20, and 24 msec in various regions. Descending impulses from the cortex (⑨) are shown to produce a potential in the ventral root in the subcortical region with a latency of 4.7 msec; this event (represented as ⑩ A) was recorded by Bernhard, Bohm, and Petersen (1953) resulting from a stimulus (S_{10}) in the primate motor cortex. We illustrate this neural circuit continuing on from the cortex discharge (⑨ to S_{10}) to the forearm to produce an EMG event in the forearm (⑨) with latency of 7 msec from cortical stimulation (Evarts, 1973).

To summarize this particular circuit, the stimuli ($S_{8,9}$) in the arm produced reactions (⑨) in the sensory motor cortex with latencies between 10 to 24 msec; resulting cortical stimulation S_{10} produced a ventral root reaction at 4.7 msec (⑩), continuing on to an arm EMG reaction, at 7 msec (⑨); there is also Evarts' EMG response at 3040 msec ⑨ , similar to Hammond's response (⑧) with a latency of 50 msec to S_8. Evart's conclusion is that the sensory motor cortex can play a role in mediating this hand-arm circuit and possibly account for the 30 to 40 msec EMG responses recorded by himself, and also for the 50 msec response recorded in man by Hammond. Emanating from the cortical event represented by ⑨ we also indicate a circuit descending to the arm with unknown mediation that results in the reaction (⑧) to $S_{8,9}$ with a latency of 80 msec.

To continue the reaction to an auditory stimulus, we represent an impulse from the subcortical region (①) to the middle ear muscle producing a response (⑪) with latencies ranging between 40 and 100 msec (Goldstein, 1968). A stimulus resulting from middle ear contraction may set off a response in the vocal folds from 65 to 100 msec later; this is represented as starting with S_{12} in the middle ear region resulting in the response represented by ⑫ (Shearer and Simmons, 1965).

The speech, ear, and eye musculature are the most refined of all the skeletal muscle, capable of producing very precise and localized responses. Many motor units in these regions consist of but two or three muscle fibers, suggesting the relatively great capability of these systems to function in the transmission of highly refined units of information. Some representative speech muscle events are as follows.

McCall and Rabuzzi (1973) stimulated the internal laryngeal nerve of the cat (s_{13}) and noted middle ear muscle responses indicated by ⑬ (in the tensor tympani with a latency of 13 msec, in stapedius with a latency of 13 msec, and in cricothyroid with a latency of 11 msec). They concluded that these reflex responses are mediated by a central reflex arc between the internal laryngeal nerve and the motor supply to the tympanic muscles. One interpretation is that the tympanic muscle reflex may have a function in vocalization, such as that it is responsible for the contraction of the middle ear muscle in association with speaking. McCall and Rabuzzi summarized a number of references that support the conclusion that contraction of middle ear muscles precedes the production of sound. It is interesting to note in this connection that middle ear muscles also contract with rapid eye movements in the dream state.

To further illustrate the great rapidity of neuromuscular circuits, particularly those involving the speech muscles, Bowman and Combs (1969) stimulated the distal portion of the hypoglossal nerve in the tongue (S_{14}) and recorded a reaction in the contralateral sensory-motor cortex with a latency of 4 to 5 msec (⑭). We have also noted the 123 msec reaction time to tactile stimulation of the tongue of 123 msec measured by Siegenthaler and Hochberg (1965)—if we subtract a motor period of perhaps 50 msec, we have a speech muscle circuit that operates in the neighborhood of 70 msec which, as they suggested, may well serve a speech function.

In psychology (and elsewhere) we use the term "response," *both overt and covert,* as if a response were a simple, instantaneous, on-off event. Such abstraction and categorization is often necessary, but we must not obscure the fact that what we abstract as a response, be it overt or covert, is a part of an extremely complex on-going stream of events. Earlier we discussed the covert buildup of muscle activity, measured by EMG, that "bursts" into an overt response. But even that covert antecedent of an overt response, or even a covert response that is not an immediate antecedent of an overt response, is extremely complex and can be studied in great detail at molecular levels. The measurement of excitation-contraction latency in human muscles by Gatev and Ivanov (1972) is illustrative. The excitation-contraction latency is the interval between the onset of the action potential and the *onset* of the muscle contraction; it is the time during which the electrical activity of the muscle changes into mechanical activity, which is an essential stage in the transmission of neural impulses to the contractile elements of the muscle. For the two muscles they studied, the excitation contraction latency of *flexor carpi ulnaris* was 8.7 msec and of *gastrocnemius lateralis* 13.1 msec. The contraction time was also shorter in *ulnaris,* 63.6 msec as compared to 109.1 msec. We represent at the bottom right of Fig. 9.7 by 15 the 8.7 msec excitation-contraction latency in the *lateralis* for ulnaris; the contraction time of 63.6 msec is also shown. The similar values for the leg region are also specified by ⑮ for the Gatev and Ivanov reference.[6]

---

[6] A related phenomenon is the miniature end plate potential which has been recorded from mammaliam myoneural junctions in vivo by Hoekman, Dretchen, and Standaert (1974). They found a mean amplitude of .95 millivolts, a mean frequency of 1.01 per second, and a mean duration of 4.44 msec.

Values for the motor period, the time between onset of the skeletal muscle contraction and the overt response, are indicated to the right of the skeletal muscle region of Fig. 9.7 as ⑯ . For arm and hand muscles, the onset of the covert response occurred some 50 to 120 msec prior to the onset of the overt response; these values for the motor period are not individually repeated, but are summarized under reference 16 in Table 9.3. The time by which covert EMG onset in speech muscles occurs prior to audible speech sound has been measured as 200-500 msec by several investigators. These references are collectively summarized under reference ⑰ in Table 9.3.

part five

Technology of Covert Processes

10

Measurement of Covert Processes as an Explication of "Higher Mental Events," and Other Practical Problems

The Higher Mental Processes

In Chapter 1, the importance of concepts of mind and mental processes was emphasized, and we certainly affirm that there are referents for reports of individuals about their "immediate experiences," "awareness," and "consciousness." In fact, these presumed problems of mind were the initial motivation for this book, as they constitute the original problems of psychology as a science. Mentalistic terms, we have noted, were inherited by contemporary behavioristic psychology from the introspectionists (among whom we number particularly the Structuralists, the Functionalists, the Psychoanalysts and the Gestaltists). The introspectionists in turn had inherited such mentalistic terms from philosophers, and from the vernacular in general. That the inheritance has been complete is attested to by the fact that there are few academic psychology departments which have not recently offered courses which include such words as "thought," "consciousness," or "emotions" in their titles. The question of mind is thus now squarely before us and we seek to ascertain the scientific status of mentalistic notions, if in fact, they should have such. One cannot disagree with Lashley's notion that if there is no consciousness, then we at least have to explain how we have the illusion that there is. Our approach in this chapter shall be to directly confront mentalistic notions with methods of analysis and empirical conclusions considered up to this point. The reader may make special reference to electropsychological measurement of mental phenomena in the data Chapters 5, 6, 7, and 8.

We have noted that Watson and other classical behaviorists dismissed "consciousness" as a commonsense notion having no scientific merit; they did, however, offer scientifically acceptable definitions for such terms (Chapter 2). Such serious scientific consideration of mentalistic questions is admirable because the public requests (at least implicitly) scientific answers to them, and it is society that supports our science. Scientists, in my opinion, should at least attempt to furnish understandable answers to popular questions, regardless of the scientific value or lack of value in doing so.

These mentalistic questions are exceedingly difficult for the scientist; the terms in everyday usage are so vaguely defined that it is hard to know how best to analyze them. In science we often have taken commonsense notions as our starting point, and through the process of explication replace the ill defined terms with (relatively) precise scientific statements. Explications of commonsense notions may or may not be scientifically fruitful, for they are judged by a complex set of criteria; an explication which is *not* fruitful in generating direct scientific progress may nevertheless have indirect heuristic or serendipitous value.

One scientifically successful (if incomplete) explication of thought was Watson's theory, as discussed in Chapter 2. Habit ("a well-worn mode of responding") was also successfuly (though not completely) explicated by Hull's (1943) definition as Habit $H = 1\text{-}10\text{-}^{A\dot{N}}$. One criterion of Hull's success is the extensive research it inspired such as the research on need-reducing conceptions of reinforcement ($\dot{N}$), and whether or not these are necessary for learning (H). As a final example of successful explication, we cite Binet's replacement of the crude notion of intelligence with one that led to an operational definition of intelligence in terms of IQ.

One possible problem with a scientist's explication, however, is that it may not satisfy the lay user of the term. There are (at least) two reasons for this. First, the consequence of the explication process (the explicatum) may not be recognized by the lay person as the original concept (the explicandum). Watson, for instance, probably satisfied few of the public when he explicated "emotion" as a visceral response phenomenon. His explication excluded quite a bit of the "personal experience." Though one psychoanalyst was said to have enthusiastically accepted that Olds' (1969) "pleasure" center in the septal region of the brain was the seat of the id, this "explication" missed much of Freud's meaning and failed to become a lasting part of psychoanalytic dogma.

The second reason why the nonscientist may not be intellectually satisfied with the scientist's reformulation of commonsense problems results from the latter's attempt to fit mentalistic notions within a materialistic, mediational process paradigm. We noted in Chapter 2 that mental events are hypothetical constructs that mediate external stimuli and overt responses. People are "conscious" to the extent that they can talk about these internal events. Consequently, an individual who is aware (conscious) of internal events can provide verbal reports about those private events. We may add that people can talk about the external, as well as the internal, world, so consciousness need not be restricted to internal events—we are conscious of external events too. That is *all* that consciousness is, by our type of explication. But some people may not be able to accept it because it constitutes a denial of the more common dualistic, nontestable view of mentalism. The position that whatever we seek to study exists physically and is observable seems absurdly obvious to the materialist, but not to the nonmaterialistic mentalist. In our discussions of idealism in Chapter 1 and the ideomotor theory in Chapter 2, we held that one who seeks to study mind as an immaterial phenomenon has subscribed to a doctrine of despair—the statement that "there *are* nonmaterial phenomena" is itself a contradiction, if by "phenomena" one means that something exists. To try to study something that is unobservable in *any* sense is an effort that boggles the imagination. If there are "mental events" that do not have *some kind* of physical basis, as in neuromuscular circuits, then questions about them are merely pseudo-statements. Pseudoquestions are not real questions at all but only sequences of words disguised as questions. Washburn's (1916) position expressed well the kind of doctrine of despair that we seek to avoid when she held that there exists an inner aspect to behavior (sensations, feelings, and thoughts) which is not identical with behavior or with any form of movement. While thoughts may accompany bodily movements, they are not identical with movement. She suggested that if a physiologist perfected an instrument by which he could observe the nervous process in the cortex that occurs when one is conscious of the sensation red, he would see nothing red about it. By watching the slight contraction of the articulatory muscles that occurs when one silently says "red" one would not see red in those contractions. The red is consciousness, and no devices for observing and registering movements will ever observe the red, though they may easily lead to the inference that it exists in consciousness. And precisely the same is true of all sensations, thoughts, and feelings, she concluded.

Using Washburn's example, our position is precisely this: Either (1) there *is* an actual redness in our consciousness that is objectively (publicly) observable, and which is quite different from the electrical characteristics of nerve impulses and electromyograms that we observe on an oscilloscope; or (2) there is no such phenomenon as "redness in one's consciousness." We believe the former to be the case, as will become most evident in discussing a thought reading machine (Chapter 11, p. 443). This "machine" is conceptualized in this instance as one which receives a person's coded psychophysiological signals and presents the decoded read-out of the actual redness for public observation. Other people can then directly observe the redness which one introspectively reports as one's "immediate experience."

Because the position that we take throughout this book is so capable of being misunderstood, perhaps it is worthwhile to emphasize several things that are not being advocated. It is easy to project notions, especially in this context, that are contradictory or irrelevant to this position. For one, the position does not deny the existence of potential phenomena in the universe which may be beyond our power to observe. While events, powers, qualities or characteristics that are untestable within our current limitations cannot be entertained within the realm of science, this fact alone does not *deny* their existence. There may be phenomena that exist but which we simply have no way of knowing about. There may well be poltergeist, but they will only be observable through poltergeist-receptors that are not now available to mere mortals. At the same time, a person may entertain all manner of *beliefs* about unobservable powers and the like, if they recognize that in so doing they are behaving as nonscientists.[1]

---

[1] I think that we humans should have great humility about our limited abilities to observe and understand the terribly complex world in which we have been placed, and that we should be tolerant of beliefs of others about supernatural phenomena. Some of us, however, are not sufficiently humble, as James Thurber observed when he said that while a man may think he amounts to a great deal, to a mosquito he is only something to eat. Robert Frost expressed his disapproval of his Maker's failure to consult him as to whether or not he should be placed in the world, and his awe at the complexity of nature. As I recall Frost's statement: Forgive me Lord for all the little tricks I have played on thee, and I will forgive you for the one grand one that you have played on me.

A strong physicalistic position can also be erroneously thought of as lessening the joys of the world by denying beauty, love, or even one's right to believe in a god. However, one does not need to be a subjective idealist to appreciate beauty in the world!

Nor is the materialist's position excessively restrictive—it does not set any answerable question "off limits for science." For example, the materialist need not deny the existence of extrasensory perception, and in fact should encourage such research, providing that *meaningful* statements about such parapsychic phenomena are formulated. If one does conclude that there is a firm data base for ESP (that a sufficient number of methodologically sound experiments have resulted in positive conclusions), then one would seek a physicalistic interpretation. It is not beyond the limits of imagination, for instance, to hypothesize ESP transmitter-receptor systems within the body that have simply not yet been empirically specified. While perhaps of low priority, the hypothesis that there is a unique physicalistic energy that is transmitted as "ESP" by at least some individuals and received by at least some others *is* testable. A testable corollary is that ESP energy travels at the speed of electromagnetic waves and is perhaps even specifiable within that spectrum; such a corollary would account for the reports (if they are reliable) of "instantaneous" transference of thoughts across great distances. In short, scientific materialism encourages a flexible attitude in order to avoid prematurely restricting the possibility of new discoveries. When scientists have been inflexible, the discovery of new knowledge has been sharply retarded. The depressing story of Gregory Mendel is appropriate here—because a great "geneticist" of his day could not conceive of sweet peas as an object of experimentation he caused the young Mendel to discontinue experimenting with sweet peas, whereupon Mendel labored fruitlessly with other specimens for the rest of his life (cf. McGuigan, 1978a). In recent times, we have witnessed many inflexible positions. Often we note failures to reach sound conclusions because social as opposed to scientific criteria have been employed, as in emotionally loaded debates about the relative contributions of heredity vs. environment to intelligence. A flexible scientific materialism even allows for the empirical investigation of religious questions, such as a hypothesis that prayer influences one's daily life (cf. McGuigan, 1978a), though apparently few are interested in the development of a science of religion.

While thus remaining flexible with regard to what are often erroneously considered "non-materialistic issues," we must also maintain skepticism—one cannot soundly embrace the phenomena of extrasensory perception or prayer without sufficient empirical justification. Even our most highly regarded scientific journals should be read skeptically. Just because an experiment is reported in a prestigious journal does not mean that all errors have been eliminated or the conclusion should be uncritically accepted.

The approach taken in this chapter, then, is to discuss instances of the higher mental processes as they are referred to in everyday language—imagination, nocturnal dreams, hallucinations, silent reading, etc. We shall also consider some related practical problems like "lie detection" and tension control. The mental processes are covert events (in that they typically occur when the person is silent, not overtly behaving), and they are susceptible to explication by means of psychophysiological measures. This general approach can be illustrated by the scientific study of nocturnal dreams, as a consequence of which we have sizeably advanced our understanding of the dream state by means of psychophysiological variables. We are thus able to furnish sound information about dreams, and to some extent even ascertain dream content from the psychophysiological measures. Societal supporters of science thus benefit by the dispelling of "old wives tales," such as that dreams occur rapidly within several seconds, that many people never dream, and so forth; there are therapeutic consequences too.

The strategy has been to employ verbal reports as the criterion of occurrence or non-occurrence of a dream, and to relate those verbal reports to immediately preceding psychophysiological events. Rapid eye movements and other psychophysiological measures have allowed us to objectively and reliably define the dream state so that we can dispense with the criterion of the verbal report. The advantage of this strategy is that, while the verbal report may suffice for the early stages of research, it is not sufficiently reliable for the more advanced stages, e.g., an awakened subject may not be reporting the immediate dream, but may be recalling one from earlier in the night, from a previous night, or maybe perhaps one that did not occur at all.[2] The same general strategy was successful for Binet when he employed loose, unreliable criteria of intelligence as his starting point; on that basis we have now advanced to highly refined, reliable measures of intelligence, (e.g., Guilford, 1968).

In short, mental processes (like dreams) *are* sequences of bodily events which occur under specifiable external and internal conditions and *nothing more*. In principle, once we have measured *all* of those bodily events, we have completely specified the mental process in question, e.g., a dream is a certain sequence of patterns of EEG reactions, covert oral responses, covert eye responses, contractions of the colon, etc. The verbal report of the mental process occurs because the individual can name ["internally tact" in Skinner's (1957) terms] some of these covert processes. This ability to name the bodily circuits no doubt occurs when the speech system is engaged. That is, when circuits involving the speech musculature, the linguistic regions of the brain, etc., are activated the individual can tact (is aware or conscious of) certain speech and non-speech contents or activities. When circuits that the individual cannot name (is not aware of) reverberate, there may be only nonspeech (nonoral) information processing. The person's tact (verbal report) of the activation of the various neuromuscular circuits may become overt under certain conditions, as when requested by the experimenter to verbally report on what was "in your mind."

---

[2] Thanks to Dean Foster for this point, and also for the excellent students that he has sent me over the years who have helped me with this work.

The phenomenon of memory is relevant to the process of internal tacts. That is, one can orally identify a number of circuits for a given mental process, but one becomes less successful at this as times passes. For instance, most people can identify the mediational processes that occur during, or up to about 10 minutes after, a dream. However, far fewer seem to recall dreams if interrogated the next morning (Goodenough, Shapiro, Holden, and Steinschriber, 1959).

An important question is how we acquire the ability to name internal events, to verbally describe some of the activated sensory-neural-motor circuits. It's quite likely that, through operant conditioning, the activation of certain circuits comes to produce internal discriminative stimuli (S^D's) that set the occasion for covert oral language responses, the occurrence of which constitute the tacting process. If the occasion demands, the covert response may become an overt verbal report. Keller and Schoenfeld (1950) commented on such a process as follows:

What makes us decide that some introspective tacts are valid and others not? Why, for example, do we question "mind" if a person says, "My mind is working"? To this and many similar questions, we can reply that there is no doubt the speaker is *saying* something, but he is not necessarily tacting what he *supposes* he is. Thus, a person who says "I am thinking" does not have ghostly thoughts as his S^D, but rather muscular responses of the vocal apparatus (and perhaps other parts of the body) which he tacts as "thinking." A child wrestling with a problem is told by his parent "My, but you're thinking hard, aren't you?" and he gropingly replies "Am I *thinking?*"; thereafter, similar activity will also be called thinking although he learns in later life to make vague statements about the "nature of thought." We all think, but we do so with our muscles which provide the only S^D's for the tact "thinking." If we are asked, however, to *describe* thinking we do so incorrectly because we have learned to talk about thinking in a certain way. We may say that we "feel our brains working," but this is not a valid tact since neural activity in the brain is not itself perceptible and no discriminative response can be anchored to it. We could examine in this manner all the misconceptions about themselves that men evidence in their verbal responding (p. 390–91).

With this general consideration let us now turn to: (1) descriptions in everyday language of a variety of higher mental processes, and similar practical problems; and (2) some illustrative psychophysiological data (from Chapters 5–8) that have been recorded when individuals were engaged in these various activities.

THINKING AND CONSCIOUSNESS

The terms "thinking" and "consciousness" from everyday language are probably the most indicative of the higher mental process. To set the introduction, we consider these terms to be mediational processes that we can name or talk about in some way. "Thinking," "thought," "consciousness," also have ambiguous statuses in everyday usage, typically referring to something that goes on "in the mind" like a belief, an opinion, or a judgment. With regard to thinking, a sample of statements by psychologists suggests that they generally consider three categories of thought: (1) reasoning processes, (2) imagination processes, and (3) contents of the mind. Reasoning is typically said to be that type of thought employed during problem solving. Imagination concerns processes in which we combine old experiences in new ways, when we are to a large extent free from controlling external stimuli. Of the third category, Johnson (1955) considered "Thought as the content of consciousness. This is the classical usage of the term in psychology. This is what people mean when they ask, 'What's on your mind?' or 'What are you thinking about?' or when they offer 'A penny for your thoughts.' These thoughts are observable only to the thinker of them; the method of investigation is self-observation" (p. 19).

Thought was, of course, a central concept for Wundt and Titchener, who believed that it consists of sensations, images, and feelings. Their major controversy with the Würzburg School (Külpe, Marbe, Bühler, etc.) occurred when the latter group reported from their introspections that there was no trace of imagery content in thought. For the Würzburg School, the task (Aufgabe) provides a set which influences associative sequences of mental contents by unconscious determining tendencies. These tendencies guide the thinking process through to the completion of the task. Later, in developing his sensitive methods of internal sensory observation, Edmund Jacobson (1929) concluded that imageless thought was merely due to inadequate introspection on the part of the Würzburg School.

The Gestaltists (Wertheimer, Köhler, Koffka, etc.) conceived of thought in a manner somewhat similar to the Würzburg School, as a unitary creative process by which one solves problems through the action of intrinsic stresses.

In his classic book, *Thinking,* Humphrey (1951) emphasized the problem-solving nature of thought, holding essentially that thinking consists of those processes which occur when an organism confronts and solves a problem. (John Dewey, in various of his writings, also emphasized the problem-solving nature of thought, characterizing it primarily as a logical process in which one formulates possible solutions and attempts to verify those hypotheses through observation.)

This brief sample of statement about thought is sufficient to indicate the fruitlessness of further endeavor along these commonsense lines, but does provide a starting point for scientific consideration. In an effort to strip the term of its ambiguity and non-physical connotations, we define "thinking" as the composite of bodily activity (neural, muscular, etc.) that necessarily results from the presentation of a language stimulus.[3] The variety of task conditions and of measurements of covert processes

---

[3] By "language stimulus" we mean words of a language that are understood by a responder, though this is but one of several indicators of "thinking"—additional indicators are demanded when similar bodily processes occur in the absence of a specifiable external stimulus or when they occur in the presence of a non-language stimulus, topics which we considered in Chapter 9.

which have been taken is illustrated by the research on problem solving in normal subjects, summarized in the data Chapters 5, 6, 7, and 8. For instance, heightened covert oral behavior (tongue EMG, lip EMG, etc.) has been recorded when normal subjects engage in a wide variety of verbal and mathematical ("mental") problems, as in the work of Jacobson (1932), and Bassin and Bein (1961). Using a mediational paradigm, McGuigan, Culver, and Kendler (1971) found that amplitude of tongue EMG increased during verbal mediation and that arms and eyes were possible loci of directional, non-verbal mediational behavior (see Fig. 2.9). These psychophysiological responses may be direct measures of verbal and nonverbal mediational responses.

In his classical work on problem solving by deaf subjects, Max (1937) hypothesized that the activity of the linguistic mechanisms in the fingers of deaf subjects would increase during the solution of "thought problems." He found that abstract thought problems elicited action-current responses in the arms, and he concluded that: "these manual responses in the deaf are more than adventitious effects of irradiated tensions . . . and . . . have some specific connection with the thinking process itself. . . . Our results thus lend some support to the behavioristic form of the motor theory of consciousness" (Max, 1937, pp. 336–37). Max's work received some confirmation from Novikova (1961). In conformity with the findings of Max and Novikova, McGuigan (1971) concluded that the manual and oral regions were covertly functioning as a common linguistic system during thinking (Fig. 10.1).

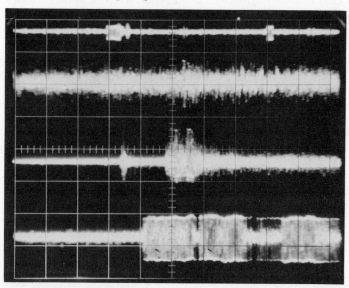

FIG. 10.1 Sample traces from a deaf subject while engaged in problem solving. The two events in top trace indicate presentation of the problem and subject's report of its solution. Increases in EMG can be noted from top down from lips, left arm, and right arm. Horizontal scale is 2 sec/division, and vertical scale is 100 μV/division.

These illustrations of covert oral and covert non-oral language responses during several kinds of "thought processes" exemplify our basic hypothetical construct paradigm (Fig. 3.4) and fit well with the neuromuscular circuit models of Chapter 9 (e.g., Fig. 9.5). In a mature science of covert processes, "thinking" should thereby be sufficiently explicated through the direct measurement of hypothetical constructs as neuromuscular circuits that it should disappear from our scientific, and perhaps from our everyday language. In its typical usage in the vernacular and in the laboratory the term "thinking" has been sufficiently vague that it has had little scientific value, other than providing us with a starting place. The classical behavioristic approach to thought in terms of mediational paradigms, though highly successful, has been incomplete in that it has not employed direct measurement of the hypothetical constructs. The wedding of psychophysiology and behavior theory that we have discussed in various places in this book should thus lead to a more complete and satisfactory explication of thought, as well as to a more complete psychology (Chapter 1). Ultimately, then, we can expect such terms as "thinking" to be replaced by equations of the type presented at the end of Chapter 3 (Fig. 3.4).

DURING SILENT READING

General Research.   In Chapter 9 we noted the major cultural advances that resulted when we first learned to write and read speech. For the individual, too, the process of reading begins when a child develops proficiency in spoken language, after which one learns to discriminate and produce various written symbols. In close connection with this, one learns to decode the written symbols into their original speech sounds; this is reading, and it may be overt (aloud) or covert (silent). This intimate relation between spoken language and the process of decoding graphic symbols suggests that covert activation of speech muscle functioning with linguistic regions of the brain are circuits of principle importance during reading, as in visual information processing within Fig. 9.5. Silent reading thus is another important cognitive activity, and one that has a major advantage for the researcher, viz., the individual's thought processes are controlled by the external linguistic stimuli that constitute the prose being read, so that the researcher knows what the reader is thinking about. The topic of covert oral responses, treated as "subvocalization," has especially interested educators and psychologists who have studied the reading process, and cognition in general.[4] Typi-

---

[4] Cole (1938) defined subvocalization as including the saying or whispering of words, faint whispering of some words, pronounced lip movements but no sound, no lip movements or sound but palpable movements of the tongue, or no lip movements, sound, or palpable movement of the tongue, but palpable movements of the throat. As noted in Chapter 3, we employ the term "covert oral behavior" to include activation of any of the speech musculature; if functioning for linguistic processing, we refer to covert oral *language* behavior.

cally, educators have held that subvocalization during silent reading is detrimental to reading proficiency, e.g., Betts has stated that ". . . any observable form of vocalization—such as silent lip movement . . . retards the rate of silent reading [which] has been common professional knowledge since the early scientific studies of reading" (1950, p. 450). Judd (1927) said "It has been shown in all recent investigations of reading that silent reading not only is more rapid than oral reading but is also likely to be correlated with a higher degree of comprehension of meaning. Lip movements during silent reading and movements in the larynx are signs of immaturity" (pp. 313–22). In contrast to this widespread view of the function of covert oral behavior, Schilling concluded from his research that "Motor expression of speech movements favours the understanding of what is read. Suppression inhibits the understanding of what is read" (1929, p. 223). Watson (1914) hypothesized that implicit speech might be physiologically required in the process of reading. More recently, Edfeldt (1960) concluded it is likely that ". . . silent speech actually constitutes an aid toward better reading comprehension" (p. 154). But this issue is an empirical one. To decide between these conflicting hypotheses one should first determine whether or not the covert oral response does reliably occur during silent reading; the next step would be to see how and under what conditions it changes—by specifying the environmental and subject variables of which covert oral behavior is a function, we should gain some insight into whether it is detrimental or beneficial during silent reading. Eventually we should determine whether covert behavior is a *necessary* part of reading.

While speculations about the function of "inner speech" (subvocalization) during silent reading are literally ancient (cf. Langfeld, 1933), Curtis (1900) reported the first effort to directly record covert oral responses. The studies that followed culminated with the work of Thorson (1925) using mechanical techniques for measuring behavior that were (necessarily) so crude that one is surprised when researchers thought they had obtained positive evidence of such miniscule events as covert responses. These mechanical techniques were replaced by the extremely sensitive procedures of quantitative electromyography, pioneered by Jacobson in 1927. Apparently, the first electromyographic measures were made by Faaborg-Andersen and Edfeldt (1958), though Jacobson and Kraft in 1942 had studied a non-oral measure (leg EMG) during silent reading. McGuigan, Keller, and Stanton (1964) electromyographically measured covert oral behavior during silent reading in children and college students using surface electrodes and also subvocalizations studied through refined audio amplification. These selected findings are illustrative of the numerous results cited in Chapter 6 that covert oral behavior typically increases during silent reading and in Chapter 6 we summarized some positive evidence that the increased level of covert oral responding was relatively localized in the speech region. For the first step mentioned above, then, localized covert responses in the speech musculature is associated with silent reading and apparently is general among language proficient people. The second step proposed above in ascertaining the function of covert oral behavior during silent reading is to specify the variables of which response amplitude is a function.

Systematic Changes in the Amplitude of Covert Oral Behavior. Two categories of variables will be considered—subject characteristics and environmental variables. Two subclasses of the former will be changes in covert oral behavior as a function of characteristics as they are *selected* in subjects, and as a function of *experimentally* produced changes in subjects.

Subject Variables. The earliest EMG study of covert oral behavior during silent reading as a function of selected characteristics of subjects was by Faaborg-Andersen and Edfeldt (1958). These researchers selected Danish subjects who were accustomed to reading a foreign language (Swedish) and subjects who could read Swedish but were not accustomed to it. They found that silent speech (vocal and mylohyoid EMG) was substantially greater for those who were unaccustomed to reading the foreign language. Adults selected on the basis of their poor reading and writing proficiency emit larger amplitudes of covert oral behavior during silent reading and writing than do adults who are good readers and writers (Edfeldt, 1960; McGuigan, 1970a). Similarly, more covert oral behavior occurs in children while reading than in adults, who were (obviously) the more proficient readers (McGuigan et al., 1964; McGuigan and Pinkney, 1973). Furthermore, children selected on the basis of especially high levels of covert oral behavior while reading naturally decreased their covert oral response amplitude over the years, as reading proficiency improved, but response amplitude stabilized at about the normal adult level (McGuigan and Bailey, 1969b); furthermore, audible subvocalizations were prominent in the first test but none were detected after three years. In Chapter 6 we discussed a replication of the McGuigan and Bailey (1969b) study in which it was shown that the natural decrease in covert oral behavior during silent reading was not artifactual due to repeated testing. We may thus conclude that amplitude of covert oral behavior is inversely related to reading proficiency of *selected* subjects.

Two possible experimental strategies for deciding whether the covert oral response is beneficial or detrimental are to: (1) increase reading proficiency and note any consequences on covert oral behavior, and (2) manipulate amplitude of covert oral behavior and note consequences on reading proficiency. If increased reading proficiency results in reduced amplitude of covert oral behavior, the theory that the response is detrimental would be supported; no change or an increase in response amplitude would suggest that the response is beneficial (strategy 1). By strategy 2, should reduction in response amplitude result in decreased reading proficiency, one could conclude that the response is beneficial; an increase in reading proficiency would suggest that the response is detrimental.

When adult reading rates were experimentally improved by 149 wpm (confirmed by systematic changes in electrically measured eye movements) the amplitude of tongue EMG significantly increased; a similar increase in tongue EMG occurred in children as a result of increased rate (increases of 172 wpm and 220 wpm in two experiments). But perhaps because amplitude of covert oral behavior for the children was relatively large at the start of the experiment, the effect was not as pronounced for the children as it was for the adults. Tongue EMG, incidentally, decreased for all three control groups in these three experiments (McGuigan and Pinkney, 1973). Similar results occurred in a remedial reading case (McGuigan and Shepperson, 1971), i.e., a child's reading proficiency was increased from the 5.6 grade level to the 7.3 grade level, as measured by a standardized test. Tongue and chin EMG also sizeably increased from before to after the treatment. These apparent behavioral consequences of improving reading proficiency thus seem to be more consonant with the theory that covert oral behavior facilitates reading proficiency.

For the second strategy, external feedback techniques have successfully reduced amplitude of covert oral behavior during silent reading (cf., Hardyck, Petrinovich, and Ellsworth, 1966; McGuigan, 1967; Hardyck and Petrinovich, 1970; and McGuigan, 1971). The only study in which reduced amplitude was shown to affect reading proficiency was that by Hardyck and Petrinovich (1970); these experimenters reduced laryngeal EMG (surface electrodes) through external feedback while college subjects read easy and difficult passages. Relative to two other groups who did not receive laryngeal feedback, Hardyck and Petrinovich found that "the laryngeal feedback group did significantly less well on comprehension of the difficult material" (1970, p. 647), leading them to conclude that ". . . subvocal speech . . . is a useful stimulus input capable of mediating a cognitive response" (p. 651). Data reported by McGuigan (1971) indicate, though, that reduced amplitude of covert oral behavior is temporary and dependent on the presence of the feedback signal [though this conflicts with the statements of Hardyck et al. (1966, 1969) that the reduction is rapidly accomplished and permanent]. In conclusion for the second strategy, reduced covert oral behavior seems to reduce reading proficiency; but due to the complexity of the methodological problems and to the crudeness of measures of reading proficiency as rate in words per minute and comprehension as a percentage, more extensive research on this matter has high priority.

In summary, the purposive manipulation of reading proficiency by increasing rate seems to increase amplitude of covert oral behavior, but in any event it does not decrease; furthermore, experimental reduction of response amplitude seems to decrease reading proficiency.

Environmental Variables. As far as external stimuli are concerned, amplitude of covert oral behavior is increased by increasing the level of difficulty of the prose being read, and by increasing the blurriness of the letters (Edfeldt, 1960). While their subjects were silently reading, McGuigan and Rodier (1968) systematically introduced white noise, auditory prose different from that being read, and that auditory prose played backwards. They concluded that presentation of prose and of backward prose led to a significantly greater amplitude of covert oral behavior than while reading during silence, but noise did not have that effect. These results on environmental variables thus indicate that amplitude of covert oral behavior becomes exaggerated as the text and conditions become more demanding.

In summary, the findings indicate that amplitude of covert oral behavior is inversely related to reading proficiency of selected subjects, and is a direct function of the degree of the textual and environmental demands. In experimental manipulation of reading rate and of amplitude of covert oral behavior, it seems that amplitude of covert oral behavior and reading proficiency are directly related. The following picture thus emerges. While reading, one orally responds to the words that constitute the prose being read. In first learning to read, the child necessarily makes large articulatory movements while attempting to pronounce the written word. Like any motor skill, as proficiency increases, the gross amount of muscular activity becomes reduced and efficiency increases—as one learns to read, swim, or ride a bicycle, initial large scale and erratic movements become woven into smooth, highly coordinated response chains. In reading, these response chains are most efficiently run off at the covert level (Chapter 3). Hence, the covert oral response persists in the adult, and continues to function while reading, be it overt or silent. During silent reading, when conditions demand, the response increases in amplitude—presumably, the poor reader and the person reading under demanding conditions enhance the reading process by exaggerating their amplitude of covert oral behavior.

Similarly, by suddenly increasing one's reading rate, there are demands for increased amplitude of covert oral behavior; presumably, as one practices at the faster rate, amplitude of response will decrease, just as it naturally does with young children.

As detailed in Chapter 9, the increased amplitude of covert oral behavior during silent linguistic processing facilitates silent reading because the speech muscle generates a verbal code which is carried through neuromuscular circuits to the brain. The nature of the code is a phonetic one, based in part on the findings of a discriminative relationship between class of covert oral behavior and the phonemic system (e.g., Locke and Fehr, 1970a; McGuigan and Winstead, 1974). In Chapter 9, we have considered such a code in detail, based on the findings of the discriminative relationship between class of covert oral behavior and phonemic system (e.g., Locke and Fehr, 1970a; McGuigan and Winstead, 1974). Consistent with a principle of behavioral efficiency, the accomplished reader typically generates a minimal amount of afferently carried verbal information in the oral region. But the poorer reader, or the good reader under distracting conditions, requires a greater amount of verbal information, perhaps needs to send a redundancy of information to the brain. *The implication for teachers, therefore, is that they should not tamper with the child's subvocalization—it is likely that the child* needs *to subvocalize while reading and, in any event, the subvocalization naturally becomes reduced in time.* Yet the fact that even a reduced amount of covert oral behavior is measurable in the adult means that the muscular response still serves a linguistic processing function regardless of the stage of life.

DURING CURSIVE HANDWRITING

Writing is of course another kind of cognitive behavior in which there is complex linguistic functioning. While cursive writing is often a process in which one copies some linguistic input (dictation), it is more common for the source of the written output to be internally generated (composition). Presumably the processing function in either case involves the running off of neuromuscular circuits, as diagrammed in Fig. 9.5. Though the writer is typically silent, the speech musculature is covertly activated when prose is written by the hand. Covert oral behavior should also increase when selected symbols are presented for one who types on the typewriter, sends Morse Code by means of a telegraph key, gives input instructions to a computer, functions on an abacus (Hatano, Miyake, and Binks, 1977), etc. Lepley (1952) made a common observation, also noticed often when one silently listens to hours of lectures, that after "approximately seven hours at intensive hurried, writing tasks . . . he was clearly aware of a marked 'stiffness' and soreness in the reacting mechanisms involved in speech; and this particularly in the region of the larynx" (p. 597). Lepley then conducted an experiment in which he found that subjects who said they subvocalized had poorer handwriting

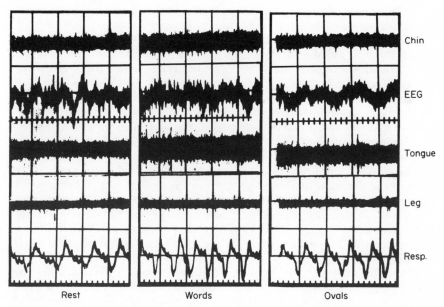

FIG. 10.2   Chin and tongue EMG increase from rest more while silently writing words than for comparison tasks (e.g., drawing ovals). Leg EMG changed little.

than those who said they did not subvocalize. Stimulated by Lepley's work, we found that heightened tongue and chin EMG occurred during cursive writing, and the increased covert oral behavior was significantly larger than during the performance of the non-linguistic comparison tasks (McGuigan, 1970b). Handwriting is thus another instance of a cognitive activity in which the output may be known to the researcher through the overt response that produces a permanent record. Of course, all of the thought processes of a writer are not captured in the resulting prose, for there must be many rapidly occurring thoughts which are not written down.

NOCTURNAL DREAMS IN THE SEEING AND BLIND

In everyday language, dreams are selective series of sleep thoughts or images, states of mind that are marked by a release from reality. Through the centuries they have been variously interpreted, such as a temporary departure of the soul, to guide armies and determine political destinies of nations, or to indicate systems of symbolism by which latent content becomes understandable through manifest content. Certainly they are among the more curious of our cognitive processes, having yielded numerous folk tales such as that people never dream, that dreams are extended episodes compressed into instants of time, that we dream but once a night, that dreams are expressions of wish fulfillment, that dreams are directed by external events, and that the mind shuts down at night during sleep. One of the major accomplishments of psychophysiology has been to further our understanding of which of these ancient beliefs might be true, as well as to precisely define the dream state in an objective manner. In Chapters 5-8 we reviewed the literature on dreaming, and noted the old observation that eye movements accompany dreams, e.g., Ladd's (1892) speculation that the eyeballs move during dreaming so that when we dream we focus our attention as we would when making the same observation during the waking life. Jacobson (1938b) discussed the electrical measurement of eye movements during dreaming, a technique which since flourished as a result of the work of Kleitman and his associates (see Chapter 5).

The strategy employed in the psychophysiology of dreams has been to awaken the dreamer during rapid eye movement (REMs) and non-REM periods, and request verbal reports about the dreams. With a very high degree of probability, the subject when awakened will report having been dreaming during REM periods but not having been dreaming during non-REM periods (though there is less vivid imagery during non-REM).

While the early psychophysiological dream research concentrated on the electrical recording of eye and brain activity, as with mental activity during waking life it was found that there was widespread activation of other bodily systems during nocturnal dreams as well. During the REM stage, for example, there occur increases in pulse and respiration rates, widespread changes in cardiovascular activity, galvanic skin responses, and activation of the sexual organs in both males and females. Dewson, Dement, and Simmons (1965) reported that middle ear muscle activity in the cat coincides with REM sleep, but in other stages of sleep these muscles were relatively inactive. Pessah and Roffwarg (1972) reported similar results in humans.

Another especially prominent research variable during dreaming has been muscle activity. Berger (1961) reported a striking decrease in muscle tonus of the extrinsic laryngeal muscles at the onset of each REM period. Jacobson, Kales, Lehmann, and Hoedemaker (1964) showed that tonus of most head and neck muscles studied decreased with onset of REM sleep, but that trunk and limb muscles exhibited stable levels of tonic activity throughout the night with no change of level associated with REM periods. Larson and Foulkes (1969) concluded that a momentary deepening of sleep in which there is less memorable and vivid mental content appeared to accompany the pre-REM suppression of neck and chin EMG potential.

With regard to covert responses during dreams, we expect, of course, that rather than tonic, it is phasic activity (which carries verbal coding) that is important for the mental content, and phasic activity has been measured by a number of dream researchers (e.g., Pivik and Dement, 1970). In Chapter 6 we also noted that there was a significant correlation between bodily location of movement and the location and amount of dreamed activity.

Baldridge, Whitman, and Kramer (1965), in studying the concurrence of fine muscle activity and REMs during sleep, found that activation of small body movements was an integrated process which appeared simultaneously from all locations sampled. They found that body movement patterns predicted REM periods in 32 out of 41 instances.

Dement and Wolpert (1958) sought to find gross overt bodily movements associated with specific dream content (such as running, fighting, or punching movements) with negative results. One would expect, however, that heightened covert EMG responses could be detected where no overt responses are made.

Molinari and Foulkes (1969) sought to replace the sleep model of REM and nonREM sleep with a tonic-phasic model. In this model contrast is made between sleep periods of phasic activity with those having none, regardless of the REM-nonREM status. They confirmed the hypothesis that phasic and nonphasic episodes within stage REM are associated with qualitatively different mental activity, and that nonphasic stage REM is associated with mental activity qualitatively similar to that of nonREM sleep. During REM-phasic awakenings, there were reports of primary visual experience while REM-nonphasic and nonREM awakenings were associated with reports of secondary cognitive elaboration.

McGuigan and Tanner (1971) measured changes in visual vs. conversational dreams. Covert oral behavior (lip and chin electromyograms) was elevated during conversational dreams, while during visual dreams there were only minor and nonsignificant changes in covert oral behavior. Little change occurred for neck responses, suggesting that those behavioral changes were not generalized throughout the body and were localized in the speech region. These findings suggest that covert oral behavior may serve a linguistic function during conversational dreams (see Figs. 10.3, 10.4, 10.5) as it does during the waking performance of linguistic activities. Among autonomic measures, penile tumescence would be a major variable in the explication of Watson's concept of emotion, which he defined as visceral responding. Studies of smooth muscle activity during dreams indicate that the sexual organs participate intimately in the dream state, e.g., Karacan, Hursch, Williams, and Thornby (1972) found that 91% of all tumescence episodes occurred at least in part during a REM period.

We have, then, a rather impressive sample of psychophysiological measures that define the dream state, and we can even use those measures to ascertain to some extent the content of the dream, due to the close relationship between directions of eye movements and dream content (Chapter 5). In spite of these successes, however, there are a number of serious problems and methodological difficulties in dream research, such as the necessity of relying on the verbal report as the criterion of whether or not the subject dreamed. Whitman, Kramer, and Baldridge (1963), for instance, reported a number of differences between dream reports rendered during the night and the reports later given to their therapists. Baekland and Lasky (1968) also reported that subjects failed to recall the next day numerous dreams that had been successfully reported at night, and Goodenough et al. (1959) concluded that dreams do occur even in individuals who claim that they never dream, suggesting that individuals should be classifed as "recallers" vs. "non-recallers." Wolpert and Trosman (1958) reported that 25 of 26 subjects had no memory of dreaming when they were questioned more than 10 minutes after the termination of the REM stage. Finally, we should note that REMs do not occur exclusively in one period, but some

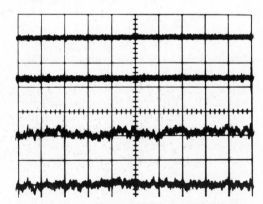

FIG. 10.3   Illustration of signals during NREM periods. Reading from top down, signals are lip EMG, chin EMG, from horizontal eye placement, and frontal EEG. Amplitude for the top three traces is 50 μV/division, and 100 μV/division for EEG. Time is 1/sec/division.

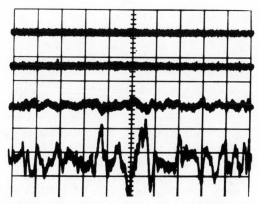

FIG. 10.4   Illustration of signals during a visual dream, as in Fig. 10.3.

often occur during the other stages of sleep and, conversely, mental activity is also present during non-REM periods, though of a less vivid nature (Foulkes, 1962).

Laboratory technique can be extremely important in reaching proper conclusions about dream results. For instance, Jacobs, Feldman, and Bender (1972) pointed out that previous investigators who found positive relationships between visual action in dreams and eye movements have used ac electrooculography. With dc electrooculography, however, Jacobs et al. found that only a minority of eye movements during stage REM are in the direction of the visual action of the dream. Of importance here, however, was their finding that when they considered only single, large amplitude, prominent eye movements, most of these were related to the colorful, compelling visual action that occurs as a prominent single visual response. These researchers reasoned that ac recording emphasizes these isolated movements, which perhaps explains the disparity of results with regard to direction of eye movements and mental content (Chapter 5).

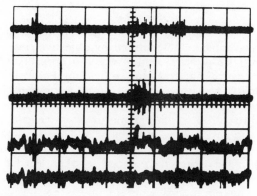

FIG. 10.5   Illustration of signals during a conversational dream, as in Fig. 10.3.

415

A particularly interesting theoretical question for us is whether or not there is eye activity during the dreams of blind subjects, and if so, what is the nature of that activity. Our expectation from the model of Chapter 9 is that in any mental activity, peripheral components of neuro-muscular circuits are activated; if there is visual imagery during dreaming, the eyes should be especially active, though the eyes also participate to some extent in nonvisual imagery. Berger, Olley, and Oswald (1962) cited the conclusion of Jastrow that people who became blind later than early childhood maintained visual imagery, but there was a progressive decline of reports of visual imagery as the individual became older. After 40 years of blindness only a few subjects were said to still report some visual imagery. Berger et al. studied some blind subjects who had been blind for life and some who had been blind for 30 to 40 years. These subjects showed no REMs and had no visual imagery in their dreams. Other subjects who had been blind for only 3 to 15 years claimed no visual imagery, but they exhibited REMs just like normals, and when wakened they reported visual dreams. The conclusion of Berger et al. was that REMs are related to visual dreams only. On the other hand, Amadeo and Gomez (1966) reported that seven of eight subjects who had been blind for life exhibited REMs during emergent Stage 1. However, there were differences in terms of overall EOG configuration, REM frequency, amplitude and cojugateness compared to the same patterns of normally sighted subjects.

Gross, Byrne, and Fisher (1965) recorded eye movement with a movement transducer (ceramic strain gauge) together with direct observation of subjects blind since birth. These subjects reported no waking visual imagery, but like normals they showed recurring rapid eye movements periods during emergent Stage 1. At the same time EOG corneofundal potentials were absent or greatly diminished. Gross et al. suggested that this finding may resolve the earlier contradictory ones in that REMs are present if measured by a movement transducer and that the reported absence of REMs may be an artifact of the EOG method.

HALLUCINATIONS

Hallucinations are regarded as "false" perceptions that are confused with "real" perceptions, as determined by objective observers. The response is evidently to internal stimuli which are mistakenly ascribed to external sources by the hallucinating individual. Hallucinations may involve any modality, and they may be positive, or negative (failure to perceive obvious external stimuli). Hysterical anesthesia is one instance of negative hallucination which may occur when reactions to an entire mode of stimulation are absent, as when a child does not pay attention to a nagging parent. Motor hallucinations have also been studied, as in patients who think that they have overtly spoken but have not (Levin, 1957, 1960). Levin also discussed the reverse case of confusion between unspoken and spoken speech wherein one is speaking and thinking overtly, believing that the thinking is silent, e.g., demented persons who walk the streets talking to themselves, or when a man may "remember" that he either mailed a letter or thought of mailing it, he is not sure which. Levin (1957, 1960) considered such motor phenomena during hallucinations as instances of the more general phenomenon of muscle activity during thought. As such, these instances are quite consonant with our general model of cognitive processing.

Other "normal" hallucinations are images of dreaming, or during waking life when a normal person experiences emotional states, sleep deprivation, or periods of deep preoccupation (cf. Forrer, 1960a).

Hallucinations also occur as a result of such pathological conditions as schizophrenia and brain tumors, and they may be produced experimentally by means of drugs, hypnosis, and conditioning. Particularly during paranoid schizophrenia auditory hallucinations are most frequent, the patient hearing one or several voices simultaneously "emanating" from such different locales as their stomach or the walls of the room. Brain tumors have been associated with hallucinations of all modalities, and for our model may be interpreted as information processing dysfunctions in the cerebral component of the neuromuscular circuits. A common finding in the literature on sensory and perceptual deprivation is that subjects report hallucinations of a variety of sorts, occurring often in front of them rather than in the head (Bexton, Heron, and Scott, 1953). Similarly, patients treated in tank-type respirators for poliomyelitis reported various kinds of hallucinations (Mendelson, Solomon, and Lindemann, 1958). There is also an extensive literature on hallucinations produced by mescaline from the plant *Anhalonium Lewinii,* from LSD (lysergic acid diethylamide), nitrous oxide, and alcohol.

Hypnosis is a useful technique for experimentally producing hallucinations (cf. Brady and Rosner, 1966; Graham, 1970b; Evans, Reich, and Orne, 1972). We employed the technique to induce oral dreams (silent recitation of "The Lord's Prayer"), "leg dreams" (riding a bicycle), and "relaxation dreams" (doing nothing) as shown in Fig. 10.6 and Fig. 10.7. Tongue EMG dramatically increased during hypnosis while silently reciting "The Lord's Prayer," while in neither of the non-oral dreams was there an apparent increase in covert oral activity. As is the case with the night linguistic dream, it seems that the oral mechanism is covertly active during the hypnotic linguistic dream also.

Considering our reliance on conditioning principles for understanding the development of covert oral language behavior, it is valuable for us to note here the variety of conditioning approaches that have been employed to produce hallucinations. For instance, Leuba and Dunlap (1951) associated a click as a stimulus with a diamond drawn on a blank piece of paper. Later to the click they reported visually "hallucinating" the diamond. One would expect that there would be increased eye activity during such visual hallucinations, just as there is increased covert oral activity during auditory hallucinations (see above). Ellson (1941a, b) successfully conditioned "hallucinations" by pairing a light and a tone and later testing subjects without the tone. Subjects nevertheless indicated that they "heard" the tone when the light was presented. Hefferline and

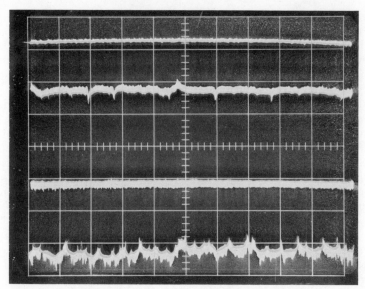

FIG. 10.6 Sample tracings typical of six college students while resting when hypnotized. From top down: left arm EMG, horizontal eye, tongue EMG, and frontal EEG. Horizontal scale is 1 sec/division; vertical scale is 100 μV/division for EMG and 50 μV/division for EEG.

Perera (1963) successfully conditioned the hallucination of a tone through an operant conditioning paradigm. (Some years later Perera informed me that one of the subjects of that early experiment *still* experienced some hallucinations, presumably concurrent with the proprioceptive feedback from the thumb twitch.) One could replace the tone in this paradigm with an orally administered language stimulus like "ali oop," as one of my students once tried, and look for covert oral language behavior immediately following the thumb twitch, but prior to the subject's key-press.

Our general interpretation is that hallucinations, like all cognitive activities, occur during the activation of selective neuromuscular circuits. Visual hallucinations would involve the occipital lobe of the brain, among others, and the eyes, especially the ocular muscles. Auditory hallucinations would similarly involve the various auditory and linguistic regions of the brain in addition to the ears and the speech musculature. Similar reasoning would apply for other classes of hallucinations, including the most interesting motor hallucinations discussed earlier. However, only in the case of auditory hallucinations have there been empirical efforts to psychophysiologically measure subvocal speech and heightened EMG from the vocal musculature during the presumed hallucinatory experience. Gould (1949, 1950) was apparently the first to successfully record covert oral language behavior prior to the overt oral report of the presence of hallucinations. McGuigan (1966b) reported significantly increased amplitude of the chin EMG and pneumogram associated with slight whisperings that corresponded roughly to the con-

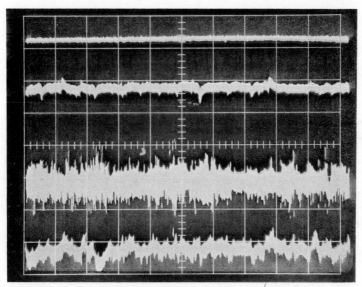

FIG. 10.7   Sample tracings during induced hypnotic verbal dream, as in Fig. 10.6.

tent of the hallucination, immediately prior to the report of having heard voices. Malmo (1975) mentioned positive results that had been recorded some years earlier that were of a similar nature, viz., heightened EMG activity during auditory hallucinations. Inouye and Shimizu (1970) similarly reported that verbal hallucinations were often accompanied by an increase in speech muscle EMG. They measured the time lag between the onset of the increased EMG discharge and the verbal hallucination as being within 1.5 seconds, with the duration of the EMG increase being positively correlated with the duration of the report of the verbal hallucination. Furthermore, the loudness of the verbal hallucination was related positively to the amount of the EMG increase. Their conclusion was that subvocal speech is a part of inner speech that is produced at the moment of experiencing verbal hallucinations.

The general notion is, then, that the patient produces the auditory hallucinations by the activation of the person's own speech musculature, though covertly. One consequence is that if the covert oral response is interfered with, the patient should fail to report an hallucination. Forrer (1960a) presented evidence that is consistent with this prediction, i.e., he reported that when a patient engages in various kinds of oral activities such as brushing or swallowing, reports of hallucinations are eliminated or reduced in frequency.

MENTAL PRACTICE IN THE ACQUISITION OF MOTOR SKILLS

A long line of research began about 1937, demonstrating that the mental practice of various motor skills results in improvement when those skills are performed overtly (Richardson, 1967). For instance,

419

Vandell, Davis, and Clugston (1943) reported that subjects who mentally practiced dart throwing by imagining throwing darts at a visible target improved their accuracy as effectively as through physical practice. Jones (1965) concluded that subjects without previous experience may learn gross bodily skills such as gymnastic skills without physical practice. Similar positive results were reported by Corbin (1967a, b) with juggling. Vandell et al. (1943) explained this phenomenon with reference to Jacobson's (1932) experimentation on imagination, viz., the process of imagining movement results in an actual, if minimal, contraction of muscles used in the overt motor skill. Perhaps covert response practice can substitute for overt response practice and even be superior (Jones, 1965). One implication for athletic training programs is that coaches help their athletes "mentally reinstate" appropriate physical conditions, and in the form of tension control, to thereby just "let the play happen." Otherwise often the athlete merely chokes, due to excessive tension, and performs tensely with muscles tightened not in accordance with his mental practice regimen.

INTROSPECTION AND VERBAL REPORT

The original uses (and they were many) of the term "introspection" had in common the feature that they constituted *the* unique method for observing an immaterial consciousness. In the later transition from the study of the self to the study of "the other one," behaviorists tended to abandon the scientific study of consciousness and the introspective[5] method, though they still maintained an interest in these mentalistic terms as they were redefined behaviorally. Hence, when forced by his critics, Watson defined consciousness as the naming of one's world inside and out. Later Skinner followed Watson, substituting the terms "external" and "internal tacts" for the processes of labeling external and internal events. Watson considered unconsciousness to be those behavioral events which one cannot name, and even went so far as to explain the process of psychoanalysis as *learning* to name internal events. Emotional difficulties involve visceral responses that the patient cannot name (recall

---

[5] As detailed in Chapter 2, we should emphasize that behaviorists typically do not deny consciousness or even hold that it is necessarily a meaningless concept. The point most often made by the more radical behaviorists is that its espousal adds nothing to our ability to predict and control behavior beyond that encompassed by the concept of the verbal report. Consciousness is regarded simply as behavior in which the subject verbally responds to other aspects of his behavior. Since S-R laws can include the verbal report merely as a naming variable, the addition of a concept or variable of consciousness is redundant, by this view, adding nothing to understanding of behavior or to the advancement of our goals in psychology. I appreciate Ralph Hefferline's elaboration of this point of view in a discussion with me; the position is not inconsistent with our model. The emphasis is merely different, in that we hold that these mentalistic terms (consciousness, etc.) do have empirical referents, and provide us with a starting point for explication. Eventually, though, we can dispense with the vague common sense terms replacing them with equations of the nature of those represented in Figs. 3.3 and 3.4. Instead, then, of including the "verbal report *merely* as a naming variable," the addition of equations to take into account covert verbal *and* non-verbal processes should greatly enhance our ability to predict and control *all behavior,* including covert.

that emotion for Watson was a matter of visceral responding). Consequently in psychoanalysis, the patient learns to attach verbal labels to visceral and other internal events. But the differences between "verbal reports" and "introspection" were important to the behaviorists in at least two ways. First, they accepted the verbal report aspect of one's introspection as data itself. Perhaps Watson's greatest achievement was his proposal that verbal behavior is no different in principle from any other kind of behavior and thus deserves a legitimite place for study within psychology. A second major difference is that the verbal report names internal events which are bodily events (e.g., kinesthetic stimuli) rather than introspective products of an immaterial consciousness. While 20th century American psychology thus progressed principally with the study of overt behavior as a function of external stimuli, essentially all behaviorists have seriously considered the process of naming internal events, which one might formulate (analogously to S-R laws) as s-R laws. One of the major theses of this book concerns behavior as a function of internal stimulation and, after making considerable progress in this century with the S-R paradigm, psychology is increasingly turning to the study of the internal environment. The consequence of this change in psychology should be tremendous, as we note later in this chapter and especially in Chapter 11. Murphy (1968) has referred to this trend as perhaps the major development of psychology in the year 2000. A manifestation of this zeitgeist is the recent rapid development of biofeedback, a topic to which we shall soon turn.

While the behaviorists have thus recognized the importance of overtly naming one's internal world (s-R laws), they have failed to develop appropriate techniques of study, as they did for S-R laws. However, such technology has been available independently of (but compatible with) the behavioristic movement. Starting about 1908 Jacobson (e.g., 1929) commenced his development of the extremely sensitive techniques of internal sensory observation for the purpose of observing one's own slight muscle sense signals. In the process of learning progressive relaxation, one goes through extensive and highly specialized training, and can eventually become extremely skilled in observing the small scale internal events known as the muscle sense of (Sir Charles) Bell. These muscle sense events, not typically observable by untrained persons, are actually afferent neural volleys generated by receptors which are activated when muscles contract. Through electromyography and verbal reports, Jacobson has shown us how to make these small scale private events publicly observable. Further development of the techniques of internal sensory observation will be evidenced as we now turn to the topics of volition, tension control, and biofeedback.

VOLITION, FREE WILL, AND WILLPOWER

Volition, the act of choosing, willing, or deciding, is an important common sense term with many ramifications for society. The very nature of most of our societal institutions, in fact, is based on the premise that humans do have a free will and are capable of exercising it to the betterment or detriment of themselves and society. Few psychological concepts have such complex histories, abounding in such confusion, contradiction, and ambiguity as the concept of the will. Seemingly endless arguments have been waged over the centuries as with the question of whether to believe in free will or determinism, terms that have little to do with one another; to relate them merely multiplies the confusion. Determinism, a principle assumed by those who seek lawful relationships (knowledge), holds that there is order in the universe. To the extent that there is lack of order in Nature, scientists must lower the probability values of proposed empirical relationships. On a determinism-indeterminism continuum, then, a complete determinism represents a universe in which there is 100% order, while a complete indeterminism would be a state of total chaos in which there are no reliable empirical relationships. The issue of free will is, therefore, obviously independent of the determinism-indeterminism issue.

The common assumption that citizens should employ their willpower is associated with one kind of culture, the present one in which we have overcrowded mental hospitals, prisons, and psychological clinics. The principle that if one commits a crime, one will be punished, embodies the common concepts of blame and fault. How often in our everyday lives do these concepts appear—the woman who takes too long to dress is *to blame* for the couple being late to the party; the child who knocks over a precariously placed lamp who instantaneously declares that it's not his *fault*. Skinner (1953) is indeed right in pointing out that society is primarily run by punitive techniques of control. A society designed on the basis of wise and effective behavioral engineering principles in which punitive techniques are largely replaced by positive psychological principles would have numerous different consequences indeed.

In considering the contemporary usage of the concept of volition or willpower, let us ask how one should exercise control over one's own behavior. The prescription is: "To stop smoking cigarettes, use your willpower!" What this principle actually says is: "To stop smoking, stop smoking!" It is a tautology in which there is no antecedent variable by means of which the individual can manipulate his or her own consequent response. The major problem of volition, then, is to provide an individual with a causal variable by which the behavior to be modified can be controlled. In his mechanistic account,[6] Sechenov (1863) suggested such an antecedent variable in terms of the sensory stimulation that results from muscle activity. An antecedent muscle response can thus produce sensory stimulation in the form of kinesthetic feedback that can control a later response, thus making that later response voluntary and conscious.

Sechenov's conception fits well with the model advanced by Alexander Bain (1859). Bain's basic notion was that the striated (voluntary) muscles

---

[6] Richardson (1930) developed an interesting mechanistic conception of volition in terms of an analogy between mental images and sparks. His electrical model illustrates a mind that has a will, though it is capable of only two ideas.

are the instrument of the will and only through them can volitional control be exercised over other mental and bodily processes. The speech musculature is the principle component of the striated musculature that is the antecedent variable with which we can control the desired response. Incipient movements, especially of the speech musculature, can therefore be used to will the appearance of sensations and ideas (see Chapter 2). If the antecedent controlling variable for the behavior to be modified is the class of responses of the skeletal musculature (principally covert speech muscle responses), how then is the connection between the two responses (controlling and controlled) made? Tuke's (1884) description of cases of acquisition of voluntary control over pupillary movements, gastro-intestinal activities and the like are illustrative of the question. Especially interesting was the case of Professor Beer who was "able in the same light to contract or dilate his pupil at will. This change in the size of the pupil, however, he brings about only through certain ideas; when, for example, he thinks of a very dark space, the pupil dilates. When, on the contrary, he thinks of a very light place, the pupil contracts" (pp. 167-68). By our model the controlling "ideas" would consist principally of initiating covert language responses. The behaviorists Hunter and Hudgins (1934) similarly developed this theme by holding that verbal processes (language responses) are the antecedents for controlling voluntary behavior—voluntary behavior, they concluded, consists of conditional responses that are under the control of self-excited receptors. Laboratory studies that have been successful in the use of covert language responses for controlling other responses include the subvocal saying ("thinking") of words and nonsense syllables to produce pupillary contraction and dilation (Hudgins, 1933, though this finding has apparently never been confirmed), in heightened electrodermal responding (Henneman, 1941; Noble, 1950), in vasodilation and vasoconstriction (Menzies, 1937; Roessler and Brogden, 1943; also Skinner, 1938, though his initiating response was apparently depth of breathing, still a covert oral response by our definition), and pulse retardation (Kotliarevsky, 1936). William James also emphasized that voluntary behavior is learned. His view was that feedback from a muscular response produces an image (which is an idea of the response to be performed). The image consists of memories of feedback and cause (will) the act of interest to occur by providing the initiating stimulus for the voluntary behavior. Kimble and Perlmuter (1970), in an incisive treatment of the problem of volition, pointed out that James' concept of the idea of a response to be performed is similar to the image of Miller, Galanter, and Pribram (1960) and to Luria's (1966a) "plan" or "motor plan." Kimble and Perlmuter developed the learning aspect of volition by considering how the initially involuntary behavior becomes voluntary. They pointed out that speech is important early in the mastery of the act to be brought under automatic control. Hence one can verbally guide the sequence of steps to better perform the act of interest, as well as to inhibit incompatible acts. With practice, the verbalizations disappear, and verbal control is unnecessary as the reaction becomes automatized. A highly practiced act thus recedes from consciousness becoming automatic and involuntary. Such automatic acts that have left the center of attention reenter attention only if they are blocked, such as zipping a jacket is attended to only if the zipper sticks, at which time the behavior at once loses its automatic character. As to the precise technique for acquiring voluntary control, we can employ the methodology developed by Jacobson (1929) in which one can learn self-operations control (progressive relaxation) by identifying the internal control signal (the signal of Bell). As we previously pointed out, the control signal consists of kinesthetic feedback from the response of interest.

The history of the scientific study of volition and willpower, as presented here, is one of the development of principles of control through the skeletal musculature. An antecedent response (typically a covert oral language response) is made which produces internal sensory stimulation that then controls the act of interest. The techniques by which one develops self-operations control lead us now to the more general topic of muscular tension control.

Some Other Technological Matters

TENSION CONTROL

The Problem. In our preceding discussion of volition, the very contemporary-sounding statements of Sechenov (1863) and Bain (1859) were summarized to the effect that the will is exercised through the control of the skeletal musculature, a principle that has great relevance for some of the contemporary problems of society. In particular, stresses of the modern world produce tension states that wreak havoc on the human biological system. Of the numerous techniques which presume to control tension, we shall consider the two which are in the scientific mainstream. The first is progressive relaxation (Jacobson, 1929) and the second is biofeedback.

One of the difficulties in studying tension and relaxation is that these terms have a variety of definitions in the vernacular; for example, "relaxation" can mean going on a picnic, playing a game of golf, or "putting the mind at rest." For our purposes, we will follow the standard scientific definitions of tension and relaxation as muscular states: Relaxation is the lengthening of muscle fibers and tension is the contraction (shortening) of muscle fibers. The consequences of these simple operational definitions are enormous, as we shall show throughout this section.

The stresses of modern society make it difficult for one to efficiently relax and tense as one moves throughout daily life. Most individuals have not learned to use their muscles efficiently, and, in fact, most have learned very effectively how to misuse them. In view of the extremely large number of muscles and muscle fibers throughout our bodies that have been misused for years (we have some 1030 separate striated muscles which comprise about half the body weight) we can well understand why the task of learning tension control is not an easy one. In most of us, massive muscle re-education is required, and often the results of a lifetime of excessive and unwise muscle tension are manifested in such pathological conditions as hypertension, colitis, anxiety, excessive fatigue, headaches, constipation, and diarrhea. Fig. 10.8 is an attempt to illustrate how contracted skeletal musculature can indirectly drive various of the autonomic systems through intervening central nervous system activity. The precise physiological mechanisms by which the skeletal musculature can control the cardiovascular and other systems must be extremely complex, and at present are poorly understood. One hint as to the physiological pathways was provided by Gellhorn and Kiely (1972) who suggested that muscular relaxation reduces proprioceptive input to the hypothalamus, with resulting lessening of hypothalamic-cortical discharges.

What do people who need to control their tensions do? Patients often

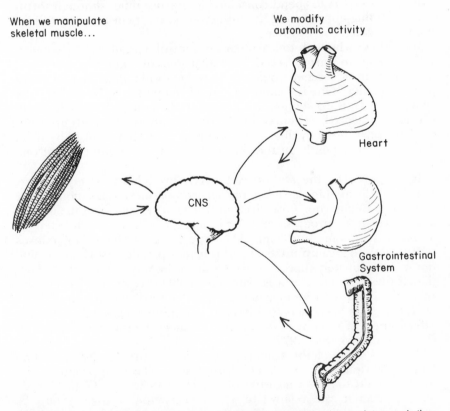

When we manipulate skeletal muscle...

We modify autonomic activity

Heart

CNS

Gastrointestinal System

FIG. 10.8   A model of the functional relationship between the skeletal musculature and other bodily functions. As tension increases, central nervous system and autonomic functions are heightened. Relaxation of the skeletal musculature produces a tranquil state throughout the body.

consult their physicians for help with their tension disorders, and are frequently advised to "go and relax," without being told how. Perhaps tranquilizing drugs are prescribed. Tranquilizers, of course, often satisfy the patient, and their effects are prompt, which contrasts with learning tension control. Patients seek instant success—they want instant "cures" of their "nervous conditions." Such wishes no doubt contribute to the enormous popularity of tranquilizing drugs, and also help account for the economic success of various faddish movements which offer easy solutions in minimum time. In view of the large number of years during which one may have misused one's muscles, "short-cut" techniques that rely on drugs, suggestion, hypnotism, mysticism, religion, and the like probably have all of the solidity of quicksand. In view of all of the maladaptive muscular habits one learns over the decades, muscle reeducation requires much time and patience. In order to learn to automatically control the entire set of neuromuscular systems and to move through daily activities with a cultivated state of psychophysiological rest, one should expect to spend considerable practice time, although fortunately nothing approaching the numerous years spent learning to misuse the muscles.

Individuals who wish to learn tension control typically ask "How long will it take me to learn to relax?" The analogous question that one might direct to a music teacher would be "How long will it take me to learn to play the piano?" One is reminded here of the tourist in New York City who asked "How do you get to Carnegie Hall?" and was advised "Practice, lady, practice." Of course, one part of the answer depends upon the level at which the individual starts and how good they want to become. Another part depends on the effectiveness of the technique that one selects.

In response to the widespread need throughout society a large number of techniques have been proposed to achieve relaxation. These techniques range from those directed strictly to the control of the musculature (such as progressive relaxation) through those directed to localized symptoms and employing apparatus (such as biofeedback techniques), to Eastern mystical and religious practices (such as meditation). Unfortunately there has been little in the way of scientific validation of these various practices, with the notable exception of progressive relaxation, and, to a lesser extent, muscle biofeedback. Recently, however, there has been increased interest in objective measurement of the effectiveness of some techniques, yet few meet the standard criteria of evaluation (Borkovec, 1977).

As one sample of the scientific validation of progressive relaxation Paul (1969) found that training in progressive relaxation produced significant reductions in a measure of anxiety, forearm EMG, heart rate, and respiration rate relative to a "self-relaxation" control group. A group that was given hypnotic suggestion of relaxation had significant decreases in the anxiety measure and in respiration rate relative to the controls. Furthermore, progressive relaxation led to a significantly greater decrease in heart rate and forearm EMG than did the hypnotized group: 85% of the subjects trained in progressive relaxation significantly reduced their anxiety, forearm EMG, heart rate and respiration rate, while 30% of the hypnotized subjects produced this change. These results are particularly impressive in view of the fact that the progressive relaxation subjects received only two one-hour sessions of training.

Progressive Relaxation (Self-Operations Control). Years of clinical and scientific validation have guided Edmund Jacobson's work, dating from his tenure as a graduate student at Harvard University in 1908. Jacobson sought to develop a method to help people to learn to behave more rationally to the stressful conditions of modern society. His broad technological goal has been to increase everyday human efficiency, including clinical treatment of pathological conditions. In progressive relaxation one learns to observe the internal sensory world, just as one observes the external world.

Learning Internal Sensory Observation. The principles are simple: (1) learn to recognize (observe) the state of tension, and (2) contrast that with the elimination of tension (relaxation). In muscular re-education, each of the major muscle groups is systematically tensed so that the learner can identify the unique sensation produced by the muscular contraction of that group. This unique sensation is the control signal, a signal which occurs when the contracting muscles activate their muscle spindle receptors to generate volleys of afferent neural impulses which are directed to the brain (Fig. 10.9). The process of internal sensory observation allows one to observe the control signals that are signs of tension in the muscle groups. Eventually the learner comes to automatically monitor all internally generated control signals, coming to recognize them instantaneously as the sensations of tension. If the tensions are undesired they may be relaxed away.

A more generalized, widespread kind of tension occurs throughout an entire limb, and in fact throughout the entire skeletal musculature. To learn to reduce this general tension, which of course most people are not aware of, one is taught to very gradually and uniformly stiffen an entire limb for a matter of some minutes, and then very gradually reverse the process, taking the limb "down to zero."

One might speculate that the two types of tension—the momentarily localized tension detected by isolated control signals, and the generalized steady residual tension—are functions of the two types of skeletal muscle fibers discussed in Chapter 9. In particular, it is possible that the rapid acting phasic fibers function in generating the control signals (which incidentally carry the linguistic coding discussed in Chapter 9), while the contraction of the tonic fibers is responsible for general tension. If this is true, it is reasonable that two different techniques are necessary for learning to control these two types of tension, and the two types of muscle fibers are perhaps innervated by different neural systems.

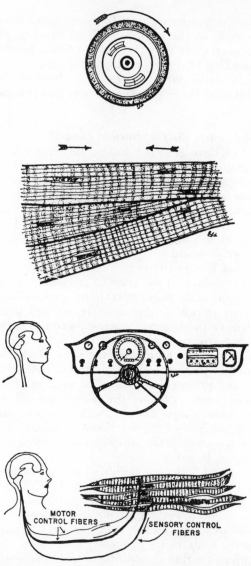

FIG. 10.9 "You run your car by manipulating the controls on and near the dashboard, whereby you make the wheels move at the rate and in the direction you desire. Likewise, you can run yourself by going on and off with the power in the controls which lie in your muscles, whereupon your muscles contract and relax in the patterns which suit your effort-purposes" (Jacobson, 1964, p. 2).

Differential Relaxation. The activities of our everyday life require numerous muscle tensions. If one is driving an automobile, one needs to depress the accelerator and steer. But in so doing, we do *not* need to grip the wheel extremely tightly, furrow the eyebrows, grit the teeth, or *lean*

428

vigorously on the door (or horn). Such extra tensions are not necessary for the primary purpose, which is driving the automobile. People who are untrained in relaxation are usually unaware of these useless wasted efforts and yet they often develop complaints of "a crick in the neck," a headache, being fatigued, etc. A well-trained individual, on the other hand, automatically relaxes those muscles which are not necessary for the act being performed, having learned that the control signals for the muscles operate analogously to the accelerator control pedal in automobiles (Fig. 10.9). To use gasoline energy, the driver depresses the accelerator pedal and keeps it depressed as long as energy expenditure is required. Analogously, individuals driving their own bodies keep the control signals operating for those muscles necessary for the act being performed, but selectively (differentially) relax those muscles not required for the daily repertoire of movements. In driving a car one relaxes the jaw muscles (ceasing to grit the teeth), moderately grips the steering wheel, and "goes negative" to relax the brow musculature. This process of contracting the muscles necessary for the activity at hand, but relaxing all others in the body, is called *differential relaxation*. To become more efficient in the use of one's energies by relaxing the muscles differentially, one can develop his or her own personal inventory of acts that are not now performed efficiently. Perhaps a professional person talking to a client wastes energy by needlessly sitting on the edge of a chair clasping the desk or writing pen; all that this act requires is the use of the speech musculature. Some persons while silently reading may vigorously grip the book with the hands, yet what is mainly required is the use of the eye and speech muscles. Busy executives, after spending hours on the telephone, often complain of bodily fatigue being totally unaware that they have been trying to "talk" with their legs all day by wastefully pressing their feet against the floor, or wrapping the legs about the chair legs.

Perhaps nowhere is differential relaxation more successfully used than in sports—the long distance runner who uses only those muscles necessary for running can run farther with less fatigue than one who has not acquired differential relaxation (Burke, 1975). By continuously monitoring the muscular control signals through internal sensory observation, the trained individual automatically practices personal energy conservation 24 hours a day including at night to promote restful sleep.

Jacobson advocates that one not only learn how and when to spend one's energies, but that one also estimate the amount of energy required for a given purpose in order to decide whether or not that purpose is worthwhile. Often it is clear, for example, that an ongoing conversation is simply not worth the effort—particularly if it is emotionally wasteful. One who is well trained in progressive relaxation does not argue heatedly or castigate the driver in front of him, or the like, as such activities merely waste energy and accomplish nothing. Cost estimation is important, and people can become quite skilled in estimating their moment-to-moment energy expenditure.

To consider how to learn differential relaxation, imagine that you are stretching your arm out to lift a weight. With this muscular contraction you are exerting effort.[7] But suppose that you don't bother to lift the weight and instead let your muscles relax. Relaxing is *not bothering to contract your musculature*—relaxation is the negative of exertion. It should be easy to relax, and difficult to exert oneself, but many people have acquired habits of exerting themselves in *everything* they do so that they contract some muscles even when trying to relax. In this way they make something difficult that is not naturally so.

"Mental Work" Is Physical Work.   Often individuals wear themselves out through needless worry in which the same thoughts recur over and over again. Such useless "mental activity" can be responsible for insomnia, as well as for daytime fatigue. A. J. Carlson, considered by physiologists to be a skeptic, once commented to Jacobson about his research on the electrical measurement of mental activity.

"Well! You have proved that mental activities are physical acts!" (Jacobson, personal communication). As Jacobson said, "It might be naive to say that we think with our muscles, but it would be inaccurate to say that we think without them" (1967, p. 110).

The conclusion that muscles are intimately involved in thought is technologically important for several reasons. For one, differential relaxation of skeletal muscles when one eliminates undesired thoughts (as in worries or insomnia) is an energy conservation measure. With our skeletal muscles we control both our external and internal worlds—they are effectors because they produce effects on the external and internal environment. By skeletal muscle manipulation we thus indirectly orchestrate brain and autonomic activites as we systematically and efficiently guide our thoughts and emotions.

Controlling Hypertension and Coronary Heart Disease.   Our heart associations are pointing out that cardiovascular diseases have now reached epidemic proportions, with 1,000,000 cardiovascular disease fatalities and 700,000 heart attack fatalities each year, with the disease progressing to earlier age levels. Progressive relaxation has been successfully applied in the control of hypertension (Hillman, 1976). In the pressures of everyday life, activities of the skeletal muscles increase, thereby increasing cardiovascular activity. The skeletal musculature requires continuous cardiovascular activity for energy supplies and for the removal of metabolic products. As states of effort and emotion increase, there are increasingly greater demands on the cardiovascular system, especially increased blood pressure that is biologically necessary to increase the supply of sugar and oxygen required by the muscles. Accordingly, there is hypertonia of the musculature of the arterioles (small arteries), which are responsible for hypertension (cf. Jacobson, 1939). If the individual continues to engage in over-effortful living, the initially intermittent smooth muscle overexertion of the arterioles can become chronic. If the cardiovascular system becomes organically damaged, the high blood

[7] Bigland-Ritchie and Woods (1974) showed that integrated EMG as a measure of the combined number and frequency of muscle fibers used in a contraction in that integrated EMG can be an index of average energy expenditure (oxygen consumption) per fiber action potential.

pressure is irreversible. However, if an individual seeks proper treatment prior to organic damage, blood pressure can be lowered, as with clinical progressive relaxation (see Fig. 10.10).

Bruxism ("Teeth Grinding"). One very common tension problem among "normal" people is the habit of grinding the teeth, especially

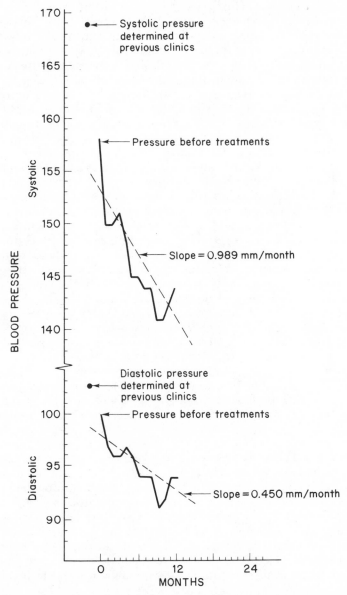

FIG. 10.10 Mean decrease of blood pressure in selected patients treated with clinical progressive relaxation. Follow-up data indicate that the decrease is lasting.

during sleep. Frequently, the problem becomes so intense that the individual wears away considerable of their teeth which in turn may lead to a variety of other disorders. Marvin P. Levine, D.D.S., and William Ayer, D.D.S. at the U.S. Army Institute of Dental Research, Walter Reed Army Medical Center, Washington, D.C., had 14 bruxism patients clinch their teeth together as hard as possible for five seconds, and then they relaxed the jaw for five seconds. The subjects repeated this procedure five times and continued the practice six times daily for two weeks. Levine and Ayer reported that within 10 days, 11 of the 14 had successfully eliminated the grinding and that in the six month follow-up, the patients had not resumed the habit. This practice is a specific instance of the application of progressive relaxation, though it is not clear that that was the motivation for this interesting work. In the application of progressive relaxation, special attention is paid to the relaxation of the masseter and as a result, bruxism is one of the earliest tension problems to be eliminated.

Gentz (1972) longitudinally studied bruxism during sleep and developed an apparatus which automatically records four simultaneous items of information using the following information transmitters: (1) an accelerometer which picks up vibrations from teeth-grinding that are propagated by way of the bone tissue; (2) a dynamometer in a dental splint which records biting and all horizontal positions of a mandible; (3) a sensitive microphone; (4) an electronic time marker. With this apparatus one can analyze biting incidents during sleep in coordination with electromyography, electroencephalography, telemetry, and psychophysical bite force measurements. The apparatus appears useful in diagnosis and treatment of nocturnal bruxism.

Colitis (Spastic Colon), Ulcers, Constipation and Diahrrea, Chronic Fatigue, and Other Applications of Clinical Progressive Relaxation. Through the years Jacobson has reported on numerous successful applications of progressive relaxation for treating these types of problems. In treating gastrointestinal problems, the clinician concentrates especially on abdominal relaxation, though one still relaxes the entire body. Jacobson has estimated that perhaps 90% of the instances of constipation and diarrhea result from tension problems concentrated in the intestinal region.

Conclusion.   The aim of progressive relaxation is to help the learners become self-reliant and to help them program themselves so that they can better carry out their individual purposes, not becoming dependent on the teacher. For the greatest benefit of society Jacobson (1973) advocates the teaching of progressive relaxation to children who, incidentally, acquire the skills more efficiently and rapidly than do adults, and thus are able to automatically employ the technique throughout their entire lives. Great advances in preventative medicine and clinical psychology could thereby be achieved. Just as we eventually learned to brush our teeth and to bathe our bodies frequently, we will eventually learn to differentially relax.

Biofeedback. Biofeedback has recently had a sizeable impact on the nation. Like many other scientific techniques, it has values and potential pitfalls. As a phenomenon to be investigated in the laboratory, the study of biofeedback has yielded valuable findings. The potential danger lies in the way the public has seized on the phenomenon as a "cure all" for its problems.

By transducing bodily signals and presenting them externally the observer can become aware of internal events that are perhaps not otherwise knowable. Through biofeedback procedures, one can see, hear, or otherwise monitor one's own brain waves, cardiovascular activity, galvanic skin response, skin temperature, and essentially any other bodily organ that can generate a signal. No doubt basic scientific findings with the use of biofeedback will have great significance for the further development of our science.

Clinically, the first use of biofeedback was apparently about 1950 by Jacobson (cf. 1957) who transduced electromyographic signals, displaying them on a cathode ray oscilloscope so that his patients could visually monitor their tension signals. After working with the technique for some time, Jacobson finally abandoned it for clinical use, apparently for two reasons. First, the learner became dependent upon the feedback signal, relaxing selected muscle groups only in the presence of that signal. The preferable technique is progressive relaxation wherein the individual monitors all tension signals under all life circumstances, without the necessity of auxiliary equipment. A second apparent problem with biofeedback concerns the permanence of the effect. Not only might it not transfer to everyday life situations, but the behavioral modification might not be permanent (McGuigan, 1971). Another problem with muscle biofeedback is that the skeletal musculature does not act as a unified system, i.e., if through biofeedback one learns to relax one muscle (such as the forehead muscle) this localized relaxation is independent of the remainder of the skeletal muscles, each of which must be relaxed in its turn. In a sense one might say after successful tension reduction of one muscle through biofeedback, there are only some 1,029 yet to go.

Biofeedback may eventually find useful and even powerful application in the public domain as a clinical technique, but to date there is little scientific validation for the procedure. Yet we are witness to numerous biofeedback clinics which are actively engaged in therapy throughout the country. While patients report relief of symptoms through various biofeedback procedures, these reports are not sufficient to justify their technological application. Biofeedback like any relaxation technique should be well validated. As Wolpe (1975) pointed out a valid therapy should produce a success rate in excess of the 50 to 60% one can expect from *any* therapy as a simple result of the "placebo effect."

In the application of clinical progressive relaxation for the treatment of a phobia, the patient imagines fearful acts of increasing intensity, then relaxes the musculature. In 1934, Jacobson (1957) had a patient who feared heights, started by imagining a feather dropping and gradually worked up to imagining looking down from tall heights. Eventually, the patient rented an office high up in a skyscraper.

Behavior modification has derived in part from principles of operant conditioning, as in the work of Wolpe (1975) and Cautela (1973). Cautela employed methods referred to as "covert conditioning" in clinical situations where the assumption is that empirical generalizations of overt operant conditioning apply to the manipulation of covert processes as well. In the application of such conditioning procedures as covert sensitization, covert positive reinforcement, covert negative reinforcement, and covert extinction, presumably small scale muscular behavior is systematically manipulated to eliminate the pathological condition. A similar approach is Homme's (1965) system of contingency management in which he assumed that private events obey the same laws as public events, and that knowledge of the topography of a response is not required in order to control its frequency. Homme's approach is a blend of three sources: operant conditioning (Skinner, 1953), the Premack principle (Premack, 1965), and contiguity theory (Guthrie, 1952). These procedures are used to systematically manipulate coverants, which are covert responses that are unlocated but nevertheless can be systematically manipulated.

The entire field of behavior modification and associated enterprises is so enormormous that we will only pay lip service to it here. The consequences for society are indeed great, and these technological approaches deserve our continued observation and study within the context of a science of covert processes.

RAPID INFORMATION PROCESSING:
"SPEED READING" AND "SPEED LISTENING"

An interesting question is whether or not we can sizeably increase the rate at which humans normally process externally presented linguistic information. Auditory information processing can be increased through training, as in individuals (especially the blind) who have learned to comprehend "compressed speech" (cf. Foulke and Sticht, 1969). The burgeoning of "speed reading courses" is an illustration of the public's desire for rapid visual information processing. Claims have been made for rates of reading of 10,000 or 25,000 words per minute.

Basic to the issue of whether there really is a legitimate speed reading phenomenon is the question of whether or not there are physiological limits to the rate at which humans can process visually presented information. Some empirical research suggests that there is such a limit, e.g., Pauk (1964) concluded that beyond about 500 words per minute, there was a loss of comprehension, which suggests that there is a physiological limit beyond which "reading" becomes merely "scanning" or "skimming." Poulton (1958) similarly concluded that there is a limit to the amount of reading material that can be understood within a given time period. Such a physiological limit, often estimated at about 1,000 words per minute, would help us to define "reading" per se, since that would constitute a criterion for maximum efficiency of visual information processing.

In reading, the eyes fixate at selected words, whereupon information from the written symbols within the perceptual span enters short-term memory. During that perceptual phase, the circuits depicted in Fig. 9.5 are activated including especially the eyes and the speech musculature. If the eyes do not sufficiently fixate on selected words, some of the visual information fails to be received, so that as we increase our efforts to read faster, we apparently read less. Anderson, Goldberg, and Hidde (1971) showed that even reading aloud each word in a sentence did not lead to complete comprehension of the meaning of the sentence. Hence, claims of "reading rates" of many thousands of words per minute should better be called scanning rather than reading. In scanning ("speed reading") one selects certain words out of each page to process, and uses those words to infer "the whole story," which one can often do because the selected words evoke recall of previously acquired and stored information, e.g., one merely needs to select the words "Mary" and "lamb" in order to reinstate the entire nursery rhyme. A learned professor thus does not need to *read* the new textbook along with the students, but only to scan it, selecting critical words in order to reinstate what the introductory students must diligently acquire for the first time. A comprehension test given to the professor who thus scans an introductory textbook for the first time at the rate of 30,000 words per minute would show no loss in comprehension. When reading novel material, though, we expect information processing limitations, as expressed by Woody Allen: "I took a speed-reading course, learning to read straight down the middle of the page, and I was able to go through War and Peace in 20 minutes. It's about Russia" (cited by Carver, 1972, p. 22).

Typically in speed reading courses attempts are made to eliminate "subvocalization," and have the reader engage in strictly "visual reading." By our model (Chapter 9), such elimination of the speech muscle component of the neuromuscular circuits would prevent comprehension. Actually, faster reading increases, rather than decreases, amplitude of "subvocalization" (tongue and chin EMG, McGuigan and Pinkney, 1973). As we have reported in a number of places in this book, "subvocalization" is useful to the reader. Parents and teachers should recognize that children need to subvocalize while reading and that when the need fades, so does the lipmoving.

The "polygraph" and related techniques are widely used for such purposes as espionage and the identification of criminals. The basic assumption is that neural and probing questions evoke different emotional states (covert response patterns) of an involuntary nature, and that these states can be psychophysiologically differentiated.

Erasistratus apparently was first to associate the emotions with psychophysiological changes by concluding that emotions alter the pulse rate. Perhaps the earliest lie detection procedure called on supernatural powers to expose the suspect's guilt. Thus frightened, the guilty would then incriminate themselves. Contemporary lie detector procedures often substitute "scientific instruments" for supernatural powers, similarly leading the suspect to confess. Other early psychophysiological lie detector techniques measured salivation with cotton or rice in the mouth, the assumption being that the guilty who lie would be frightened and therefore have a dry mouth.

Probably the first scientific investigation of deception was by the Italian criminologist Lombroso who reported reliable differences in blood pressure changes between guilty and innocent suspects. Marston (1917), a student of Münsterberg, added the important concepts of making several simultaneous psychophysiological measurements and of establishing the reliability of those measurements. Benussi (1914) concluded that a respiration ratio was indicative of truthful vs. false answers. Larson (1932) was apparently the first to employ a polygraph which measured blood pressure, pulse rate, and respiration changes. The widely used Keeler (1930) polygraph added GSR and in 1945 the Reid polygraph added an electromyographic channel. Reid had noted that individuals undergoing interrogation tensed the muscles of their arms during questioning [McGuigan and Pavek (1972) concluded that electromyographic arm measures differentiated between yes-no thoughts on a probabilistic basis]. Darrow (1936) noted that palmar sweating increases tactile sensitivity and one's ability to grasp with the hands, and that both reactions have evolutionary significance for primates moving among the trees. Hence Darrow conceived of deception responses as emotional reactions to the possibility of being detected. Such deception responses thus function to facilitate adjustment, and are psychophysiologically measurable.

Negative evidence for the cardiogram and pneumogram for lie detection was found by Bitterman and Marcuse (1947). Though their subjects *did* differentially respond to relevant and irrelevant questions, all were innocent.

Lacey (1950) found that systolic and diastolic blood pressure, pulse rate, and palmar conductance were not reliably correlated within a given subject. The implication for lie detection techniques is negative in that any given psychophysiological response cannot be considered to be representative of the general psychophysiological activity of the body. Lykken (1960) obtained positive results using GSR with the "guilty knowledge technique" in which the interrogator seeks involuntary "give away" responses to stimuli when a guilty person recalls a crime. However, this technique has limited technological application, since the interrogator must know pertinent facts about the crime which may not be available to anyone other than the guilty individual.

E. N. Sokolov (1963) psychophysiologically distinguished between reactions to probing vs. neutral questions by noting that the orienting response to neutral questions adapts rather easily. Probing questions, on the other hand, require more processing of information with more attendant decision-making requirements.

Kugelmass and Lieblich (1966) concluded that GSR detection results under stress were essentially similar to those obtained in mildly stressful experimental situations. Combined GSR and heart rate measures were far superior in detection efficiency than heart rate alone, though normal inflation of the blood pressure cuff reduced the detection efficiency of the GSR channel. Further positive results with GSR were obtained by Kugelmass, Lieblich, and Bergman (1967) and by Kugelmass and Lieblich (1968).

This sample of studies is illustrative of efforts to develop a deception detection technology, and we conclude that the field lacks generalized validity. Yet polygraphs as "lie detectors" are extensively used by the federal government. As the Committee on Government Operations pointed out, over four million dollars was spent in one fiscal year to administer nearly 20,000 polygraph tests in spite of the Committee's conclusion that "there is no 'lie detector,' neither machine nor human. People have been deceived by a myth that a metal box in the hands of an investigator can detect truth or falsehood"[8] (see also Bigland-Ritchie and Woods, 1974).

While the Committee on Government Operations based its negative conclusion on such autonomic indicators as GSR, heart rate, and respiration, they similarly concluded that alternative techniques also lack validity. One, the psychological stress evaluator (PSE-1) graphically displays inaudible frequency modulations in speech superimposed on overt audible modulations. Presumably, internal stresses are thereby involuntarily manifested and thus detectable by the system. This system is simpler to operate than the polygraph and does not have to be used at the time of interrogation since a tape recorder is employed. A second technique, the Mark II Voice Stress Analyzer, measures energy changes in the lower and middle range of speech frequencies. Rapid variations in the tremolo or vibrato amplitude of speech are electronically extracted and instantaneously displayed as presumed changes in emotional stress. Other possible detection systems are based on measures of face temperature, EKG, or EEG. An interesting system the Committee examined was the use of a retinoscope to observe changes in retinal color, pupil size,

---

[8] Committee on Government Operations, 94th Congress, 2nd Session, House Report No. 94-795, The use of polygraphs and similar devices by federal agencies. Washington, D.C.: U.S. Government Printing Office, 1976.

and eye focus as indices of emotional responses. The retinoscope is allegedly successful on intoxicated or drugged individuals. Finally, the Committee noted a "microwave respiration monitor" to detect lying through increased rate of respiration, as indicated by increased palpitation of the stomach. This system can be used remotely without the knowledge of the suspect, and could be employed for remote and surreptitious truth verification at border crossings, airports, and police lineups. The Committee's general conclusion was that "Evidence presented in the hearings upon which this report is based demonstrates that such devices have even less scientific validity than the polygraph."[9]

In view of the paucity of scientific evidence to establish the validity and reliability of polygraphy and other available systems, the position of Orne, Thackray, and Paskewitz (1972) and Orne (1973) that "lie detection" is a misnomer is fitting. While these authors granted that psychophysiological changes are recordable in emotionally loaded situations, those changes are held to be unrelated to lying. When lie detection is successful it is due to non-scientific practices. As Orne (personal communication, March 23, 1976) put it, so much depends "upon the extensive experience, skill, and integrity of the examiner, and therefore the use of the polygraph to detect deception is perhaps best considered a clinical art. . . . In its simplest terms, a good interrogator aided by the polygraph is more effective in detecting deception than a good interrogator without the polygraph. It is crucial to remember, however, that a fool, even with the aid of the polygraph, remains a fool."

What is the future of deception detection? Past technology has been almost exclusively based upon the Keeler polygraph which principally measures respiration, cardiovascular activity and GSR. Other psychophysiological measures have received little systematic attention, and our science of covert processes contains sufficient data such that, in all probability, we could now develop advanced and effective deception detection systems. The strategy would be to employ a large number of psychophysiological measures, as the arm EMG and eye measures that were successfully used by McGuigan and Pavek (1972) to probabilistically diagnose yes vs. no thoughts. Similarly Cutrow, Parks, Lucas, and Thomas (1972) measured eye blink latency and rate, breathing amplitude and rate, heart rate, palmar and volar forearm GSR, and voice latency when subjects were instructed to always answer "no" to questions. Eye blink rate and latency significantly increased during questions in which the "no" response constituted a lie, compared to truthful "no's." All other concomitant measures also significantly increased during deception. Cutrow et al. concluded that each measure is useful for the detection of deception, but an index combining more than one psychophysiological variable holds advantages over independent measures (see also Podlesny and Raskin, 1977).

The societal implications of a successful deception detection system

[9] Ibid., p. 437.

are enormous, as will be discussed in the next chapter. For now we note that certain countermeasures *are* available to the individual.

Conclusion

We may well ask whether there *are* different mental processes: Is thinking a different internal information processing phenomenon than dreaming? Is a night dream different in this sense from a day dream? Is a waking hallucination different from a dream or a series of rational thoughts? Certainly the various mental processes occur under a variety of external stimulating conditions—the night dream occurs during sleep in contrast to the day dream. But are different processes (quantitatively or qualitatively) set off in these cases, or do quite similar processes occur under different conditions? We can specify certain variables that influence the nature of our mental processes, such as temporary or permanent bodily condition. Temporary changes may influence mental content as when a hungry person dreams about food. Permanent states would be influential as when a diseased state of the temporal lobe produces hallucinations. Mental content can be limited by bodily condition, as in the case of congenitally blind individuals lacking visual content in their dreams.

External conditions may influence mental content, depending on the content of the sensory input and on which sensory modalities are activated. And finally, we may note that the conditioning histories (experiences) clearly influence our mental content, i.e., a person who has never heard of or seen snow would certainly not dream about snow.

While we can in such ways as specified above account for various differences in our mental processes, there is no reason to think that the various common sense terms (thoughts, hallucinations, dreams) are actually indicative of different kinds of internal information processes. They all involve activation of neuromuscular circuits, following the model of Fig. 9.5. Nocturnal dreams, hallucinations, daydreams, problem-solving thought thus all involve the same kinds of bodily processes, differing merely according to such variables as specified above. The nocturnal dream, for instance, differs from directed thought processes while awake primarily in that it lacks guiding control from external environmental stimuli. In short, the various mental phenomena are all instances of the same general explicandum, so that similar psychophysiological patterns are recordable for all. Accordingly, the higher mental processes identified by various common sense terms have little scientific value other than providing us with a starting point. As we become increasingly successful in explicating these common sense terms, they lose their value and will be replaced by equations such as those represented in Figs. 3.3 and 3.4. However, the scientific study of mental processes has important implications for society, about which we shall now speculate.

11

Consequences of a Science
of Covert Behavior
for Institutions of Society

Robert Oppenheimer, the physicist who was so important in the technological development of nuclear energy, addressed the 1955 meeting of the American Psychological Association and prophesized the future social consequences of psychology as follows:

In the last ten years the physicists have been extraordinarily noisy about the immense powers which . . . have come into the possession of man, powers notably and strikingly for very large-scale and dreadful destruction. We have spoken of our responsibilities and of our obligations to society in terms that sound to me very provincial, because the psychologist can hardly do anything without realizing that for him the acquisition of knowledge opens up the most terrifying prospects of controlling what people do and how they think and how they behave and how they feel. . . . As the corpus of psychology gains in certitude and subtlety and skill, I can see that the physicist's pleas that what he discovers be used with humanity and be used wisely will seem rather trivial compared to those pleas which you will have to make and for which you will have to be responsible (1956, p. 128).

In a lighter vein, Toda (1972), considered possible roles of psychology in the *very* distant future, stating that "According to my speculations, psychology will make tremendous progress in the coming century, comparable to the progress made by physics in the last century. In contrast to cultural progress, biological progress is slow" (p. 311). "In the very distant future, psychology will be the master science. Psychology will be the most important of all the sciences. The reason? Very simple. Otherwise, mankind will not survive. And if no people survive, there will be no psychology . . . we will then have to learn, somehow, how to live with our fellowman; and, in order to accomplish this very difficult task, our attention must inevitably be oriented toward the inner world within ourselves" (p. 312).[1]

In this chapter we shall speculate about some of the technological consequences of psychology, the science of behavior, which might be especially important for the future of the human race. Though one of the younger sciences, psychology is one of the most rapidly developing. Today it is regarded as the queen of the social sciences, in part because of its relatively advanced methodological sophistication. Among the consequences of an advanced science of psychology for our every day world are those for the functioning of our social institutions, for our morals and ethics, and for our general modes of behavior. Numerous possibilities have been considered in futuristic novels, foremost among which are Thomas Moore's *Utopia,* Aldous Huxley's *Brave New World,* George Orwell's *1984* and B. F. Skinner's *Walden II.* Many people today consider it a realistic possibility that yesterday's fiction will be tomorrow's fact. Not without reason, some see society accelerating its rush toward *Brave New World* and *1984.*

B. F. Skinner (1953, 1971) has directly addressed the question of the social consequences of a refined science of psychology from his vantage point as one of the leading neobehaviorists. Apparently influenced strongly by Thorndike and Watson, Skinner professes to be appalled by the widespread use of punitive techniques in society for controlling behavior. His highly successful *Science and Human Behavior* was an agile and talented analysis of the social institutions of contemporary western society and included recommendations for improvements through the cogent application of scientifically established principles. Skinner's major strategy is to generally substitute operations of reinforcement for those of punishment, though punishment still has its place in behavioral en-

---

[1] Among the techniques for exploring our inner world are those of internal sensory observation developed by Jacobson (1929) and biofeedback, as discussed in Chapter 10 and this chapter.

gineering. In teaching children to study, for example, it is preferable
(because it is both more effective and more pleasant for all) to reward
them when they emit desirable behavior than to spank them when they
have not. Skinner's (1971) major philosophical effort, *Beyond Freedom and
Dignity,* attracted widespread attention to his message, as well as a broad
side of criticism. The criticisms resulted because of misunderstandings
of Skinner's intent, and because society is not yet ready to broadly accept
and incorporate empirically based psychological principles.

One major problem that helped to foster the attack on Skinner's position centered around his use of the word "control." He was consistent
with his use of "control" as it is scientifically defined, i.e., the purpose of
psychology is to predict and control behavior wherein "control" means to
change a response by systematically manipulating stimulus conditions.
"Control" in this sense means the learning process in education, or the
elimination of a phobia through behavior therapy. Unfortunately,
surplus meaning was read into his use of the word, bringing the worst of
Orwellian *1984* "mind control" erroneously into Skinner's context. Had
Skinner employed a neutral or novel term (like "modify") he would have
been less likely to be accused of advocating the establishment of an
autocratic society with a psychologist king.

The problem of acceptance of the application of behavioral principles
for the improvement of society is probably unavoidable by *any* psychologist at this stage of our development. Ours is a world in which there
is much cultural lag, and the general public is simply unaware of the
technical aspects of psychological principles. For instance, a common
error is to think of permissiveness as the opposite of punishment; or that
positive reinforcement is the equivalent of permissiveness or laissez
faire. It will be a *long* time before punitive techniques for modifying
behavior are replaced with those of reinforcement, as many of our institutions still function on the basis of principles of the Old Testament—
"An eye for an eye and a tooth for a tooth." Together with the concepts
of "blame" and "fault," these form cornerstones of society's behavior,
and even the bases of foreign policy among some nations. The educational process will continue to be slow and often painful, but if we are to
develop a truly enlightened populace, we must vigorously work at improving our school systems, our universities, and our scientific and
technological institutions.

For the classical psychology of overt behavior, the questions and issues
we raise are not new. Neither are they new for the developing science of
covert processes, for they have been raised over the centuries by highly
respected science fiction writers, among others. What *is* new in the present context is that the achievements of a science of covert behavior now
make science fiction speculations about technological consequences of
psychology, if not as present realities, as accomplishments that can be
realized in the foreseeable future.

We have noted two reasons governing the need for a science of covert
processes: (1) scientists must hypothesize logical constructs that inter-

vene between external stimuli and overt responses, as a consequence of which a wide variety of covert processes have been formalized (Chapter 3); (2) the empirical science of psychophysiology (electropsychology) has been developing rapidly on its own. The combination of these two reasons (the power of formal behaviorist models and the richness of psychophysiological empiricism) yields many potentially fruitful applications for society. The need now is to formulate a basis for rational action so that these achievements can be used wisely. In an effort to advance toward that formulation, we now shall examine some of the well-recognized problems for which society has long sought solutions, though we follow no order of priority.

There are two general categories of technological applications that we shall consider. The first is that of "diagnosis" of an individual's covert processes, and the second is that of modifying, manipulating, controlling or in some way putting those covert processes to use.

Diagnosis of Covert Processes or the Development of a "Thought Reading Machine"

We have witnessed many mechanical reproductions and representations of mental processes, as in Capek's (1923) classical *Rossum's Universal Robots;* Richardson's (1930) machine of a mind that has a will and is capable of two ideas; and Hebb's (1954) diagram of a machine that could introspect upon itself. More popularly, the development of versatile computers has led to many electronic analogies of the mind (cf. especially Wiener's 1948 *Cybernetics*). The computer as a psychophysiological tool would be a major component in the development of a general thought reading machine. In this regard Dewan's (1967) tour de force is impressive. The subject emitted Morse Code as dots and dashes of alpha waves through control of the eyes; the brain signals were then computer decoded and printed out as meaningful prose.

The following general paradigm for reading thoughts electromechanically is straight forward in principle; it's feasibility merely awaits refined development of the kinds of empirical relationships specified in Chapters 5-8. The theoretical basis was sketched out in our discussion of the formal status of covert processes in Chapter 3, the technological application of which is presented in Fig. 11.1. Represented at the top is an external linguistic stimulus (S_L) that evokes patterns of (1) covert oral behavior; (2) covert nonoral behavior; (3) electrically measured neurophysiological reactions; and (4) a culminating overt language response. The subject has sensors placed appropriately about the body. Complex patterns of covert reactions as a function of class of stimulus input (the empirical relationships developed in Chapters 5-8) are stored in the computer's memory. By continuously monitoring the covert reaction inputs, the continuously searching computer identifies those patterns and relates them to the "thoughts" generated as a function of the

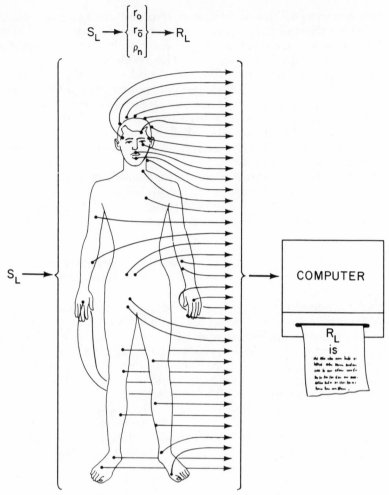

$$S_L \rightarrow \left\{ \begin{array}{c} r_o \\ r_{\bar{o}} \\ \rho_n \end{array} \right\} \rightarrow R_L$$

$S_L \rightarrow$

COMPUTER

R_L
is

FIG. 11.1 Representation of the basic paradigm for developing a "Thought Reading Machine."

stimulus input. Continuous readouts from the computer then allow the stream of mental processes to become public. Let us see in greater detail how this system might be constructed. Our immediate discussion will be limited to language processes, after which we shall briefly consider non-linguistic processes (pictorial imagery, etc.).

We assume that classes of external linguistic stimuli have been conditioned to unique states of a person's effector system, and the totality of these states constitutes one's repertoire of covert language reactions (Chapter 4). Among those covert language responses, a certain number produce internal stimuli which can be adequately discriminated if one is a trained, astute observer of one's own bodily processes (as in Progressive

Relaxation). That smaller class of covert language responses constitutes the possibile instances of internal tacts (verbal reports) the person can successfully emit overtly (R_L in Fig. 11.1). Now, our problem consists of the following. What are the specific connections between external stimuli and covert language responses that have been built up? By systematically presenting words (and/or their associated stimulus objects where possible), and measuring all possible bodily reactions of an implicit nature, it should be possible to explicitly formulate existing S_L-r associations. Hopefully, we would not need to actually measure reaction patterns to all of the words in a language, so that we might reduce the enormity of this task through some linguistic classification system. Perhaps we could group words into classes and subclasses as a function of common covert language behavior patterns which they evoke. The general procedure, though, would be to present word X and measure covert language response pattern #1. By asking the person "What were you thinking about?" after each word presentation, data on the class of verbal reports (R_L) that are available to that person can be accumulated. In short, relationships between external stimuli, covert reaction patterns and overt tacts can be ascertained in the form of $S_L \rightarrow r \rightarrow R_L$ laws.

Up to this point the patterns of covert language processes and the subjects' descriptions (tacts) of those response patterns have been controlled by the experimenter through the presentation of external stimuli. To simplify matters, we would hope that a given pattern of covert language responses would be the same, regardless of whether that pattern was evoked by an external stimulus or an internal one. In this way, we could assume that thought processes are similarly controlled by the dominant external and internal stimuli. The remaining feat would be to leave the person alone with instructions to think about whatever he desires, as Travis (1937) had his subjects let their "minds wander" while studying the "temporal course of consciousness." The computer would monitor the patterns of covert reactions fed into it as the subject is "lost in thought." It would then continuously identify the various external stimulus conditions that had been previously associated with those successive covert patterns. The computer could thus postdict the previous stimulus conditions and also predict the tacting response on the basis of the covert language reaction patterns. In this way we could, at least in principle, obtain a continuous record of what a person is thinking about. During the final, applied phase of thought diagnosis, we would not need to have subjects verbally report their thoughts. Consequently, thought records could be obtained regardless of a subject's cooperativeness (other than his "agreement" to be "strapped" into the apparatus).

To obtain the continuous thought record of a person, we have made a few assumptions! For one, we have assumed adequate knowledge of the stimulus-response relationships for a specific individual. Another assumption is that the relationships ascertained for a given individual are general in that they obtain among members of a particular culture. The implication from this assumption is that, without preliminary investigation of an individual, it would be possible to infer thoughts (potential tacting activity) of any given individual. As to how general stimulus-covert language response patterns would actually be among individuals of a given culture, it is reasonable to expect *some* similarities as well as some differences. To the extent to which individuals within a given culture have a common conditioning history, they would yield similar response patterns to any given stimulus. We expect a word like *wristwatch* to frequently evoke heightened EMG activity in the left wrist of individuals in the U.S., but a word like "cat" would evoke a variety of different response patterns among people. The conditioning history in the case of these two stimuli would be quite different. Jacobson (1932) showed that there is some response communality for words such as "Eiffel Tower," so that we could expect to specify a class of words (like "Empire State Building" or "flagpole") that principally evoke vertical patterns in electrical measures of eye responses. Through factor analysis, we might find factors that contain common eye and speech response components as a function of certain common linguistic stimuli, but with differences that would serve to differentiate members of a common class. For instance, we should have common vertical eye responses to "Empire State Building" and to "Eiffel Tower," but slightly different tongue reactions when these two different linguistic stimuli are presented.

Another assumption is that our laboratory system is adequate to record and relate all of the necessary data. Perhaps we will require additional technological development of laboratory systems to reach a high level of probability for our inferences, though contemporary systems appear adequate for predictions that at least exceed chance. Conceivably the technique of applying electrodes to localized regions of the body might be improved on. The individual in Fig. 11.1 is emitting many responses that are obviously missed by this electrode-point system. Perhaps a system could be developed for continuous recording of signals over the entire surface of the body. Rather than point-by-point regional measurement, a continuous sensor system might simultaneously examine all outputs from the entire body.

We are also assuming sufficient knowledge about bodily systems, but only an overly optimistic scientist would deny that there are as yet undiscovered bodily reactions that would be important for this project. It would be surprising indeed if the amazingly complex organism homo sapiens does not yield future response measures that we have not yet even begun to conjecture about. Berger reported electroencephalograms only a half century ago, and vague suspicions of the existence of the phenomenon are limited to the preceding 50-year period. We are still developing novel response measures [infrared radiation of the body, capillary responses (Taylor, 1959), magnetic reactions from the brain (Kolta, 1973)], and we might even measure unique signals that constitute a basis for possible psychic phenomena like extrasensory perception.

The process of internalization or abbreviation of responses (Chapter

4) presents another possible difficulty. With practice, motor responses become abbreviated as there develops increased speed of performance and skill. The same probably occurs for vocal activity as it becomes covert: "even if we could roll out the implicit processes they would be so abbreviated, short circuited and economized that they would be unrecognizable unless their formation has been watched from the transition (to implicitization)" (Watson, 1919 p. 325). Presumably Watson meant that the subvocal activity of saying a word becomes so different from the muscular activity when the word is said aloud that one would have difficulty in telling what word was subvocally pronounced from speech muscle electromyograms. We might follow Watson's suggestion and study such a transition to implicitization, or we might be merely satisfied with the establishment of relationships between covert speech muscle responses (*whatever* they are) and the consequent tact of the individual's thoughts.

A somewhat less expansive "Thought Reading Machine" might be constructed on the basis of global acts, rather than linguistic units. In Table 11.1, a number of reactions are plotted as a function of target area for selected stimuli. For example, if we present stimuli that are targeted to excite primarily the visual modality, we expect primarily covert activity in the eyes. Hence, if we instruct the subject to imagine the Eiffel Tower, we expect the main reaction to be in the eyes rather than, say, in the legs or arms. On the other hand, if one is instructed to ride a bicycle, we would expect the response pattern depicted for that activity in Table 11.1; and similarly for other areas, such as those involved in merely thinking of abstract words (Ohm's Law). We expect that the eyes and the speech region are active during any imagination task, as indicated by the pluses for all acts in the rows for those regions. However, there should be relatively more activity in certain bodily regions for certain imagination tasks, as indicated by the double pluses.

TABLE 11.1   Plan for a Relatively Primitive "Thought Reading Machine"

Major Covert Language Response Expected in the:	Target Stimulus for Imagined Gross Motor Acts		
	Visual (e.g., Eiffel Tower)	(e.g., Ride a bicycle)	Language (e.g., "Ohm's Law")
Eyes	++	+	+
Arms		++	
Legs		++	
Speech region	+	+	++

The relationships of the nature illustrated in Table 11.1 are thus at a more molar level than for the preceding plan which was based on detailed linguistic analyses. Nevertheless that molar plan would still be useful in rather generally identifying what a person is thinking. A more limited "Thought Reading Machine" could function now, based on the work of McGuigan and Pavek (1972); with it, we could ascertain whether a person was silently answering questions as yes vs. no. On the basis of electrical measurements of eye activity and of differential arm electromyograms they probablistically detected "yes vs. no" thoughts to questions, suggesting a technique that would even be applicable in a field situation, i.e., thanks to the effective development of solid state, miniaturized electronics it would be possible to construct a small sensor system that could be attached to critical regions of the body (the eyes and the arms in this instance). Signals could then be sent from the body by telemetry for laboratory analysis and processing. A subject would be presented with a sequence of "yes-no" questions. A simple readout, perhaps in the form of coded banks of lights, could indicate combined reaction patterns that predict whether the subject has just silently answered the question with "yes" or "no."

The technological applications of thought reading machines are numerous. They will always be probabilistic in nature, but with the combination of multiple electropsychological measurements, we should eventually be able to develop a system which diagnoses an individual's thoughts with a high degree of probability. Several illustrative studies suggest a variety of directions for future development.

Dream research has been especially productive in yielding relationships between various measures of covert behavior and specific dream content parameters as we noted in the data Chapters 5-8. For example, horizontal REMs are related to reports of horizontal "dream activities," and vertical REMs to vertical "dream activities" (e.g., Dement and Kleitman, 1957), unique eye movement patterns are related to reports of unique dream episodes (Roffwarg, Dement, Muzio, and Fisher, 1962); and active and passive rapid eye movements relate strongly to dream reports that were judged, respectively, to be active and passive (Berger and Oswald, 1962b). One specific example of the close correspondence between a specific covert behavior pattern and a unique overt oral language response vividly illustrates the point: during sleep one of Wolpert's subjects gave heightened EMG in the right arm, then in the left arm and then in a leg; his later oral report was that he dreamed of lifting a bucket with his right arm, transferring the bucket to his left arm, then proceeding to walk (Kleitman, 1960). In another kind of study, Schwartz et al. (1973) diagnosed differential emotional status from facial electromyograms, using multiple electrode placements on the face. Let us now turn to some more specific applications of the diagnosis of covert processes.

CLINICAL APPLICATIONS

A diagnostic system such as that described above would have impressive clinical applications, as in determining what a noncommunicative depressive or schizophrenic is thinking. Such a system would help with the difficult task of deciding whether a child is autistic or feebleminded. At present the diagnosis depends upon the therapist's success: if we can modify the child's behavior, we conclude the child was autistic; if not, we conclude that the child is feebleminded.

Traditionally the psychotherapist has employed detection techniques for clinical purposes in a variety of ways, so the principle of thought detection per se is not at issue. What *is* at issue is whether or not the clinician should be provided with a more successful detection system than the present word association tests or projective techniques.

INTELLIGENCE OPERATIONS

As we noted in Chapter 10, detection systems have been employed in a variety of ways with numerous social consequences. We note as an example the unfortunate possibility of their use in an autocratic society for ascertaining loyalty: "Do you love me?" said Big Brother. "Yes, I do, Big Brother." "You lie," was the instant answer, "You lie."[2]

With remotely monitored "bugging" equipment we can analyze conversations at a distance without the knowledge or consent of the speakers. This system is already effective, as demonstrated in football games where the television viewer can sometimes hear the signals being called by the quarterback, or a coach's discussion of his strategy. Voice analyzers or other systems of monitoring psychophysiological signals could be employed to monitor the activities of foreign policy makers, for example, in estimating the degree of confidence that should be placed in what is actually being said during international negotiations. In this way it might be possible to "authenticate" or disconfirm the truthfulness of what negotiators are saying. If such an application became effective, it might be that diplomats would refuse to speak and would engage only in written or coded interchange.

The storage of voice signals or other bodily signals on magnetic tape allows for delayed analysis, which might be more effective than on-line monitoring. There would be benefits for historians too in later interpretation of semantically important public statements.

LEGAL APPLICATIONS:
LIE DETECTION (OR THE DETECTION OF DECEPTION)

From the point of view of a practicing attorney, the following statement represents well the need for an effective "lie detector."

Courts, prosecutors, law enforcement agencies, and defense attorneys are all interested in the polygraph or some other accurate indicator of deception in speeding up the administration of the system of justice and in insuring more accurate results. Often, many men are charged with the commission of the same crime. A large temptation exists for one or more of these defendants to give testimony against his co-defendants in return for a dismissal of the charge or some other leniency. The law of this State is that a man can be convicted upon the uncorroborated testimony of an accomplice. At this point, without the poly-

---

[2] From *Washington Watch*, vol. 3, no. 3, October 17, 1975, p. 3.

graph or some other way of testing the truth or falsity of the testifying accomplice's veracity, the judge or the jury can only rely upon the demeaner and apparent straightforwardness of the testifying witness. I have personally observed at least one miscarriage of justice in such a situation.

In addition, use of the polygraph or a similar accurate device would be of great aid to law enforcement agencies in solving crime. Very often, a suspect is arrested upon certain circumstantial evidence (which can also be used to convict). If the suspect keeps insisting that he is innocent, it is indeed in the best interests of justice that he be given every opportunity to clear himself in order that the law enforcement agency in question can look further for the real culprit.

In still other situations, the courts waste much time in hearing felony cases which, if the defendant had been believed from the outset, the charge would only have been a misdemeaner speedily and readily handled by guilty plea in lower court. I have seen many cases where a reduction in charge was brought about by a lengthy trial on evidence discovered only after long and diligent work by the defense attorney. Often, that defense attorney is an appointed defense attorney, and the money for his appearance in Circuit Court on a felony charge comes from the taxpayers. Accordingly, I believe the continued study of the polygraph and your study to be of great importance to the fair and accurate administration of justice (Rebecca H. Hanslin, personal communication, August 1, 1975).

While the application of a thought reading system to deception detection can thus be beneficial, the possible dangers can be viewed with alarm. A rather dramatic illustration is the following passage from the 1952 science fiction story *Player Piano* by Kurt Vonnegut, Jr.[3]

"DO YOU SWEAR to tell the truth, the whole truth and nothing but the truth, so help you God?"

"I do," said Paul.

The courtroom television cameras dollied back from his face, to reveal on fifty million television screens the table of the Illium Federal Courtroom's south wall.

The accused, seated on the witness stand, resembled less a man than an old fashioned switchboard, with wires running from temperature-, pressure-, and moisture-sensitive instruments at his wrists, armpits, chest, temples, and palms. These in turn, ran to a grey cabinet under the witness stand, where their findings were interpreted and relayed to a dial a yard in diameter over Paul's head.

[Prosecutor] "Could it be, Doctor, that this hate of what you describe as an injustice to humanity is in fact a hate of something a good bit less abstract?

"Maybe. I don't quite follow you."

"I'm talking about hate for some*one*, Doctor."

"I don't know who you're talking about."

"The needle says you *do* know Doctor—that you *do* know your red-white-and-blue patriotism is really an expression of hate and resentment for one of the greatest patriots in American history, your father!"

"Nonsense."

"The needle says you lie!" The prosecutor turned away from Paul in seeming disgust.

[3]Excerpted from the book *Player Piano* by Kurt Vonnegut, Jr. Copyright © 1952 by Kurt Vonnegut, Jr. Reprinted by permission of Delacorte Press/Seymour Lawrence.

Contemporary society is greatly concerned with the multiple invasions of privacy which computer technology has allowed, and lie detection may be no less an invasion of privacy. Other instances of possible invasion of privacy include psychometric screening for school admission of students and employment selection, mandatory medical tests, such as those for venereal disease which are required for food handlers, tests for alcoholic content of the blood in automobile drivers, fingerprints, and access to private records such as the Internal Revenue Service's access to personal financial accounts (by studying a record of one's checks and credit card charges, a great deal can be ascertained about an individual's past movements and personal life). How these issues will be resolved constitutes a difficult question for society. On the one hand, some of these efforts are for the welfare of society, but on the other they may be unjustified invasions of privacy of our citizenry. One help is that often the individual has available certain countermeasures. For instance, one can control certain bodily processes such as pulse rate, heart beat, temperature, or status of the skeletal muscle to some extent, so that one may "hide one's thoughts from the machine." Countermeasures for voice analyses could include scramblers, and we do have monitors that can detect the presence of tape recorders, bugs, and the like.

Systematic Manipulation of Covert Processes

In the preceding section we considered the *diagnosis* of various mental processes through psychophysiological measurement of covert events. In this section we shall consider how the *modification* of covert processes might be beneficially (or detrimentally) applied for society.

CLINICAL APPLICATIONS IN GENERAL

In Chapter 10 we considered the area of behavior modification in which methods of progressive relaxation and principles of operant conditioning have been used for clinical purposes. As we noted, the emphasis is on changing behavior without specifying the cause (the current rejection of the medical model of "mental disease"). Consequently, a major advantage of behavioral therapeutic approaches is that one may apply the principles without knowing the bodily locus of the pathology, if in fact there is such. Nevertheless, when a client reports problems which involve certain bodily areas therapy can often be enhanced, e.g., if an individual's complaint is principally of colitis, one would clinically apply progressive relaxation to include the entire body with concentration on the abdominal region. Similarly, if the client's major complaint concerns headaches, the clinical application would be for extensive attention to the eye region (including the neck muscles which are "extensions of the eyes"). With continued application and refinement of these behavioral methodologies, our therapies should become increasingly effective. While there are few validating data for any therapeutic method, there is an increasing indication that such behavioral technologies *are* more effective than placebo comparison conditions (cf. Wolpe, 1975). One can confidently expect that in the not too distant future, behavioral approaches to traditional "psychological" and "psychiatric" problems will be extremely effective so that a large number of contemporary syndromes can be treated with dispatch. However, there will probably remain a large number of other behavioral problems, such as manic depressive psychoses or alcoholism, for which these approaches are non-specific and alternative methods will need to be developed.

CONTROLLING HALLUCINATIONS

Since we have obtained objective data of psychophysiological processes (principally of the speech musculature) occurring during auditory hallucinations, one may speculate about how to control pathological hallucinations through conditioning or relaxation methodologies. If, as we concluded in Chapters 6, 9, and 10, the speech musculature is a critical component of the neuromuscular circuits which produce hallucinations, then elimination of the muscular component should eliminate the hallucinations. In this instance, by conditioning the speech musculature to be otherwise involved, or, perhaps more simply, merely teaching the patient to relax the speech musculature, we expect that the patient's hallucinations could be eliminated through voluntary control. We have also speculated that there is heightened covert eye activity during visual hallucinations, so that the same principle of control would apply to the eyes (McGuigan, 1966b). That is, by relaxing the eyes the visual muscle component of the relevant neuromuscular circuits would be removed, thus eliminating the visual hallucination.

These principles have been well established in the practice of clinical progressive relaxation for the control of "normal" thoughts, as in worry and insomnia. We can more generally speculate about the control of thoughts through conditioning principles or relaxation of other psychophysiological events than those of the skeletal musculature. We should also include the indirect control of visceral and central nervous system activity through the skeletal musculature (Fig. 10.8). Thought control could be quite effective.

SEMANTIC PROCESSING AND TRACERS[4]

Available psycholinguistic data (cf. Osgood and Richards, 1973; Osgood and Hoosain, 1974) on the nature and functioning of semantic features suggest that we can obtain some "external handles" on meaning in the form of psychophysiological tracers. One important consequence of a successful wedding of Osgood's semantic theory and psychophysiology would be our ability to study the development of meaning longitudi-

---

[4] My reliance on Charles E. Osgood in this section is apparent and appreciated.

nally. Such a project would have special significance for the possible process of response abbreviation or internalization (transition of overt responses to covert responses) and possible central representations, as discussed in Chapter 4.

Some encouraging progress has already been made on the development of a technology of electropsychological tracers of semantic processes. Following Basmajian (1963 a, b), we used auditory biofeedback to allow subjects to monitor and isolate a small response in the right thumb (cf. Osgood and McGuigan, 1973). With some success, we then attempted to bring that covert response under external stimulus control to the visual presentation of the word CLICK (Chapter 4). There also was some generalization to "click-like" words ("bang," "pop," "crack") during the same "unintentional" period. While this is certainly not the way mediating reactions would be conditioned during language acquisition in children, it does give us a start on a tracer of some kind of semantic process denoted by the concept of "click."

In our next step, we attempted to attach artificial (arbitrary) tracers to "old" (already developed) semantic features presented in an artificial language (Osgood and McGuigan, 1973). We made some progress in conditioning[5] a small right thumb response to the word "future" and a left thumb response to the word "past." The successful findings in this preliminary research suggest that we should employ a more extensive artificial language. For instance, we might use three features which could form a basis for developing an artificial language as follows: (1) terminable-interminable; (2) future-past; (3) dynamic-incipient. By thus attaching known covert linguistic responses to critical features of this simplified language, we might enhance our study of internal linguistic events. For example, using such an artificial (but true) language we would know better where to place our peripheral electrodes, and thus facilitate our study of temporal relationships among EEG and response events; we thus should be better able to trace the important linguistic feedback loops specified earlier (Fig. 9.5). Furthermore, we might allow two individuals to covertly communicate with each other, as perhaps by observing oscilloscopes that monitor critical responses in the other person's body.

In seeking "natural" tracers of "new" meanings, we could study possible semantic features like Tighten/Loosen (screwing-in vs. screwing-out rotation with right hand), Collect/Discard (pincing-together vs. separating-apart movements of the left hand) and perhaps Oriental/Occidental (eye squinting vs. eye widening!) to a variety of both visual and written sign materials. In this case, it would be necessary to "shape" and then differentially reinforce these motor reactions in the process of reacting to the visual or verbal training materials, then produce semantic

---

[5] Whether or not this is conditioning that obeys classical laws of conditioning is a difficult question to answer, but there certainly is some resemblance to operant learning (cf. Chapter 4; McGuigan, 1973b).

generalization and discrimination by the use of differential reinforcement with appropriate signs, and finally test with novel stimulus materials in a relaxed state. The tests for centralization would require correct
verbal reactions to novel sign combinations at various stages in the "conditioning" process while demonstrating that the amplitudes of the *tracer*
reactions decrease. In such ways it would be valuable to develop covert
nonoral responses as tracers for complex semantic bodily states. With
such motor tracers we could monitor complex states while one is processing meanings, an endeavor that would facilitate the development of our
thought reading machine (Fig. 11.1) and contribute to our understanding of the development of linguistic processes, and to the mechanisms of
internal information processing.

THOUGHT CONTROL AND SELF-MANAGEMENT

In our discussion of the diagnosis of covert processes for the development of a "thought reading machine," and in this general section on the
manipulation of covert processes, we have been considering a variety of
applications of the control of thoughts (control of hallucinations, worry,
insomnia, etc.). Just as the diagnosis can be beneficial or detrimental, the
control process can too. To eliminate an individual's "normal" worries,
his excessive fears, his distressing hallucinations can only be regarded as
beneficial for society, particularly through self-management procedures.
Thought control, as in the Orwellian sense, is yet another matter. We are
well aware of the methods used by the Hitlers and Stalins of the world,
and of the brainwashing techniques developed and applied so effectively
by the Chinese, especially as brought to our attention during the Korean
War. It is truly amazing how one's mind can be swayed by those who
have sufficient control. We have many excellent accounts and studies of
brainwashing techniques in all of their variations.

Three critical elements in changing "a person's mind," including one's
belief system and perception of the world, appear to be those of (1)
presenting a substantial threat[6] to one's well being mentally or physically; (2) submerging the individual in a pool of misinformation so that
the individual loses anchoring to reality; and (3) reinforcing some belief
that is different from and incompatible with a present one. This general
procedure is somewhat consonant with a discriminative stimulus training
paradigm wherein there is punishment of the person's present belief
system (the response to be suppressed) and reinforcement of an alternative belief system (the low strength response to be made dominant) with
misinformation generously sprinkled throughout the stages. As a consequence, extremely amazing "flips of the mind" can be achieved. The
belief systems, the loyalties, and even the apparently sincere states of
affection of Patty Hearst obtained national prominence. One can see

---

[6] The strength of the threat factor in controlling minds was well expressed by Charles
Colson, as it came to light around the termination of the Nixon presidential administration with his principle that "if you get them by the balls, their hearts and minds will
follow" (from Bernstein and Woodward, *All The President's Men,* 1974).

these elements operating quite effectively through the succession of threats and applied punishment, and in swamping her with various kinds of information and misinformation. As a consequence, Miss Hearst went through a dramatic series of changes in her apparent states of love and affection and in her belief systems—she apparently expressed frequent changes in loyalty and love to several men, her family, institutions of society, and her colleagues in alleged crime. Such dramatic changes in feelings and beliefs are rather common in everyday life. A woman psychologist once suggested to me that these changes in loyalty and belief systems occur more readily in women than in men, and she offered an interesting evolutionary hypothesis. To illustrate with excessive brevity, one can imagine the problems that early cave woman faced as she was "dragged off by the hair" by a new cave man who had just conquered her pairmate. Those cave women who could not easily switch their loyalties to the new man probably did not have great survival value so that possessers of those genes became extinct. Early women who *could* switch loyalties easily thus had greater survival value, and it is their distant progeny we observe in our world today as in Chekov's "Little Darling." Regardless of whether or not there is truth in these speculations, it still is amazing to watch a person (woman or man) who vigorously (and ceremoniously) announces loyalty, love, and the like to another. And then, when the individual is subjected to trying circumstances, with reinforcement of alternative behaviors and given misinformation (the three factors specified above), there is abandonment of the pairmate, perhaps even with hostility.[7] The case was made well by Orwell in *1984*. Such dramatic changes are to be understood partially in terms of emotional behavior. The problem of rehabilitating such "brain washed" individuals is a difficult one indeed.

Ways in which thought might be controlled in the future are so numerous as to stagger the imagination. Conditioning methods such as we have suggested above in the control of hallucinations, or in brain washing techniques are of course quite possible. One can imagine even more extreme techniques such as Big Brother continuously monitoring a target individual's thoughts through a thought reading machine and, when the desired thought appeared, electrical stimulation of the septal region could be administered à la Olds (1969) to produce immediate reinforcement by activating the "pleasure center." Perhaps to be aware of such possibilities might help to forestall them.

COVERT CONTROL OF ELECTROMECHANICAL SYSTEMS THROUGH BIO SERVO LOOPS

We have witnessed the development of a variety of effective and sensitive control systems involving bioelectromechanical servo loops (e.g., Ford and White, 1959). Systematically emitted electrical signals from a region of the body (as in the case of specific eye movements or localized

---

[7] Another important variable allegedly applied by the "Moonies," the Chinese, and others, is to make the victim feel intense guilt.

electromyographical signals) can be amplified and directed to drive electromechanical systems. Dewan (1967), for instance, might have had his Morse code alpha wave signals drive such an electromechanical system rather than merely being decoded by a computer. Possible applications are enormous, as in assisting an amputee or paraletic to manipulate himself through life. The pattern of psychophysiological signals might allow space astronauts to control their space ship, perhaps when overt movements (as under the stress of high Gs) are not possible. Similarly, through the development of a suitable language (as we discussed under "Tracers"), astronauts could communicate with each other by presenting linguistic readouts of their various psychophysiological systems to each other. One could imagine for instance a digital readout of selected EEG and EMG patterns from one individual to another to linguistically communicate, as well as serving as a monitor for control of electromechanical systems.

SOCIETAL CONSEQUENCES OF TENSION CONTROL

Because techniques of tension control have much wider applicability than merely in the clinical area, we shall more generally discuss this topic here. In Chapter 10 we noted the needs of people in our modern world to learn to differentially relax, and we considered how one can learn to move through life more efficiently. The wise application of techniques of tension control, we saw, have prophylactic as well as therapeutic values. By learning to spend one's energies primarily for the accomplishment of the highest priority goals, thus ignoring relatively unimportant matters including those negative incidents in life that merely drain your resources, a healthy person should be able to noticeably increase his or her achievements. If, for instance, one is an academician, the job, typically defined, is that of teaching students and conducting scholarly activities. One's self-programming task is to reduce to a minimum the extent to which energies are diverted for subsidiary tasks. In academia such tasks are many: excessively frequent meetings of academic committees that concentrate on relatively trivial matters; completing endless pedantic bureaucratic forms; responding to a constant flood of memoranda about trivia; finding paper clips for unknown students who have discovered an open office door; and answering phone calls from those who wish to find Professor X who doesn't answer his own phone. In the face of frustrating situations, such as when one finds oneself in a line of traffic from which there is no escape, the trained individual accepts the inevitable and merely relaxes, instead of pounding the horn and yelling at the driver in front. When an official or administrator with limited vision imposes bureaucratic rules that may have originally served a purpose but are now merely functionally autonomous, the efficient responder does not emotionally unload, but merely leaves the situation with as little loss of energy as possible. While being aggressed toward, it would typically be inefficient for one to counteraggress, unless of course such is necessary for survival—quite often the aggressioncounteraggression cycle that typically escalates can be prevented if one of the members of the circuit merely ceases to respond. This principle has been espoused by religious leaders, as in the phrase that councils the "turning of the other cheek." In less lofty form, one representation was expressed by the Irishman who was observed to have been repeatedly kicked and knocked down by the Jackass he was trying to lead. Each time the Irishman merely picked himself up and continued his progress. When asked why he never got mad and responded in kind, the Irishman replied that he just regarded the nature of the source. Like the Irishman, one should seldom respond emotionally, or with anger, particuarly to primitive social behaviors. When one does it is only after careful deliberation (instead of being a reflexive act), in which the energy expenditure is calculated and it is decided that the expenditure is justified for the accomplishment of the desired purposes. Once the anger is expressed, though, the individual immediately becomes calm and unemotional again.

In such ways, then, one who has learned to systematically control internal tensions can be expected to increase one's achievement and prevent the development of pathological conditions. We also saw in Chapter 10 that those who have already become victimized by tension disorders can often reduce or eliminate the pathological condition by applying tension control principles. The life of the afflicted can thus often become more joyous and productive. One can speculate about the nature of a world in which everyone applies these principles. Not only would the quality of life be improved at the level of the individual, but application at the level of nations might contribute to a more peaceful world (McGuigan, 1970c).

Conclusion

It is reasonable to expect that the science of psychology will yield exponentially increasing applications for society. The scientist traditionally has had little interest in how society uses the pure knowledge that is acquired, but the question of use has now become critical for determining the kind of world in which we live, and even for the survival of civilization. The choice is not the scientist's. The choice is society's. The question is whether society will use the fruits of science wisely or unwisely, whether use will be made for the benefit of the many or for the privileged few? Traditionally the scientist as citizen has exercised but one vote in determining how scientific findings are to be used. And at that, the scientist frequently has not voted, preferring to stay removed from everyday problems in an effort to maintain objectivity. Whether or not the world will be able to continue to exist with one vote for one person, weighing the qualifications of every individual equally, is a question worthy of consideration. On the one hand, a benevolent autocracy is probably the most efficient form of government (though even a benevolent dictator may not stay benevolent when power corrupts). On the other hand, with one vote for one person, the assumption is that the opinion of Plato is not more valuable than that of a person with perhaps an IQ of 80 whose education terminated at the third grade, or of a psychopath. The futuristic novelist Shute in *On the Beach* attacked this problem with the concept of the multiple vote such that, according to the number of criteria one satisfied, his or her vote was more heavily weighted. The multiple vote led to the emergence of Australia as a superior nation.

Sometimes a scientist testifies in his or her area of expertise, thereby exercising relatively great influence over the application of the scientist's findings. But such influence is often only informal, and frequently ignored by the public. Perhaps the scientist should relinquish the traditional role and actively engage in the technological application of scientific findings, while at the same time the public formalizes the roles of the scientist for greater participation in everyday society. Perhaps the scientist as a scientist-citizen should have greater voice in how scientific findings are to be used for the engineering of a better world. More generally, perhaps the wise scientists *and* non-scientists should exercise more control over the development of society, the extreme being that those who engage in barbaric and primitive behavior to the detriment of society should be disenfranchised. Perhaps in these ways, and hopefully in others too, some of the uses of a science of covert processes can be employed for the betterment of the world.

Acronyms

AEP	Average Evoked Potentials
AER	Auditory Evoked Reaction (response)
BCD	Binary Coded Decimal
CNS	Central Nervous System
CNV	Contingent Negative Variation
CPS	Cycles Per Second (see Hz, Preferred)
CRO	Cathode Ray Oscilloscope
CRT	Cathode Ray Tube
EAP	Eye Artifact Potentials
ECG	Electrocardiogram (see EKG)
EEG	Electroencephalogram
EKG	Electrocardiogram
EMG	Electromyogram
EOG	Electrooculogram
EP	Evoked Potentials
ERG	Electroretinogram
ERP	Event-Related Potentials
GSR	Galvanic Skin Response
Hz	Hertz (CPS, cycles per second)
MAP	Muscle Action Potential (see EMG)
MP	Motor Potential
RP	Readiness Potential
SEP	Somatic Evoked Potential
SER	Somatic Evoked Response
SPS	Steady Potential Shifts

VEP	Visual Evoked Potential
VER	Visual Evoked Response
r_G	Hull's fractional antedating goal reaction
r_M	Osgood's meaning reaction ("response")
R_L	Overt Linguistic Response
r_L	Covert Linguistic Response
r_O	Covert oral response
$r_{\bar{O}}$	Covert nonoral response
s_L	Internal Linguistic Stimulus
S_L	External Linguistic Stimulus

Glossary[1]

Ablation: The surgical removal of portions of the brain, traditionally in search of localized functions such as those of memory or speech.

Action potential: A localized electrical change in membrane permeability which is propogated along a neuron or muscle fiber (MAP).

Afferent neural activity: Neural impulses from receptors directed to the central nervous system.

Allophone: Phonemes which are subtly different but the difference in the distinctive feature has no effect on the meaning in a given language. Allophones in one language may be separate phonemes in another.

Alpha (Berger) waves: EEG rhythms between about 8 and 13 Hz, most easily recordable during relaxation in a dark room and easily disrupted by light and/or mental activity.

Analog: A continuous (vs. discrete) signal that may assume any value within a specified range, e.g., electrical or speech signals are analog signals.

Aphasia: Loss or impairment of the ability to use language due to a brain lesion. Varieties of aphasia include sensory aphasia (the inability to understand words) and motor aphasia (the inability to speak or to speak an intended word).

Autokinetic illusion: A visual illusion of movement of a stationary point light source when viewed against a dark background.

Average evoked potential (AEP): The repetitive presentation of a stimulus produces a consistent signal that may be recorded from the scalp through signal averaging. It is thought that impulses from sensory nerves produce these slow potentials, with the primary evoked potential occurring in the sensory representation areas. Secondary average evoked potentials are recordable from any scalp location.

---

[1] Thanks to Brad Davis for his help with this, and in numerous other ways too.

Base line: In psychophysiology, usually a steady, standard, normal condition such as resting or relaxation when a variable, or set of variables, is recorded prior to the administration of a special treatment. The effect of the treatment is then measured by comparison with the base line level.

Behavior: A composite of responses where "response" is defined as activity of muscles and glands.

Behaviorism: Contemporary psychology wherein psychology is defined as the study of behavior. The typical approach is to seek lawful relationships among internal and external stimuli on the one hand, and overt and covert responses on the other.

Beta waves: EEG signals from about 14 to 30 Hz, thought to be present during thinking and arousal in general.

Bilabial: Referring to both lips, the term is used to describe a specific characteristic of speech. The phoneme /p/ is bilabial.

Bilabial stops: A distinctive feature of certain phonemes such as /p/ and /b/ wherein the lips hold air back, allowing for an explosive release either voiced or unvoiced.

Binary: Having to do with "2." The number system with a radix (base) of two. Information may be represented in binary arithmetic as in 0 or 1.

Binary coded decimal (BCD): A number code in which individual decimal digits are each represented by a group of binary digits; in the 8-4-2-1 BCD notation, each decimal digit is represented by a four-place binary number, weighted in sequence as 8, 4, 2, and 1.

Biofeedback: Process of transducing internal bodily signals to present them to the behaver as external stimuli. In this way the behaver can become aware of internal functioning, and in some cases develops control over those internal systems.

Broca's area: A brain region generally held to be important for the production of speech. Its location in the left frontal lobe (more specifically on the caudal portion of the inferior frontal convolution) of the dominant hemisphere. Lesions in this area have been thought to result in "expressive aphasia."

Buccal tract: The mouth cavity.

Cathode ray tube (CRT): A display device in which controlled electron beams are used to present signals on a luminescent screen.

Cell assembly: A hypothetical construct proposed by D. O. Hebb that consists of closed circuits of neurons in the cortex. Excitation of series of cell assemblies is hypothesized to be responsible for such mental processes as perception and images.

Centralism: The position that non-cerebral systems of the body, such as muscle and autonomic systems, have no function in cognition.

Closed loop: A signal path in which outputs are fed back to inputs. In some circuits there is comparison with desired values to regulate system behavior, as in servo loops.

CNS: Central nervous system consisting of the brain, spinal cord, and associated nerves.

Common mode rejection: The ability of a differential-input circuit to discriminate against a voltage appearing at both input terminals, expressed as a ratio or log ratio.

Common mode rejection ratio: Applied to differential amplifiers, a measure of the amplifier's ability to reject ambient noise such as 60 Hz interference.

Common mode voltage: A signal which appears at both terminals of a differential input device, like an amplifier.

Conditional response: A response which can be evoked by a previously neutral stimulus, the latter of which originally could not evoke the response.

Confound: Confounding occurs when an extraneous variable is systematically related to an independent variable, and it might differentially affect the dependent variable. Consequently one cannot conclude that the independent variable affects the dependent variable if there are positive results in the experiment. In the vernacular, confounding result in an invalid experiment. Other definitions are common, especially in statistics.

Contingent negative variation (CNV): A DC shift measured at the scalp which is recorded when responses to stimuli are required in a decision-making paradigm. Also called a "readiness potential" or "expectancy wave."

Coverants: Topologically unspecified covert responses of an operant variety.

Covert processes: Bodily events which are not readily observable without the use of equipment or apparatus to extend the scope of our senses. The process may be behavioral (muscular or glandular) or neural (as when electroencephalographically observable). A synonym would be covert events.

Cricoarytenoid: Pertaining to the cartilage of the larnyx articulated by the arytenoid cartilage.

Curare strategy: The attempt to determine the degree of involvement of the voluntary musculature by blocking this system using curare (d-turbocurarine). The uses of this strategy have in general failed to control for very small muscle events. Thus the finding that the subjects of such experiments could "think" when paralyzed is not conclusive.

Cybernetics: The study of regulatory mechanisms involving feedback developed by N. Wiener. These mechanisms were hypothesized to occur in machines, individuals, and large social groups and institutions.

Delta waves: EEG waves of less than about 4 Hz. Delta waves are abnormal in a waking adult, but present at various times of sleep.

Distinctive features: Those characteristics of speech sounds that define a phoneme. A set of minimal distinctive features are those features (microphonemes) that uniquely define each phoneme, as specified in Table 9.2, p. 333.

Donovan's brain theory: *Donovan's Brain* is a novel in which the brain of a man named Donovan is maintained in a living state so as to continue functioning cognitively. This is an extreme centralist theory apparently not advocated by any prominent thinker (Chapter 2).

Dualism: The notion that mind and body are of different stuff with independent existence. The conception is of a mental (non-physically defined) world on the one hand and of a strictly materialistic one on the other. This conception of the universe is meaningless and has resulted in centuries of fruitless argument. For instance, the notion has raised the question of how the mental and physical worlds relate to each other, spawning such notions as psychophysical parallelism, and psychophysical interactionism.

Efferent neural activity: Neural impulses from the brain to effectors.

Electrocardiogram: (ECG or EKG, the former anglicized, the latter from the

German.) An electrical measure of heart activity consisting of a complex of signals.

Electrodermal events: An electrical measure of changes in skin potential or resistance, principally the galvanic skin response.

Electroencephalogram (EEG): An unprocessed recording of the electrical activity of the brain taken from electrodes placed on the scalp.

Electromyogram (EMG): See Muscle action potential.

Electrooculogram (EOG): Strictly, a recording of the slow DC shift of the standing potential between the retina and the cornea of the eye when the eye moves. More loosely, the term refers to any electrical recording of activity of the eyes.

Epistemic correlation: A relation joining an unobserved component of anything designated by a concept by postulation to its directly inspected component, denoted by a concept by intuition. (A concept espoused by Northrup.)

Equipotentiality: Lashley's conception of the cortex as lacking well-defined areas that function differentially. Rather, various areas of the cortex can serve various functions equally well. The concept followed from research in which extirpation of portions of the cortex resulted in a general loss of ability rather than specific losses.

Exteroceptor: A sense organ which is stimulated directly by energy changes outside the body.

Frontalis muscle: The muscle across the forehead which is often used to measure tension in humans. Tension here is *not* indicative of tension elsewhere in the body.

Galvanic skin response: The change in the resistance of the skin to the flow of electrical current which results from changes in sweat gland activity.

Gamma efferents: The feedback control of muscular tension is modified by the activity of gamma motor fibers, which innervate the intrafusal muscle spindles. Activation produces a contraction of the intrafusal fiber and thus a stretching and activation of the spindle receptors. This activates the positive feedback system of type 1 afferents and biases type 2 afferents; in turn, there is a change in tension in associated extrafusal fibers, and finally activation of the negative feedback system of the Golgi tendon organs.

Gamma waves: EEG of about 35 to 50 Hz. This pattern is seldom encountered, and its existence is not generally accepted.

Gating: The process whereby afferent signals are controlled by efferent processes so that certain inputs are not passed to higher centers. Gating may occur while attending to one sensory modality so completely that others are excluded.

Glottis: The opening between the free margins of the vocal cords.

Hertz (Hz): Cycles per second (CPS), as in 60 Hz.

Higher mental processes: An inexact term used to distinguish cognition from reflex or sensation (both of which are components of cognition).

Hologram: A hologram has the unique property that the entire scene of a tri-dimensional photograph may be recovered from any small portion ot it, there being some loss of clarity but not of the entire area. A holographic theory of memory suggests that memory is stored simultaneously throughout the cerebral cortex in a manner analogous to a hologram. Thus removal of any portion of the brain which didn't destroy recall would leave all memory more or less available if somewhat less clear (which is consistent with Lashley's classical research).

Homunculus: Literally, a little man, usually thought of as being within the head. The term arises from dualistic psychology with the conception that the "little man" directs actions of the body, as one would control a marionette through strings. Any notion of feedback is thereby negated. Consistent with Donovan's brain theory.

Hypothetical construct: See Mediating processes.

Ideomotor theory of consciousness: The dualistic (and therefore meaningless) position that ideas occur in a non-materialistic mind and exert directing influences on behavior through motor consequences.

Implicit language habits: See covert language response. This is literally Watson's term that defines thought in terms of covert reactions of muscle responses throughout the body.

Integrator: An instrument which sums electrical activity over time to yield an amplitude measure. Principally used in electromyography.

Internal information processing: The interactive functioning of various systems of the body, principally neuromuscular circuits, to process externally and internally generated information.

Internalization: The process by which overt behavior becomes reduced in amplitude to the covert level through experience or practice, e.g., children typically read aloud, then read silently but with noticeable subvocalization, and then eventually with no overtly noticeable lip movement. In this instance the overt motor behavior evoked during reading becomes more effecient through abbreviation.

Intervening variable: See Mediating processes.

Kappa waves: An EEG rhythm of about 10 Hz found in about 30% of normal subjects, presumably evoked during problem solving.

Kinesthesis: An internal sense that generates knowledge of bodily movements. Proprioceptors are in joints, tendons, and muscles to provide the input for kinesthesis.

Kymograph: A system of recording psychophysiological data that was employed during early research. The record was produced by a stylus moving on a slowly turning drum which often had been blackened by smoke.

Lingual-alveolar: Lingual refers to the tongue and alveolar refers to the sockets of the teeth, thus the combination involves the tongue and the forward portion of the roof of the mouth. Phonemes which fall into this category include /d/, /n/, /t/, /s/, and others.

Linguistic response (R_L): A response that is a component of a language, and is meaningful. The response may be overt as in an audible speech utterance (R_L), or it may be covert as in slight electromyographically recordable activities of the speech or non-speech musculature (r_L).

Linguistic stimulus (S_L): Any stimulus which is a component of a language, typically a natural language, and is in some sense meaningful (such as evoking a meaning reaction).

Mediating processes: Processes which are postulated as occurring between stimulus onset and the occurrence of a response when there are lawful relations among the three events. The mediating process may be a hypothetical construct (having some physiological or psychophysiological reality) or an intervening variable (a fictitious process hypothesized merely to account for given behavior). All such mediating processes are also referred to as logical constructs.

Micron (μ): One millionth of a millimeter.

Micro-phonemes: See Distinctive features.

Microvolt (μv): One millionth of a volt, (10^{-6}). The order of magnitude of the signal measured in most covert measures. Far less than the power that can be measured in the atmosphere from such radiating sources as power lines and radio stations.

Millisecond (Msec, or ms.): One thousandth of a second (.001 sec).

Mind: A self-programming operation of the body which consists of, and only of, the activation of complex neuromuscular circuits.

Monads: In Leibnitz's doctrine, these atomic units (monads) that are ultimate units of being compose the self or soul and the material world.

Monism: The conception of the universe as consisting of one and only one kind of "stuff." Reality may thus be either materialistic or non-materialistic. Materialism forms the basis of science. A non-materialism may also form a logically consistent model of reality, as in Berkeley's subjective idealism.

Muscle action potential (MAP): An electrically sensed signal that results when a localized disturbance is transmitted along a muscle cell membrane. The disturbance then results in contraction of the fibers of the muscle. See Action potential. Synonymous with electromyogram.

Mylohoid: A muscle that forms the muscular floor of the mouth and raises the hyoid and the tongue. The muscle is active in the initial phases of swallowing. Technically, its origin is the inner aspect of the mandible, and it fuses with the fibers on either side in a median line that extends from near the symphysis back to the hyoid bone.

Neural codes: Components of the nervous systems when activated conduct neural impulses that transmit information throughout the body. The relationship between externally presented information and the neural coding in the receptor and immediately following has been extensively studied. Particularly relevant to the neuromuscular concept of internal information processing is how information is generated in the neuromuscular components.

Neurobiotaxis: A notion about systematic decrease of synaptic resistance to account for a variety of psychological phenomena such as learning. Primitive forms were suggestions that components of neurons grow closer to each other with repeated stimulation. More sophisticated notions concern activities of boutons, as in Hebb.

Neuromuscular circuit: A circuit consisting of central neural components, efferent pathways, musculature components, and afferent pathways back to the central nervous system. Reverberation of these neuromuscular circuits is the essential operation in internal information processing. The processing of information received externally that is stored internally cna explicate common sense terms such as thinking and creativity. In these circuits the musculature and brain thus interact by way of the afferent and efferent nervous pathways. Thinking is thus not just a central phenomenon, but a process that involves the entire body.

Neuromuscular junction: The surfaces where motor neurons come in contact with the musculature they innervate.

Nystagmus: An involuntary rapid movement of the eyeballs, which may be lateral, vertical, rotary, or mixed.

Occipital lobe: The posterior cortical portion of the cerebral hemisphere which contains the main projection areas for vision.

Orienting reflex: The complex widespread covert response pattern that alters an organism's status with respect to stimulus.

Parietal lobe: The cortical area forward of the occipital lobes above the temporal lobes, and posterior to the central fissue. Its function is primarily sensory.

Parsimony, principle of: The principle that we prefer to explain phenomena with simpler principles than with more complex principles when either will suffice. Specific instances are Occam's razor and Morgan's canon.

Patellar tendon reflex: A reflex response evoked by a sudden tap just below the kneecap (synonymously, the knee-jerk reflex).

Peripheral: A vague term referring to those portions of the body outside of the brain and spinal cord. The term causes confusion of what was traditionally referred to as the "peripheralist position" on the higher mental processes.

Peripheralist: A traditional position asserting that systems in the body other than the brain are involved in cognitive processing. Often incorrectly applied to suggest that a peripheralist doesn't ascribe cognitive functions for the brain.

Phoneme: A group of similar sounds which are regarded as having the same sound in a given language and having a distinct function in determining meaning.

Phonemic level: At this level phonemes are defined only by their distinctive features.

Phonetic alphabet: An alphabet wherein each symbol represents a speech sound. It may be used to define the pronunciation of each letter in a word.

Phrenology: The notion that mental traits can be assessed by the structure of the skull. The presumption was that various mental characteristics are highly localized in specific brain regions. The under- or overdevelopment of the brain in those particular regions could then be assessed according to the depressions or heightenings of the skull at that point.

Physical phonetic level: The measurement of acoustic stimuli into its physical components via sound spectrograms or wave form analysis from an oscilloscope. That is, the physical measurement of the acoustic signal.

Placebo: A treatment condition in a research project which has no specific direct effect on the dependent variable itself. Rather, the placebo may affect the dependent variable through suggestion and is used as a control for that extraneous variable. Consequently the effects of suggestion may be assessed so that validity of the experimental treatment may be more accurately ascertained.

Plethysmograph: An instrument used to measure changes in the volume of a portion of the body, especially components of the cardiovascular system.

Pneumogram: A breathing record of both frequency and amplitude (volume), classically accomplished by strain gauges attached to a flexible strap which is placed around the chest.

Polygraph: A common synonym for "lie detector," it is a system which includes several ink writing pens which record psychophysiological events on a slowly moving roll of paper. The pens are driven by small motors which respond to the input of any of several signals such as GSR, EEG. Because of mechanical limitations polygraphs do not provide a linear response to input signals over 200 Hz.

Progressive relaxation: The technique developed by Edmund Jacobson for controlling tension. The technique resulted in the demonstration that zero muscle tonus is achievable.

Projection areas: Those areas of the brain which are primarily associated with a particular sensory modality. The occipital region is the main projection area for vision and presumably is involved in the interpretation of visual stimuli.

Proprioceptors: Those receptors that are sensitive to changes in position of portions of the body. These include receptors which signal the positions of limbs, as well as vestibular senses.

Psyche: The Greek conception of a life principle, approximately translated as "soul."

Psycholinguistics: The study of the manner in which language is related to characteristics of the language user, and includes the processes by which one emits or interprets components of the language.

Psychophysiology: The study of those response and neural events which require laboratory apparatus for their observation. Electrical measures of psychophysiological events are the most prominent and include such covert processes as electroencephalograms, electromyograms, and electro-oculograms.

Pulse: A short-duration change in the level of a variable.

Range: The difference between the upper and lower values that can be measured.

Rapid eye movements (REM): Unique eye movements occurring during emergent Stage 1 of sleep associated with dreaming. Recording is from the external canthi for horizontal movements, and electrodes placed just above and below the eye for vertical movements.

Read: To acquire data from a source.

Reference electrode: An EEG electrode placed on a subject in monopolar recording to allow potential differences to be sensed between that location (e.g., ear lobe) and a variety of others.

Representational response: The covert response one makes upon perceiving a word. It may be measured electromyographically.

Reticular activating system (RAS): A diffuse system of nuclei in the central and lower brain which are components of a neural circuit involving the cortex. The RAS affects levels of arousal by bombarding the cortex which in turn stimulates the RAS. During sleep the RAS does not accept external stimulation.

Semantic theory: Having to do with the meaning of words and how meanings develop.

Semantic tracers: A peripheral bodily event, perhaps electromyographically measurable, that indexes a more basic meaning reaction as in Osgood's r_M.

Sense: To detect the presence of an event.

Sensitivity: The ratio of a change in steady-state output to the corresponding change of input, often measured in percent of span.

Sensor: A device (e.g., electrode) especially and directly responsive to a measurable event.

Signal averaging: A process by which a signal is recovered from signal and noise through repeated processing of many samples which contain the signal. The noise "randomizes out" leaving only the signal, as with an average evoked potential.

Speech signals: Those sounds which are interpreted as linguistic units (e.g., words) and have meanings.

Stimulus: Any energy that excites a receptor whereupon afferent neural impulses are generated. A stimulus may be external (outside the skin of the organism) or internal, as in neural impulses. Any stimulus results in some (overt or covert) response.

String galvanometer: An instrument which is sensitive to minute changes in current flow. Its sensitivity is a function of the low friction in the string from which the indicator is suspended, along with a coil which develops a magnetic field based on the flow of current.

Tact: A vocal naming response. An external tact names an external event; an internal tact, one within the skin.

Tambour: A device, consisting of an elastic membrane, to communicate pressure changes to a recording pen.

Temporal lobe: The cortical area of the brain below the lateral fissure containing auditory regions.

Theta waves: EEG patterns of 4 to 7 Hz, found primarily in young children.

Vagus nerve: The tenth cranial nerve which contains many of the fibers of the autonomic nervous system and thus innervates much of the viscera.

V.o.a.: The ventral lateral nucleus of the dentathalmic fibers.

V.o.p.: The terminal nucleus of the dentathalmic fibers.

Wernicke's area: A cerebral area in the temporal region on the dominant side of the brain. Its relation to the understanding of speech is exceedingly complex. Lesions in this area are said to result in irreversible aphasia.

Zeitgeist: Spirit of the time.

References

Aarons, L. Subvocalization: Aural and EMG feedback in reading. *Perceptual and Motor Skills*, 1971, *33*, 271–306.

Abbs, J. H. The influence of the gamma motor system on jaw movements during speech: A theoretical framework and some preliminary observations. *Journal of Speech and Hearing Research*, 1973, *16*, 175–200.

Acker, L. E. and Edwards, A. E. Transfer of vasoconstriction over a bipolar meaning dimension. *Journal of Experimental Psychology*, 1964, *67*, 1–6.

Adams, J. A. A closed-loop theory of motor learning. *Journal of Motor Behavior*, 1971, *3*, 111–49.

Adams, J. A., Goetz, E. T., and Marshall, P. H. Response feedback and motor learning. *Journal of Experimental Psychology*, 1972, *92*, 391–97.

Adams, J. A., McIntyre, J. S., and Thorsheim, H. I. Response feedback and verbal retention. *Journal of Experimental Psychology*, 1969, *82*, 290–96.

Adatia, A. K. and Gehring, E. N. Proprioceptive innervation of the tongue. *Journal of Anatomy*, 1971, *110*, 215–20.

Adrian, E. D., and Matthews, B. H. C. The Berger rhythm: Potential changes from the occipital lobes of man. *Brain*, 1934, *57*, 355–85.

Alpern, M., Lawrence, M., and Wolsk, D. *Sensory Processes.* Belmont, Calif: Brooks/Cole, 1967.

Amadeo, M. and Gomez, E. Eye movements, attention and dreaming in subjects with lifelong blindness. *Canadian Psychiatric Association Journal*, 1966, *11*, 501–7.

Amadeo, M., and Shagass, C. Eye movements, attention, and hypnosis. *Journal of Nervous and Mental Disease*, 1963, *136*, 139–45.

Amadeo, M. and Shagass, C. Brief latency click-evoked potentials during waking and sleep in man. *Psychophysiology*, 1973, *10*, 244–50.

Amassian, V. E., and Weiner, H. The effect of (+)-tubocurarine chloride and of acute hypotension on the electrical activity of the cat. *Journal of Physiology*, 1966, *184*, 1–15.

Anderson, R. C., Goldberg, S. R., and Hidde, J. L. Meaningful processing of sentences. *Journal of Educational Psychology,* 1971, *62,* 395–99.

Andreassi, J. L., Mayzner, E. S., Beyda, D. R., and Davidovics, S. Effects of induced muscle tension upon the visual evoked potential and motor potential. *Psychonomic Science,* 1970, *20,* 245–47.

Angel, R. W., Hollander, M., and Wesley, M. Hand-eye coordination: The role of "motor memory." *Perception and Psychophysics,* 1973, *14,* 506–10.

Anokhin, P. K. A new conception of the physiological architecture of conditioned relfex. In J. F. Delafresnaye (ed.), *Brain mechanisms and learning.* Springfield, Ill.: Charles C Thomas, 1961.

Anokhin, P. K. Cybernetics and the integrative activity of the brain. In M. Cole and I Maltzman (eds.), *A handbook of contemporary Soviet psychology.* New York: Basic Books, 1969.

Antrobus, J. S. Rapid eye movements during signal detection performance. *Proceeding of the International Colloquium* on "The oculomotor system and brain function." The Slovak Academy of Science, Bratislava, Czechoslovakia, 1970.

Antrobus, J. S. Eye movements and non-visual cognitive tasks. In Zikmund, V. (ed.) *The oculomotor system and brain functions.* London: Butterworths & Bratislava, Czechoslovakia: Slovak Academy of Sciences, 1973.

Antrobus, J. S. and Antrobus, J. S. Rapid eye movements and rapid eye movement periods. *Psychophysiology,* 1969, *6,* 45–48.

Antrobus, J. S., Antrobus, J. S., and Singer, J. L. Eye movements accompanying daydreaming, visual imagery, and thought suppression. *Journal of Abnormal and Social Psychology,* 1964, *69,* 244–52.

Arey, L. B. *Developmental anatomy,* 7th ed. Philadelphia: Saunders, 1965.

Arkin, A. M., Lutzky, H., and Toth, M. F. Congenital nystagmus and sleep: A replication. *Psychophysiology,* 1972, *9,* 210–17.

Arkin, A. M., Weitzman, E. D., and Hastey, J. M. An observational note on eye movement patterns during REM and non-REM sleep in subjects with congenital nystagmus. *Psychophysiology,* 1966, *3,* 69–72.

Armington, J. *The electroretinogram.* New York: Academic Press, 1974.

Arnold, F. Obstructed breathing and memory. *Psychological Clinic of Philadelphia,* 1915, *8,* 234–46.

Aserinsky, E. and Kleitman, N. Regularly occurring periods of eye motility, and concomitant phenomena during sleep. *Science,* 1953, *118,* 273–74.

Aserinsky, E. and Kleitman, N. Two types of ocular motility occurring in sleep. *Journal of Applied Physiology,* 1955, *8,* 1–10.

Averback, E. and Coriell, A. S. Short-term memory in vision. *The Bell System Technical Journal,* 1961, *40,* 309–28.

Bacon, J. *Eye movements and detection of sequence patterns in an auditory detection task.* Unpublished B. A. Honors Thesis. The City College of the City University of New York, 1970.

Baekeland, F. and Lasky, R. The morning recall of rapid eye movement period reports given earlier in the night. *Journal of Nervous & Mental Disease,* 1968, *147,* 570–79.

Baginsky, R. G. Voluntary control of motor unit activity by visual and aural feedback. *Electroencephalography and Clinical Neurophysiology,* 1969, *27,* 724.

Bain, A. *The senses and the intellect.* London: Parker, 1855.

Bain, A. *The emotions and the will.* London: Parker, 1859.

Bakan, P. Hypnotizability, laterality of eye-movements and functional brain asymmetry. *Perceptual and Motor Skills,* 1969, *28,* 927–32.

Bakan, P. and Shotland, R. L. Lateral eye movement, reading speed, and visual attention. *Psychonomic Science,* 1969, *15,* 93–94.

Baldridge, B. J., Whitman, R. M., and Kramer, M. The concurrence of fine muscle activity and rapid eye movements during sleep. *Psychosomatic Medicine,* 1965, *27,* 19–26.

Baldridge, B. J., Whitman, R. M., Kramer, M., and Ornstein, P. H. The effect of induced eye movements on dreaming. *Psychophysiology,* 1968, *5,* 230.

Ballet, G. *Le langage interieur et les diverses formes de l'aphasie* (1886). In R. Pintner (ed.), Inner speech during silent reading. *Psychological Review,* 1913, *20,* 129–53.

Barlow, M. C. The role of articulation in memorizing. *Journal of Experimental Psychology,* 1928, *11,* 306–12.

Bartlett, N. R. A comparison of manual reaction times as measured by three sensitive indices. *Psychological Record,* 1963, *13,* 51–56.

Bartoshuk, A. K. Electromyographic gradients and electroencephalographic amplitude during motivated listening. *Canadian Journal of Psychology,* 1956, *10,* 156–64.

Basmajian, J. V. *Muscles alive: Their functions revealed by electromyography.* Baltimore: © 1962 The Williams & Wilkins Co.

Basmajian, J. V. Control and training of individual motor units. *Science,* 1963, *141,* 440–441. (a)

Basmajian, J. V. Conscious control of single nerve cells. *New Scientist,* 1963, *20,* 662–64. (b)

Basmajian, J. V. Electromyography comes of age. *Science.* 1972, *176* 603–9.

Basmajian, J. V., Baeza, M., and Fabrigar, C. Conscious control and training of individual spinal motor neurons in normal human subjects. *The Journal of New Drugs.* 1965, *5,* 78–85.

Basmajian, J. V., and Simard, T. G. Effects of distracting movements on the control of trained motor units. *American Journal of Physical Medicine,* 1967, *46,* 1427–49.

Bassin, F. V. and Bein, E. S. Application of electromyography to the study of speech. In N. O'Connor (ed.), *Recent Soviet psychology.* New York: Liveright Publishing, 1961.

Bechterev, V. M. *Foundations of general reflexology of man.* Moscow: Gosizdat, 1923.

Begleiter, H., Gross, M. M., and Kissin, B. Evoked cortical responses to affective visual stimuli. *Psychophysiology,* 1967, *3,* 336–44.

Begleiter, H., Gross, M. M., Porjesz, B., and Kissin, B. The effects of awareness on cortical evoked potentials to conditioned affective stimuli. *Psychophysiology,* 1969, *5,* 517–29.

Begleiter, H., and Platz, A. Cortical evoked potentials to semantic stimuli. *Psychophysiology,* 1969, *6,* 91–100.

Begleiter, H. and Platz, A. Evoked potentials: Modifications by classical conditioning. *Science,* 1969, *166,* 769–71.

Begleiter, H. and Porjesz, B. Evoked brain potentials as indicators of decision-making. *Science,* 1975, *187,* 754–55.

Begleiter, H., Porjesz, B., Yerre, C., and Kissin, B. Evoked potential correlates of expected stimulus intensity. *Science,* 1973, *179,* 814–16.

Beh, H. C. and Hawkins, C. A. Effect of induced muscle tension on acquisition and retention of verbal material. *Journal of Experimental Psychology,* 1973, *98,* 206–8.

Bell, Sir C. On the necessity of the sense of muscular action to the full exercise of the organs of the senses. *Proceedings of the Royal Society of Edinburgh*, 1842, pp. 361–63.

Belmaker, R., Proctor, E., and Feather, B. W. Muscle tension in human operant heart rate conditioning. *Conditional Reflex*, 1972, 7, 97–106.

Benussi, V. Die Atmungssymptome der Lüge. *Archiv für die gesamte Psychologie*, 1914, 31, 244–73.

Berger, H. Uber das elektrekephalogramm des Menschen. *Archiv fur Psychiatrie Nervenkrankheiten*, 1929, 87, 527–70.

Berger, R. J. Tonus of extrinsic laryngeal muscles during sleep and dreaming. *Science*, 1961, 134, 840.

Berger, R. J., Olley, P., and Oswald, I. The EEG, eye movements and dreams of the blind. *Quarterly Journal of Experimental Psychology*, 1962, 14 183–86.

Berger, R. J. and Oswald, I. Effects of sleep deprivation on behaviour, subsequent sleep, and dreaming. *Journal of Mental Science*, 1962, 108, 457–65. (a)

Berger, R. J. and Oswald, I., Eye movements during active and passive dreams. *Science*, 1962, 137, 601. (b)

Berger, S. M., Irwin, D. S., and Frommer, G. P. Electromyographic activity during observational learning. *American Journal of Psychology*, 1970, 83, 86–94.

Berger, S. M. and Hadley, S. W. Some effects of a model's performance on an observer's electromyographic activity. *American Journal of Psychology*, 1975, 88, 263–76.

Berger, T. W. and Thompson, R. F. Limbic system interrelations: Functional division among hippocampal-septal connections. *Science*, 1977, 197, 587–89.

Bergmann, G. The contribution of John B. Watson. *Psychological Review*, 1956, 63, 265–76.

Bergum, B. and Lehr, D. Prediction of stimulus approach: Core measures Experiment II. Research and Advanced Engineering Division, Fundamental Research Laboratory, Xerox. Report No. R66-36, July 1966.

Bernal, G. and Berger, S. M. Vicarious eyelid conditioning. *Journal of Personality and Social Psychology*, 1976, 34, 62–68.

Bernhard, C. G., Bohm, E., and Petersen, I. Investigations on organization of corticospinal systems in monkeys (Macaca mulatta). *Acta Physiologica Scandinavica*, 1953, 29, 79.

Bernstein, N. A. *Sketches of physiology of locomotions and physiology of activity*. Moscow: Medicina, 1966.

Berry, R. N. and Davis, R. C. Muscle responses and their relation to rote learning. *Journal of Experimental Psychology*, 1958, 55, 188–94.

Berry, R. N. and Davis, R. C. The somatic background of rote learning. *Journal of Experimental Psychology*, 1960, 59, 27–34.

Betts, E. A. *Foundations of reading instruction*. New York: American, 1950.

Bexton, W. H., Heron, W., and Scott, T. H. Effects of decreased variation in the sensory environment. *Canadian Journal of Psychology*, 1954, 8, 70–76.

Bickford, R. G., Jacobson, J. L., and Cody, D. T. R. Nature of average evoked potentials to sound and other stimuli in man. *Annals of the New York Academy of Sciences*, 1964, 112, 204–18.

Bigland-Ritchie, B. and Woods, J. J. Integrated EMG and oxygen uptake during dynamic contractions of human muscles. *Journal of Applied Physiology*, 1974, 36, 475–79.

Bills, A. G. The influence of muscular tension on the efficiency of mental work. *American Journal of Psychology*, 1927, 38, 227–51.

Binet, A. *L'Etude expérimentale de l'intelligence.* Paris, 1903. (Sokolov, A. N. *Inner speech and thought.* New York: Plenum Press, 1972.)

Bird, C. and Beers, F. S. Maximum and minimum inner speech in reading. *Journal of Applied Psychology,* 1933, *17,* 182–97. (Edfeldt, A. W. *Silent speech and silent reading.* Chicago: University of Chicago Press, 1960.)

Birk, L., Crider, A., Shapiro, D., and Tursky, B. Operant electrodermal conditioning under partial curarization. *Journal of Comparative and Physiological Psychology,* 1966, *62,* 165–66.

Bitterman, M. E. and Marcuse, F. L. Cardiovascular responses of innocent persons to criminal investigation. *American Journal of Psychology,* 1947, *60,* 407–12.

Black, A. H. Cardiac conditioning in curarized dogs: The relationship between heart rate and skeletal behavior. In William F. Prokasy (ed.), *Classical conditioning.* New York: Appleton-Century-Crofts, 1965.

Black, A. H. Transfer following operant conditioning in the curarized dog. *Science,* 1967, *155,* 201–3.

Black, A. H. The direct control of neural processes by reward and punishment. *American Scientist,* 1971, *59,* 236–45.

Black, A. H., Carlson, N. J., and Solomon, R. L. Exploratory studies of the conditioning of autonomic responses in curarized dogs. *Psychological Monographs,* 1962, *76,* 1–31.

Black, A. H. and Dalton, A. J. The relationship between the avoidance response and subsequent changes in heart rate. In W. F. Proskasy (ed.), *Classical conditioning.* New York: Appleton-Century-Crofts, 1965.

Black, A. H. and Lang, W. M. Cardiac conditioning and skeletal responding in curarized dogs. *Psychological Review,* 1964, *71,* 80–85.

Blumenthal, M. Lingual myographic responses during directed thinking. Unpublished doctoral dissertation, University of Denver, 1959.

Bond, G. L. and Tinker, M. A. *Reading difficulties: Their diagnosis and correction.* New York: Appleton-Century-Crofts, 1957. (Edfeldt, A. W. *Silent speech and silent reading.* Chicago: University of Chicago Press, 1960.)

Borden, G. J., Harris, K. S., and Catena, L. Electromyographic study of speech musculature during lingual nerve block. Paper presented at the American Speech and Hearing Association Convention, San Francisco, Calif., November 1972.

Borkovec, T. D. Thereapy outcome research: Group design and methodology. In F. J. McGuigan (ed.), *Tension Control: Proceedings of the Third Meeting of the American Association for the Advancement of Tension Control.* Louisville: AAATC, 1977.

Boros, J. Biopotential recordings of the tongue with EMG during listening to texts with various contents *Studia Psychologica,* 1972, *14,* 94–96.

Botwinick, J. and Thompson, L. W. Premotor and motor components of reaction time. *Journal of Experimental Psychology,* 1966, *71,* 9–15.

Bousfield, W. A., Whitmarsh, G. A., and Danick, J. J. Partial response identities in verbal generalization. *Psychological Reports,* 1958, *4,* 703–13.

Bower, G. Mental imagery and associative learning. In L. Gregg (ed.), *Cognition in learning and memory.* New York: John Wiley, 1972.

Bowman, J. P. and Combs, C. M. Discharge patterns of lingual spindle afferent fibers in the hypoglossal nerve of the rhesus monkey. *Experimental Neurology,* 1968, *21,* 105–19.

Bowman, J. P. and Combs, C. M. The cerebrocortical projection of hypoglossal afferents. *Experimental Neurology,* 1969, *23,* 291–301.

Brady, J. P. and Levitt, E. E. Nystagmus as a criterion of hypnotically induced visual hallucinations. *Science,* 1964, *146,* 85–86.

Brady, J. P. and Levitt, E. E. Hypnotically induced visual hallucinations. *Psychosomatic Medicine*, 1966, *28*, 351–63.

Brady, J. P. and Rosner, B. S. Rapid eye movements in hypnotically induced dreams. *Journal of Nervous and Mental Disease*, 1966, *143*, 28–35.

Brain, W. R. In P. Laslett (ed.), *The physical basis of mind*. Oxford: Basil Blackwell, 1950.

Breed, G. and Colaiuta, V. Looking, Blinking and sitting. Nonverbal dynamics in the classroom. *Journal of Communication*, 1974, *24*, 75–81.

Breese, B. B. On inhibition. *Psychological Review Monographs*, 1899, *3*, 47–48.

Brenner, D., Williamson, S. J., and Kaufman, L. Visually evoked magnetic fields of the human brain. *Science*, 1975, *190*, 480–82.

Brenner, F., Moritz, F., and Benignus, V. The EEG correlates of attention in humans. *Neuropsychologia*, 1974, *10*, 467–69.

Brinley, F. J., Jr., Kandel, E. R., and Marshall, W. H. The effect of intravenous d-tubocurarine on the electrical activity of the cat cerebral cortex. *Transactions of the American Neurological Association*, 1958, *83*, 53–58.

Brown, B. B. Visual recall ability and eye movements. *Psychophysiology*, 1968, *4*, 300–306.

Brown, B. B. Recognition of aspects of consciousness through association with EEG alpha activity represented by a light signal. *Psychophysiology*, 1970, *6*, 442–52.

Brown, R. and Bellugi, U. Three processes in the child's acquisition of syntax. In E. H. Lenneberg (ed.), *New directions in the study of language*. Cambridge, Mass.: MIT Press, 1964.

Brown, R. W. and McNeill, D. The "tip of the tongue" phenomena. *Journal of Verbal Learning and Verbal Behavior*, 1966, *5*, 325–37.

Brumlik, J., Richeson, W. B., and Arbit, J. The origin of certain electrical cerebral rhythms. *Brain Research*, 1966/1967, *3*, 227–47.

Bruner, J. S., Olver, R. R., and Greenfield, M. *Studies in cognitive growth; a collaboration at the Center for Cognitive Studies*. New York: John Wiley, 1966.

Buchsbaum, M. S. and Drago, D. Hemispheric asymmetry and the effects of attention on visual evoked potentials. *Progress in Clinical Neurophysiology*, in press.

Buchsbaum, M. and Fedio, P. Visual information and evoked responses from the left and right hemispheres. *Electroencephalography and Clinical Neurophysiology*, 1969, *26*, 266–72.

Buchsbaum, M. and Fedio, P. Hemispheric differences in evoked potentials to verbal and nonverbal stimuli in the left and right visual fields. *Physiology and Behavior*, 1970, *5*, 207–10.

Buchwald, J. S., Standish, M., Eldred, E., and Halas, E. S. Contribution of muscle spindle circuits to learning as suggested by training under Flaxedil. *Electroencephalography and Clinical Neurophysiology*, 1964, *16*, 582–94.

Bullock, T. H. Signals and neuronal coding. T. Melnechuk and F. O. Schmitt (eds.). In G. C. Quarton, *The Neurosciences: A Study Program*. New York: Rockefeller University Press, 1967.

Burke, T. R. Relaxed running. In F. J. McGuigan (ed.), *Proceedings of the First Meeting of the American Association for the Advancement of Tension Control*. Chicago: University Publications, 1975.

Burrows, D. and Okada, R. Parallel scanning of semantic and formal information. *Journal of Experimental Psychology*, 1973, *97*, 254–57.

Busciano, G. A., Spadetta, V., Carella, A., and Caruso, G. A study of the visomotor components of dreaming in subjects with impaired ocular mobility. *Acta Neurologica*, 1971, *26*, 1–6.

Campbell, D., Sanderson, R. E., and Laverty, S. G. Characteristics of a conditioned response in human subjects during extinction trials following a simple traumatic conditioning trial. *Journal of Abnormal and Social Psychology*, 1964, *68*, 627–39.

Cannon, W. B. *Bodily changes in pain, hunger, fear and rage*, rev. ed. New York: Appleton-Century-Crofts, 1929.

Capek, K. *R.U.R. (Rossum's Universal Robots)*. Garden City, N.Y.: Doubleday, 1923.

Carlsöö, S. S. and Edfeldt, A. W. Attempts at muscle control with visual and auditory impulses as auxiliary stimuli. *Scandinavian Journal of Psychology*. 1963, *4*, 231–35.

Carr, H. *Psychology*. New York: Longmans, Green, 1925.

Carver, R. P. Speed readers don't read; they skim. *Psychology Today*, 1972, p. 22.

Caton, R. The electric currents of the brain. *British Medical Journal*, 1875, *2*, 278.

Cautela, J. R. Covert processes and behavior modification. *Journal of Nervous and Mental Disease*, 1973, *157*, 27.

Chapman, R. M. Spectral sensitivity of single neural units in the bullfrog retina. *Journal of the Optical Society of America*, 1961, *51*, 1102–12.

Chapman, R. M. Spectral sensitivities of neural impulses and slow waves in the bullfrog retina. *Vision Research*, 1962, *2*, 89–102.

Chapman, R. M. Evoked responses to relevant and irrelevant visual stimuli while problem solving. *Proceedings of the 73rd Annual Convention of the American Psychological Association—1965*, pp. 177–78.

Chapman, R. M. Discussion of the specification of psychological variables in an average evoked potential experiment. In E. Donchin and D. D. Lindsley (eds.), *Average evoked potentials: Methods, results, and evaluations*. Washington, D.C.: Government Printing Office, NASA SP-191, 1969, pp. 262–75.

Chapman, R. M. Kappa waves and intellectual abilities. *Electroencephalography and Clinical Neurophysiology*, 1972, *33*, 254.

Chapman, R. M. and Bragdon, H. R. Evoked responses to numerical and non-numerical visual stimuli while problem solving. *Nature*, 1964, *203*, 1155–57.

Chapman, R. M., Cavonius, C. R., and Ernest, J. J. Alpha and Kappa electroencephalogram activity in eyeless subjects. *Science*. 1971, *171*, 1159–61.

Chase, W. G. (ed.). *Visual information processing*. New York: Academic Press, 1973.

Cherry, C. *On human communication*. Cambridge, Mass.: MIT Press, 1957.

Chomsky, N. and Halle, M. *The sound pattern of English*. New York: Harper & Row, 1968.

Clark, R. S. An experimental study of silent thinking. *Archives of Psychology*, 1922, *48*, 5–100.

Clites, M. S. Certain somatic activities in relation to successful and unsuccessful problem solving. Part I. *Journal of Experimental Psychology*, 1935, *18*, 708–24.

Clites, M. S. Certain somatic activities in relation to successful and unsuccessful problem solving. Part III. *Journal of Experimental Psychology*, 1936, *19*, 172–92.

Cofer, C. N. and Foley, J. P. Mediated generalization and the interpretation of verbal behavior: I. Prolegomena. *Psychological Review*, 1942, *49*, 513–40.

Cohen, G. How are pictures registered in memory? *Quarterly Journal of Experimental Psychology*, 1973, *25*, 557–64.

Cohen, J. Very slow brain potentials relating to expectancy: The CNV. In E. Donchin and D. B. Lindsley (eds.), *Average evoked potentials*. Washington, D.C.: NASA SP-191, 1969.

Cohen, J. and Walter, W. G. The interaction of responses in the brain to semantic stimuli. *Psychophysiology*, 1966, *2*, 187–96.

Cohen, M. J. and Johnson, H. J. Relationship between heart rate and muscular activity within a classical conditioning paradigm. *Journal of Experimental Psychology*, 1971, *90*, 222–26.

Cohn, R. Differential cerebral processing of noise and verbal stimuli. *Science*, 1971, *172*, 599–601.

Cole, L. *The improvement of reading.* New York: Farrar & Rinehart, 1938.

Cole, R. A. Perceiving syllables and remembering phonemes. *Journal of Speech and Hearing Research*, 1973, *16*, 37–47.

Cole, M. and Maltzman, I. *A handbook of contemporary Soviet psychology.* New York: Basic Books, 1969.

Cole, R. A. and Scott, B. Distinctive feature control or decision time: Same-different judgments of simultaneously heard phenomes. *Perception and Psychophysics*, 1972, *12*, 91–94.

Cole, R. A. and Young, M. Effect of subvocalization on memory for speech sounds. *Journal of Experimental Psychology: Human Learning and Memory*, 1975, *1*, 772–79.

Colle, H. A. Rehearsal as inner speech. Paper presented at the meetings of the American Psychological Association, September 2-8, 1972, Honolulu, Hawaii.

Collins, W. E. Effects of mental set upon vestibular nystagmus. *Journal of Experimental Psychology*, 1962, *63*, 191–97.

Collins, W. E. and Posner, J. B. Electroencephalogram alpha-activity during mild vestibular stimulation. *Nature*, 1963, *199*, 933–34.

Colvin, S. S. and Meyer, E. J. The development of imagination in school children and the relation between educational types and retentivity of material appealing to various sense departments. *Psychological Review*, 1909, *11*, (1, Pt. 2).

Conrad, R. C. Acoustic confusions in immediate memory. *British Journal of Psychology*, 1964, *55*, 75–83.

Corbin, C. B. Effects of mental practice on skill development after controlled practice. *Research Quarterly* (American Association for Health, Physical Education, and Recreation), 1967, *38*, 534–38. (a)

Corbin, C. B. The effects of covert rehearsal on the development of a complex motor skill. *Journal of General Psychology*, 1967, *76*, 143–50. (b)

Costell, R. M., Lunde, D. T., Kopell, B. S., and Wittner, W. K. Contingent negative variation as an indicator of sexual object preference. *Science*, 1972, *177*, 718–20.

Courten, H. C. Involuntary movements of the tongue. *Yale Psychological Studies*, 1902, *10*, 93–95.

Curtis, H. S. Automatic movements of the larynx. *American Journal of Psychology*, 1900, *11*, 237–39.

Cutrow, R. J., Parks, A., Lucas, N., and Thomas, K. The objective use of multiple physiological indices in the detection of deception. *Psychophysiology*, 1972, *9*, 578–88.

Cutting, J. E. Two left-hemisphere mechanisms in speech perception. *Perception and Psychophysics*, 1974, *16*, 601–12.

Dallett, K. M. Intelligibility and short-term memory in the repetition of digit strings. *Journal of Speech and Hearing Disorders*, 1964, *7*, 362–68.

Darley, F. L., Aronson, A. E., and Brown, J. R. Clusters of deviant speech dimensions in the dysarthrias. *Journal of Speech and Hearing Research*, 1969, *12*, 462–96. (a)

Darley, F. L., Aronson, A. E., and Brown, J. R. Differential diagnostic patterns of dysarthria. *Journal of Speech and Hearing Research*, 1969, *12*, 246–69. (b)

Darrow, E. W. The galvanic skin reflex (sweating) and blood pressure as preparatory and facilitative functions. *Psychology Bulletin*, 1936, *33*, 73–94.

Darrow, C. W. and Hicks, R. G. Interarea electroencephalographic phase relationships following sensory and ideational stimuli. *Psychophysiology*, 1965, *1*, 337–46.

Darwin, E. *Zoonomia, or the laws of organic life*, vol. 1, sect. xiv. London, 1794.

Dashiell, J. F. A physiological-behavioristic descripton of thinking. *Psychological Review*, 1925, *32*, 54–73.   Copyright 1925 by the American Psychological Association.   Reprinted by permission.

Dashiell, J. F. Is the cerebrum the seat of thinking? *Psychological Review*, 1926, *33*, 13–29.

Dashiell, J. F. *Fundamentals of objective psychology*. Cambridge, Mass.: Riverside Press, 1928.

Dashiell, J. F. *Fundamentals of general psychology*, 3rd ed. Boston: Houghton-Mifflin, 1949.

Davis, H. Enhancement of evoked cortical potentials in humans related to a task requiring a decision. *Science*, 1964, *145*, 182–83.

Davis, H. Classes of auditory evoked responses. *Audiology*, 1973, *12*, 464–69.

Davis, R. C. The relation of certain muscle action potentials to "mental work." *Indiana University Publications Science Series*, 1937, *5*, 5–29.

Davis, R. C. The relation of muscle action potentials to difficulty and frustration. *Journal of Experimental Psychology*, 1938, *23*, 141–58.

Davis, R. C. Patterns of muscular activity during "mental work" and their constancy. *Journal of Experimental Psychology*, 1939, *24*, 451–65.

Davis, R. C. Response patterns. *Transactions of the New York Academy of Sciences*, 1957, *19*, 731–39.

Davis, R. C., Buchwald, A. M., and Frankmann, R. W. Autonomic and muscular responses, and their relation to simple stimuli. *Psychological Monographs*, 1955, *69*, 1–71.

Davis, R. C., Garafolo, L., and Gault, F. P. An exploration of abdominal potentials. *Journal of Comparative and Physiological Psychology*, 1957, *50*, 519–23.

Davis, R., and Schmit, V. Visual and verbal coding in the interhemispheric transfer of information. *Acta Psychologica*, 1973, *37*, 229-40.

Dawson, G. D. Cerebral responses to electrical stimulation of peripheral nerves in man. *Journal of Neurology and Neurosurgical Psychiatry*, 1947, *10*, 134–40.

Day, M. E. An eye movement phenomenon relating to attention, thought and anxiety. *Perceptual and Motor Skills*, 1964, *19*, 443–46.

Day, M. E. An eye-movement indicator of individual differences in the physiological organization of attentional processes and anxiety. *Journal of Psychology*, 1967, *66*, 51–62.

Deckert, G. H. Pursuit eye movements in the absence of a moving stimulus, *Science*, 1964, *143*, 1192–93.

Delafresnaye, J. F. *Brain mechanisms and consciousness*. Oxford: Blackwell Scientific Publications, Ltd., 1954.

Dement, W. C. and Kleitman, N. The relation of eye movements during sleep to dream activity: An objective method for the study of dreaming. *Journal of Experimental Psychology*, 1957, *53*, 339–46. (a)

Dement, W. C. and Kleitman, N. Cyclic variations in EEG during sleep and their relation to eye movements, bodily motility and dreaming. *Electroencephalography and Clinical Neurophysiology*, 1957, *9*, 673–90. (b)

Dement, W. and Wolpert, E. A. The relation of eye movements, body motility, and external stimuli to dream content. *Journal of Experimental Psychology*, 1958, *55*, 543–53.

Descartes, R. (1650) in R. Herrnstein and E. G. Boring (eds.), *Source Book in the History of Psychology*. Cambridge, Mass.: Harvard University Press, 1965.

Dewan, E. M. Occipital alpha rhythm, eye position and lens accommodation. *Nature*, 1967, *214*, 975–77.

Dewan, E. M. A demonstration of the effect of eye position and accommodation on the occipital alpha rhythm. *Electroencephalography and Clinical Neurophysiology*, 1968, *24*, 188.

Dewson, J. H., Dement, W. C., and Simmons, F. B. Middle ear muscle activity in cats during sleep. *Experimental Neurology*, 1965, *12*, 1–8.

DiCara, L. V. and Miller, N. E. Changes in heart rate instrumentally learned by curarized rats as avoidance responses. *Journal of Comparative and Physiological Psychology*, 1968, *65*, 8–12. (a)

DiCara, L. V. and Miller, N. E. Instrumental learning of peripheral vasomotor responses by the curarized rat. *Communications in Behavioral Biology*, 1968, *1*, 209–12. (b)

DiCara, L. V. and Miller, N. E. Instrumental learning of systolic blood pressure responses by curarized rats: Dissociation of cardiac and vascular changes. *Psychosomatic Medicine*, 1968, *30*, 489–94. (c)

DiCara, L. V. and Miller, N. E. Instrumental learning of vasomotor responses by rats: Learning to respond differentially in the two ears. *Science*, 1968, *159*, 1485–86. (d)

DiCara, L. V. and Miller, N. E. Heart-rate learning in the noncurarized state, transfer to the curarized state, and subsequent retraining in the noncurarized state. *Physiology and Behavior*, 1969, *4*, 621–24. (a)

DiCara, L. V. and Miller, N. E. Transfer of instrumentally learned heart-rate changes from curarized to noncurarized state: Implications for a mediational hypothesis. *Journal of Comparative and Physiological Psychology*, 1969, *68*, 159–62. (b)

DiCara, L. V. and Stone, E. A. Effect of instrumental heart-rate training on rat cardiac and brain catecholamines. *Psychosomatic Medicine*, 1970, *32*, 359–68.

DiCara, L. V. and Weiss, J. M. Effect of heart-rate learning under curare on subsequent noncurarized avoidance learning. *Journal of Comparative and Physiological Psychology*, 1969, *69*, 368–74.

Dinges, D. F. and Klingaman, R. L. Effects of induced muscle tension upon the visual-evoked potential and motor potential: A replication. *Psychonomic Science*, 1972, *28*, 303–5.

DiVesta, F. J. and Rickards, J. P. Effects of labeling and articulation on the attainment of concrete, abstract, and number concepts. *Journal of Experimental Psychology*, 1971, *88*, 41–49.

Dodge, R. *Die Motorischen Wortvorstellungen*. 1896. (Jacobson, E. The electrophysiology of mental activities. *American Journal of Psychology*, 1932, *44*, 677–94.)

Doehring, D. G., Conditioning of muscle action potential responses resulting from passive hand movement. *Journal of Experimental Psychology* 1957, *54*, 292–96.

Donchin, E. Data analysis techniques in average evoked potential research. In E. Donchin and D. B. Lindsley (eds), *Average evoked potentials*. Washington, D.C.: NASA SP-191, 1969.

Dorman, M. F. Auditory evoked potential correlates of speech sound discrimination. *Perception and Psychophysics*, 1974, *15*, 215–20.

Douglas, W. W. Autocoids. In L. S. Goodman and A. Gillman (eds.), *Pharmacological basis of therapeutics*, New York: Macmillan, 1970.

Duffy, E. *Activation and behavior*. New York: John Wiley, 1962.

Duke, J. D. Lateral eye movement behavior. *Journal of General Psychology*, 1968, *78*, 189–95.

Dunlap, K. *A system of psychology*. New York: Scribner's, 1912.

Dunlap, K. *The elements of scientific psychology.* St. Louis: C. V. Mosby, 1922.

Dunlap, K. The short-circuiting of conscious responses. *Journal of Philosphy,* 1927, *24,* 263–67.

Dunlap, K. In C. Murchison (ed.), *A history of psychology in autobiography, vol. II.* Worcester, Mass.: Clark University Press, 1932. Reissued New York, Russell & Russell, 1961.

Durrell, D. C. *Improvement of basic reading abilities.* New York: World, 1940. Cited by Edfeldt (1960).

Eason, R. G., Aiken, L. R., Jr., White, C. T., and Lichtenstein, M. Activation and behavior. II. Visually evoked cortical potentials in man as indicants of activation level. *Perceptual and Motor Skills,* 1964, *19,* 875–95.

Eccles, J. C. *Brain and conscious experience.* New York: Springer-Verlag, 1966.

Edfeldt, A. W. *Silent speech and silent reading.* Chicago: University of Chicago Press, 1960.

Egger, La parole interieure (1881). In R. Pintner, Inner speech during silent reading. *Psychological Review,* 1913, *20,* 129–53.

Ellingson, R. J. Brain waves and problems of psychology. *Psychological Bulletin,* 1956, *53,* 1–34.

Ellson, D. G. Hallucinations produced by sensory conditioning. *Journal of Experimental Psychology,* 1941, *28,* 1–20. (a)

Ellson, D. G. Experimental extinction of an hallucination produced by sensory conditioning. *Journal of Experimental Psychology,* 1941, *28,* 350–61. (b)

Ellson, D. G., Davis, R. C., Saltzman, I. J., and Burke, C. J. *A report of research on detection of deception.* Contract N6onr-18011, Indiana University, 1952.

Elul, R. Gaussian behavior of the electroencephalogram: Changes during performance of mental task. *Science,* 1969, *164,* 328–31.

Ericksen, C. W., Pollack, M. D., and Montague, W. E. Implicit speech: Mechanism in perceptual encoding? *Journal of Experimental Psychology,* 1970, *84,* 502–7.

Ertl, J. and Schafer, E. W. P. *Erratum*-Cortical activity preceding speech. *Life Sciences,* 1967, *6,* 473–79. (a)

Ertl, J. and Schafer, E. W. P. Cortical Activity preceding speech. *Life Sciences,* 1967, *6,* 473–79. (b)

Estable, C. Curare and Synapse. In D. Bovet, F. Bovet-Nitti, and G. B. Marini-Bettolo (eds.), *Curare and curare-like agents.* Amsterdam: Elsevier, 1959.

Estes, W. K., Phonemic coding and rehearsal in short-term memory for letter strings. *Journal of Verbal Learning and Verbal Behavior,* 1973, *12,* 360–72.

Evans, F. J., Gustafson, L. A., O'Connell, D. N., Orne, M. T., and Shor, R. E. Verbally induced behavioral responses during sleep. *Journal of Nervous and Mental Disease,* 1970, *150,* 171–87.

Evans, F. J., Reich, L. H., and Orne, M. T. Optokinetic nystagmus, eye movements and hypnotically induced hallucinations. *Journal of Nervous and Mental Disease,* 1972, *154,* 419–31.

Evarts, E. V. Pyramidal tract activity associated with a conditioned hand movement in the monkey. *Journal of Neurophysiology,* 1966, *29,* 1011–27.

Evarts, E. V. Motor cortex reflexes associated with learned movement. *Science,* 1973, *179,* 501–3.

Ewert, P. H. Eye-movements during reading and recall. *Journal of General Psychology,* 1933, *8,* 65–84.

Faaborg-Andersen, K. and Edfeldt, A. W. Electromyography of intrinsic and extrinsic laryngeal muscles during silent speech: Correlation with reading activity. *Acta oto-laryngologica,* 1958, *49,* 478–82.

Fair, P. L., Schwartz, G. E., Friedman, M. J., Greenberg, P. S., Klerman, G. L., and Gardner, E. A. Facial expression and emotion: An electromyographic study. Paper presented at the 45th annual meeting of Eastern Psychological Association, Philadelphia, April, 1974.

Fedio, P. and Buchsbaum, M. Unilateral temporal lobectomy and changes in evoked responses during recognition of verbal and nonverbal material in the left and right visual fields. *Neuropsychologia*, 1971, *9*, 261–71.

Feldman, R. M., and Goldstein, R. Averaged evoked responses to synthetic syntax sentences (3S). *Journal of Speech and Hearing Research*, 1967, *10*, 689–96.

Fenwick, P. B. C. and Walker, S. The effect of eye position on the alpha rhythm. In C. R. Evans and T. B. Mulholland (eds.), *Attention in neurophysiology.* New York: Appleton-Century-Crofts, 1969.

Ferrier, D. *The functions of the brain.* London: Smith Elder, 1876.

Ferrier, D. *The functions of the brain,* 2nd ed. New York: Putnam, 1886.

Fessard, A. E. Mechanisms of nervous integration and conscious experience. In Delafresnaye, J. F. (ed.), *Brain mechanisms and consciousness.* Springfield, Ill.: Charles C Thomas, 1954.

Festinger, L. and Easton A. M. Inferences about the efferent system based on a perceptual illusion produced by eye movements. *Psychological Review,* 1974, *81*, 44–58.

Festinger, L. and Maccoby, N. On resistance to persuasive communications. *Journal of Abnormal and Social Psychology,* 1964, *68*, 359–66.

Fields, C. Instrumental conditioning of the rat cardiac control system. *Proceedings of the National Academy of Sciences,* 1970, *65*, 293–99.

Fienberg, S. E. Stochastic models for single neuron firing trains: A survey. *Biometrics,* 1974, *30*, 399–427.

Filbey, R. A. and Gazzaniga, M. S. Splitting the normal brain with reaction time. *Psychonomic Science,* 1969, *17*, 335–36.

Fink, J. B. Conditioning of muscle action potential increments accompanying an instructed movement. *Journal of Experimental Psychology.* 1954, *47*, 61–68.

Fink, J. B. and Davis, R. C. Generalization of a muscle action potential response to tonal duration. *Journal of Experimental Psychology,* 1951, *42*, 403–8.

Fitts, P. M. and Posner, M. I. *Human performance.* Monterey, Calif.: Brooks/Cole, 1967.

Fjeld, S. P. Motor response and muscle action potential in the measurement of sensory threshold. *Psychophysiology,* 1965, *1*, 277–81.

Ford, A. Bioelectric potentials and mental effort: I. Cardiac effects. *Journal of Comparative and Physiological Psychology,* 1953, *46*, 347–51.

Ford, A. Bioelectrical potentials and mental effort: II. Frontal lobe effects. *Journal of Comparative and Physiological Psychology,* 1954, *47*, 28–30.

Ford, A. and White, C. T. The effectiveness of the eye as a servo-control mechanism (Research and Development Report 934). San Diego, Calif.: U.S. Navy Electronics Laboratory, 1959.

Forrer, G. R. Effect of oral activity on hallucinations. *American Journal of Psychiatry,* 1960, *2*, 110–13. (a)

Forrer, G. R. Benign auditory and visual hallucinations. *American Journal of Psychiatry,* 1960, *3*, 119–22. (b)

Foss, D. J. and Swinney, D. A. On the psychological reality of the phoneme: perception, identification, and consciousness. *Journal of Verbal Learning and Verbal Behavior,* 1973, *12*, 246–57.

Foulke, E. and Sticht, T. G. Review of research on the intelligibility and comprehension of accelerated speech. *Psychological Bulletin,* 1969, *72*, 50–62.

Foulkes, W. D. Dream reports from different stages of sleep. *Journal of Abnormal and Social Psychology*, 1962, *65*, 14–25.

Freeman, G. L. Changes in tonus during completed and interrupted mental work. *Journal of General Psychology*, 1930, *4*, 309–34.

Freeman, G. L. Mental activity and the muscular processes. *Psychological Review*, 1931, *38*, 428–449. (a)

Freeman, G. L. The spread of neuro-muscular activity during mental work. *Journal of General Psychology*, 1931, *5*, 479–494. (b)

Freeman, G. L. The facilitative and inhibitory effects of muscular tension upon performance. *American Journal of Psychology*, 1933, *45*, 17–52.

Fremont-Smith, F. Discussion section. In H. A. Abramson (ed.), *Problems of Consciousness*. New York: Corlies, Macey, 1951.

Fruhling, M., Basmajian, J. V., and Simard, T. G. A note on the conscious controls of motor units by children under six. *Journal of Motor Behavior*, 1969, *1*, 65–68.

Fryer, D. H. Articulation in automatic mental work. *American Journal of Psychology*, 1941, *54*, 504–17.

Fucci, D. J. Oral vibrotactile sensation: An evaluation of normal and defective speakers. *Journal of Speech and Hearing Research*, 1972, *15*, 179–84.

Fujimura, O. Acoustics of speech. In J. H. Gilbert (ed.), *Speech and cortical functioning*. New York: Academic Press, 1972.

Galin, D., and Ornstein, R. Lateral specialization of cognitive mode: An EEG study. *Psychophysiology*, 1972, *9*, 412–18.

Galindo, A. Curare and pancuronium compared: Effects on previously undepressed mammalian myoneural junctions. *Science*, 1972, *178*, 753–55.

Gall, F. J. and Spurzheim, G. *Recherches sur le systeme nerveux en général, et sur celui du cerveau en particulier*. Paris: Institute de France, 1809.

Galperin, P. Y. Stages in the development of mental acts. In M. Cole and I. Maltzman (eds.), *A handbook of contemporary Soviet psychology*. New York: Basic Books, 1969.

Galzigna, L., Manani, G., Mammano, S., Gasparetto, A., and Deana, R. Experimental study on the neuromuscular blocking action of procaine amide. *Agressologie*, 1972, *13*, 107–16.

Gammon, S. A., Smith, P., Daniloff, R., and Kim, G. Articulation and stress/ juncture production under oral anesthetization and masking. *Journal of Speech and Hearing Research*, 1971, *14*, 271–82.

Gardner, R., Grossman, W. I., Roffwarg, H. P., and Weiner, H. Does sleep behavior appear in the dream? *Psychosomatic Medicine*, 1973, *35*, 450–51.

Garrity, L. I. An electromyographical study of subvocal speech and recall in preschool children. *Developmental Psychology*, 1975, *11*, 274–81. (a)

Garrity, L. I. Measurement of subvocal speech: Correlations between two muscle leads and between two recording methods. *Perceptual and Motor Skills*, 1975, *40*, 327–30. (b)

Gates, A. J. *The improvement of reading*. New York: Macmillan, 1947.

Gatev, V. and Ivanov, I. Excitation-contraction latency in human muscles. *Agressologie*, 1972, *13*, 7–12.

Geldard, F. A. Some neglected possibilities of communication. *Science*, 1960, *131*, 1583–88.

Geldard, F. A. cutaneous coding of optical signals: The optohapt. *Perception and Psychophysics*, 1966, *1*, 377–81.

Gellhorn, E. and Kiely, W. F. Mystical states of consciousness: Neurophysical and clinical aspects. *Journal of Nervous and Mental Disease*, 1972, *154*, 399–405.

Gentz, R. Apparatus for recording of bruxism during sleep. *Swedish Dental Journal*, 1972, *65*, 327–42.

Germana, J. Psychophysiological correlates of conditioned response formation. *Psychological Bulletin*, 1968, *70*, 105–14.

Giannitrapani, D. Electroencephalographic differences between resting and mental multiplication. *Perceptual and Motor Skills*, 1966, *22*, 399–405.

Gibson, J. J. *The senses considered as perceptual systems.* Boston: Houghton-Mifflin, 1966.

Glanzer, M., Chapman, R. M., Clark, W. H., and Bragdon, H. R. Changes in two EEG rhythms during mental activity. *Journal of Experimental Psychology*, 1964, *68*, 273–83.

Glaros, A. G. and Rao, S. M. Bruxism: A critical review. *Psychological Bulletin*, 1977, *84*, 767–81.

Glass, A. and Kwiatkowski, A. W. Normal power spectral density changes in the EEG during mental arithmetic and eye opening. *Electroencephalography and Clinical Neurophysiology* 1968, *25*, 507.

Glass, A. and Kwiatkowkski, A. W. Power spectral density changes in the EEG during mental arithmetic and eye-opening. *Psychologische Forschung*, 1970, *33*, 85–99.

Goff, W. R., Matsumiya, Y., Allison, T., and Goff, G. D. Cross-modality comparisons of average evoked potentials. In E. Donchin and D. B. Lindsley (eds.), *Average evoked potentials.* Washington, D.C.: NASA SP-191, 1969.

Goldstein, Moise, H., Jr. The auditory periphery. In V. B. Mouncastle (ed.), *Medical physiology*, vol. II. Saint Louis: C. V. Mosby, 1968.

Goldwater, B. C. Psychological significance of pupillary movements. *Psychological Bulletin*, 1972, *77*, 340–55.

Golla, F. L. The objective study of neurosis. *Lancet*, 1921, *2*, 115–22.

Golla, F. L. and Antonovitch, S. The relation of musclar tonus and the patellar reflex to mental work. *Journal of Mental Science*, 1929, *75*, 234–41.

Golla, F., Hutton, E. L., and Walter, W. G. The objective study of mental imagery. I. Physiological concomitants. *Journal of Mental Science*, 1943, *89*, 216–22.

Goodenough, D. R., Shaprio, A., Holden, M., and Steinschriber, L. A comparison of "dreamers" and "nondreamers": Eye movements, electroencephalograms, and the recall of dreams. *Journal of Abnormal and Social Psychology*, 1959, *59*, 295–302.

Goodwin, G. M., McCloskey, D. I., and Matthews, P. B. C. Proprioceptive illusions induced by muscle vibration: Contribution by muscle spindles to perception? *Science*, 1972, *175*, 1382–84.

Goss, A. E. Early behaviorism and verbal mediating responses. *American Psychologist*, 1961, *16*, 285–98.

Goto, H. Studies on "inner speech." I. Reading and speech movement. *Folia Psychiatrica et Neurologica Japonica*, 1968, *22*, 65–77. (a)

Goto, H. Studies on "inner speech." II. Hearing and speech movement. *Folia Psychiatrica et Neurologica Japonica*, 1968, *22*, 79–88. (b)

Goto, H. Auditory perception by normal Japanese adults of the sounds "L" and "R." *Neurophychologia*, 1971, *9*, 317–23.

Gould, L. N. Auditory hallucinations and subvocal speech. *Journal of Nervous and Mental Disease*, 1949, *109*, 418–27.

Gould, L. N. Verbal hallucinations as automatic speech. *American Journal of Psychiatry*, 1950, *107*, 110–19.

Gould, J. D. and Carn, R. Visual search, complex backgrounds, mental counters, and eye movements. *Perception and Psychophysics*, 1973, *14*, 125–32.

Grabow, J. D. and Elliott, F. W. The electrophysiologic assessment of hemispheric asymmetries during speech. *Journal of Speech and Hearing Research,* 1974, *17,* 64-72.

Graham, K. R. Optokinetic nystagmus as a criterion of visual imagery. *Journal of Nervous and Mental Disease,* 1970, *151,* 411–14. (a)

Graham, K. R. Eye movements as a criterion of visual hypnotic hallucinations. Paper presented at the meeting of the American Psychological Association, Miami Beach, September 1970. (b)

Granit, R. *Receptors and sensory perception.* New Haven: Yale University Press, 1955.

Granit, R. *The Basis of motor control.* New York: Academic Press, 1970.

Granit, R. *Mechanisms regulating the discharge of motoneurons.* Springfield, Ill.: Charles C Thomas, 1972.

Greenberg, S. *Elicited optokinetic nystagmus during problem-solving and day-dreaming.* Unpublished doctoral dissertation. City University of New York, 1970.

Greenberg, S. In J. L. Singer, S. Greenberg, and J. S. Antrobus. Looking with the mind's eye: Experimental studies of ocular motility during daydreaming and mental arithmetic. *Transactions of the New York Academy of Sciences,* 1971, *33,* 694–709.

Greenwald, A. G. Sensory feedback mechanisms in performance control with special reference to the ideo-motor mechanism. *Psychological Review.* 1970, *77,* 73–99.

Griffith, D. and Johnston, W. A. An information-processing analysis of visual imagery. *Journal of Experimental Psychology,* 1973, *100,* 141–46.

Grings, W. W. The role of consciousness and cognition in autonomic behavior change. In F. J. McGuigan and R. A. Schoonover (eds.), *The psychophysiology of thinking.* New York: Academic Press, 1973. (a)

Grings, W. W. Cognitive factors in electrodermal conditioning. *Psychological Bulletin,* 1973, *79,* 200–210. (b)

Grob D. Neuromuscular blocking drugs. In W. S. Root and F. G. Hoffman (eds.), *Physiological pharmacology, vol. 3.* New York: Academic Press, 1967.

Gross, J., Byrne, J., and Fisher, C. Eye movements during emergent Stage 1 EEG in subjects with lifelong blindness. *Journal of Nervous and Mental Disease,* 1965, *141,* 365–70.

Guilford, J. P. *The nature of human intelligence.* New York: McGraw-Hill, 1967.

Guilford, J. P. Intelligence has three facets. *Science,* 1968, *160,* 615–20.

Gullickson, G. R. and Darrow, C. W. The rapidity of EEG time changes during mental function. *Electroencephalography and Clinical Neurophysiology,* 1968, *24,* 281.

Guthrie, E. R. *The psychology of learning,* rev. ed. New York: Harper & Row, 1952.

Hahn, W. W. and Slaughter, J. Heart rate responses in curarized rats. *Psychophysiology,* 1970, *7,* 429–35.

Haider, M. Vigilance, attention, expectation and cortical evoked potentials. *Acta Psychologica,* 1967, *27,* 245–52.

Haider, M., Spong, P., and Lindsley, D. B. Attention, vigilance, and cortical evoked potentials in humans. *Science,* 1964, *145,* 180–82.

Hall, D. C. Eye movements in scanning iconic imagery. *Journal of Experimental Psychology,* 1974, *103,* 825–30.

Halle, M. and Stevens, K. N. *Analysis by synthesis. (Proceedings of the seminar on speech compression and processing,* vol. 2, Paper D-7, Technical Report 59-198). Cambridge, Mass: Air Force Cambridge Research Center, 1959.

Hammond, P. H. Involuntary activity in biceps following the sudden application of velocity to the abducted forearm. *Journal of Physiology,* 1955, *127,* 23–25.

Hansen, F. C. C. and Lehmann, A. Ueber unwillkürliches Flüstern. *Philos. Studien*, 1895, *11*, 471–530.

Hardyck, C. The elimination of sub-vocal speech activity during reading by continuous feedback. *Psychophysiology*, 1969, *5*, 564.

Hardyck, C. D., and Petrinovich, L. F. Treatment of subvocal speech during reading. *Journal of Reading*, 1969, *12*, 361–68, 419–22.

Hardyck, C. D. and Petrinovich, L. F. Subvocal speech and comprehension level as a function of the difficulty level of reading material. *Journal of Verbal Learning and Verbal Behavior*, 1970, *9*, 647–52.

Hardyck, C. D., Petrinovich, L. F., and Ellsworth, D. W. Feedback of speech muscle activity during silent reading: Rapid extinction. *Science*, 1966, *154*, 1467–68.

Harris, K. S. *Vowell stress and articulatory reorganization* (Status Report on Speech Research, pp. 167–78). New Haven: Haskins Laboratories, October-December 1971.

Harris, K. S. Psychological aspects of articulatory behavior. In T. A. Sebeok (ed.), *Current trends in linguistics, vol. 12.* The Hague: Mouton, 1974.

Harrison, V. F., and Mortensen, O. A. Identification and voluntary control of single motor unit activity in the tibialis anterior muscle. *Anatomical Record*, 1962, *144*, 109–16.

Hartman, G. W. II. Changes in visual acuity through simultaneous stimulation of other sense organs. *Journal of Experimental Psychology*, 1933, *16*, 393–407.

Hasselt, P. V. A short latency visual evoked potential recorded from the human mastoid process and auricle. *Electroencephalography and Clinical Neurophysiology*, 1972, *33*, 517–19.

Hassler, R. Thalamic regulation of muscle tone and the speech of movements. In D. P. Purpura and M. D. Yahy (eds.), *The thalamus.* New York: Columbia University Press, 1966.

Hatano, G., Miyake, Y., and Binks, M. G. Performance of expert abacus operators. *Cognition*, 1977, *5*, 47–55.

Hathaway, S. R. An action potential study of neuromuscular relations. *Journal of Experimental Psycology*, 1935, *18*, 285–98.

Head, H. *Aphasia and kindred disorders of speech, vol. 1.* New York: Macmillan, 1926.

Hebb, D. O. Studies of the organization of behavior: II. Changes in the field orientation of the rat after cortical destruction. *Journal of Comparative Psychology*, 1938, *26*, 427–44.

Hebb, D. O. *The organization of behavior.* New York: John Wiley, 1949.

Hebb, D. O. The role of neurological ideas in psychology. *Journal of Personality*, 1951, *20*, 39–55.

Hebb, D. O. The problem of consciousness and introspection. In J. F. Delafresnaye (ed.), *Brain mechanisms and consciousness.* Oxford: Blackwell Scientific Publications, Ltd., 1954.

Hebb, D. O. *Psychology.* New York: Saunders, 1958.

Hebb, D. O. The semiautonomous process: Its nature and nurture. *American Psychologist*, 1963, *18*, 16–27.

Hebb, D. O. *A textbook of psychology.* Philadelphia: W. B. Saunders, 1966.

Hebb, D. O. Concerning imagery. *Psychological Review*, 1968, *75*, 466–77.

Hebb, D. O. *Textbook of psychology*, 3rd ed. Philadelphia: W. B. Saunders 1972.

Hefferline, R. F. and Keenan, B. Amplitude-induction gradient of a small human operant in an escape-avoidance situation. *Journal of the Experimental Analysis of Behavior*, 1961, *4*, 41–43.

Hefferline, R. F. and Keenan, B. Amplitude-induction gradient of a small-scale (covert) operant. *Journal of the Experimental Analysis of Behavior*, 1963, *6*, 307–15.

Hefferline, R. F., Keenan, B., and Harford, R. A. Escape and avoidance conditioning in human subjects without their observation of the reponse. *Science*, 1956, *130*, 1338–39.

Hefferline, R. F., Keenan, B., Harford, R. A., and Birch, J. Electronics in psychology. *Columbia Engineering Quarterly*, 1960, *13*, 10–15.

Hefferline, R. F. and Perera, T. B. Proprioceptive discrimination of a covert operant without its observation by the subject. *Science*, 1963, *139*, 834–35.

Heinemann, L. G. and Emrich, H. Alpha activity during inhibitory brain processes. *Psychophysiology*, 1971, *7*, 442–50.

Henderson, L. Spatial and verbal codes and the capacity of STM. *Quarterly Journal of Experimental Psychology*, 1972, *24*, 485–96.

Henmon, V. A. C. Relation between mode of presentation and retention. *Psychological Review*, 1912, *19*, 79–96.

Henneman, R. H. An attempt to condition the GSR to sub-vocal stimuli. *Psychological Bulletin*, 1941, *38*, 571.

Hernandez-Peón, R., Scherrer, H., and Jouvet, M. Modification of electric activity in cochlear nucleus during "attention" in unanaesthetized cats. *Science*, 1956, *123*, 331–32.

Herrick C. J. *Neurological foundations of animal behavior*. New York: Henry Holt, 1924.

Herrnstein, R. S. and Boring, E. G. (eds.). *Source book in the history of psychology*. Cambridge, Mass.: Harvard University Press, 1965.

Hilden, A. H. An action current study of the conditioned hand withdrawal. *Psychological Monographs*, 1937, *49*, 173–204.

Hillman, E. C., Jr. The effect of tension control on blood pressure. In F. J. McGuigan (ed.), *Tension control: Proceedings of the second meeting of the American association for the advancement of tension control*. Chicago: University Publications, 1976.

Hillyard, S. A. and Galambos, R. Effects of stimulus and response contingencies on a surface negative slow potential shift in man. *Electroencephalography and Clinical Neurophysiology*, 1967, *22*, 297–304.

Hillyard, S. A., Hink, R. F., Schwent, V. L., and Picton, T. W. Electrical signs of selective attention in the human brain. *Science*, 1973, *182*, 177–80.

Hintzman, D. L. Classification and aural coding in short-term memory. *Psychonomic Science*, 1965, *3*, 161–62.

Hintzman, D. L. Articulatory coding in short-term memory. *Journal of Verbal Learning and Verbal Behavior*. 1967, *6*, 312–16.

Hirano, M. and Ohala, J. Use of hooked-wire electrodes for electromyography of the intrinsic laryngeal muscles. *Journal of Speech and Hearing Research*, 1969, *12*, 362–73.

Hirose, H. and Gay, T. *The activity of the intrinsic laryngeal muscles in voicing control: An electromyographic study* (Status Report on Speech Research, 115–42). New Haven: Haskins Laboratories, October–December 1971.

Hirsh, S. K. Vertex potentials associated with an auditory discrimination. *Psychonomic Science*, 1971, *22*, 173–75.

Hodes, R. Electrocortical synchronization resulting from reduced proprioceptive drive caused by neuromuscular blocking agents. *Electroencephalography and Clinical Neurophysiology*, 1962, *14*, 220–32.

Hoekman. T. B., Dretchen, K. L., and Standaert, F. G. Miniature end plate potentials recorded from mammalian myoneural junctions in vivo. *Science,* 1974, *183,* 213–15.

Holland, M. K. and Tarlow, G. Blinking and mental load. *Psychological Reports,* 1972, *31,* 119–28.

Holt, E. B. Materialism and the criterion of the psychic. *Psychological Review,* 1937, *44,* 33–53.

Homme, L. E. Perspectives in psychology: XXIV. Control of coverants, the operants of the mind. *Psychological Record,* 1965, *15,* 501–11.

Horridge, G. A. The electrophysiological approach to learning in isolatable ganglia. *Animal Behavior,* 1965, Suppl. 1, 163–82.

Hothersall, D. and Brener, J. Operant conditioning of changes in heart rate in curarized rats. *Journal of Comparative and Physiological Psychology,* 1969, *68,* 338–42.

Howard, J. L., Galosy, R. A., Gaebelein, C. J., and Obrist, P. A. Some problems in the use of neuromuscular blockage. In P. A. Obrist, A. H. Black, J. Brener, and L. V. DiCara (eds.), *Cardiovascular psychophysiology: Current issues in response mechanisms, biofeedback and methodology.* Chicago: Adline-Atherton, 1974.

Hudgins, C. V. Conditioning and voluntary control of the pupillary light reflex. *Journal of General Psychology,* 1933, *8,* 3–51.

Hull, C. L. Knowledge and purpose as habit mechanisms. *Psychological Review,* 1930, *37,* 511–25.

Hull, C. L. Goal attraction and directing ideas conceived as habit phenomena. *Psychological Review,* 1931, *38,* 487–506.

Hull, C. L. *Principles of behavior.* New York: Appleton-Century-Crofts, 1943.

Hull, C. L. *A behavior system.* New Haven: Yale University Press, 1952.

Hull, C. L. Psychology and the scientist: IV. Passages from the idea books of Clark L. Hull. *Perceptual and Motor Skills,* 1962, *15,* 807–82.

Humphrey, G. *Thinking.* New York: John Wiley, 1951.

Humphrey, G. and Coxon, R. V. *The chemistry of thinking.* Springfield, Ill.: Charles C Thomas, 1963.

Hunter, W. S. The problem of consciousness. *Psychological Review,* 1924, *31,* 1–37. (a)

Hunter, W. S. The symbolic process. *Psychological Review,* 1924, *31,* 478–97. (b)

Hunter, W. S. Muscle potentials and conditioning in the rat. *Journal of Experimental Psychology,* 1937, *21,* 611–24.

Hunter, W. S. and Hudgins, C. V. Voluntary activity from the standpoint of behaviorism. *Journal of General Psychology,* 1934, *10,* 198–204.

Inouye, T. and Shimizu, A. The electromyographic study of verbal hallucination. *Journal of Nervous and Mental Disease,* 1970, *151,* 415–22.

Inouye, T. and Shimizu, A. Visual evoked response and reaction time during verbal hallucination. *Journal of Nervous and Mental Disease,* 1972, *155,* 419–26.

Ishihara, T., and Yoshii, N. Multivariate analytic study of EEG and mental activity in juvenile delinquents. *Electroencephalography and Clinical Neurophysiology,* 1972, *33,* 71–80.

Isley, C. L., Jr., and Basmajian, J. V. Electromyography of the human cheeks and lips. *The Anatomical Record,* 1973, *176,* 143–47.

Ivanov-Smolensky, A. G. *Works of the institute of higher nervous activity: Pathophysiological series, vol. 2.* Moscow: Academy of Science, 1956.

Jackson, J. H. *Selected writings of John Hughlings.* London: Hodder & Stoughton, 1931-1932.

Jacobs, L. D., Feldman, M., and Bender, M. B. The pattern of human eye movements during sleep. *Transactions of the American Neurological Association,* 1970, *95,* 114–19. (a)

Jacobs, L. D., Feldman, M., and Bender, M. B. Are the position and movements of the eyes during rapid eye movement sleep (REM) related to dream content? *Federal Proceedings,* 1970, *29,* 453. (b)

Jacobs, L., Feldman, M., and Bender, M. B. Are the eye movements of dreaming sleep related to the visual images of the dreams? *Psychophysiology,* 1972, *9,* 393–401.

Jacobson, A., Kales, A., Lehmann, D., and Hoedemaker, F. S. Muscle tonus in human subjects during sleep and dreaming. *Experimental Neurology,* 1964, *10,* 418–24.

Jacobson, E. Consciousness under anaesthetics. *American Journal of Psychology,* 1911, *22,* 333–45.

Jacobson, E. Voluntary relaxation of the esophagus. *American Journal of Physiology,* 1925, *72,* 387–94.

Jacobson, E. Action currents from muscular contractions during conscious processes. *Science,* 1927, *66,* 403.

Jacobson, E. *Progressive relaxation.* Chicago: University of Chicago Press, 1929.

Jacobson, E. Electrical measurements of neuromuscular states during mental activities. I. Imagination of movement involving skeletal muscle. *American Journal of Physiology,* 1930, *91,* 567–608. (a)

Jacobson, E. Electrical measurements of neuromuscular states during mental activities. II. Imagination and recollection of various muscular acts. *American Journal of Physiology,* 1930, *94,* 22–34. (b)

Jacobson, E. Electrical measurements of neuromuscular states during mental activities. III. Visual imagination and recollection. *American Journal of Physiology,* 1930, *95,* 694–702. (c)

Jacobson, E. Electrical measurements of neuromuscular states during mental activities. IV. Evidence of contraction of specific muscles during imagination. *American Journal of Physiology,* 1930, *95,* 703–12. (d)

Jacobson, E. Electrical measurements of neuromuscular states during mental activities. V. Variation of specific muscles contracting during imagination. *American Journal of Physiology,* 1931, *96,* 115–21. (a)

Jacobson, E. Electrical measurements of neuromuscular states during mental activities. VI. A note on mental activities concerning an amputated limb. *American Journal of Physiology,* 1931, *96,* 122–25. (b)

Jacobson, E. Electrical measurements of neuromuscular states during mental activities. VII. Imagination, recollection and abstract thinking involving the speech musculature. *American Journal of Physiology,* 1931, *97,* 200–209. (c)

Jacobson, E. Electrophysiology of mental activities. *American Journal of Psychology,* 1932, *44,* 677–94.

Jacobson, E. *Progressive relaxation,* rev. ed. Chicago: University of Chicago Press, 1938. (a)

Jacobson, E. *You can sleep well.* New York: McGraw-Hill, 1938. (b)

Jacobson, E. Variations of blood pressure with skeletal muscle tension and relaxation. *Annals of Internal Medicine,* 1939, *12,* 1194–1212.

Jacobson, E. *You must relax, 4th ed..* New York: McGraw-Hill, 1957.

Jacobson, E. *Self-operations control.* Philadelphia: Lippincott, 1964.

Jacobson, E. *Biology of emotions.* Springfield, Ill: Charles C Thomas, 1967.

Jacobson, E. Electrophysiology of mental activities and introduction to the psychological process of thinking. In F. J. McGuigan and R. A. Schoonover (eds.), *The psychophysiology of thinking.* New York: Academic Press, 1973.

Jacobson, E. and Kraft, F. L. Contraction potentials (right quadriceps femoris) in man during reading. *American Journal of Physiology,* 1942, *137,* 1–5.

Jakobson, R., Fant, C. G. M., and Halle, M. *Preliminaries to speech analysis. Acoustical Lab. Report 13.* Cambridge, Mass.: MIT Press, 1952.

Jakobson, R., Fant, C. G. M., and Halle, M. *Preliminaries to speech analysis.* Cambridge, Mass.: MIT Press, 1963.

Jakobson, R. C. and Halle, M. *Fundamentals of language.* The Hague, Netherlands: Mouton, 1956.

Jakobson, R. and Halle, M. *Fundamentals of language,* 2nd ed. The Hague, Netherlands: Mouton, 1971.

James, W. *The principles of psychology.* New York: Holt, 1890.

Jenness, D. Auditory evoked-response differentiation with discrimination learning in humans. *Journal of Comparative and Physiological Psychology,* 1972, *80,* 75–90.

Jewett, D. L., Romano, M. N., and Williston, J. S. Human auditory evoked potentials: Possible brain stem components detected on the scalp. *Science,* 1970, *167,* 1517–18.

John, E. R., Herrington, R. N., and Sutton, S. Effects of visual form on the evoked response. *Science,* 1967, *155,* 1439–42.

Johnson, D. M. *The psychology of thought and judgment.* New York: Harper & Row 1955.

Johnson, L. C. Nonspecific galvanic skin response and respiration. *Psychology Reports,* 1961, *9,* 516.

Johnson, L. C., Ulett, G. A., Sines, J. O., and Stern, J. A. Cortical activity and cognitive functioning. *Electroencephalography and Clinical Neurophysiology.* 1960, *12,* 861–74.

Jones, B. Is there any proprioceptive feedback? Comments on Schmidt (1971). *Psychological Bulletin,* 1973, *79,* 386–88.

Jones, J. G. Motor learning without demonstration of physical practice under two conditions of mental practice. *Research Quarterly,* 1965, *36,* 270–76.

Judd, C. H. Reduction of articulation. *American Journal of Psychology,* 1927, *39,* 313–22.

Kadochkin, L. N. The role of speech kinesthesis in the formation of certain othographic habits. *Voprosy Psikhologii,* 1955, *3.* (Cole, M. and Maltzman, I. *A handbook of contemporary Soviet psychology.* New York: Basic Books, 1969.)

Kamiya, J. Conscious control of brain waves. *Psychology Today,* 1968, *1,* 56–60.

Kantor, J. R. An objective interpretation of meaning. *American Journal of Psychology,* 1921, *32,* 231.

Kaplan, I. T. and Schoenfeld, W. N. Oculomotor patterns during the solution of visually displayed anagrams. *Journal of Experimental Psychology,* 1966, *72,* 447–51.

Kappers, C. U. A. On the structural laws in the nervous system. The principles of neuro-biotaxis. *Brain,* 1921, *44,* 125.

Karacan, I., Hursch, C. J., Williams, R. L., and Thornby, J. I. Some characteristics of nocturnal penile tumescence in young adults. *Archives of General Psychiatry,* 1972, *26,* 351–56.

Karlin, L. Cognition, preparation, and sensory-evoked potentials. *Psychological Bulletin,* 1970, *73,* 122–36.

Keeler, L. A method for detecting deception. *American Journal of Police Science,* 1930, *1,* 38–51.

Keen, S. My new carnality. *Psychology Today.* 1970. *4,* 59–61.

Kekcheev, K. K., Kravkov, S. V., and Shvarts, L. A. On factors reducing the activity of the visual and auditory organs. In I. D. London (ed.), Research on sensory interaction in the Soviet Union. *Psychological Bulletin*, 1954, *51*, 531–68.

Keller, F. and Schoenfeld, W. N. *Principles of Psychology*. New York: Appleton-Century-Crofts, 1950.

Kendler, H. H. Verbal factors in problem solving behavior. *Transactions of the New York Academy of Sciences, Ser. II*, 1954, *16*, 348–53.

Kendler, H. H. and Kendler, T. S. Reversal-shift behavior: Some basic issues. *Psychological Bulletin*, 1969, *72*, 229–32.

Kendler, T. S. An ontogeny of mediational deficiency. *Child Development*, 1972, *43*, 1–17.

Kennedy, J. L., Gottsdanker, R. M., Armington, J. C., and Gray, F. E. A new electroencephalogram associated with thinking. *Science*, 1948, *108*, 527–29.

Kesner, R., A neural system analysis of memory storage and retrieval. *Psychological Bulletin*, 1973, *80*, 177–203.

Keul, J., Doll, E., and Keppler, D. *Energy metabolism of human muscle*. Baltimore: University Park Press, 1972.

Kiang, N. *Discharge patterns of single fibers in the cat's auditory nerve*. Cambridge, Mass: MIT Press, 1966.

Kimble, G. A. and Perlmuter, L. C. The problem of volition. *Psychological Review*, 1970, *77*, 361–84.

Kimmel, H. D. and Davidov, W. Classical GSR conditioning with concomitant EMG measurement. *Journal of Experimental Psychology*, 1967, *74*, 67–74.

Kinsbourne, M. Eye and head turning indicates cerebral lateralization. *Science*, 1972, *176*, 539–41.

Kirman, J. H. Tactile communication of speech: A review and an analysis. *Psychological Bulletin*, 1973, *80*, 54–74.

Kleitman, N. The sleep-wakefulness cycle. In H. A. Abramson (ed.), *Problems of consciousness*. New York: Corlies, Macey, 1951.

Kleitman, N. Patterns of dreaming. *Scientific American*, 1960, *203*, 82–103.

Knott, J. R. Brain potentials during silent and oral reading. *Journal of General Psychology*, 1938, *18*, 57–62.

Knott, J. R. Some effects of "mental set" on the electrophysiological processes of the human cerebral cortex. *Journal of Experimental Psychology*, 1939, *24*, 384–405.

Kocel, K., Galin, D. Ornstein, R., and Merrin, E. L. Lateral eye movement and cognitive mode. *Psychonomic Science*, 1972, *27*, 223–24.

Kodman, F., Jr. Validity of GSR conditioning. *Psychological Reports*, 1967, *21*, 813–18.

Koelle, G. B. Neuromuscular blocking agents. In L. S. Goodman and A. Gillman (eds.), *Pharmacological basis of therapeutics*. New York: Macmillan, 1960.

Kolta, P. Strong and permanent interaction between peripheral nerve and a constant inhomogeneous magnetic field. *Acta Physiologica Academiae Scientiarum Hungaricae*, 1973, *43*, 89–94.

Koltsova, M. M. *On formation of the highest nervous activity of the child*. Moscow: MEDGIZ, 1958.

Kornilov, K. N., 1921. In M. G. Yaroshevsky. *Istoriya psichologii*. Moscow: Mysl'. 1966.

Kotliarevsky, L. I. Cardio-vascular conditioned reflexes to direct and to verbal stimuli. *Fiziologicheskii Zhurnal SSSR*, 1936, *20*, 228–42. (*Psychological Abstracts*, 1939, *13*, 4046.)

Koukkou, M. and Lehmann, D. EEG and memory storage in sleep experiments with humans. *Electroencephalography and Clinical Neurophysiology*, 1968, *25*, 455–62.

Koulack, D. Rapid eye movements and visual imagery during sleep. *Psychological Bulletin*, 1972, *78*, 155–58.

Kugelmass, S. and Lieblich, I. Effects of realistic stress and procedural interference in experimental lie detection. *Journal of Applied Psychology*, 1966, *50*, 211–16.

Kugelmass, S. and Lieblich, I. Relation between ethnic origin and GSR reactivity in psychophysiological detection. *Journal of Applied Psychology*, 1968, *52*, 158–62.

Kugelmass, S., Lieblich, I., and Bergman, Z. The role of "lying" in psychophysiological detection. *Psychophysiology*, 1967, *3*, 312–15.

Külpe, O. *Outlines in Psychology* (1895). In E. Jacobson, *Progressive Relaxation*, rev. ed. Chicago: University of Chicago Press, 1938.

Lacey, J. I. Individual differences in somatic response patterns. *Journal of Comparative and Physiological Psychology*, 1950, *43*, 338–50.

Lacey, B. C., and Lacey, J. I. Studies of heart rate and other bodily processes in sensorimotor behavior. In P. A. Obrist, A. H. Black, J. Brener, and L. V. DiCara (eds.), *Cardiovascular psychophysiology: Current issues in response mechanisms, biofeedback, and methodology*. Chicago: Aldine-Atherton, 1974.

Lachman, J., Aarons, L., and Erikson, J. Nystagmus: A parameter of mental function. *Perceptual and Motor Skills*, 1968, *26*, 943–50.

Ladd, G. T. Contribution to the psychology of visual dreams. *Mind*, 1892, *1*, 299–304.

Ladefoged, P. Sub-glottal activity during speech. *Proceedings of the Fourth International Congress of Phonetic Sciences, Helsinki, 1961*. The Hague: Mouton, 1962.

Ladefoged, P. Linguistic phonetics. *Working Papers in Phonetics*, 6, Phonetics Lab., UCLA, 1967.

La Mettrei, J. O. *Man a machine*. Chicago: Open Court, 1912.

Langfeld, H. S. A response interpretation of consciousness. *Psychological Review*, 1931, *38*, 87–108.

Langfeld, H. S. The historical development of response psychology. *Science*, 1933, *77*, 243–50.

Larson, J. A. *Lying and its detection*. Chicago: University of Chicago Press, 1932.

Larson, J. D. and Foulkes, D. Electromyogram suppression during sleep, dream recall, and orientation time. *Psychophysiology*, 1969, *5*, 548–55.

Lashley, K. S. Basic neural mechanisms in behavior. *Psychological Review*, 1930, *37*, 1–24.

Lashley, K. S. The problem of serial order in behavior. In L. A. Jeffress (ed.), *Cerebral mechanisms in behavior: The Hixon Symposium*. New York: John Wiley, 1951.

Lashley, K. S. In J. F. Delafresnaye, *Brain mechanisms and consciousness*. Springfield, Ill.: Charles C Thomas, 1954.

Lashley, K. S. Cerebral organization and behavior. *Association for Research in Nervous and Mental Disease. Research Publications*, 1958, *36*, 1–18.

Lashley, K. S. Cerebral organization of behavior. *The neuropsychology of Lashley; selected papers*. New York: McGraw-Hill, 1960.

Lawrence, M. Hearing. *Annual Review of Psychology*, 1957, *8*, 29–60.

Lehman, R. S. Eye-movements and the autokinetic illusion. *American Journal of Psychology*, 1965, *78*, 490–92.

Lehmann, D., Beeler, G. W., Jr., and Fender, D. H. EEG responses to light flashes during the observation of stabilized and normal retinal images. *Electroencephalography and Clinical Neurophysiology*, 1967, *22*, 136–42.

Lenneberg, Eric H. *Biological foundations of language.* New York: John Wiley, 1967.

Lenox J. R., Lange, A. F., and Graham, K. R. Eye movement amplitudes in imagined pursuit of a pendulum with eyes closed. *Psychophysiology*, 1970, *6*, 773–77.

Leontiev, A. N. *Problems of psychic development.* Moscow: APN RSFSR Press, 1959.

Lepley, W. M. The participation of implicit speech in acts of writing. *American Journal of Psychology*, 1952, *65*, 597–99.

Leshner, S. S. Effects of aspiration and achievement on muscular tensions. *Journal of Experimental Psychology*, 1961, *61*, 133–37.

Leuba, C., Birch, L., and Appleton, J. Human problem solving during complete paralysis of the voluntary musculature. *Psychological Reports*, 1968, *22*, 849–55.

Leuba, C. and Dunlap, R. Conditioning imagery. *Journal of Experimental Psychology*, 1951, *41*, 352–55.

Levin, M. Motor hallucination: some motor aspects of mentation. *American Journal of Psychiatry*, 1957, *113*, 1020–3.

Levin, M. Motor function in mentation; imagery and hallucination; the independence of the highest cerebral centers. *American Journal of Psychiatry*, 1960, *117*, 142–46.

Lewis, D. J. Sources of experimental amnesia. *Psychological Review.* 1969, *76*, 461–72.

Lewis, D. J. A cognitive approach to experimental amnesia. *American Journal of Psychology* (in press).

Lewis, S. A., Jenkinson, J., and Wilson, J. An EEG investigation of awareness during anaesthesia. *British Journal of Psychology*, 1973, *64*, 413–15.

Liberman, A. M., Cooper, F. S., Shankweiler, D. P., and Studdert-Kennedy, M. Perception of the speech code. *Psychological Review*, 1967, *74*, 431–61.

Liberman, A. M., Cooper, F. S., Harris, K. S., MacNeilage, P. F., and Studdert-Kennedy, M. Some observations on a model for speech perception. In W. Wathen-Dunn (ed.), *Models for the perception of speech and visual form.* Cambridge, Mass.: MIT Press, 1967.

Liberman, A. M. and Studdert-Kennedy, M. Phonetic perception. In R. Held, H. Leibowitz, and H. L. Teuber (eds.), *Handbook of sensory physiology. Vol. VIII, "Perception."* Heidelberg: Springer-Verlag, 1977.

Lifshitz, K. The averaged evoked cortical response to complex visual stimuli. *Psychophysiology*, 1966, *3*, 55–68.

Light, J. S. and Gantt, W. H. Essential part of reflex arc for establishment of conditioned reflex: Formation of conditioned reflex after exclusion of motor peripheral end. *Journal of Comparative Psychology*, 1936, *21*, 19–36.

Lille, F., Pottier, M., and Scherrer, J. Influence in man of the level of mental activity on evoked potentials. *Electroencephalography and Clinical Neurophysiology*, 1968, *25*, 512.

Lindsay, P. H. and Norman, D. A. *Human information processing. An introduction to psychology.* New York: Academic Press, 1972.

Lindsey, J. W. The auditory evoked potential in man: A review. *T.-I.-T. Journal of Life Sciences*, 1971, *1*, 91–110.

Lindsley, D. B. Electroencephalography. In J. McV. Hunt (ed.), *Personality and the behavior disorders, vol. 2.* New York: Ronald, 1944.

Lindsley, D. B. Discussion re: The phenomena of hypnosis. In H. A. Abramson (ed.), *Problems of consciousness*. New York: Corlies, Macey, 1951.

Lindsley, D. B. Average evoked potentials—achievements, failures and prospects. In E. Donchin and D. B. Lindsley (eds.), *Average evoked potentials*. Washington, D.C.: NASA SP-191, 1969.

Lippold, O. Origin of the alpha rhythm. *Nature*, 1970, *226*, 616–18. (a)

Lippold, O. Bilateral separation in alpha rhythm recording. *Nature*, 1970, *226*, 459–60. (b)

Lippold, O. Are alpha waves artefactual? *New Scientist*, 1970, 12 March, 506–7. (c)

Lippold, O. C. J., and Novotny, G. E. K. Is alpha rhythm an artefact? *Lancet*, 1970, *1*, 976–79.

Lishman, J. R., and Lee, D. N. The autonomy of visual kinaesthesis. *Perception*, 1973, *2*, 287–94.

Lloyd, A. J. and Leibrecht, B. C. Conditioning of a single motor unit. *Journal of Experimental Psychology*, 1971, *88*, 391–95.

Locke, J. L. Children's language coding in short-term memory. *Language and Speech*, 1969, *12*, 187–91.

Locke, J. L. Short-term memory encoding strategies of the deaf. *Psychonomic Science*, 1970, *18*, 233–34. (a)

Locke, J. L. Phonetic analysis of pronounceability. *Psychological Reports*, 1970, *27*, 583–87. (b)

Locke, J. L. Subvocal speech and speech. *Asha*, 1970, *12*, 7–14. (c)

Locke, J. L. Phonemic processing in silent reading. *Perceptual and Motor Skills*, 1971, *32*, 905–6. (a)

Locke, J. L. Phonetic mediation in four-year-old children. *Psychonomic Science*, 1971, *23*, 409. (b)

Locke, J. L. Acoustic imagery in children's phonetically mediated recall. *Perceptual and Motor Skills*, 1971, *32*, 1000–1002. (c)

Locke, J. L. and Fehr, F. S. Phonetic coding of aurally and visually presented words with oral and graphic recall. *American Journal of Psychology*, in press.

Locke, J. L. and Fehr, F. S. Young children's use of the speech code in a recall task. *Journal of Experimental Child Psychology*, 1970. *10*, 367–73. (a)

Locke, J. L. and Fehr, F. S. Subvocal rehearsal as a form of speech. *Journal of Verbal Learning and Verbal Behavior*, 1970, *9*, 495–98. (b)

Locke, J. L. and Fehr, F. S. Phonetic correlates of graphic recall. *Perceptual and Motor Skills*, 1971, *33*, 1040–42. (a)

Locke, J. L. and Fehr, F. S. Subvocalization of heard or seen words prior to spoken or written recall. *American Journal of Psychology*, 1972, *85*, 63–68.

Locke, J. L. and Fehr, F. S. Electromyographic studies of subvocal rehearsal in learning. In R. Karrer (ed.), *Developmental psychophysiology of mental retardation*. Springfield, Ill. Charles C Thomas, 1976.

Locke, J. L. and Ginsburg, M. Electromyography and lipreading in the detection of verbal rehearsal. *Bulletin of the Psychonomic Society*, 1975, *5*, 246–48.

Locke, J. L. and Kutz, K. J. Memory for speech and speech for memory. *Journal of Speech and Hearing Research*, 1975, *18*, 176–91.

Locke, J. L. and Locke, V. L. Recall of phonetically and semantically similar words by 3-year-old children. *Psychonomic Science*, 1971, *24*, 189–90. (a)

Locke, J. L., and Locke, V. L. Deaf children's phonetic, visual, and dactylic coding in a grapheme recall task. *Journal of Experimental Psychology*, 1971, *89*, 141–46. (b)

Lockhart R. D. and Brandt, W. Length of striated muscle fibres. *Journal of Anatomy*, 1937–1938, vol. 72.

Loftus, G. R. Eye fixations and recognition memory for pictures. *Cognitive Psychology*, 1972, *3*, 525–51.

Lorens, S. A., Jr., and Darrow, C. W. Eye movements, EEG, GSR and EKG during mental multiplication. *Electroencephalography and Clinical Neurophysiology*, 1962, *14*, 739–46.

Lucretius, C. T. *On nature.* New York: Bobbs-Merrill, 1965.

Luria, A. R. *The role of speech in the regulation of normal and abnormal behavior.* New York: Liveright Publishing, 1961.

Luria, A. R. *Human higher cortical functions and their disturbance in local brain desctruction.* Moscow: Izdatelstvo Moskovskogo Universiteta, 1962. (Cole, M. and Maltzman, I. *A handbook of contemporary Soviet psychology.* New York: Basic Books, 1969)

Luria, A. R. *Higher cortical functions in man.* New York: Basic books, 1966. (a)

Luria, A. R. *Human brain and psychological processes.* New York: Harper & Row, 1966. (b)

Luria, A. R. The origin and cerebral organization of man's conscious action. Lecture to the XIX International Congress of Psychology, London, 1969.

Luria, A. R. and Polyakova, A. G. Observations on the development of voluntary actions in early childhood. I-II, *Proceedings Acad. Ped. Sci.*, 1959, *3*, 4 (Russian).

Lyakh, G. S. Features characterizing conditioned connections in response to mimicoarticulatory and acoustic components of speech stimuli in children during the first year of life. *Zhurnal Vysshei2 Nervnoi2 Deyatel' Nosti*, 1968, *18*, 1069–71.

Lykken, D. T. The validity of the guilty knowledge technique: The effects of faking. *Journal of Applied Psychology*, 1960, *44*, 258–62.

Lykken, D. T., Rose, R., Luther, B., and Maley, M. Correcting psychophysiological measures for individual differences in range. *Psychological Bulletin*, 1966, *66*, 481–84.

Lynch, J. J., Paskewitz, D. A. and Orne, M. T. Some factors in the feedback control of human alpha rhythm. *Psychosomatic Medicine*, 1974, *36*, 399–410.

MacCorquodale, K. and Meehl, P. E. On a distinction between hypothetical constructs and intervening variables. *Psychological Review*, 1948, *55*, 95–107.

Mackworth, J. F. The visual image and the memory trace. *Canadian Journal of Psychology*, 1962, *16*, 55–59.

Mackworth, J. F. The duration of the visual image. *Canadian Journal of Psychology*, 1963, *17*, 62–81.

Mackworth, N. H. and Morandi, A. J. The gaze selects informative details within pictures. *Perception and Psychophysics*, 1967, *2*, 547–52.

MacNeilage, P. F Changes in electroencephalogram and other physiological measures during serial mental performance. *Psychophysiology*, 1966, *2*, 344–53. (a)

MacNeilage, P. F. EEG amplitude changes during cognitive processes involving similar stimuli and responses. *Psychophysiology*, 1966, *2*, 280–86. (b)

MacNeilage, P. F. Motor control of serial ordering of speech. *Psychological Review*, 1970, *77*, 182–95.

MacNeilage, P. F., and MacNeilage, L. A. Central processes controlling speech production during sleep and waking. In F. J. McGuigan and R. A. Schoonover (eds.), *The psychophysiology of thinking: Studies of covert processes.* New York: Academic Press, 1973.

Magoun, H. W. Discussion in J. F. Delafresnaye, *Brain Mechanisms and Consciousness*. Springfield, Ill.: Charles C Thomas, 1954.

Mah, C. S. and Albert, D. J. Electroconvulsive shock induced amnesia: An analysis of the variation in the length of the amnesia gradient. *Behavioral Biology*, 1973, *9*, 517–40.

Malmo, R. B. Physiological gradients and behavior. *Psychological Bulletin*, 1965, *64*, 225–34.

Malmo, R. B. *On emotions, needs, and our archaic brain*. New York: Holt, Rinehart and Winston, 1975.

Maltzman, I. The orienting reflex and thinking as determiners of conditioning and generalization to words. In H. H. Kendler and J. T. Spence (eds.), *Essays in neobehaviorism*. New York: Appleton-Century-Crofts, 1971.

Marg, E. Development of electro-oculography. *A.M.A. Archives of Ophthamology*, 1951, *45*, 169–85.

Marshall, J. E. Eye movements and the visual autokinetic phenomenon. *Perceptual and Motor Skills*, 1966, *22*, 319–26.

Marston, W. M. Systolic blood pressure systems of deception. *Journal of Experimental Psychology*, 1917, *2*, 117–63.

Marteniuk, R. G. and Ryan, M. L. Psychophysics of kinesthesis: Angular movement. *Journal of Motor Behavior*, 1972, *4*, 135–42.

Marteniuk, R. G., Shields, K. W., and Campbell, S. Amplitude, position, timing, and velocity as cues in reproduction of movement. *Perceptual and Motor Skills*, 1972, *35*, 51–58.

Massaro, D. W. Preceptual images, processing time, and perceptual units in auditory perception. *Psychological Review*, 1972, *79*, 124–45.

Massaro, D. W. Perceptual units in speech recognition. *Journal of Experimental Psychology*, 1974, *102*, 199–208.

Matin, E. Saccadic suppression: A review and an analysis. *Psychological Bulletin*, 1974, *81*, 899–917.

Matsumiya, Y., Tagliasco, V., Lombroso, C. T., and Goodglass, H. Auditory evoked response: Meaningfulness of stimuli and interhemispheric asymmetry. *Science*, 1972, *175*, 790–92.

Mattingly, I. G. and Kavanagh, J. F. *The relationships between speech and reading* (Status Report on Speech Research, SR-29/30). New Haven: Haskins Laboratories, January–June 1972.

Maudsley, H. *The physiology of mind*, 3rd ed. New York: Appleton, 1883.

Max, L. W. An experimental study of the motor theory of consciousness. *Psychological Bulletin*, 1933, *30*, 714.

Max, L. W. An experimental study of the motor theory of consciousness: I. Critique of earlier studies. *Journal of General Psychology*, 1934, *11*, 112–25.

Max, L. W. An experimental study of the motor theory of consciousness: III. Action-current responses in deaf mutes during sleep, sensory stimulation and dreams. *Journal of Comparative Psychology*, 1935, *19*, 469–86.

Max, L. W. An experimental study of the motor theory of consciousness: IV. Action-current responses in the deaf during awakening, kinaesthetic imagery and abstract thinking. *Journal of Comparative Psychology*, 1937, *24*, 301–44.

McAdam, D. W. and Whitaker, H. A. Language production: Electroencephalographic localization in the normal human brain. *Science*, 1971, *172*, 499–502. (a)

McAdam, D. W. and Whitaker, H. A. Electrocortical localization of language production. *Science*, 1971, *174*, 1359–61. (b)

McCall, G. N. and Rabuzzi, D. D. Reflex contraction of middle-ear muscles secondary to stimulation of laryngeal nerves. *Journal of Speech and Hearing Research*, 1973, *16*, 56–61.

McCormack, P. D. and Clemence, G. D. Monitoring eye movements during paired-associate learning in a retroactive inhibition setting. *Canadian Journal of Psychology/Canadian Psychologist*, 1970, *24*, 184–93.

McCroskey, R. L., Jr., The relative contribution of auditory and tactile cues to certain aspects of speech. *Southern Speech Journal*, 1958, *24*, 84–90.

McCulloch, W. S. Why the mind is in the head. In L. A. Jeffress (ed.), *Cerebral mechanisms in behavior; The Hickson Symposium*. New York: John Wiley, 1951.

McDade, J. E. A hypothesis for non-oral reading: Argument, experiment, and results. *Journal of Educational Research*, 1937, *30*, 489–503.

McDougall, W. The physiological factors of the attention process, I. *Mind*, 1902, *11*, 316–51.

McGaugh, J. L., Time dependent processes in memory storage. *Science*, 1966, *153*, 1351–58.

McGuigan, F. J. *Thinking: Studies of covert language processes*. New York: Appleton-Century-Crofts, 1966. (a)

McGuigan, F. J. Covert oral behavior and auditory hallucinations. *Psychophysiology*, 1966, *3*, 73–80. (b)

McGuigan, F. J. Feedback of speech muscle activity during silent reading: Two comments. *Science*, 1967, *157*, 579–80.

McGuigan, F. J. Subvocal speech during silent reading. U.S. Department of Health, Education and Welfare, Final Report, Project No. 2643, Contract No. OE J-10-073, 1967.

McGuigan, F. J. Covert oral behavior during the silent performance of language tasks. *Psychological Bulletin*, 1970, *74*, 309–26. (a)

McGuigan, F. J. Covert oral behavior as a function of quality of handwriting. *American Journal of Psychology*, 1970, *83*, 377–88. (b)

McGuigan, F. J. Reduccion de la tension internacional por metodos psicologicos. *Revista Latinoamericana de Psicologia*, 1970, *2*, 327–41. (c)

McGuigan, F. J. Covert linguistic behavior in deaf subjects during thinking. *Journal of Comparative and Physiological Psychology*, 1971, *75*, 417–20.

McGuigan, F. J. External auditory feedback from covert oral behavior during silent reading. *Psychonomic Science*, 1971, *25*, 212–14.

McGuigan, F. J. Covert linguistic behavior in deaf subjects during thinking. *Journal of Comparative and Physiological Psychology*, 1971, *75*, 417–20.

McGuigan, F. J. Electrical measurement of covert processes as an explication of "higher mental events." In F. J. McGuigan and R. A. Schoonover (eds.), *The psychophysiology of thinking*. New York: Academic Press, 1973. (a)

McGuigan, F. J. Conditioning of covert behavior: Some problems and some hopes. In F. J. McGuigan and D. B. Lumsden (eds.) *Contemporary approaches to conditioning and learning*. Washington, D.C.: V. H. Winston & Sons, 1973. (b)

McGuigan, F. J. The function of covert oral behavior ("silent speech") during silent reading. *International Journal of Psycholinguistics*, 1973, *2*, 39–47. (c)

McGuigan, F. J. Review of A. N. Sokolov, *Inner speech and thought* (G. T. Onischenko, trans. D. B. Lindsley, ed., Plenum Press). *American Scientist*, 1973, *61*, 98–99. (d)

McGuigan, F. J. The function of covert oral behavior in linguistic coding and internal information processing. In Kurt Salzinger (ed.), Psychology in Progress: An Interim Report. *Annals of the New York Academy of Sciences*, 1976, *270*, 57–89.

McGuigan, F. J. *Experimental psychology*, 3rd ed. Englewood Cliffs, N.J.: Prentice-Hall, 1978. (a)

McGuigan, F. J. *Psychophysiological measurement of covert behavior: A guide for the laboratory*. Hillsdale, N.J.: Erlbaum, 1978. (b)

McGuigan, F. J. Imagery and thinking: Covert functioning of the motor system. In G. E. Schwartz and D. Shapiro (eds.), Consciousness and self regulation: Advances in Research II. New York: Plenum, in press.

McGuigan, F. J. and Bailey, S. C. Covert response patterns during the processing of language stimuli. *Interamerican Journal of Psychology*, 1969, *3*, 289–99. (a)

McGuigan, F. J. and Bailey, S. C. Longitudinal study of covert oral behavior during silent reading. *Perceptual and Motor Skills*, 1969, *28*, 170. (b)

McGuigan, F. J. and Bertera, J. In F. J. McGuigan and D. B. Lumsden (eds.), *Contemporary approaches to conditioning and learning*. Washington, D.C.: V. H. Winston & Sons, 1973.

McGuigan, F. J. and Boness, D. J. What happens between an external stimulus and an overt response? A study of covert responses. *Pavlovian Journal of Biological Science*, 1975, *10*, 112–19.

McGuigan, F. J., Culver, V. I., and Kendler, T. S. Covert behavior as a direct electromyographic measure of mediating responses. *Conditional Reflex*, 1971, *6*, 145–52.

McGuigan, F. J. and Keller, B. The effect of muscular inhibition and interference on thought. Unpublished manuscript, 1962.

McGuigan, F. J., Keller, B., and Stanton, E. Covert language responses during silent reading. *Journal of Educational Psychology*, 1964, *55*, 339–43.

McGuigan, F. J., Osgood, C. E., and Childress, A. R. Conditioning of muscular tracers to semantic features. In C. E. Osgood and F. J. McGuigan, Psychophysiological correlates of meaning: Essences or tracers? In F. J. McGuigan and R. A. Schoonover (eds.), *The psychophysiology of thinking*. New York: Academic Press, 1973.

McGuigan, F. J., Osgood, C. E., and Hadley, S. Perceptual clarification of auditory signals with simultaneous visual input—the Gilbert and Sullivan effect. In C. E. Osgood and F. J. McGuigan, Psychophysiological correlates of meaning: Essences or tracers? In F. J. McGuigan and R. A. Schoonover (eds.), *The psychophysiology of thinking*. New York: Academic Press, 1973.

McGuigan, F. J. and Pavek, G. V. On the psychophysiological identification of covert nonoral language processes. *Journal of Experimental Psychology*, 1972, *92*, 237–45.

McGuigan, F. J., and Pinkney, K. B. Effects of increased reading rate on covert processes. *Interamerican Journal of Psychology*, 1973, *7*, 223–31.

McGuigan, F. J. and Rodier, W. I. III. Effects of auditory stimulation on covert oral behavior during silent reading. *Journal of Experimental Psychology*, 1968, *76*, 649–55.

McGuigan, F. J. and Schoonover, R. A. *The psychophysiology of thinking: Studies of covert processes*. New York: Academic Press, 1973.

McGuigan, F. J. and Shepperson, M. H. The effect of remedial reading on covert oral behavior. *Journal of Clinical Psychology*, 1971, *27*, 541–43.

McGuigan, F. J. and Tanner, R. G. Covert oral behavior during conversational and visual dreams. *Psychonomic Science*, 1971, *23*, 263–64.

McGuigan, F. J. and Winstead, C. L., Jr., Discriminative relationship between covert oral behavior and the phonemic system in internal information processing. *Journal of Experimental Psychology*, 1974, *103*, 885–90.

McIntyre, A. R., Bennett, A. L., and Hamilton, C. Recent advances in the pharmacology of curare. In A. R. McIntyre (ed.), Curare and anticurare agents. *Annals of the New York Academy of Sciences,* 1951, *54,* 297–530.

McKee, G., Humphrey, B., and McAdam, D. W. Scaled lateralization of alpha activity during linguistic and musical tasks. *Psychophysiology,* 1973, *10,* 441–43.

Melton, A. W. and Martin, E. *Coding processes in human memory.* Washington, D.C.: V. H. Winston, 1972.

Mendelson, J., Solomon, P., and Lindemann, E. Hallucinations of poliomyelitis patients during treatment in a respirator. *Journal of Nervous and Mental disorders,* 1958, *126,* 421–28.

Menzies, R. Conditioned vasomotor responses in human subjects. *Journal of Psychology,* 1937, *4,* 75–120.

Meumann, E. *Lectures on experimental teaching.* 1917, Part 3. (Sokolov, A. N. *Inner speech and thought.* New York: Plenum Press, 1972.)

Millenson, J. R. *Principles of behavioral analysis.* New York: Macmillan, 1967.

Miller, G. A., Galanter, E., and Pribram, K. H. *Plans and the structure of behavior.* New York: Holt, Rinehart & Winston, 1960.

Miller, G. A. and Nicely, P. E. An analysis of perceptual confusions among some English consonants. *Journal of the Acoustical Society of America,* 1955, *27,* 338–52.

Miller, N. E. and Banuazizi, A. Instrumental learning by curarized rats of a specific visceral response, intestinal or cardiac. *Journal of Comparative and Physiological Psychology,* 1968, *65,* 1–7.

Miller, N. E. and DiCara, L. V. Instrumental learning of heart rate changes in curarized rats: Shaping, and specificity to discriminative stimulus. *Journal of Comparative and Physiological Psychology,* 1967, *63,* 12–19.

Miller, N. E. and DiCara, L. V. Instrumental learning of urine formation by rats, changes in renal blood flow. *American Journal of Physiology,* 1968, *215,* 677–83.

Molinari, S. and Foulkes, D. Tonic and phasic events during sleep: Psychological correlates and implications. *Perceptual and Motor Skills,* 1969, *29,* 343–68. Monograph Supplement 1-V29.

Moore, K. C. The mental development of a child. *Psychological Review Monograph.* 1896, *1,* 150.

Morgan, A. H., MacDonald, H., and Hilgard, E. R. EEG alpha: Lateral asymmetry related to task, and hypnotizability. *Psychophysiology,* 1974, *11,* 275–82.

Morgan, C. T., Cook J. S. III, Chapanis, A., and Lund, M. W. *Human engineering guide to equipment design.* New York: McGraw-Hill, 1963.

Morgan, A. H., McDonald, P. J., and McDonald, H. Differences in bilateral alpha activity as a function of experimental task, with a note on lateral eye movements and hypnotizability. *Neuropsychologia,* 1971, *9,* 459–69.

Morrell, L. K. and Salamy, J. G. Hemispheric asymmetry of electrocortical responses to speech stimuli. *Science,* 1971, *174,* 164–66.

Moskowitz, E. and Berger, R. J. Rapid eye movements and dream imagery: Are they related? *Nature,* 1969, *224,* 613–14.

Mould, M., Treadwell, L., and Washburn, M. F. Minor studies from the psychological laboratory of Vassar College: XXVII. The influence of suppressing articulation on the favorable effect of distributing repetitions. *American Journal of Psychology,* 1915, *26,* 286–88.

Mowrer, O. H. *Learning theory and the symbolic processes.* New York: John Wiley, 1960. (a)

Mowrer, O. H. *Learning theory and behavior.* New York: John Wiley, 1960. (b)

Mueller, F. M. *The science of thought.* London: Longmans Green, 1887.

Mulholland, T. The concept of attention and the electroencephalographic alpha rhythm. In C. R. Evans and T. B. Mulholland (eds.), *Attention in neurophysiology*. New York: Appleton-Century-Crofts, 1969.

Müller-Freienfels, R. Beiträge zum problem des wortlosen denkens. *Archiv für die gesamte psychologie*, 1912, *23*, 334.

Mundy-Castle, A. C. The electroencephalogram and mental activity. *Electroencephalography and Clinical Neurophysiology*, 1957, *9*, 643–55.

Münsterberg, H. Die Association successiver Vorstellungen. *Zeitschrift fur Psychologie*, 1890, *1*, 99–107.

Münsterberg, H. The physiological basis of mental life. *Science* 1899, *9*, 442–47.

Murdock. B. B., Jr. The effects of noise and delayed auditory feedback on short-term memory. *Journal of Verbal Learning and Verbal Behavior*, 1967, *6*, 737–43.

Murphy, G. *Psychology in the year 2000*. Wayne State University Centennial, May 10, 1968.

Murray, D. J. The effect of white noise upon the recall of vocalized lists. *Canadian Journal of Psychology*, 1965, *19*, 333–45.

Murray, D. J. The role of speech responses in short-term memory. *Canadian Journal of Psychology*, 1967, *21*, 263–76.

Mysak, E. D. *Speech pathology and feedback theory*. Springfield, Ill.: Charles C Thomas, 1966.

Nazarova, L. K. On the role of speech kinesthesis in writing. *Sovet Pedag.*, 1952, No. 6. Cited by Cole and Maltzman (1969).

Nebes, R. D. Hemispheric specialization in commissurotomized man. *Psychological Bulletin*, 1974, *81*, 1–14.

Neisser, U. Visual imagery as process and as experience. In J. S. Antrobus (ed.), *Cognition and effect*. Boston: Little, Brown, 1970.

Nelson, D. and Brooks, D. H. Independence of phonetic and imaginal features. *Journal of Experimental Psychology*, 1973, *97*, 1–7.

Neumann, E. And Blanton. R. The early history of electrodermal research. *Psychophysiology*, 1970, *6*, 453–75.

Neville, H. Electrographic correlates of lateral asymmetry in the processing of verbal and nonverbal auditory stimuli. *Journal of Psycholinguistic Research*, 1974, *3*, 151–63.

Noble, C. E. Conditioned generalization of the galvanic skin response to a subvocal stimulus. *Journal of Experimental Psychology*, 1950, *40*, 15–25.

Northrop, F. S. C. *The logic of the sciences and the humanities*. New York: Macmillan, 1948.

Novikova, L. A. Electrophysiological investigation of speech. Conference on Psychology, 1–6 July, 1955, pp. 337–51. In N. O'Connor (ed.), *Recent Soviet psychology* New York: Pergamon Press, 1961.

Novikova, L. A. Electrophysiological investigation of speech. In N. O'Connor (ed.), *Recent Soviet psychology*. New York: Liveright Publishing Co., 1961.

O'Brien, J. A. *Silent reading*. New York: Macmillan, 1921.

Ohman, A. and Lader, M. Selective attention and "habituation" of the auditory averaged evoked response in humans. *Physiology and Behavior*, 1972, *8*, 79–85.

Ohtani, A., Kuchinomachi, Y. and Yagi, A. A simple device for detecting saccades and judging their intervals. *Behavior Research Methods and Instrumentation*, 1974, *6*, 547–49.

Ojemann, G. A. Language and the thalamus: Object naming and recall during and after thalamic stimulation. *Brain and Language*, 1975, *2*, 1.

Ojemann, G. A. and Ward, A. A., Jr. Speech representation in ventrolateral thalamus. *Brain*, 1971, *94*, 669–80.

Okuma, T., Fujmori, M., and Hayashi, A. The effect of environmental temperature on the electrocortical activity of cats immobilized by neuromuscular
blocking agents. *Electroencephalography and clinical neurophysiology*, 1965, *18*,
392–400.

Olds, J. The central nervous system and the reinforcement of behaviour. *American Psychologist*, 1969, *24*, 114–32.

Oppenheimer, R. Analogy in science. *American Psychologist*, 1956, *11*, 127–35.

Orne, M. T. Implications of laboratory research for the detection of deception.
Polygraph, 1973, *2*, 169–99.

Orne, M. T. and Paskewitz, D. A. Aversive situational effects on alpha feedback
training. *Science*, 1974, *186*, 458–60.

Orne, M. T., Thackray, R. I., and Paskewitz, D. A. On the detection of
deception—A model for the study of the physiological effects of psychological
stimuli. In N. Greenfield and R. Sternbach (eds.), *Handbook of psychophysiology*.
New York: Holt, Rinehart & Winston, 1972.

Osgood, C. E. *Method and theory in experimental psychology*. New York: Oxford
University Press, 1953.

Osgood, C. E. A behavioristic analysis of perception and meaning as cognitive
phenomena. In J. S. Bruner (ed.), *Contemporary approaches to cognition*. Cambridge, Mass.: Harvard University Press, 1957. (a)

Osgood, C. E. Motivational dynamics of language behavior. In M. R. Jones (ed.),
Nebraska Symposium on Motivation. Lincoln: University of Nebraska Press, 1957.
(b)

Osgood, C. E. On understanding and creating sentences. *American Psychologist*,
1963, *18*, 735–51.

Osgood, C. E. Where do sentences come from? In D. Steinberg and L. Jakobovits
(eds.), *Semantics*. New York: Cambridge University Press, 1971.

Osgood, C. E. and Hoosain, R. Salience of the word as a unit in the perception of
language. *Perception and Psychophysics*, 1974, *15*, 168–92.   Reprinted by permission of *Perception and Psychophysics*.

Osgood, C. E. and McGuigan, F. J. Psychophysiological correlates of meaning:
Essences or tracers? In F. J. McGuigan and R. A. Schoonover (eds.), *The
psychophysiology of thinking*. New York: Academic Press, 1973.

Osgood, C. E. and Richards, M. M. From Yang and Yin to *and* or *but*. *Language*,
1973, *49*, 380–412.

Paivio, A. *Imagery and verbal processes*. New York: Holt, Rinehart and Winston,
1971.

Paivio, A. Psychophysiological correlates of imagery. In F. J. McGuigan and R.
A. Schoonover (eds.), *The psychophysiology of thinking: Studies of covert processes*.
New York: Academic Press, 1973.

Palágyi, M. *Naturphilosophische Vorlesungen uber die Grundprobleme des Bewusstseins
und des Lebens*, 2nd ed. Leipzig: Barth, 1924.

Pappas, B. A., DiCara, L. V., and Miller, N. E. Learning of blood pressure
responses in the noncurarized rat: Transfer to the curarized state. *Physiology
and Behavior*, 1970, *5*, 1029–32.

Pauk, W. Speed reading? *Journal of the Reading Specialist*, 1964, *4*, 18–19.

Paul, G. L. Physiological effects of relaxation training and hypnotic suggestion.
Journal of Abnormal Psychology, 1969, *74*, 425–37.

Pavlov, I. P. *Lectures on conditioned reflexes. Vol. II. Conditioned reflexes and psychiatry*.
New York: International Publishers, 1941.

Penfield, W. Some mechanisms of consciousness discovered during electrical
stimulation of the brain. *Proceedings of the National Academy of Sciences*, 1958, *44*,
51–66

Penfield, W. Consciousness, memory, and man's conditioned reflexes. In Karl H. Pribram (ed.), *On the biology of learning.* New York: Harcourt Brace Jovanovich, 1969.

Penfield, W. and Jasper, H. *Epilepsy and the functional anatomy of the human brain.* Boston: Little, Brown, 1954.

Penfield, W. and Roberts, L. *Speech and brain mechanisms.* Princeton, N.J.: Princeton University Press, 1959.

Pepin, A. C., Kibbee, M., and Wells, C. A. Brain potentials during silent and oral reading: A critical note. *Journal of General Psychology,* 1952, *46,* 99–102.

Perkel, D. H. Spike trains as carriers of information. In F. O. Schmitt (ed.), *The Neurosciences: Second study program.* New York: Rockefeller University Press, 1970.

Perky, C. W. An experimental study of imagination. *American Journal of Psychology,* 1910, *21,* 422–52.

Pessah, M. A. and Roffwarg, H. P. Spontaneous middle ear muscle activity in man: A rapid eye movement sleep phenomenon. *Science,* 1972, *178,* 773–76.

Petajan, J. H. and Philip, B. A. Frequency control of motor unit action potentials. *Electroencephalography and Clinical Neurophysiology,* 1969, *27,* 66–72.

Petrinovich, L. F. and Hardyck, C. D. Generalization of an instrumental response between words and pictures. *Psychonomic Science,* 1970, *18,* 239–41.

Piaget, J. and Inhelder, B. *Mental imagery in the child.* New York: Basic Books, 1971.

Picton, T. W. and Low, M. D. The CNV and semantic content of stimuli in the experimental paradigm: Effects of feedback. *Electroencephalography and Clinical Neurophysiology,* 1971, *31,* 451–56.

Pintner, R. Inner speech during silent reading. *Psychological Review,* 1913, *20,* 129–53.

Pishkin, V. Electromyographic variation concomitant with concept identification parameters. *Perceptual and Motor Skills,* 1964, *18,* 649–52.

Pishkin, V. Electromyography in cognitive performance by schizophrenics and normals. *Perceptual and Motor Skills,* 1973, *37,* 382.

Pishkin, V. and Shurley, J. T. Electrodermal and electromyographic parameters in concept identification. *Psychophysiology,* 1968, *5,* 112–18.

Pivik, T. and Dement, W. C. Phasic changes in muscular and reflex activity during non-REM sleep. *Experimental Neurology,* 1970, *27,* 115–24.

Podlesny, J. A. And Raskin, D. C. Physiological measures and the detection of deception. *Psychological Bulletin,* 1977, *84,* 782–99.

Pollack, I. and Ficks, L. Information of elementary multidimensional auditory displays. *Journal of The Acoustic Society of America,* 1954, *26,* 155–58.

Poon, L. W., Thompson, L. W., Williams, R. B., Jr., and Marsh, G. R. Changes of antero-posterior distribution of CNV and late positive component as a function of information processing demands. *Psychophysiology,* 1974, *11,* 660–73.

Porjesz, B. and Begleiter, H. The effects of stimulus expectancy on evoked brain potentials. *Psychophysiology,* 1975, *12,* 152–57.

Posch, J. *Phenomena of our mind and their nature: Project of a realistic psychology.* Budapest: Pfeifer, 1915.

Poulton, E. C. Time for reading and memory. *British Journal of Psychology,* 1958, *49,* 230–45.

Premack, D. Reinforcement theory. In D. Levine (ed.), *Nebraska symposium on motivation.* Lincoln: University of Nebraska Press, 1965.

Pribram, K. H. *Languages of the brain.* Englewood Cliffs, N.J.: Prentice-Hall, 1971.

Prosser, C. L. and Hunter, W. S. The extinction of startle responses and spinal reflexes in the white rat. *American Journal of Psychology*, 1936, *117*, 609–18.

Pushkin, V. N. The study of thinking as a process. *Voprosy Psikhologii*, 1969, *15*, 20–35.

Putnoky, J. Measuring the motor evoking capacity of words by a rating procedure. *Magyar Pszichológiai Szemle*, 1975, *32*, 383–95.

Putnoky, J. "Motority" as a correlate of word abstractness: A rating procedure. *Studia Psychologica*, 1976, *18*, 51–64.

Pylyshyn, Z. W. What the mind's eye tells the mind's brain: A critique of mental imagery. *Psychological Bulletin*, 1973, *80*, 1–24.

Quarton, G. C., Melnechuk, T., and Schmitt, F. O. (eds.), *The neurosciences: A study program*. New York: Rockefeller University Press, 1967.

Raphael, L. J. *An electromyographic investigation of the feature of tension in some American English vowels* (Status Report on Speech Research, 179–91). New Haven: Haskins Laboratories, October–December, 1971.

Ray, R. *Classical conditioning of heart rate in restrained and curarized rats*. Unpublished doctoral dissertation, University of Tennessee, 1969.

Razran, G. H. S. Semantic, syntactic, and phonetographic generalization of verbal conditioning. *Psychological Bulletin*, 1939, *90*, 89–90.

Razran, G. H. S. A quantitative study of meaning by a conditioned salivary technique (semantic conditioning). *Science*, 1939, *90*, 89–90. (a)

Reder, S. M. On-line monitoring of eye-position signals in contingent and noncontingent paradigms. *Behavior Research Methods and Instrumentation*, 1973, *5*, 218–28.

Reed, H. B. The existence and function of inner speech in the thought processes. *Journal of Experimental Psychology*, 1916, *1*, 365–92.

Regan, D. *Evoked potentials in psychology, sensory physiology and clinical medicine*. London: Chapman and Hall, 1972.

Reichenbach, H. *Atom and cosmos*. London: Allen & Unwin, 1932.

Reiser, O. L. The structure of thought. *Psychological Review*, 1924, *31*, 51–73.

Reuder, M. E. The effect of ego orientation and problem difficulty on muscle action potentials. *Journal of Experimental Psychology*, 1956, *51*, 142–48.

Reyher, J. and Morishige, H. Electroencephalogram and rapid eye movements during free imagery and dream recall. *Journal of Abnormal Psychology*, 1969, *74*, 576–82.

Ribot, T. Les mouvements et leur importance psychologique. *Revue Philosophie*, 1879, *8*. (Trans. by Thorson, A. M. The relation of tongue movements to internal speech. *Journal of Experimental Psychology*, 1925, *8*, 1–32.)

Richardson, A. Mental practice: A review and discussion. Part I. *Research Quarterly*, 1967a, *38*, 95–107.

Richardson, L. F. The analogy between mental images and sparks. *Psychological Review*, 1930, *37*, 214–27.

Riggs, L. A., Ratliff, F., Cornsweet, J. C., and Cornsweet, T. N. The disappearance of steadily-fixated objects. *Journal of the Optical Society of America*, 1953, *43*, 495–501.

Ringel, R. L. and Steer, M. D. Some effects of tactile and auditory alterations of speech output. *Journal of Speech and Hearing Research*, 1963, *6*, 369–78.

Ritter, W. and Vaughan, H., Jr., Average evoked responses in vigilance and discrimination: A reassessment. *Science*, 1969, *164*, 326–28.

Roberts, B. H., Greenblatt, M., and Solomon, H. C. Movements of the vocal apparatus during auditory hallucinations. *American Journal of Psychiatry*, 1951, *108*, 912–14.

Robinson, J. E. The effect of speech musculature movement on reading comprehension (Doctoral dissertation, L.S.U., 1964). *Dissertation Abstracts,* 1964, *25,* 4866.

Roessler, R. L. and Brogden, W. J. Conditioned differentiation of vasoconstriction to subvocal stimuli. *American Journal of Psychology,* 1943, *56,* 78–86.

Roffwarg, H. P., Dement, W. C., Muzio, J. N. and Fisher, C. Dream imagery: Relationship to rapid eye movements of sleep. *Archives of General Psychiatry,* 1962, *7,* 235–58. In F. J. McGuigan (ed.), *Thinking: Studies of covert language processes.* New York: Appleton-Century-Crofts, 1966.

Rohrbaugh, J. W., Donchin, E., and Eriksen, C. W. Decision making and the P300 component of the cortical evoked response. *Perception and Psychophysics,* 1974, *15,* 368–74. Reprinted by permission, *Perception and Psychophysics.*

Roland, B. C. Eye-movements of stutterers and non-stutterers during silent, oral, and choral reading. *Perceptual and Motor Skills,* 1972, *35,* 297–98.

Rollins, H. A. and Thibadeau, R. The effects of auditory shadowing on recognition of information received visually. *Memory and Cognition,* 1973, *1,* 164–68.

Rosen, S. and Czech, D. The conditioning of EOG (electrooculogram) responses through conflict-producing situations. *Journal of Experimental Research in Personality,* 1965, *1,* 71–77.

Rosen, S. and Czech, D. The use of electrooculography for identifying phases of cognitive process. *Psychophysiology,* 1966, *3,* 203–12.

Rosenfeld, J. P. The meaning of operantly conditioned changes in evoked responses. In G. E. Schwartz and J. Beatty (eds.). *Biofeedback: Theory and research.* New York: Academic Press, 1977.

Rosenfeld, J. P. and Hetzler, B. E. Operant-controlled evoked responses: Discrimination of conditioned and normally occurring components. *Science,* 1973, *181,* 767–70.

Rosenfeld, J. P. Hetzler, B. E., Birkel, P. A., Kowatch, R. A., and Antoinetti, D. N. Operant conditioned potentials, centrally evoked at random intervals. *Behavioral Biology,* 1976, *16,* 305–17.

Rosenfeld, J. P., Rudell, A. P., and Fox, S. S. Operant control of neural events in humans. *Science,* 1969, *165,* 821–23.

Rossi, A. M., Furhman, A., and Solomon, P. Sensory deprivation: Arousal and rapid eye movement correlates of some effects. *Perceptual and Motor Skills,* 1964, *19,* 447–51.

Rossi, A. M., Furhman, A., and Solomon, P. Arousal levels and thought processes during sensory deprivation. *Journal of Abnormal Psychology,* 1967, *72,* 166–73.

Roth, W. T., Kopell, B. S., and Bertozzi, P. E. The effect of attention on the average evoked response to speech sounds. *Electroencephalography and Clinical Neurophysiology,* 1970, *29,* 38–46.

Rounds, G. H., and Poffenberger, A. T. The measurement of implicit speech reactions. *American Journal of Psychology,* 1931, *43,* 606–12.

Rouvray, D. H. The search for useful topological indices in chemistry. *American Scientist,* 1973, *61,* 729–35.

Rubenstein, H., Lewis, S. S., and Rubenstein, M. A. *Evidence for phonemic recording in visual word recognition.* Bethlehem, Pa.: Center for the Information Sciences, Lehigh University, 1971.

Ruchkin, D. S. and Sutton, S. Visual evoked and emitted potentials and stimulus significance. *Bulletin of the Psychonomic Society,* 1973, *2,* 144–46.

Runquist, W. N. and Blackmore, M. Phonemic storage of concrete and abstract words with auditory presentation. *Canadian Journal of Psychology,* 1973, *27,* 456–63.

Ruth, J. S. and Giambra, L. M. Eye movements as a function of attention and rate of change in thought content. *Perceptual and Motor Skills,* 1974, *39,* 475–80.

Sandler, L. S. and Schwartz, M. Evoked responses and perception: Stimulus content versus stimulus structure. *Psychophysiology,* 1971, *8,* 727–39.

Saraga, E. and Shallice, T. Parallel processing of the attributes of single stimuli. *Perception and Psychophysics,* 1973, *13,* 261–70.

Sasmor, R. M. Operant conditioning of a small-scale muscle response. *Journal of the Experimental Analysis of Behavior,* 1966, *9,* 69–85.

Sassin, J. F. and Johnson, L. C. Body motility during sleep and its relation to the K-complex. *Experimental Neurology,* 1968, *22,* 133–44.

Sauerland, E. K. and Mizuno, N. Hypoglossal nerve afferents: Elicitation of a polysynaptic hypoglossal-laryngeal reflex. *Brain Research,* 1968, *10,* 256–58.

Savin, H. B. and Bever, T. G. The nonperceptual reality of the phoneme. *Journal of Verbal Learning and Verbal Behavior,* 1970, *9,* 295–302.

Scheck, M. G. Involuntary tongue movements under varying stimuli. *Proceedings of the Iowa Academy of Science,* 1925, *32,* 385–91.

Schiff, S. K., Bunney, W. E., Jr., and Freedman, D. X. A study of ocular movements in hypnotically induced dreams, *Journal of Nervous and Mental Disease,* 1961, *133,* 59–68.

Schilling, R. *Z. Psychol.,* 1929, *111,* 204–46. In G. Humphrey, *Thinking, an introduction to its experimental psychology.* New York: John Wiley, 1951.

Schliesser, H. F. and Coleman, R. Effectiveness of certain procedures for alteration of auditory and oral tactile sensation for speech. *Perceptual and Motor Skills,* 1968, *26,* 275–81.

Schmidt, B. Changing patterns of eye movement. *Journal of Reading,* 1966, *9,* 379–85.

Schmidt, R. A. Proprioception and the timing of motor responses. *Psychological Bulletin,* 1971, *76,* 383–407.

Schmidt, R. A., Proprioception versus motor outflow in timing: A reply to Jones. *Psychological Bulletin,* 1973, *79,* 389–90.

Schmitt, F. O. (Ed.-in-Chief). *The neurosciences: Second study program.* New York: The Rockefeller University Press, 1970.

Schoenfeld, W. N. and Cummings, W. W. Behavior and perception. In S. Koch (ed.), *Psychology: A study of a science, vol. 5.* New York: McGraw-Hill, 1963.

Schwartz, G. E. Biofeedback, self-regulation, and the patterning of physiological processes. *American Scientist,* 1975, *63,* 314–24.

Schwartz, G. E., Fair, P. L., Greenberg, P. S., Friedman, M. J., and Klerman, G. L. Facial electromyography in the assessment of emotion. Paper presented at the meeting of the Society for Psychophysiological Research, Galveston, Texas, October 1973.

Schwartz, G. E., Fair, P. L., Greenberg, P. S., Mandel, M. R., and Klerman, G. L. Facial expression and depression: An electromyographic study. Paper presented at the meeting of the American Psychosomatic Society, Philadelphia, March, 1974.

Scott, C. M. and Ringel, R. L. Articulation without oral sensory control. *Journal of Speech and Hearing Research,* 1971, *14,* 804–18.

Scully, H. E. and Basmajian, J. V. Motor-unit training and influence of manual skill. *Psychophysiology,* 1969, *5,* 625–32.

Seamon, J. G. and Gazzaniga, M. S. Coding strategies and cerebral laterality effects. *Cognitive Psychology,* 1973, *5,* 249–56.

Sechenov, I. M. *Reflexes of the brain.* In I. M. Sechenov, *Selected works.* Moscow and Leningrad: State Publishing House for Biological and Medical Literature,

1935. Originally published in St. Petersburg, 1863, in R. J. Herrnstein and E. G. Boring (eds.), *A source book in the history of psychology*. Cambridge, Mass.: Harvard University Press, 1965.

Sechenov, I. M. *Physiology of the nervous system*. St. Petersburg, 1866.

Sechenov, I. M. *Elements of thought*. St. Petersburg, 1878.

Sechenov, I. M. *Collected works*. Moscow: State Publishing House, 1935.

Secor, W. B. Visual reading: A study in mental imagery. *American Journal of Psychology*, 1900, *11*, 225–36.

Serafetinides, E. A., Shurley, J. T., Brooks, R., and Gideon, W. P. Electrophysiological changes in humans during sensory isolation. *Aerospace Medicine*, 1971, *42*, 840–42.

Shagass, C. *Evoked brain potentials in psychiatry*. New York: Plenum Press, 1972.

Shallice, T. Mental states and processes. *Science*, 1974, *183*, 1072–73.

Sharrard, G. A. W. Evoked responses—Introductory studies on their relationship to the perception of language. *Journal of Laryngology and Otology*, 1969, *83*, 947–58.

Shaw, W. A. The distribution of muscular action potentials during imaging. *Psychological Record*, 1938, *2*, 195–216.

Shaw, W. A. The relation of muscular action potentials to imaginal weight lifting. *Archives of Psychology*, 1940, *35*, 50.

Shearer, W. M. and Simmons, F. B. Middle ear activity during speech in normal speakers and stutterers. *Journal of Speech and Hearing Research*, 1965, *8*, 203–7.

Sheatz, G. C. and Chapman, R. M. Task relevance and auditory evoked responses. *Electroencephalography and Clinical Neurophysiology*, 1969, *26*, 468–75.

Shelburne, S. A., Jr. Visual evoked responses to word and nonsense syllable stimuli. *Electroencephalography and Clinical Neurophysiology*, 1972, *32*, 17–25.

Shelburne, S. A., Jr. Visual evoked responses to language stimuli in normal children. *Electroencephalography and Clinical Neurophysiology*, 1973, *34*, 135–43.

Sherrington, C. S. Postural activity of muscle and nerve. *Brain*, 1915, *38*, 191–234.

Sherrington, C. S. *The integrative action of the nervous system*. New Haven: Yale University Press, 1947.

Sherrington, C. S. and Sowton, S. C. M. Observations on reflex responses to single break-shocks. *Journal of Physiology*, 1915, *49*, 331–48.

Sherrod, D. R. Lateral eye movements and reaction to persuasion, *Perceptual and Motor Skills*, 1972, *35*, 355–58.

Shevrin, H. and Fritzler, D. Visual evoked response correlates of unconscious mental processes. *Science*, 1968, *161*, 295–98.

Shevrin, H. and Rennick, P. Cortical response to a tactile stimulus during attention, mental arithmetic and free associations. *Psychophysiology*, 1967, *3*, 381–88.

Shevrin, H., Smith, W. H., and Fritzler, D. E. Average evoked response and verbal correlates of unconscious mental processes. *Psychophysiology*, 1971, *8*, 149–62.

Sidlauskas, A. E. Language. The ideas of Dr. Alfred Tomatis. Unpublished manuscript, University of Ottawa, 1970.

Siegenthaler, B. M. and Hochberg, I. Reaction time of the tongue to auditory and tactile stimulation. *Perceptual and Motor Skills*, 1965, *21*, 387–93.

Simard, T. G. Fine sensorimotor control in healthy children: An electromyographic study. *Pediatrics*, 1969, *43*, 1035–41.

Simard, T. G. and Basmajian, J. V. Methods in training the conscious control of motor units. *Archives of Physical Medicine and Rehabilitation*, 1967, *48*, 12–19.

Simard, T. G. and Ladd, W. L. Conscious control of motor units with thalidomide children: An electromyographic study. *Developmental Medicine and Child Neurology,* 1969, *11,* 743–48.

Simon, H. A. and Barenfeld, M. Information-processing analysis of perceptual processes in problem solving. *Psychological Review,* 1969, *76,* 473–83.

Simpson, H. M. and Climan, M. H. Pupillary and electromyographic changes during an imagery task. *Psychophysiology,* 1971, *8,* 483–90.

Singer, J. L. Daydreaming and the stream of thought. *American Scientist,* 1974, *62,* 417–25.

Singer, J. L. and Antrobus, J. S. Eye movements during fantasies. Imagining and suppressing fantasies. *Archives of General Psychiatry,* 1965, *12,* 71–76.

Singer, J. L., Greenberg, S., and Antrobus, J. S. Looking with the mind's eye: Experimental studies of ocular motility during daydreaming and mental arithmetic. *Transaction of the New York Academy of Sciences,* Series II, 1971, *33,* 694–709.

Skinner, B. F. *The behavior of organisms. An experimental analysis.* New York: Appleton-Century-Crofts, 1938.

Skinner, B. F. *Science and human behavior.* New York: Macmillan, 1953.

Skinner, B. F. *Verbal behavior.* New York: Appleton-Century-Crofts, 1957.

Skinner, B. F. Behaviorism at fifty. *Science,* 1963, *140,* 951–58.

Skinner, B. F. *Beyond freedom and dignity.* New York: Knopf, 1971.

Skinner, B. F. and Delabarre, E. B. In B. F. Skinner (ed.), *Behavior of organisms.* New York: Appleton-Century-Crofts, 1938.

Slatter, K. H. Alpha rhythms and mental imagery. *Electroencephalography and Clinical Neurophysiology,* 1960, *12,* 851–59.

Slaughter, J., Hahn, W., and Rinaldi, P. Instrumental conditioning of heart rate in the curarized rat with varied amounts of pretraining. *Journal of Comparative and Physiological Psychology,* 1970, *72,* 356–59.

Small, A. M. Psychoacoustics. In F. D. Minifie, T. J. Hixon, and F. Williams (eds.), *Normal aspects of speech, hearing and language.* Englewood Cliffs, N.J.: Prentice-Hall, 1973.

Smith, A. A., Malmo, R. B., and Shagass, C. An electromyographic study of listening and talking. *Canadian Journal of Psychology,* 1954, *8,* 219–27.

Smith, A. D. Input order and output interference in organized recall. *Journal of Experimental Psychology,* 1973, *100,* 147–50.

Smith, C. U. M. *The brain: Toward an understanding.* New York: Putnam's, 1970.

Smith, D. B. D., Donchin, E., Cohen, L., and Starr, A. Auditory averaged evoked potentials in man during selective binaural listening. *Electroencephalography and Clinical Neurophysiology,* 1970, *28,* 146–52.

Smith, E. E. Choice reaction time: An analysis of the major theoretical positions. *Psychological Bulletin* 1968, *69,* 77–110.

Smith, K. Conditioning as an artifact. *Psychological Review,* 1954, *61,* 217–25.

Smith, K. U. and Henry, J. P. Cybernetic foundations for rehabilitation. *American Journal of Physical Medicine,* 1967, *46,* 379–467.

Smith, M. O. History of the motor theories of attention. *Journal of General Psychology,* 1969, *80,* 243–57.

Smith, P. T. Feature-testing models and their application to perception and memory for speech. *Quarterly Journal of Experimental Psychology,* 1973, *25,* 511–34.

Smith, P. T. and Jones, K. F. Phonemic organization and search through long-term memory. In P. M. A. Rabbitt and S. Dormic (eds.), *Attention and Performance,* vol. 5. New York: Academic Press, 1975.

Smith, S. M., Brown, H. O., Toman, J. E. P., and Goodman, L. S. The lack of cerebral effects of *d*-tubocurarine. *Anesthesiology,* 1947, *8,* 1–14.

Smith, T. L. On muscular memory. *American Journal of Psychology,* 1896, *7,* 453–90.

Smith, W. G. The relation of attention to memory. *Mind,* 1895, *4,* 47–73.

Smith, W. M. Visual recognition: Facilitation of seeing by saying. *Psychonomic Science,* 1965, *2,* 57–58. (a)

Smith, W. M. Visual recognition: Facilitation of seeing by hearing. *Psychonomic Science,* 1965, *2,* 157–58. (b)

Society Proceedings, American Electroencephalographic Society. Bloomington, Minnesota, September 16-18, 1971. *Electroencephalography and Clinical Neurophysiology,* 1972, *33,* 237–55.

Sokolov, A. N. The speech mechanisms of mental activity. *Izvestiia Akademiia Pedagogicheskikh Nauk RSFSR,* 1956, *81.* (Cole, M. and Maltzman, I., *A handbook of contemporary Soviet psychology.* New York: Basic Books, 1969.)

Sokolov, A. N. *The dynamics and function of inner speech (concealed articulation).* Izv. APN RSFSR, No. 113, Moscow, 1960.

Sokolov, A. N. Inner speech as a mechanism of thought. *18th International Conference on Psychology, Abstracts,* Vol. 2, Moscow, 1966.

Sokolov. A. N. Speech-motor afferentation and the problem of brain mechanisms of thought. *Voprosy Psikhologii,* 1967, *13,* 41–54.

Sokolov, A. N. *Internal speech and thinking.* Moscow, USSR: Prosveshchenie, 1968.

Sokolov, A. N. Studies of the speech mechanisms of thinking. In M. Cole and I. Maltzman (eds.), *A handbook of contemporary Soviet psychology.* New York: Basic Books, 1969.

Sokolov, A. N. Internal speech and thought. *International Journal of Psychology,* 1971, *6,* 79–92.

Sokolov, A. N. *Inner speech and thought.* New York: Plenum Press, 1972.

Sokolov, E. N. *Perception and the conditioned reflex.* New York: Macmillan, 1963.

Solberg, K. B., Tyre, T. E., and Stinson, G. M. Ivanov-Smolensky conditioning in adults and children using an electromyographic response measure. *Psychonomic Science,* 1970, *18,* 365–66.

Solomon, R. L. and Turner, L. H. Discriminative classical conditioning in dogs paralyzed by curare can later control discriminative avoidance responses in the normal state. *Psychological Review,* 1962, *69,* 202–19.

Souriau, P. La perception des Faits psychiques. *Annee Psychologique,* 1907, *13,* 56.

Sperling, G. The information available in brief visual presentations. *Psychological Monographs,* 1960, *74* (Whole No. 498).

Sperry, R. W. Neurology and the mind-brain problem. *American Scientist,* 1952, *40,* 291–312.

Sperry, R. W. Lateral specialization of cerebral function in the surgically separated hemispheres. In F. J. McGuigan and R. A. Schoonover (eds.), *The psychophysiology of thinking.* New York: Academic Press, 1973.

Spreng, L. F., Johnson, L. C., and Lubin, A. Autonomic correlates of eye movements bursts during stage REM sleep. *Psychophysiology,* 1968, *4,* 311–23.

Stein, R. B. The role of spike trains in transmitting and distorting sensory signals. In F. O. Schmitt (Ed.-in-Chief), *The Neurosciences: Second study program.* New York: Rockefeller University Press, 1970.

Steinbach, M. J. Eye tracking of self-moved targets: The role of efference. *Journal of Experimental Psychology,* 1969, *82,* 366–76.

Stennett, R. G. The relationship of performance level to level of arousal. *Journal of Experimental Psychology,* 1957, *54,* 54–61.

Stevens, K. N. and Halle, M. Remarks on analysis by synthesis and distinctive features. In W. Wathendenn (ed.), *Models for the perception of speech and visual form.* Cambridge, Mass.: MIT Press, 1967.

Stevens, K. N. and House, A. S. Speech perception. In J. V. Tobias (ed.), *Foundations of modern auditory theory*, vol. 2. New York: Academic Press, 1972.

Stoy, E. G. A preliminary study of ocular attitudes in thinking of spatial relations. *Journal of General Psychology*, 1930, *4*, 379–85.

Stoyva, J. M. Finger electromyographic activity during sleep: Its relation to dreaming in deaf and normal subjects. *Journal of Abnormal Psychology.* 1965, *70*, 343–49.

Stricker, S. S. Studien uber die Sprachvorstellungen (1880). In R. Pintner, Inner speech during silent reading. *Psychological Review*, 1913, *20*, 129–53.

Strømnes, F. J. Memory models and language comprehension, *Scandinavian Journal of Psychology*, 1974, *15*, 26–32.

Strother, G. B. The role of muscle action in interpretative reading. *Journal of General Psychology*, 1949, *41*, 3–20.

Studdert-Kennedy, M. The perception of speech. In T. A. Sebeok (ed.), *Current trends in linguistics*, vol. 12. The Hague: Mouton, 1974.

Sussman, H. M. The role of sensory feedback in tongue movement control. *Journal of Auditory Research*, 1970, *10*, 296–321.

Sussman, H. M. The laterality effect in lingual-auditory tracking. *Journal of the Acoustical Society of America*, 1971, *49*, 1874–80.

Sussman, H. M. What the tongue tells the brain. *Psychological Bulletin*, 1972, *77*, 262–72.

Sutton, S. The specification of psychological variables in an average evoked potential experiment. In E. Donchin and D. B. Lindsley (eds.), *Average evoked potentials: Methods, results, and evaluations.* Washington, D.C.: National Aeronautics and Space Administration, SP-191, 1969.

Sutton, S. Braren, M., Zubin, J., and John, E. R. Evoked-potential correlates of stimulus uncertainty. *Science*, 1965, *150*, 1187–88.

Sutton, D. and Kimm, J. Reaction time of motor units in biceps and triceps. *Experimental Neurology*, 1969, *23*, 503–15.

Sutton, S., Tueting, P., Zubin, J., and John, E. R. Information delivery and the sensory evoked potential. *Science*, 1967, *155*, 1436–39.

Symmes, D. and Eisengart, M. A. Evoked response correlates of meaningful visual stimuli in children. *Psychophysiology*, 1971, *8*, 769–78.

Szegal, B. *The EMG-study of certain forms of mental activity.* Unpublished dissertation, Budapest, Eötvös Loránd University, 1973.

Szentagothai, J. The "module-concept" in cerebral cortex architecture. *Brain Research*, 1975, *95*, 475–96.

Tani, K., Atsushi, C., and Nakai, M. Mental activities and electroencephalograms. *Reports of the Science of Living*, 1968, *16*, 183–89. (Ishihara, T. and Yoshii, N. Multivariate analytic study of EEG and mental activity in juvenile delinquents. *Electroencephalography and Clinical Neurophysiology*, 1972, *33*, 71–80.)

Taub E. and Berman, A. J. Movement and learning in the absence of sensory feedback. In S. J. Freedman (ed.), *The neurophysiology of spatially oriented behavior.* Homewood, Ill.: Dorsey Press, 1968.

Taylor, S. E. A report on two studies of the validity of eye-movement photography as a measurement of reading performance. *Reading in a Changing Society.* International Reading Association Conference Proceedings, vol. 4 (edited by J. Allen Figurel). New York: Scholastic Magazine, 1959, pp. 240–45.

Tecce, J. J. Contingent negative variation and individual differences: A new approach in brain research. *Archives of General Psychiatry*, 1971, *24*, 1–16. Copyright 1971, American Medical Association.

Tecce, J. J. Contingent negative variation (CNV) and psychological processes in man. *Psychological Bulletin*, 1972, *77*, 73–108.

Teichner, W. H. and Krebs, M. J. Laws of visual choice reaction time. *Psychological Review,* 1974, *81,* 75–98. (a)

Teichner, W. H. and Krebs, M. J. Visual search for simple targets. *Psychological Bulletin,* 1974, *81,* 15–28. (b)

Teichner, W. H. and Price, L. M. Eye aiming behavior during the solution of visual patterns. *Journal of Psychology,* 1966, *62,* 33–38.

Teitelbaum, H. Spontaneous rhythmic ocular movements: Their possible relationship to mental activity. *Neurology,* 1954, *4,* 350–54.

Telford, C. W. and Thompson, N. Some factors influencing voluntary and reflex eyelid responses. *Journal of Experimental Psychology,* 1933, *16,* 524–39.

Tepas, D. I. Computer analysis of the electroencephalogram: Evoking, promoting, and provoking. *Behavior Research Methods and Instrumentation,* 1974, *6,* 95–110.

Terzuolo, C. A. Data transmission by spike trains. In F. O. Schmitt (ed.), *The neurosciences: Second study program.* New York: Rockefeller University Press, 1970.

Teyler, T. J., Roemer, R. A., Harrison, T. F., and Thompson, R. F. Human scalp-recorded evoked-potential correlates of linguistic stimuli. *Bulletin of the Psychonomic Society,* 1973, *1,* 333–34. By permission of *Bulletin of Psychonomic Society.*

Thorndike, E. L. Animal intelligence: An experimental study of the associative processes in animals. *Psychological Review Supplements,* 1898, *2* (Whole No. 8).

Thorndike, E. L. Ideo-motor action. *Psychological Review,* 1913, *20,* 91–106.

Thorson, A. M. The relation of tongue movements to internal speech. *Journal of Experimental Psychology,* 1925, *8,* 1–32.

Thysell, R. V. Reaction time of single motor units. *Psychophysiology,* 1969, *6,* 174–85.

Titchener, E. B. *Lectures on the experimental psychology of the thought-processes.* New York: Macmillan, 1909.

Titchener, E. B. *A textbook of psychology.* New York: Macmillan, 1910.

Tobias, J. V. (ed.). *Foundations of modern auditory theory,* vol. 2. New York: Academic Press, 1972.

Toda, M. Possible roles of psychology in the very distant future. In F. J. McGuigan and P. J. Woods (eds.), *Contemporary studies in psychology.* New York: Meredith Corporation, 1972.

Tolman, E. C. *Purposive behavior in animals and men.* New York: Appleton-Century-Crofts, 1932.

Tomatis, A. In A. E. Sidlauskas, *Language. The ideas of Dr. Alfred Tomatis.* Unpublished manuscript, University of Ottawa, 1970.

Totten, E. Eye-movement during visual imagery. *Comparative Psychology Monographs,* 1935, *11,* 1–46.

Travis, L. E. and Knott, J. R. Brain potential studies of perseveration; II. Perseveration time to visually presented words. *Journal of Experimental Psychology,* 1937, *21,* 353–58.

Travis, R. C. and Kennedy, J. L. Prediction and automatic control of alertness. I. Control of lookout alertness. *Journal of Comparative and Physiological Psychology,* 1947, *40,* 457–61.

Trowill, J. A. Instrumental conditioning of the heart rate in the curarized rat. *Journal of Comparative and Physiological Psychology,* 1967, *63,* 7–19.

Tuke, D. H. *The influence of the mind upon the body, II,* 2nd ed. London: Churchill, 1884.

Tuttle, W. W. The effect of attention or mental activity on the patellar tendon reflex. *Journal of Experimental Psychology,* 1924, *7,* 401–19.

Tversky, B. Eye fixations in prediction of recognition and recall. *Memory and Cognition,* 1974, *2,* 275–78.

Twaddell, W. F. On defining the phoneme. *Language Monographs,* 1935, *16,* 1–62.

Ulett, G. A., Akpinar, S., and Itil, T. M. Quantitative EEG analysis during hypnosis. *Electroencephalography and Clinical Neurophysiology,* 1972, *33,* 361–68.

Ulett, G. A. and Johnson, L. C. Pattern, stability, and correlates of photic electroencephalographic activation. *Journal of Nervous and Mental Disorders,* 1958, *126,* 153–68.

Underwood, B. J. Articulation in verbal learning. *Journal of Verbal Learning and Verbal Behavior,* 1964, *3,* 146–49.

Underwood, B. J. False recognition produced by implicit verbal responses. *Journal of Experimental Psychology,* 1965, *70,* 122–29.

Underwood, B. J. *Experimental psychology,* 2nd ed. New York: Appleton-Century-Crofts, 1966.

Unna, K. R. and Pelikan, E. W. Evaluation of curarizing drugs in man. VI. Critique of experiments on unanesthetized subjects. In A. R. McIntyre (ed.), Curare and anti-curare agents. *Annals of the New York Academy of Sciences,* 1951, *54,* 297–530.

Uttal, W. R. Do compound evoked potentials reflect psychological codes? *Psychological Bulletin,* 1965, *64,* 377–92.

Uttal, W. R. (ed.), *Sensory coding. Selected readings.* Boston: Little, Brown, 1972.

Vandell, R. A., Davis, R. A., and Clugston, H. A. The function of mental practice in the acquisition of motor skills. *Journal of General Psychology,* 1943, *29,* 243–50.

Van Liere, D. W. Characteristics of the muscle tension response to paired tones. *Journal of Experimental Psychology,* 1953, *46,* 319–24.

Van Riper, C. and Irwin, J. *Voice and articulation.* Englewood Cliffs, N.J.: Prentice-Hall, 1962.

Vaughan, H. G., Jr. The relationship of brain activity to scalp recordings of event-related potentials. In E. Donchin and D. B. Lindsley (eds.), *Average evoked potentials.* Washington, D.C.: NASA SP-191, 1969.

Vaughan, A. O., and McDaniel, J. W. Electromyographic gradients during complex visual discrimination learning. *Psychonomic Science,* 1969, *16,* 203–4.

Vigotsky, L. S. *Thinking and speech.* Moscow: OQIZ-SOTSEKGIZ, 1934.

Vigotsky, L. S. *Selected psychological studies.* Moscow: APN RSASR Press, 1956.

Vigotsky, L. S. *Thought and language.* New York: John Wiley, 1962.

Vogel, W., Broverman, D. M., and Klaiber, E. L. EEG and mental abilities. *Electroencephalography and Clinical Neurophysiology,* 1968, *24,* 166–75.

Vogel, W., Broverman, D. M., Klaiber, E. L., and Kun, K. J. EEG response to photic stimulation as a function of cognitive style. *Electroencephalography and Clinical Neurophysiology,* 1969, *27,* 186–90.

Volavka, J., Matoušek, M., and Roubiček, J. Mental arithmetic and eye opening. An EEG frequency analysis and GSE study. *Electroencephalography and Clinical Neurophysiology* 1967, *22,* 174–76.

Volkova, V. D. On certain characteristics of the formation of conditioned reflexes to speech stimuli in children. *Fiziologicheskii Zhurnal SSSR,* 1953, *39,* 540–48.

Wallerstein, H. An electromyographic study of attentive listening. *Canadian Journal of Psychology,* 1954, *8,* 228–38.

Walter, W. G. The contingent negative variation. An electrical sign of significant association in the human brain. *Science,* 1964, *146,* 434. (a)

Walter, W. G. The convergence and interaction of visual, auditory and tactile responses in human nonspecific cortex. *Ann. N.Y. Acad. Science.*, 1964, *112*, 320–61. (b)

Walter, W. G. Slow potential waves in the human brain associated with expectancy, attention, and decision. *Archiv fur psychiatrie und Nervenkrankheiten*, 1964, *206*, 309–22. (c)

Washburn, M. F. The function of incipient motor processes. *Psychological Review*, 1914, *21*, 376–90.

Washburn, M. F. *Movement and mental imagery*. Boston: Houghton-Mifflin, 1916.

Washburn, M. F. *The animal mind*, 4th ed. New York: Macmillan, 1936.

Waszak, M. and Obrist, W. D. Relationship of slow potential changes to reponse speed and motivation in man. *Electroencephalography and Clinical Neurophysiology*, 1969, *27*, 113–20.

Watson, J. B. Psychology as the behaviorist views it. *Psychological Review*, 1913, *20*, 158–77.

Watson, J. B. *Behavior: An introduction to comparative psychology*. New York: Holt, 1914.

Watson, J. B. *Psychology from the standpoint of a behaviorist*. Philadelphia: Lippincott, 1919.

Watson, J. B. Is thinking merely the action of language mechanisms? *British Journal of Psychology*, 1920, *11*, 87–104.

Watson, J. B. *Behaviorism*, rev. ed. Chicago: University of Chicago Press, 1930. Reissued New York, W. W. Norton & Co., 1970.

Watson, J. B. In C. Murchison (Ed.), *A history of psychology in autobiography, Vol. III*. Worcester, Mass.: Clark University Press, 1936.

Wechsler, D. E. Engrams, memory storage, and mnemonic coding. *American Psychologist*, 1963, *18*, 149–53.

Weerts, T. C. and Lang, P. J. The effects of eye fixation and stimulus and response location on the contingent negative variation (CNV). *Biological Psychology*, 1973, *1*, 1–19.

Wegmann, M. and Weber, R. Blink rate and imagined letters. *Bulletin of the Psychonomic Society*, 1973, *2*, 370–72.

Weinberg, H. and Cole, R. E. Averaged evoked potentials to classes of visual stimuli. *Psychonomic Science*, 1968, *11*, 71–72.

Weinberg, H., Walter, W. G., Cooper, R., and Aldridge, V. J. Emitted cerebral events. *Electroencephalography*, 1974, *36*, 1–8.

Weiss, A. P. Behavior in the central nervous system. *Psychological Review*, 1922, *29*, 329–43.

Weiss, A. D. the locus of reaction time change with set, motivation, and age. *Journal of Gerontology*, 1965, *20*, 60–64.

Weiten, W. and Etaugh, C. Lateral eye-movement consistency is related to academic aptitude. *Perceptual and Motor Skills*, 1974, *38*, 1203–6.

Weitzenhoffer, A. M. A case of pursuit-like eye movements directly reflecting dream content during hypnotic dreaming. *Perceptual and Motor Skills*, 1971, *32*, 701–2.

Weitzenhoffer, A. M. and Brockmeier, J. D. Attention and eye movements. *Journal of Nervous and Mental Disease*, 1970, *151*, 130–42.

Wells, L. An EMG investigation of subvocalization during the silent reading process. Unpublished doctoral thesis. The Ontario Institute for Studies in Education. University of Toronto, 1976.

Wenger, M. A., Baggchi, B. K., and Anand, M. D. Experiments in India on "voluntary" control of the heart and pulse. *Circulation*, 1961, *24*, 1319–25.

Westcott, M. R. and Huttenlocher, J. Cardiac conditioning: The effects and implications of controlled and uncontrolled respiration. *Journal of Experimental Psychology,* 1961, *61,* 353–59.

Whitman, R. M., Kramer, M., and Baldridge, B. Which dream does the patient tell? *Archives of General Psychiatry,* 1963, *8,* 277–82.

Wickelgren, W. A., and Berian, K. M. Dual trace theory and the consolidation of long-term memory. *Journal of Mathematical Psychology,* 1971, *8,* 404–17.

Wiener, N. *Cybernetics.* New York: John Wiley, 1948.

Wilson, J. R. and DiCara, L. V. Influence of neuromuscular blocking drugs on recovery of skeletal electromyographic activity in the rat. *Psychophysiology,* 1975, *12,* 249–53.

Wolpe, J. Relaxation as an instrument for breaking adverse emotional habits. In F. J. McGuigan (ed.), *Tension control.* Blacksburg, Va.: University Publications, 1975.

Wolpert, E. A. Studies in psychophysiology of dreams, II. An electromyographic study of dreaming. *A.M.A. Archives of General Psychiatry,* 1960, *2,* 231–41.

Wolpert, E. A., and Trosman, H. Studies in psychophysiology of dreams: I. Experimental evocation of sequential dream episodes. *A.M.A. Archives of Neurology and Psychiatry,* 1958, *79,* 603–6.

Wood, C. C. Parallel processing of auditory and phonetic information in speech discrimination. *Perception and Psychophysics,* 1974, *15,* 501–8.

Wood, C. C. Average evoked potentials and phonetic processing in speech perception. *Progressive Clinical Neurophysiology,* in press.

Wood, C. C., Goff, W. R., and Day, R. S. Auditory evoked potentials during speech perception. *Science,* 1971, *173,* 1248–51.

Woodworth, R. S. and Schlosberg, H. *Experimental psychology,* rev. ed. New York: Henry Holt, 1954.

Wyczoikowska, A. Theoretical and experimental studies in the mechanism of speech. *Psychological Review,* 1913, *20,* 448–58.

Yamaguchi, Y. and Niwa, K. Feedback training and self-control of frontal theta burst of EEG appearing during mental work. *J. Jap. Psychosom. Soc.,* 1974, *14,* 344–53.

Young, R. M. *Mind brain and adaptation in the nineteenth century.* New York: Oxford University Press, 1970.

Zhinkin, N. I. Investigation of internal speech using the methods of central speech obstacles. *Izv. Akad. Pedag. Nauk. REFSR,* 1960, No. 113. Cited by Cole and Maltzman (1969).

Zhinkin, N. I. Code transfers in internal speech. *Vop. Yazik.,* 1964, No. 6 Cited by Cole and Maltzman (1969).

Zhinkin, N. I. *Mechanisms of Speech.* The Hague: Mouton, 1968.

Zikmund, V. Oculomotor activity during visual imagery of a moving stimulus pattern. *Studia Psychologica,* 1966, *4,* 254–73.

Zubek, J. P. and MacNeill, M. Effects of immobilization: Behavioral and EEG changes. *Canadian Journal of Psychology,* 1966, *20,* 316–36.

Zubek, J. P. and MacNeill, M. Effects of immobilization: Behavioral and EEG changes. *Canadian Journal of Psychology,* 1966, *20,* 316–36.

Zwosta, M. and Zenhausern, R. Application of signal detection theory to subliminal and supraliminal accessory stimulation. *Perceptual and Motor Skills,* 1969, *28,* 699–704.

Author Index

Subject Index